'*Studying English Literature in Context* will undoubtedly advance the theory and practice of cultural materialist pedagogy in higher education. I recommend this lively and enjoyable volume as a valuable resource for teachers and students of English literature, and as an excellent anthology of scholarly essays in its own right.'

Caroline Franklin, Swansea University

'*Studying English Literature in Context* helps to ease students' transition from second- to third-level study by offering scholarly essays that are written specifically for students. This makes academic writing and argument more accessible to students coming to such material for the first time, with the further resources offering the additional benefit of helping students to think more critically about what they are reading. *Studying English Literature in Context* offers new university students much-needed support as they work towards the broader/ deeper critical inquiry in which they will engage at later stages of their programme. It is likely to be widely assigned in undergraduate survey courses, and much used.'

Naomi McAreavey, University College Dublin

'Driven by the conviction that texts are fruitfully understood within the context of their time, this enormously adaptable book manages, without strain, to appeal both to scholars and to students, to bookworms and to neophytes. It covers the entire history of English literature and drama with an ease and dexterity matched only by ambition and range. Critical reflections accompanying each essay inform students, without dryness, of the scholarly tradition to which they contribute. This collection deserves a place on reading lists wherever English literature is nurtured and cherished.'

Ronan McDonald, The University of Melbourne

'*Studying English Literature in Context* is a superb collection of essays by leading scholars that will foster stimulating response, reignite debate, and demand intellectual engagement by readers of representative texts from the long history of English. The authors recognise that, from *The Dream of the Rood*'s multivalence to Aphra Behn's colonial novel *Oroonoko* and Grace Nichols' feminist poetry, literature both contributes to, and reflects, sociocultural critique, linking past modes of creative expression with current conversations

about form, textual ambiguity, literary resistance, and periodisation. In addition to this impressive set of critical interpretations, generous resources are provided to situate the student in the long chronology and complex range of generic, stylistic, material, and performative possibilities offered by literature. The whole volume works to ensure enhanced understanding of the significance of poetry, prose, and drama, both to authors and creators and to audiences globally; as Poplawski anticipates, this book offers *contextured* readings, encouraging connections between eras, affect, and modalities to amplify the power of the written and spoken word.'

Elaine Treharne, Stanford University

'An impeccable selection of wide-ranging but sharply focused texts in their historical and cultural contexts by seasoned scholars with a keen sense of the past as well as a sharp eye for essential contemporary issues such as feminism, environmentalism, immigration, and politics. The crisp and succinct essays are packed with engaging questions that suggest lively classroom discussion as well as thoughtful critical examination.'

Stephen Kern, Ohio State University

Studying English Literature in Context

Ranging from early medieval times to the present, this diverse collection explores the myriad ways in which literary texts are informed by their historical contexts. The thirty-one essays draw on varied themes and perspectives to present stimulating new readings of both canonical and non-canonical texts and authors. Written in a lively and engaging style by an international team of experts, these specially commissioned essays collectively represent an incisive contribution to literary studies; they will appeal to scholars, teachers and graduate and undergraduate students. The book is intended to complement Paul Poplawski's previous volume, *English Literature in Context*, and incorporates additional study elements designed specifically with undergraduates in mind. With an extensive chronology, a glossary of critical terms and a study guide suggesting how students might learn from the essays in their own writing practices, this volume provides a rich and flexible resource for teaching and learning.

Paul Poplawski taught at the University of Wales and the University of Leicester, where he was Director of Studies at Vaughan College and Senior Lecturer in English. He was the general editor of the two editions of *English Literature in Context* (2008, 2017), to which he also contributed the chapters 'The Twentieth Century, 1901–39' and 'Postcolonial Literature in English'. He is a member of the editorial board of the Cambridge Edition of the Works of D. H. Lawrence and co-author of the third edition of *A Bibliography of D. H. Lawrence* (2001). In addition to several other books and essays on Lawrence, he has published a book on Jane Austen (1998) and was the editor of *Encyclopedia of Literary Modernism* (2003). Most recently, he was guest editor for the MHRA *Yearbook of English Studies* for 2020, entitled *Back to the Twenties: Modernism Then and Now*.

Studying English Literature in Context
Critical Readings

Edited by

Paul Poplawski

CAMBRIDGE
UNIVERSITY PRESS

CAMBRIDGE
UNIVERSITY PRESS

University Printing House, Cambridge CB2 8BS, United Kingdom

One Liberty Plaza, 20th Floor, New York, NY 10006, USA

477 Williamstown Road, Port Melbourne, VIC 3207, Australia

314–321, 3rd Floor, Plot 3, Splendor Forum, Jasola District Centre,
New Delhi – 110025, India

103 Penang Road, #05–06/07, Visioncrest Commercial, Singapore 238467

Cambridge University Press is part of the University of Cambridge.

It furthers the University's mission by disseminating knowledge in the pursuit of
education, learning, and research at the highest international levels of excellence.

www.cambridge.org
Information on this title: www.cambridge.org/9781108479288
DOI: 10.1017/9781108782999

© Cambridge University Press 2022

First published 2022

Printed in the United Kingdom by TJ Books Limited, Padstow Cornwall

A catalogue record for this publication is available from the British Library.

ISBN 978-1-108-47928-8 Hardback
ISBN 978-1-108-74957-2 Paperback

Contents

Figures

Notes on Contributors

SUE ASBEE recently retired as Senior Lecturer at the Open University, UK, and is now an Honorary Associate there. She was the editor of *Yellow Book Writers* – the third volume of Jane Spirit et al. (eds), *The Women Aesthetes: British Writers 1870–1900* (2013) – which focuses on the last decade of the nineteenth century and includes women writers like Charlotte Mew, Vernon Lee, John Oliver Hobbs and Ella D'Arcy and others whose work appeared in the *Yellow Book*. She has also published work on American novelists from the same era, Kate Chopin and Edith Wharton, and later American poets, Langston Hughes, Claude McKay, Allen Ginsberg and Frank O'Hara.

IZABEL F. O. BRANDÃO recently retired as Professor of Literatures in English and Contemporary Brazilian Women Writers at the Federal University of Alagoas, Brazil. Her publications include a book on D. H. Lawrence (2009) and several books and essays on feminist literary criticism in both Portuguese and English. She is one of the editors of a feminist anthology in translation, *Traduções da cultura: perspectivas críticas feministas 1970–2010* (*Translations of Culture: Feminist Critical Perspectives 1970–2010*) (2017). Her latest book, in collaboration, is *Literatura e ecologia: trilhando novos caminhos críticos* (*Literature and Ecology: Tracking New Critical Paths*) (2019). She is also a poet; her latest collection is *As horas da minha alegria* (*The Hours of My Joy*) (2013).

ANNA BUDZIAK is Associate Professor at the University of Wrocław, Poland. She has co-edited a book on Richard Shusterman's somaesthetics and written three monographs: *Historia u T. S. Eliota*, in Polish (2002), *Text, Body and Indeterminacy: Doppelgänger Selves in Pater and Wilde*, shortlisted for the ESSE Book Award 2008–2010, and *T. S. Eliot's Ariel Poems: Making Sense of the Times* (2021).

FIONNUALA DILLANE is Professor in Nineteenth-Century Literature at the School of English, Drama and Film, University College Dublin, Ireland. She researches and publishes on George Eliot and more generally in the fields of Victorian print cultures, genre history and memory studies. She is the vice president of the Research Society for Victorian Periodicals.

MARIA FRAWLEY is Professor of English at the George Washington University, USA, where she teaches courses in nineteenth-century British literature and chairs the Department of English. She is the author of three books: *A Wider Range: Travel Writing by Women in Victorian England* (1994), *Anne Brontë* (1996) and *Invalidism and Identity in Nineteenth-Century Britain* (2004). In addition, she has prepared an edition of Harriet Martineau's *Life in the Sick-Room* for Broadview Press (2003). She is co-editor of Routledge's *Companion to Jane Austen* (2021), and is currently working on several projects related to nineteenth-century life writing.

TERRY GIFFORD is a former chair of the Ted Hughes Society, a visiting research fellow in Environmental Humanities at Bath Spa University, UK, and Profesor Honorifico at the Universidad de Alicante, Spain. He is the author/editor of seven books on Ted Hughes and his other published works include *Pastoral* (2020), *Reconnecting with John Muir* (2006) and *Green Voices* (2011).

JANE GROGAN is Associate Professor in Renaissance Literature at University College Dublin, Ireland. She is the author of two monographs, two edited collections of essays, a critical edition of the first English translation of Xenophon's *Cyropaedia*, and numerous articles. A past president of the International Spenser Society, her most recent research on Spenser looks at his reception in Irish literature from Yeats onwards, and at auto-fiction as a potential resource for rethinking Spenser's corpus.

INA HABERMANN is Professor of English Literature at the University of Basle, Switzerland, and acted as director of the Centre of Competence Cultural Topographies from 2009 to 2017. Her publications include *Staging Slander and Gender in Early Modern England* (2003), *Myth, Memory and the Middlebrow: Priestley, du Maurier and the Symbolic Form of Englishness* (2010) and, as editor with Michelle Witen, *Shakespeare and Space: Theatrical Explorations of the Spatial Paradigm* (2016). She ran the Swiss National Science Foundation project British Literary and Cultural Discourses of Europe (2014–17), and her research interests include middlebrow writing, Britishness and Englishness, literary otherworlds and discourses of Anglophilia.

KATIE HALSEY is Professor of Eighteenth-Century Literature at the University of Stirling, Scotland, and the director of its Centre for Eighteenth-Century Studies. She is the principal investigator of the project Books and Borrowing, 1750–1830: An Analysis of Scottish Borrowers' Registers, funded by the AHRC, and the author, among other works, of *Jane Austen and Her Readers, 1786–1945* (2012).

ODDVAR HOLMESLAND is Professor of English Literature at the University of Agder, Kristiansand, Norway. He teaches courses in literature and culture ranging over the sixteenth to the twentieth centuries, and his research interests include early modern as well as modern literature. He is the author of *Utopian Negotiation: Aphra Behn and Margaret Cavendish* (2013), *Form as Compensation for Life: Fictive Patterns in Virginia Woolf's Novels* (1998) and *A Critical Introduction to Henry Green's Novels: The Living Vision* (1986).

CHRISTA JANSOHN is Professor of British Culture at the University of Bamberg, Germany. Her publications include a monograph on the 'Shakespeare Apocrypha' and its reception in Germany (2000) and bilingual editions of *Shakespeare's Sonnets* (1992), *A Lover's Complaint* and the narrative poems (1993). She is editor of *German Shakespeare Studies at the Turn of the Twenty-first Century* (2006); together with Richard Fortheringham and Robert White of *Shakespeare's World/World Shakespeares* (2006); with Lena Cowen Orlin and Stanley Wells of *Shakespeare without Boundaries* (2011); and with Dieter Mehl of *Shakespeare Jubilees: 1769–2014* (2015).

RICHARD J. JONES is Senior Lecturer in English Literature at the Open University, UK. He is the author of *Tobias Smollett in the Enlightenment: Travels through France, Italy and Scotland* (2011) and recent articles on Smollett's work in the *Journal of Eighteenth-Century Studies* (2018), *Literature Compass* (2018) and *The Eighteenth Century: Theory and Interpretation* (2019).

JORDAN KISTLER is Lecturer in Victorian Literature at the University of Strathclyde, Scotland. Her work explores the intersections between science and literature in the nineteenth century, and she has published on a range of topics in this area, including blindness, mesmerism and museum display.

FILIP KRAJNÍK is a lecturer in English literature at the Department of English and American Studies, Faculty of Arts, Masaryk University in Brno, Czech Republic. His main research interests are late medieval English poetry and early modern English theatre. He is currently co-editing a volume on medieval female piety entitled *Women across Borders* (forthcoming). With his research team, he is also working on a project focusing on the transnational and multi-genre aspects of the English theatre of the Restoration period. An edited volume, tentatively entitled *Restoration Reshaping*, is expected in 2022.

JOEL KUORTTI is Professor of English at the University of Turku, Finland. His major research interests are postcolonial theory, Indian literature in English, transnational identity, transculturation and translocality, gender and cultural studies, and ordinariness. His books include *Fictions to Live In: Narration as an Argument for Fiction in Salman Rushdie's Novels* (1998), *Tense Past, Tense Present: Women Writing in English* (2003), *Writing Imagined Diasporas: South Asian Women Reshaping North American Identity* (2007), *Reconstructing Hybridity* (co-edited with J. Nyman; 2007), *Changing Worlds/Changing Nations: The Concept of Nation in the Transnational Era* (co-edited with O. P. Dwivedi; 2012), *Critical Insights: Midnight's Children* (2014), *Transculturation and Aesthetics* (2015) and *Thinking with the Familiar in Contemporary Literature and Culture 'Out of the Ordinary'* (co-edited with K. Ilmonen, E. Valovirta and J. Korkka; 2019).

STEFANIA MICHELUCCI is Professor of English Studies at the University of Genoa, Italy. As a visiting scholar, she has also taught in many other universities around the world, including the University of California, Berkeley, USA, and Kyoto Tachibana University, Japan. Her publications include *Space and Place in the Works of D. H. Lawrence* (2002), *The Poetry of Thom Gunn: A Critical Study* (2009) and many essays on writers of the nineteenth and twentieth centuries, with particular attention on the relationship between literature and the visual arts. With Ian Duncan and Luisa Villa she has recently co-edited a volume of essays entitled *The British Aristocracy in Popular Culture, Essays on 200 years of Representations* (2020). She is now working on a new book on Thom Gunn.

F. FIONA MOOLLA is a lecturer in the English Department at the University of the Western Cape, South Africa. Among other academic and non-academic publications, her works include, as author, *Reading Nuruddin Farah: The Individual, the Novel & the Idea of Home* (2014), and, as editor, *Natures of Africa: Ecocriticism and Animal Studies in Contemporary Cultural Forms* (2016). Her current consuming passion is the study of the literary and social significance of eros in African and other cultures.

BEN MOORE is Assistant Professor in English Literature at the University of Amsterdam, Netherlands, where he teaches a range of undergraduate and postgraduate courses. His research focuses mainly on cities, architecture and money in the nineteenth-century novel. He has published in journals including *Modernism/modernity*, *Journal of Victorian Culture*, *Gaskell Journal*, *Modern Language Review*, *Victorian Literature and Culture* and *Dickens Quarterly*. He is presently working on a monograph entitled *Invisible Architecture in Nineteenth-Century Literature: Rethinking Urban Modernity*.

LEE MORRISSEY, Professor and Alumni Distinguished Professor of English at Clemson University, USA, is the author of *From the Temple to the Castle: An Architectural History of British Literature, 1660–1760* (1999) and *The Constitution of Literature: Literacy, Democracy, and Early English Literary Criticism* (2007). He is the editor of *Debating the Canon: A Reader from Addison to Nafisi* (2005) and associate editor of the *Encyclopedia of British Literature, 1660–1789* (2015). He has been a Fulbright Scholar at the National University of Ireland Galway and a McCarthy Fellow at Marsh's Library, Dublin, and is currently writing a monograph on John Milton.

JUDITH PALTIN is an associate professor in the Department of English Language and Literatures at the University of British Columbia, Canada. She has published *Modernism and the Idea of the Crowd* with Cambridge University Press (2020), articles in the *James Joyce Quarterly*, *The Conradian*, *Conradiana*, *The Wildean* and *Interdisciplinary Studies in Literature and Environment*, and a chapter in *Affective*

Materialities: Reorienting the Body in Modernist Literature (2019; edited by Kara Watts, Molly Volanth Hall and Robin Hackett).

ALESSANDRA PETRINA is Professor of English Literature at the University of Padua, Italy. Her research focuses primarily on late medieval and early modern intellectual history, and on Anglo-Italian cultural relations. Her publications include *The Kingis Quair* (1997), *Cultural Politics in Fifteenth-Century England: The Case of Humphrey, Duke of Gloucester* (2004) and *Machiavelli in the British Isles: Two Early Modern Translations of the Prince* (2009). She has edited and co-edited a number of volumes, including (with Clara Calvo) *Shakespeare and Popular Culture* (2018), and (with Ian Johnson) *The Impact of Latin Culture on Medieval and Early Modern Scottish Writing* (2018). Her latest book is *Petrarch's Triumphi in the British Isles* (MHRA Tudor and Stuart Translation Series, 2020).

FIONA PRICE is author of *Reinventing Liberty: Nation, Commerce and the Historical Novel from Walpole to Scott* (2016) and *Revolutions in Taste 1773–1818: Women Writers and the Aesthetics of Romanticism* (2009), and editor, with Benjamin Dew, of *Historical Writing in Britain, 1688–1830: Visions of History* (2014). She has edited two historical novels, Jane Porter's *The Scottish Chiefs* (1810; 2007) and Sarah Green's *Private History of the Court of England* (1808; 2011). She is currently working on a monograph on the idea of the 'real' in the Romantic period novel. She is Professor in English Literature at the University of Chichester, UK.

ULLA RAHBEK is Associate Professor of Postcolonial Literatures at Copenhagen University, Denmark. Her most recent publications are *Refugee Talk: Propositions on Ethics and Aesthetics,* with Eva Rask Knudsen (Pluto, 2022), *British Multicultural Literature and Superdiversity* (2019), *In Search of the Afropolitan*, with Eva Rask Knudsen (2016), and *Global Voices* (Gyldendal, 2016).

CATHERINE RILEY is a writer and the director of Primadonna Festival, the first literary festival in the UK to give prominence specifically to work by women, as well as to writers of all genders, economic statuses and ethnicities whose voices are not usually heard. She is an expert on contemporary feminist publishing in the UK. She has published *Feminism and Women's Writing: An Introduction* (with Lynne Pearce) (2018) and *The Virago Story: Assessing the Impact of a Feminist Publishing Phenomenon* (2018), as well as numerous journal articles and chapters. She has taught English Literature and Gender Studies at Lancaster and Northumbria Universities and Birkbeck College, London.

DANIEL SANJIV ROBERTS studied English at Chennai, Hyderabad and Cambridge, and teaches at Queen's University Belfast, Northern Ireland. He is the author of *De Quincey, Coleridge and the High Romantic Argument* (2000) and has edited texts by Thomas De Quincey, Robert Southey and Charles Johnston for major critical editions. His edited collections (with Robert Morrison) include *Thomas De Quincey: New Theoretical and Critical Directions* (2007), *Romanticism and Blackwood's Magazine: 'An Unprecedented Phenomenon'* (2013), and (with Jonathan Wright) *Ireland's Imperial Connections, 1775–1947* (2019).

LORETTA STEC is Professor of English at San Francisco State University, USA, where she teaches twentieth-century literatures in English with an emphasis on women writers, as well as animal studies. She has published on, among others, Virginia Woolf, Rebecca West, Djuna Barnes, D. H. Lawrence, Gertrude Stein, Naomi Mitchison and Bessie Head. She is currently at work on a project on contemplative pedagogy, linking meditation practices with modernist representations of consciousness.

EMILY V. THORNBURY is currently Associate Professor of English at Yale University, USA, specialising in Old English and Anglo-Latin poetry and poetics. Her first book, *Becoming a Poet in Anglo-Saxon England* (2014), explored pre-Conquest poetry as a fundamentally social practice; her second monograph, *The Virtue of Ornament*, will consider theories of labour and value in early medieval literature and art. Before moving to Yale, she taught at the University of California at Berkeley.

CLARE WALLACE is Associate Professor at the Department of Anglophone Literatures and Cultures at Charles University in Prague, Czech Republic. Her teaching is mainly focused on Irish studies and theatre studies. She is author of *The Theatre of David Greig* (2013) and *Suspect Cultures: Narrative, Identity and Citation in 1990s New Drama* (2006). She has edited a number of books, including *Monologues: Theatre, Performance, Subjectivity* (2008), *Stewart Parker: Television Plays* (2008) and (with Anja Müller) *Cosmotopia: Transnational Identities in David Greig's Theatre* (2011). She is a member of research group British Theatre in the Twenty-First Century: Crisis, Affect, Community, funded by the Spanish Ministry of Economy and Competitiveness and FEDER (European Union). She is also Key Researcher in the European Regional Development Fund project Creativity and Adaptability as Conditions of the Success of Europe in an Interrelated World, which has supported this work.

K. S. WHETTER is Professor of Medieval English at Acadia University, Nova Scotia, Canada, and Past President of the North American Branch of the International Arthurian Society. His principal teaching and research interests are the romance and epic-heroic genres and the medieval Arthurian legend, particularly Malory's *Morte Darthur*. His Arthurian publications include articles in *Arthuriana*, *Arthurian Literature* and *Speculum* as well as the books *The Manuscript and Meaning of Malory's Morte Darthur: Rubrication, Commemoration, Memorialization* (2017), *Understanding Genre and Medieval Romance* (2008), *Re-Viewing Le Morte Darthur:*

Texts and Contexts, Characters and Themes (co-edited with Raluca L. Radulescu; 2005) and *The Arthurian Way of Death: The English Tradition* (co-edited with Karen Cherewatuk; 2009).

ROBERT WILCHER retired as Reader in Early Modern Studies in the English Department at the University of Birmingham, UK, in 2007. In addition to *The Writing of Royalism 1628–1660* (2001), he has published many articles on early modern literature and twentieth-century drama, and books on Andrew Marvell, Arnold Wesker and Sir John Suckling. He is a joint editor of *The Works of Henry Vaughan* (Oxford University Press, 2018) and the author of *Keeping the Ancient Way: Aspects of the Life and Work of Henry Vaughan* (2021). He is an honorary fellow of the Shakespeare Institute.

PAUL WRIGHT is a former assistant dean of the University of Wales Trinity Saint David and now a part-time lecturer in English and creative writing and a bookseller. He has researched and published on British Romanticism and contemporary poetry, and particularly on the connections between science and poetry.

Preface, Volume Outline and Rationale

What do you get if you take the text out of context? A con? Well, perhaps not a confidence trick exactly, but surely some kind of sleight of hand which creates the illusion of something entirely self-contained, whose meanings and significance are magically self-generated without any apparent connection to history and the complex swirling networks of language, culture and society that shape and inform all our lives.

It may be true that, as long as we can understand the language it is written in, a text can appear to be perfectly comprehensible without our knowing too much about the particular historical circumstances out of which it grew and without thinking too much about how our own contexts as active readers might influence the meanings we derive from it. But this apparent autonomy of signification obscures the fact that individual texts in themselves would have no meaning at all without the historically evolved frameworks of language, culture and society that have brought them into being as signifying entities in the first place. It also obscures the individual's crucial 'activation' of meaning in the very process of reading, a process that inevitably has its own contexts and associated frameworks of interpretation.

Whether or not we are consciously aware of it, we are constantly drawing on 'contextual' information to make sense of the many material and symbolic 'texts' around us. In decoding and processing symbolic written texts in particular, we draw from our internalised store of information, knowledge, beliefs, assumptions and understanding about the world. And even if that store of 'ready-made' contextual resources is lacking in some way, we will still, as meaning-making creatures, automatically smooth over any gaps or anomalies to try to make sense of things as best we can – or as best suits us – even if this is based on a sort of creative guesswork. In this way most of us can make reasonably good sense of most of the texts we read, even if they were written at some distance from us, chronologically, geographically or culturally, in times, places or cultures where our grasp of relevant contexts must be largely uncertain. It is here that the sleight of hand I mentioned comes into play most obviously – that is, when we take the text out of context and simply assimilate what we read to our own inner and often unexamined 'map' of the world. And it is here, therefore, where critically contextualised readings of texts such as are presented in this collection can help not only to provide us with richer, fuller contextual understanding of particular texts, but also to sensitise us to all the things *we don't know* we don't know about many of the texts we read and believe we understand. Imagine, for instance, what a reader in thirty years' time might make of these final words from a recent poem by Grace Nichols: '*I can't breathe*' ('Breath', 2020). Most of us today, in 2022, will immediately understand the connotations of these words because of the contexts of the continuing coronavirus pandemic and the brutal police murder of George Floyd in 2020. Detached from these contexts, however, readers in 2052 will probably miss the full significance of the line on first reading (even if, unfortunately, they are still likely to recognise its echoing of the climate emergency). Nichols's poem was written to commemorate the 1977 Battle of Lewisham and would therefore have another specific historical context to be retrieved and explored as well (see www.explore.gold/breath).

There are, in fact, myriad complex ways in which texts depend for their meanings on 'contextual' factors, and this volume's richly diverse collection of essays, spanning the whole of English literary history, seeks to explore and elucidate some of these ways by setting a wide range of texts and contexts in illuminating dialogue with one another. 'Context' may seem to be a simple concept, but this is far from the case, as will be seen, and one aim of this volume is to refine our understanding of how texts and contexts feed off each other by considering some of the many material, institutional and symbolic contexts that have dialogically informed English literature from its beginnings in Anglo-Saxon times through to the globalised present.

Taking in all the main literary genres and considering a balanced mixture of both well-known and lesser-known texts and authors, the essays range variously across social, political, economic, religious, scientific and literary-critical contexts. They engage with many topics and issues of contemporary relevance – such as social crisis and precarity, migration, racial and gender inequalities, and the threat to our environment – and draw on a number of critical fields and perspectives, including anthropology, cultural materialism, ecocriticism, everyday life studies, feminism, genre studies, life writing, New Historicism, postcolonialism and print culture studies.

The volume's emphasis on texts and contexts should be seen as an equal emphasis on both elements; in turn, its overall approach presupposes a view of literature as a form of active social critique where literary texts are seen as shaping contexts as much as they are shaped by them. The dialogue between the two is not always neatly balanced and generally not directly synchronous in time, but one of the most highly valued qualities of literature has always been its ability to hold up a critical mirror to society, and the analysis of this function of texts naturally plays a major role here. Moreover, as already suggested, in looking into the mirror of texts in their own historical periods, many of the essays also refract critical light on facets of our own contemporary society – and this in turn reflects an overarching aspiration of this volume to convey a compelling sense of the always *immediate* relevance of studying English literature in context.

Volume Outline and Rationale

As will become clear, there is an important distinction to be noted between the essays and the book's supplementary study support elements. The essays, that is, have been conceived as contributions to critical scholarship within literary studies and have been written, accordingly, at the levels of sophistication that one would normally expect to find in scholarly journals and other essay anthologies (such as the well-known series of Cambridge Companion volumes, for example). The study support elements, on the other hand, have been conceived and written especially with students (and their teachers) in mind, with the intention of helping students to make the most of the essays and to draw lessons from them in terms of developing their own critical practice. There is no reason why serious students should not find most of the essays in this volume readily accessible – especially if they are read in conjunction with the book's study support elements and, where relevant, with advice and guidance from teachers – but the key point here is that, unlike those study support elements, the essays are not written solely for students, but are intended as mainstream scholarly essays for a broad academic audience. The sense in which the essays *are* particularly intended for students, when seen together as an integral part of the whole book, is in the sense of offering students a varied range of models of how criticism is generally conducted within English studies which they can then draw upon in their own evolving essay writing practice.

Following a general introduction, the volume presents thirty-one essays organised, as follows, into seven broad chronological parts and an eighth part on postcolonial literature (whose period span has conventionally been seen as similar to that of the immediately preceding section, though it has roots going back much further in time, as several of the essays in earlier sections here testify):

I   Medieval English, 500–1500
II   The Renaissance, 1485–1660
III   The Restoration and Eighteenth Century, 1660–1780
IV   The Romantic Period, 1780–1832
V   The Victorian Age, 1832–1901
VI   The Twentieth Century, 1901–1939
VII   The Twentieth and Twenty-First Centuries, 1939–2020
VIII Postcolonial Literature in English

The grouping of the essays into these traditional literary periods, along with a final part on postcolonial literature, is partly a matter of convenience as it mirrors the structure of my earlier Cambridge volume, *English Literature in Context* (2nd edn, 2017), and will facilitate cross-referencing between the two books for those who wish to use the two together (for example, to set the focused readings here against the general historical contexts there). However, as suggested above, many of the essays address issues which cut across chronological lines, and it is part of the purpose of the book positively to suggest thematic continuities between the essays and links across the periods they represent. This is not to suggest that there are continuous lines of argument from essay to essay, or any narrowly prescribed set of themes for the book. The essays are unified first and foremost by their common critical concern to explore texts in relation to their contexts – but, as far as subject matter goes, each individual essay can be approached entirely on its own terms, if the reader so wishes. In that respect, the volume should be seen more as a 'miscellany' of critical readings rather than as a strongly themed anthology. Nevertheless, for readers who *do* want to pursue thematic links, there is plenty of scope to do so. To aid in this, each of the eight parts is preceded by an introductory note section which, in addition to introducing the individual essays within that part of the book, specifically draws attention to such links and continuities throughout the volume and suggests some ways in which readers might set essays from different periods in fruitful dialogue with one another.

Beginning students in particular will find it helpful to refer to *English Literature in Context* if they would like to consolidate their knowledge and understanding of the broad historical and cultural backgrounds to English literature which the essays here generally take for granted. I do, however, also signal clearly in my introductory notes where there are especially useful links in the former volume to specific parts or individual essays in the present book.

Each essay is immediately preceded by a short abstract summarising the main focus and argument of the essay. Among other things, it is hoped that this will be a helpful browsing feature for readers who wish to read selectively within what is clearly a large collection. Notes and references are found at the end of each individual essay. After these endnotes, each essay then has its own short supplementary section entitled 'Critical Reflections and Further Study' in which contributors reflect on the development of their essays and offer some questions and suggestions for further thought, research and reading. These sections have been designed with undergraduate students (and their teachers) particularly in mind, and one anticipated use of them is as a stimulus for classroom or seminar discussion following a careful independent reading of the related essay. An additional aim here has been to add a personal dimension to the essays in which contributors can share something of their own development as critical practitioners and thus perhaps 'demystify' the process of academic writing for students a little. It is for this reason that these sections vary somewhat according to the contributor's preferred style of engagement with the reader, although there are some standard features common to them all. For example, no endnotes have been used in these sections and all references are given fully either within the running text or in a further reading list at the end of the piece (although occasionally cross-references to a relevant endnote in the essay itself are given).

Further related aids to study in the volume are provided by the chronology at the start of the book and the three appendices at the end. The chronology presents a selective list of historical and cultural events alongside literary developments and is designed to help readers situate the main subjects of the essays in their broad historical and literary contexts. To help in mapping out the waypoints of the essays within a long history, I have highlighted at first mention any authors who are the principal focus of discussion in an essay, along with the key texts that are discussed. The glossary of critical terms in Appendix A provides short definitions of some of the key terms that appear within the volume. Appendix B presents a study guide for students, exploring the various ways in which they might optimise their learning from the essays and draw on them as models in their own academic practice, especially in their essay writing. In this, the study guide highlights one important ambition of the book as a whole, which, as mentioned earlier, is to offer a convenient source of exemplary contextualised critical readings that can be selectively mapped on to a range of study programmes and used flexibly at a number of levels to enhance and consolidate learning, teaching and research. Appendix C offers two alternative and non-chronological orderings of the essays – one organised according to genre and one according to theme. This offers an additional aid to considering the links and continuities across essays and periods, and, of course, this appendix can also be used in conjunction with the book's index in order to plot analytical routes through the essays.

Despite the large size of this collection, it should go without saying that, even with so many essays, it cannot pretend to cover all relevant aspects of English literary history, nor to deal comprehensively with the mass of topics and issues which that long history has inevitably thrown up. While the book does offer generous coverage of authors, topics, texts and contexts, there are inevitably many gaps and discontinuities in this provisional 'story' of English literature in context – and, of course, all the essays are merely 'essays' (explorative, speculative 'attempts') on their subjects and not the last word. Nevertheless, I sincerely hope that the volume establishes a sufficiently coherent overall narrative to provide a firm basis for those who wish to undertake further critical explorations along similar lines.

Acknowledgements

First and foremost I would like to thank my contributors for their superb scholarship and professionalism in helping me to bring this project to fruition. It has been a great pleasure and privilege to work with such a talented and supportive group of colleagues and I thank them sincerely for their enthusiastic cooperation and encouragement throughout the long process of this volume's development. I am particularly grateful to Terry Gifford and Ulla Rahbek for starting things off at a brisk pace with their early submissions, and to Robert Wilcher for stepping in so helpfully at a relatively late stage in the project. My warm thanks, too, to contributors Anna Budziak, Katie Halsey, Judith Paltin and K. S. Whetter for their extra work in contributing to the book's glossary. I am indebted to Emily Hockley at Cambridge for entrusting me with this project in the first place and for helping to shape and advance it in its early stages. I am also sincerely grateful to several other people at the Press for their invaluable assistance: to Natasha Burton for help during the book's early gestation and then, as its production manager, for steering it smoothly through to publication; to George Laver for his careful administrative work and in helping to finalise the book's images; to Rachel Blaifeder for earlier administrative assistance; to Dino Costi for the excellent index; and to Alex Wright for his good offices in ensuring the book's timely publication. Hilary Hammond, the book's copy-editor, deserves special thanks for her meticulous attention to detail and for her many felicitous suggestions for improving the text. Sincere thanks for their meticulous work are also due to the indefatigable Denesh Shankar and the typesetting team of Integra, India. The anonymous reviewers of the book's original proposal made many very helpful and encouraging comments which helped to advance the project and for which I am extremely grateful; and my thanks, too, for similarly helpful comments, to the anonymous reviewers of the later manuscript. I would like to thank my fellow contributors to the 'parent' volume, *English Literature in Context*, for laying there such an excellent foundation for this book, and I am grateful to them also for various forms of direct support with this project: my warm thanks, then, to Valerie Allen, Andrew Hiscock, Peter Kitson and John Brannigan – and double thanks to Maria Frawley and Lee Morrissey who, I am delighted to say, were also able to contribute essays here. Warm thanks too to Lynne Pearce for long-standing and continuing intellectual and ideological inspiration as well as for her immediate help with this book. For their help, I would also like to thank Lynda Prescott and Helen Wilcox. For, among other things, invaluable technological support, my love and thanks to Emily and Simon and grandchildren Poppy, Oscar and Charlie. For just about everything else, my love and gratitude to my wife, Angie.

Chronology

The following chronology is highly selective and aims simply to provide a point of quick historical reference and literary orientation in relation to the main texts and issues considered in this volume. Most of the works and authors referred to in the essays are included here. The titles of works which feature prominently in the volume are in boldface and the names of authors who feature prominently are in boldface at first mention. The entries in the left-hand column relate primarily, though not exclusively, to British history and culture.

In creating this resource, I have often drawn on the more detailed chronologies to be found in my earlier edited volume *English Literature in Context* (2nd edn, 2017), and I therefore gratefully acknowledge their help in this task of my co-contributors to that volume.

	HISTORY AND CULTURE	LITERATURE
55 BCE–CE 410	Romans in Britain	
449	Bede's date for arrival of Germanic mercenaries to Britain; piecemeal Anglo-Saxon settlement from now	
Late 400s / early 500s		Gildas, *The Ruin of Britain* (L), source for Bede
597	St Augustine brings Roman Christianity (and script) to Kent	
635	St Aidan from Iona founds Lindisfarne monastery, Northumbria	
657–80		'Cædmon's Hymn'
674	Founding of Monkwearmouth monastery, Northumbria, where Bede (672/3–735) was educated as a child before moving to the twin monastery of Jarrow (founded 682)	
c. 678	English Christian missions to the Continent	*Battle of Finnsburgh* Earliest original date for *Beowulf*
c. 698		***Dream of the Rood*** Lindisfarne Gospels (L)
c. 730–50	Ruthwell Cross, Scotland: stone monument with runic inscriptions from *Dream of the Rood*	
731		Bede, *Ecclesiastical History of the English People* (L)
793	Danish invasions begin; Lindisfarne monastery sacked	
800	Charlemagne, Holy Roman Emperor	Approximate date for 'Cynewulf' poems: *Juliana*, *Christ II* (in Exeter Book, c. 950), *Fates of the Apostles*, *Elene* (in Vercelli Book, c. 950) Old English (OE) riddles
871	Alfred the Great, King of Wessex, then of Anglo-Saxons	Possible date of *Andreas*
c. 880	Kingdom of the Anglo-Saxons and boundaries of Danelaw established.	*Anglo-Saxon Chronicle* begun
924	Æthelstan, King of Anglo-Saxons, then of English (927)	
937	Battle of Brunanburh: Æthelstan defeats Norsemen and Scots	*Battle of Brunanburh* recorded as poem in *Anglo-Saxon Chronicle*

Date		
939	Edmund, first king of all England	
c. 950		Exeter Book (–c. 1000), Vercelli Book (containing earliest homilies), Junius manuscript, *Beowulf* manuscript
c. 980	Second wave of Viking invasions (–1066)	
991	Battle of Maldon Danegeld first paid	*Battle of Maldon* composed within twenty years
c. 998		Ælfric, Latin *Grammar* in OE; *Colloquy* (L)
1014		Wulfstan, Archbishop of York, *Sermo Lupi ad Anglos* in OE
1066	Battle of Hastings: William of Normandy defeats Harold	
1086	Domesday land survey completed.	
1096–99	First Crusade (Jerusalem stormed 1099)	
c. 1100		*Chanson de Roland*
c. 1137		Geoffrey of Monmouth, *History of the Kings of Britain* (L): first sustained account of King Arthur
1154	Henry II	OE Peterborough Chronicle ends
1169–71	Invasion of Ireland	
1170	Murder of Thomas Becket	
1177–81		Chrétien de Troyes, *Chevalier au lion* (or *Yvain*)
1189	Richard I	(–1216) Approximate date for *The Owl and the Nightingale*
1199	John I	
1215	Pope Innocent III, Fourth Lateran Council John signs Magna Carta	
1216	Henry III	
c. 1220		*Ancrene Riwle* (or *Ancrene Wisse*)
c. 1230–75		*Roman de la Rose* composed in two stages, from the 1230s by Guillaume de Lorris and by Jean de Meun about forty years later
c. 1250		First English (metrical) romances: *King Horn*, *Floris and Blauncheflur*

	HISTORY AND CULTURE	LITERATURE
1272	Edward I	
1275	First formal meeting of Parliament	Approximate date for English fabliaux, *Dame Sirith*, *Fox and the Wolf*
1282–83	Conquest of Wales by Edward I	
c. 1285	Hereford *Mappa Mundi*	
1290	Jews expelled from England	
c. 1290s?		*Of Arthour and of Merlin* (in Auchinleck manuscript, c. 1330), non-alliterative romance Metrical romances: *Havelok the Dane, Arthour and Merlin, Kyng Alisaunder, Sir Tristrem, Amis and Amiloun*
1296	Edward I invades Scotland; Wars of Scottish Independence ensue	
early–mid 1300s		*Ywayne and Gawayne*
1307	Edward II	
c. 1308–21		Dante, *The Divine Comedy*
1314	Battle of Bannockburn: Robert Bruce defeats English; his kingship of Scotland recognised by Treaty of Northampton, 1328	
1327	Edward III	
c. 1330		Auchinleck manuscript: large miscellany of religious and didactic poetry and including *Sir Orfeo* and several other romances Petrarch, *Il Canzioniere* (–74)
1337	Hundred Years War begins	
c. 1338		Boccaccio, *Il Filostrato*
1340		(–70) fl. Dafydd ap Gwilym, Welsh poet (–41) Boccaccio, *Il Teseida*
1348–50	Black Death widespread; estimated population loss in Britain at 30–50 per cent	Boccaccio, *The Decameron* (–52)
c. 1350	First paper-mill built in England	Romances: *Tale of Gamelyn, Athelston, William of Palerne,* and others

Date	Events	Literary works
1362	English declared official language of law courts	
c. 1365–1400	Jean Froissart, *Chroniques*	William Langland, *Piers Plowman*, A-text (approximate date)
c. 1370–87		Geoffrey Chaucer, *The Book of the Duchess* (1370), *The House of Fame*, **The Parliament of Fowls**, *Troilus and Criseyde*, *The Legend of Good Women*
1377	Richard II accedes, aged 10	Earliest record of York mystery plays; *Piers Plowman*, B-text (approximate date)
1378	Great Schism (–1417): rival popes in Rome and Avignon	
1381	Peasants' Revolt (or Great Revolt)	
1382	Marriage of Richard II to Anne of Bohemia	Complete translation of Bible into Middle English
c. 1386–90		John Gower, *Confessio Amantis*
c. 1387–1400		Geoffrey Chaucer, *Canterbury Tales*
c. 1390		*Piers Plowman*, C-text; Alliterative *Morte Arthure*; (–c. 1425) **The Awntyrs off Arthure**
1390s		*Sir Gawain and the Green Knight*, *Pearl*, *Patience*, *Cleanness*; Vernon manuscript: compilation of earlier vernacular religious works
1399	Richard II deposed and murdered; Henry IV	
c. 1400		*Sir Gawain and the Carle of Carlisle*, *Stanzaic Morte Arthur*
1413	Henry V	
1415	Battle of Agincourt	
1418		(–c. 1509) Paston letters
1422	Henry VI accedes (nine months old)	
c. 1424		James I of Scotland, *Kingis Quair*
1428–29	Joan of Arc lifts siege of Orléans in turning point of Hundred Years War	
1431	English burn Joan of Arc as witch in Rouen	(–38) John Lydgate, *The Fall of Princes*

	HISTORY AND CULTURE	LITERATURE
1430s	Portuguese navigators explore west coast of Africa; enslaved Africans first introduced into Portugal (1434)	Osbern Bokenham, *Legendys of Hooly Wummen*
1445	Jack Cade's rebellion	
1450		
1453	Hundred Years War ends; English retain only Calais. Fall of Constantinople and end of eastern Roman empire	
1455	First book printed in Europe using movable lead type – the 42-line Bible, printed in Mainz, Germany, by Johannes Gutenberg (c. 1400–68)	
1455–85	Wars of the Roses	
c. 1456		William Dunbar (–c. 1513), Scots poet
1461	Edward IV, House of York, made king	
c. 1470		Sir Thomas Malory, *Morte Darthur*
1470–1	Henry VI briefly reinstated; deposed and murdered 1471; Edward IV resumes reign	
1477	William Caxton (c. 1420–91) introduces printing to England	Caxton's printed works include *Reynard the Fox, Canterbury Tales, Order of Chivalry, The Golden Legend, Morte Darthur*
1483	Edward V murdered; Richard III accedes	
1485	Battle of Bosworth Field and death of Richard III. Henry VII accedes	
1487	Cape of Good Hope rounded by Bartholomew Diaz	
1492	Arrival of Columbus in the Caribbean	
1497	Vasco da Gama sails round Africa to India (–99), opening a new trade route to the east	
1501	Amerigo Vespucci voyages to the New World (–02); his later account is basis of name 'America' and of its identification as a separate continent	
1508	Michelangelo begins work on the Sistine Chapel	Scottish poet Gavin Douglas completes translation of *The Aeneid* by Virgil (70–19 BCE)
1508	Henry VIII accedes	Erasmus, *In Praise of Folly*

Year	Event	Works
1510	Spain grants royal charter for trade of enslaved Africans to New World	
1513	Portuguese explorers begin contact with China	Niccolò Machiavelli, *The Prince*; Sir Thomas More, *History of Richard III*
1516	Erasmus's Latin translation of New Testament published in Basle	More, *Utopia* (L); Ludovico Ariosto, *Orlando Furioso*
1517	Martin Luther, *Wittenberg Theses*	
1519	Invasion of Mexico by Cortés and defeat of Aztec empire (–21); Magellan begins his voyage around the world (–22)	
1525		William Tyndale, *New Testament*
1533	English Church separates from Rome, Henry VIII is excommunicated	
1534	Act of Supremacy: Henry becomes head of the Church of England	Rabelais, *Gargantua*
1535	Sir Thomas More and Bishop Fisher executed	First entire translation of Bible in English published by Miles Coverdale, building on work of Tyndale
1536	Union of England and Wales; Dissolution of monasteries begins	
1541	Henry proclaims himself King of Ireland	
1542	James V of Scotland dies, leaving his days-old daughter, Mary, as Queen of Scots	
	Early Tudor propaganda argues for Anglo-Scottish union and invokes concept of an empire of 'Great Britain'; Inquisition established in Rome	
1543	Copernicus, *On the Revolutions of the Heavenly Spheres*	
1545–63	Council of Trent	
1547	Death of Henry VIII; Edward VI	
1549		Book of Common Prayer (principally by Thomas Cranmer)
1550	Giorgio Vasari, *Lives of the Most Excellent Painters, Sculptors and Architects*	
1553	Mary I	
1558	Elizabeth I	

	HISTORY AND CULTURE	LITERATURE
1559	Act of Uniformity to settle the state of the Church in England	John Foxe, *Acts and Monuments of the Christian Church* (Foxe's *Book of Martyrs*) William Baldwin, George Ferrers et al., *Mirror for Magistrates*
1561		Sir Thomas Hoby's translation of Castiglione's *The Courtier* (1528) Jasper Heywood's translation of **Hercules Furens** by Seneca (c. 4 BCE–CE 65)
1562	Privateer Sir John Hawkins leads first British participation in the growing transatlantic slave trade between West Africa and the New World	Thomas Norton and Thomas Sackville, *Gorboduc* first performed (printed 1565)
1564		**William Shakespeare** and Christopher Marlowe born
1567		Arthur Golding's translation of Ovid's *Metamorphoses* (c. CE 8)
1569	Mercator's map of the world published	
1576	The Theatre – first purpose-built playhouse in London	
1577	Sir Francis Drake begins circumnavigation of the globe (–81)	Raphael Holinshed, *The Chronicles of England, Scotland and Ireland* (–78)
1578	Elizabeth I grants royal patent to Sir Humphrey Gilbert allowing for the colonisation of any 'remote, heathen and barbarous lands'	John Lyly, *Euphues: The Anatomy of Wit* **John Florio**, *First Fruites*
1579		Sir Thomas North's translation of Plutarch's *Lives* **Edmund Spenser**, *The Shepherd's Calendar*
1580	Union of Spanish and Portuguese crowns	Torquato Tasso, *Gerusalemme Liberata* Michel de Montaigne, *Essais* I–II John Stow, *The Chronicles of England*
1581		**Thomas Newton (ed.), Seneca: His Tenne Tragedies Translated into English**
1582		Richard Hakluyt, *Diverse Voyages*
1584	Attempted first colonial settlement in America, at Roanoke Island, 'Virginia' (named by Sir Walter Ralegh after Queen Elizabeth I)	Giordano Bruno, *Cena de le Ceneri*
1586		**William Warner, Albions England** (chronicle enlarged in further editions until 1612)

Year		
1587	Execution of Mary, Queen of Scots Pope proclaims crusade against England	Thomas Kyd, *The Spanish Tragedy*, Marlowe, *Tamburlaine* I performed
1588	Spanish Armada defeated	
1589		Hakluyt, *The Principal Navigations, Voyages and Discoveries of the English Nation* Marlowe, *The Jew of Malta* performed George Puttenham, *The Art of English Poesy*
1590		Sir Philip Sidney, *Countess of Pembroke's Arcadia* Spenser, **The Faerie Queene** I–III (IV–VI, 1596)
1591		Sidney, *Astrophil and Stella*
1592		Anon., **Arden of Faversham** Samuel Daniel, *Delia* Marlowe, *Dr Faustus*, Shakespeare, *Comedy of Errors* performed Mary Sidney, *Tragedy of Antony*
1593		Shakespeare, *Richard III* performed Death of Marlowe
1594	Nine Years' War in Ireland (–1603)	Shakespeare, *The Taming of the Shrew* performed
1595	Ralegh sails to South America; on return, publishes *The Discoverie of the Large, Rich and Beautiful Empire of Guiana* (1596)	Daniel, *Civil Wars* Shakespeare, *Richard II* and possibly *Romeo and Juliet* performed Sidney, *An Apology for Poetry* (or *The Defence of Poesy*) Spenser, *Amoretti*
1597	New Poor Law Early opera productions in Europe Dowland, *First Book of Songs*	Francis Bacon, *Essays* Shakespeare, *Henry IV, Part I* performed
1599	Globe theatre built At least 700,000 enslaved Africans in the New World by this time	William Scott, **The Modell of Poesy** Shakespeare, **Henry V**, *Julius Caesar* performed
1600	East India Company chartered	Shakespeare, *Hamlet* written around this time (published 1603)
1603	Death of Elizabeth I. James VI of Scotland accedes to English throne as James I	John Florio, translation of Montaigne's *Essais*
1605	The Gunpowder Plot	Bacon, *The Advancement of Learning* Cervantes, *Don Quixote*, part 1 (part 2, 1615)

	HISTORY AND CULTURE	LITERATURE
1606		Ben Jonson, *Volpone*, Shakespeare, *King Lear*, Cyril Tourneur, *The Revenger's Tragedy* performed
1607	Founding of Jamestown, Virginia, the first permanent British settlement in America	Francis Beaumont and John Fletcher, *The Knight of the Burning Pestle*
1608	East India Company gains trade concessions in India and first trading stations established by 1613 Plantation of Ulster begins	Birth of John Milton
1609		Shakespeare, *Pericles*; *Sonnets* Spenser, *The Faerie Queene* (first complete edition)
1610	Henry Hudson explores seas of Canada Galileo, *The Starry Messenger*	Jonson, *The Alchemist* performed
1611	Authorised Version of the Bible	Chapman, translation of Homer's *Iliad* Shakespeare, *The Tempest* performed
1612		John Webster, *The White Devil* performed
1613		Webster, *The Duchess of Malfi* performed Elizabeth Cary, *Tragedy of Mariam*
1614–15	Transportation of convicts begins from Britain to Virginia as condition of pardon from death sentence	Chapman, translation of Homer's *Odyssey*
1616	Lectures on the circulation of the blood by William Harvey in London	Jonson, *Works* Deaths of Shakespeare and Cervantes
1620	*Mayflower* Pilgrims sail to America	Bacon, *Novum Organum*
1621	John Donne becomes Dean of St Paul's Cathedral	Robert Burton, *The Anatomy of Melancholy* Mary Wroth, *The Countess of Montgomerie's Urania, Part I* Performances of Philip Massinger, *A New Way to Pay Old Debts*; Thomas Middleton, *Women Beware Women*
1623		Shakespeare, *First Folio*
1624	Ascendancy of Cardinal Richelieu in France (–42)	John Donne, *Devotions upon Emergent Occasions*
1625	Charles I	
1629	Charles dissolves Parliament; period of personal rule lasts till 1640	Lancelot Andrewes, *XCVI Sermons*

Date	Event	Literary works
1633		John Ford, *'Tis Pity She's a Whore* George Herbert, *The Temple* Posthumous publication of Donne (d. 1631), *Poems*
1637	Charles's attempt to impose prayer book on Scotland leads to Bishops' Wars Descartes, *Discours de la méthode*	Milton, *Lycidas*
1639–40	English defeated by Scots in two Bishops' Wars	
1640	Parliament recalled; dissolved only in 1660 (the Long Parliament)	
1641	Rebellion in Ireland	
1642	(–49) Civil War between Royalists and Parliamentarians; first (inconclusive) military engagement at the Battle of Edgehill	
1644	Battle of Marston Moor secures North of England for Parliament	Milton, *Areopagitica*
1645	New Model Army established; defeats main Royalist army at Battle of Naseby	
1646		Milton, *Poems* **Henry Vaughan**, *Poems*
1649	Trial and execution of Charles I; abolition of monarchy and England declared a Commonwealth Descartes, *The Passions of the Soul*	
1650	Defeat of Scots at Battle of Dunbar; Cromwell replaces Fairfax as Lord General	Andrew Marvell, 'An Horatian Ode' Vaughan, ***Silex Scintillans*** (enlarged edn, 1655)
1651	Charles II crowned at Scone but defeated at Battle of Worcester Navigations Act: first in series protecting Britain's trade monopoly with its colonies	Marvell, 'Upon Appleton House' Thomas Hobbes, *Leviathan*
1653	Cromwell named Lord Protector	Margaret Cavendish, *Poems and Fancies* Izaak Walton, *The Compleat Angler*
1656		John Bunyan, *Some Gospel-Truths Opened* Sir William D'Avenant, *The Siege of Rhodes* James Harrington, *The Commonwealth of Oceana*

	HISTORY AND CULTURE	LITERATURE
1660	Restoration of Charles II Royal Society founded Theatres reopened	Milton, *A Ready and Easy Way to Establish a Free Commonwealth* John Dryden, *Astraea Redux*
1665	Plague in London	
1666	Great Fire of London	
1667		Dryden, *Annus Mirabilis* Milton, *Paradise Lost*
1670	Hudson's Bay Company chartered by Charles II with rights over huge areas of Canada	
1673	Test Act excludes Catholics from public office Royal Africa Company establishes forts on West African coast, trading in enslaved Africans and gold	
1675		William Wycherely, *The Country Wife*
1676		George Etheredge, *The Man of Mode* performed
1677		**Aphra Behn**, *The Rover* performed
1678	Popish Plot	Bunyan, *Pilgrim's Progress*
1679–81	Exclusion Crisis: Bill of 1679, aimed at Charles II's Roman Catholic heir, James, leads to Charles dissolving Parliament three times in succession	Lucy Hutchinson, *Order and Disorder* (1679) Dryden, *Absalom and Achitophel* (1681)
1684		Behn, *A Voyage to the Isle of Love*
1685	Charles II dies, James II accedes Monmouth's Rebellion	
1688	Glorious Revolution; James II replaced by William and Mary (–1702)	Behn, *Oroonoko*
1689	(–97) King William's War, principally against France but also against Jacobites in Scotland and Ireland seeking restoration of James II; Jacobites effectively defeated by 1691 Toleration Act modifies laws against Dissenters Henry Purcell, *Dido and Aeneas* (opera)	Behn, *The Widow Ranter* performed John Locke, *A Letter Concerning Toleration*

Year		
1690	Battle of the Boyne, Ireland: William defeats James II and Catholic Irish	Locke, *An Essay Concerning Human Understanding*, *Two Treatises of Government*
1694	Bank of England established	
1698		Jeremy Collier, *A Short View of the Immorality and Profaneness of the English Stage*
1700		William Congreve, *The Way of the World* performed
1701	Act of Settlement ensures Protestant (and thus Hanoverian) royal succession	
1702	William dies; Queen Anne accedes / War of the Spanish Succession (–13) involves Britain once more in wide-ranging war with France and Spain	
1704	Battle of Blenheim	Daniel Defoe, *The Review* (–13) / Jonathan Swift, *Tale of A Tub*, *The Battle of the Books*
1707	Act of Union with Scotland	
1709		*The Tatler* (–11)
1711		*The Spectator* (–12) / Alexander Pope, *An Essay on Criticism*
1713	Treaties of Utrecht between Britain and both France and Spain	
1714	Queen Anne dies without male heir; George I accedes	Bernard de Mandeville, *Fable of the Bees* (first published as *The Grumbling Hive*, 1705)
1715	James Stuart, Old Pretender, fails in Jacobite uprising from Scotland	
1717	George Friedrich Handel, *Water Music*	
1718	Transportation Act extends transportation to non-capital offences	
1719		Defoe, *Robinson Crusoe*
1720	South Sea Bubble / Sir Robert Walpole rises to power	Pope, translation of Homer's *Iliad*
1722	Atterbury Plot attempts to restore Jacobites (–23) / Johann Sebastian Bach, *Well-Tempered Clavier* I	Defoe, *Moll Flanders*; *A Journal of the Plague Year*

	HISTORY AND CULTURE	LITERATURE
1724		Defoe, *Roxana*; *A Tour through the Whole Island of Great Britain*
1726		Swift, *Gulliver's Travels*
1727	George II	
1728		Pope, *The Dunciad*; John Gay, *Beggar's Opera* performed
1730	Britain now world's main slave-trading nation: c. 3 million enslaved people will be transported by 1807	Henry Fielding, *Tom Thumb* performed
1731		George Lillo, *The London Merchant* performed
1732	William Hogarth, *The Harlot's Progress*	Covent Garden Theatre opens
1733		Pope, *An Essay on Man* (–34)
1734		Fielding, *Don Quixote in England*
1739–48	Wars of Jenkins' Ear and Austrian Succession, including Anglo-French conflicts in India	
1740		Samuel Richardson, *Pamela*
1742	Walpole loses majority and resigns; Handel, *Messiah*	Fielding, *Joseph Andrews*; Pope, *New Dunciad*
1745	Charles Edward Stuart ('Young Pretender') leads Jacobite Rebellion in Scotland; Hogarth, *Marriage à la Mode*	
1746	Battle of Culloden: Jacobites defeated	William Collins, *Odes*
1747	Hogarth, *Industry and Idleness*	Richardson, *Clarissa* (–48)
1748	Treaty of Aix-la-Chapelle, ends War of Austrian Succession	Tobias Smollett, *Roderick Random*
1749		Fielding, *Tom Jones*
1750	Hogarth, *Beer Street, Gin Lane*	Samuel Johnson, *The Rambler* (–52)
1751	(–72) Denis Diderot et al., *Encyclopédie*	Thomas Gray, *Elegy Written in a Country Church Yard*; Smollett, *Peregrine Pickle*
1752	Benjamin Franklin invents lightning conductor	Fielding, *Amelia*; Charlotte Lennox, *The Female Quixote*

1753	British Museum opens	Richardson, *Sir Charles Grandison* (–54) Smollett, *The Adventures of Ferdinand Count Fathom*
1755		Johnson, *A Dictionary of the English Language* Smollett, translation of *Don Quixote*
1756	(–63) Seven Years' War: Britain allied with Prussia against France, Austria, Russia and, later, Spain, with fighting in Europe, India and the Americas; Britain's victory establishes her naval supremacy and makes her the leading world power	Smollett co-founds *The Critical Review* (–60)
1757	Battle of Plassey: British victory signals beginning of overall British rule in India; Robert Clive becomes Governor of Bengal (–60)	Edmund Burke, *A Philosophical Inquiry into the Origin of Our Ideas of the Sublime and Beautiful*
1758	William Battie, *Treatise on Madness*	Johnson, *Idler* (–60)
1759	Wolfe conquers French Canada (Quebec) for Britain Voltaire, *Candide*	Alexander Gerard, *Essay on Taste* Johnson, *Rasselas* Laurence Sterne begins publishing *Tristram Shandy* (–67)
1760	George III Major rebellion of enslaved people in Jamaica	Anon, *Battle of the Reviews* (satirical pamphlet) Oliver Goldsmith, *The Citizen of the World* (–61) Smollett's *The British Magazine* begins publication (–67); includes serial publication of *The Life and Adventures of Sir Launcelot Greaves* (–61)
1764	Voltaire, *Philosophical Dictionary*	Horace Walpole, **The Castle of Otranto**
1765	Stamp Act imposes direct taxation on New World colonies	Smollett, *Travels in France and Italy*
1768–71	Captain Cook charts coasts of New Zealand, eastern Australia and southern New Guinea; later voyages chart parts of Antarctica (1772–75) and the Pacific coast of America (1776–79)	Sterne, *A Sentimental Journey* (1768)
1771	First edition of *Encyclopaedia Britannica*	Smollett, *The Expedition of Humphrey Clinker* Henry Mackenzie, *The Man of Feeling*
1772	Lord Mansfield, in the Somerset case, rules that enslaved people are free on English soil	Samuel Foote, *The Nabob*

	HISTORY AND CULTURE	LITERATURE
1773	Warren Hastings first Governor-General of India East India Company gains monopoly on Indian opium production and rapidly expands illicit trade to China John Harrison's chronometer wins Longitude Prize	Goldsmith, *She Stoops to Conquer* Phyllis Wheatley (c. 1753–84), *Poems on Various Subjects, Religious and Moral*
1775–83	American War of Independence ends in defeat for Britain and the loss of her thirteen American colonies	
1777	Joseph Priestley, *Disquisitions Relating to Matter and Spirit*	Richard Brinsley Sheridan, *The School for Scandal*
1778	Scottish court rules slavery illegal Founding of Royal Academy Vernacular printing press established in India and publishes a *Grammar of the Bengali Language* by Nathaniel Halhed	Fanny Burney, *Evelina*
1780	Gordon Riots	
1781	The *Zong* massacre: over 130 enslaved people thrown overboard by crew of slave-trade ship *Zong*; ensuing court case adds momentum to abolitionist movement	
1782		Ignatius Sancho (1729–80), *Letters of the Late Ignatius Sancho, an African*
1783	William Pitt the Younger becomes prime minister (PM) and remains in office until 1801	Sophia Lee, *The Recess* (–85)
1784	India Act to regulate East India Company **Sir William Jones** founds Bengal Asiatick Society to promote study of Indian culture	Charlotte Smith, *Elegiac Sonnets*
1785	Hastings returns to Britain, accused of corruption; acquitted after long impeachment trial (1788–95)	William Cowper, *The Task* **Sir Charles Wilkins** translates *Bhagavad Geeta* from Sanskrit Clara Reeve, *The Progress of Romance*
1786	Wolfgang Amadeus Mozart, *The Marriage of Figaro*	William Beckford, *Vathek* Robert Burns, *Poems, Chiefly in the Scottish Dialect*
1787	Society for the Abolition of the Slave Trade founded 'Am I Not a Man and a Brother', anti-slavery medallion by Josiah Wedgwood with image of kneeling black man in chains, arms raised in appeal (see 2016, 'taking the knee')	Ottobah Cugoanoa, *Thoughts and Sentiments on the Evil and Wicked Commerce of the Human Species* Jones, 'The Enchanted Fruit; or the Hindu Wife'

Year	Historical events	Literary works
1788	First British settlement at Botany Bay, Australia The African Association established to promote exploration of Africa *The Times*	
1789	Wilberforce introduces twelve resolutions against the slave trade French Revolution begins	William Blake, *Songs of Innocence* Olaudah Equiano, *The Interesting Narrative of the Life of Olaudah Equiano, or Gustavus Vassa, the African,* Jones translates Indian drama, *Shakuntala*, by Kalidasa
1790	Edmund Burke, *Reflections on the Revolution in France* Immanuel Kant, *Critique of Judgement*	**Ann Radcliffe**, *Sicilian Romance* Joanna Baillie, *Poems*
1791	Thomas Paine, *Rights of Man*, part 1 (part 2, 1792) Haitian Revolution (–1804), led by Pierre Toussaint L'Ouverture Galvani publishes results of electrical experiments with frogs' legs	Erasmus Darwin, *The Botanic Garden* Mary Robinson, *Poems* (–93)
1792	French Republic declared London Corresponding Society formed Commons resolves on gradual abolition of slavery by 1796 Baptist Missionary Society founded	William Gilpin, *Essay on Picturesque Beauty* Smith, *Desmond* Mary Wollstonecraft, *A Vindication of the Rights of Woman*
1793	Execution of Louis XVI and French Terror French Revolutionary Wars begin (–1802)	Blake, *America*; *Visions of the Daughters of Albion* Reeve, *The Memoirs of Roger de Clarendon* William Wordsworth, *Descriptive Sketches*; *An Evening Walk*
1794	Habeas corpus suspended Execution of Robespierre	Blake, *Songs of Innocence and of Experience* William Godwin, *Caleb Williams* Radcliffe, **The Mysteries of Udolpho**
1795	Treasonable Practices and Seditious Meetings Acts Britain siezes Dutch Cape Colony in South Africa British navy introduces lime juice to combat scurvy James Hutton, *Theory of the Earth*	Maria Edgeworth, *Letters for Literary Ladies* Hannah More, *Cheap Repository Tracts*
1796	Edward Jenner develops vaccination against smallpox Turner's first oil paintings exhibited	Beckford, *Modern Novel Writing* Burney, *Camilla* S. T. Coleridge, *Poems on Various Subjects* Elizabeth Hamilton, *Translation of the Letters of a Hindoo Rajah* Matthew Lewis, *The Monk*

	HISTORY AND CULTURE	LITERATURE
1797	Bank Restriction Act (–1821) Invasion scares Naval mutinies at Spithead and Nore	Radcliffe, *The Italian*
1798	Irish rebellion suppressed Thomas Malthus, *Essay on the Principle of Population* Joseph Haydn, *The Creation*	Coleridge, *Fears in Solitude*; *France: An Ode*; *Frost at Midnight* F. C. Patrick, *More Ghosts!* More, *Strictures on the Modern System of Female Education* Wordsworth and Coleridge, *Lyrical Ballads*
1799	Six Acts against radical activities Introduction of income tax Victory over French-backed Tipu Sultan of Mysore gives Britain control over most of south and west India	Lewis, *Tales of Terror* Anna Seward, *Original Sonnets* Wordsworth, *Two-Part Prelude* (manuscript)
1800	Baptist Mission at Serampore, India, establishes printing press; soon prints translations of Bible and grammars and dictionaries in several Indian languages Volta generates electricity Beethoven, First Symphony	Edgeworth, *Castle Rackrent*
1801	Act of Union with Ireland Pitt resigns; Henry Addington PM First census of England and Wales Thomas Jefferson elected US president	Robert Southey, *Thalaba the Destroyer*
1802	Peace of Amiens William Paley, *Natural Theology*	*Edinburgh Review* founded Walter Scott, *Minstrelsy of the Scottish Border* (–03)
1803	Napoleonic Wars begin (–15) Richard Trevithick builds first working railway steam engine	Thomas Chatterton, *Collected Works* Jane Porter, *Thaddeus of Warsaw*
1804	Pitt returns as PM Napoleon crowned Emperor	Blake, *Milton* Hamilton, *Memoirs of the Life of Agrippina, Wife of Germanicus*
1805	Battle of Trafalgar; death of Nelson Richard Payne Knight, *Principles of Taste*	Scott, *Lay of the Last Minstrel* Wordsworth, *The Prelude* completed Mary Tighe, *Psyche; or, The Legend of Love*

Year	Events	Literary works
1806	Death of Pitt	Robinson, *Poetical Works*
1807	Act passed abolishing the slave trade in British colonies Geological Society founded	Charles and Mary Lamb, *Tales from Shakespeare* Thomas Moore, *Irish Melodies* Wordsworth, *Poems in Two Volumes*
1808	Peninsular War begins Adam Dalton, *New System of Chemical Philosophy*	Scott, *Marmion* Felicia Hemans, *England and Spain*
1809	First use of gas-lighting in central London	More, *Coelebs in Search of a Wife* *Quarterly Review* founded
1810	George III suffers mental breakdown	George Crabbe, *The Borough* Porter, **The Scottish Chiefs** Scott, *The Lady of the Lake* Southey, *The Curse of Kehama*
1811	Prince of Wales becomes Regent Luddite Riots Charles Bell, *Idea of a New Anatomy of the Brain*	**Jane Austen**, *Sense and Sensibility* Sydney Owenson, *The Missionary: An Indian Tale* Percy Shelley, *The Necessity of Atheism*
1812	Assassination of PM Spencer Perceval Napoleon invades Russia War between Britain and America Elgin marbles arrive in London	Anna Laetitia Barbauld, *Eighteen Hundred and Eleven* **Lord Byron**, *Childe Harold's Pilgrimage* I and II Crabbe, *Tales* Jane West, *The Loyalists*
1813	Execution of Luddite leaders Napoleon loses Battle of Leipzig	Austen, *Pride and Prejudice* Eaton Stannard Barrett, *The Heroine; or, Adventures of a Fair Romance Reader* Byron, ***The Giaour; The Bride of Abydos*** Shelley, *Queen Mab*
1814	Napoleon defeated, exiled to Elba Robert Stephenson builds steam locomotive	Austen, *Mansfield Park* Byron, *The Corsair* Scott, **Waverley** Wordsworth, *The Excursion*

	HISTORY AND CULTURE	LITERATURE
1815	Napoleon escapes to raise army again; finally defeated at Battle of Waterloo; Congress of Vienna peace treaty	Byron, *Hebrew Melodies*
		John Jea, *The Life, History, and Unparalleled Sufferings of John Jea*
	Corn Law passed	Thomas Love Peacock, *Headlong Hall*
	From now to 1914, c. 21.5 million Britons will emigrate to the colonies	Scott, *Guy Mannering*
	Humphry Davy's miners' safety lamp	Wordsworth, *Poems*
	First major Chinese–English dictionary (6 vols) by Robert Morrison of the London Missionary Society	
1816	Severe economic depression	Austen, *Emma*
	Spa Field Riots	Byron, *Childe Harold's Pilgrimage III*
	Gold Standard introduced	Coleridge, *Kubla Khan*
	William Cobbett, *Political Register*	Scott, *The Antiquary*
1817	Habeas Corpus suspended	*Blackwood's Edinburgh Magazine*
	Manchester 'Blanketeers' march to London	Byron, *Manfred*
	Pentrich armed uprising, Derbyshire	Coleridge, *Sibylline Leaves; Biographia Literaria*
	David Ricardo, *Principles of Political Economy*	William Hazlitt, *Characters of Shakespeare's Plays*
		John Keats, *Poems*
		Thomas Moore, *Lalla Rookh*
		Porter, *The Pastor's Fireside*
		Southey, *Wat Tyler*
1818	Habeas corpus restored	Austen, *Northanger Abbey; Persuasion*
	Defeat of Sir Francis Burdett's motion for parliamentary reform	Byron, *Beppo; Childe Harold's Pilgrimage IV*
		Keats, *Endymion*
		Charles Lamb, *Works*
		Scott, *Rob Roy*
		Mary Shelley, *Frankenstein*
1819	Peterloo Massacre, Manchester	Byron, *Don Juan I and II*
	Six Acts	Scott, *Ivanhoe; The Bride of Lammermoor*
	Factory Act	Shelley, *The Mask of Anarchy*
	William Lawrence, *Lectures on Physiology, Zoology and the Natural History of Man*	Wordsworth, *Peter Bell; The Wagoner*
	Schubert, *The Trout Quintet*	

1820	George IV Cato Street Conspiracy Hans Christian Oersted discovers electromagnetism Royal Astronomical Society founded *London Magazine* (–29)	John Clare, *Poems Descriptive of Rural Life* Keats, *Lamia and Isabella; The Eve of St Agnes and other Poems* Lamb, 'Elia' essays in *London Magazine* (–23) Charles Robert Maturin, *Melmoth the Wanderer* Shelley, *Prometheus Unbound*
1821	Greek War of Independence	Baillie, *Metrical Legends* Byron, *Cain; Sardanapalus; Don Juan III–V* Clare, *The Village Minstrel* **Thomas De Quincey, *Confessions of an English Opium-Eater*** Shelley, *Adonais; Epipsychidion*
1822	Royal Academy of Music founded	Byron, *The Vision of Judgement* Hemans, *Welsh Melodies* Shelley, *Hellas* Wordsworth, *Ecclesiastical Sketches*
1823	Anti-Slavery Society founded Royal Asiatick Society of Great Britain and Ireland meets Mechanics Institute founded *The Lancet* appears	Byron, *The Age of Bronze; The Island; Don Juan VI–XIV* Lamb, **'Old China'** Mary Shelley, *Valperga*
1824	Repeal of Combination Act gives trade unions right to exist (–26) Britain defeats Burma (Myanmar) in war and annexes Assam Royal Society for the Prevention of Cruelty to Animals founded National Gallery founded	Byron, *Don Juan XV–XVI* James Hogg, *Confessions of a Justified Sinner* Scott, *Redgauntlet* Robert Wedderburn, *The Horrors of Slavery*
1825	Stockton–Darlington Railway opens	Hazlitt, *The Spirit of the Age*
1826	London Zoological Society founded	Scott, *Woodstock* Mary Shelley, *The Last Man*
1827	University of London founded	Clare, *The Shepherd's Calendar*
1828	Repeal of Test and Corporation Acts Schubert, Ninth Symphony	Hemans, *Records of Woman*
1829	Catholic Emancipation Act Robert Peel creates Metropolitan police force	Hogg, *The Shepherd's Calendar*

	HISTORY AND CULTURE	LITERATURE
1830	William IV Earl Grey's Whig reforming government 'Captain Swing' rural riots Cobbett, *Rural Rides* Opening of Manchester–Liverpool Railway Royal Geographical Society founded, influential in promoting exploration of Africa John Hershel, *Preliminary Discourse on the Study of Natural Philosophy* Charles Lyell, *Principles of Geology* vol. I	Hemans, *Songs of the Affections* Alfred Tennyson, *Poems, Chiefly Lyrical*
1831	(–32) First major cholera outbreak in Britain (further epidemics, 1848–49, 1853–54, 1866) (–32) 'Baptist War' rebellion of enslaved people in Jamaica Michael Faraday discovers electromagnetic induction Voyage of *Beagle* begins (–36)	Ebenezer Elliot, *Corn-Law Rhymes* Peacock, *Crotchet Castle* Mary Prince, *The History of Mary Prince, a West Indian Slave*
1832	Great Reform Act Morse invents the telegraph	Tennyson, *Poems*
1833	Abolition of Slavery Act (enacted in British Empire, 1834); alternative indentured labour from India begins Factory Reform Act	Thomas Carlyle, *Sartor Resartus* (–34) First of John Henry Newman's *Tracts for the Times*
1834	Poor Law Amendment Act	
1835	Macaulay's Minute on Education establishes English as India's official language for government and education	
1836		Charles Dickens, *Sketches by Boz; The Pickwick Papers* (–37)
1837	Victoria becomes queen Smallpox epidemic Brunel, Great Western Railway	Carlyle, *The French Revolution*; Dickens, *Oliver Twist* (–38)
1838	People's Charter Anti-Corn Law League	Dickens, *Nicholas Nickleby* (–39)
1839	(–42) First Opium War with China and first Afghan War Sarah Stickney Ellis, *The Women of England: Their Social Duties and Domestic Habits*	Carlyle, *Chartism* Charles Darwin, *The Voyage of the Beagle* Edgar Allan Poe, 'The Fall of the House of Usher'

Year	Events	Literature and the arts
1840	Victoria marries Albert Penny post established J. M. W. Turner, *The Slave Ship* (based on the *Zong*; see 1781)	Dickens, *The Old Curiosity Shop* Frances Trollope, *Michael Armstrong, Factory Boy*
1841	Robert Peel becomes PM David Livingstone's first expedition to Africa *Punch* begins	Robert Browning, *Pippa Passes* Carlyle, *On Heroes* Dickens, *Barnaby Rudge*
1842	Poor Law renewed Copyright Act Mudie's Lending Library opens Edwin Chadwick, *Report on the Sanitary Condition of the Labouring Population* *Illustrated London News* begins	Browning, *Dramatic Lyrics* Tennyson, *Poems* (2 vols)
1843	Theatre Regulation Act	Carlyle, *Past and Present* Dickens, *A Christmas Carol* John Ruskin, *Modern Painters* (vol. 1) Wordsworth named Poet Laureate
1844	Factory Act limits working hours for women and children Railway mania begins Robert Chambers, *Vestiges of the Natural History of Creation* J. M. W. Turner, *Rain, Steam and Speed – the Great Western Railway*	Benjamin Disraeli, *Coningsby, or The New Generation* G. W. M. Reynold, *Mysteries of London* (–48)
1845	Irish potato famine begins (–50)	Disraeli, *Sybil, or The Two Nations* Edward Lear, *Book of Nonsense*
1846	Corn Laws repealed	
1847	Ten Hours' Factory Act	**Charlotte Brontë**, *Jane Eyre* Emily Brontë, *Wuthering Heights* Anne Brontë, *Agnes Grey* W. M. Thackeray, *Vanity Fair* (–48)
1848	Chartist rebellion Public Health Act Pre-Raphaelite Brotherhood founded Marx and Engels, *Communist Manifesto*	Elizabeth Gaskell, *Mary Barton*

	HISTORY AND CULTURE	LITERATURE
1849	Henry Mayhew, *London Labour and the London Poor* series begins in *Morning Chronicle* Bedford College for Women founded	Dickens, *David Copperfield* (–50)
1850	Public Libraries Act Dickens starts *Household Words* (–59)	Elizabeth Barrett Browning, *Sonnets from the Portuguese* Charlotte Brontë, *Shirley* Charles Kingsley, *Alton Locke* Tennyson, **In Memoriam**
1851	Great Exhibition at the Crystal Palace Harriet Taylor Mill, *The Enfranchisement of Women*	Gaskell, *Cranford*
1852		Dickens, *Bleak House* (–53)
1853	(–56) Crimean War	Matthew Arnold, *Poems* Charlotte Brontë, *Villette*
1854		Coventry Patmore, **The Angel in the House** Dickens, *Hard Times* Gaskell, *North and South* (–55)
1855	Repeal of stamp duty on newspapers *Daily Telegraph* begins	Browning, *Men and Women* Dickens, *Little Dorrit* (–57) Gaskell, *The Life of Charlotte Brontë*
1856	(–60) Second Opium War	Barrett Browning, *Aurora Leigh*
1857	Indian Rebellion (–58) Divorce and Matrimonial Causes Act Social Science Association founded David Livingstone, *Missionary Travels and Researches In South Africa*	George Eliot, *Scenes of Clerical Life* Thomas Hughes, *Tom Brown's Schooldays* Mary Seacole, *The Wonderful Adventures of Mary Seacole in Many Lands* Anthony Trollope, *Barchester Towers*
1858	India Act abolishes East India Company and places India under direct crown rule *English Woman's Journal*	Robert Ballantyne, *Coral Island* Dion Boucicault, *Jessie Brown; or, The Relief of Lucknow*
1859	Darwin, *On the Origin of Species* Dickens, *All the Year Round* John Stuart Mill, *On Liberty* Samuel Smiles, *Self-Help*	Wilkie Collins, *The Woman in White* Eliot, *Adam Bede* Dickens, *A Tale of Two Cities*

Year	Events	Literature
1860	*Cornhill Magazine*	Eliot, *The Mill on the Floss* Dickens, **Great Expectations** (–61)
1861	Death of Prince Albert Isabella Beeton, *Book of Household Management*	Eliot, *Silas Marner* Mrs Henry Wood, *East Lynne*
1862		George Meredith, **Modern Love** Christina Rossetti, 'Goblin Market' Tennyson, *Idylls of the King*
1863	Charles Lyell, *Antiquity of Man* Thomas Henry Huxley, *Man's Place in Nature*	Kingsley, *The Water-Babies* Thackeray, *The Roundabout Papers*
1864	First Contagious Diseases Act	John Henry Newman, *Apologia Pro Vita Sua* Dickens, *Our Mutual Friend* (–65) **Sheridan Le Fanu**, *Uncle Silas*
1865	Women's Suffrage Campaign Joseph Lister establishes antiseptic surgery Transatlantic cable laid St Pancras railway station completed	Arnold, *Essays in Criticism* (1st series) Lewis Carroll, *Alice in Wonderland* Meredith, *Rhoda Fleming*
1866		Eliot, *Felix Holt, the Radical* Ruskin, *The Crown of Wild Olives* Algernon Charles Swinburne, *Poems and Ballads*
1867	Second Reform Act Fenian Rising in Ireland Canada becomes self-governing Dominion Marx, *Das Kapital* (–83)	Trollope, *Last Chronicle of Barset*
1868	Disraeli, PM (Feb.) Gladstone, PM (Dec.) Huxley, *On the Physical Basis of Life*	Browning, *The Ring and the Book* (–69) Collins, *The Moonstone*
1869	Suez Canal opens Diamond rush in South Africa Girton College, Cambridge founded John Stuart Mill, *The Subjection of Women* *The Graphic* founded	Arnold, *Culture and Anarchy* R. D. Blackmore, *Lorna Doone* Leo Tolstoy, *War and Peace*

	HISTORY AND CULTURE	LITERATURE
1870	First Married Women's Property Act (further Acts, 1882, 1884) Forster's Education Act Herbert Spencer, *Principles of Psychology* British trading vessels sail up the Niger	Dickens, *The Mystery of Edwin Drood*
1871	Trade Union Act Darwin, *The Descent of Man* Stanley meets Livingstone	Eliot, *Middlemarch* (–72) Le Fanu, **Carmilla** (–72, serial; then in *In a Glass Darkly* (1872))
1874	Disraeli, PM British colony of Gold Coast formed Claude Monet, *Impression, Sunrise*	Thomas Hardy, *Far From the Madding Crowd* James Thomson, 'The City of Dreadful Night'
1876	Telephone invented	Eliot, *Daniel Deronda*
1877	Queen Victoria named Empress of India Britain annexes the Transvaal	Harriet Martineau, *Autobiography*
1878	Gilbert and Sullivan, *HMS Pinafore*	Hardy, *The Return of the Native*
1879	Britain invades Zululand Second Afghan War (–81) Electric light bulb invented	Browning, *Dramatic Idylls* Meredith, *The Egoist* Henrik Ibsen, *A Doll's House*
1880	Gladstone, PM First Anglo-Boer War (–81) London University admits women to degrees	Eliot, *Daniel Deronda*
1881	'The scramble for Africa' begins as European powers compete for new colonial territories	Henry James, *Portrait of a Lady* Arthur O'Shaughnessy, *Songs of a Worker* (incl. 'The Line of Beauty') Robert Louis Stevenson, *Treasure Island* (–82)
1882	Britain invades Egypt	
1883	Maxim invents machine gun	Olive Schreiner, *The Story of an African Farm*
1884	Third Reform Act (–85) Berlin Conference, to agree rules on European territorial claims in Africa Fabian Society founded Robert Koch describes cholera bacillus	

Year	Events	Literature
1885	Founding of the Indian National Congress	Rider Haggard, *King Solomon's Mines*
1886	Repeal of Contagious Diseases Acts Gold rush in Transvaal	Hardy, *The Mayor of Casterbridge* Stevenson, *Dr Jekyll and Mr Hyde*
1887	Queen Victoria's golden jubilee British South Africa Company founded by Cecil Rhodes Friedrich Nietzsche, *The Genealogy of Morals*	Arthur Conan Doyle, *A Study in Scarlet* Haggard, *Allan Quatermain* May Kendall, *Dreams to Sell* Constance Naden, *A Modern Apostle* (includes 'Evolutional Erotics')
1888	Arts and Crafts Exhibition Society 'Jack the Ripper' murders in London	Hardy, *Wessex Tales* Rudyard Kipling, *Plain Tales from the Hills* Mary Augusta Ward, *Robert Elsmere*
1889		Mathilde Blind, *The Ascent of Man* George Gissing, **The Nether World** Amy Levy, *A London Plane and Other Verses*
1890	First underground railway in London Moving-picture shows appear Rhodes's 'Pioneer Column' invades Mashonaland in Southern Rhodesia William Booth, *In Darkest England and the Way Out* William James, *Principles of Psychology*	Sir James Frazer, *The Golden Bough* begins publication (–1915) William Morris, *News from Nowhere* Oscar Wilde, *The Picture of Dorian Gray*
1891	William Morris, Kelmscott Press	Ella D'Arcy, 'The Smile' Gissing, *New Grub Street* John Oliver Hobbes (Pearl Richards), *Some Emotions and a Moral* Dollie Radford, *A Light Load*
1893	Independent Labour Party formed British forces conquer whole of Southern Rhodesia Britain annexes Yorubaland, Nigeria Gandhi in South Africa (–1915), campaigning against racism and segregation, develops principles of civil disobedience Women gain the vote in New Zealand	Gissing, **The Odd Women** George Bernard Shaw, *Mrs Warren's Profession* (first produced 1902) Wilde, *A Woman of No Importance*
1894	*Yellow Book* first published	Hobbes, *A Sinner's Comedy* Edith Nesbit, **'Miss Lorrimore's Career'** Charlotte Mew, **'Passed'** (in *Yellow Book*)

	HISTORY AND CULTURE	LITERATURE
1895	Oscar Wilde imprisoned for homosexuality	Hardy, *Jude the Obscure* Radford, *Songs and Other Verses* Wilde, *The Importance of Being Earnest*; *An Ideal Husband*
1897	Queen Victoria's diamond jubilee British troops invade Benin, looting its bronze treasures	Mona Caird, *The Morality of Marriage* Mary Kingsley, *Travels in West Africa* Bram Stoker, *Dracula*
1898	British force led by Kitchener defeats Mahdist regime in Sudan and establishes Anglo-Egyptian condominium (–1956) Britain forces granting of lease for strategic port of Weihaiwei in China	Hardy, *Wesser Poems*
1899	(–1902) Second Anglo-Boer War First petrol motor bus in London First wireless transmission across the English Channel Magnetic (tape) recording invented William James, *Talks on Psychology*	Henrik Ibsen, *When We Dead Awaken* Arthur Symons, *The Symbolist Movement in Literature* H. G. Wells, *Tales of Space and Time* W. B. Yeats, *The Wind among the Reeds* Irish Literary Theatre founded
1900	Conservative government re-elected Relief of Mafeking (Boer War) Northern and Southern Nigeria established as British protectorates Max Planck's quantum theory Sigmund Freud, *The Interpretation of Dreams* *Daily Express*	Joseph Conrad, *Lord Jim* Wells, *Love and Mr Lewisham*
1901	Death of Queen Victoria; Edward VII accedes Funeral of Queen Victoria filmed B. S. Rowntree's *Poverty: A Study of Town Life* Federation of Australia established Marconi's first transatlantic radio communication	Hardy, *Poems of the Past and Present* (–02) Kipling, *Kim* Thomas Mann, *Buddenbrooks* Shaw, *Three Plays for Puritans* Wells, *The First Men in the Moon*
1902	Treaty of Vereeniging ends Boer War Balfour Education Act establishes state system of secondary schools Midwives Act Georges Méliès, *Voyage to the Moon* (film) First recordings by Enrico Caruso	Arnold Bennett, *Anna of the Five Towns* Conrad, *Heart of Darkness* Doyle, *The Hound of the Baskervilles* Kipling, *Just So Stories* *Times Literary Supplement* Yeats, *Cathleen ni Houlihan*

Year		
1903	Workers' Educational Association founded Women's Social and Political Union (WSPU) founded *Daily Mirror* Wright brothers make first powered flight (–04) British forces invade Tibet	Samuel Butler, *The Way of All Flesh* Erskine Childers, *The Riddle of the Sands* Conrad, *Typhoon* James, *The Ambassadors* Shaw, *Man and Superman*
1904	Entente Cordiale between Britain and France 8,465 cars licensed in Britain Manchester Empire is first large music hall to be used as cinema Ernest Rutherford, *Radioactivity* Thorstein Veblen, *The Theory of Business Enterprise* Die Brücke, Dresden group of expressionist artists Building of Panama Canal begins (–14)	Abbey Theatre, Dublin, founded J. M. Barrie, *Peter Pan* Conrad, *Nostromo* James, *The Golden Bowl* J. M. Synge, *Riders to the Sea*
1905	Suffragette agitation begins Unemployed Workmen Act Aliens Act restricts immigration Sinn Féin founded; Ulster Unionist Council formed Swadeshi ('home-produced') movement begins in India Russo-Japanese War Albert Einstein's special theory of relativity	Doyle, *The Return of Sherlock Holmes* E. M. Forster, *Where Angels Fear to Tread* Shaw, *Major Barbara* Wells, *Kipps* Wilde, *De Profundis*
1906	Liberal landslide in general election; 29 Labour MPs elected and Labour Party constituted Education (Provision of Meals) Act HMS *Dreadnought*, world's largest battleship, launched Founding of Muslim League in India	Walter de la Mare, *Poems* Everyman's Library series begins John Galsworthy, *The Man of Property* performed William Le Queux, *The Invasion of 1910* Nesbit, *The Railway Children* Yeats, *Poetical Works*
1907	Education Act allows for medical inspections in schools Qualification of Women Act allows women to stand for local councils Pablo Picasso, *Les Demoiselles d'Avignon*, introduces cubism Henri Bergson, *Creative Evolution*	Ethel Carnie Holdsworth, *Rhymes from the Factory* Conrad, *The Secret Agent* Forster, *The Longest Journey* Edmund Gosse, *Father and Son* James Joyce, *Chamber Music* *The New Age*, ed. A. R. Orage Synge, *The Playboy of the Western World*

	HISTORY AND CULTURE	LITERATURE
1908	Old Age Pensions Act introduces state pensions for over seventies Children's Act (to tackle negligence) Unemployed hunger march Ford's Model T car sold in Britain Pathé's first regular newsreel First aeroplane flight in Britain Edward Carpenter, *The Intermediate Sex*	Bennett, *The Old Wives' Tale* W. H. Davies, *Autobiography of a Super-Tramp* Ford Madox Ford founds *The English Review* Forster, *A Room with a View* Wells, *The War in the Air*
1909	Lloyd George's 'People's Budget' C. F. G. Masterman, *The Condition of England* Louis Blériot flies across English Channel North Pole reached by Robert Peary F. T. Marinetti, first Futurist manifesto	Galsworthy, *Strife* Hardy, *Time's Laughingstocks* Ezra Pound, *Personae* Wells, *Ann Veronica; Tono-Bungay*
1910	George V Liberals re-elected to minority governments in two general elections; Labour wins forty seats Hunger strike of Suffragettes in prison South Wales miners' strike South Africa becomes dominion First Post-Impressionist exhibition in London Freud, *On Psychoanalysis* Scott's Antarctic expedition (–12)	Bennett, *Clayhanger* Forster, *Howards End* Galsworthy, *Justice* Wells, *The History of Mr Polly* Yeats, *The Green Helmet*
1911	Strike of rail workers and London dockers National Insurance Act (provision for sickness and unemployment) Parliament Act removes Lords' veto Model T Ford assembly plant opens in Manchester Roald Amundsen reaches South Pole Franz Boas, *Primitive Mythology* Der Blaue Reiter, Munich group of Expressionist artists	Bennett, *Hilda Lessways* Rupert Brooke, *Poems* Conrad, *Under Western Eyes* D. H. Lawrence, *The White Peacock* Katherine Mansfield, *In a German Pension* Wells, *The New Machiavelli*

Year	Events	Works
1912	Widespread strikes in Britain Irish Home Rule Bill and ensuing Ulster crisis Women's Franchise Bill rejected; suffragettes riot in London *Titanic* sinks on maiden voyage *Daily Herald*, 'The Labour Daily Newspaper' Harriet Quimby flies across English Channel c. 400 cinemas in London African National Congress (ANC) founded in South Africa	Robert Bridges, *Poetical Works* de la Mare, *The Listeners* Lawrence, *The Trespasser* Mann, *Death in Venice* Edward Marsh (ed.), *Georgian Poetry* *Poetry: A Magazine of Verse* (Chicago) *Poetry Review* (London) Pound, *Ripostes*
1913	Triple Alliance of rail, transport and miners' unions Ulster Volunteer Force formed Suffragette Emily Davison dies after throwing herself under horse at Epsom Derby Freud, *Totem and Taboo* and *Interpretation of Dreams* (1900) first translated into English Igor Stravinsky, *The Rite of Spring*	Carnie Holdsworth, *Miss Nobody* Lawrence, *Sons and Lovers*; *Love Poems* Compton Mackenzie, *Sinister Street* Marcel Proust, *A la recherche du temps perdu* (*Remembrance of Things Past*), first of seven volumes (–27)
1914	Home Rule Act passed but then suspended because of war Suffragette riots in London First World War begins (28 June) Germans bomb Yorkshire coast	*The Egoist* (formerly, *The New Freewoman*) Wyndham Lewis (ed.), *Blast: A Review of the Great English Vortex* Hardy, *Satires of Circumstance* Joyce, *Dubliners* Pound, *Des Imagistes*
1915	'Shells Scandal' and collapse of Liberal administration: coalition government formed under Herbert Asquith War intensifies with huge losses on all fronts, including Gallipoli campaign; poison gas used for first time at Second Battle of Ypres; Zeppelin attacks on London German submarine blockade of Britain lifted after sinking of passenger liner, *Lusitania* Gandhi returns to India and begins to advocate for home rule ('swaraj') Einstein's general theory of relativity	Richard Aldington, *Images* Bennett, *These Twain* Brooke, *1914 and Other Poems* John Buchan, *The Thirty-Nine Steps* Ford, *The Good Soldier* Franz Kafka, *Metamorphosis* Lawrence, *The Rainbow* Amy Lowell (ed.), *Some Imagist Poets: An Anthology* Dorothy Richardson, *Pointed Roofs*, first in thirteen-novel sequence *Pilgrimage* (–38; thirteenth posthumous, 1967) **Virginia Woolf**, *The Voyage Out*

	HISTORY AND CULTURE	LITERATURE
1916	David Lloyd George forms second coalition government Conscription introduced Battle of the Somme kills over 1 million; theories of shell shock develop from treatment of casualties Easter Rising in Dublin suppressed; 450 killed; leaders executed Dada art movement launched in Zurich Carl Jung, *Psychology of the Unconscious*	Hardy, *Selected Poems* H. D. (Hilda Doolittle), *Sea Garden* Joyce, *A Portrait of the Artist as a Young Man* Lawrence, *Twilight in Italy* Charlotte Mew, *The Farmer's Bride* Shaw, *Pygmalion*
1917	USA enters the war Russian Revolution Third Battle of Ypres (Passchendaele) Freud, *Introduction to Psychoanalysis*	Carnie Holdsworth, *Helen of Four Gates* (film adaptation, 1920, dir. Cecil Hepworth) T. S. Eliot, *Prufrock and Other Observations* Edward Thomas, *Poems* Yeats, *The Wild Swans at Coole*
1918	First World War ends (11 November) Influenza pandemic kills over 21 million worldwide by 1920 4th Reform Bill gives vote to all men over 21 and women over 30 Ministry of Health established Maternity and Child Welfare Act Marie Stopes, *Married Love; Parenthood* Rutherford splits atom Oswald Spengler, *Decline of the West* (vol. II, 1922)	Brooke, *Collected Poems* Joyce, *Exiles* Wyndham Lewis, *Tarr* Mansfield, *Prelude* Siegfried Sassoon, *Counter-Attack* Edward Thomas, *Last Poems* Rebecca West, *The Return of the Soldier*
1919	Versaille Peace Conference Anglo-Irish War begins Nancy Astor becomes first woman MP Sex Disqualification Removal Act opens professions to women c. 1,000 strikes (–20) British troops kill c. 400 demonstrators at Amritsar in the Punjab Government of India Act (concessions towards self-government) First transatlantic flight by John Alcock and Arthur W. Brown	Aldington, *Images of War* *Coterie* (–21) *English Studies* journal (–present) Somerset Maugham, *The Moon and Sixpence* Shaw, *Heartbreak House* Sassoon, *War Poems* Woolf, *Night and Day*

Year		
1920	League of Nations first meets Government of Ireland Act partitions Ireland Unemployment Insurance Act British Communist Party founded Oxford admits women to degrees Jung, *Psychological Types*	Agatha Christie, *The Mysterious Affair at Styles* Eliot, *The Sacred Wood* Lawrence, *Women in Love* Wilfred Owen, *Poems* Pound, *Hugh Selwyn Mauberley* Yeats, *Michael Robartes and the Dancer*
1921	Economic slump National Unemployed Workers' Movement established Anglo-Irish Treaty establishes Irish Free State Marie Stopes opens first birth-control clinic in London	Aldous Huxley, *Crome Yellow* Luigi Pirandello, *Six Characters in Search of an Author* Shaw, *Back to Methuselah*
1922	Unemployment at 2 million First of series of 'hunger marches' throughout the 1920s and 1930s Geddes Committee axes government spending Irish Civil War (–23) Mussolini comes to power in Italy Egypt regains independence Radio broadcasting begins Major Jack C. Savage develops skywriting	*Criterion* (ed. T. S. Eliot) Eliot, *The Waste Land* Frazer, *The Golden Bough* (one-volume abridged edn) Galsworthy, *The Forsyte Saga* Hardy, *Late Lyrics and Earlier* Joyce, *Ulysses* published in Paris (US, 1933; UK, 1936) Lawrence, *Studies in Classic American Literature* Mansfield, *The Garden Party* Woolf, *Jacob's Room*
1923	British empire at its largest-ever extent Matrimonial Causes Act allows women same rights as men to sue for divorce	E. E. Cummings, *Tulips and Chimneys* Huxley, *Antic Hay* Lawrence, *Birds, Beasts and Flowers* Rose Macaulay, *Told by an Idiot* Sean O'Casey, *The Shadow of a Gunman*
1924	First Labour government in Britain under Ramsay MacDonald (January) Housing Act (for subsidised public housing) Conservative government re-elected (December) First manifesto of surrealism Freud, *The Ego and the Id*	Ford, *Some Do Not* (first book of *Parade's End* tetralogy) Forster, *A Passage to India* T. E. Hulme, *Speculations* Mann, *The Magic Mountain* O'Casey, *Juno and the Paycock* Shaw, *Saint Joan*

	HISTORY AND CULTURE	LITERATURE
1925	Pensions Act for pensions at 65 Guardianship of Infants Act gives women equal rights to their children	Carnie Holdsworth, *This Slavery* H. D., *Collected Poems* Scott Fitzgerald, *The Great Gatsby* Ernest Hemingway, *In Our Time* Lawrence, *St Mawr* Hugh MacDiarmid, *Sangschaw* Woolf, *Mrs Dalloway*; *The Common Reader* Yeats, *A Vision*
1926	General Strike Electricity (Supply) Act initiates supply through national grid (completed by 1936) Television first demonstrated by John Logie Baird; British Broadcasting Corporation (BBC) established	Lawrence, *The Plumed Serpent* T. E. Lawrence, *Seven Pillars of Wisdom* MacDiarmid, *Penny Wheep*; *A Drunk Man Looks at the Thistle* O'Casey, *The Plough and the Stars*
1927	Trade Disputes Act makes general strikes illegal Charles Lindbergh, first solo transatlantic flight	Forster, *Aspects of the Novel* Robert Graves and Laura Riding, *A Survey of Modernist Poetry* Jean Rhys, *The Left Bank* Woolf, *To the Lighthouse*
1928	Minimum voting age for women reduced to 21 from 30 Alexander Fleming discovers penicillin (fully exploited from 1940) First films with sound in Britain	Lawrence, *Lady Chatterley's Lover*; *Collected Poems*; *The Woman Who Rode Away* R. C. Sheriff, *Journey's End* first produced (published 1929; film version, 1930) Evelyn Waugh, *Decline and Fall* Woolf, *Orlando* Yeats, *The Tower*
1929	General election returns minority Labour government; Margaret Bondfield becomes first woman Cabinet member New York Wall Street Crash and start of international economic depression	Aldington, *Death of a Hero* William Faulkner, *The Sound and the Fury* Graves, *Goodbye to All That* J. B. Priestley, *The Good Companions* Erich Maria Remarque, *All Quiet on the Western Front* (film version, 1930) Woolf, *A Room of One's Own*

Year		
1930	Coal Mines Act reduces underground working to 7½ hours a day Gandhi leads mass campaign of civil disobedience in India Britain returns Weihaiwei to China Amy Johnson, solo flight to Australia Jet engine invented Freud, *Civilisation and Its Discontents*	W. H. Auden, *Poems* Eliot, **Marina**; *Ash Wednesday* Faulkner, *As I Lay Dying* Hardy, *Collected Poems* Lawrence, *The Virgin and the Gipsy* Sol T. Plaatje, *Mhudi* (written 1920)
1931	Economic crisis and escalating unemployment cause collapse of government; MacDonald forms National (coalition) Government Ford Dagenham plant expands mass production of cars in Britain Statute of Westminster makes key shift from empire to Commonwealth	Elizabeth Bowen, *Friends and Relations* Ivy Compton-Burnett, *Men and Wives* Lawrence, *Apocalypse* Woolf, *The Waves*
1932	Unemployed hunger march to London British Union of Fascists formed by Sir Oswald Mosley BBC Empire Service established	Eliot, *Sweeney Agonistes; Selected Essays* Huxley, *Brave New World* Lawrence, *Last Poems* Woolf, *Second Common Reader*
1933	Hitler becomes German chancellor	Auden, *The Dance of Death* Vera Brittain, *Testament of Youth* George Orwell, *Down and Out in London and Paris* Yeats, *The Winding Stair*
1934	Special Areas Act provides limited assistance to alleviate unemployment in depressed areas	Orwell, *Burmese Days* Pound, *Make it New* Dylan Thomas, *18 Poems*
1935	National Government re-elected Italy invades Ethiopia Radar invented Nylon invented	Mulk Raj Anand, *Untouchable* Eliot, *Murder in the Cathedral* Louis MacNeice, *Poems* R. K. Narayan, *Swami and Friends* Penguin Books launched

	HISTORY AND CULTURE	LITERATURE
1936	Death of George V; accession of Edward VIII, who abdicates later in the year; his brother becomes King George VI Jarrow March of unemployed 'Battle of Cable Street': Mosley's British Union of Fascists try to march in East End of London but are forcibly stopped by anti-fascist demonstrators Spanish Civil War begins Arab revolt over Jewish settlement in Palestine gathers pace with attacks also on British troops	Anand, *Coolie* Auden, *Look, Stranger!* Winifred Holtby, *South Riding* Huxley, *Eyeless in Gaza* Orwell, *Keep the Aspidistra Flying* Dylan Thomas, *25 Poems*
1937	PM Neville Chamberlain pursues policy of appeasement towards Italy and Germany Charles Madge and Tom Harrison start 'Mass Observation' project to document lives of the masses (−38) Riots in Caribbean colonies Irish Free State renamed Eire	Auden and MacNeice, *Letters from Iceland* Christopher Isherwood, *Sally Bowles* David Jones, *In Parenthesis* Lewis Jones, *Cwmardy* Orwell, *The Road to Wigan Pier* Priestley, *Time and the Conways* Woolf, *The Years*
1938	Chamberlain's Munich agreement with Hitler ('peace in our time') Continuing Arab revolt in Palestine suppressed by British	Idris Davies, *Gwalia Deserta* C. Day-Lewis, *Overtures to a Death* Orwell, *Homage to Catalonia* Raja Rao, *Kanthapura* Waugh, *Scoop* Woolf, *Three Guineas*
1939	Second World War begins after Germany invades Czechoslovakia and then Poland Spanish Civil War ends Electron microscope invented	Eliot, *The Family Reunion* Isherwood, *Goodbye to Berlin* Joyce, *Finnegans Wake* Flann O'Brien, *At Swim-Two-Birds* Rhys, *Good Morning, Midnight*
1940	Winston Churchill succeeds Neville Chamberlain as PM Dunkirk evacuation and Battle of Britain	D. Thomas, *A Portrait of the Artist as a Young Dog* Graham Greene, *The Power and the Glory*
1941	USA and USSR (Allies) enter the war against Germany and Japan (Axis) Rowntree Report on Poverty	Noel Coward, *Blithe Spirit*

Year	Events	Culture
1942	Battle of El Alamein, North Africa Japan overruns Singapore, occupies British Malayan territories and Burma (–45) and reaches eastern borders of India Anti-British 'Quit India' campaign begins; Gandhi and other leaders imprisoned (–44) Beveridge Report on Social Security	Eliot, 'Little Gidding'
1943	Allied invasion of Italy Fall of Mussolini	Coward, *This Happy Breed* Henry Green, *Caught*
1944	D-Day invasions of Normandy Allies recapture France Butler Education Act Michael Tippett, *A Child of Our Time* (oratorio) Miners' Strike	H. E. Bates, *Fair Stood the Wind for France* Compton-Burnett, *Elders and Betters* Eliot, *Four Quartets*
1945	Atomic bombs dropped on Hiroshima and Nagasaki (respectively, c. 100, 000 and c. 75, 000 killed at once) End of Second World War Labour government formed under PM Clement Attlee Fifth Pan-African Congress, Manchester In Palestine, armed Jewish campaign against British gathers pace Benjamin Britten, *Peter Grimes* (opera)	John Betjeman, *New Bats in Old Belfries* Green, *Loving* Philip Larkin, *The North Ship* Nancy Mitford, *The Pursuit of Love* Orwell, *Animal Farm* Elizabeth Taylor, *At Mrs Lippincote's* Waugh, *Brideshead Revisited*
1946	National Health Act Bank of England nationalised Arts Council founded First meeting of United Nations In China, war between communists and nationalists renewed (–49) In Palestine, Jewish forces bomb British headquarters at the King David Hotel, killing 91 people	Peter Abrahams, *Mine Boy* Larkin, *Jill* Eric Linklater, *Private Angelo* Taylor, *Palladian* D. Thomas, *Deaths and Entrances*
1947	Coal industry nationalised US Marshall Aid for European recovery 15 August: partition and independence of India and Pakistan; partition causes millions of people to flee their homes and huge loss of life in intercommunal violence	Albert Camus, *La Peste* Malcolm Lowry, *Under the Volcano* Arthur Miller, *All My Sons* Tennessee Williams, *A Streetcar Named Desire*

	HISTORY AND CULTURE	LITERATURE
	Britain refers Palestine mandate back to the United Nations	
1948	National Health Service founded	G. V. Desani, *All About H. Hatterr*
	Railways nationalised	Eliot, *Notes Towards a Definition of Culture*
	British Nationality Bill defines all Commonwealth and empire	Christopher Fry, *The Lady's Not for Burning*
	citizens as British subjects; *Empire Windrush* brings first Caribbean	Greene, *The Heart of the Matter*
	migrants to work in Britain	F. R. Leavis, *The Great Tradition*
	Britain withdraws from Palestine; Arab–Israeli War follows and	Alan Paton, *Cry, the Beloved Country*
	state of Israel established	Terence Rattigan, *The Browning Version*
	Riots in Accra on the Gold Coast (Ghana) push Britain to accelerate	
	moves towards independence	
	Assassination of Gandhi by Hindu extremist	
	Afrikaaner National Party comes to power in South Africa and	
	inaugurates era of apartheid	
1949	Iron and steel industries nationalised	**Dannie Abse**, *After Every Green Thing*
	Eire becomes the Irish Republic	Bowen, *The Heat of the Day*
	North Atlantic Treaty Organisation (NATO) formed	Eliot, *The Cocktail Party*
	Communist People's Republic of China established	Mitford, *Love in a Cold Climate*
		Orwell, *Nineteen Eighty-Four*
1950	Labour returned to government, with small majority	Greene, *The Third Man*
	Korean War (–53)	Doris Lessing, *The Grass is Singing*
1951	Conservatives form government, with Churchill as PM	Keith Douglas, *Collected Poems*
	British spies Burgess and Maclean defect to USSR	Larkin, *Poems*
	First free elections in Gold Coast: Kwame Nkrumah becomes PM	Olivia Manning, *School for Love*
		J. D. Salinger, *The Catcher in the Rye*
1952	George VI dies; Elizabeth II accedes	Christie, *The Mousetrap*
	Britain produces own atomic bomb	Jones, *The Anathemata*
	State of emergency in Kenya (–60)	Lessing, *Martha Quest*
	First contraceptive pills made	Amos Tutuola, *The Palm-Wine Drinkard*
1953	Coronation of Elizabeth II	Ray Bradbury, *Fahrenheit 451*
	Cuban Revolution begins (–59)	Ian Fleming, *Casino Royale*
	Ascent of Everest by Hillary and Tenzing	L. P. Hartley, *The Go-Between*
		George Lamming, *In the Castle of My Skin*

Year	Events	Literary works
1954	Post-war food rationing ends Vietnam War (–75)	Abrahams, *Tell Freedom* Kingsley Amis, *Lucky Jim* William Golding, *Lord of the Flies* Martin Carter, *Poems of Resistance* Lamming, *The Emigrants* D. Thomas, *Under Milk Wood*
1955	Churchill retires; Anthony Eden becomes PM; Conservatives returned to government in election Women gain equal pay in civil service State of emergency in Cyprus (–59) Treaty for European Union	Samuel Beckett, *Waiting for Godot* Larkin, *The Less Deceived* Vladimir Nabokov, *Lolita* R. S. Thomas, *Song at the Year's Turning* Patrick White, *The Tree of Man*
1956	Suez Crisis Hungarian uprising suppressed by USSR Transatlantic telephone service begins	Robert Conquest (ed.), *New Lines* John Osborne, *Look Back in Anger* Sam Selvon, *The Lonely Londoners* Khushwant Singh, *Train to Pakistan* J. R. R. Tolkien, *The Lord of the Rings*
1957	Eden resigns over Suez; Harold Macmillan becomes PM Britain tests its first hydrogen bomb European Economic Community Gold Coast gains independence as Ghana	Janet Frame, *Owls Do Cry* **Ted Hughes, The Hawk in the Rain** Larkin, *A Girl in Winter* Iris Murdoch, *The Sandcastle* V. S. Naipaul, *The Mystic Masseur* White, *Voss*
1958	Race riots in Nottingham and Notting Hill Campaign for Nuclear Disarmament (CND) founded First stereo recordings J. K. Galbraith, *The Affluent Society* Raymond Williams, *Culture and Society*	**Chinua Achebe, Things Fall Apart** Brendan Behan, *The Hostage* Rose Macaulay, *The World My Wilderness* Harold Pinter, *The Birthday Party* Nayantara Sahgal, *A Time to Be Happy* Alan Sillitoe, *Saturday Night and Sunday Morning*

	HISTORY AND CULTURE	LITERATURE
1959	Conservatives returned to government Aldermaston–London CND march First part of M1 motorway opened C. P. Snow, *Two Cultures* Fidel Castro comes to power in Cuba	John Arden, *Serjeant Musgrave's Dance* Malcolm Bradbury, *Eating People is Wrong* Laurie Lee, *Cider with Rosie* Sillitoe, *The Loneliness of the Long Distance Runner* Arnold Wesker, *Roots*
1960	Nigeria and Cyprus gain independence Sharpeville Massacre in South Africa; large anti-apartheid demonstrations in Trafalgar Square *New Left Review* *Lady Chatterley* trial TV soap opera *Coronation Street*	Achebe, *No Longer at Ease* Lawrence Durrell, *The Alexandria Quartet* Wilson Harris, *The Palace of the Peacock* Hughes, **Lupercal** Pinter, *The Caretaker* Sylvia Plath, *The Colossus*
1961	Abortive US invasion of Cuba South Africa leaves Commonwealth; the ANC moves from passive resistance to strategic armed struggle *Private Eye* (satirical magazine)	Thom Gunn, *My Sad Captains* Naipaul, *A House for Mr. Biswas* Narayan, *The Man-Eater of Malgudi* Muriel Spark, *The Prime of Miss Jean Brodie* Waugh, *Sword of Honour Trilogy*
1962	Commonwealth Immigrants Act ends right to free entry from Commonwealth (further related Acts, 1968, 1971) National military service ends Jamaica, Trinidad & Tobago, Uganda become independent US–Soviet Cuban Missile Crisis	Al Alvarez (ed.), *The New Poetry* Anthony Burgess, *A Clockwork Orange* Lessing, *The Golden Notebook* Derek Walcott, *In a Green Night*
1963	Macmillan resigns as PM, replaced by Alec Douglas-Home Robbins Report on Higher Education leads to major expansion of universities Kenya gains independence Organisation of African Unity founded President J. F. Kennedy assassinated in the USA Nuclear Test Ban Treaty Britten, *War Requiem*	Dennis Brutus, *Sirens Knuckles Boots* Anita Desai, *Cry the Peacock* Athol Fugard, *Blood Knot* Nadine Gordimer, *Occasion for Loving* B. S. Johnson, *Travelling People* John Le Carré, *The Spy Who Came in from the Cold* Plath, *The Bell Jar*
1964	Labour forms government under Harold Wilson In South Africa, Nelson Mandela and other ANC leaders sentenced to life imprisonment	Achebe, *Arrow of God* Larkin, *The Whitsun Weddings* Ngũgĩ wa Thiong'o, *Weep Not, Child* Joe Orton, *Entertaining Mr Sloane*

Year	Events	Literature
1965	Race Relations Act to curb racial discrimination Death penalty abolished Unilateral Declaration of Independence by government of Rhodesia, deemed illegal by Britain and the UN Emergency in Aden (Yemen) (–67) The Beatles awarded MBE	Michael Anthony, *The Year in San Fernando* Edward Bond, *Saved* Margaret Drabble, *The Millstone* Ngũgĩ, *The River Between* Pinter, *The Homecoming* Plath, *Ariel* Wole Soyinka, *The Interpreters*
1966	Labour returned as government Barbados, Bechuanaland (as Botswana) and British Guiana (as Guyana) become independent British Colonial Office merged into Commonwealth Office *Cathy Come Home* (landmark TV play on homelessness) England wins football World Cup	Achebe, *A Man of the People* Elechi Amadi, *The Concubine* Basil Bunting, *Briggflatts* John Fowles, *The Magus* Orton, *Loot* Jean Rhys, *Wide Sargasso Sea* Tom Stoppard, *Rosencrantz and Guildenstern are Dead*
1967	Abortion legalised Homosexuality decriminalised Biafra's secession sparks Nigerian–Biafran civil war (–70) Aborigines granted citizenship in Australia after referendum World's first heart transplant	Angela Carter, *The Magic Toyshop* Hughes, *Wodwo* Kamau Brathwaite, *Rights of Passage* Naipaul, *The Mimic Men* Ngũgĩ, *A Grain of Wheat*
1968	Race Relations Act outlaws discrimination Commonwealth Immigration Act Enoch Powell makes anti-immigration 'rivers of blood' speech in Birmingham Commonwealth Office merged into Foreign Office Prague Spring in Czechoslovakia ended by Soviet invasion May revolts in Paris Steve Biko establishes South African Students' Organisation In US, assassinations of Martin Luther King and Robert Kennedy Theatre censorship ends in Britain	Ayi Kwei Armah, *The Beautyful Ones Are Not Yet Born* Bond, *Early Morning* Brathwaite, *Masks* Brutus, *Letters to Martha and Other Poems from a South African Prison* **Bessie Head**, *When Rain Clouds Gather* Barry Hines, *A Kestrel for a Knave* Hughes, *The Iron Man* Alice Munro, *Dance of the Happy Shades* Spark, *The Public Image*

	HISTORY AND CULTURE	LITERATURE
1969	UK miners' strike Northern Ireland 'troubles' begin US moon landings Booker Prize for fiction begins	Maya Angelou, *I Know Why the Caged Bird Sings* Margaret Atwood, *The Edible Woman* Brathwaite, *Islands* Fowles, *The French Lieutenant's Woman* B. S. Johnson, *The Unfortunates* Bernice Rubens, *The Elected Member* Walcott, *The Gulf*
1970	Conservatives form government under Edward Heath Equal Pay Bill Women's Liberation Movement Voting age reduced to 18 Biafra surrenders in Nigerian Civil War	Nuruddin Farah, *From a Crooked Rib* Hughes, *Crow* C. P. Snow, *Strangers and Brothers*
1971	Immigration Act Decimalisation of sterling Greenpeace founded Bangladesh gains independence from Pakistan Military coup in Uganda begins nine years of dictatorship by Idi Amin	Achebe, *Beware, Soul Brother* Bond, *Lear* Head, *Maru* Geoffrey Hill, *Mercian Hymns* Naipaul, *In a Free State* Taylor, *Mrs Palfrey at the Claremont*
1972	Miners' strike leads to State of Emergency Northern Ireland placed under direct rule from London Guerrilla warfare intensifies in Rhodesia In Uganda, the Amin regime summarily expels 60, 000 Asians	Achebe, *Girls at War and Other Stories* Angela Carter, *The Infernal Desire Machines of Doctor Hoffman* Thomas Keneally, *The Chant of Jimmie Blacksmith* Stoppard, *Jumpers*
1973	UK joins European Economic Community Oil and energy crisis Caribbean Community (CARICOM) established	Abse, *Funland and Other Poems* Martin Amis, *The Rachel Papers* J. G. Ballard, *Crash* Head, *A Question of Power* John McGrath, *The Cheviot, the Stag, and the Black, Black Oil* Peter Shaffer, *Equus* Soyinka, *Season of Anomy* Walcott, *Another Life*

Year		
1974	After first inconclusive election, Labour elected under Harold Wilson Invasion of northern Cyprus by Turkey Watergate scandal in US First evidence of ozone depletion	J. M. Coetzee, *Dusklands* Larkin, *High Windows* Soyinka, *Collected Plays* (2 vols)
1975	Sex Discrimination Bill Inflation at 25 per cent North Sea oil production begins End of Vietnam War	Achebe, *Morning Yet on Creation Day: Essays* Amis, *Dead Babies* Ruth Prawer Jhabvala, *Heat and Dust* Linton Kwesi Johnson, *Dread Beat and Blood* David Lodge, *Changing Places* **Salman Rushdie**, *Grimus* Selvon, *Moses Ascending* Iain Sinclair, *Lud Heat* Paul Scott, *The Raj Quartet*
1976	Wilson retires and James Callaghan becomes PM Race Relations Act strengthens anti-discrimination laws Notting Hill riots Soweto uprising in South Africa	David Edgar, *Destiny* Hughes, *Season Songs* Emma Tennant, *Hotel de Dream*
1977	Battle of Lewisham, London: planned march of racist National Front Party blocked by thousands of counter-demonstrators; many injured following violent clashes; police use baton charges and riot shields Death of Steve Biko in police custody further galvanises anti-apartheid movement in South Africa and internationally Virago Press begins publishing Tom Nairn, *The Break-Up of Britain*	**Ama Ata Aidoo**, *Our Sister Killjoy* Angela Carter, *The Passion of New Eve* Head, **The Collector of Treasures and Other Botswana Village Tales** Hughes, *Gaudete*; *Orts*
1978	(–79) Winter of Discontent with widespread strikes and severe winter conditions First IVF 'test-tube baby' born Edward Said, *Orientalism*	Desai, *Games at Twilight and Other Stories* **David Hare**, *Plenty* Hughes, **Cave Birds** Ian McEwan, *The Cement Garden* Fay Weldon, *Praxis*

	HISTORY AND CULTURE	LITERATURE
1979	Winter of Discontent contributes to Conservative election victory; Margaret Thatcher becomes PM	**Caryl Churchill**, *Cloud Nine*
	Idi Amin ousted in Uganda	Buchi Emecheta, *The Joys of Motherhood*
	Iran Hostage Crisis	Penelope Fitzgerald, *Offshore*
	Soviet invasion of Afghanistan (Dec.)	Hughes, *Moortown Diary*; **Remains of Elmet**
		Earl Lovelace, *The Wine of Astonishment*
1980	Major recession begins bringing steady rise in unemployment	Howard Brenton, *The Romans in Britain*
	Riots in Bristol	Coetzee, *Waiting for the Barbarians*
	Zimbabwe gains independence; Robert Mugabe becomes PM	Desai, *Clear Light of Day*
		Golding, *Rites of Passage*
		L. K. Johnson, *Inglan is a Bitch*
		Caryl Phillips, *Strange Fruit*
		Tom Phillips, *The Humument*
		Graham Swift, *The Sweet-Shop Owner*
1981	Government privatises British Aerospace, first in a growing programme of privatisations	Farah, *Sardines*
	British Nationality Bill restricts the definition of British citizenship	Alasdair Gray, *Lanark*
	Riots in London, Liverpool and Manchester	Head, **Serowe: Village of the Rain Wind**
	Anti-nuclear Greenham Common Women's Peace Camp protests begin	Ngũgĩ, *Detained: A Writer's Prison Diary; Writers in Politics: Essays*
	AIDS first positively identified in US	Rushdie, **Midnight's Children**
	IBM launches first personal computer	D. M. Thomas, *The White Hotel*
1982	Falklands War	Pat Barker, *Union Street*
		Bruce Chatwin, *On the Black Hill*
		Churchill, *Top Girls*
		Michael Frayn, *Noises Off*
		Timothy Mo, *Sour Sweet*
1983	Conservative government re-elected	Coetzee, *The Life and Times of Michael K*
	Unemployment rises to over 3 million	Shashi Deshpande, *Roots and Shadows*
		Hughes, **River**
		Jamaica Kincaid, *At the Bottom of the River*
		Grace Nichols, **i is a long memoried woman**
		Rushdie, **Shame**
		Alice Walker, *The Color Purple*

Year	Events	Literary works
1984	UK miners' strike (–85) IRA Brighton hotel bombing during Conservative Party conference Golden Temple at Amritsar stormed by Indian troops with large Sikh death toll; Indira Gandhi assassinated later in year; anti-Sikh riots follow Major famine in Ethiopia (–85)	Iain Banks, *The Wasp Factory* Julian Barnes, *Flaubert's Parrot* David Dabydeen, *Slave Song* Head, *A Bewitched Crossroad: An African Saga* Ted Hughes becomes Poet Laureate Nichols, **The Fat Black Woman's Poems**
1985	Riots in London and Birmingham Live Aid concerts for Ethiopia	Peter Ackroyd, *Hawksmoor* Atwood, *The Handmaid's Tale* Tony Harrison, *v.* Keri Hulme, *The Bone People* Kincaid, *Annie John* C. Phillips, *The Final Passage* Jeanette Winterson, *Oranges Are Not the Only Fruit* Benjamin Zephaniah, *The Dread Affair*
1986	Chernobyl explosion Laptop computers introduced	Coetzee, *Foe* Kazuo Ishiguro, *An Artist of the Floating World* Nichols, *Whole of a Morning Sky* Ngũgĩ, *Decolonising the Mind* Ben Okri, *Incidents at the Shrine*
1987	Conservatives returned to government Black Monday stock market crash Paul Gilroy, *There Ain't No Black in the Union Jack*	Achebe, *Anthills of the Savannah* Chatwin, *The Songlines* Abdulrazak Gurnah, *Memory of Departure* Toni Morrison, *Beloved*
1988	President Zia of Pakistan dies in plane crash; Benazir Bhutto elected PM Stephen Hawking, *A Brief History of Time*	Achebe, *Hopes and Impediments: Selected Essays 1965–1987* Jean 'Binta' Breeze, *Riddym Ravings* André Brink, *States of Emergency* Peter Carey, *Oscar and Lucinda* Dabydeen, *Coolie Odyssey* Tsitsi Dangarembga, *Nervous Conditions* Gurnah, *Pilgrim's Way* Rushdie, **The Satanic Verses** Soyinka, *Mandela's Earth and Other Poems*

	HISTORY AND CULTURE	LITERATURE
1989	Revolutions in eastern Europe and continuing liberalisation in USSR signal end of Cold War P. W. Botha replaced by F. W. de Klerk as president of South Africa Iranian death threats against Salman Rushdie arising from *Satanic Verses*	Simon Armitage, *Zoom!* Ishiguro, *The Remains of the Day* Head, **Tales of Tenderness and Power** Gita Mehta, *Raj* Nichols, **Lazy Thoughts of a Lazy Woman** M. G. Vassanji, *The Gunny Sack* Winterson, *Sexing the Cherry*
1990	Margaret Thatcher resigns as PM, replaced by John Major Reunification of Germany Release of Nelson Mandela (11 Feb.) and unbanning of ANC signals end of apartheid era in South Africa	A. S. Byatt, *Possession* Head, *A Woman Alone: Autobiographical Writings* Kincaid, *Lucy* Hanif Kureishi, *The Buddha of Suburbia* Rushdie, *Haroun and the Sea of Stories* Walcott, *Omeros*
1991	(First) Gulf War	Aidoo, **Changes: A Love Story** Okri, *The Famished Road* Rushdie, *Imaginary Homelands: Essays and Criticism*
1992	Conservatives returned to government Sterling devalued European single market formed	Hughes, *Shakespeare and the Goddess of Complete Being* Michael Ondaatje, *The English Patient* Barry Unsworth, *Sacred Hunger* Yvonne Vera, *Why Don't You Carve Other Animals?*
1993	Stephen Lawrence killed in racist attack in south London Nelson Mandela and F. W. de Klerk share Nobel Peace Prize Australian Native Title Act formally recognises Aboriginal land rights Paul Gilroy, *The Black Atlantic*	Fred D'Aguiar, *British Subjects* Farah, *Gifts* Head, *The Cardinals* Hughes, *The Iron Woman* Mehta, *A River Sutra* C. Phillips, *Crossing the River* Walcott, *The Odyssey*

1994	Northern Ireland Peace Process begins Church of England ordains first women priests National Lottery begins First fully multiracial elections in South Africa give clear victory to the ANC: Nelson Mandela becomes president	Brathwaite, *Barabajan Poems* Jonathan Coe, *What a Carve Up!* Dabydeen, *Turner* (on Turner's painting *The Slave Ship*; see 1840) D'Aguiar, *The Longest Memory* Romesh Gunesekera, *Reef* Gurnah, *Paradise* Hughes, *Winter Pollen*; *Elmet* Rushdie, *East, West*
1995	Channel Tunnel opens between Britain and France Military government in Nigeria executes Ogoni civil and environmental rights activists, including writer Ken Saro-Wiwa	Barker, *Regeneration Trilogy* Hare, **Skylight** Sarah Kane, *Blasted* Rushdie, *The Moor's Last Sigh*
1996	First mammal cloned (Dolly the sheep) at Roslin Institute, Edinburgh	Aidoo, *The Girl Who Can and Other Stories* Breeze, *Riding on de Riddym* Helen Fielding, *Bridget Jones's Diary* Rohinton Mistry, *A Fine Balance* Nichols, *Sunris* Pinter, *Ashes to Ashes* Mark Ravenhill, *Shopping and Fucking* Swift, *Last Orders*
1997	Tony Blair becomes PM as Labour returns to power for first time since 1979 Referenda decide in favour of devolution for Scotland and Wales Britain hands back Hong Kong and New Territories to China Princess Diana dies in car crash	Carey, *Jack Maggs* Vikram Chandra, *Love and Longing in Bombay* Richard Flanagan, *The Sound of One Hand Clapping* Hughes, *Tales From Ovid* Kincaid, *The Autobiography of My Mother* Mehta, *Snakes and Ladders: A View of Modern India* Arundhati Roy, *The God of Small Things* Walcott, *The Bounty*

	HISTORY AND CULTURE	LITERATURE
1998	The Belfast or Good Friday Agreement heralds political settlement in Northern Ireland	D'Aguiar, *Feeding the Ghosts* (see 1781, the *Zong* massacre) Kiran Desai, *Hullabaloo in the Guava Orchard* Hughes, *Birthday Letters* Kamila Shamsie, *The City by the Sea* Walcott, *What the Twilight Says* (essays)
1999	Macpherson Report arising from Stephen Lawrence's murder (1993) highlights institutional racism in Metropolitan police and makes seventy recommendations to combat racism Scottish Parliament and Welsh Assembly open	Armitage, *Killing Time* Coetzee, *Disgrace* Joanne Harris, *Chocolat* Ravenhill, **Some Explicit Polaroids** Rushdie, *The Ground beneath Her Feet* Sarah Waters, *Tipping the Velvet*
2000	Millennium celebrations Paul Gilroy, *Against Race*	Achebe, *Home and Exile* (essays) Churchill, *Far Away* D'Aguiar, *Bloodlines* Amitav Ghosh, *The Glass Palace* Jhumpa Lahiri, *Interpreter of Maladies* Ondaatje, *Anil's Ghost* Shamsie, *Salt and Saffron* Zadie Smith, *White Teeth*
2001	Labour returned to government 9/11 terrorist attacks in USA	Bernardine Evaristo, *The Emperor's Babe* Gurnah, *By the Sea* McEwan, *Atonement* Zephaniah, *Too Black, Too Strong*
2002	US-led coalition forces (including UK) invade Afghanistan	Churchill, *A Number* Coetzee, *Youth* Frayn, *Spies* Alice Oswald, *Dart* Shamsie, *Kartography*

Year	Events	Literary works
2003	Second Gulf War David Crystal, *English as a Global Language* (1997) 2nd edn suggests around a quarter of the world's population can communicate usefully in English	Chimamanda Ngozi Adichie, *Purple Hibiscus* Monica Ali, *Brick Lane* Rachel Cusk, *The Lucky Ones* **debbie tucker green, *born bad; dirty butterfly***
2004	Ten countries join European Union to bring total to twenty-five	Achebe, *Collected Poems* Sarah Hall, *The Electric Michelangelo* Hollinghurst, *The Line of Beauty* Andrea Levy, *Small Island* David Mitchell, *Cloud Atlas*
2005	Labour returned to government Terrorist attacks in London kill fifty-two people Paul Gilroy, *Postcolonial Melancholia*	Leila Aboulela, *Minaret* **Diana Evans**, *26a* Sebastian Faulks, *Human Traces* Kathleen Jamie, *Findings* Nichols, ***Startling the Flying Fish*** Rushdie, *Shalimar the Clown* Shamsie, *Broken Verses* Ali Smith, *The Accidental* Z. Smith, *On Beauty*
2006	Terrorist plot to use explosives on transatlantic flights thwarted Murder of Russian dissident Alexander Litvinenko in London	Adichie, *Half of a Yellow Sun* Aidoo (ed.), ***African Love Stories*** Breeze, *The Fifth Figure* Kiran Desai, *The Inheritance of Loss* Tom McCarthy, *Remainder* Anthony Neilson, *Realism* Bapsi Sidhwa, *Water: A Novel* Dangarembga, *The Book of Not*
2007	Tony Blair steps down and Gordon Brown becomes PM Global banking crisis begins Northern Ireland Assembly meets, with Unionist and Nationalist partners in government Scottish National Party wins Scottish parliamentary elections	Achebe wins Man Booker International Prize Anne Enright, *The Gathering* Hall, *The Carhullan Army* **Mohsin Hamid, *The Reluctant Fundamentalist*** Oswald, *A Sleepwalk on the Severn*

	HISTORY AND CULTURE	LITERATURE
2008	Global recession begins, lasting until 2012, and causing sharp rise in unemployment, credit crises and housing market collapse Government announces bailout of £400bn for failing banks in UK Barack Obama elected US president and will be first African-American president	Aravind Adiga, *The White Tiger* Ghosh, *Sea of Poppies* Hilary Mantel, *Wolf Hall* Rushdie, *The Enchantress of Florence*
2009	Parliamentary expenses scandal Unemployment reaches 2.5 million Protests against G20 summit in London	Armitage, *Sir Gawain and the Green Knight* Tim Crouch, *The Author* Evans, *The Wonder* Ngũgĩ, *Something Torn and New: An African Renaissance* Nichols, *Picasso, I Want My Face Back* Shamsie, *Burnt Shadows*
2010	Conservatives and Liberal Democrats form coalition government, with David Cameron as PM Student protests against rising tuition costs Catastrophic earthquake in Haiti	Brathwaite, *Elegguan* Aminatta Forna, *The Memory of Love* Helon Habila, *Oil on Water* Jon McGregor, *Even the Dogs* Andrea Levy, *The Long Song* Nadifa Mohamed, *Black Mamba Boy* Rushdie, *Luka and the Fire of Life*
2011	Protests in London against government austerity measures Widespread rioting in English cities British troops withdrawn from Iraq Civil war in Syria (–present)	Adiga, *Last Man in Tower* Barnes, *The Sense of an Ending* Breeze, *Third World Girl: Selected Poems* Deborah Levy, *Swimming Home* A. Smith, *There But For The*
2012	London hosts Olympic Games	Churchill, *Love and Information* Faulks, *A Possible Life* Jamie, *Sightlines* Robert Macfarlane, *The Old Ways* Mantel, *Bring up the Bodies* Z. Smith, *NW* Soyinka, *Of Africa*

Year	Events	Literature
2013	Succession to the Crown Act ends male gender bias in succession rules Obama re-elected as US president	Tash Aw, *Five Star Billionaire* Adichie, *Americanah* NoViolet Bulawayo, *We Need New Names* Evaristo, *Mr Loverman* **David Greig, The Events** Lahiri, *The Lowland* Mohamed, *The Orchard of Lost Souls* **Yvonne Adhiambo Owuor, Dust**
2014	Referendum on Scottish independence: 55% vote against Same-sex marriage legalised in UK, except Northern Ireland British troop withdrawals from Afghanistan	Adichie, *We Should All Be Feminists* Armitage, *Paper Aeroplane: Selected Poems 1989–2014* Cusk, *Outline* Flanagan, *The Narrow Road to the Deep North* Shamsie, *A God in Every Stone* A. Smith, *How To Be Both* tucker green, *Second Coming* (film) Walcott, *The Poetry of Derek Walcott, 1948–2013*
2015	Conservatives form government, with David Cameron as PM European 'migrant crisis' reaches a peak with around a million displaced people (largely from Syria and Afghanistan) seeking refuge Paris Agreement: international treaty on climate change with goal of limiting global warming to 2°C, and ideally 1.5°C, as soon as possible	Hall, *The Wolf Border* Sarah Howe, *Loop of Jade* Ishiguro, *The Buried Giant* Marlon James, *A History of Seven Killings* McCarthy, *Satin Island* Lisa McInerney, *The Glorious Heresies*
2016	Labour MP Jo Cox shot and stabbed in street by killer with far-right profile In referendum, UK votes 51.9% to 48.1% to leave EU; England and Wales vote leave while Scotland, Northern Ireland and London vote remain; 'Brexit' divisions continue to dominate political affairs for next four years PM David Cameron resigns, replaced by Theresa May Donald Trump elected US president Growing awareness of spread of 'fake news', conspiracy theories and far-right terrorist narratives on internet platforms	Adiga, *Selection Day* **Churchill, Escaped Alone** Kit de Waal, *My Name is Leon* D. Levy, *Hot Milk* Z. Smith, *Swing Time* Amy Liptrot, *The Outrun*

	HISTORY AND CULTURE	LITERATURE
	Contemporary 'taking the knee' anti-racism movement initiated by Colin Kaepernick, who kneels during national anthem before game of American football; the gesture has antecedents possibly going back to Wedgwood's famous anti-slavery image (see 1797) David Olusoga, *Black and British: A Forgotten History*	
2017	Terror attacks in London and Manchester General election returns a hung parliament but Conservatives still largest party with Theresa May PM Launch of UN project Tech against Terrorism in partnership with Global Internet Forum to Counter Terrorism Myanmar Rohingya refugee crisis Spread of #MeToo movement in wake of Weinstein sexual abuse case Jane Austen (d. 1817) features on new Bank of England £10 note	Helen Dunmore, *Inside the Wave* Hamid, *Exit West* Kazuo Ishiguro wins Nobel Prize in Literature Le Carré, *A Legacy of Spies* McGregor, *Reservoir 13* McInerney, *The Blood Miracles* Sally Rooney, *Conversations with Friends* Will Self, *Phone* Shamshie, *Home Fire*
2018	Seventieth anniversary of NHS Large protests in UK against visit of US President Trump Mass march in London for a people's vote on outcome of Brexit negotiations	Pat Barker, *The Silence of the Girls* Barnes, *The Only Story* Dangarembga, *This Mournable Body* de Waal, *The Trick to Time* Evans, **Ordinary People** Forna, *Happiness* Guy Gunaratne, **In Our Mad and Furious City** D. Levy, *The Cost of Living* Rooney, *Normal People* tucker green, *ear for eye*
2019	Fire at Notre-Dame de Paris destroys spire and much of roof Second London People's Vote march Paul Gilroy wins Holberg Prize for research in the humanities	Kevin Barry, *Night Boat to Tangier* Evaristo, **Girl, Woman, Other** Habila, **Travellers** Jamie, *Surfacing* D. Levy, *The Man Who Saw Everything* Owuor, **The Dragonfly Sea** Rushdie, *uichotte*

Year	Events	Literature
2020	UK formally leaves EU Covid-19 global pandemic; c.2 million deaths worldwide by Jan. 2021 with widespread long-term lockdowns; vaccines developed by end of 2020 Police killing of George Floyd in US sparks worldwide protests and surge in Black Lives Matter movement (officer responsible found guilty of murder, April 2021) Footballer and anti-racism and anti-poverty campaigner Marcus Rashford awarded MBE for continuing initiatives to end child food poverty in the UK Joe Biden elected US president; Kamala Harris first female vice president, and first African- and Asian-American to hold the post Padraic X. Scanlan, *Slave Empire: How Slavery Built Modern Britain*	Adiga, *Amnesty* Armitage, *Magnetic Field: The Marsden Poems* Atwood, *Dearly* Mantel, *The Mirror and the Light* Nichols, *Passport to Here and There* Maggie O'Farrell, *Hamnet* Douglas Stuart, *Shuggie Bain* Gurnah, *Afterlives* Dora McAnulty, *Diary of a Young Naturalist* Susanna Clarke, *Piranesi*
2021	6 Jan.: far-right mob attacks US Capitol in Washington DC in failed attempt to overturn presidential election; second impeachment of President Trump for inciting insurrection; Joe Biden inaugurated as US president Afghanistan: in May, US announces withdrawal of troops by 11 Sept.; Taliban henceforth make rapid military advances and take power again by 15 Aug.; US, UK and other NATO countries scramble to evacuate tens of thousands of personnel and vulnerable Afghan citizens Postponed UEFA Euro 2020 football tournament and Japan Olympic Games take place Haiti hit by another catastrophic earthquake (see 2010), and then by large tropical storm	Aw, *Strangers on a Pier* Barker, *The Women of Troy* Cusk, *Second Place* Evaristo, *Manifesto* Faulks, *Snow Country* Amanda Gorman, *Call Us What We Carry* Hall, *Burntcoat* Ishiguro, *Klara and the Sun* D. Levy, *Real Estate* McInerney, *The Rules of Revelation* Mohamed, *The Fortune Men* Rooney, *Beautiful World, Where Are You* Rushdie, *The Seventh Wave* (novella to be published serially, weekly, on digital platform Substack)

HISTORY AND CULTURE	LITERATURE
Record-breaking heatwaves, wildfires and floods experienced across northern hemisphere; report of Intergovernmental Panel on Climate Change (IPCC) says past five years have been hottest on record since 1850; described by UN secretary general as 'code red for humanity', report cites 'unequivocal' evidence of human-induced global warming, warns of continuing life-threatening climate extremes across the globe, and calls for urgent emissions cuts to keep warming below critical tipping-point levels	Soyinka, *Chronicles from the Land of the Happiest People on Earth*
	Damon Galgut, *The Promise*
	Lauren Groff, *Matrix*
	Gurnah wins Nobel Prize in literature
Covid-19 pandemic: highly transmissible 'Delta' variant of virus becomes dominant strain worldwide by mid-year with yet another variant, 'Omicron', starting a third major wave of the pandemic in December; global (and UK) statistics Jan. 2020–Jan. 2022: c. 381 million cases (UK, c. 10 m); c. 5.7 million deaths (UK, c. 150 k); c. 53 % of total population fully vaccinated (UK, c. 75 %)	Nichols awarded Queen's Gold Medal for Poetry
	James Rebanks, *English Pastoral*
UN Climate Change Conference (COP26) held in Glasgow (November)	
Barbados becomes a republic	
Sathnam Sanghera, *Empireland: How Imperialism Shaped Modern Britain*	
British Black Lives Matter, ed. Lenny Henry and Marcus Ryder	
2022 February 24: Russia's President Putin orders invasion of Ukraine in start of unprovoked and globally condemned war of aggression; Ukraine offers strong resistance; by April, c. 10 million people displaced with c. 4.5 million seeking external refuge.	

Introduction

PAUL POPLAWSKI

With thirty-one essays covering such a broad range of topics, authors, texts and contexts, it would be impractical, and probably of limited use, to try to present a full introductory summary of all this material in one single general introduction. I have instead provided separate introductory notes at the start of each of the period sections, before each group of essays, in the hope that this will be of more immediate practical use to readers in relating my comments to the essays as they are about to be read. Nevertheless, having already explained the overall rationale and principles of organisation for the book in my preface, I would like to take this opportunity to outline just some of its key thematic contours and some of the shared features of the essays beyond their many individual differences of focus and approach – and then also to reflect briefly on the concept of 'context' and on the complexity of the relationship between texts and contexts.

Time, Space, Print Culture, Language

As one might expect with a book about historical contexts, the essays are organised in a broadly chronological sequence and they are grouped according to conventional English literary periodisation. Such periodisation has been the subject of much critical debate in recent years, but one paradoxical effect of following the evolving history of texts and contexts sequentially through these essays is precisely to be reminded that period contexts are not only constantly carried forwards in many complex ways (and often by literary texts themselves of course) but also operate retroactively in their own time by framing, shaping and colouring how previous periods are understood and interpreted. This is an understanding that all the contributors share, I think, and almost every single essay has the potential to send the reader shuttling backwards and forwards across all the other essays – and therefore backwards and forwards across English literary history. Consider, as one brief example, the trajectory from K. S. Whetter's early essay on medieval metrical romance through to Fiona Moolla's later consideration of romance elements in the fiction of modern-day Africa, passing by way of, among others, the Gothic romance of Austen's *Northanger Abbey* discussed by Katie Halsey. Such a relay of connections will, I hope, reinforce the sense that once we begin to look closely at texts in relation to their contexts, it becomes difficult to separate them off categorically from other texts and contexts shadowing them within the same broad cultural history, however far separated in time they may be and however carefully one tries to divide or periodise that history. Thus, despite the book's conventionally periodised structure (or perhaps partly because of it), the essays themselves, cumulatively, offer critical resistance to being corralled in this way and certainly to any suggestion of a mechanistic relationship among texts, contexts and periods.

Individually, too, most of the essays reflect at least implicitly on questions of period and on how we might negotiate transhistorical networks of connections and continuities in an adequately flexible and nuanced way. Lee Morrissey's essay is particularly helpful here in that it takes the issue of literary periodisation directly as its main theme and explores it in some sophisticated detail. Anna Budziak's essay on T. S. Eliot is also noteworthy in this respect for its meticulous placing of a text both within its own contemporaneous contexts and, in a sort of palimpsestic reading, in relation to texts and contexts from different past periods. Eliot's own famous concern for tradition is of course highly pertinent to all this, but Budziak almost out-Eliots him in a reading which subtly brings to focus one of the main realisations that I hope readers will take away from this book; that contexts operate synchronically *and* diachronically – *and* at the same time!

If questions of time are an inescapable feature of a project concerned with historical contexts, so too are questions of space, place, travel and mobility: again, almost every essay here touches on such questions in some way or other. Given that one basic definition of 'context' is 'setting', this could hardly be otherwise; and, of course, literature has had travels and journeying in its DNA from the very earliest human narratives. Significantly, the first essay in this collection, by Emily Thornbury, begins by addressing René Wellek's question 'What and where is a poem?' before embarking on a hugely absorbing tour of the many places of the peculiarly mobile Old English poem, *The Dream of the Rood*. Among many other things, her essay suggests how, in Anglo-Saxon culture, sacramental places and objects, pilgrimages, processions, performance and poetry all appear to have been interdependent and interwoven phenomena, simultaneously both artistic texts and material social contexts. In a rather different way Ulla Rahbek's final essay, too, in its consideration of postcolonial fiction and contemporary migrant narratives, and dealing with questions of mobility and community, identity and belonging, makes us think about how we negotiate our place in the world by negotiating literal places in the world, whether locally or globally. Global and transnational perspectives underpin the discussions of several other essays (e.g. those by Petrina, Grogan, Roberts and Kuortti) and the anthropology of space, place and travel is helpfully adumbrated by Stefania Michelucci's essay on Lawrence's *Women in Love*; while Terry Gifford's ecocritical study of the poetry of Ted Hughes reminds us of our fundamental placement on the earth and of the precarious future that now faces the human story-text within *its* defining context.

Related in some complex ways to questions of time and space, the broad theme of material print culture can be seen as a further permeating background for the whole collection. Several essays focus on the subject directly, but it also indirectly informs many, if not most, of the others. Clearly, the practical, material contexts involved in the production, circulation and consumption of literary texts, along with their transmission and reception through time, are of central importance to understanding how English literature has evolved and, crucially, how it has interacted at different times and in different places with pertaining social, cultural, economic, and ideological forces. The essays by Filip Krajník, Alessandra Petrina, Jane Grogan, Richard Jones, Katie Halsey, Ben Moore, Fionualla Dillane, Sue Asbee and Catherine Riley are particularly relevant here in providing a vivid sense of some of the complex networks of relationships that have been involved in material print culture through the ages and that continue to shape English literary history to the present.

My title claims that this is a book about *English* literature. But, in standing back to make this brief review of the collection, I see now just how much the essays have tended to contextualise English texts and traditions by reference to *non*-English texts and traditions. This may have something to do with the international nature of the team of contributors, but it is perhaps only natural, too, bearing in mind the mixed linguistic roots of the English language, still so clearly evident in the Anglo-Saxon and medieval periods, and bearing in mind the language's phenomenal global spread from colonial and postcolonial times to the present. At almost every turn, it seems, 'English' literature has developed out of, or in close interaction with, literature from other cultures and in other languages. The obvious early importance of translations and pan-European literary interchange is made very clear here in several of the essays (see, for example, Krajník's essay on Chaucer as translator). Even such a very British-seeming author as Tobias Smollett drew in a major way from European classics such as Cervantes's *Don Quixote*, as Richard Jones shows in his essay. Smollett was in fact Scottish, and we also need to remember that when we talk of English literature we often too easily elide Scottish, Irish and Welsh literary, linguistic and cultural influences with those of England. Grogan's essay makes this clear in relation to Ireland, while the essays by Fiona Price on Walter Scott and Jane Porter and by Robert Wilcher on Henry Vaughan draw attention to Scottish and Welsh contexts respectively. From Aphra Behn's Guianas-based *Oroonoko* in Oddvar Holmesland's essay to Izabel Brandão's reading of the contemporary work of Guyana-born British poet Grace Nichols, and from the early influences of India on English literature explored by Daniel Sanjiv Roberts to the 'chutnification' of English in Salman Rushdie's fiction discussed in Joel Kuortti's essay, this volume clearly bears strong witness to the supra-Englishness of English literature. One might even be inclined to adapt Wellek's question above and ask: what and where, then, is English literature?

Texts, Contexts, Contexture

As the orthography of the words clearly announces, texts and contexts are closely related. They are, in fact, mutually defining and it is particularly useful here to remember that the *Oxford English Dictionary*'s foundational definition of 'context' is explicitly textual, referring to the parts of a text that 'immediately precede and follow a word or passage and clarify its meaning'. I stress this point because other common definitions and everyday understandings of 'context' obscure this original text-based connection in referring outwards to notions of 'setting', 'circumstances' or 'environment' – that is, to concrete notions of immediate place or location or surroundings, as, for example, in the following sentence: 'This was highly inappropriate behaviour in the context of a lecture.' Mediating between these two leading definitions we also have the discursive and obviously relational sense of 'in relation to', as in: 'In the context of environmental concerns, we should all use less plastic.' All three of these senses are important to this book and, together, they make clear that context is what *defines* any given situation, whether abstract or concrete, textual or actual.

But this only takes us so far. *How* exactly does context define the situation and which parts of the context do the defining? This is perhaps clearer in the 'textual' definition above, as we can in principle point to specific words that clarify a meaning in a given passage – but even then, with anything longer than a short phrase or two, it quickly becomes a matter of judgement and interpretation as to exactly which words are the decisive ones. And there's the rub: contexts need defining and interpreting just as much as texts and situations do. This is where the mutuality of definition comes in and where we see that contexts are defined by texts as much as the other way round and that the concept of 'context' is altogether a much more slippery and complex one than might at first appear. Indeed, its complexity in relation to literary texts will become ever clearer as this volume progresses and as each of the essays introduces new ways of understanding it. However, let me offer a brief etymological reflection on our two keywords as a means of preparing the ground for the essays to come and of helping to clarify at least the general nature of this complexity.

As already noted, the words 'text' and 'context' are lexically related and the construction 'con + text', at its simplest, means just 'with', 'together with', 'beside' or 'against' the text. We might say, then, that the context 'frames' or 'sets off' the text, complementing and/or contrasting with it, putting it into relief, as it were, and that this is how it clarifies the text's meaning. A consideration of the original Latin roots of the words can help to nuance our understanding of this relationship further. Thus, 'text' can be related back to *texere*, which means 'to weave', and to *textus*, meaning 'web', 'fabric', or 'texture'. In parallel, 'context' relates to *contexere*, 'to interweave', and *contextus*, 'woven together'.

These terms nicely evoke the *material* elements of textuality; but, most importantly for my purposes here, they suggest a useful metaphorical distinction (and relationship) between the finished 'weaving', or woven fabric, of the text and the surrounding tangle of events and circumstances – the context – from which the threads of that weaving have been drawn. As already noted, a text's contexts are often seen as its 'background' or 'setting', the various elements (historical, biographical, social, etc.) that 'frame' it and clarify its meanings, giving it definition as a discrete and apparently autonomous signifying entity. But we can now see the paradox that while a text may be 'set off' by its contexts, those contexts are also inevitably *inter*woven into the very fabric of the text and remain an inextricable part of its meanings. In this light, we need to reject any clear-cut binary distinction between texts and contexts and to think, rather, in the above terms, of a *continuous* field, or network, of signification that links texts and contexts together flexibly within an interwoven fabric or web of meanings.

This is certainly the sort of complex conception of relations that informs this volume's general approach to reading texts in context. However, it still does not quite capture the full complexity of how texts and contexts interact, partly because it does not explicitly acknowledge the complicating dimension of time. Not only are texts always subject to changing contexts of production, circulation and reception across time, to changing frameworks of analysis, understanding and interpretation, but texts themselves can also exert historical influences both on contexts and on other texts. As already noted, moreover, contexts need to be interpreted just as much as texts do and they are therefore equally subject to changing paradigms of interpretation and understanding. As also outlined earlier, this dimension of time is a prominent theme in the essays which follow, and the interwoven web of meanings mentioned above ideally needs to be understood not just in spatial terms but as extending backwards and forwards in time as well.

The terms of the above etymology have suggested to me a type of critical neologism with which I would like to conclude this introduction, and it is a neologism that I offer, in part, as a tribute to my contributors. My many hours spent immersed in their essays have left me with an almost tactile sense of interacting texts and contexts and the image I am left with is of some thickly interwoven web of fabric, with substantial breadth, depth and extension, *and* with multiple ghostly threads tracing their ways back and forth through time to conjure up yet more such webs of fabric down the ages. To describe these essays, then, merely as 'contextual readings', while perfectly accurate in some ways, now seems somehow inadequate to the task of conveying the full nature and achievement of these essays in capturing the complexities of interrelating texts and contexts. I therefore propose an alternative 'con' word, which I think better communicates the material practice of these essays: 'contextured'. This is a relatively rare word, but the noun 'contexture', while also related to 'context', has a general meaning of 'structure' and refers mainly to 'the weaving together of parts into one body' and, most appropriately here, to a style of composition in writing which entails such a weaving together of parts into one whole.

These essays, then, I suggest, are best considered not so much as contextual but as contextural or *contextured* readings, readings which, as they explore complex webs of interacting meanings, weave texts and contexts tightly together into what is effectively one indivisible but richly textured body of discourse.

PART I
Medieval English, 500–1500

INTRODUCTORY NOTE

Emily Thornbury's study of *The Dream of the Rood* provides the perfect opening for this collection in immediately highlighting the fluid boundaries and intricate interdependencies between texts and contexts in the early medieval period. Thornbury's quest to discover the answer to exactly what and where the poem is, is in itself an immediate challenge to our usual contemporary understanding of texts as discrete and self-contained entities largely defined by the physical borders of page and book. In her discussion of the various manifestations of *The Dream of the Rood*, we are effectively asked if the poem is a monument or a manuscript, a performance or a devotional practice, and we gain a sense of a mobile, shape-shifting type of textuality always inextricably intermingled with its various surrounding contexts. (In this, it might be interesting to consider if there are any possible analogies here with contemporary digital textuality; and see, for example, Essay 19 for the different mediations of Fionnuala Dillane's discussed text, *Carmilla*, from Victorian serial to digital blog.)

If Thornbury's essay raises the question of where texts and contexts begin and end, Filip Krajník's essay might be understood to ask the additional question of where 'authorship' begins and ends. For us, the relationship between author and text, and the status of the author *as* author, as 'original creator', are generally taken for granted as relatively straightforward matters. But, as we know, and as Krajník's title suggests, the medieval writer was not seen in the individualistic terms of the 'creative genius' figure we have inherited from the Romantic era, a figure who supposedly creates a text *ab initio*, but as someone more akin to a scribe, an editor or translator, someone seen to be passing on some form of pre-existing text, even if newly 'processed' in one way or another. As Krajník's carefully contextualised argument develops, moreover, the importance of Chaucer's *actual* translations of works from other languages emerges, too, as a central feature of Chaucer's own sense of 'authorship' and as it fed intertextually (along with other people's translations) into works such as *The Parliament of Fowls*, which is the textual focus of the essay. Krajnik's reflections on medieval models of authorship and the elucidation of background linguistic and cultural influences emphasise again the permeable boundaries between texts and contexts – and, in exploring some of the possible historical occasions for which *The Parliament* may have been written, Krajnik also stresses the important connection for Chaucer between his text and its informing social function. *The Parliament of Fowls* may not exhibit quite the pronounced textual 'mobility' as *The Dream of the Rood*, especially as the text appears to have a more definite anchor in a known 'author', but, coming to Krajnik's essay in the immediate light of Thornbury's essay, we still see some of the same factors of fluidity between text and context in the inevitably intertextual notion of the 'translator'.

Chaucer's translation of the *Roman de la Rose* and his own significant contribution to medieval romance literature make a natural bridge to the next essay where K. S. Whetter expertly sketches out the evolution of the genre from twelfth-century France onwards, before turning to a sustained analysis of two representative examples of Arthurian romance, *Ywayne and Gawayne* and *The Awntyrs off Arthure*. Whetter neatly maps out the social, cultural and political terrain informing medieval romance, with special attention to how the genre absorbed and expressed issues to do with kingship and loyalty, with local lordship and feudal estate management, and with the roles and rights of aristocratic and gentry women. He suggests at the conclusion of his essay that the ability of romance to explore key aspects of social life may or may not have been a major reason for its *initial* emergence as a genre, but that this was almost certainly a major reason for its subsequent growth and popularity from medieval times to the present – and evidence of this ongoing popularity is not hard to find among other essays in this collection as one proceeds through the different period sections, especially if we are alert to the various ways in which the romance genre constantly evolves and reinvents itself. Lee Morrissey in Essay 9 reminds us of the genre's influence on the emergence of the novel ('roman') and Oddvar Holmesland's Essay 10 discusses Aphra Behn's *Oroonoko* specifically in terms of romance. It is useful, further, to consider ways in which the concept and genre of romance might be seen to be absorbed and reworked in Romanticism. As I mentioned in my introduction, too, Fiona Moolla's postcolonial essay on romance in modern African fiction provides an interesting contemporary coordinate here (see Essay 27 and note that Moolla's references to critical works on romance helpfully complement Whetter's).

All three essays in this section, in very different ways, concern themselves with the transmission, mediation and circulation (if not recycling) of texts. It might be instructive then to see them in the light of the contemporary concept within print culture studies of a 'communications circuit' and to set them in dialogue with later essays which discuss related issues (in particular, Essays 4, 5, 11, 14 and 19).

1

Finding *The Dream of the Rood* in Old English Literature

EMILY V. THORNBURY

Abstract

The Old English poem called *The Dream of the Rood* has challenged audiences for more than a thousand years. It is precocious in content, using the dream vision to open up a fictional space for contemplation; within that space, it demands that readers emotionally re-experience the central mystery of the Christian religion. In this way it anticipates much later medieval literary trends. *The Dream of the Rood* is also formally challenging, using wordplay, complex shifts in metre and haunting repetitions to weave a complex web of affect and meaning. It is a triumph of craft, which perhaps explains why it seems to have been popular across early medieval England.

The poem is also elusive, multiform. One text appears in a tenth-century manuscript; others, close kin, are engraved on objects – a monumental stone cross and a gold reliquary. Still other echoes of *The Dream of the Rood* appear across the corpus of Old English verse.

Which is the real poem? How can we, today, read a text that presents to us such varied faces, especially when none of them can be tied to any author whose name and life we know?

This essay considers modern scholars' varied answers to these questions, answers which help us perceive how early literature's voices – and its silences – can echo or reply to much later concerns. In the medieval reception of *The Dream of the Rood* and its tradition, we will also see ways to pose these questions altogether differently – and thus to rethink the way we understand poetry's place in the world.

The Old English poem we call *The Dream of the Rood* challenges modern assumptions about the nature of a literary text in space and time. René Wellek's counterintuitive but revealing question in *Theory of Literature* – 'What and where is a poem?' – takes on new resonance in an early medieval context.[1] One poem which we call *The Dream of the Rood* appears in a tenth-century manuscript called the Vercelli Book. It is a copy, made from another text now lost, and may have been copied from a copy – and perhaps rewritten along the way. A poem which is too

Figure 1.1 The Ruthwell Cross, Dumfries and Galloway, Scotland. The cross is now housed in Ruthwell parish church.

much like *The Dream of the Rood* to be unrelated, yet too different to be called the same poem, is carved in runes on the sides of an early eighth-century stone monument in the village church of Ruthwell, in south-west Scotland (Figure 1.1). Yet another artefact – this one a gold reliquary cross now in Brussels, Belgium – is engraved with two lines of Old English poetry nearly identical to lines in the Vercelli and Ruthwell texts. Which is the real poem? What and where is *The Dream of the Rood*?

In the wider context of ancient literature, our poem does not appear especially elusive. The copy in the Vercelli Book is clear and undamaged; and though parts of the Ruthwell Cross inscription have been broken off, most of the surviving runes are intact and legible. In this our texts contrast with such poems as *The Ruin*, large sections of which have been burned out of the only manuscript copy we have, and even *Beowulf*, whose manuscript has been badly damaged. Likewise, the Bewcastle

Cross, a close stylistic cousin of the Ruthwell monument, has an inscription panel worn away to a bumpy sandstone plane. Moreover, unlike (say) the corpus of ancient Etruscan, Old English is well understood by modern scholars, and we can be quite confident that we know what the words in these texts mean.

The poem's story is also relatively clear. In the 156-line Vercelli Book text an unnamed speaker relates what he saw in 'the middle of the night', when a vast, terrifying and beautiful Cross appeared to him and described what it saw and felt when Christ was executed upon it. Despite its pain and grief, the Cross could do nothing to stop the execution, and was left to mourn its Lord's death; but this horror, it explains, paradoxically became the source of its present glory. The Cross goes on to urge the dreamer to tell what he has seen, so that everyone can know that the Cross will help them on the Day of Judgement. After the Cross's speech has ended, the dreamer reflects on his hopes for its aid; on his own death; and on Christ's triumph when he rescued the patriarchs from Hell. While the Ruthwell text is much shorter – only about fifteen lines of verse, some so damaged that only a few words or letters can be read – it contains much of the Cross's description of the Crucifixion, spoken in its own voice:

> [Ahof] ic riicnæ kyninc
> heafunæs hlafard   hælda ic ni dorstæ
> bismærædu unket men ba ætgad[re]   ic [wæs] miþ blodæ bistemid[2]

> [I lifted up] the mighty king, the Lord of heaven: I dared not bow down. People mocked us two both together; I was soaked in blood ...

This is a transliteration of the runes visible on the left-hand side of the east face of the monument. These verses correspond closely to lines 44–9 of the Vercelli text:

> Rod wæs ic ærered: ahof ic ricne cyning,
> heofona hlaford;   hyldan me ne dorste.
> Þurhdrifan hi me mid deorcan næglum;   on me syndon þa dolg gesiene,
> opene inwidhlemmas.   Ne dorste ic hira ænigum sceððan.
> Bysmeredon hie unc butu ætgædere;   eall ic wæs mid blode bestemed,
> begoten of þæs guman sidan,   siððan he hæfde his gast onsended.[3]

> A cross I was raised up: I lifted up the mighty king, the Lord of heaven; I dared not bow down. They pierced me through with dark nails; upon me those wounds are visible, the public marks of treachery. I dared not injure any of them. They mocked us two both together; I was entirely covered in blood, drenched from that man's side when he had sent forth his spirit.

Even in these two short passages, we can perceive some of the essential qualities of the poem. The speaking Cross is immobile – it repeatedly says it could not move – yet it feels deeply, and seems to relive the suffering it experienced during the Crucifixion as it tells its story to the Dreamer. It thinks of Christ not merely as the Lord but as *its* lord, and wishes to serve him properly. These aspects are shared by both the Ruthwell and Vercelli texts. Yet the differences between the two – in language, in length – are just as clear.

To try to understand the *Dream*'s many facets, we must begin with a tour of the places in which we find it. The most expansive of these sites is undoubtedly the Vercelli Book. Written in southern England in the second half of the tenth century, this manuscript is now in Vercelli, Italy – though precisely how it came there, no one knows.[4] The Vercelli Book contains twenty-three prose homilies along with six poems, all in Old English.[5] The homilies treat a range of subjects, including preparation for death and Doomsday, the necessity of suffering and labour, and the miracles of Christ and his apostles; they seem to have been put together from several different sources. The poems, too, are highly varied, ranging from a long account of St Andrew's adventures in the land of the cannibals (*Andreas*), through shorter penitential poems (*Soul and Body I, Homiletic Fragment I*) and a verse list of the apostles' mission fields (*Fates of the Apostles*). This last poem includes a runic 'signature' passage by the poet Cynewulf, whose signature also appears in *Elene*, a long poem about the finding of the True Cross.[6] The Vercelli Book, then, seems to have been a multipurpose tool whose texts were designed for preaching, teaching and private devotion. As a setting for *The Dream of the Rood*, the manuscript draws attention to several of the poem's features: its focus both on New Testament history and the end of the world; its power to inspire penitential feeling; and its status as a written work of Old English literature.

Though its verse text is closely related, the Ruthwell Cross presents a distinctively different view of the poem. The cross itself is a carved sandstone monument more than five metres (about seventeen feet) high, which now stands in a parish church in Ruthwell, Dumfriesshire, Scotland, a region which was once part of the medieval kingdom of Northumbria.[7] Because it was broken and buried during the Protestant Reformation, and its surviving pieces reassembled during the eighteenth century, there is some debate about whether the Ruthwell Cross (as it is now) was originally an obelisk, the present cross-piece being a modern restoration.[8] The stone carving was once brightly painted; its style links the Ruthwell Cross to another eighth-century monument at Bewcastle, and ultimately to the monastery of Wearmouth-Jarrow, whose leaders, inspired by Roman art, supported the creation of many ambitious stone artworks.[9] As it currently stands, the north and south faces of the Ruthwell Cross depict saints as well as scenes from the life of Christ; the unique range of images shows a preference for penitential and eremitic themes, identified by Latin inscriptions in the surrounding borders. On the sides, panels of vine scrolls inhabited by birds and beasts are surrounded by runes: the *Dream of the Rood* text (Figure 1.2).

The Ruthwell poem thus at first seems local in a way the Vercelli Book's text does not. Cut in runic letters, written in the Northumbrian dialect, and set at a

Figure 1.2 East face middle section of the Ruthwell Cross, with the runes visible on the edges bordering the central interlace carvings.

distance from major towns and settlements, it would appear on every level to be restricted to a small audience. Yet this is partly an illusion created by a modern perspective trained on ubiquitous print and ethereal electronic media. As Seeta Chaganti has pointed out, inscribed objects – not books – were the paradigmatic experience of written language for most people in early medieval England.[10] This point is underscored by a third instantiation of the poem, engraved on silver plates affixed to a wooden reliquary cross that was once fully encased in gems and precious metals, and is now in the treasury of the Cathedral of St Michael and St Gundula in Brussels. Beginning from the base of its right side, the inscription encircling the cross's outer edge reads:

+ Rod is min nama   Geo ic ricne cyning
bær byfigynde   blode bestemed
Thas rode het Æþlmær wyrican and Adhelwold hys beroþor
Criste to lofe for Ælfrices saule hyra beroþo[r][11]

Cross is my name: formerly I bore the mighty king, trembling and soaked in blood. Æthelmær and his brother Æthelwold commanded this cross be made to honour Christ, for the soul of their brother Ælfric.

On the back of the cross is also inscribed '+ Drahmal me worhte' (Drahmal made me). For the Brussels Cross, then, words and object give each other meaning: the main inscription both defines the object's borders and allows it to voice its own name as well as those of its makers and dedicatees, so that the words on metal 'shape and delineate physically the identity of the object', as Chaganti writes. Though the poem takes different shapes on metal, stone and parchment, it is a significant part of the experience of each object.

Moreover, neither the Brussels Cross nor the Ruthwell monument were intended to be contemplated in solitude from a distance, as if they were museum objects. Éamonn Ó Carragáin reads close ties in the Ruthwell Cross's set of images to the yearly and daily cycles of monastic religious observance, and concludes that the monument itself was likely to have been physically incorporated into liturgical events that included the whole community.[13] The Brussels Cross, too, would have actively participated in communal life: as a processional cross, it would have been carried within and outside the church during major rites.[14] Performance – as Catherine E. Karkov and Chaganti have argued – was thus an essential, constitutive aspect of both objects, in which the inscribed poem plays its part for, and with, the reading and listening audience.[15]

While the physical portability of the Vercelli Book and Brussels Cross would seem to give their texts greater mobility, recognising the performative aspect of the Ruthwell inscription allows us to perceive that its *Dream* text was not in practice fixed to its site either. The stone cross was not its limit but rather the centre from which experience of the poem radiated outwards through the community and perhaps from one community to another. With a shift in perspective, we can see that the Ruthwell Cross combined the familiar – incised runes, Old English verse – with the daringly exotic – an immense stone monument carved in a foreign style. It is thus similar to the poem, which locates itself in several cultural contexts simultaneously, and synthesises them into something new.

The Dream of the Rood – and its Crucifixion narrative in particular – is saturated with the heroic language and motifs familiar to us from poems like *Beowulf* and *The Battle of Maldon*. As many scholars have shown, Christ is portrayed as a warrior facing combat with courage; his disciples, and the Cross itself, are his loyal retainers and the instruments of his conquest.[16] For the Cross, the experience is a painful (if ultimately triumphant) one, and through its suffering the heroic ethos itself is represented in complex and ambivalent terms.[17] The combination of martial imagery with religious subjects is not unique to the *Dream*; indeed, it is so common that it may be considered the normal mode of religious discourse in Old English narrative verse. But it has caused a good deal of difficulty for modern critics, who have sometimes struggled to reconcile the fact of the poem's heroic diction with the equally apparent fact of its Latin learning. In 1949 Margaret Schlauch connected the literary device of the speaking Cross with a school exercise commonly given to young people learning Latin.[18] Since then, scholars have traced the poem's many ties to the early medieval discipline of *grammatica*, which encompassed everything from elementary Latin to advanced analysis of literary and religious texts, and shaped the way all educated people approached language.[19] It is clear, moreover, that the *Dream*'s understanding of Christianity is learned and sophisticated, encompassing a thorough knowledge of the Gospels' narrative but also a considerable acquaintance with Latin liturgy and hagiographical texts.[20]

Like the Cross that appears to the Dreamer alternately covered in treasure and blood (lines 21–3), the *Dream* challenges us to perceive the essential unity of the apparently irreconcilable. We can, if we wish, decide that the poem is 'really' in one place or another – within secular, Old English-speaking heroic culture, or within learned, Latinate Christian culture – and accordingly consider the incompatible parts of it as somehow 'unreal': rhetorical sugar-coating for a resistant audience, perhaps, or tedious and unnecessary elaboration. But accepting the *Dream of the Rood*'s inherent multiplicity, and the implications of that multiplicity, can provide us with a fruitful way of understanding this poem and poetry more generally.

Wellek's reflections on the nature of poetry are again useful. He compares a poem and particular texts, readings, memories or recitations of that poem to Saussure's distinction between *langue* and *parole*:

> The system of language (*langue*) is a collection of conventions and norms whose workings and relations we can observe and describe as having a fundamental coherence and identity in spite of very different, imperfect, or incomplete pronouncements of individual speakers. In this respect at least, a literary work of art is in exactly the same position as a system of language. We as individuals shall never realize it completely, for we shall never use our own language completely and perfectly. ... We shall never know an object in all its qualities, but still we can scarcely deny the identity of objects even though we may see them from different perspectives.[21]

Viewed in this way, a poem, like a language, is an emergent phenomenon: given shape by its instantiations across time and space, and yet transcending any individual manifestation. While a particular version may gain ascendance and authority for all sorts of reasons – it is a popular edition, a widely heard recitation, a common schoolroom assignment – all poems thus exist as part of a complex ecosystem. The three written or inscribed versions of *The Dream of the Rood* do not force us to choose which one is 'real', then. All are, and each instance presents a distinctive interpretation that expands the poem's capacity for meaning. The radically different scales of the Vercelli, Brussels and Ruthwell texts need not disturb us here: consider, for instance, the several versions of 'Poetry' that Marianne Moore wrote, ranging from twenty-nine lines to three.[22]

A modern case like Moore's, presenting several distinct authorial versions of the 'same' poem, helps us perceive that textual multiplicity and fluidity are not simply a medieval phenomenon ended by the advent of print. That said, scholars have long recognised a real difference in the scale of variation found in medieval texts. Paul Zumthor used the word *mouvance* to describe the way medieval French romances changed from manuscript to manuscript: comparing any two passages, one might find minor variations in wording, or a few lines in one book but not the other, or radical differences in length or content.[23] *Mouvance*, Zumthor believed, was a function of medieval literature's fundamentally oral character: each text of a romance was in essence a separate performance.

Over the last century or so a great deal of creative research has helped those steeped in highly literate societies to better understand the mindset of primarily oral cultures.[24] Scholars of early medieval England quickly recognised the explanatory power of oral theory, especially for Old English poetry. Very soon, these researchers realised that – contrary to the assumptions of the earliest scholarship on oral verse – orality and literacy were not mutually exclusive; learning to read and write did not immediately affect one's ability to compose in an oral style. By studying the differences between texts of Old English poems, Katherine O'Brien O'Keeffe was able to show that even scribes who were primarily concerned with the word-for-word copying of texts before them, were also, in some sense, performing: many of the changes they introduced were not mistakes, but variations based on knowledge of many other poems.[25] *Mouvance* in Old English was thus what happened when literate people continued to work within the framework of oral culture.[26]

Fluidity is not the same thing as evanescence, however. Verbal art in oral cultures is capable of stability over many years or, indeed, generations.[27] To return to Wellek's metaphor, the 'language' of such a poem permits a larger range of possible expressions than we (in late print culture) are used to hearing from a single work; yet the core idiom remains recognisably the same. Each instantiation – whether spoken or sung aloud, written in ink, carved, incised, or even embroidered on some other material – constitutes a separate performance, and each performance represents a new interaction between the choices, knowledge and capacities of the performer; the resistances and opportunities offered by the medium; and the desires and capacities of the audience. Moreover, the single truly universal recording medium – memory – allows for the layering and coexistence of many performances across time: this allows us to perceive how rich the experience of the Ruthwell and Brussels inscriptions could have been for people who encountered them repeatedly, through many modes of communal performance. For each person, the real poem would have been the emergent knowledge produced by a succession of encounters.

We can thus understand literary allusion as a kind of double performance, reinstantiating the prior text while also creating something new. This phenomenon, I believe, is at play in the poem called *Guthlac B*. The second of the Exeter Book's two poems about the hermit Guthlac of Crowland, *Guthlac B* recounts the saint's death.[28] While drawing on later chapters of the Latin life of Guthlac by Felix, the Old English poem boldly reframes its narrative. It begins not with the saint's birth and early years, but with Adam and Eve's sin and expulsion from Paradise, before turning to Guthlac as the saint prepares for his death. The onset of his fatal illness is described thus:

> Ða se ælmihtiga
> let his hond cuman   þær se halga þeow,
> deormod on degle   domeadig bad,
> heard ond hygerof.   Hyht wæs geniwad,
> blis in breostum.   Wæs se bancofa
> adle onæled,   inbendum fæst,
> lichord onlocen.   Leomu hefegedon,
> sarum gesohte.   He þæt soð gecneow
> þæt hine ælmihtig   ufan neosade,
> meotud fore miltsum. (*Guthlac B* 950b–959a)

Then the Almighty placed his hand where the holy servant awaited, courageous in the desert, eager for glory, resolute and bold in spirit. Hope was renewed, joy in his heart. The bone-coffer, secure in its inward bonds, was kindled with its funeral flame, the body's treasure unlocked. His limbs grew heavy; he was visited by pains. He recognised indeed that the Almighty sought him from above, the Creator in his mercy.

Guthlac's experience echoes the final lines of the Vercelli Book *Dream* text:

> Hiht wæs geniwad
> mid bledum ond mid blisse   þam þe þær bryne þolodan.
> Se Sunu wæs sigorfæst   on þam siðfate,
> mihtig ond spedig   þa he mid manigeo com,
> gasta weorode   on Godes rice,
> Anwealda ælmihtig,   englum to blisse
> ond eallum ðam halgum   þam þe on heofonum ær
> wunedon on wuldre,   þa heora Wealdend cwom,
> ælmihtig God,   þær his eðel wæs. (*DR* 148b–56)

Hope was renewed with glory and joy for those who there endured the flame. The Son was victorious on the raid, mighty and prosperous when he came with the multitude, a host of spirits, into God's kingdom, the almighty Monarch, to the joy of the angels and all those holy ones who already dwelt in glory in the heavens, when their ruler, almighty God, came to his homeland.

The passage from the *Dream* describes the Harrowing of Hell. This event – in which Christ, before his resurrection, descended into Hell to free the souls of the righteous – is both a standard part of the medieval Passion narrative, and arresting and strange in the context of the *Dream* because of its placement at the end of the poem, outside both the Cross's speech and the Dreamer's framing account of it. The re-enactment of the Harrowing in *Guthlac B* is in its way equally startling, as the flames of original sin from which the patriarchs in the *Dream* were saved meld with the burning fever that preceded Guthlac's death. As a literary allusion, the invocation of the *Dream* makes clear that Guthlac's fatal illness is both (like the patriarchs' suffering) a natural consequence of the Fall described in the poem's opening, and, for Guthlac himself, a welcome liberation. Imagined as a double performance, however, the *Guthlac B* passage does something rather more complicated. It unbinds the Harrowing from the historical moment of the Crucifixion and envisions the event itself as continually present – not echoed by the death of a saint, but actually occurring at each such moment. As such, it presents a compelling interpretation of the Harrowing passage in the *Dream*. As reprised in *Guthlac B*, the final lines of the *Dream* are not a displaced fragment of history, but a depiction of the Dreamer's longed-for death and triumphant entry into heaven alongside Christ, whose story he has at last fully joined.

Seeing *Guthlac B* as performing *The Dream of the Rood* at certain key moments dovetails with Robert E. Bjork's argument that one of the poem's major goals is to demonstrate the mystic unity of Guthlac and Christ.[29] This purpose seems to come to the fore as *Guthlac B* depicts the beam of light that Guthlac's disciple Beccel sees surrounding the dead saint's house:

> Ða wæs Guðlaces   gæst gelæded
> eadig on upweg.   Englas feredun
> to þam longan gefean,   lic colode,
> belifd under lyfte.   Ða þær leoht ascan,
> beama beorhtast.   Eal þæt beacen wæs
> ymb þæt halge hus,   heofonlic leoma,
> from foldan up   swylce fyren tor
> ryht aræred   oð rodera hrof ... (*Guth B* 1305–12)

Then Guthlac's blessed spirit was lifted along the upward path. Angels conducted him to the eternal joy; his body cooled, abandoned beneath the sky. Then a light shone forth there, the brightest of beams. That sign was entirely around that holy house, a heavenly radiance raised up like a fiery tower from the ground to the skies' roof ...

This echoes the Dreamer's opening account of his vision:

> Þuhte me þæt ic gesawe   syllicre treow
> on lyft lædan,   leohte bewunden,
> beama beorhtost.   Eall þæt beacen wæs
> begoten mid golde ... (*DR* 4–7a)

It seemed to me that I saw a very wonderful tree lifted up in the air, wound about with light, the brightest of beams. That sign was entirely suffused with gold ...

Guthlac's soul, 'lifted' (*gelæded*) up like the Cross, seems to meld with the supernatural radiance and, in turn, the Cross. As in modern English, Old English *beam* may refer to rood or light; the *Dream* makes overt use of that double meaning, and by invoking the *Dream*, *Guthlac B* makes the Cross present in what, on the surface, is not a cross at all.[30] This effect is intensified by the final line of the quoted passage, 'ryht aræred ô rodera hrof' ('raised up straight to the heavens' roof'), which seems to allude, via a favourite Old English pun, to 44a of the Vercelli text: 'Rod wæs ic aræred'.[31]

From this double performance emerges a complex and profound theory of sanctity. The co-presence of the Cross with the light arising from Guthlac's hermitage implies that the quiet death of a confessor was as holy as a martyr's violent end; and it suggests that Guthlac, too, partakes of the Cross's cosmic grandeur and the intercessory power it promises (*DR* 117–21). Most of all, the invocation of the *Dream* allows *Guthlac B* to build towards one of its goals: a kind of glimpse of the eternal present of divine temporality. By integrating Guthlac's death with Christ's, the co-presence of the two poems obliges the audience to experience them simultaneously, and so to understand that – like Adam and Eve's first sin – they were not discrete, now past historical events. All were, and are, part of the same act of divine salvation.

This reading of *Guthlac B* entails that both poet and presumed audience knew *The Dream of the Rood* well, and in a form fairly similar to the Vercelli Book text. Given that Andy Orchard has produced persuasive evidence that *Andreas* and Cynewulf's *Elene* also allude to the *Dream*, it seems increasingly likely that the poem was well known, and an important part of early English literary culture.[32] This of course does not mean that everyone's *Dream of the Rood* would have been identical: we have already seen how different the Ruthwell, Brussels and Vercelli texts are from one another, and it is possible that the Vercelli Book text represents multiple stages of composition by different authors.[33] We might even suggest that the more popular and beloved an early medieval artwork was, the more likely it was to be multiple: to be performed differently, repeatedly, in many media and for many purposes.

The Dream of the Rood thus helps us to perceive that the quest for a singular, original or even 'best' text or interpretation can obscure as often as it reveals, and that a poem's multiplicity need not be a barrier to a shared experience and knowledge of it. Found in manuscript, stone and metal – and in the memories of other Old English poets, and of countless modern readers of Old English too – the *Dream* forms a kind of limit case for the dispersal of a medieval text across space, time and media. It is nowhere, and everywhere; and this allows us to perceive the liberatory potential in Wellek's idea of the emergent text. Just as the many different performances of *The Dream of the Rood* did not compromise the 'real' medieval poem but gave it life, so can creative modern interpretations become part of the ongoing life and performance history of this text, and of all others.

NOTES

1. René Wellek and Austin Warren, *Theory of Literature*, 3rd edn (New York: Harcourt, Brace, Jovanovich, 1977), pp. 142–57.
2. Michael Swanton (ed.), *The Dream of the Rood* (Liverpool University Press, 1996), p. 94 (with some transliteration); all translations are mine.
3. Ibid., pp. 95–7 (punctuation slightly altered).
4. Its shelfmark is Vercelli, Biblioteca Capitolare CXVI. A useful overview of the manuscript can be found in the editors' introduction to *New Readings in the Vercelli Book*, ed. Samantha Zacher and Andy Orchard (University of Toronto Press, 2009), pp. 3–11; for a more detailed study of its language and handwriting, see the introduction to D. G. Scragg (ed.), *The Vercelli Homilies and Related Texts*, Early English Text Society OS 300 (Oxford University Press, 1992).
5. For the prose, see Scragg (ed.), *Vercelli Homilies*; for the poems see George Philip Krapp (ed.), *The Vercelli Book*, Anglo-Saxon Poetic Records 2 (New York: Columbia University Press, 1932).
6. Besides the two Vercelli Book poems, Cynewulf's signature appears in two poems in the Exeter Book (Exeter Cathedral Library MS 3501): see Robert E. Bjork (ed. and trans.), *The Old English Poems of Cynewulf*, Dumbarton Oaks Medieval Library (Cambridge, MA: Harvard University Press, 2013).
7. Swanton (ed.), *Dream* describes the Ruthwell monument and inscription at pp. 9–38. For an indispensable recent account, including detailed plates and drawings, see also Éamonn Ó Carragáin, *Ritual and the Rood: Liturgical Images and the Old English Poems of the Dream of the Rood Tradition* (Toronto: British Library, 2005).
8. Ó Carragáin, *Ritual*, pp. 12–32. Ó Carragáin argues that the monument was indeed originally cross-shaped; for the contrary view see Fred Orton, 'Northumbrian Sculpture (the Ruthwell and Bewcastle Monuments): Questions of Difference', in Jane Hawkes and Susan Mills (eds), *Northumbria's Golden Age* (Stroud: Sutton, 1999), pp. 216–26.
9. Jane Hawkes, 'Reading Stone', in Catherine E. Karkov and Fred Orton (eds), *Theorizing Anglo-Saxon Stone Sculpture* (Morgantown: West Virginia University Press, 2003), pp. 5–30 (pp. 26–9); Jane Hawkes, '*Iuxta morem Romanorum*: Stone and Sculpture in Anglo-Saxon England', in Catherine E. Karkov and George Hardin Brown (eds), *Anglo-Saxon Styles* (Albany: State University of New York Press, 2003), pp. 69–99.
10. Seeta Chaganti, 'Vestigial Signs: Inscription, Performance, and *The Dream of the Rood*', *PMLA* 125 (2010), 48–72 (50).
11. Text transcribed from Ó Carragáin, *Ritual*, fig. 55 (p. 340).
12. Chaganti, 'Vestigial Signs', 55.
13. Ó Carragáin, *Ritual*, esp. pp. 280–2.
14. Ibid., pp. 339–54.
15. Catherine E. Karkov, 'Naming and Renaming: The Inscription of Gender in Anglo-Saxon Sculpture', in Karkov and Orton (eds), *Theorizing*, pp. 31–64; Chaganti, 'Vestigial Signs'.
16. See, e.g., Michael D. Cherniss, 'The Cross as Christ's Weapon: The Influence of Heroic Literary Tradition on *The Dream of the Rood*', *Anglo-Saxon England* 2 (1973), 241–52; Carol Jean Wolf, 'Christ as Hero in *The Dream of the Rood*', *Neuphilologische Mitteilungen* 71 (1970), 202–10; Anne L. Klinck, 'Christ as Soldier and Servant in *The Dream of the Rood*', *Florilegium* 4 (1982), 109–16.

17. See especially Klinck, 'Christ as Soldier', and Mary Dockray-Miller, 'The Feminized Cross of *The Dream of the Rood*', *Philological Quarterly* 76 (1997), 1–18.

18. Margaret Schlauch, '*The Dream of the Rood* as Prosopopoeia', in *Essays and Studies in Honor of Carleton Brown* (New York University Press, 1949), pp. 23–34.

19. See, e.g., Martin Irvine, *The Making of Textual Culture: 'Grammatica' and Literary Theory, 350–1100* (Cambridge University Press, 1994), esp. pp. 437–49. Andy Orchard, '*The Dream of the Rood*: Cross-References', in Zacher and Orchard (eds), *New Readings*, pp. 225–53, connects the *Dream* to the popular teaching mode of *enigmata* (literary riddles), which in turn often incorporated prosopopoeia.

20. See, e.g., Rosemary Woolf, 'Doctrinal Influences on *The Dream of the Rood*', *Medium Ævum* 27 (1958), 137–53; Earl R. Anderson, 'Liturgical Influence in *The Dream of the Rood*', *Neophilologus* 73 (1989), 293–304; Ó Carragáin, *Ritual*; Thomas D. Hill, 'The *Passio Andreae* and *The Dream of the Rood*', *Anglo-Saxon England* 38 (2009), 1–10.

21. Wellek and Warren, *Theory of Literature*, p. 152.

22. For the earlier versions see Marianne Moore, *Observations*, ed. Linda Leavell (New York: Farrar, Strauss & Giroux, 2016), pp. 26–8; for the latest, her *The Complete Poems* (New York: Macmillan, 1967), p. 36.

23. Paul Zumthor, *Toward a Medieval Poetics*, trans. Philip Bennett (Minneapolis: University of Minnesota Press, 1991).

24. Some accessible foundational works include Albert Bates Lord, *The Singer of Tales*, 2nd edn (Cambridge, MA: Harvard University Press, 2000); Walter J. Ong, *Orality and Literacy: The Technologizing of the Word* (London: Routledge, 1991); and John Miles Foley, *How To Read an Oral Poem* (Urbana: University of Illinois Press, 2002).

25. Katherine O'Brien O'Keeffe, *Visible Song: Transitional Literacy in Old English Verse* (Cambridge University Press, 1990).

26. This phenomenon was not restricted to poetry: for instance, in 'Crying Wolf: Oral Style and the *Sermones Lupi*', *Anglo-Saxon England* 21 (1992), 239–64, Andy Orchard showed that the eleventh-century archbishop Wulfstan of York's sermons varied in similar ways.

27. Comparing the texts of widely spaced performances of the same poem by the same singers in Lord, *Singer of Tales*, for instance, shows not only considerable stability of content but, often, word-for-word verbal identity alongside frequent variation.

28. The text here is from George Philip Krapp and Elliot van Kirk Dobbie (eds), *The Exeter Book*, Anglo-Saxon Poetic Records 3 (New York: Columbia University Press, 1936). For more thorough notes and discussion, see Jane Roberts (ed.), *The Guthlac Poems of the Exeter Book* (Oxford: Clarendon Press, 1979).

29. Robert E. Bjork, *The Old English Verse Saints' Lives: A Study in Direct Discourse and the Iconography of Style* (University of Toronto Press, 1985), pp. 90–109 (pp. 91–3).

30. If the Ruthwell monument were indeed an obelisk originally (see note 8), then we may see a shade of similarity in this third beam.

31. On the *rod* 'Cross'/*rodor* 'heaven' pun, see Roberta Frank, 'Some Uses of Paronomasia in Old English Scriptural Verse', *Speculum* 47 (1972), 207–26 (210–11).

32. Orchard, 'Cross-References', pp. 248–53. Many scholars have argued on stylistic grounds that *Guthlac B*, like *Elene*, was composed by Cynewulf: the poem's ending has been lost from the manuscript, along with any runic signature that once existed. See Bjork (ed.), *Poems of Cynewulf*, which includes *Guthlac B*.

33. Many scholars have suggested that the first and second part of the Vercelli text are by different authors: see most recently Leonard Neidorf, 'The Composite Authorship of *The Dream of the Rood*', *Anglo-Saxon England* 45 (2016), 51–70.

CRITICAL REFLECTIONS AND FURTHER STUDY

Rather like its (now) titular speaking Cross, *The Dream of the Rood* maintains a curious double existence. To readers of Old English, it is among the handful of best-known and most studied poems, not least because it appears in popular textbooks like Bruce Mitchell and Fred C. Robinson, *A Guide to Old English*, 8th edn (Oxford: Blackwell, 2011) and Peter S. Baker, *Introduction to Old English*, 3rd edn (Oxford: Wiley-Blackwell, 2012). Unlike *Beowulf*, however, the *Dream* has not yet found a broad modern audience through translation. Several, however, are available, including that of Ciaran Carson in Greg Delanty and Michael Matto (eds), *The Word Exchange* (New York: W. W. Norton, 2011), pp. 366–77, and Mary Clayton in *Old English Poems of Christ and His Saints*, Dumbarton Oaks Medieval Library (Cambridge, MA: Harvard University Press, 2013), which allow non-specialist readers to glimpse its strange and remarkable qualities.

The density and richness of the *Dream*'s language are one reason it is beloved by readers of Old English and little known to others, since many of its more complex techniques are difficult to render in modern English. Carol Braun Pasternack, for instance, has traced the variations in mode created by shifts in verb placement, in 'Stylistic Disjunctions in *The Dream of the Rood*', *Anglo-Saxon England* 13 (1984), 167–86. Meanwhile Susan Irvine showed how a single ambiguous pronoun embodied a profound theological point in 'Adam or Christ? A Pronominal Pun in *The Dream of the Rood*', *Review of English Studies* 48 (1997), 433–47. While verbal repetition is more readily translated than the twists of Old English's word order and syntax, its significance is easy to overlook: however, scholars like Constance B. Hieatt, in 'Dream-Frame and Verbal Echo in *The Dream of the Rood*', *Neuphilologische Mitteilungen* 72 (1971), 251–63, have shown how recurrent words and phrases held together the poem's concentric structure. These are but a handful of the many excellent readings of *Dream*; a glance over the yearly bibliographies published by the *Old English Newsletter* will demonstrate how intensely this poem's language has been studied.

Although close reading remains perhaps the most popular critical method, the *Dream* rewards many different approaches. In '*The Dream of the Rood*: Cross-References', in Samantha Zacher and Andy Orchard (eds), *New Readings in the Vercelli Book* (Toronto University Press, 2009), pp. 225–53, Andy Orchard combines close reading with a corpus-based approach akin to distant reading. This enables him to track the poem's verbal entanglements with the genre of riddles (popular in both Latin and Old English), and to argue that the poem

Elene makes extensive literary allusion to the *Dream*. Many other recent critics have also been inclined to see the *Dream* as part of a learned, literary culture. Martin Irvine, for instance, in *The Making of Textual Culture: 'Grammatica' and Literary Theory, 350–1100* (Cambridge University Press, 1994), at pp. 437–49 reads it as part of a wider early medieval practice of biblical commentary. More recently, in '*The Dream of the Rood* as Ekphrasis', in *Text, Image, Interpretation: Studies in Anglo-Saxon Literature and Its Insular Context in Honour of Éamonn Ó Carragáin*, ed. Alastair Minnis and Jane Roberts (Turnhout: Brepols, 2007), pp. 267–88, Paul E. Szarmach places the *Dream*'s alternation of description and narrative within the context of Christian Patristic theories of how to interpret visual art. Even as they locate the *Dream* within the tradition of Latin learning, however, these critics – like most others – have also stressed the creativity of the poem's approach, and its synthesis of Old English as well as Latinate poetics. In this vein, Heather Maring shows in 'Two Ships Crossing: Hybrid Poetics in *The Dream of the Rood*', *English Studies* 91 (2010), 241–55, that a word long assumed to be a scribe's mistake is instead an ingenious fusion of a Latinate theological metaphor with an Old English poetic type-scene.

Much of the best recent criticism has thus proceeded on the assumption that the poets and visual artists engaged in constructing the *Dream of the Rood* complex were both skilled in, and conscious of, the work of integrating multiple cultural strands. In particular, Éamonn Ó Carragáin's many publications – culminating in *Ritual and the Rood: Liturgical Images and the Old English Poems of* The Dream of the Rood *Tradition* (Toronto: British Library, 2005) – have worked towards a cumulative picture of a multidimensional artwork inseparable from the life, as well as the thought, of early medieval monasticism. His painstaking study of every aspect of the Ruthwell monument and the Brussels Cross shows that they were constructed to demand of their audiences the same full physical, spiritual and intellectual presence required of participants in the liturgy, as well as knowledge of the liturgy itself. Ó Carragáin's work draws on and engages with recent art-historical scholarship that seeks to revise traditional assumptions about the Ruthwell monument and related sculptures, of which Catherine E. Karkov and Fred Orton (eds), *Theorizing Anglo-Saxon Stone Sculpture* (Morgantown: West Virginia University Press, 2003) and Fred Orton, Ian Wood and Clare A. Lees, *Fragments of History: Rethinking the Ruthwell and Bewcastle Monuments* (Manchester University Press, 2007) are particularly notable examples. In recent years literary scholars have been increasingly open to exploring the very different affordances of inscribed art, as compared to manuscripts; Martin Foys takes up this question in *Virtually Anglo-Saxon: Old Media, New Media, and Early Medieval Studies in the Late Age of Print* (Gainesville: University Press of Florida, 2007), as does Seeta Chaganti in

'Vestigial Signs: Inscription, Performance, and *The Dream of the Rood*', *PMLA* 125 (2010), 48–72.

This overview covers only a few of the most important directions in which studies of the *Dream of the Rood* complex seem to me to be tending. Though I have lacked space to mention many important areas of scholarship (such as source studies), the notes of the works cited here should help orient the curious reader. For a glimpse of the possible range of critical approaches to the period more generally, see Jacqueline Stodnick and Renée R. Trilling (eds), *A Handbook of Anglo-Saxon Studies* (Chichester: Wiley–Blackwell, 2012).

2 The Translator as Author: The Case of Geoffrey Chaucer's *The Parliament of Fowls*

FILIP KRAJNÍK

Abstract

In the Middle Ages the concept of authorship differed greatly from that of the present day and the profession of an author often involved activities which would nowadays be termed copying, rewriting, compiling or translating. The borders between these were not strict and the classification of a work in terms of its originality or derivativeness could be – and often was – highly subjective. This essay discusses the case of perhaps the most ambitious of late medieval English poets and the 'father of English poetry', Geoffrey Chaucer. Focusing on one of Chaucer's finest shorter poems, *The Parliament of Fowls*, it describes how Chaucer treated old authorities in developing his own reputation and what strategies he employed to establish a harmony among the multiple authorial voices his works incorporated. Lastly, the essay proposes that, at least for Chaucer, medieval authorship was not necessarily defined solely by the level of the writer's creative input, but also by the occasion for which the work was written, its original context and purpose, as well as its actual or anticipated audiences.

Chaucer the Translator

At some point in the late 1380s Eustache Deschamps (1346–1406), a French poet closely associated with the courts of Charles V and his sons Charles VI and Louis of Orléans, sent Chaucer, at the latter's request, copies of some of his and, possibly, other French authors' poems via both men's common friend, the courtier, soldier and diplomat Sir Lewis Clifford (c. 1330–1404). Included as a cover letter of sorts was the famous 'Ballade adressé à Geoffrey Chaucer', in which Deschamps praised his colleague across the Channel, calling him 'Socrates versed in philosophy', 'Seneca in morals', 'Ovid in your poetry', as well as the 'worldly God of Love in Albion'.[1] Besides other things, Deschamps lauded Chaucer as sole possessor of the spring of Helicon and for having started a great flower bed of English poetry, to which he, Deschamps, was humbly sending 'some plants of mine' that would 'only be a nettle in your garden'. What may be quite surprising for a modern reader is the fact that, at a time when Chaucer would have already penned works such as *The Book of the Duchess*, *The House of Fame*, *The Parliament of Fowls* and, perhaps, *Troilus and Criseyde* and *The Legend of Good Women*, the only achievement of the English writer that Deschamps found worthy of mention was the former's partial English translation of the famed French dream romance *Le Roman de la Rose*, through which Chaucer 'will spread light to those who do not know French' (Figure 2.1). Moreover, the refrain of the ballad, repeated four times throughout the poem, calls Chaucer not a poet (although the word does ultimately appear in the poem's envoi) but rather the 'great

Figure 2.1 Miniature from a 1353 manuscript of *Le Roman de la Rose* by Guillaume de Lorris and Jean de Meun. The work was written in two stages, first in *c.* 1230 by de Lorris and completed *c.* 1275 by de Meun. There are over 250 extant manuscripts, and this image is taken from one in the Bibliothèque de Genève, MS fr. 178, folio 1r.

translator, noble Geoffrey Chaucer'. For Deschamps, Chaucer's greatest achievement was thus his ability to convey the works of Continental authors to English audiences, maintaining that the beginning of the great English poetic tradition was an act of translation rather than an independent creative process.

Influenced by the post-Romantic concept of the author as sole genius, modern readers tend rather simplistically to associate translation with mediation rather than creation and with derivation rather than originality. For Chaucer, however, whose ambition it was to occupy a place next to such European literary figures as Dante (c. 1265–1321), Boccaccio (1313–75) or Guillaume de Machaut (c. 1300–77), who all wrote their greatest works in the vernacular, the title of 'great translator' was not at all impertinent; indeed, even he himself characterised some of his literary efforts as 'translations'. In the prologue to *The Legend of Good Women*, the God of Love chastises the speaker of the poem (who is a fictionalised version of Chaucer himself), 'of myn olde sevauntes thow mysseyest, / And hynderest hem with thy translacioun, / And lettest folk from hire devocioun / To serve me, and holdest it folye / To serve love' ('you speak ill of my old servants and plague them with your translations and hinder people from their devotion in my service and consider it foolish to serve love') (F version, 323–7).[2] According to the God, by writing or adapting stories such as *Le Roman de la Rose* or *Troilus and Criseyde*, Chaucer committed a heresy against the religion of love and he especially wronged women, whom he depicted as treacherous and unworthy of men's trust. The narrator, however, finds an ally in Lady Alceste, the God of Love's consort (probably inspired by King Richard II's wife, Anne of Bohemia, who was known for being able to control her husband's temper), who intervenes and explains to the God that 'this man ys nice, / He myghte doon yt, gessyng no malice, / But for he useth thynges for to make; / Hym rekketh noght of what matere he take' ('this man is foolish, he might have done it without malice since he is used to writing works without paying attention to the matter that he chooses') (F 362–5). By merely translating older works, Alceste argues, Chaucer 'ne hath nat doon so grevously amys ... / As thogh that he of malice wolde enditen / Despit of love, and had himself yt wroght' ('has not done such a great sin ... as if he himself had written scornfully about love out of malice') (F 369–72). As Andrew Kraebel has pointed out, medieval authors, especially those writing in the vernacular, frequently disavowed their authorial responsibility, with well-known names such as John Gower (1330–1408), John Lydgate (1370–1451) or Osbern Bokenham (1393–1463) often envisioning themselves as 'compilers' or 'translators' rather than 'authors' or 'poets'.[3] It is, however, significant that Chaucer puts the issue of authorship at the centre of his fictional quarrel with the God of Love, a quarrel which ultimately serves as the pretext for the narrator's composition of the collection of stories about ancient heroines.

Following St Bonaventure's mid-thirteenth-century categorisation of authorship, the Middle Ages distinguished between four modes of writing (or writers): (1) the scribe, 'who copies a text without altering it in any way'; (2) the compiler, 'who joins texts together, but without adding anything of his own'; (3) the commentator, 'who accompanies the text he is copying with words of his own by way of explication and gloss'; and (4) the author, 'who blends words from other writers with his own words, using theirs so as to confer authority of his'.[4] Despite this seemingly clear-cut hierarchy of literary roles the medieval notion of authorship was a rather grey area, often defying straightforward classification. If we return to the Prologue to Chaucer's *Legend*, while the English poet's version of *Le Roman* mentioned by the God of Love can easily be called a translation both by medieval and modern standards, his *Troilus*, another work that becomes the cause of the dispute, arguably transcends the category. As Piero Boitani has observed in his analysis of the poem and its Italian models (chiefly Boccaccio's *Il Filostrato*), 'Chaucer's translations from Italian in the *Troilus* are not so much translations, or even adaptations – they are true *rewritings*', often restructuring the story and offering original themes and elements.[5] As such, Chaucer might have easily claimed the status of new authority for his text but decided not to.

On the other hand, when Lady Alceste defends Chaucer's writing before the God, she mentions several of his apparently non-translative works to prove the poet's true devotion to love. These include 'the Hous of Fame' (F 417), indeed a largely original work; 'the Deeth of Blaunche the Duchesse' (i.e., *The Book of the Duchess*, F 418), which contains substantial borrowings from Jean Froissart's *Le Paradys d'Amours* (1361–2) and incorporates the story of Ceyx and Alcyone from Ovid's *Metamorphoses*; 'the love of Palamon and Arcite' (i.e., 'The Knight's Tale', F 420), which is basically a retelling of Boccaccio's *Il Teseida*; and 'the lyf also of Seynt Cecile' (i.e., 'The Second Nun's Tale', F 426), which in *The Canterbury Tales* is called 'the legend in translacioun' (prologue to 'The Second Nun's Tale', line 25), while Alceste simply asserts that Chaucer 'maad' (made = wrote) the story (F 425). It appears that in the Middle Ages, at least with Chaucer, the definition of what constituted a translation and what an original work was rather fluid and the borders between the individual modes of authorship were blurred and permeable. Taking as an example another poem by Chaucer mentioned by Alceste in defence of the poet (F 419), *The Parliament of Fowls*, this essay will argue that, besides the manner and the level of the writer's actual contribution to the text, the decisive factors of the work's position within the literary hierarchy of the time could also be the context in which it was received, its purpose and its (imagined or actual) audience.

The Parliament of Fowls and Its Sources

Of all Chaucer's shorter poems, *The Parliament of Fowls* has received most critical attention. One of four dream visions by Chaucer, *The Parliament* is the first significant work to employ rhyme royal, Chaucer's own stanzaic form that quickly became a mark of poetic prestige (it was later used by figures such as James I of Scotland and William Shakespeare). It is also credited as the first work to mention St Valentine as the patron of lovers, effectively starting the saint's amorous cult in Europe.[6] Kathryn L. Lynch, a recent editor of Chaucer's lesser poems, has called *The Parliament* 'a dazzling little poem' which, 'like a multifaceted gem, deftly brings together disparate literary and philosophical traditions without ever losing its artistic poise or integrity'.[7] With its multiplicity of themes and subjects, however, the work has also posed a riddle for literary critics, who have tried to find harmony among the voices of Chaucer's narrator and those of old authorities, whom he comments on, translates and rewrites.

Even the very first line of *The Parliament*, 'The lyf so short, the craft so long to lerne', is a translation of Hippocrates' aphorism 'Ὁ βίος βραχύς, ἡ δὲ τέχνη μακρή', known in the Middle Ages in its reversed Latin form *Ars longa, vita brevis* ('Art is long, life is short'). While Hippocrates used this phrase as an opening for his observation on the vastness of medical expertise,[8] Chaucer deploys it to draw a contrast between *auctoritas* and lived experience, in this case in the matters of romantic love. Chaucer's persona introduces himself as a poet who prefers old works to his own observations ('I knowe nat Love in dede ... Yit hapeth me ful ofte in bokes reede / Of hys myrakles and his crewel yre' ('I do not know love in person ... yet I often happen to read in books of its miracles and cruel ire') (8, 10–11)) – a common Chaucerian strategy as an opening approach to his audience. Then he goes on to inform us that one of the books which he has recently read was 'Tullyus of the Drem of Scipioun' (31), a fragment from Book VI of Cicero's *De re publica* (mid first century BCE), a political treatise popular all over Europe at the time.[9] What follows is a close, albeit compressed, summary of Cicero's work (including some of the direct speeches from the original), which can be called the first ever translation of the Latin story into English. Even here we see how Chaucer manipulates his models for his own ends: while Cicero's political and didactical text is pervaded by the idea of Neo-Platonic asceticism (Scipio the Elder explicitly advises his grandson, Scipio the Younger, to 'fix your attention upon the heavens and contemn what is mortal'),[10] Chaucer's Scipio above all advises the future statesman to 'loke ay besily thow werche and wysse / To commune profit' ('look that you industriously work and instruct towards common profit') (74–5), providing a template for a medieval king rather than an ancient politician.

Finishing the reading and falling asleep, the speaker has a dream that occupies the largest part of the poem. With Scipio the Elder as his guide, he appears in front of a garden wall (a motif borrowed from *Le Roman*), on which there is a double inscription 'of gold and blak iwriten' (141), echoing the words on the gates of hell in Canto III of Dante's *Inferno*, informing the visitors that, inside, they can find both a 'blysful place' (127) and 'mortal strokes of the spere' (135). When the speaker finally enters (or is rather unceremoniously shoved inside by Scipio), he finds himself in a beautiful park, whose description closely follows the garden of Venus in *Il Teseida*, including its architecture and inhabitants. From time to time Chaucer diverges from his model, for instance by removing the ubiquitous myrtle, an attribute of Venus which, in the Italian work, links the garden exclusively to the Goddess,[11] while in the English poem the park serves as a common *locus amoenus* or pleasant place. Similarly, the name of Cupid's daughter, who arranges her father's arrows 'after they shoulde serve' ('according to how they should serve') (216), is changed from Voluptuousness (It. Voluttà)[12] to 'Wille' ('Will') (214).

This section of the speaker's visit to the garden culminates in his entering the temple of Venus, which is full of 'sykes hoote as fyr' ('sights hot as fire') (246), representing the passionate, carnal side of love. Still following Boccaccio's model, the speaker learns from frescoes in the temple of classical stories of lovers who were punished for their trespasses and he even meets the goddess Venus herself. Somewhat mischievously, Chaucer changes the description of the temple's statue of the god of fertility Priapus from Boccaccio's 'in such a garb [It. 'in abito'] that anyone who wanted to see him at night could do so, as when, with its braying, the most slothful of animals aroused Vesta whom Priapus desired not a little and toward whom he was advancing',[13] to the double entendre 'In swich aray as whan the asse hym shente / With cri by nighte' ('in such guise as when the ass shamed him with its braying at the night') (255–6) – with 'aray' possibly meaning both clothes and a 'position' or 'state' (that is, with an erect penis, ready to rape Vesta).[14]

Leaving the temple, the speaker finds himself on a grassy clearing, where birds have assembled to find themselves partners, as they do every year 'on Seynt Valentynes day' (309). While this final section of *The Parliament* is largely original, the allegorical figure of Lady Nature, who presides over the birds' assembly, is borrowed from French theologian Alanus ab Insulis's *De planctu Naturae* (c. late 1160s), as the speaker announces: 'And right as Aleyn, in the Pleynt of Kynde, / Devyseth Nature of aray and face, / In swich aray men myghte hire there fynde' ('and exactly as Alanus, in his *Plaint of Nature*, describes Nature's clothes and face, in such a state people could find her there') (316–18). Although Chaucer does not literally 'translate' the text of *De planctu*, the reference is significant not only in stirring the audience to visualise Nature's appearance (Alanus spends the entirety of Prose I of his work describing her in detail), but also in offering a key to *The Parliament*'s interpretation. In Alanus's treatise, Venus, who is supposed to assist Nature in preserving order in the matters of love, leaves her lawful husband Hymenaeus and, from an affair with Antigenius, a son named Jocus is born, from whom all sorts of perversions originate. By juxtaposing Boccaccio's Venus and Alanus's Nature, Chaucer presents the audience with two forms of love: one based on libido and self-interest, the other on virtue and common good.

The discussion itself among the birds follows in the tradition of the anonymous Middle English debate poem *The Owl and the Nightingale*, Jean de Condé's ream vision *La Messe des oiseaux* and, possibly, the anonymous *Li Fablel dou ieu d'amors*, which Chaucer might have known and in which birds discuss the alue and meaning of love and lovers.[15] Among the birds of various classes (from ie lowest water fowls to the aristocratic birds of prey), a beautiful formel (female) agle stands out, whose three suitors (a royal eagle and two lower tercels) try to onvince her of their respective merits. As the discourse does not seem to draw to a ear conclusion and the other birds grow impatient (offering various more or less xtravagant ways of solving the eagles' dilemma), Lady Nature lets the formel de- ide, advising her to chose her royal suitor. The formel, however, decides to ask for year's extension, maintaining that 'I wol nat serve Venus ne Cupide, / Forsothe s yit, by no manere weye' ('in truth I will not serve Venus or Cupid as yet in any anner') (652–3).

The birds are then relieved and permitted to choose their mates, upon which the peaker wakes up at their singing and shouting. Finally, when he briefly reflects pon his experience, he promises the audience to read more books to have better reams in the future, playfully indicating that his dream about the parliament of owls (and, by extension, Chaucer's entire poem) might be read as nothing more an an amalgamation of older works.

Chaucer the Compiler?

The Parliament of Fowls thus consists of three distinct parts, each of which is ased on one of the poem's three main sources: (1) the 'Proem', which largely etells the *Somnium Scipionis* episode from Cicero; (2) the first half of the dream, vhich closely follows an episode from Boccaccio's *Il Teseida*; and (3) the parlia- ient of fowls itself, which is largely original, but whose contents are framed by Alanus ab Insulis's *De planctu Naturae*, the knowledge of which, on the part of the udience, Chaucer took for granted. Among the lesser, but still important, sources or the English poem are Guillaume de Lorris and Jean de Meung's *Le Roman de a Rose*, which was a model for all late medieval dream visions,[16] and Dante's *Commedia*, whose text Chaucer had brought to England from Italy and for which, s Boitani puts it, the English poet's interest was 'gradually deepening' throughout iis career.[17]

'[O]ut of old bokes ... / Cometh al this newe science', argues the narrator at he beginning of *The Parliament* (24–5). The question that long plagued Chau- er's commentators was what 'science' could possibly stand behind such disparate ources that would grant the poet the mark of independent authority and allow iim to author such a new and coherent work. Bertrand H. Bronson saw the bridge etween the seemingly unrelated moral-theological world of Cicero and the secu- ar garden of love in irony, 'sometimes so delicate as to be almost imperceptible',[18] which ultimately unifies the individual parts of the poem – a similar sort of irony that, as has been once suggested, also unifies the two distinct parts of *Le Roman de la Rose*.[19] According to R. M. Lumiansky, the gap between the two worlds 'reflects the uneasiness which Chaucer feels because of his inability to reconcile his writing of love poetry with his hope for perfect bliss in the after-life'.[20] To his mind, the speaker strives for harmony between two kinds of felicity: the 'true' one, which is represented by the salvation of the soul, and the 'false' one, represented by worldly love and secular writing. In contrast, John P. McCall found any attempts to search for unity in *The Parliament* a misunderstanding of the poem's message, as the tension between the individual parts of the work, to his mind, emphasises the medieval view of the world, which is 'chaotic, transitory and yet somehow lovely and lasting'.[21] M. H. Leicester elaborated on McCall's theory, seeing the apparent disharmony of the poem as an (intentionally) unsuccessful attempt to fathom complex individual experience through authorities – religious, philosophical or literary – which, after centuries of development and refinement, were at odds with each other to an extent that, by Chaucer's time, 'the situation had begun to assume the dimensions of a cultural crisis'.[22]

While none of these interpretations seem to give a straightforward answer to the question of the underlying philosophy of the poem, they all assume that, by prefacing the conventional love-vision with Cicero's story, Chaucer set forth a thematic plan for the whole piece and a philosophical framework within which the dream portion of the poem should be understood. Such philosophical unity and a clear, original message would confer upon *The Parliament* a strong enough claim for its own artistic meaning beyond being a mere compilation.

The most persuasive interpretation of the poem in terms of its philosophical coherence has been suggested by Kathryn L. Lynch, who opines that the central problem of *The Parliament* is the issue of the will in respect to both love and all other spheres of human life – especially in terms of medieval debates regarding deterministic and voluntaristic concepts of the will and the relationship between the will and the intellect.[23] Indeed, the notions of the will and choice permeate the entire poem: the speaker has to decide whether he will prefer experience to old authorities and whether he will or will not enter the allegorical garden of love; Scipio the Younger needs to choose between aspiring to higher places or clinging to Earth; the formel eagle is supposed to pick one of her suitors; and the audience needs to choose between Venus's and Nature's concepts of love. The emphasis on the choice itself, rather than the object of it, would indeed explain the baffling ending of *The Parliament*, when the formel decides *not* to make a decision, while asking 'to have my choys al fre' (649), which breaks the genre convention of the medieval debate.[24] Furthermore, the aforementioned change of Cupid's daughter's name from Boccaccio's Voluptuousness to Will – stressing that it is she who prepares Cupid's arrows, 'Some for to sle, and some to wounde and kerve' ('some to slay, some to wound and cut') (217) – redefines love from a predominantly sensual experience in Boccaccio to one of free will and deliberate choice, even if it entails suffering.

Yet, given that Valentine poetry and Valentine's cult of love quickly became associated with courtly audiences,[25] the question remains whether, in *The Parliament*, the love becomes a vehicle for Chaucer's complex philosophical purpose or whether the philosophy serves mainly to link together elements of the discussion of love in its various forms, becoming the poem's secondary rather than primary concern. To put it from a different perspective, what kind of audience did Chaucer envision for *The Parliament* and what kind of contribution would elevate the poet in that audience's eyes from a translator or a compiler to a true author, or *actoritas*, as Alceste seems to consider him?

The Translator as the Author

Before examining this question, let us once more return to Lady Alceste's defence of Chaucer in the Prologue to *The Legend of Good Women* and quote it *in extenso*:

Al be hit that he kan nat wel endite,
Yet hath he maked lewed folk delyte
To serve yow, in preysinge your name.
He made the book that hight the Hous of Fame,
And eke the Deeth of Blaunche the Duchesse,
And the Parlement of Foules, as I gesse,
And al the love of Palamon and Arcite
Of Thebes, thogh the storye ys knowen lyte;
...
And maad the lyf also of Saynt Cecile. (F 414–21, 426)

Although he cannot write well, in praise of your name he has caused lay people to rejoice in serving you. He wrote a book called the House of Fame and also the Death of Blanche the Duchess and the Parliament of Fowls, I believe, and all the love of Palamon and Arcite from Thebes, although the story is little known. ... And also wrote the life of Saint Cecilia.

As mentioned above, these works that Chaucer arguably 'made' differ from one another in terms of the poet's actual contribution, some being close translations of older works, some original compositions and some combinations of both. What, however, links all the pieces together is the likely purpose for which they were written. *The House of Fame*, the most original of the group, deals with a topic which was perhaps very personal to Chaucer – that is, how a man can obtain fame. Recently, Alfred Thomas has pointed out that the image of Chaucer as a celebrated poet, to whose recitations the English royal court, including King Richard himself listened carefully (as depicted in the Corpus Christi College MS 61 of *Troilus and Criseyde*) is a later construct and that, in his lifetime, Chaucer competed (presumably with no major success) with a number of other poets to win the attention of the king and the queen.[26] It is then only logical that, in the Prologue to *The Legend* Chaucer imagines Queen Anne as Lady Alceste, who has received and appreciated a work confessing his ambitions and who, like the Goddess Fame herself, decided about the writer's reputation.

The remaining works, too, seem to be linked in one way or another to the royal court. *The Book of the Duchess* is an elegy on the death of Blanche of Lancaster (d. 1368), wife of John of Lancaster, the fourth son of King Edward III and one of the most powerful men in England, from whom Chaucer received a pension for unspecified services;[27] the story of Palamon and Arcite (which later became 'The Knight's Tale') is on the one hand a condensed retelling of *Il Teseida*, while at the same time it contains a number of details which obviously flatter Anne of Bohemia and even bears a striking similarity to the old Bohemian legend of the War of the Maidens (Czech 'Dívčí válka'), which, in some form, the queen's Bohemian entourage could easily have brought to England.[28] Moreover, Henry Ansgar Kelly maintains that Chaucer's reference to 3 May in the story is a commemoration of the betrothal of King Richard and Queen Anne, the poet's tribute to the royal couple.[29] Finally, Chaucer's life of St Cecilia closely follows two medieval martyrologies offering very little to support the assertion that Chaucer 'made' the story.[30] What seems to be of great significance is that, when Chaucer later decided to incorporate the text into *The Canterbury Tales* as 'The Second Nun's Tale', not only did he call it a 'translacioun', as mentioned above, but his anonymous nun asks for forgiveness for doing 'no diligence / This ilke storie subtilly to endite' ('no diligence artfully to compose this same story') (79–80). If we are to believe Thomas's hypothesis, the life of St Cecilia was probably composed as another attempt on the part of Chaucer to win the favour of Queen Anne by means of writing a story paralleling her chaste marriage with King Richard, as well as paying homage to her as a member of family with a long tradition of learned and pious women (Figure 2.2).[31] The form which Chaucer decided to employ in the poem, rhyme royal, surely testifies to the work's importance for the poet. If this was the case, boasting of the poem's authorship through Lady Alceste would make sense originally, but when attributing it to nun in a literary collection years later, the same text could easily become in his eyes a not particularly skilful retelling, or translation, of a well-known story.

It appears that in the case of all these works, important as the level of his actual creative input was, Chaucer's motivation in openly declaring himself as their author was to enhance his reputation within the cultural sphere in which he operated. The fact that the common denominator of all the works from Alceste's list is Chaucer's ambition to gain recognition as a court writer seems to provide

Figure 2.2 King Richard II and Anne of Bohemia, his queen. From the fourteenth-century Coronation Order of Service, the Liber Regalis.

good framework within which the notion of *The Parliament*'s authorship should be examined. Since John Koch's 1877 study,[32] it has been a staple of Chaucer criticism that the formel eagle 'of shap gentilleste' ('of a noblest shape'), in whom 'was everi vertu at his reste' ('every virtue had its place') (373, 376), represents Anne of Bohemia, while the royal tercel, 'The wyse and worthi, secre, trewe as stel' ('the wise and worthy one, discreet and true as steel') (395), stands for King Richard II, and that the poem records, in a fictionalised form, Richard's wooing of Anne. Kelly even maintains that it was for this occasion that Chaucer invented the cult of love, which he attributed to a local Genoese saint named Valentine whom he learned about during his travels to Italy and whose feast day, 3 May, coincided with the date of Richard's ratification of the marriage treaty. In 1389 Richard II would pick the same date to pronounce himself to be of age and claim the right to the full rule of the country.[33]

It is obvious that this date had a special significance for the King, both in personal and political terms, and Chaucer seems to have been fully aware of the fact. Larry D. Benson maintains that in *The Parliament* Chaucer wanted first and foremost to give the young king advice as to what constitutes a good ruler. While in the story about the young Scipio Chaucer 'provides a tactful exhortation to Richard to "werche and wysse" the good of the commonwealth',[34] the dream portion had to show the king 'what love is, both good and evil, if he is to … serve the commonwealth in the manner expected of a king'.[35] *The Parliament*, therefore, is not just an allegorical wedding poem flattering the king and his new wife, whom Chaucer envisions as the primary sponsors of his work, but also a form of instruction for the young ruler in a vein similar to medieval 'mirrors for magistrates'. Of all Chaucer's courtly poems, *The Parliament* is the most ambitious and also the one in which Chaucer addresses the king and the queen in the most straightforward manner. As such, Chaucer must have been proud of his work, especially as it gave rise to a whole tradition of Valentine poetry both in England and on the Continent.[36] In the light of Chaucer's ambitions to become a major court writer – and in the context of other of his works which he hoped would win him royal favour and secure him fame – *The Parliament of Fowls* could be read as a prime example of how a medieval author could promote a sense of his own authorial independence even while involved in the copying, retelling and translating of 'old bokes' along the way.

Through the lens of this observation we might also approach Chaucer's 'Retraction', an epilogue to *The Canterbury Tales* written perhaps not long before Chaucer's death, in which the author symbolically rejects his works of 'wordly vanitees', including 'the book of Troilus; the book also of Fame; the book of XXV. Ladies [i.e., *The Legend of Good Women*]; the book of the Duchesse; the book of Seint Valentynes day of the Parlement of Briddes … and many another book' (1086–7). 'But the translacion of Boece de Consolacione [i.e., Boethius's *De consolatione Philosophiae*]', Chaucer continues, 'and othere bookes of legendes of seintes, and omelies, and moralitee, and devocioun, that thanke I oure Lord Jhesu Crist and his blisful Mooder, and alle the seintes of hevene' (1088–90).

These words were written years after Queen Anne's death (1394) and probably shortly after the deposition of her husband, King Richard II (1399). By that time, Chaucer had long abandoned his ambitions to secure royal patronage and focused on other, more realistic (albeit no less ambitious) projects. It appears that at the end of his life, with his courtly dreams gone, Chaucer the translator, who had worked so hard to become Chaucer the author, once again embraced his reputation of being a 'great translator'.

NOTES

1. Eustache Deschamps, quoted from James I. Wimsatt's translation, *Chaucer and His French Contemporaries: Natural Music in the Fourteenth Century* (University of Toronto Press, 1991), p. 250.
2. All quotations from Chaucer are drawn from *The Riverside Chaucer*, 3rd edn, gen. ed. Larry D. Benson (Oxford University Press, 2008). References are incorporated within the main text and are to the lines of the work.
3. See Andrew Kraebel, 'Modes of Authorship and the Making of Medieval English Literature', in Ingo Berensmeyer, Gert Buelens and Marysa Demoor (eds), *The Cambridge Handbook of Literary Authorship* (Cambridge University Press, 2019), pp. 98–114 (pp. 99–100).
4. Roger Ellis, 'Translation', in Peter Brown (ed.), *A Companion to Chaucer* (Oxford: Blackwell, 2000), pp. 443–58 (p. 451).
5. Piero Boitani, 'Chaucer Translates from Italian', in Denis Renevey and Christiania Whitehead (eds), *Lost in Translation?* (Turnhout: Brepols, 2009), pp. 93–107 (p. 98, original italics).
6. For a discussion of Chaucer's contribution to St Valentine's love cult, see Henry Ansgar Kelly, *Chaucer and the Cult of Saint Valentine* (Leiden: Brill, 1986).
7. Geoffrey Chaucer, *Dream Visions and Other Poems*, ed. Kathryn L. Lynch (New York: W. W. Norton, 2007), p. 93.
8. *Hippocratic Writings*, ed. G. E. R. Lloyd, trans. J. Chadwick, W. N. Mann, I. M. Lonie and E. T. Withington (Harmondsworth: Penguin, 1983), p. 206.
9. Scipio's dream is alluded to several times in Chaucer's works and appears in the opening lines of *Le Roman de la Rose* as 'the avysioun / That whilom mette kyng Cipioun' (Chaucer's translation, lines 9–10).
10. Macrobius, *Commentary on the Dream of Scipio*, trans. William Harris Stahl, 2nd edn (New York: Columbia University Press, 1990), p. 74.
11. Giovanni Boccaccio, *The Book of Theseus*, trans. Bernadette Marie McCoy (New York: Medieval Text Association, 1974), p. 176.
12. Ibid., p. 177.
13. Ibid., p. 178. The story of Priapus's attempted rape of Vesta, frustrated by the braying of an ass, comes from book VI of Ovid's *Fasti*.
14. Indeed, a huge erect penis was a common feature of Roman statues and pictures of Priapus.
15. See Kelly, *Chaucer and the Cult of Saint Valentine*, pp. 99–100.
16. Kathryn L. Lynch calls the period between the twelfth and fourteenth centuries in Europe the 'Age of Dream Vision', comparing the genre's popularity in the high Middle Ages to the prevalence of the novel in the modern era (Kathryn L. Lynch, *The High Medieval Dream Vision: Poetry, Philosophy and Literary Form* (Stanford University Press, 1988), p. 1).
17. Boitani, 'Chaucer Translates from Italian', 103. According to Paget Toynbee, *Dante in English Literature from Chaucer to Cary*, 2 vols (London: Methuen, 1909), vol. I, even for Chaucer's learned contemporary and friend Gower, 'Dante appears to have been little more than a name' (p. xvii); the acquaintance with Dante of Chaucer's follower

Lydgate 'was not much more extensive than that of Gower', while Lydgate's contemporary Occleve 'apparently had no knowledge of him whatever' (p. xviii). The first post-Chaucerian author to show significant knowledge of Dante was apparently Milton (Toynbee, *Dante*, vol. I, pp. xxiv–xxvii).

18. Bertrand H. Bronson, 'In Appreciation of Chaucer's *Parlement of Foules*', *University of California Publications in English* 3 (1935), 193–224 (198).

19. See Guillaume de Lorris and Jean de Meun, *Romance of the Rose*, trans. Charles Dahlberg, 3rd edn (Princeton University Press, 1995), pp. 5–10.

20. R. M. Lumiansky, 'Chaucer's *Parlement of Foules*: A Philosophical Interpretation', *Review of English Studies* 25 (1948), 81–89 (87).

21. John P. McCall, 'The Harmony of Chaucer's *Parliament*', *Chaucer Review* 5 (1970), 22–31 (31).

22. H. M. Leicester Jr, 'The Harmony of Chaucer's *Parlement*: A Dissonant Voice', *Chaucer Review* 9 (1974), 15–34 (19).

23. See Kathryn L. Lynch, *Chaucer's Philosophical Vision* (Cambridge: D. S. Brewer, 2000), pp. 83–109.

24. Edith Rickert, 'A New Interpretation of *The Parlement of Foules*', *Modern Philology* 18 (1920), 1–29 (3): '[I]n no other *demande d'amours*, as far as I have been able to observe, has the balance of the argument been completely upset by throwing all the stress on the first suitor, and the problem shifted from Which will she choose? to Why does she not choose the first?'

25. As Jack B. Oruch points out, on St Valentine's Day of 1400, the *cour amoureuse* was formed in Paris with six hundred members, including King Charles VI ('St. Valentine, Chaucer, and Spring in February', *Speculum* 3 (1981), 534–65 (558)).

26. See Alfred Thomas, *Reading Women in Late Medieval Europe: Anne of Bohemia and Chaucer's Female Audience* (New York: Palgrave Macmillan, 2015).

27. See A. C. Spearing, *Medieval Dream-Poetry* (Cambridge University Press, 1976), p. 50.

28. Thomas, *Reading Women*, pp. 111–37.

29. Kelly, *Chaucer and the Cult of Saint Valentine*, p. 127.

30. For the discussion of the sources of 'Second Nun's Tale' see Sherry L. Reames, 'The Sources of Chaucer's "Second Nun's Tale"', *Modern Philology* 76 (1978), 111–35; and Sherry L. Reames, 'A Recent Discovery concerning the Sources of Chaucer's "Second Nun's Tale"', *Modern Philology* 87 (1990), 337–61.

31. See Thomas, *Reading Women*, pp. 79–110.

32. John Koch, 'Ein Beitrag zur Kritik Chaucer's', *Englische Studien* 1 (1877), 287–9.

33. See Kelly, *Chaucer and the Cult of Saint Valentine*, p. 125. According to Kelly, the Genoese Valentine was superseded by his more famous Roman namesake as the patron saint of lovers by the end of the fourteenth century.

34. Larry D. Benson, 'The Occasion of *The Parliament of Fowls*', in Larry D. Benson and Siegfried Wenzel (eds), *The Wisdom of Poetry: Essays in Early English Literature in Honor of Morton W. Bloomfield* (Kalamazoo: Medieval Institute Publications, 1982), pp. 123–44 (p. 130).

35. Ibid., 132.

36. See Kelly, *Chaucer and the Cult of Saint Valentine*.

CRITICAL REFLECTIONS AND FURTHER STUDY

In my essay I have paid most attention to three issues concerning Chaucer's *The Parliament of Fowls*: (1) the question of its employment of older sources in the context of medieval notions of literary authorship; (2) the work's underlying philosophical and thematic reading, which contributes to its artistic unity; and (3) the occasion for which the poem was written and its importance for the work's declared status as an original text. There is, however, one more issue whose understanding is important for an informed reading of *The Parliament*, as well as a number of other medieval works, and that is its employment of dreams, a subject rich with potential for further exploration.

The Parliament of Fowls is a dream vision, an immensely popular and productive genre of the high and late Middle Ages, popularised in the early thirteenth century by the French allegorical romance *Le Roman de la Rose*. In a dream vision, the narrator of the work usually falls asleep to find himself in a beautiful allegorical place, where from an authoritative person he learns some doctrine that he can apply in the waking world. Besides mentioning dreams in a number of other works (such as 'The Nun's Priest's Tale'), Chaucer wrote four such dream visions: *The Book of the Duchess*, *The House of Fame*, *The Parliament of Fowls* and the Prologue to *The Legend of Good Women*.

In ancient and medieval Europe, dreams were a subject of many heated scientific, moral and theological debates. Greek physician Hippocrates (*c.* 460–*c.* 370 BCE), whose aphorism opens *The Parliament*, used dreams as a diagnostic tool. Roman neo-Platonist Macrobius (fl. *c.* 400 CE), whose work Chaucer probably knew, wrote a commentary on the 'dream of Scipio' episode from Cicero's *De re publica*, in which he distinguished between non-significative and significative dreams, the former being *nightmares* (caused by mental or physical distress) and *apparitions* (the transitional moments between wakefulness and slumber), the latter *enigmatic dreams* (symbolical representations of the future), *prophetic visions* (literal dreams about future events) and *oracular dreams* (dreams in which an authoritative figure reveals what will or will not happen). As Walter Clyde Curry maintains (*Chaucer and the Mediaeval Sciences*, pp. 207ff.), a frequent medieval appropriation of this system was a threefold division of dreams into the *somnium naturale* (caused by bodily complexions and humours), *somnium animale* (springing from waking thoughts) and *somnium coeleste* (a dream coming from a supernatural agent). When *The Parliament*'s narrator reflects on his own dream of Scipio, he suspects it might have been a meaningless *somnium animale* based on his previous reading of Cicero, since

The wery huntere, slepynge in his bed,
To wode ayeyn his mynde goth anon;
The juge dremeth how his plees been sped;

> The cartere dremeth how his cart in gon;
> The riche, of gold; the knyght fight with his fon;
> The syke met he drynketh of the tonne;
> The lovere met he hath his lady wonne. (99–105)

> When the weary hunter sleeps in his bed, his mind soon goes back to the woods, the judge dreams of how his cases are sped, the carter dreams of how his carts go, the rich dreams of gold, the knight fights with his foe, the sick dreams that he drinks from a tun, the lover dreams he has won his lady.

Similar lists of dreamers and their archetypal dreams had been a literary commonplace since classical antiquity and are to be found in works of Claudian, Petronius, Boccaccio and, two centuries after Chaucer, in the famous Queen Mab monologue in Shakespeare's *Romeo and Juliet* (I.iv.53–95). At the same time, *The Parliament*'s speaker's prayer to Venus (113–19), who subsequently appears in his dream, indicates that the dream portion of the poem might be a significative *somnium coeleste*. By creatively incorporating medieval dream lore, Chaucer leaves his audience in oblivion as to whether the content of his work has any special meaning and whether it is at all worthy of their attention.

It is not surprising that Chaucer's dream visions appear to be closely linked to courtly culture. While dreaming in the Middle Ages was usually a journey into suspect territory, several classes of privileged dreamers were recognised, such as saints and Christian rulers. One of the latter was Anne of Bohemia's father, Bohemian King and Holy Roman Emperor Charles IV (1316–78), who had the reputation of being an avid dream observer. In his autobiography *Vita Caroli* he devotes an entire chapter to a dream which he had at the age of 17 and which he considered as God's warning against lechery. At the Prague court of Charles's son and Anne's brother, King Wenceslaus IV (1361–1419), an opulent Czech translation of one of the most popular medieval dream interpretation manuals, the so-called *Oneirocriticon of Achmet*, was commissioned, possibly by Wenceslaus himself as its sponsor. By placing royal or royal-like figures in his literary dreams, Chaucer again refers to a medieval commonplace; yet, by attributing the dreams to ignorant narrators, who are not capable of fully understanding their content, the poet also playfully reverses the tradition of royal dreamers.

Just as there were no clear boundaries between medieval translators and authors, we cannot completely separate medieval philosophy, science, politics and art. Medieval authors, including Chaucer, knew how to make the most of this fact and, by employing dreams in their works, they were able to create complex and multivalent intersections of various different spheres of medieval life and thinking.

FURTHER READING

Brown, Peter (ed.), *Reading Dreams: The Interpretation of Dreams from Chaucer to Shakespeare* (Oxford University Press, 1999)

Curry, Walter Clyde, *Chaucer and the Mediaeval Sciences*, 2nd edn (New York: Barnes & Noble, 1960)

Kruger, Steven F., *Dreaming in the Middle Ages* (Cambridge University Press, 1992)

Le Goff, Jacques, 'Rêves', in Jacques Le Goff and Jean-Claude Schmitt (eds), *Dictionnaire raisonné de l'Occident medieval* (Paris: Fayard, 1999), pp. 950–68

Phillips, Helen, 'Chaucer's Love Visions', in Corinne Saunders (ed.), *A Companion to Medieval Poetry* (Oxford: Wiley-Blackwell, 2010), pp. 414–34

Rupprecht, Carol Schreier (ed.), *The Dream and the Text* (Albany: State University of New York Press, 1993)

Russell, J. Stephen, *The English Dream Vision: Anatomy of a Form* (Columbus: Ohio State University Press, 1988)

Winny, James, *Chaucer's Dream-Poems* (London: Chatto & Windus, 1973)

3 Arthurian Romance as a Window on to Medieval Life: The Case of *Ywayne and Gawayne* and *The Awntyrs off Arthure*

K. S. WHETTER

Abstract

Part of the popularity and endurance of medieval romance rests in the ways that the genre speaks to the interests of late medieval society. Sometimes the interests and motifs of French and English romancers are similar: the anonymous *Ywayne and Gawayne* is a shorter but reasonably faithful English redaction of Chrétien's *Chevalier au lion*. Accordingly, both texts highlight romance's defining generic features of adventure, love (with and without courtship), women (of the gentry or nobility and who play various roles) and a happy ending. Yet *Ywayne and Gawayne* also displays greater concern with reconciling chivalric display with the duties of local government and the rights of aristocratic or gentry women, including their roles in managing familial estates. The problems of local lordship that are writ small in *Ywayne and Gawayne* are expanded in *The Awntyrs off Arthure* (also anonymous) to cover all of Arthur's kingdom and the means by which that kingdom is maintained. Like *Sir Gawain and the Carle of Carlisle* or the episode of the rebellion of the twelve kings in Thomas Malory's *Morte Darthur*, *Awntyrs* highlights the problems an English king could face when confronted with recalcitrant regional lords in Scotland, Wales and the North. In *Awntyrs*, Gawain and Arthur are accused of taking lands unjustly, but Gawain's single combat with the challenger allows Arthur to create a happy ending that avoids any immediate political problems. Romance thus offers modern readers a window on to late medieval culture, just as (it seems) it offered its original authors and audiences a venue in which to explore some of the major social, cultural and political questions of the day.

The genre of medieval romance was the single most popular form of *secular* literary entertainment in the Middle Ages, a popularity confirmed by the fact that even today romances survive in all of the major European languages, including French, German, Dutch, English, Welsh and Norse. The popularity and evolution of medieval romance are, however, easier to discern than its origins. Several prominent romances survive from Hellenistic literature, though classicists often refer to them as 'ancient novels' and it is difficult, in contrast to classical epic or drama, to judge how popular they were in their day.[1] Notably, however, the centuries immediately following the Roman departure from Britain attest to nothing resembling romance: authors writing in Old English produced various genres, including wisdom poetry, dream visions, elegies and heroic literature – but not romance. According to J. R. R. Tolkien, medieval English literature is marked near its beginning and end by 'two poets that study at length the heroic and chivalrous': the *Beowulf*-poet and the *Gawain*-poet.[2] *Beowulf* (generally though not universally dated to the eighth century) epitomises the epic-heroic kind of story, albeit one that is also markedly elegiac; *Sir Gawain and the Green Knight* (generally dated to somewhere in the last quarter of the fourteenth century) is often said to epitomise the romance kind, albeit with considerable generic manipulation.[3] Tolkien's conjoining of these two poems is but one example of the oft-noted similarities between the epic-heroic and romance genres, including the similarities between their heroes – particularly the hero's quest for adventure and fame (variously termed *los*, *pris*, *worshyp*). Ultimately, however, epic-heroic literature is bleaker than romance, with its hero being more isolated and tragic than the romance hero. In contrast, romance combines the hero's quest for adventure and name with a much greater interest in manners and amorous love than is common in the more martial epic-heroic genre. Romance is also broadly comic in its drive towards reconciliation and the aversion of catastrophe, both of which elements are notably lacking in epic-heroic stories.

The generic evolution occurred in the twelfth century when, to use the traditional subject divisions, romancers suddenly turned their attention to the story matter of antiquity (Graeco-Roman subjects), of France (especially Charlemagne) and of Britain (King Arthur); eventually romancers also turned to what modern scholars term the Matter of England. Scholars can easily discern the early popularity and favourite subjects of the new romance genre, but not why it suddenly emerges in twelfth-century France. Northrop Frye contends that, in the history of fictional genres, romance keeps re-emerging in those 'transitional phase[s]' when the older and dominant genres start to stagnate.[4] Eugène Vinaver links romance's rise with secular exegesis: the French *chanson* was driven by plot, action and emotional affect, typifying epic's tendency to raise imponderable questions about the universe or human motivation; romance provides *meaning* to adventure, particularly in exploring love.[5] These scholars are compelling, and are best augmented by R. W. Southern's association of romance with twelfth-century humanism: changes to medieval thinking that foreground the importance of self-knowledge, love and pity, and devotion. The romance emphasis on individual adventure, quests and love thus becomes the secular encapsulation of the late medieval emphasis on spirituality, pilgrimage, divine love and the Passion, a theological doctrine that supersedes the resigned fortitude and tragedy of epic.[6] Romance and humanism highlight increasing acceptance of secular attitudes, particularly an interest in the individual, the rise of chivalry and the idealisation of women and love. Although other origins have been offered, the (multifaceted) explanation given here has the advantage of helping to explain why the new romance genre quickly exploded across Europe into every major nation and language.

In Middle English alone, depending on how one counts the various fragments and cognates, and depending on whether one includes Chaucer's romances, there are around one hundred and twenty extant romances.[7] Fully a quarter are Arthurian. As I have suggested elsewhere, a fruitful approach to genre study is to determine which literary features an audience deemed *essential* to a genre and which were merely commonly recurring but unessential.[8] Romance's essential and defining generic features are the combination of adventure, love (sometimes as part of courtship but sometimes between friends or family), gentry or noble women (in various roles), and a happy ending (Figure 3.1). One of the notorious difficulties of genre study, however, is that there are always exceptions to the established generic rules, and in late medieval England the unknown poets of *Sir Gawain and the Green Knight* and the stanzaic *Le Morte Arthur*, together with Sir Thomas Malory, are notable for combining the generic features of epic and romance in such a fashion as to create tragic-romance hybrids.[9] Such hybrids, though, like Chaucer's literary experimentations, come in the fourteenth and fifteenth centuries, when certainties are again being questioned. Nevertheless, both early and late romances provided a wider application of literature to life than did epic, especially in the greater role romance gives to women.

Accordingly, here I explore the ways in which Arthurian romance provides a window on to prominent late medieval sociopolitical and cultural issues. For reasons of space I shall focus on just two representative examples. *Ywayne and Gawayne* displays a concern with reconciling chivalric display with the duties of marriage, local government, and the rights of aristocratic and gentry women. The problems of local lordship that are writ small in *Ywayne and Gawayne* are expanded in *The Awntyrs off Arthure* to cover all of King Arthur's kingdom and the martial means by which that kingdom is maintained. *Awntyrs* thus focuses on the problems an English king could face when confronted with recalcitrant regional lords in Scotland, Wales and the North – an issue that also appears in Sir Thomas Malory's *Morte Darthur*.

Ywayne and Gawayne, from the early to mid fourteenth century, is noteworthy both for its own artistic excellence and for being the only direct Middle English adaptation/translation of a French romance by Chrétien de Troyes.[10] The poem's date and northern provenance conceivably situate *Ywayne* among the contentious Anglo-Scottish border relations discussed below. Certainly the English poet's emphasis on Arthur's court as the epitome of truth and chivalry (7–46) and the linking of Arthur's justice to English laws of female inheritance (3729–72) not only make 'Arthur a predecessor to ... English Kings', but support Tony Hunt's contention that Arthur in this poem – King of England and conqueror of Wales

Figure 3.1 Set of three panels from an ivory casket carved with scenes from courtly romances, produced in France, *c.* 1330–50, clearly for an aristocratic clientele. The centre panel depicts a jousting tournament and, to the right, knights assaulting the Castle of Love, a favourite allegory of chivalric love. The lower panel shows Sir Gauvain and a lion and Lancelot crossing the sword bridge.

and Scotland (7–9) – may well be 'a symbol for Edward I';[11] if not Edward I, who died in 1307, the English poet may have modelled his Scottish-conquering king on Edward's knightly grandson Edward III (r. 1327–77), who continued these territorial claims. As for romance essentials, the adventure element is most emphatically symbolised by the magical well that instigates first Colgrevance's and then Ywayne's quest for adventure (320–438, 619–94) and whose guardian is the Lady Alundyne's first husband, killed in his adventurous combat with Ywayne (655–62). Nevertheless, all of Ywayne's adventures are undertaken for love (love of his cousin Colgrevance; love of Gawayne; love of Alundyne), and women (including Lunet, Alundyne, and the lady and her handmaiden who cure Ywayne's madness (1709–866)) likewise play a key role in this romance.[12] Alundyne, however, is also subject to the adventures of the fountain. She suffers emotionally when her first husband is killed (821–36) and especially when Ywayne fails to return to her (1591–628); but for all of the thunder and lightning associated with the magical well (e.g., 320–88), the real challenge of the fountain explicitly involves a threat to Alundyne's control over her lands (e.g., 940–1256). This threat is telling, and *Ywayne and Gawayne* presents several more cases of gentry women whose inheritance is threatened but, with Ywayne's assistance, eventually restored. In this as in other matters, it reflects, if at times it also exaggerates and idealises, historical reality.

The role of women in estate management and concerns with suitable marriage prospects are issues that recur throughout *Ywayne and Gawayne* as they also recurred in medieval life. The Pastons were a fifteenth-century English family who rose from humble origins to gentry status; their voluminous correspondence provides an invaluable resource for historical investigation of various key cultural and political issues, including gentry land disputes, concerns with good lordship, and suitable marriage prospects.[13] The Paston letters are dominated by Margaret (via clerkly amanuenses). As Peter Coss points out, several Paston letters reveal Margaret's 'ability to handle the tenantry and the practical defence of the family's interests', a fact that helps to illustrate some of the power that some medieval women could wield, even if filtered through their husbands' names.[14] In this example Margaret is running the estate in her husband's absence, but the evidence of other letters, wills and court records illustrates that many wives likewise worked cooperatively with their husbands in such fashion, and many more no doubt worked behind the scenes.[15]

In *Ywayne and Gawayne*, although Alundyne is introduced as the grieving widow of the first Knight of the Fountain, it quickly becomes apparent that it is Alundyne and Lunet, more than her husband or male counsellors, who run her demesne. Alundyne is not free to seek adventure but she – and her lands – are certainly *subject* to adventure (see the connections drawn between the well's defence and her rule and property at 943–9, 1021–4, 1079–88, 1183–5, 1211–24). Alundyne thus requires a champion to defend the fountain and her lands; nevertheless, Ywayne must seek Alundyne's permission in order temporarily to leave her side 'Armes forto haunte a stownde' ('to practise and pursue tournaments and fighting for a time') (1496), and it is she who sets a twelve-month limit on his adventuring ways (1500–14). He is accordingly devastated by her messenger's denunciation of him when he fails to return within the stipulated year's time (1583–656). It is clearly Alundyne rather than Ywayne who controls the relationship. The ring she chooses to give to Ywayne and expressly had not given to her first husband (1525–44) strongly suggests her equal authority in that previous marriage. Furthermore, her husband and Ywayne excepted, the male members of her court are all inept, if not also cowardly (see, e.g., 711–12, 952–4, 1179–250). In the Middle Ages, 'most major landowners … relied heavily on [a] council' to help manage the estates and finances.[16] It is also clear from the surviving records that armigerous husbands and wives had a common purpose in maintaining and advancing their familial interests, including their manorial interests.[17] In *Ywayne and Gawayne*, however, this management pattern is inverted, with several gentry or noble women wielding considerably more power than most of their counterparts in real life. As Alundyne remarks at the story's climax, the idea that any of her household knights might defend her lands is not worth speaking of: 'For wele I wate, so God me mend, / I have na knight me mai defend' ('For well I know, so help me God, / I have no knight who can defend me') (3879–80). Alundyne's council, too, is at best self-seeking, and instead of administering the household, her steward is notable only for trying to have Lunet killed (2130–88, 2507–645) – presumably out of jealousy.

Taking Chrétien's *Yvain* as his model (Figure 3.2), Erich Auerbach influentially defined medieval romance as an idealised 'self-portrayal of feudal knighthood', and although he states that love and '[w]omen play an important part', his 'Knight Sets Forth' chapter title indicates the extent to which his argument prioritises male ideals and male adventure.[18] There is, however, especially in the English *Ywayne*, an ideal of *female* power evident in the many armigerous women who assist Ywayne or whose rights Ywayne champions. The narrator's comment at lines 3767–8, reflecting the legal practice of partitioning land inherited by female heirs, as opposed to the exclusive inheritance of male primogeniture, is original to the Middle English poet and not found in Chrétien's influential progenitor of this story, a romance that was popular enough to be translated into Middle High German, West Norse, Old Swedish, Welsh and the Middle English version under consideration here. Although this addition to *Ywayne* highlights the English poet's concern with female rights, a variation on his principal theme of truth, the most important of the poem's prominent women, in terms of power, is Lunet. Alundyne controls her own lands, however much those lands are under threat; but Lunet is described as 'al [Alundyne's] maystres, / Her keper and hir cownsaylere' ('all her teacher, / Her protector and her counsellor') (936–7). Significantly, this description occurs

Figure 3.2 A fourteenth-century manuscript image from Chrétien de Troyes's twelfth-century *Yvain*, the French version of the *Ywayne and Gawayne* story: Lunet in prison, talking to Yvain; Yvain fighting a giant; Yvain and his lion championing Lunet against her accusers. The original is multicoloured. All three scenes are narrated in *Ywayne and Gawayne*, but the Middle English poem in its single MS has only minimal decoration (see Guddat-Figge, *Catalogue*, pp. 173–6).

after the audience's first introduction to Lunet in her first two meetings with the imprisoned Ywayne, meetings that showcase Lunet's quick thinking and ability to control the situation by helping Ywayne evade capture and secure the affections of Alundyne, with whom he has fallen in love at first sight (691–930). This sort of protection and assistance enacts the female form of *worshyp* so desired by the romance knight, but modified to Lunet's less martial theatre of operations.[19] Lunet's plan involves bringing Alundyne and Ywayne together, thereby solving Ywayne's lovesickness and Alundyne's need of a champion. Modern readers sometimes succumb to the stereotype that all medieval marriages were unloving political arrangements, but lines 1077–260 illustrate the spectrum of medieval marriages that included unloving arranged marriages, arranged marriages based on or developing into affection, and companionate marriages. Alundyne must marry 'Els had hyr lande bene destruyt' ('Or else her land had been destroyed') (1256), but her initial query to Lunet about whether the knight Lunet is proposing for marriage 'be cumen of gentil kyn' ('is descended from noble kin') (1048), like her subsequent acknowledgement of Ywayne's being both 'A king son and a noble knyght' (1194), highlights the concern among the gentry and armigerous classes for a spouse of suitable rank.[20] *Ywayne and Gawayne* thus typifies many medieval romances in its portrait of the marriage concerns of the knights and gentry and noble women who comprise the genre's main characters and much of its audience; it also considerably idealises reality in giving several women considerable control over their own estates – provided they can find a truthful knight to champion their cause.

The explicit emphasis on truth and land ownership in *Ywayne* recurs elsewhere in medieval romance, including in another northern romance, *The Awntyrs off Arthure at the Terne Watheleyne* (first quarter of the fifteenth century).[21] A notorious difficulty for defining medieval romance is the genre's structural variety. Superficially, the *Awntyrs* seems quite different from *Ywayne and Gawayne*: *Ywayne* is a little over four thousand lines, is closely based on a Chrétien source, survives in a single manuscript, and uses couplets; the *Awntyrs* is barely seven hundred lines, conflates elements from several source traditions, survives in four manuscripts, and employs a complex alliterative verse form augmented by concatenation, stanzas and rhyme. Although there is some debate about the genre of *Awntyrs*, the defining role in the narrative given to the combination and interaction of the essential romance features of knights, gentry or noble women, adventure and love (of various kinds) render it a romance.[22] Both *Ywayne* and *Awntyrs* share concerns with mercy, marriage, magnate rights and land ownership; but whereas *Ywayne* focuses on truth and female land rights, the *Awntyrs* focuses on the justness of Arthur's and Gaynour's (Guenevere's) and Gawayn's actions. The critical commonplace that *Awntyrs* castigates Arthurian excess and immorality notwithstanding, I agree with A. C. Spearing that the poem is instead a celebration of Arthurian splendour.[23]

After a supernatural storm separates Gaynour and Gawayn from Arthur's hunting party, the queen and her nephew are confronted by the *memento mori* ghost of Gaynour's mother, who warns Gaynour of the dangers of sinful living (74–260). The ghost also criticises Arthur's covetousness and alludes to another poem, the alliterative *Morte Arthure*, while prophesying his downfall (265–312). When the ghost and storm fade away, the hunters reassemble at Arthur's hunting court, whereupon they are visited by Sir Galeron, who accuses Arthur and Gawayn of unjustly seizing his lands (339–433). Influenced by the belief that the poem comprises two unconnected stories rather artlessly stitched together, a conviction entrenched by Hanna's critical edition, scholars assume that Gaynour and Gawayn ignore the ghost's warning and remain proud and ostentatious, while Arthur's interactions with Galeron epitomise his greed and 'militaristic overexpansion'; such faults, it is said, secure the inevitable Arthurian doom.[24] I argue the exact opposite: the *Awntyrs* obviously glances towards the final destruction of the Arthurian world, but it ends happily with the characters managing to avert destruction through noble action.

Spearing perspicaciously illustrates both the structural and thematic cohesion of *Awntyrs* and its poet's artistry.[25] Helen Phillips makes an equally convincing case for the poem's 'unifying themes' of 'lordship ... and mutability', adding that the manuscript evidence does not support a bipartite division of *Awntyrs*.[26] Rather, the encounter between Gaynour and the ghost and the battle between Galeron and Gawayn (495–648) are quite effectively joined by a briefer middle section highlighting Arthur's lordship and power.[27] Significantly, *Awntyrs* introduces Arthur as 'that conquerour kydde' ('renowned conqueror') (3), an epithet that runs throughout the alliterative *Morte Arthure* – long considered a source for *Awntyrs* – but that also introduces this focus on Arthur's kingship.[28] Both alliterative poems emphasise connections between Arthur's kingship and conquest, but whereas the alliterative *Morte* focuses on Arthur's imperial wars on the Continent as he fights Rome, the *Awntyrs* looks inward to the consolidation of power at the borders of Arthur's insular domains.

Randy P. Schiff makes much of the setting of *Awntyrs* in the contested and 'militarized Anglo-Scottish border', arguing that *Awntyrs* (like the alliterative *Morte* and *Golagros and Gawane*) condemns 'imperialist expansionism'.[29] Gawayn's famous query to the ghost in *Awntyrs* – 'How shal we fare ... þat fonden to fight, / And þus defoulen þe folke on fele kinges londes' ('How shall we conduct ourselves ... who test ourselves in combat / And thus treat harshly the people of many kings' lands') (261–2) – thus vocalises the border counties' anxiety about violence and the poet's anti-imperial, anti-war message.[30] Schiff is laudably wary of outmoded nineteenth-century associations of medieval literature with the rise of modern nation states, but the strong regional identity of the borders does not automatically translate into anti-imperial sentiment, Arthur's conquering status is not necessarily corrupt in medieval eyes, and Gawayn and Galeron's bloody combat is hardly unique to 'the staged duels of marcher culture'.[31] The *Awntyrs* does reflect the warfare and reiving (or raiding) typical of the borders; but it also reflects the choreographed violence typical of both romance descriptions of fighting and the pan-European knightly ideology. As for Schiff's thesis that border affinities and regional identity meant that 'medieval England and Scotland ... did not imagine themselves as sovereign ... entities',[32] the idea is untenable. As the Scottish Wars of Independence (1296–328, 1332–56/7) reveal, these were different kingdoms with different rulers and peoples aware of distinct political realms, however much some of the peoples in those realms might have in common. Moreover, '[n]owhere in medieval Europe was the potential of a nation state realised at an earlier date than in England'; yet '[b]y 1400' Scotland had a similar identity and '[t]he period 1306–1488 is a crucial one in what used to be called Scotland's "national development"'.[33] It is true that the centuries prior to 1296 witnessed considerable cross-border acculturation evident in everything from landholding and marriage to a shared dialect; but by the fourteenth and fifteenth centuries, when the *Awntyrs* was composed, the Anglo-Scottish border had long been a 'sharply defined ... political boundary': hence Andy King's well-documented conclusion that, 'in the fourteenth century, the imperatives of warfare, politics and administration ensured that the marcher gentry on either side of the border thought of themselves as Englishmen or Scots first, and marchers only second'.[34] The point is thus not whether Galeron's self-identification as 'Þe grettest of Galwey[,] ... Of Connok, of Carrak, of Conyngham, of Kyle' ('The greatest of Galloway, ... Of Cumnock, of Carrick, of Cunningham, of Kyle') (417–18) associates him with actual Scottish locations but that he claims lands that are also claimed – and successfully defended – by Gawayn and Arthur, thereby furthering the theme of lordship in the poem.

As with modern criticism contending that the alliterative *Morte* is an anti-war poem,[35] scholarly insistence on *Awntyrs*'s supposed aversion to violence or kingdom-making is anachronistic, imposing the well-justified modern abhorrence of war on to an age and region dominated by violent competitiveness. It has long been recognised that the late medieval English nobility equated war with profit, and the Percies especially benefited from northern violence.[36] Scottish lords were equally concerned with honour and personal gain, and border lords regularly employed raiding to maintain prestige and acquire wealth.[37] Tellingly, then, Galeron is willing to cede the contested lands to Gawayn and Arthur provided that their champion can 'wyn hem in were' ('win them [the contested lands] in single combat') (421–33). Gawayn of course answers the challenge, but only after ensuring Galeron's comfort (439–59). Both the challenge and the mutual willingness to abide by the outcome of the combat recall and answer Gawayn's earlier question to the ghost (discussed above). There is a concern here with keeping truth, but Gawayn also accepts Galeron's challenge in the belief that he 'counter[s] with þe knight / In defence of my riȝt' ('encounters in combat with the knight / In defence of my [moral] right') (466–7) and that God will give victory to the just (471). The defeated Galeron likewise keeps his word, acknowledging Gawayn's 'makeles ... might' ('matchless ... power'), releasing his land claim, and offering fealty to Arthur (638–48). Arthur himself 'commaunde[s] pes' ('orders and prescribes peace') by giving Gawayn lands in Wales; he (or Gawayn, depending on the manuscript reading) gifts Galeron several Scottish lands, and Galeron joins the Round Table (649–702). It bears repeating that the precise location or reality of the lands in question is less important than their symbolism. Both in literature and in life the medieval gentry and nobility accepted violence as a way of life – but a capable king was expected to maintain peace and security at home. One way that such peace happened was through preventing or quelling rebellion, extending the kingdom, and rewarding one's vassals. In *Awntyrs*, contrary to the ghost's warning and much moralistic scholarship, Arthur and Gawayn secure the safety of Arthur's borders through the dual benefit of (1) acquiring a powerful new vassal who rules his own lands yet (2) recognises Arthur's greater sovereignty. This successful resolution is entirely in keeping with the late medieval governmental system of affinity and mutual obligation; but the collective abiding by agreed-upon procedures also recalls the concern with truth emphasised in *Ywayne and Gawayne* (33–44) and in the ghost's self-identification earlier in *Awntyrs* (205–6).

My defence of Arthur's kingship in *Awntyrs* supports and is supported by Spearing's and Phillips's work on the poem, including their insightful arguments about its unity and artistry. The ghost, for instance, advocates 'Mekenesse and mercy' and 'pité' (250–1). Appropriately, it is pity that later causes Gaynour to agree to Galeron's lady's request to 'Haf mercy on yondre kniȝt' ('Have mercy on yonder knight') by 'meekly' requesting that Arthur stop the battle before Galeron dies (619–37), and it is Arthur's willingness to enact royal 'mercy' and pity that enables the happy ending.[38] Chaucer repeatedly observes that 'pitee renneth soone in gentil herte' ('pity moves without delay in gentle heart'), *gentil* meaning both *kind* or *gracious* and *belonging to the noble or gentry* class.[39] This enacting of *gentil hertes* is why I contend, contrary to many scholars, that the behaviour of Gaynour and Arthur in *Awntyrs* is entirely to their credit. Although it has been argued that Galeron's joining Arthur's polity merely postpones further violence and proves the impossibility of Arthur and his court avoiding the final prophesied destruction,[40] the poem's happy ending testifies otherwise. It is precisely Arthur's strength and action, prompted by Gaynour and the message of the ghost (330–4, the Douce MS reading), that showcase his 'political maturity and power', his ability successfully to govern 'several peoples rather than one'.[41] This same royal power allows Arthur to avoid the deposition dangers faced by England's Richard II or Henry VI, for as K. B. McFarlane observes, 'only under-mighty kings … have over-mighty subjects'.[42] By thus emphasising Arthur's avoidance of destruction, the *Awntyrs*-poet both unifies his narrative and displays considerable artistic 'genius' in placing 'the glorification of what was doomed … after the [ghost's] prophecy of doom'.[43]

Analysing English chivalric culture, Nigel Saul concludes that '[i]t is difficult not to see in the Gawain of the English romances something of the chivalric ideal to which English knighthood aspired in the age of the Hundred Years War'.[44] Yet chivalric ideology, both in literature and life, was built on '[t]ension and paradox', interrogation and 'valorization'.[45] Such tension is evident in the romances under scrutiny here. It is partly by following Gawayne's advice about married knights not giving up chivalry and the pursuit of arms (1452–98), and especially by failing to keep his word, that Ywayne is denounced by Alundyne in *Ywayne and Gawayne*. Gawayne is thus *partly* responsible for Ywayne's crisis; yet paradoxically, in medieval English Arthuriana as a whole Gawain is so prominent and heroic that the anonymous English poet of *Ywayne* likely added Gawayne's name to this English adaptation of Chrétien's French *Yvain* story to capitalise on the popularity of the beloved English Gawain figure.[46] Gawain's reputation for truth in English Arthurian romance as a whole is epitomised by the pentangle on his shield in *Sir Gawain and the Green Knight*,[47] and although the question of how seriously or lightly Gawain fails to keep his word in this alliterative masterpiece is a major critical controversy, it is certainly true that the English Gawain in general is noted (by both medieval and modern audiences) for his courtesy and honour and prowess:[48] all traits that he reveals in the texts under discussion here. I thus agree with Saul, but contend further that romance authors regularly explore not merely chivalric ideals, but each of the principal sociopolitical relationships undergirding the complex system of affinities and alliances, duties, vassalage and rewards by which the armigerous classes governed late medieval England.[49]

Ywayne and Gawayne approaches the sociopolitical problems of martial and marital alliances, duties and rewards with a focus on landholding women of gentry or even noble rank. This female focus should not surprise modern readers: women are such a defining feature of the romance genre that Malory's Round Table Oath gives women a prominent position in the *Morte Darthur*'s chivalric enterprise.[50] Malory's Oath has a chivalric and military function, enjoining knights to avoid wrongdoing, murder, and treason, to grant mercy and always to assist women; failure to abide by the Oath's precepts will cost knights their reputation and any political or personal patronage from Arthur. Malory also several times throughout the first half of the *Morte* emphasises the extent of Arthur's polity, how 'he was hole kynge of Ingelonde, Walys, Scotlande' ('king of all England, Wales, Scotland') and elsewhere.[51] These comments are all original to Malory, but the example of *The Awntyrs off Arthure* reveals how other English Arthurian romancers were probing similar issues regarding the creation and maintenance of Arthur's realm, including the problems an English king could face when confronted with recalcitrant regional lords in those border areas of Scotland, Wales and the North. Medieval romance in general and Arthurian romance in particular are thus notable for the elasticity and variety of the genre, allowing the better storytellers to retune stock tropes and even characters to harmonise with new textual or historical circumstances. If the opportunities romance afforded authors for exploring key issues of society do not completely explain the origins of the genre, they certainly help explain its attractiveness to medieval and modern audiences.

NOTES

1. An excellent overview and bibliography is provided by Elizabeth Archibald, 'Ancient Romance', in Corinne Saunders (ed.), *A Companion to Romance: From Classical to Contemporary* (Oxford: Blackwell, 2004), pp. 10–25.

2. J. R. R. Tolkien, 'The Homecoming of Beorhtnoth Beorhthelm's Son', *Essays and Studies* 6 (1953), 1–18 (16).

3. For the significance of this manipulation see K. S. Whetter, '"Oft leudlez alone": The Isolation of the Hero and Its Consequences in *Sir Gawain and the Green Knight*', in Larissa Tracy and Geert H. M. Claassens (eds), *Medieval English and Dutch Literatures: The European Context: Essays in Honour of David F. Johnson* (Cambridge: D. S. Brewer, 2022), pp. 251-72.

4. Northrop Frye, *The Secular Scripture: A Study of the Structure of Romance* (Cambridge, MA: Harvard University Press, 1976), pp. 28–9. Cf. W. P. Ker, *Epic and Romance: Essays on Medieval Literature*, 2nd edn (London: Macmillan, 1908), pp. 321–4.

5. Eugène Vinaver, *The Rise of Romance* (Oxford University Press, 1971), pp. 1–32 (p. 17).

6. R. W. Southern, *The Making of the Middle Ages* (London: Hutchinson, 1953), pp. 209–34. *Contra* Vinaver, *Romance*, pp. 2–3.

7. For dates, manuscripts and sources see *A Manual of the Writings in Middle English 1050-1500: Fascicule 1. Romances*, ed. J. Burke Severs (New Haven: Connecticut Academy of Arts and Sciences, 1967). For descriptions and contents of the principal manuscripts of English romance see Gisela Guddat-Figge, *Catalogue of Manuscripts containing Middle English Romances* (Munich: Fink, 1976).

8. See K. S. Whetter, *Understanding Genre and Medieval Romance* (Farnham: Ashgate, 2008).

9. See K. S. Whetter, 'The Stanzaic *Morte Arthur* and Medieval Tragedy', *Reading Medieval Studies* 28 (2002), 87–111; Whetter, *Understanding Genre*, pp. 99–149; and Whetter, '"Oft leudlez alone"'. For the contrary view, that unhappy endings do not change a romance's genre, see Helen Cooper, *The English Romance in Time: Transforming Motifs from Geoffrey of Monmouth to the Death of Shakespeare* (Oxford University Press, 2004), pp. 361–408. Readers not familiar with the Middle English Arthurian tradition need to be warned that there are two anonymous poems and a prose work with confusingly similar titles: *Le Morte Arthur* (written in stanzas and often called 'the stanzaic *Morte*'); *Morte Arthure* (an alliterative poem often therefore called 'the alliterative *Morte*'); and Malory's *Le Morte Darthur* (in prose and sometimes called 'Malory's Arthuriad' and sometimes corrected to modern grammar with 'D'Arthur'). To add to the confusion, modern scholars sometimes italicise 'stanzaic' and 'alliterative' and sometimes do not, just as they may or may not distinguish the verse forms with an initial capital.

10. All references will be made parenthetically in the text, citing line numbers from Albert B. Friedman and Norman T. Harrington (eds), *Ywain and Gawain*, Early English Text Society OS 254 (Oxford University Press, 1964). The English romance is a shorter but faithful adaptation of Chrétien de Troyes's *Chevalier au lion* (or *Yvain*) of 1177–81. Throughout the essay I maintain the Middle English spellings of characters' names and textual titles, using standardised (modern) forms only when speaking of generalities.

The titles of many medieval texts are editorial, but *Ywayne and Gawayne* is clearly titled – in the spelling I use – at line 4.

11. Respectively, Dieter Mehl, *The Middle English Romances of the Thirteenth and Fourteenth Centuries* (London: Routledge, 1968), pp. 182–3; Tony Hunt, 'Beginnings, Middles, and Ends: Some Interpretative Problems in Chrétien's *Yvain* and Its Medieval Adaptations', in Leigh A. Arrathoon (ed.), *The Craft of Fiction: Essays in Medieval Poetics* (Rochester, MI: Solaris Press, 1984), pp. 83–117 (pp. 90–1).

12. Whetter, *Understanding Genre*, pp. 66–70.

13. Norman Davis (ed.), *Paston Letters and Papers of the Fifteenth Century*, 2 vols (Oxford: Clarendon Press, 1971 and 1976); vol. III, ed. Richard Beadle and Colin Richmond (Oxford University Press, 2005). On lordship, see Raluca L. Radulescu, *The Gentry Context for Malory's Morte Darthur* (Cambridge: D. S. Brewer, 2003).

14. *Paston Letters*, vol. I, pp. 131–4, Letter 73; Peter Coss, *The Lady in Medieval England 1000–1500* (Stroud: Sutton, 1999), pp. 1–2. See also Coss, *Lady*, pp. 31–3 and 110–11; and Jennifer Douglas, '"Kepe wysly youre wrytyngys": Margaret Paston's Fifteenth-Century Letters', *Libraries & the Cultural Record* 44.1 (2009), 29–49.

15. See Eileen Power, *Medieval Women*, ed. M. M. Postan (Cambridge University Press, 1975), pp. 35–52; Rowena E. Archer, '"How ladies ... who live on their manors ought to manage their households and estates": Women as Landholders and Administrators in the Later Middle Ages', in P. J. P. Goldberg (ed.), *Woman is a Worthy Wight: Women in English Society c. 1200–1500* (Stroud: Sutton, 1992), pp. 149–81.

16. Coss, *Lady*, p. 63.

17. See, e.g., the sources in notes 14 and 15. The armigerous classes are those '[b]earing, or entitled to bear, heraldic arms' (*OED*, s.v.).

18. Erich Auerbach, *Mimesis: The Representation of Reality in Western Literature*, trans. Willard R. Trask (Princeton University Press, 1953), pp. 123–42 (p. 131).

19. For an insightful comparative study of gender in all medieval adaptations of the story, see Evelyn Meyer, 'Manuscript versus Edition: The Multiple Endings of *Yvain/Iwein/Iven/Ywayne* and Their Gender Implications', *Amsterdamer Beiträge zur älteren Germanistik* 68 (2011), 97–141. Meyer emphasises the greater role given to female political power in *Ywayne* (110–12).

20. The issue is fruitfully discussed in relation to Malory by Karen Cherewatuk, *Marriage, Adultery, and Inheritance in Malory's Morte Darthur* (Cambridge: D. S. Brewer, 2006).

21. All references will be made parenthetically in the text, citing line numbers from Ralph Hanna III (ed.), *The Awntyrs off Arthure at the Terne Wathelyn: An Edition based on Bodleian Library MS. Douce 324* (Manchester University Press, 1974). I follow most editors in adding a final *e* to *Watheleyne*. My spelling of character names again follows those in the poem.

22. For details of the debate and a fuller discussion of the *Awntyrs*' romance features, see Whetter, *Understanding Genre*, pp. 85–8.

23. A. C. Spearing, '*The Awntyrs off Arthure*', in Bernard S. Levy and Paul E. Szarmach (eds), *The Alliterative Tradition in the Fourteenth Century* (Kent State University Press, 1981), pp. 183–202 (pp. 191, 200); revised in Spearing, *Medieval to Renaissance in English Poetry* (Cambridge University Press, 1985), pp. 121–42.

24. See, e.g., Chelsea S. Henson, '"Under a holte so hore": Noble Waste in *The Awntyrs off Arthure*', *Arthuriana* 28.4 (2018), 3–24 (3). Henson provides a representative recent example of this type of interpretation, though her conclusions partly rework the older complaints of Arthurian immorality through the new lenses of ecocriticism and waste theory. On the poem's (supposed) morality, see David N. Klausner, 'Exempla and *The Awntyrs of Arthure*', *Mediaeval Studies* 34 (1972), 307–25.

25. See notes 23 and 27.

26. Helen Phillips, '*The Awntyrs off Arthure*: Structure and Meaning. A Reassessment', *Arthurian Literature* 12 (1993), 63–89 (71).

27. Ibid., 71–81. Spearing also highlights how the imagerial and numerological centre of the poem is Arthur in royal splendour: A. C. Spearing, 'Central and Displaced Sovereignty in Three Medieval Poems', *Review of English Studies* 33.131 (1982), 247–61 (250–2).

28. Phillips, '*Awntyrs*', 79. On the valorising nature of Arthur's 'kyde conquerour' epithet in the *Morte*, see Fiona Tolhurst and K. S. Whetter, 'Memories of War: Retracting the Interpretive Tradition of the Alliterative *Morte Arthure*', *Arthuriana* 29.1 (2019), 88–108.

29. Randy P. Schiff, *Revivalist Fantasy: Alliterative Verse and Nationalist Literary History* (Columbus: Ohio State University Press, 2011), pp. 100–19 (p. 105).

30. Ibid., pp. 105–11. It is impossible here fully to account for the nuances of the ME in a single modernisation. Since translation is also interpretation, it should be admitted that, notwithstanding my thesis that the *Awntyrs* is not a critique of Arthurian chivalry, an equally possible rendering of these lines is 'How shall we behave/prosper ... who venture to fight / And thus trample underfoot the people of many kings' lands'.

31. *Contra* ibid., pp. 109–19.

32. Ibid., p. 109.

33. R. R. Davies, 'The Peoples of Britain and Ireland 1100–1400 I: Identities', *Transactions of the Royal Historical Society* 4 (1994), 1–20 (1 and 18); Katie Stevenson, *Power and Propaganda: Scotland 1306–1488* (Edinburgh University Press, 2014), p. 12.

34. Andy King, 'Best of Enemies: Were the Fourteenth-Century Anglo-Scottish Marches a "Frontier Society"?', in Andy King and Michael A. Penman (eds), *England and Scotland in the Fourteenth Century: New Perspectives* (Woodbridge: Boydell, 2007), pp. 116–35 (pp. 131–2, 135). Other essays in this volume support King's conclusion. I am indebted to R. Andrew McDonald for this reference.

35. For details and rebuttal, see Tolhurst and Whetter, 'Memories', 88–108.

36. Respectively, K. B. McFarlane, *The Nobility of Later Medieval England: The Ford Lectures for 1953 and Related Studies* (Oxford: Clarendon Press, 1973), pp. 19–40; J. A. Tuck, 'War and Society in the Medieval North', *Northern History* 21 (1985), 33–52.

37. Tuck, 'War and Society', 33–52.

38. Spearing, *Medieval to Renaissance*, pp. 139–40; Phillips, '*Awntyrs*', 81.

39. In Geoffrey Chaucer, *The Riverside Chaucer*, ed. Larry D. Benson, 3rd edn (Boston: Houghton Mifflin, 1987), see, e.g., *Canterbury Tales* I.1761; IV.1986; V.479.

40. Schiff, *Fantasy*, pp. 116–19; Henson, 'Noble Waste', 16–20.

41. Adapted from Davies, 'Peoples', 11.

42. McFarlane, *Nobility*, p. 179.

43. Spearing, *Medieval to Renaissance*, p. 141.

44. Nigel Saul, *For Honour and Fame: Chivalry in England, 1066–1500* (London: Bodley Head, 2011), p. 310.

45. Adapted from Richard W. Kaeuper, *Holy Warriors: The Religious Ideology of Chivalry* (University of Pennsylvania Press, 2009), p. 26.

46. Friedman and Harrington, eds, *Ywain and Gawain*, pp. 108–10, *Commentary* to the English poem's title.

47. *Sir Gawain and the Green Knight*, ed. J. R. R. Tolkien and E. V. Gordon, 2nd edn Norman Davis (Oxford: Clarendon Press, 1967), lines 619–65.

48. On the hero's overwhelming success and minimal failure in *Sir Gawain and the Green Knight*, see Whetter, '"Oft leudlez alone"'. On Gawain's reputation in general, see B. J. Whiting's classic 'Gawain: His Reputation, His Courtesy and His Appearance in Chaucer's *Squire's Tale*', *Mediaeval Studies* 9 (1947), 189–234.

49. This system was long called *feudalism*, but historians now avoid that term, regarding it as anachronistic and incapable of dealing with local and temporal variations. See especially Susan Reynolds, *Fiefs and Vassals: The Medieval Evidence Reinterpreted* (Oxford: Clarendon Press, 1994).

50. Sir Thomas Malory, *Le Morte Darthur*, ed. P. J. C. Field (Cambridge: D. S. Brewer, 2013), vol. I, 97.27–98.3.

51. Ibid., vol. I, 12.30–3; 47.1–5; 289.12–20. Given some romancers' explorations of key sociopolitical issues, it is tempting to link Malory's emphasis on Arthur's extensive kingship to the attempts by Edward I and Edward III to extend English control to Scotland, Wales and France; Arthur looks all the greater for the historical parallels.

CRITICAL REFLECTIONS AND FURTHER STUDY

Northrop Frye labels romance *The Secular Scripture* (see my essay, note 4). What is it about romance, especially medieval romance, that makes it so enduring? Do you agree with those archetypal or psychological approaches like Frye's (and see also Barron and Frye in Further Reading) that present romance as the genre nearest to wish-fulfilment? Personally, I find that many romances *can* fruitfully be read in this way; however, I am also continually drawn back to romance's contexts: notably its literary contexts (sources and genre), manuscript contexts, and historical contexts. For me, these contexts, albeit traditional, illuminate the genre's popularity with both medieval and modern audiences.

In my case study of two Arthurian romances I contend, among other things, that romance's success partly hinges upon its presentation of relations between ruler and ruled: not just between king and subject-knights but between the royal court and rural courts of powerful magnates, and even between women and their estates. The following questions continue these investigations.

The crisis in *Ywayne and Gawayne* is caused by Ywayne's failure to return to Alundyne at the promised time. The fault is Ywayne's, but it is Gawayne who initially urges Ywayne temporarily to leave marriage in favour of pursuing knightly adventure. Gawayne's reasoning reflects his well-known status as a lover-errant: a reference not only to Gawayne's own amorous reputation in Arthurian romance but also to the generic expectation that knightly adventure and prowess are closely interconnected with love, courtship, and women. Might readers today consider this connection between love and prowess a window on to medieval gender relations, woeful proof of medieval patriarchy, or perhaps a possibility for female empowerment?

As he struggles to reclaim his true love and true identity, Ywayne becomes known as the Knight with the Lion. The lion has been seen as everything from a glorified pet to a representation of the loyalty or truth that Ywayne must learn, or even to a symbol of divine grace. Since space did not permit a detailed discussion of the lion on my part, what do you think *is* its meaning?

The Yvain story was highly successful in the Middle Ages, starting in Old French (*c*. 1177–81) but being translated into Middle High German (*c*. 1190–1200), Old Norse (during King Hákon Hákonarson's reign, 1217–63), and Middle English (1300–50). Might it be the variety of female roles in this text, including female friendship, that make it work?

Several critics of *Awntyrs* (e.g., Robson; see Further Reading) argue that Gaynour and Gawayn ignore the ghost's warning and that Arthur remains ignorant of the apparition; lines 331–4 imply, and in one manuscript categorically state, otherwise. Why might critics want to disallow the king's awareness of the ghost's message? My interpretation of *Awntyrs* runs counter to the more fashionable Arthur-bashing that has dominated scholarship since the mid twentieth century (e.g., Matthews, in Further Reading, and Henson (see my essay, note 24)), but it is a reading that is supported both by historical contexts and the poem's own artistic structure. How convinced are you that *Awntyrs* is unified? If it is unified, does Arthur's ability to convert Galeron to his political retinue reflect his capabilities as a successful king? Does it aid your understanding of the poet's portrait of Arthur to study medieval attitudes to violence and kingship?

The Awntyrs is typical of English romance in surviving today in manuscript anthologies: books that contain several different kinds of stories as well as other written artefacts, sometimes secular, sometimes religious, frequently both. Are the miscellaneous contents of many prominent romance manuscripts merely contingency, or were at least some medieval users attempting to create personal libraries in the form of anthologies whose contents reflect personal and familial interests? Against this variegated reading background, consider how successfully the *Awntyrs* balances an awareness of historical loss, including the traditional tragic ending of the Arthurian world, with the hope 'that human reform can temper … misfortune' (Whitman, 'Envisioning the End', 89).

The creation and study of character in English literature is frequently said to be a post-medieval phenomenon. Might we consider romance's popularity as stemming in part from its nascent interest in character and situation? Is part of romance's durability and affect – whether medieval or modern – due to its exposure of the audience to strange new worlds via an idealised version of our own world and behaviour? That is, might the romance protagonist's adventures be successfully likened to both 'an early form of travel literature' (Rouse, 'Walking (between) the Lines', p. 137) and to identity formation (Crane, 'Knights in Disguise'?

FURTHER READING

Archibald, Elizabeth, 'Women and Romance', in Henk Aertsen and Alasdair A. MacDonald (eds), *Companion to Middle English Romance* (Amsterdam: VU University Press, 1990), pp. 153–69

Barron, W. R. J., *English Medieval Romance* (London: Longman, 1987)

Crane, Susan, 'Knights in Disguise: Identity and Incognito in Fourteenth-Century Chivalry', in F. R. P. Akehurst and Stephanie Cain Van D'Elden (eds), *The Stranger in Medieval Society* (University of Minnesota Press, 1997), pp. 63–79

Finlayson, John, 'Definitions of Middle English Romance', *Chaucer Review* 15.1 (1980), 44–62, and 15.2 (1980), 68–81

Finlayson, John, 'Reading Romances in Their Manuscript: Lincoln Cathedral Manuscript 91 ("Thornton")', *Anglia* 123.4 (2006), 632–66

Frye, Northrop, *Anatomy of Criticism: Four Essays* (Princeton University Press, 1957)

Jensen, Christopher, 'The Role of the Lion in the Middle English *Ywain and Gawain*', *Arthuriana* 30.1 (2020), 104–24

Johnston, Michael, *Romance and the Gentry in Late Medieval England* (Oxford University Press, 2014)

Matthews, William, *The Tragedy of Arthur: A Study of the Alliterative 'Morte Arthure'* (Berkeley: University of California Press, 1960)

Robson, Margaret, 'From Beyond the Grave: Darkness at Noon in *The Awntyrs off Arthure*', in Ad Putter and Jane Gilbert (eds), *The Spirit of Medieval English Popular Romance* (Harlow: Longman, 2000), pp. 219–36

Rouse, Robert, 'Walking (between) the Lines: Romance as Itinerary/Map', in Rhiannon Purdie and Michael Cichon (eds), *Medieval Romance, Medieval Contexts* (Cambridge: D. S. Brewer, 2011), pp. 135–47

Vishnuvajjala, Usha, '"Me rewes sore": Women's Friendship, Affect and Loyalty in *Ywain and Gawain*', *Arthurian Literature* 35 (2020), 117–32

Whitman, Jon, 'Envisioning the End: History and Consciousness in Medieval English Arthurian Romance', *Arthuriana* 23.3 (2013), 79–103

PART II
The Renaissance, 1485–1660

INTRODUCTORY NOTE

Alessandra Petrina's essay sounds an important chord for the volume in its eloquently elaborated analysis of the Renaissance as a pan-European 'crossroads' of linguistic, cultural and material exchange and interanimation – as, in some ways, an age of 'globalisation' *avant la lettre*. The importance of travel and trade, including the growth of the international book trade at this time, and the imaginings and representations of international networks of relationships, are all keynotes in this essay. The striking allegorical map illustrating the essay nicely captures the roving spirit of the age (and also testifies to the growth of map-making at the time) and it provides an immediate visualisation of how Europeans were thinking strategically beyond local borders. The position of Britain within the map's iconography is worth studying and will surely suggest some contemporary relevance in the light of Petrina's discussion (and its conclusion in particular) as well as some links to other essays in this section and to later essays.

Jane Grogan's essay picks up the baton of global cultural exchange in her tracing of the dialogic growth and development of the epic in this period. Focusing in careful detail on an important treatise from the period which has only recently come to prominence in the field, Grogan provides an illuminating commentary on the poetics of the epic genre as these were evolving in tandem with new global perspectives and with new political configurations in Britain and Ireland. Among other things, by drawing on this relatively new material, Grogan's essay significantly expands our understanding of the literary-critical contexts of the period and provides a useful early perspective on the institution of literary criticism.

The social and political contexts of Renaissance Britain are skilfully mediated through close textual analysis in the following three essays by Christa Jansohn, Ina

Habermann and Robert Wilcher. Jansohn turns the focus from epic poetry to domestic drama in her lively account of the popular anonymous play *Arden of Faversham* and its place in the history of this theatrical genre as it rapidly developed throughout the age of Shakespeare and beyond. In exploring the actual events on which the play is based, along with how these were later represented in Holinshed's influential history, *Chronicles of England, Scotland and Ireland*, which was probably the main source for the play, Jansohn provides valuable insights into both the social background of the play and the complex nature of its contexts. Jansohn's analysis of the play draws attention to its relative sophistication, for the time, in its treatment of character and motivation and her discussion focuses in particular on the sexual politics of the play and how it may have reflected changing attitudes towards marriage during the period. In attending closely to questions of genre, style and stagecraft in Renaissance drama, Jansohn's essay connects neatly to the next essay in this section, and both obviously relate generically to Clare Wallace's on contemporary drama (Essay 26).

In her essay here, Ina Habermann presents a finely detailed analysis of Shakespeare's language and stagecraft in *Henry V*. The play is carefully contextualised within the trajectory of Shakespeare's other history plays and in relation to broader political history. In the wake of the UK's withdrawal from the European Union in 2020, this is an especially timely discussion of a play which, as Habermann points out, has often been framed in nationalistic terms. Her critically nuanced approach to this aspect of the play provides a good basis for further discussion along these lines, perhaps especially in relation to the contexts established earlier by Petrina and Grogan (Essays 4 and 5); and Ulla Rahbek's essay (31) also provides some directly pertinent contemporary reflections on questions of national identity.

Wilcher's meticulously observed analysis of certain stylistic and thematic developments in Henry Vaughan's poetry is carefully related to the politico-religious context of south Wales in the period of the English Civil Wars, in the years when Vaughan's collection of religious lyrics, *Siler Scintillans*, was written and first published. But, in addition, Wilcher also establishes further contexts for the poems by considering their later transmission and reception in the late Romantic and early Victorian eras and how this in turn coloured present-day interpretations of his work, especially by obscuring important aspects of their original seventeenth-century context. Wilcher's sophisticated analysis thus lays bare some of the complexities of fully contextualised reading and sheds light not just on Vaughan's poetry but also on the intricacies involved in the web of contexts out of which any text is woven. In everyday life, Vaughan was a practising physician and this provides an interesting line of connection to Paul Wright's essay (15) where he discusses another poet-physician, John Keats, partly in relation to yet another, Vaughan's later Welsh compatriot, Dannie Abse.

4

The Renaissance in England: A Meeting Point

ALESSANDRA PETRINA

Abstract

This essay deals with the concept of 'Renaissance', proposing a definition of the term as a meeting point, in both historical and geographical terms. It then focuses on its etymology, in the context of the investigation of other keywords such as 'humanism' and 'Middle Ages'. The very flexibility of this concept in historical terms suggests we should look at it not as a starting point, but rather as a long period of transformation, marked by a number of events, such as the Black Death, the establishment of printing in Europe, and the Protestant Reformation. Such events are often distant in time, but their interaction brings about the passage from medieval to early modern. The essay then moves on to discuss the Renaissance in England against the background of its relationship with other European countries. The claim underlying this section is that the uniqueness of Tudor literature is the result of a multiplicity of voices: by opening itself to texts from other cultures, the English canon acquires its identity. Encouraged by the development of printing and the spread of education, translation becomes a primary concern for Tudor writers: it develops both vertically, by importing classical texts as well as works from the Latin and vernacular Middle Ages, and horizontally, by acquiring contemporary classics from other countries. Thanks to the proliferation of translations, the English language becomes a rich and flexible instrument. At the same time, the greater ease of travel and the intensifying exchanges between England and the rest of Europe promote the circulation of ideas and texts at an international level, and help put England on the early modern cultural map.

The title of this essay is indebted to a definition of the Renaissance offered by the Belgian historian Jo Tollebeek in 2001: 'The Renaissance was a new beginning, a turning point'.[1] In the second part of my discussion I shall focus on England, and on English literature, as the specific object of this analysis of the Renaissance; but it is important at this stage to reflect on the concept of Renaissance since debates, and sometimes controversies, about the term and its meaning go well beyond the English case, and embrace the Renaissance as a more general idea.

The term is generally used as a univocal definition of a phase in western European thought that may be said to have had its first manifestations in fifteenth-century Italy, and to be still applicable to something as far in time and place as seventeenth-century England. However, the volatility of the concept is shown by the application of the same term to periods or cultural movements other than the one discussed here: we can talk, for instance, of a Hellenistic Renaissance focused on Alexandria and its famed library; of a twelfth-century Renaissance that finds its most powerful symbols in the Gothic cathedrals; of a Harlem Renaissance in the 1920s. What the word indicates is therefore a moment not in time but in the collective spirit. Of all terms used to designate a historical period or a cultural movement, 'Renaissance', together perhaps with 'Romanticism', is one of the most loaded, so much so that it has been repeatedly challenged, repudiated, or, in recent times, substituted with the more neutral 'early modern'. Even its spelling – whether or not it should be written with a capital R – is an object of discussion.[2] It is clear that by choosing to adopt it to designate the passage from the medieval to the modern era in Europe, we are offering not simply a definition but an assessment. It is therefore important to understand how it came to be adopted.

The word itself was first coined in France in the fourteenth century, with the meaning of 'rebirth', and only in the eighteenth century did it acquire, in France first and in the following century in England, the meaning of a 'revival of the arts and high culture under the influence of classical models', to use the definition provided by the *Oxford English Dictionary*. This very definition tells us that we can understand the Renaissance only in relation to other concepts: the Middle Ages, of which the Renaissance is a consequence, and humanism, which gave the impulse to the revival. The late Middle Ages brought with them a new reckoning with the large and complex cultural inheritance of the classical world. For centuries, monastic institutions had preserved, copied and perpetuated classical (especially Latin) literature in manuscripts, saving it from the destruction caused by the fall of the Roman empire and the civil and political unrest that followed throughout Europe. As commercial routes expanded and facilitated the exchange not only of goods but also of information, intellectual culture, in the form of books and other artefacts, began to circulate independently of religious authority. Towards the end of the twelfth century we also see the beginning of a new phenomenon, the universities, which began to develop in different parts of Europe, starting with locations as far apart as Bologna, Oxford, Paris, Salamanca and Coimbra; with their growth and multiplication they presented a model of learning that could be autonomous from monastic education. Such institutions offered to an expanding segment of the population an opportunity for upward mobility through learning and intellectual ability; the idea of the *clericus* – the man who can not only read and write but uses his intellectual assets to make a living (the male-only noun and pronouns are unfortunately inevitable here) – developed from designating somebody closely connected to a religious institution to indicating the kind of professional Geoffrey Chaucer had in mind when he described the Clerk of Oxford, concluding his portrait with a memorable touch: 'And gladly wolde he lerne, and gladly teche'.[3]

Like 'Renaissance', the term 'humanism' is also a very late coinage, first used in 1808, and in its creation expressing admiration and perhaps nostalgia for a moment in the past in which classical, pre-Christian texts were not only studied, but became models of humane, as opposed to divine, learning.[4] But as is the case with 'Renaissance', this definition of humanism speaks of German idealism rather than of the practical approach of fifteenth-century intellectuals to a new profession. It is no surprise, therefore, that while 'humanism' is a nineteenth-century word, 'humanist' is first attested in the fifteenth century,[5] and indicates a teacher or student of *studia humanitatis*, subjects promoting the knowledge of humanity and humanity's intellectual development.[6] Humanists were in fact professional readers, writers and teachers, entrusted with the increase and dissemination of learning rather than with political theory or philosophy.[7] Such intellectuals could approach the classical legacy (received thanks to the medieval copyists) with a renewal of curiosity, bringing to their reading their changed perception of the world, and perhaps recovering a fuller sense of the cultural contexts in which these ancient texts had been composed. If the Middle Ages had kept Latin literacy in the west alive, the knowledge of ancient Greek had steeply declined since the fifth century, and philosophers such as Aristotle were known mainly thanks to Arabic translations; by the fourteenth century this almost forgotten language was the object of a revival of interest, and Greek philosophers and poets could be approached afresh.

We could thus identify the Renaissance with the phase in which various impulses, from the secularisation of learning and the professionalisation of the intellectual to new approaches to classical texts, gathered and flowed, resulting in a resetting of intellectual attitudes. Yet we should exercise care when assessing this movement. The idea of a revival brings with it positive connotations, and this is particularly evident if we look at the early scholarly attempts to define this period. We normally identify in Jacob Burckhardt's hugely influential *Civilization of the Renaissance in Italy* (1860) the first comprehensive attempt to describe the 'passage to the modern world';[8] Burckhardt expressed unreserved admiration for the Renaissance, contrasting it to a medieval period beset by ignorance and superstition. One of the most famous sections from this book can be used to discuss the complex connotations of the term. After a first chapter devoted to a historical exploration of late medieval Italy, the scholar turns to his core concern, the development of the individual, starting with 'the Italian ... the firstborn among the sons of modern Europe':

In the Middle Ages both sides of human consciousness – that which was turned within as that which was turned without – lay dreaming or half awake beneath a common veil. The veil was woven of faith, illusion, and childish prepossession, through which the world and history were seen clad in strange hues. Man was conscious of himself only as member of a race, people, party, family, or corporation – only through some general category. In Italy this veil first melted into air; an *objective* treatment and consideration of the state and of all the things of this world became possible. The *subjective* side at the same time asserted itself with corresponding emphasis; man became a spiritual *individual*, and recognized himself as such.[9]

These words have been echoed in recent times by another scholar who has consciously taken up the Burckhardtian legacy, Stephen Greenblatt:

> Something happened in the Renaissance, something that surged up against the constraints that centuries had constructed around curiosity, desire, individuality, sustained attention to the material world, the claims of the body ... The key to the shift lies not only in the intense, deeply informed revival of interest in the pagan deities and the rich meaning that once attached to them. It lies also in the whole vision of a world in motion, a world not rendered insignificant but made more beautiful by its transience, its erotic energy, and its ceaseless change.[10]

Both passages speak of something they do not attempt to define in terms of time and place, but in terms of spiritual impulse. When we say that the Victorian age covers the period of Queen Victoria's reign, from 1837 to 1901, we define this period by giving it a beginning and an end: however debatable, these boundaries allow us to locate the period with a degree of precision. But it is very difficult to attempt something similar with the Renaissance. The two scholars quoted above share a vocabulary of active verbs, of *melting, asserting, surging up*: in both cases we perceive the sense of sudden shift that liberates energy and change, expressed in almost messianic tones.

 However, such an attempt tells us more about the scholars who offered these definitions, and the times in which they lived, than about the actual Renaissance. We seem to long for a change, especially when the times we live in are obscure, or uncertain, so we look back at the past trying to identify a moment in which human beings found in themselves the freedom to think and to act independently of religious or political constrictions. But the definition of Renaissance in terms of an awakening, a change, a swerve, clashes not only with common sense but with the coordinates of space and time in which we locate this phenomenon. Its chronology is flexible and vast: there is common agreement that the first writer we may take as a reference point for our understanding of the Renaissance is the fourteenth-century poet Petrarch; Burckhardt sees the end of the Italian Renaissance in the *sacco di Roma* (1527); but by that time English literature was only just taking its first, tentative steps away from its medieval period, and entering a phase that, after a transitional fifteenth and early sixteenth century, would culminate in William Shakespeare, John Donne and perhaps John Milton – that is to say, well into the seventeenth century. An analogous distance in time as well as in cultural climate may be perceived if we attempt, for instance, a comparison between the sixteenth-century poets of the French Pléiade, active mainly in the 1540s and 1550s, and the greatest writer of the Spanish Renaissance, Miguel de Cervantes (1547–1616), whose *Don Quijote* was published in two parts in 1605 and 1615.

It is perhaps more useful to think of the Renaissance not as a period, or a shift, or a moment, but in terms of *movement*, also in the literal sense, which would help us to understand why its chronology and geography should be so flexible: its impetus literally moves from Italy to France, to the Low Countries, to England, and as it expands to northern Europe it gathers momentum from historical events that are generated outside Italy, the most important being the establishment of the first printing presses, the Protestant Reformation and the scientific revolution. Many definitions of the Renaissance suggest that it is a dynamic concept. Antonio Gramsci used a water metaphor when describing it, while also radically antedating its beginning: 'I agree with the opinion that the Renaissance is a movement indicating a great flow, beginning after the year 1000; Humanism and Renaissance *stricto sensu* are its two concluding moments, mainly located in Italy, while the more general historical process is European and not simply Italian'.[11] So, complementing the idea of movement, it is perhaps also useful to think of the Renaissance as a meeting point or point of confluence, in both historical and geographical terms. We will find that, in spite of great differences in cultural attitudes and ideology, many theoreticians of the Renaissance offer the same approach. Many of the great technological innovations that have been seen to characterise the Renaissance, from the use of gunpowder to the printing press, had in fact been invented long before, and elsewhere outside of Europe. Attention to the classics, and attempts to recover the lost Greek inheritance, had characterised the efforts of a number of scholars throughout the Middle Ages. The universities had first appeared, albeit in a very tentative form, in the twelfth century, while the city-states first established in Italy around the eleventh century became a model that was being assimilated in central Europe in the following centuries. But by the end of the fourteenth century another element entered the equation: the Black Death. As far as is known, it appears to have been the deadliest pandemic ever known, killing 30 to 60 per cent of the population of Europe. While it brought with it terror, desolation, civil unrest and religious fanaticism, it also forced a redrawing of social boundaries and a resetting of the economy. The growing demand for specialised labour during this period further reduced the straitened circumstances of some segments of the population, but at the same time opened up the possibility of increased social mobility for others. We therefore see an unpredictable concatenation of historical events introducing the transition into the modern world. The pandemic brought with it the end of a cultural age, and in the long run favoured a process of change.

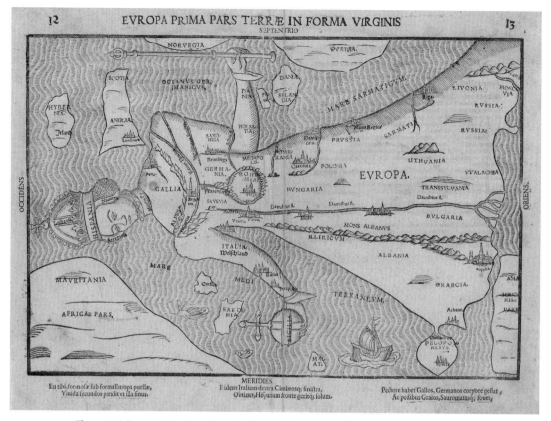

Figure 4.1 *Europa Prima Pars Terrae In Forma Virginis*. Map of Europe in the form of a queen or maiden, by Heinrich Bünting, 1582.

Within this vast landscape, the place of the British Isles, especially in the early stages of the European Renaissance, seems to have been rather marginal (Figure 4.1). This does not necessarily impinge upon the quality of its literary production: the late fourteenth century in England saw the emergence of English as a literary language (a phenomenon which would be followed, in the fifteenth century, by the establishment of English as the language of Chancery)[12] mainly thanks to some of the most significant poets of the canon: Geoffrey Chaucer, William Langland and the *Pearl*-poet. In the following century, while English writers seemed to be struggling under the great shadow of Chaucer, Scottish literature experienced a moment of great flourishing, with the poetic output of James I, Robert Henryson and, later, Gavin Douglas and William Dunbar. But both these phases, extraordinary as they were, found little echo in the European cultural world.

It has become a commonplace to refer to English cultural isolation by mentioning a famous passage appearing in John Florio's *First Fruites*, when he has one of his speakers note that the English language is 'a useful language here in England, but beyond Dover it is worthless'.[13] A few years later, in the opening lines of the third dialogue of his *Cena de le Ceneri*, first published in London in 1584, Giordano Bruno has one of his characters, Theophilo, ask Nolano (the writer's alter ego) whether he understands English. The answer is a supercilious negative: 'There is nothing to force him to learn it, since any honourable gentleman with whom he would converse knows either Latin, or French, or Spanish, or Italian; as they know that the English language is not used except within their island, they would believe themselves wild men, if they knew no language but their own.'[14] We might simply read the former quotation as an astute marketing ploy on the part of somebody who aspired to become a teacher of Italian for the elite, and the latter as one more example of Bruno's complete want of diplomatic finesse. But these passages also reveal the attitude of English intellectuals: just as Florio was meeting a desire, on the part of his contemporaries, to acquire a competence in Italian, so Bruno, in spite of his condescending tone, was noting the effort made by English gentlemen to learn foreign languages. This was partly motivated by status anxiety,[15] as the English language was still struggling to find international recognition. But there was also a genuine desire to enter the European cultural arena. Early sixteenth-century intellectuals in England had found that Latin could answer their need for intercultural exchange: thus Thomas More would write his main work in Latin, and in the same language correspond with Erasmus and other humanists outside England. By the same token George Buchanan, the foremost Scottish humanist, wrote exclusively in Latin, since his interlocutors were likely to be French and Portuguese intellectuals rather than his countrymen. Yet this choice was consciously elitist, as shown by the prefatory section of More's *Utopia*, in which the author states his intention not to publish his work, as 'most men know nothing of learning; many despise it'.[16] The alternative seemed to be between writing in English, thus condemning oneself to insularity, and writing in Latin, thus leaving one's work confined to a restricted (if European) circle. The desire to learn contemporary vernaculars – above all French, Italian, Spanish – was the answer to this perplexity. Genuine cultural intent and social aspirations are fused in the *cri de cœur* the writer and bibliophile Gabriel Harvey inserts on the margins of his copy of Florio's *First Fruites*: 'How fluently the Earl of Leicester, Master Hatton, Sir Philip Sidney and many of our renowned nobles speak the Italian language. Why couldn't Axiophilus speak it with the same dexterity?'[17]

This aspiration is symptomatic of a wider embracing of classical and contemporary foreign cultures, which is one of the distinguishing traits of the English Renaissance. If the image we can use with reference to the Italian Renaissance is one of confluence of different streams, in the case of England we may rather evoke the image of the crossroads. In his previously mentioned work, *The Swerve*, Stephen Greenblatt identifies the turning point from the Middle Ages to the Renaissance in the discovery, on the part of the humanist Poggio Bracciolini, of a 500-year-old manuscript of Lucretius' *De rerum natura*, a Latin poem written in the first century BCE, proposing an analysis of the fundamental structures of the universe as based upon physical laws rather than divine intervention. While we may dispute the actual impact of a book that had, after all, been copied more than once and was therefore known in the Middle Ages, it is important here to note that another scholar, Roberto Weiss, writing seventy years before Greenblatt, had attributed Bracciolini an equally pivotal role, this time with reference to England. In his hugely influential *Humanism in England During the Fifteenth Century*, Weiss went so far as to state that 'before Poggio came to England in 1418, it is quite impossible to find ... any humanistic manifestations in this country'.[18] Equally interesting is the fact that the meeting between Bracciolini and his English patron, Henry Beaufort, bishop of Winchester, took place between 1414 and 1417 at the Council of Constance: not only a political and religious occasion but also a moment of international cultural exchange and 'a large and thriving book-market'.[19] It may be argued that Poggio was of little use to the bishop's household, concluding his English sojourn after only four years. But what is interesting is the fact that this meeting, seen as a forerunner to the English Renaissance, is identified with an act of cultural appropriation of a foreign model. Poggio himself profited from his visit, as shown by recently edited fragments which reveal his interest for recent English history,[20] and by the fact that he pursued his favourite activity of manuscript hunting while at the service of Henry Beaufort.

Book exchange is one of the markers of this new climate; cultural acquisition, whether through patronage or translation, would become one of the distinguishing traits of English humanism first, and then of the English Renaissance. Towards the end of the fifteenth century the rise of printing, generally (and correctly) seen as a great incentive to the spread of literacy and knowledge, also gave an enormous boost to the idea of intellectual exchange. Having (almost) exactly the same copy of a book in different corners of Europe meant that scholars who were far apart could rely on the same source for comparing their inferences and observations. Printing also widened access to texts since books were now more numerous and much less expensive, and it dramatically increased the demand for translations. In England in particular, with the strong impulse given to the advancement of education in the early decades of the Tudor dynasty, there was a strengthening of humanism, in the sense of a professionalisation of intellectual labour. This development had a religious dimension related to the rise of Protestantism. While, in Catholic Rome, Michele Ghislieri (the future Pope Pius V) showed his mistrust of printing by associating it with storm and desolation, and the office of the Maestro del Sacro Palazzo noted despairingly that the Holy Church would have profited from the disappearance of printing,[21] the English Protestant John Foxe, in his *Acts and Monuments*, welcomed printing, in a language echoing Luther's celebration,[22] as the sign of God's might: 'not with sword and tergate to subdue his exalted aduersary, but with Printing, writing, and reading to conuince darkenes by light, errour by truth, ignorance by learning'.[23]

The uniqueness of Tudor literature is thus the result of a multiplicity of voices: by opening itself to texts from other cultures, the English canon acquired its identity. Encouraged by the development of printing and the spread of education, translation became a primary concern for Tudor writers: it developed both vertically, by importing classical texts as well as works from the Latin and vernacular Middle Ages, and horizontally, by acquiring contemporary classics in modern vernaculars. Thanks to the proliferation of translations, the English language became a rich and flexible instrument, and gradually reduced the use of Latin in academia and eventually in religious and scientific discourse. As the idea of the nation was rising and beginning to be established in early modern consciousness across Europe, the intellectual community in England awoke to the parallel awareness of the construction of a national library of the mind: acquiring new books for this library meant employing translation to give classical sources or contemporary vernacular texts a new citizenship. At the same time, the greater ease of travel and the intensifying exchanges between England and the rest of Europe promoted the circulation of ideas and texts at an international level, and helped put England on the early modern cultural map. The universities played their role in this process of cultural exchange: Jonathan Woolfson notes how one of the main points of reference for English intellectuals on the Continent was the University of Padua, and observes that 'far from making Italy irrelevant, the humanism of Erasmus and his north European *familia* reinvigorated Padua's place as a centre for these studies'.[24] Religious differences could be overcome by the urgent and practical desire for learning.

Translation has often been hailed as one of the keys to understanding English Renaissance literature; this was the claim made, as early as 1931, by Francis Otto Matthiessen, who significantly entitled his most important work as *Translation: An Elizabethan Art*.[25] Once again, there is no doubt that the impulse to practise translation as a form of cultural acquisition originated much earlier: Geoffrey Chaucer, the foremost English medieval poet, had been hailed by his contemporary Eustace Deschamps with the words *grant translateur*, and described as the man who enriched the English literary garden by planting foreign flowers.[26] The fifteenth century was also notable for great translations that drew from disparate sources to offer an encyclopaedia of learning – for example John Lydgate's *Fall of Princes* (1431–8) – as well as works that presented a gathering and rewriting of disparate literary traditions, as in the case of Thomas Malory's *Morte Darthur* (c. 1470). But the sixteenth century saw a substantial increase in translation activity, a trend favoured by the arrival of printing. In 1476 William Caxton brought from Bruges, where he had learned his trade, not only the technology of printing, but also a tradition of French romances that would meet the favour of his customers. Caxton understood that the acquisition of foreign literary models through translation might gain him a readership. Besides, when he started working in

Westminster, in 1476, the late arrival of this trade in England in comparison with what was happening on the Continent triggered a heightened interest on the part of English readers for the importation of printed books (a similar phenomenon can be observed in Scotland, where printing began in the early sixteenth century). The considerable demand for foreign books, which increased after 1476, helped sharpen the attention of English and Scottish readers for the cultural offerings of the Continent. The information that can be found in the Renaissance Cultural Crossroads digital catalogue speaks eloquently to this development. Based on the English Short Title Catalogue, the database catalogues all translations printed in England from the onset of printing to 1641, and offers interesting details not only about the languages translators most frequently drew upon (a large majority of the translations come from Latin, closely followed by French, while Italian covers little more than 8 per cent of the total), but also on the prevailing practice of using intermediary translations.[27] It clearly reflects a culture that found its identity through translation (Figure 4.2).

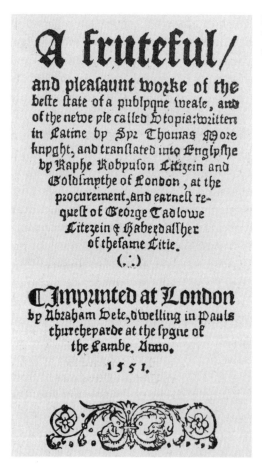

Figure 4.2 Title page of Ralph Robinson's 1551 translation into English of Thomas More's *Utopia* (1516)

Translators 'were eager to enrich their language with the *res*, i.e. the know-ledge or wisdom heretofore available only in the foreign tongue'.[28] In this, English translators were following a trend common to early modern Europe, as the de-veloping vernacular literatures made use of translation to find their own identity and definition: in this sense we can read Umberto Eco's famous dictum that 'the language of Europe is translation'.[29] But we might also argue that in the case of England great attention was devoted to contemporary works in the vernacular, and to intermediary translations of both vernacular and classical works. Fol-lowing the example of contemporary French intellectuals, English readers and writers accorded an enthusiastic reception to contemporary classics, as in the case of the wave of English Petrarchism and sonnet-writing that followed the circulation of his *Canzoniere* and *Trionfi* and brought a spate of translations in its wake. Such translations opened the way to works that define for us the English Renaissance lyric: Philip Sidney's *Astrophil and Stella*, Samuel Daniel's *Delia* and Edmund Spenser's *Amoretti*. But English writers also received, mainly through French intermediary translations, classical works such as Ovid's *Meta-morphoses* and Plutarch's *Lives*, or the great Italian tradition of the Renaissance novella, and they duly imitated and rewrote these models giving them new life in a drastically changed form. Much of this material would help shape the works of William Shakespeare, Ben Jonson and the other great Elizabethan and Jacobean playwrights.

The very pragmatic attitude of the translators who made this appropriation possible is evident in the words of Thomas North, who was translating Amyot's preface to *his* translation of Plutarch's *Lives*:

> If it so fortune that men find not the speech of this translation so flowing, as they
> have found some other of mine ... I beseech the reader to consider, that the office of a
> fit translater, consisteth not onely the faithfull expressing of his authors meaning, but
> also in a certain resembling and shadowing out of the forme of his style and the maner
> of his speaking ... For how harsh or rude soever my speech be, yet am I sure that my
> translation will be much easier to my countrymen, than the Greeke copie is, even to
> such as are best practised in the Greeke tonge, by reason of Plutarkes peculiar maner of
> inditing, which is rather sharpe, learned, and short, than plained, polished, and easie.[30]

Perhaps unconsciously, North was echoing words William Caxton had used for his translation of Virgil's *Aeneid*, once again undertaken via a French intermedi-ary. For Caxton, the lexical choices implicit in the act of translation had become a source of reflection on the appropriateness of the language he would use: 'And thus bytwene playn rude | & curious I stande abashed. but in my Iudgemente | the comyn termes that be dayli vsed ben lyghter to be vnderstonde than the olde and auncyent englysshe'.[31] Translation thus becomes a linguistic as well as a cultural key for understanding the English Renaissance.

Renaissance England was a meeting point in more ways than one. Just as the exchange of books was gaining momentum so the nation began to lose its marginality and to find itself closer to the centre of European culture and politics. This shift was partly the result of decades of Tudor policy, but it was also the consequence of the more frequent travelling of people as well as of goods. The foreigners who arrived in England from the mid sixteenth century onwards generally belonged to the middle class, and, when not forced to seek refuge in England for religious reasons, were drawn there because of commercial interests. Small communities of foreigners began to form in London, often with their own church, each creating a network of relations within the city and sometimes within the Court. Towards the end of the century relations with Scotland also intensified, as English people became more and more aware that the most probable successor of Queen Elizabeth was to be the present king of Scotland. At the same time, English people began to discover new forms of travelling: they followed an itinerary through various European courts, or were prompted by book circulation, or even motivated by the desire to see the great cities of the Continent, such as Paris, Venice or Rome. English and Scottish students started to attend the Continental universities, with a particular predilection for Paris and Padua; international events such as the Frankfurt book fair saw an increasing participation of English printers and booksellers, eager to insert England within the European cultural networks. The European perception of the English began to change, as the nation was at the same time acquiring a more specific national identity, losing its marginality, and entering European politics more and more decidedly.

England's autonomy and its isolation are defined and challenged in the sixteenth century. Referring to the French conquest of Calais (1558), the historian Fernand Braudel noted that it was then that England became an island.[32] As such, it would be famously celebrated by John of Gaunt in the deathbed monologue Shakespeare wrote for him in *Richard II* (1597): the evocation of the 'sceptered isle' has generated a series of misreadings on the part of scholars who did not perceive the irony of Shakespeare's stance. Commenting on the Shakespearean passage, Andrew Hadfield notes that 'of course, England is not an island and the speech should be read as a potential reminder that its boundaries are exceptionally porous and liable to be penetrated';[33] a reminder that was all the more necessary at the end of the sixteenth century. Literary and philosophical reflection warned the English reader as to the risk of enclosing oneself in isolation, whether in cultural, political, or existential terms, and we may read in this light John Donne's statement: 'No man is an *Iland*, intire of it selfe; every man is a peece of the *Continent*, a part of the *maine*; if a *Clod* bee washed away by the *Sea, Europe* is the lesse'.[34] The Renaissance established a new relation between England and the rest of Europe.

NOTES

1. Jo Tollebeek, '"Renaissance" and "Fossilization": Michelet, Burckhardt, and Huizinga', *Renaissance Studies* 15 (2001), 354–66 (354).

2. Tison Pugh, 'A Copyeditor's Introduction', *Exemplaria* 25 (2014), 313–14 (313).

3. Geoffrey Chaucer, *The Canterbury Tales*, general prologue, line 308, from David Lawton (ed.), *The Norton Chaucer* (New York: W. W. Norton, 2019).

4. F. J. Niethammer, a German educator, coined the term 'to express the emphasis on the Greek and Latin classics in secondary education, as against the rising demands for a more practical and more scientific training'. Paul Oskar Kristeller, *Renaissance Thought: The Classic, Scholastic, and Humanist Strains* (New York: Harper Torch-books, 1961), p. 9.

5. The *OED* dates its first attestation to 1484.

6. Augusto Campana, 'The Origin of the Word "Humanist"', *Journal of the Warburg and Courtauld Institutes* 9 (1946), 60–73.

7. James Hankins, 'Humanism and the Origins of Modern Political Thought', in Jill Kraye (ed.), *The Cambridge Companion to Renaissance Humanism* (Cambridge University Press, 1996), pp. 118–41 (p. 118).

8. Jules Michelet, *Cours au Collège de France*, ed. P. Viallaneix (Paris: Gallimard, 1995), vol. I, p. 351.

9. Jacob Burckhardt, *The Civilization of the Renaissance in Italy*, trans. S. G. C. Middlemore, 2nd edn (London: Allen & Unwin, 1890), p. 129.

10. Stephen Greenblatt, *The Swerve: How the Renaissance Began* (New York: W. W. Norton, 2011), pp. 9–10.

11. Antonio Gramsci, *Quaderni del carcere*, 17 (IV) §(8): https://quadernidelcarcere.wordpress.com/2015/02/12/umanesimo-e-rinascimento-3/ (accessed 9 February 2022).

12. On this phenomenon see John H. Fisher, *The Emergence of Standard English* (University Press of Kentucky, 1996).

13. *Florio His Firste Fruites* (London: Thomas Woodcocke, 1578), sig. 50r.

14. Giordano Bruno, *La Cena de le Ceneri* (London: John Charlewood, 1584), p. 47.

15. Neil Rhodes, 'Status Anxiety and English Renaissance Translation', in Helen Smith and Louise Wilson (eds), *Renaissance Paratexts* (Cambridge University Press, 2011), pp. 107–20 (p. 108).

16. Thomas More, *Utopia*, ed. George M. Logan and Robert M. Adams (Cambridge University Press, 1989), p. 6.

17. The note appears on sig. Aiiir of Harvey's copy of John Florio's *First Fruites* (Axiophilus is Harvey's pseudonym). See Virginia F. Stern, *Gabriel Harvey: His Life, Marginalia, and Library* (Oxford: Clarendon Press, 1979), p. 156.

18. Roberto Weiss, *Humanism in England during the Fifteenth Century* (Oxford: Blackwell, 1941), p. 7.

19. Margaret Harvey, *England, Rome and the Papacy 1417–64: The Study of a Relationship* (Manchester University Press, 1993), p. 40.

20. Martin C. Davies, 'Poggio Bracciolini as Rhetorician and Historian: Unpublished Pieces', *Rinascimento* 22 (1982), 153–82.

21. Marco Santoro, 'La prassi bibliografica degli inquisitori di ancien régime: *l'Index librorum prohibitorum* nel XVI secolo', *Italica* 82 (2005), 408–25.

22. As quoted in Elizabeth Eisenstein, *The Printing Press as an Agent of Change* (Cambridge University Press, 1983), p. 147.

23. John Foxe, *Actes and Monuments* (London: Iohn Daye, 1583), p. 707.

24. Jonathan Woolfson, *Padua and the Tudors: English Students in Italy, 1485–1603* (University of Toronto Press, 1998), p. 137.

25. Francis Otto Matthiessen, *Translation: An Elizabethan Art* (Cambridge, MA: Harvard University Press, 1931). See also George Steiner, *After Babel: Aspects of Language and Translation* (Oxford University Press, 1975), p. 247.

26. T. Atkinson Jenkins, 'Deschamps' Ballade to Chaucer', *Modern Language Notes* 33 (1918), 268–78.

27. See Renaissance Cultural Crossroads digital catalogue, www.dhi.ac.uk/rcc/; and S. K. Barker and Brenda M. Hosington (eds), *Renaissance Cultural Crossroads: Translation, Print and Culture in Britain, 1473–1640* (Leiden: Brill, 2013).

28. F. M. Rener, *Intepretatio: Language and Translation from Cicero to Tytler* (Amsterdam: Rodopi, 1989), p. 222.

29. Umberto Eco, 'The Language of Europe is Translation', lecture given at the ATLAS conference Assises de la Traduction Littéraire, Arles, 14 November 1993.

30. Thomas North, 'Amiot to the Readers', in *The Liues of the Noble Grecians and Romanes, compared together by that graue learned philosopher and historiographer, Plutarke of Chaeronea* (London: Thomas Vautroullier, 1579), sig. [viir]. On this point see Tania Demetriou and Rowan Tomlinson (eds), *The Culture of Translation in Early Modern England and France, 1500–1600* (Houndmills: Palgrave Macmillan, 2015).

31. *Caxton's Eneydos, 1490, Englisht from the French Liure del Eneydes, 1483*, ed. M. T. Culley and F. J. Furnivall (London: Trübner, 1890), p. 3.

32. Fernand Braudel, *Civilisation matérielle, économie et capitalisme, XVe–XVIIIe siècles*, vol. III, *Les Temps du monde* (Paris: Armand Colin, 1979), p. 302.

33. Andrew Hadfield, 'Afterword: One of Those Days in England', in Willy Maley and Margaret Tudeau-Clayton (eds), *This England, that Shakespeare: New Angles on Englishness and the Bard* (Farnham: Ashgate, 2010), pp. 221–4 (p. 223).

34. Devotion XVII, in John Donne, *Complete Poetry and Selected Prose*, ed. John Hayward (London: Nonesuch Press, 1929), p. 538.

CRITICAL REFLECTIONS AND FURTHER STUDY

This essay is prompted by a critical debate that centres on the very meaning of the word 'Renaissance' and interrogates the term and its implications. Starting with the fundamental definitions proposed in the nineteenth and early twentieth centuries by Jules Michelet, Jacob Burckhardt and Johan Huizinga, up to the recent controversy generated by Stephen Greenblatt's *The Swerve* (2011), this word and the concept it should define have been the object of constant scrutiny and reassessment. Such scrutiny has also involved a regauging of the passage between the Middle Ages and the Renaissance since different parts of Europe experienced this at different times, along with a redefinition of the idea of humanism. Scholars such as James Simpson, in his *Oxford English Literary*

History volume of 2002 (see Further Reading) have felt that the long passage between the medieval and the early modern world, a passage marked in northern Europe by the onset of the Reformation, merits special attention and qualifies as a time of cultural revolution. In the present essay I try to set the question against the wider European background, highlighting the uniqueness of the English case by showing how, across the Continent, the very idea of Renaissance is fragmented and can thus be expressed by means of different metaphors.

In addition, in recent years the discussion of the unique features of the Renaissance in England has focused on the role of translation, whose importance and influence has been studied by Morini (*Tudor Translation*, 2006) and is also the object of the impressive Renaissance Cultural Crossroads database, while individual case studies are analysed in Fred Schurink's edited collection of essays, *Tudor Translation* (2011). We need to understand what we mean by translation, and whether Renaissance translation in any way diverges from the modern practice; and it may be posited that the early practice finds its *raison d'être* in a process of assimilation and acquisition. By being translated into English, classical and contemporary texts enrich the English language and enter the English intellectual library; by opening up to ancient and foreign influences, English culture acquires its extraordinary variety and wealth. Language learning, a practice recently studied in the case of Italian by Jason Lawrence ('*Who the Devil*', 2005), may lead to the acquisition of social status but also to the assimilation of cultural diversity.

This approach raises a number of further questions. How do we reconcile the attention to translation in Renaissance England with the country's efforts to find its own separate identity as a nation? Did the English nation build a literary heritage thanks to its acquisition of foreign models? Does the English language as used by Renaissance writers reflect this process? While the developing identification of English as the language of the nation is studied in John Fisher's *The Emergence of Standard English* (1996), the first question is central to Richard Helgerson's *Forms of Nationhood* (1992). Though starting from very different premises, both studies invite us to consider the English literary Renaissance as a phenomenon in which the single work is not simply the product of a single person, but of an intellectual community that includes sources, patrons, prospective readers, scribes, printers. Studies that take into account the role of French or of Italian culture in Tudor literature (as analysed, respectively, by Richmond and Wyatt in their monographs cited in the Further Reading) offer us precious insight into the role of contemporary foreign vernaculars, while Greg Walker's book on Henrician literature, *Writing Under Tyranny* (2005), assesses poetic production against a particularly fraught moment of English history. Within these premises, we need to ask whether our post-Romantic notion of the author as the only creator of the literary work is still tenable. It may be more profitable to think of literary production as a node in an extremely articulated network. It is also useful to adopt such a model to characterise different literary genres, connecting them with their modes of production: the milieu that produced the Elizabethan lyric is radically different from the grounds on which Elizabethan drama flourished, although a writer like William Shakespeare might be among the most significant representatives of both genres.

Another set of questions concerns the role of Scotland in the definition of the English Renaissance, as the two nations were being united under a common ruler. The two countries were still two distinct political entities, and would remain so until the Acts of Union in 1707. In 1603, at Queen Elizabeth's death, the kingdoms of England and Scotland would be ruled by one monarch, James VI and I, but before this date there is a centuries-old history of war. It is therefore inevitable to see in the two cultures widely different intellectual approaches to classical and contemporary foreign literature; by the same token, their approach to the Renaissance may be deemed to be dissimilar. Is there a Scottish Renaissance, and does it coincide in time with the English one? Is it equally founded on translation? This has been the object of recent studies by Parkinson (ed.), *James VI and I* (2013) and Verweij, *Literary Culture of Early Modern Scotland* (2016), that have focused on the last decades of the sixteenth century, and on the Scottish reign of King James: as Scotland was politically drawing closer to England, its court looked at European literary models that would reset the country on the international cultural map. Scotland and England, uneasy companions, offer striking instances of the diversification and variety of the European phenomenon that goes under the name of the Renaissance.

Studying the Renaissance means understanding the redrawing of boundaries; geography and the art of map-making were being fundamentally reconsidered as the voyages of Columbus, Magellan and Janszoon prompted the necessity to relocate Europe within the world map. The example of a Renaissance map (see Figure 4.1), in Peter Meurer's analysis of 2008, transforms the mythological memory of Europa as a princess into an ideological statement, changing over the years with the changes in the political scene. With the benefit of hindsight, we may look at it almost as a last desperate stance against an inexorable world change that progressively displaced the centrality of Europe.

FURTHER READING

Renaissance Cultural Crossroads, digital archive, www.dhi.ac.uk/rcc/

Burckhardt, Jacob, *The Civilization of the Renaissance in Italy*, trans. S. G. C. Middlemore (London: Allen & Unwin, 1890)

Fisher, John H., *The Emergence of Standard English* (Lexington: University Press of Kentucky, 1996)

Greenblatt, Stephen, *The Swerve: How the Renaissance Began* (New York: W. W. Norton, 2011)

Helgerson, Richard, *Forms of Nationhood: The Elizabethan Writing of England* (University of Chicago Press, 1992)

Huizinga, Johan, *The Waning of the Middle Ages* (London: Edward Arnold, 1924)

Lawrence, Jason, *'Who the Devil Taught Thee so Much Italian?' Italian Language Learning and Literary Imitation in Early Modern England* (Manchester University Press, 2005)

Meurer, Peter, 'Europa Regina: 16th Century Maps of Europe in the Form of a Queen', *Belgeo: Revue Belge de Géographie* 3–4 (2008), 355–70: https://doi.org/10.4000/belgeo.7711

Morini, Massimiliano, *Tudor Translation in Theory and Practice* (Farnham: Ashgate, 2006)

Parkinson, David J. (ed.), *James VI and I, Literature and Scotland: Tides of Change, 1567–1625* (Leuven: Peeters, 2013)

Richmond, Hugh M., *Puritans and Libertines: Anglo-French Literary Relations in the Reformation* (Berkeley: University of California Press, 1981)

Schurink, Fred (ed.), *Tudor Translation* (Houndmills: Palgrave Macmillan, 2011)

Simpson, James, *The Oxford English Literary History*, vol. II, *1350–1547: Reform and Cultural Revolution* (Oxford University Press, 2002)

Verweij, Sebastiaan, *The Literary Culture of Early Modern Scotland: Manuscript Production and Transmission, 1560–1625* (Oxford University Press, 2016)

Walker, Greg, *Writing under Tyranny: English Literature and the Henrician Reformation* (Oxford University Press, 2005)

Wyatt, Michael, *The Italian Encounter with Tudor England: A Cultural Politics of Translation* (Cambridge University Press, 2005)

5 'Mr Spencer's Moral Invention': The Global Horizons of Early Modern Epic

JANE GROGAN

Abstract

Spenser's *The Faerie Queene* has long been read as a key text in 'Atlantic history' and the emerging models of planter colonialism in Ireland and America. This essay argues that Spenser's work also deserves a place in the larger context of global Renaissance studies: that is, a recent critical paradigm foregrounding the global changes to political, cultural and socioeconomic formations, often (and certainly in the case of Europe) brought about by various forms of transcultural exchange or encounter.

One new angle of approach to Spenser – and indeed to early modern epic – that foregrounds these global horizons presents itself in the recently rediscovered poetic treatise of William Scott. Strongly influenced by Sidneyan poetics (as indeed Spenser was), Scott's accomplished treatise, *The Modell of Poesy* (1599), is distinguished by its attention to recent literary writing. But we find some surprises, not so much in the judgements as in the associations and connections made between key early modern texts. In Scott's treatment of epic, Spenser's *The Faerie Queene* keeps company with More's *Utopia*, Sidney's *Arcadia*, Daniel's *Civil Wars*, and, perhaps most surprisingly, Warner's *Albions England*, along with the usual suspects – Homer, Xenophon, Virgil, Heliodorus, Ariosto and Tasso. It is a salient reminder of the diverse forms and more exploratory meanings of heroic writing for early modern English readers. This essay takes what is perhaps the most obvious outlier in Scott's tally, Warner's *Albions England* (1586–1612) to argue for strong connections between the 1596 edition of this work and Spenser's epic, connections that shed new light on the global rather than primarily national horizons of early modern English epic for its first readers.

The early modern English tradition of epic is usually regarded as small but brilliant, well able to stand against its European counterparts – a narrative with which its authors would, no doubt, be pleased to agree. In the recent *Blackwell Companion to Renaissance Poetry* (2018), for example, 'Epic and Epyllion' leads the 'Forms and Genres' section, with essays on three prime examples of English epic – the first two of which are much more frequently read and discussed than the third: Edmund Spenser's *The Faerie Queene* (1590–6; 1609), John Milton's *Paradise Lost* (1667), and Lucy Hutchinson's *Order and Disorder* (1679). While the subsection on epyllion opens with an eleven-page essay explaining this contested term/form and its history, no such essay is deemed necessary for epic, traditionally the highest and best theorised of literary genres, despite the significant differences between the three exemplars presented – Spenser's chivalric, allegorical epic, and the two very different biblical epics, Hutchinson's only relatively recently regarded as the first epic written by an English woman.

The earliest of the three, Spenser's *The Faerie Queene*, stands apart (Figure 5.1). It is more European in its models, but more English in its ambitions, than the other two. More backward-looking, even old-fashioned (as allegory, as dynastic epic, with its deliberately archaic poetic language), it is also more forward-looking than them (in its poetic innovations, hybridity and collaborative engagement with readers).

The firſt Booke of
the Faerie Queene.

Contayning

The Legend of the Knight
of the Red Croſſe,
OR
Of Holineſſe.

LO I the man, whoſe Muſe whylome did maske,
　As time her taught, in lowly Shephards weeds,
　Am now enforſt a farre vnfitter taske,
For trumpets ſterne to chaunge mine Oaten reeds:
And ſing of Knights and Ladies gentle deeds,
Whoſe praiſes hauing ſlept in ſilence long,
Me, all too meane, the ſacred Muſe areeds
　To blazon broade emongſt her learned throng:
Fierce warres and faithfull loues ſhall moralize my ſong.

Helpe then, O holy virgin chiefe of nyne,
　Thy weaker Nouice to performe thy will,
　Lay forth out of thine euerlaſting ſcryne
The antique rolles, which there lye hidden ſtill,
　　　　　A 2　　　　　　Of

Figure 5.1 Title page of the first Book of *The Faerie Queene*, 1590.

But the politics of nationhood in epic remains the dominant scholarly approach to analysing post-Virgilian epic, and any introductory essay to the three would probably have discussed the ways in which they variously shaped the historical, cultural and political imaginary of nationhood. Above all other literary genres, epic is the one usually tasked with imagining the nation – and for an emerging vernacular literature like English at a time of classical revival, forging the cultural imaginary and the political imaginary went hand in hand. Even today, for a modern poet like Carol Rumens, *The Faerie Queene* remains 'an epic of national identity-building'.[1]

But *The Faerie Queene* is also distinguished from the other two epics by its author's direct and active involvement in the plantation of Ireland, and by the imbrication of Ireland in the poem's imaginary. Its 'Englishness' owes much to its dedication to Queen Elizabeth and the ways in which Spenser does or does not follow through on that promise to represent her 'realmes' to her in the 'mirrhour' of the poem (following the Virgilian model). But much critical ink has been spilled in the last thirty years on the subject of 'Spenser and Ireland', with both historians and literary scholars reading Spenser's prose dialogue/treatise, *A View of the Present State of Ireland*, alongside his poetic corpus, culminating in a wider (if differently shaded) acknowledgement of the 'near coincidence of Ireland and Fairy Land in Spenser's imagination, a magical conjunction the spell of which isn't broken until the Mutabilitie Cantos [1609], when Ireland is Ireland'.[2] This important scholarly work on Spenser's implication in colonial violence and oppression in early modern Ireland, and the complex nationalisms at play in *The Faerie Queene*, has, curiously, been set aside in more recent efforts to rethink the 'English Renaissance' in terms of 'global Renaissance studies': a recent critical paradigm foregrounding the *global* changes to political, cultural and socioeconomic formations, often brought about by various forms of transcultural exchange, connection or encounter (including trade, imperialism and international conflict).

In this essay I want to return to the 1590s, when Spenser's epic was first published in two instalments (1590; 1596), to examine anew how it was understood as epic, and to bring into focus its global horizons, including but not limited to Ireland. This will be achieved with the help of a recently rediscovered manuscript treatise on English poetics, one which was particularly attuned to questions of vernacular English literature and its ambitions with respect to established genres and models of classical and recent European literature. This was William Scott's *The Model of Poesy*. Scott includes *The Faerie Queene* among a varied set of English exemplars of epic to stand alongside the shining examples of Homer and Virgil, including, most strikingly, William Warner's once popular but now forgotten verse chronicle, *Albions England* (1586–1612). By comparing the 1596 edition of *Albions England* (the edition Scott probably knew) to *The Faerie Queene* – with a close textual comparison between Spenser's Book II and Warner's Books IX–XII, which were added in 1596 – we gain a rich new perspective on how wide and capacious the parameters of early modern epic were understood to be during the 1590s; how global (rather than simply national) its purview; and how relevant Spenser's Irish materials could be to that.

William Scott's 'all manner of heroical poems'

Written in the summer of 1599, just three years after the publication of Spenser's second instalment and Warner's 1596 edition, Scott's *The Model of Poesy* is, after many years of obscurity, now readily available in a modern edition. Its editor, Gavin Alexander, details Scott's continuities with Philip Sidney's *Defence of Poesy* (1595), to which it is clearly indebted, but notes also the new ground Scott treads.[3] The *Model* is conspicuously well attuned to the concerns of English literary culture at the very end of the sixteeenth century – and its allusions to contemporary English dramatic and non-dramatic literature are where Scott's work provides richest pickings.[4] Epic is a case in point.

For Scott, 'the heroical or epic' has to do with the narration of 'great and weighty things in weighty and high style', while aiming 'to raise the mind by admiration to some glorious good':

> The difference peculiar to [the epic poet], and that sequestereth him from all kinds else, is in that in a continued narration or discourse of weighty matter, in a worthy and grave style, he seeks by a delightful admiration to raise the mind to the affecting some more than ordinary pitch of good. And this contains in it all manner of heroical poems.

Although relatively uncontentious in its claims, it is worth noting Scott's unusual emphasis not on taxonomic exclusion from this, the apex of literary genres, but on inclusion of 'all manner of heroical poems'. When it comes to setting out illustrative examples of epic, however, Scott moves from familiar classical exemplars to some unexpected contemporary texts:

> Of the first in verse is Homer in Greek, Virgil in Latin; modern, Ariosto, Tasso, and those that be more historical and less fiction (like Lucan) – *The Disunion of Lancaster and York*, *Albions England*. Those in prose are such as Xenophon's *Cyrus*, Heliodorus, ancient; later, Sir Thomas More's *Utopia* and the *Arcadia* (except you will make the last a mixed kind as having pastoral and much verse). To these you may add Master Spencer's moral invention, shadowed so naturally and properly under the persons in his *Faerie Queene*. In some example or precedent, feigned or true, they all endeavour by an admiring emulation to direct and move us to virtue in particular or general. Xenophon (as Tully acknowledgeth) in his Cyrus hath given us "effigiem iusti imperii", the true scantling of an happy estate of government. Aeneas is an image of a perfect man for wisdom, valour, and piety, as far as Virgil could imagine; Orlando of bold hardiness.[5]

Like Sidney, Scott had no difficulty allowing for epics narrated in prose – Sidney's preferred heroic example of Xenophon's *Cyropaedia* appears once again here, alongside Heliodorus's *Aethiopica*. But to the exalted ancient ranks of Homer, Virgil, Lucan and Heliodorus, Scott adds Samuel Daniel (*The Civil Warres*), William Warner (*Albions England*), Edmund Spenser (*The Faerie Queene*), Thomas More (*Utopia*) and Sidney (*Arcadia*).[6] Scott's 'all manner of heroical' poems thus range from a verse history of the English Wars of the Roses to Sidney's 'mixed kind' of prose epic, by way of the entirely new literary-political genre of More's treatise, and, most interestingly for my purposes, Warner's chaotic, quasi-chronicle, quasi-romance *Albions England* (1586–1612). The title-page description of Warner's first edition gives some sense of how striking it is to find it in Scott's census of heroical poems:

> Albions England. Or historicall map of the same island: prosecuted from the liues, actes, and labors of Saturne, Iupiter, Hercules, and Æneas: originalles of the Brutons, and English-men, and occasion of the Brutons their first aryuall in Albion. Continuing the same historie vnto the tribute to the Romaines, entrie of the Saxones, inuasion by the Danes, and conquest by the Normaines. With historicall intermixtures, inuention, and varietie: proffitably, briefly, and pleasantly, performed in verse and prose by William Warner.

Figure 5.2 shows the slightly revised 1589 version. What could Scott have found in Warner's sprawling hybrid chronicle that reminded him of the 'more than ordinary' ambitions of a Virgil or a Spenser?

Certainly, Scott grants *The Faerie Queene* security of tenure in the category of heroical poems, or '*epopoeia*', by the proximity of his general description of epic's project to the declared method and ambitions of Spenser's poem, 'shadowed so naturally and properly under the persons in his *Faerie Queene*'. When in the next sentence Scott declares that 'In some example or precedent, feigned or true, they all endeavour by an admiring emulation to direct and move us to virtue in particular or general', it is productively unclear whether 'they all' still refers to Spenser's 'persons in his *Faerie Queene*' or to his catalogue of epics more generally, so close is the description to Spenser's explanation of his method in the 'Letter to Ralegh' appended to the first edition of *The Faerie Queene*. 'The generall end therefore of all the booke is to fashion a gentleman or noble person in vertuous and gentle discipline', Spenser wrote, acknowledging that he 'followed all the antique Poets historicall', from Homer and Virgil to Ariosto and Tasso. 'By ensample of [these] excellente Poets, I labour to pourtraict in Arthure ... the image of a braue knight, perfected in the twelue morall vertues', he continues, next identifying the individual hero-knights of each Book as 'patrones' of individual virtues. Or, as Scott had put it a little earlier, delivering 'the images of the virtues themselves in the person and actions of these heroes'.

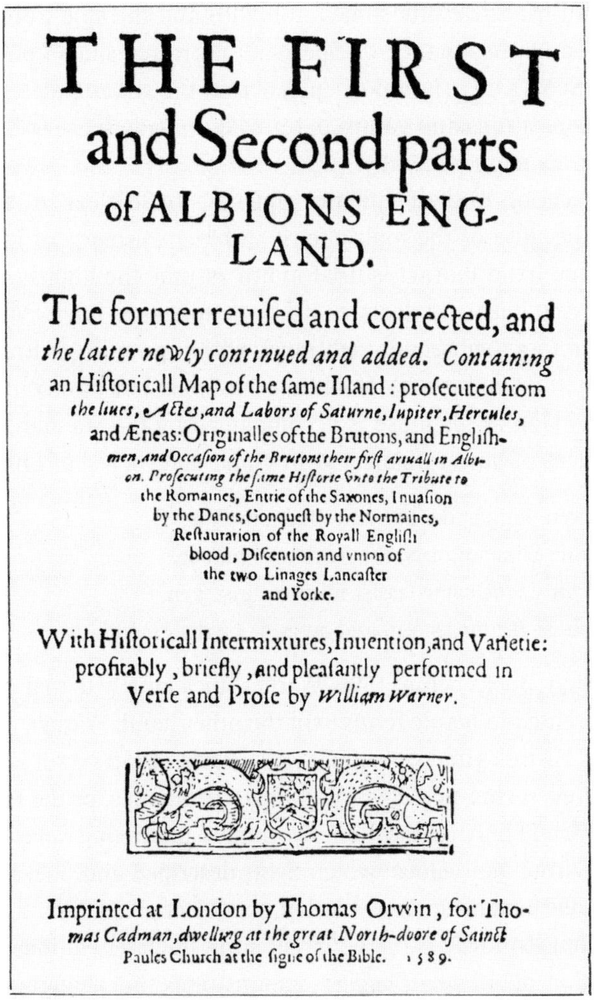

Figure 5.2 William Warner, *Albions England*: title page, 1589 edition.

Spenser's epic plan extends to 'shadow[ing]' Queen Elizabeth, too, in his aim to fashion virtuous readers: 'In that Faery Queene I meane glory in my generall intention, but in my particular I conceiue the most excellent and glorious person of our soueraine the Queene, and her kingdome in Faery land. And yet in some places els I do otherwise shadow her.' Thus, each of the six complete Books of *The Faerie Queene* stars a knight (or several knights, in Book IV) on courtly quests ultimately serving Elizabeth/the Faery Queen, quests designed to exemplify the nature and acquisition of a particular virtue. And if the chivalric trials of each Book are shaped by the trials peculiar to its allotted virtue – sexual intemperance, excess and greed, for example, faced by the hero-knight Guyon in the case of Book II, the Book of Temperance – the reader, too, is intended to benefit in parallel from those lessons and trials. Despite some anomalies and the epic's unfinished nature, the consistency and consonance of Spenser's narrative shape, poetics and moral pedagogy with Scott's description of epic, across the six completed Books, clearly signals its epic aspirations and values in terms that made sense to Scott and Spenser's contemporaries more generally.

The same dedication to these epic principles is not so clear in William Warner's work, not least because of the multiplicity and inconsistency of its forms and interests. On the one hand Warner is unafraid to assume the high style of epic in the very place where epic usually declares itself: the opening lines. Warner's work began in 1586 (and in all subsequent editions), with a promise of British (Protestant) chronicle history, beginning with Noah and his sons, but in mixed heroical terms. An invocation to God as his muse is accompanied by the standard humility trope, but also assurances of both romance 'gestes' and epic 'actes' of English destiny:

> I tell of things done long agoe, of many things in few:
> And chiefly of this Clime of ours, the Accidents pursue.
> Thou high Director of the same, assist mine artlesse pen,
> To write the gests of *Brutons* stout, and actes of English men.[7]

And in the first eight Books before 1596, Warner stuck largely to that chronicle history, occasionally presented in heroic terms.[8] On the other hand, Warner's ever-expanding 'intermixture' of 'Histories and Inventions', all 'performed in verse', identified the text less with epic or even chronicle history than with romance, or the many compendia of more colourful, and only ever notionally morally improving *novelle*. Not only that, but the 'acts of virtue and valour' which Scott described and Spenser presented are increasingly diluted among more everyday acts of conversation, and undertakings not of chivalric but expressly commercial intent in the later editions.

The 1596 edition of *Albions England* demonstrates this changing direction well; tellingly, the change arises as Warner tackles the task of narrating the reign of the incumbent monarch.[9] *Albions England* grew from eight to twelve Books, acquired a second dedicatee, and dispensed with the 1592 edition's handsome single opening page of Book IX, 'Of our now most gracious and triumphant souereign Queene Elizabeth'. Rewritten in 1596, though, this smooth panegyric of her being 'Inrich'd, Feared, Honor'd, Lou'd' becomes a testier defence of 'Elizabeth, her Persecutors, Persecution, and her passage thereout'. It does incorporate one or two phrases from the 1592 panegyric, but now focuses primarily on hostility to her rule, both internal and external. What heroic discourse prevails surrounds these 'malcontent' enemies rather than Elizabeth herself, and, to make matters less heroic still, we find in Book IX a concerted move away from chronicle history and into fictional 'histories and inventions', now more localised and vernacular than the Ovidian digressions of the 1592 edition. (Sandwiched between accounts of the attempts on Elizabeth's life, and the Spanish Armada, for example, is 'Of the Chat passed betwixt two old

Widowes, concerning new fangles now vsed by women' and 'More of their Chat'.) This tendency continues with Books X–XII, though the digressions quickly cluster around a main subplot: the romance of Sir John Mandeville and Eleanor. This, too, is indicative of the proliferation of the text's quasi-heroic energies into other kinds of national concerns – specifically, into the theme of global travel. Mandeville, of course, is the putative pseudo-English author of what we might best call 'the Mandeville text', a late medieval book of marvellous travels of uncertain provenance but great popularity across Europe right into the early modern period, and whose name became a byword for colourful, and not entirely believable travels to the Middle and Far East.[10] And yet, for all of its divergences and intermixtures, the 1596 edition of Warner's text shows clear parallels with *The Faerie Queene*, and at times even seems to be in dialogue with it, in ways that help clarify Scott's understanding of epic (and, by extension, that of his contemporaries).[11] Both shift the interests of epic from the national to the global, and identify the wider global scene as the context of British chronicle history in that moment. Both seriously engage the epistemological and political implications of the recent global 'voyages of discovery' and trade, whether in their narratives or their metaphorical resources, and both seek ways to admit these new formations of knowledge into their works. (Both also destabilise chronicle models of historical temporality and explore different forms of temporality through more conspicuously speculative or fictional modes of thought.) Both diagnose a moment of crisis – or certainly challenge – in the late years of Elizabeth's reign, stemming from national uncertainty about the dynastic future. And both take a strong interest in expanding the repertoire of techniques available to the poet to fashion a heroic poem. To clarify late sixteenth-century English understandings of the global interests of early modern epic, I want now to explore the dialogic work of Book II of *The Faerie Queene* and Books IX–XII of Warner's 1596 edition.

Scott, it should be said, was not entirely out on a limb in associating Spenser with Warner, Sidney and Du Bartas. Warner seems to have enjoyed some degree of prominence or visibility in the closing years of the sixteenth century, just as Scott was writing his treatise.[12] But none of these allusions give enough detail to substantiate Scott's categorisation of Warner's poem as heroic; the dialogue with Spenser does, and gives us a new angle of approach to how the business of early modern English epic was understood.

Spenser and Warner

Early on in *The Faerie Queene*, in the playful but significant Proem preceding Book II, Spenser had balanced Faeryland (and indeed the whole 'famous antique history' of his poem) against recent activities of global travel, trade and 'discovery'. Specifically, he had juxtaposed the reader's credence in Faeryland (and, by extension, in Spenser's heroic project conducted within it) against the credibility of reports of those global travels. It is a witty touch, given the proverbial problems with credibility that dogged early modern travellers' reports.[13]

> Right well I wote most mighty Soueraine,
> That all this famous antique history,
> Of some, th'aboundance of an idle braine
> Will iudged be, and painted forgery,
> Rather then matter of iust memory,
> Sith none, that breatheth liuing aire, does know,
> Where is that happy land of Faery ... (II.Pr.1)

To this readerly problem, Spenser suggests the solution that just as America north and south were previously unknown to Europeans, 'Why then should witlesse man so much misweene / That nothing is, but that which he hath seene?' (II.Pr.3). It was a concept he would revisit in later Books, notably in the allegory of the Giant with the Scales in Book V, but here it serves to justify the mixed fictions of Spenser's epic as 'matter of iust memory'.[14] What the Proem chiefly manages, though, is to resituate Britain-and-Ireland-as-Faeryland ('thine owne realmes in lond of Faery') and its heroic dynastic chronicle history ('And in this antique Image thy great auncestry') in a global rather than simply national context. This Proem prefaces the very Book in which the heroic national origins and destiny of Queen Elizabeth's 'realmes' are most directly and fully addressed and expounded: one of the longest cantos in the whole poem describes the contents of a chronicle called 'Briton Moniments', as read by Prince Arthur, containing 'the famous auncestries' of Queen Elizabeth (II.x.1) from 'antique times' where Britain was 'saluage wildernesse' (II.x.5–6) before being first named 'Albion'. In other words, in Book II, English chronicle history, and England's national epic, go global.

The Proem's emphasis on travel, on the domestic necessarily rewritten in global terms that cast its certainties into less certain light, remains a constant in Book II at the levels of genre, plot, allegory, language and style. Note, for example, its narrative proximity to the Homeric travels of *The Odyssey*, its use of maritime metaphors, its casting of a critical eye on its very own chivalric model of 'errant knights' (II.i.51), or even its moral–allegorical interest in the dynamics between stasis and mobility. All of these features instate global mobility rather than national concerns as the Book's driving conditions. Guyon's overly energetic destruction of the Bower of Bliss at the end of Book II that Stephen Greenblatt's reading of the poem has made notorious (and, for many readers, the ultimate colonial signature of *The Faerie Queene* more generally) is only one image of the Book's many global interests.[15] Daniel Vitkus and Michael Murrin have identified the 'hardy enterprize' of the commercial voyages invoked in the Proem as key to Book I and II's heroic logic, and to the poem's wider construction of Britain's national interests, now construed to involve outward-facing commercial, economic and diplomatic concerns rather than simply autochthonous origin tales and domestic heroes.[16] Even its allegorical referents – the Irish rebel Maleger attacking the somatic house of Alma, the faraway Circean enchantress Acrasia wreaking havoc on domestic alliances and knight-errantry globally, the gold-strewn 'huge threasury' (II.vii.4) and worldly temptations of Mammon's cave that Guyon does not quite resist – speak to global rather than simply national challenges and even emergencies. Ireland may, in the wishful terms of the day, have been part of the emerging 'empire' of Britain, but Spenser's figuration of the attack of Maleger is of a hostile external element attacking the political body of the English nation – an attack on the very site in which the privileged chronicle history encountered by Arthur is so carefully stored. In other words, systems of global exchange, knowledge and travel are written into the work of Book II from its opening words, and reframe its canto of chronicle history in complex, global terms.

Warner, too, expands the national interests and geographical purview of his poem considerably in the 1596 edition of *Albions England*, moving beyond the tally of glorious English kings to treatments of the religious wars in France, the Spanish inquisition and the recent conflicts in the Low countries in Books IX and X, as key events for Elizabeth's reign. In so doing, Warner partly follows an established pattern of setting the religious divisions within Christendom as a global conflict, one which European imperialism ensured was also distributed well beyond Europe. But he also responds to Spenser's globalising technique in other key respects, reframing traditional national interests in global terms and, in particular, insisting on global contexts in almost all of his direct addresses to Queen Elizabeth. Like Spenser, he draws on the rich metaphorical vocabulary of the voyages of trade and discovery to describe the work of describing Elizabeth – and, like Spenser, cleverly globalises more domestic or local terms. In addressing Elizabeth, for example, Warner recalls the terms of Walter Ralegh's well-known poem to her, *Ocean's Love to Cynthia*, as Spenser had done before him; but where Spenser evoked Cynthia (Elizabeth), Warner playfully redeploys Ralegh's disappointed 'Ocean' persona to express the impossibility of approaching her, even with the supporting resources of classical tradition or the exotic spoils of foreign voyages of discovery:

> For me to wreste from Hercules his Club as easie weare,
> As in the Ocean of her fame, with choysest sayles, to beare
> That fraight, [tha]t with the India[n] wealth may more than much co[m]pare ... (sig. P2v)

It is a complex, mixed image, not helped by Warner's clumsy syntax, but its Spenserianism, and triangulation with Ralegh (well known for his support for English voyages, of course), is clear.[17] Like Spenser, Warner also deploys the metaphor of maritime travel to describe the narratorial labour of his poem: concluding Book VIII, he appeals to God for help with navigating 'A prosperous Course', as do Spenser's narrator and Guyon's Palmer.[18] Similarly, Warner seems to speak directly to (and take heart from) the favour Spenser and his poem found with Queen Elizabeth, when he alludes to her having 'at wel-meant Toyes ... smilde'; Elizabeth had granted Spenser a pension, upon his presentation to her of the first instalment of *The Faerie Queene* just a few years earlier. This comment (which may not be entirely friendly) arises as Warner distinguishes his work from the 'Ridled Poesies' and cod-'intellective' poems of 'some moderne Poets' – but he then swerves to appeal to Mnemosyne, goddess of memory to 'controule ... our Muse' (sig. P2), in a move that once again recalls Spenser and Book II Proem's contention about his poem comprising 'matter of iust memory'.

Beyond these guiding metaphors of travel, ocean-going and the acquisition or exchange of precious goods, we find Warner responding warmly to Spenser's sense of the heroic potential of English trade voyages, and the possibilities they offer to reorient English dynastic epic – what it knows and tells and imagines – in global terms. The closest dialogue with Spenser's Proem to Book II can be found in Books XI and XII of *Albions England*, which shift the scene wholly from England to 'strange Countries' to follow not kings or queens any more, but 'great Achieuements done / By English, in contrarie clymes' (closing lines of Book XI (sig. V2)). These are also the Books in which Warner most vigorously pursues the travelling love affair of Mandeville and Eleanor, the poem's latest romance digression-cum-subplot, weaving its geography and fictional imaginary among the factual voyages of the English merchants.[19] In one way, it is quite a shift – from kings and queens to merchants and factors – but it is in tune not just with Spenser's epic but also with the ongoing efforts of Richard Hakluyt and others to present English merchants as national heroes of a new kind. '[S]tately be the Subiect' of the English merchants' travels, Warner insists, before going further to argue that they faced 'trewer Perils, and more braue Achieuements' (sig. [S6]v) than Jason or Ulysses.[20] Book XI treats at length of the early travels of the Muscovy Company agents (Chancellor, Willoughby, Burroughs and Jenkinson) to Russia and Persia. These were the first English corporate as well as crown-sanctioned exploratory trading travels to distant parts. Mainly known to English readers through Hakluyt's 1589 collection of edited accounts (and less widely from shorter excerpts published in the *History of Trauayle* (1577)), here they are presented for the first time within a specifically literary framework: not just as epic actors in pursuit of national causes, but alongside the romance narrative of Mandeville, whose notorious (and fictional) travels covered some of the same ground as them. Nonetheless, Warner maintains an explicit focus on the commercial motivations and focus of the English agents' voyages, but continues to inveigle a heroic narrative and vocabulary in tandem with it (e.g., 'This Marte, thus set a foote' (sig. T4v) cannily merges a standard term for trade with classical martial overtones ('mart') more befitting heroic enterprise).

The interweaving of these new English heroes with the Mandeville narrative brings us back to Spenser once again. In Warner's Mandeville we find less of the colourful traveller of late medieval tradition, who reported seeing woolly chickens, cannibals, and blemmyes (men without heads), but instead a newly chivalricised Mandeville, who uses the materials of Spenserian epic to engage the global as well as domestic scene. First encountered by Eleanor – and the reader – in a joust, Warner's Mandeville occupies a double role both in his own person and as an anonymous 'green knight', a standard medieval figure of the chivalric tradition Spenser revives. Eleanor falls for the green knight, with Mandeville as her second preference. She will only discover long after he leaves that the two are one and the same; Spenser's knights, too, find multiple identities a useful way of traversing a hostile world, as Britomart proves. After many travels, letters and trials, the pair are reunited and their love affair resolved in Rome. After further praise of English travellers (name-checking Hakluyt along the way), Warner now centres Book XII on Rome, lovingly 'discribed in her Ruines' ('Such wonders, couch't in Ruins, as vnseene might seeme vntrew' (sig. [V8])) – and the Italian city-states, together with a brief section on 'discouerers' of the 'East, South, and Southeast'. Here, Warner once again invokes Spenser's witty bargain with the reader in the Proem to Book II, but sets the notorious city of Rome (unvisited and unseen, for late sixteenth-century Elizabethan Protestants) as the glamorous stakes of domestic doubt, more so than the distant parts 'discovered' later in the Book. Warner keeps English travellers as well as the epic tradition in view as he compares the Elizabethan travellers' activities 'for Text, and Truth' to those celebrated in '[t]he Iliads, and Aeneados' (sig. P2v).[21] Thus, we have in the new Books of the 1596 edition medieval romance subplot and contemporary English chronicle history rewritten as the heroic deeds of English travellers abroad, 'intermixed' and made to serve one another's cause, and all in resonantly Spenserian terms.

Like Spenser, then, though more circuitously, and in much cloggier poetic diction, Warner argues for the necessity of accepting the national significance of global events, and the connectedness of the domestic and the global 'euen in our times'. Like Spenser, Warner stakes the credibility and persuasiveness of his poem on the voyages of discovery and even on the credibility of Mandeville's own travels:

Who reads Sir Iohn de Mandeuil his Trauels, and his Sights,
That wonders not? and wonder may, if all be true he wrights.
Yeat rather it beleeue (for most, now modernly approu'd)
Than this our Storie, whence suppose he was to Trauell mou'd ...

But where Spenser sought readerly buy-in, Warner partly eschews it, asking readers to grant only the basic premise of Warner's Mandevillian fiction – *that* he travelled – on the basis of the 'modernly approu'd' accounts. It is yet another playful, fictionalising, Spenserian move disguised as a readerly bargain for credibility, given how dubiously Mandeville's travels (and very existence) were increasingly regarded.[22] Once again, the difficulty of crediting travel accounts is enfolded into the readerly relationship with the epic poem, and with the kinds of materials it treats:

> Now let vs say the Lands, the Seas, the People and their Lore,
> This Knight did see: whome, touching which, not storie shall we more,
> But to our *English* Voyages, euen in our times, shall frame
> Our Muse and what you hear of Theirs, of his the like do ame,
> For Countries, not for Customes (then, and now, not still the same)
> Yeat interlace we shall, among, the Loue of her and him:
> Meane while, about the World, our Muse is stripped now to swim. (sigs [S8]v–T1 (Book XI))

The transformation of Warner's heroic muse into a piscine creature not of land but of sea, a (very) long-distance swimmer, nicely captures the way that Warner, in dialogue with Spenser, shifts the domain of epic from the national to the global. Deeper links with some of Scott's other examples of epic now become visible, notably Thomas More's *Utopia*: its complex fictional bargaining, its cast of historical characters credibly meeting a conspicuously fictional returned traveller who engages them in a serious scholarly dialogue/travel narrative of a distant land called Utopia with powerful lessons to teach both England and Europe.

That the genre of travel writing is a crucial part of the generic hybrid that is the *Utopia* has long been acknowledged; much less studied is the significance of travel writing to the early modern English epic imagination, the diversity of its forms and the new opportunities and challenges it presented for heroic fiction-making at poetic, political and epistemological levels. Warner's muse now prepares to plunge into the oceans of the world, new territories for English authors of 'all manner of heroical poems', but a vital new source of materials with which to imagine the heroic future of Albions England, or Spenser's Britain, beyond court, nation or the royal jousting field. If chronicle history as Warner and Spenser told it had earlier presented the nation to Elizabeth in traditional heroic terms, their work also made it clear that a separate temporal, spatial and narrative framework entirely would now be needed to imagine the nation and its heroic future after her. Warner's inclusion of the Muscovy Company travellers, entwined with Mandevillian fiction, in the imaginary of English epic, or More's English diplomats in Europe meeting a fictional traveller from a distant, better-run land, or Spenser's flagging knights, displaced from Elizabeth's court in order to serve it, each testify to the increasingly urgent sense of the necessarily *global* and more diverse horizons of English national political concerns – and the global and more diverse forms, therefore, of English epic – by the end of the 1590s. We have William Scott to thank for making that shifting scene visible to us.

NOTES

1. Carol Rumens, 'Poem of the Week: *The Faerie Queene*, by Edmund Spenser', *Guardian*, 9 August 2013, www.theguardian.com/books/2013/aug/19/poem-week-faerie-queene-edmund-spenser.

2. Gordon Teskey, *Spenserian Moments* (Cambridge, MA: Harvard University Press, 2019), p. 111.

3. William Scott, *The Model of Poesy*, ed. Gavin Alexander (Cambridge University Press, 2013).

4. The most substantial response to it so far appears in the *Sidney Journal*, special issue 33.1 (2015), featuring six essays on Scott (though none with a focus on epic), a foreword by Gavin Alexander and a review of his edition.

5. Scott, *Model*, pp. 19–20.

6. Scott also included Guillaume Salluste Du Bartas's *Judith* (translated into English by Thomas Hudson in 1584); Scott's own translation of excerpts from Du Bartas's better-known biblical epic of creation, *La Sepmaine*, followed directly on *The Model of Poesy* in the surviving manuscript. See Peter Auger, 'A Model of Creation? Scott, Sidney and Du Bartas', *Sidney Journal* 33.1 (2015), 38–52.

7. Could there also be a distant hint of the 'fierce warres and faithful loues' that Spenser promised would 'moralize my song' (I.Pr.1) in 1590? Parts of *The Faerie Queene* are known to have been circulating in London by 1588.

8. The connection with epic was probably strengthened by the inclusion of a prose epitome of the *Aeneid* immediately after the main work.

9. William Warner, *Albions England: A continued historie of the same kingdome* ... (London: by the Widow Orwin for I.B., 1596).

10. The waning authority and credibility of Mandeville's travels in the second half of the sixteenth century is captured in the inclusion of Mandeville in the 1589 edition of Hakluyt's *Principall Navigations* (albeit with some caveats), but his exclusion by the time of the second edition (1598–1600). See also Ladan Niayesh (ed.), *A Knight's Tale: Mandeville and Mandevillian Lore in Early Modern England* (Manchester University Press, 2011).

11. That one of the distinguishing features of epic is its conspicuous effort to assert its kinship and continuities with earlier epics is also worth bearing in mind.

12. See the passing mentions in Michael Drayton's posthumously published verse epistle to Henry Reynolds, Thomas Nashe's preface to Robert Greene's *Menaphon* and in two contemporary literary compendia, Francis Meres's *Palladis Tamia* (1598) and Robert Allott's *England's Parnassus* (1600), both of which testify to Warner's high favour at the turn of the sixteenth century.

13. The well-known proverb 'a traveller may lie by authority' was used by those either for *or* against travel writing, however, Claire Jowitt and David McInnis argue, putting Spenser and Warner into direct dialogue with the travel writing tradition. See *Travel and Drama in Early Modern England: The Journeying Play*, ed. Claire Jowitt and David McInnis (Cambridge University Press, 2018), p. 2.

14. Spenser also introduces the possibility of 'other worldes' within the moon (probably alluding to the infamous lunar episode in canto 34 of Ariosto's *Orlando furioso*). Early modern Protestant poetics (e.g. Sidney, Spenser, Puttenham) tend to favour affect above truth as the cardinal qualities of literature.

15. Stephen Greenblatt also makes the connection between Spenser's Irish experience and that of English planters in Virginia in his analysis of this scene. 'Spenser and the Destruction of the Bower of Blisse' appears as chapter 4 in his seminal monograph of

New Historicist approaches, *Renaissance Self-Fashioning: From More to Shakespeare* (University of Chicago Press, 1980).

16. See Daniel Vitkus, 'The New Globalism: Transcultural Commerce, Global Systems Theory and Spenser's Mammon', in *A Companion to the Global Renaissance*, ed. Jyotsna G. Singh (Oxford: Blackwell, 2009), pp. 29–49 (p. 37); and Michael Murrin, *Trade and Romance* (University of Chicago Press, 2013), pp. 183–226.

17. Besides being known for his travels to Virginia and his colonial holdings in Ireland, Ralegh also published *Discouerie of the Large, Rich, and Bewtiful empyre of Guiana*, a highly propagandistic relation of his disastrous 1595 voyage to Guiana in 1596.

18. '… in sayling through the Ocean deepe and large / Of her now Highnes Scepter' (sig. P1).

19. Warner's use of 'achievements' subtly rewrites Guyon's defence of his knight-errantry to Mammon: 'I in armes and in atchievements braue, / Do rather choose my flitting houres to spend' (II.vii.33). Guyon's point is scored against Mammon's seductive argument in favour of pursuing riches instead.

20. Sig. T1r–v. Warner's own father had travelled with the first Muscovy Company voyage (1553) to Russia, as Warner proudly declares when first introducing the voyages.

21. The likely source for this narrative seems to be the anonymous lost play, *Sir John Mandeville* – and not vice versa, as Martin Wiggins and Catherine Richardson suggest, given the play's date of 1589–92 (derived from Henslowe's Diary). See *British Drama 1533–1642: A Catalogue* (Oxford University Press, 2012), vol. III, pp. 144–5.

22. Despite his loss of reputation, Mandeville remained a popular cultural figure for travel well into the seventeenth century, as Henry Neville's *The Isle of Pines* (1668) demonstrates.

CRITICAL REFLECTIONS AND FURTHER STUDY

BIG QUESTIONS, SMALLER QUESTIONS

How should we read the poetry of Edmund Spenser, and specifically his great epic *The Faerie Queene*, if we accept his implication, both biographically and culturally, in the violent history of colonialism in Ireland? And might there be, as Seamus Heaney once suggested (*Stepping Stones*, p. 455; see Further Reading), some kind of corrective or at least 'instructive' opportunity in that? These are some of the unspoken questions behind my essay, and its attempt to shift the framework of analysis of the now well-established critical trope of 'Spenser and Ireland' into 'global Renaissance' studies, with the new opportunities and insights it affords into the early modern world. But, more immediately, this essay asks what it is to write an 'English epic' in the early modern period, and what early modern readers might have expected – or accepted – as heroical writing, the kind of writing that sought to glorify the nation, its literature and its history.

I try to explore these questions not by way of theoretical manoeuvres, but by setting as a starting point a new piece of primary evidence: a recently rediscovered treatise of poetics dating from 1599 that includes, in its knowledgeable dealings with recent English literature, *The Faerie Queene* in company with a rather surprising set of alternative English exemplars of epic writing. What unites William Scott's company of epic exemplars, I argue, is their global perspective, their formal flexibility and their willingness to use the resources of fiction to shift the field of epic enquiry from the national to the global. With this new context and intertext to guide us, perhaps we can revisit the contexts of Spenser's Irish engagements in *The Faerie Queene*, and not just in British or Irish or archipelagic terms (three of the main scholarly approaches in the last thirty years). The ethical questions are certainly important, and need to be held in view; but in the accompanying essay I aim firstly to produce a more contextually informed way of framing those questions.

THEORIES AND METHODOLOGIES

There have been earlier attempts to decentre the national agenda in Spenser's *The Faerie Queene*, notably from the historiographical movement known as the 'New British' history, which tried to move away from nationally centred – but especially Anglocentric – approaches to the history of Britain and Ireland, and instead to recognise the plurality of connections and what was shared between them. Scholars differ on quite how successful this has been in moving away from Anglocentrism. But literary scholars have taken heart from such work, and produced a wealth of important scholarship on Spenser in early modern Ireland. More recently still, in literary studies the 'archipelagic turn' has taken those 'interactive entities' (Kerrigan, p. vii; see Further Reading) and worked more diligently on peripheral figures and textual forms, focalising not just a shared history but local and national tensions around the establishing of nationhood as a cultural or political category. (On the 'archipelagic turn', see the useful essay by Murray cited in Further Reading.) Another important recent approach led by Patricia Palmer, David Baker and Willy Maley has renewed the effort to reject Anglocentrism by rejecting the use of Spenser as the focalising category through which to bring early modern Ireland into view, and instead emphasising the diverse and multicultural nature of early modern Irish society, connections and culture. My own essay follows a wider movement in early modern studies (including English) which once again seeks not just to reject Anglocentrism but to 'provincialise Europe' by attending to global connections, exchanges and traffic. Or, as the accompanying essay summarises it: 'a recent critical paradigm foregrounding the *global* changes to political, cultural and socioeconomic formations, often brought about by various forms of transcultural exchange, connection or encounter (including trade as well as imperialism and international conflict)'. It implicitly suggests that this might provide a new context for considering not just the Irish material in *The Faerie Queene* (now widely accepted), but other elements of the epic that have not yet been attended to in global terms.

THE CONTEXTUAL APPROACH

My primary approach in this essay is contextual: finding a way into Spenser's poem – and what was understood by epic writing in late sixteenth-century England – through a highly informed, roughly contemporary treatise of poetics, one that presents some significant differences to our established understanding of English Protestant poetics but is supported by intelligent and knowledgeable allusions to recent English writing. The gains of this approach are enhanced by the fact that this treatise, William Scott's *The Model of Poesy* (1599), was only rediscovered quite recently, and so offers a fresh but credible approach to early modern English poetics that we did not know that we were missing. Scott's discussion of epic, while relatively uncontroversial, ventures away from what we expect to read (based largely on the more prominent poetic treatise by Philip Sidney (1595), primarily in its choice of English exemplars of epic: a strikingly wide-ranging, formally diverse set of writings and authors). By choosing the most unlikely of these authors and texts, William Warner's *Albions England* (1586–1612), and investigating its connections with *The Faerie Queene*, one of the two primary examples of English epic accepted by Scott's contemporaries and by scholars today (the other being Milton's *Paradise Lost*), the essay hopes to shed light on a forgotten set of early modern understandings of the work, style and opportunities of epic in the later years of Queen Elizabeth's reign.

FURTHER READING

Alexander, Gavin, introduction to William Scott, *The Model of Poesy*, ed. Alexander (Cambridge University Press, 2013)

Baker, David, 'Britain Redux', *Spenser Studies* 29 (2014), 21–36

Brotton, Jerry, *The Renaissance: A Very Short Introduction* (Oxford University Press, 2006)

Hadfield, Andrew, *Spenser: A Life* (Oxford University Press, 2012)

Heaney, Seamus, *Stepping Stones: Interviews with Dennis O'Driscoll* (London: Faber & Faber, 2009)

Herron, Thomas, *Spenser's Irish Work: Poetry, Plantation, and Colonial Reformation* (Farnham: Ashgate, 2007)

Kerrigan, John, *Archipelagic English: Literature, History and Politics, 1603–1707* (Oxford University Press, 2008)

McCabe, Richard, *Spenser's Monstrous Regiment: Elizabethan Ireland and the Poetics of Difference* (Oxford University Press, 2005)

Murray, Patrick J., 'The Archipelagic Turn: Nationhood, Nationalism, and Early Modern Studies, 1997–2017', *Seventeenth Century* 33.4 (2018), 485–95

Palmer, Patricia, 'Missing Bodies, Absent Bards: Spenser, Shakespeare and a Crisis in Criticism', *English Literary Renaissance* 36.3 (2006), 376–95

Ramachandran, Ayesha, *The Worldmakers: Global Imagining in Early Modern Europe* (University of Chicago Press, 2015)

Singh, Jyotsna G. (ed.), *A Companion to the Global Renaissance: Literature and Culture in the Era of Expansion, 1500–1700*, 2nd edn (Oxford: Wiley-Blackwell, 2021)

6 *Arden of Faversham*

CHRISTA JANSOHN

Abstract

Arden of Faversham is one of the few anonymous dramas which even today enjoy a great deal of popularity both among readers and on stage. It is perhaps the best-known 'domestic tragedy' and is based on an actual murder committed in 1551. The play was written between 1588 and 1591 and printed in 1592 as a quarto edition. As was also the case with Shakespeare's history plays, *Macbeth*, parts of *King Lear* and *Cymbeline*, Holinshed's *Chronicles of England, Scotland and Ireland* (1577; rev. 1578) was the play's most important historical source; and this essay will focus primarily on the ways in which this material was used, as well as the play's ongoing reception. The essay begins with an overview of the actual historical events behind the play's action, before sketching out its genesis as a drama of intensively debated authorship. Following this, it argues that even in spite of its moralising framework, *Arden* opened English drama up to a new range of subject matters by considerably narrowing the gap between lofty subjects deemed worthy of a stylised poetic treatment, on the one hand, and the humble fare traditionally more suited to comedy, on the other. It is this innovative combination which may (at least in part) explain its enduring popularity. The essay's concluding sections consider the complex relationship between the tragedy and its source, arguing that *Arden* reflects gradual societal and moral shifts around the question of marriage in particular.

Forty-four miles from London, on Sunday, 15 February 1551, a treacherous murder was committed in the little market town of Faversham in the county of Kent: Alice Arden, together with her lover Mosby and two other accomplices, stabbed her husband from behind while he was playing backgammon in the parlour. He was fifty-nine, a wealthy landowner and former mayor of Faversham.[1] His wife, who was twelve years his junior and had been married to him for about seven years, was condemned to death for the crime, together with the other murderers, one month later. There is still a plaque on their half-timbered house (80, Abbey Street; Figure 6.1) marking the deed: 'Here lived Thomas Arden (Mayor 1548, Comptroller of the Port of Sandwich and Customer of Faversham) and herein on 15 February, 1551 he was murdered at the instigation of his wife. The House is immortalised in the Elizabethan drama "Arden of Feversham".[2] As the plaque suggests, this terrible deed and its portrayal in drama are closely bound up with the history of the town and continue to attract tourists. However, the murder also provided a rich source of material for literary and historical treatments more generally, especially since contemporary murders in the Elizabethan period proved a particularly popular element in a corpus of topics that was drawn upon repeatedly in the widely circulating ballads, pamphlets, and dramas of the time. Despite their contemporary popularity, though, only a few of the numerous plays attested to have been preserved, such as *Arden of Faversham* (1592), *A Warning for Fair Women* (1599), Robert Yarington's *Two Tragedies in One* (1601), and *A Yorkshire Tragedy* (1608). Of these, *Arden of Faversham* is almost unanimously regarded as the most successful, and one reason for this is no doubt to do with the large role given to the character of Alice Arden, whose lines take up about a quarter of the text, thereby representing one of the most substantial female roles in the Elizabethan repertoire.

Arden of Faversham, which appeared anonymously, was not written until almost forty years after the murder, and probably between 1588 and 1591.[3] On 3 April 1592 the printer Edward White (*c.* 1548–*c.* 1612) was granted the publication rights by an entry in the Stationers' Register,[4] and in the same year the play was published in a quarto edition without the name of the author being given (Figure 6.2). This

Figure 6.1 Arden's House, Faversham, Kent.

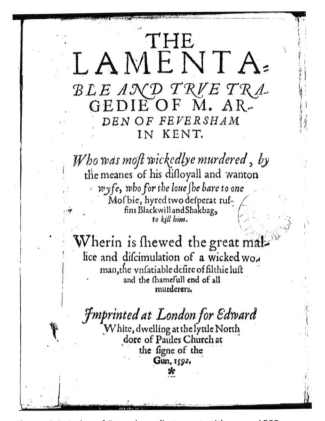

Figure 6.2 *Arden of Feversham*, first quarto title page, 1592.

edition was followed by two additional reprints in 1599 and 1633, at a time when most of the early Elizabethan dramas were practically forgotten. In 1770 it was attributed to William Shakespeare for the first time by Edward Jacob, a bookshop owner from Faversham, in the edition he published as *The Tragedy of Mr. Arden, of Feversham* (Feversham, 1770). It was subsequently treated in English-speaking countries for a long time as an apocryphal drama, whereas the German Romantics, in their assessment of Shakespeare's works, assumed that it was part of a process of literary maturation, seeing in it the early work of a young, as yet inexperienced, dramatist.[5]

In the twentieth and twenty-first centuries in particular, research has focused on further potential authors, for example Christopher Marlowe (1564–93) and Thomas Kyd (1558–94), as well as – repeatedly – William Shakespeare (1564–1616). There is more or less a consensus that Scenes 4–8 are probably by Shakespeare (but even in the case of Scene 9 the authorship is disputed). In the *New Oxford Shakespeare*, the play was listed as 'Anonymous and Shakespeare' with a detailed analysis of the authorship question; and in 2024 it will be included in the *Collected Works of Thomas Kyd*.[6]

This intensive authorship debate may be one reason why *Arden of Faversham* has continued to attract attention in literary studies and on stage, but the fascination of the play, both in the past and the present, has its roots in the enormous unscrupulousness with which the husband's murder was initiated and implemented, and also in the fact that the murder was carried out by a woman, an extraordinary deed which for contemporaries aroused 'special horror' – whereas the murder of a wife by her husband was merely accorded the status of an 'unnatural crime'. According to the provisions of the Treason Act of 1351, in common law a murder committed by a woman was 'petty treason' or 'petit treason',[7] and the murderer ended up being burnt at the stake.[8]

There is no doubt that *Arden of Faversham* enjoyed great popularity, and even in the eighteenth century it was republished and adapted by, among others, George Lillo, the author of the *London Merchant* (1731), which, as is well known, initiated the era of the 'domestic drama'. It appears that Lillo thought he was linking up his new dramatic genre with the tradition of the Elizabethan 'domestic drama'. However, *Arden of Faversham* does not have much more in common with the later domestic drama than the fact that the main characters are drawn from the middle classes rather than the ranks of kings and nobles.[9] Yet *Arden of Faversham* is much more than the domestic melodrama that the subtitle seems to suggest,[10] and it is closer to other types of Elizabethan drama than it appears at first glance.

The action is expressly narrated to act as a warning, where the individual case is taken as a generally valid instance of the eternal law of guilt and punishment. Hot on the heels of the evil deed follows retribution, a retribution which is brought about by the guilty themselves. However, the drama's representation of an egregious crime diverges starkly from Marlowe's moral heroism in good as in evil. The two villains Black Will and Shakebag are not to be read as dramatically impressive criminals who pursue their dastardly ends with particular passion. Instead, they are constantly assailed by doubt and distrust, only committing their murder half-heartedly, and immediately regretting it in the instant it is committed. In other words, not only is the simple mechanism of crime, remorse and punishment shown here, but above all the perverting power of evil, which from the outset does not permit a sense of human fellowship to develop, punishing the guilty even before the justice of the secular authorities can reach them. This is in fact probably the notable strength of this play: Alice Arden and her lover Mosby think that they can secure their love by the murder, but right from the beginning they discover that their own relationship is poisoned; their malicious plans result in each mistrusting the other. In its portrayal of the ways in which a shared guilt engenders not a mutual sense of belonging but rather quite the opposite, the play shows something approaching a psychological realism that is rare in this period of English drama.

The differentiation of the two main characters is underscored dramatically by the contrast with the much more primitive figures of the murderers, particularly the textbook villain Black Will, whose murky character is outlined at the beginning by Bradshaw (I.1–12), who also gives a catalogue of his villainies (XIV.10–29). It is precisely these scenes which reveal how effectively the actual observation of reality and the tradition of the morality plays complement each other. Black Will is both apparently a well-observed phenomenon from day-to-day life in London and also a descendant of the devil from medieval drama. We certainly find a clear mark of allegory in the scene where he and Shakebag are lying in wait for Arden in the fog, and he answers Shakebag's question 'where art thou?' with: 'almost in hell's mouth, where I cannot see my way for smoke' (XII.1–3). 'Hell's mouth' was both a prop used in the morality plays and the name of a specific part of the stage; and it is quite obvious that Black Will, who at this very point is preparing to commit murder, has already reached the place of his damnation. Thus, a certain degree of realism and a fairly simplistic moral are not mutually exclusive, as it is precisely in the medieval mystery plays that we sometimes find the most accurate reflection of reality: in other words, 'realism' is used as a possible faithful depiction of everyday life in this play too, not for its own sake, but because it always serves a higher goal, namely that of portraying the play's moral as dramatically as possible.

Furthermore, *Arden of Faversham* can demonstrate how a series of conventions have become part and parcel of Elizabethan drama and are no longer restricted to a specific form of tragedy, such as the Senecan, for example. This is particularly true of the blank verse in the play, which by now had become almost exclusively the medium of tragedy even if the technique of using different plot levels, with shifts between verse and prose, such as we find in Marlowe's *Doctor Faustus*, were still to come (although here, too, we encounter specific themes of the main plot, such as jealousy, secret love and the thought of murdering a troublesome rival, all repeated on another level).

Since it first unfolded in the drama (Norton's and Sackville's *Gorboduc* (1565) is an early example), blank verse itself had become much more flexible, not only at the hands of a poet like Christopher Marlowe but also when employed by the much more modest author of *Arden of Faversham*, whose technique is not devoid of a certain skilful craftsmanship. The play testifies, moreover, to the emergence of a common pattern in the drama of the period whereby an adeptness at blank verse and a flexible dramatic technique permitted the playwright to dramatise any kind of subject matter. As such, this period sees the development of a kind of functional drama, with numerous plays emerging which deal with a significant variety of subjects from the realms of history and legend. As is apparently the case here, they often enact a straightforward, uncomplicated moral lesson, sometimes (it appears) simply as a kind of 'justification' for staging an interesting plot. The vast majority of these plays are now forgotten or have yet to be reprinted. *Arden of Faversham* is one of the first available examples of this dramatic 'insouciance', where anything that appealed to the imagination could be dramatised; and an example, too, of the loosening of dogmatic strictures as regards dramatic technique and, importantly, the types of people deemed worthy of serious treatment on the stage. Such an evolution can also be seen stylistically in some of the play's relatively relaxed and 'natural' dialogue, even though a more formal rhetorical style is still clearly in evidence. Indeed, the language is often still markedly sententious, with general truisms quoted, carefully contrived comparisons made, and elaborate speeches staged, slowing down the dramatic pace. One good example of this is the rather stiff dialogue at the beginning of the play (though this is, in itself, quite a skilful way of introducing Arden's melancholy mood and thereby hinting at the impending disaster). Elsewhere, the dialogue is much more relaxed, with a greater sense of genuine interaction between the characters, such as occurs above all in the scenes involving Mosby and Alice. The alternation between a conventionally rhetorical style and a more naturalistic, down-to-earth style is in fact a characteristic feature of the play.

Another notable feature is that the repetition of similar types of scene – the planning scene and the persuasion scene, among others – seems designed to create a structural rhythm in the play not dissimilar to that of Thomas Kyd's *Spanish Tragedy* (written between 1582 and 1592 and whose language, too, is reminiscent of Senecan drama). At the same time it is clear that the classical tradition has been completely assimilated, and it is precisely the apparent normality of the play in this respect that shows how rapidly an indigenous dramatic style has developed. Accordingly, monologues are managed with skill and complexity, such as those recited by Michael (III.192–209 and IV.58–86), through which the threatening atmosphere in particular is emphasised. In the first of these, Arden is denounced; in the second, which is much more unconventional, the account of his dilemma is followed by his sudden outcry, which throws all sober reflection to the wind and serves as a warning to Arden.

Similarly, Mosby's carefully balanced monologue (VIII.1–43) reveals him to be a person at odds with himself, who is by no means convinced of the path he is choosing and yet who still finds himself driven towards the crime. On the other hand, Mrs Arden's monologues (e.g. I.93–103), with their excessively flowery style, are an expression of her deceitfulness. The effusive image of a great love which she describes is scarcely reflected in the play, and the murder bears a much less ideal fruit. Again, the murder scene, during the backgammon game, shows the curious combination of stylised rhetoric and completely unstylised behaviour, of presumptuous dignity and true vileness.

All this goes towards explaining the popularity of *Arden of Faversham*. It was not a pioneering breakthrough in the domestic tragedy, but what can be said of it is that it opened up drama to a new range of subject matters, with the gap being narrowed between lofty subjects seen to be worthy of stylised poetic treatment and humbler material usually considered more suited to comedy, even though the play's moralising purpose essentially remained the same. It is primarily the portrait of the murderer with her unbridled passion, her self-torment, and her doubts, which show a previously unknown psychological intensity, even though its sentimental features and heavy-handed attempts to edify the audience betray the lowbrow nature of the play.

As with Shakespeare's history plays, the source of *Arden of Faversham* is Holinshed's *Chronicles of England, Scotland and Ireland*.[11] The subject is therefore taken from a historical account, not from the author's present, and both the title and subtitle make clear that the dramatist is treating the story here as if it really is a case of significant historical importance. Even in the source itself, however, Alice is described as a 'wicked woman' (p. 155) and her behaviour in terms of 'filthy disorder' and 'evil demeanor' (pp. 149, 157). Yet the play also places greater emphasis on the social context than its source, specifically on Mosby's social climbing (I.310–14) and Arden's avarice, which is denounced very early on by the exploited Greene: 'Desire of wealth is endless in his mind' (I.474). Equally, however, it was no doubt the contracted killers Shakebag and Black Will, probably the most energetic criminal characters in Elizabethan theatre, who contributed to the play's success.

Moreover, in Holinshed the murder story is discussed on a completely different level, and Holinshed's intentions are quite different from those in the anonymous drama. Despite his very engaged discussion and the explicit reference to the authenticity of his sources, Holinshed expresses doubts as to whether this murder really does deserve a place in a broader history, while at the same time devoting several pages to it, before finally returning to his chronicle with the parenthetical, 'To Returne then where we left', even if the only other record for the year 1551 concerns the effects of the 'Sweating sickenesse'.

In justification of his extensive interpolation about Arden's murder, Holinshed very quickly finds legitimation on the flimsy grounds that he mainly wanted to record the deed on account of its 'horribleness':

> The which murther, for the horribleness thereof, although otherwise it may seeme to
> be but a priuate matter, and therefore as it were impertinent to this historie, I haue
> thought good to set it foorth somewhat at large, hauing the instructions deliuered to
> me by them, that haue vsed some diligence to gather the true vnderstanding of the
> circumstances. (p. 148)

Yet a perusal of the *Chronicles* shows that the emotionally charged argument in no way contradicts the nature of Holinshed's historiography, since he repeatedly inserted accounts of this kind, thereby breaking with the ossified conventions of a traditional chronicle. Annabel Patterson refers to these episodes as 'anecdotes', defining them as 'brief independent narratives about human behavior, short enough to be emblematic, independent enough of its surroundings to be portable, and with one or more colorful individuals at its center', nevertheless expressly excluding the murder of Arden as a paradigmatic anecdote, as it does not represent, in her view, the 'signs of the economic, social-domestic and politico-religious conditions of life of early modern England'.[12]

In my view, however, Arden's murder is an essential part of this history, used mainly to restabilise an unstable political and social situation in its portrayals of the miserable consequences of a relationship in which the woman no longer accepts the role assigned to her by nature. As a result, the microcosm of the 'natural marital relationship between the sexes' endangers the sociopolitical macrocosm, as men are after all 'lords and lawfull kings in their houses', as Richard Hooker in *Of the Laws of Ecclesiastical Polity* (1593) puts it; the husband is 'Cheefe gouernour', the wife 'fellow helper', as we are told in Dod and Cleaver (1598);[13] Henry Smith calls her 'an under-officer in his Commonwealth' (1591),[14] and a discordant marriage is compared to a disunited kingdom: 'As a kingdom cannot stand if it be divided, so a house cannot stand if it be divided ... '[15] This commonplace of marital companionship as a political microcosm is picked up by Shakespeare in the comedy *The Taming of the Shrew*, which on this point, incidentally, departs explicitly from the exclusively biblical interpretation of the anonymous play.[16]

In *Arden of Faversham*, too, the author uses a political term to give expression to Alice's criticism of her marriage to Arden. Her rebellion is directed equally at her passive position and at what she sees as an unjustified appropriation of her own personality in the marital relationship:

> And he [Arden] usurps it, having nought but this,
> That I am tied to him by marriage.
> Love is a god, and marriage is but words ... (I. 99–101)[17]

In Arden's eyes Mosby's 'usurpation' is, then, in fact bound up with his commercial acquisitiveness:

> As for the land, Mosby, they are mine
> By letters patents from his majesty.
> But I must have a mandate for my wife;
> They say you seek to rob me of her love ... (I.300–3)[18]

Alice's fate is deeply rooted in her striving for emancipation, which, however, blinds her to reality, which would only propel her from one dependent relationship to another. The anonymous author makes this patently clear when, on the one hand, he has Alice asking, 'Why should he [Arden] ... govern me that am to rule myself?' (X. 83–5), while, on the other hand, her lover at an early stage expresses the idea of a union by saying, 'If thou'lt be ruled by me' (I.224).

As the examples from contemporary sources confirm, the relationship between the sexes was often associated with constellations of political power; thus, private and public matters do have more in common than is suggested by Holinshed's pseudo-problem, namely that 'it may seem to be but a priuate matter' (p. 148). In fact, a private affair could easily be manipulated for the purposes of a cautionary social statement.

An additional aspect also seemed to have been important to Holinshed in his account, when, right from the outset, he introduces Alice as the sole person pulling the strings in the murder plot. Thus we read in his chronicle: 'Arden, most cruellie murthered and slaine by the procurement of his owne wife' (p. 148). Only then does he portray the killing particularly graphically as a joint operation:

> ... that blacke Will stept foorth, and cast a towell about his necke, so to stop his breath and strangle him. Then Mosbie hauing at his girdle a pressing iron of fourteene pounds weight, stroke him on the hed with the same, so that he fell downe, and gaue a great grone, insomuch that they thought he had beene killed.
>
> Then they bare him awaie, to laie him in the counting house, & as they were about to laie him downe, the pangs of death comming on him, he gaue a great grone, and stretched himselfe, and then blacke Will gaue him a great gash in the face, and so killed him out of hand, laid him along, tooke the monie out of his pursse, and the rings from his fingers, ... After that blacke Will was gone, mistresse Arden came into the counting house, and with a knife gaue him seuen or eight p[r]icks into the brest. (p. 155)

The murder scene reaches its markedly objectionable climax when Alice stabs her husband's dead body, with its associations of Julius Caesar's murder in Shakespeare's tragedy of 1599 (III.i.75), and Plutarch's description of the same (from which Shakespeare drew), where the bloody ritual is likewise depicted as a joint act of liberation from a tyrant: 'for it was agreed among them that every man should give him a wound, because all their parts should be in this murther'.[19] This psychological motivation is no doubt also valid for the play. Here Alice is also the last to join in the ritual; however, in contrast to Holinshed, it is she who deals the decisive fatal stab.[20] Both versions, though, are roughly comparable in their brutality.

Interestingly, the second edition of the *Chronicles* (1587) adds further emphasis to what is already a morally highly charged condemnation of the murdering wife by means of newly inserted marginalia (such marginalia is common in the first edition but limited in the Arden account to the annotation, '1551 An.reg.5 Arden murthered' (p. 1703)). Abraham Fleming, who signed himself as responsible for the annotations, was thus apparently given free rein for comments such as 'Loue and lust' or 'O importunate & bloudie minded strumpet!' (pp. 148, 154), which clearly intensified the moral censure. Apart from its subtitle, the play represents a complete departure from this morally didactic approach, although, admittedly, in modern productions the issue is almost invariably blurred by comedic elements. The passion of the lovers, the unscrupulousness of the social climber Mosby and his exploitative adversary Arden, but also the bloodthirstiness of the two hired killers with their nascent self-torment and doubts, are all frequently reduced to parody in the style of a kind of 'comedy thriller',[21] with the result that the play's psychological intensity is often lost, just as it is deprived of what is in parts quite a powerful use of rhetoric: its recourse to conventions deriving from classical tragedy serve, at least when the play is read, to confer upon it the seriousness of a poetic tragedy.

Holinshed's account of the Arden murder was in later years repeatedly cited as authoritative. Henry Goodcole, for example, in 'Adultress's Funeral Day' (1635), wrote: 'I will only remember you of Mistress Arden, who caused her husband to be murdered in her own house at Feversham in Kent, the memorable circumstances thereof deserving places in a most approved chronicle, may be very well spared in this short discourse.'[22] Even at the end of the nineteenth century Abel H. Coppinger adopts Holinshed's account (along with excerpts from the anonymous play) directly in his study, commenting that modern research has hardly anything to add to the reliable historical sources. His discourse is included in the anthology *Twelve Bad Women* (1897), which reached its third edition by 1911. It bears the curious subtitle *Illustrations and Reviews of Feminine Turpitude Set Forth by Impartial hands.*[23] Even though the collection is to be regarded as complementing Thomas Seccombé's *Lives of Twelve Bad Men: Original Studies of Eminent Scoundrels by Various Hands* (London, 1894), the subtitle, preface and the motto by Thomas Otway,[24] which was added in the second edition, clearly betray a misogynistic cast of mind: 'the purpose is to give unvarnished accounts of twelve women of whom enough is known to show that they were consistently bad, whether owing to a vicious temperament, a crooked nature, or a lack of moral perception, resulting in unscrupulousness and crime' (Preface, p. xii). The subsequent enumeration of the main characteristics of the *Twelve Bad Women* is in many respects reminiscent of the lists of women held up for condemnation in medieval sermons and literary texts.[25] In this volume, however, Alice's murder is portrayed as a mere 'crime passionel', 'sordid enough in its details, [but] redeemed from the reproach of vulgarity' (p. xiii), and the portrayal retains little of the immediate social purpose evident in Holinshed and the anonymous play.

In fact, going back to the immediate historical context, it is notable that Alice Arden's crime forms part of a group of stories occurring particularly frequently between 1590 and 1630 which involve murders of their husbands by wives, whose origin was apparently to be sought in the 'female rebellion' which was flaring up at the time and which was perceived to be linked to the growing instability of the institution of marriage.[26] The almost aphoristic statement by the character of Alice in the play, 'Love is a god, and marriage is but words' (I.101), might therefore be seen to be symptomatic of a changed attitude towards marriage in the period, an attitude which then gave rise to a variety of corrective responses in literary and historical texts and, above all, in sermons.

In the 'dialogue' between Holinshed's *Chronicles* and the drama of *Arden of Faversham* that I have been exploring, we can thus detect some of the fault lines of an evolving modern culture, especially in relation to questions of marriage, morality, power and gender. As we have seen, apart from its subtitle, the anonymous play, unlike Holinshed, generally dispenses with explicit moralising:

> Gentlemen, we hope you'll pardon this naked tragedy
> Wherein no filèd points are foisted in
> To make it gracious to the ear or eye;
> For simple truth is gracious enough
> And needs no other points of glozing stuff. (Epilogue, 14–18)

However, as suggested earlier, it is in the play's relative sophistication in its treatment of character and motivation that its main significance lies for an understanding of the development of early modern drama and society. The characters in the play are certainly subject to less moralistic finger-wagging than is evident in Holinshed's account, but, more importantly, they are also portrayed with a greater degree of psychological realism as complex individuals. Thus, the reader (if not necessarily the theatre audience) is treated to a much more nuanced image of the protagonists than the play's sources provide.

NOTES

1. For copious documentation on Faversham and on Thomas Arden in particular see Patricia Hyde, *Thomas Arden in Faversham: The Man Behind the Myth* (Faversham: Faversham Society, 1996).
2. Pictures of the house and the plaques are available on the website Waymarking.com: https://bit.ly/3LmCSrp. There are different spellings for the town, namely Faversham and Feversham(e), and the same is true for Arden (Arden and Ardern). In this essay the spellings have been standardised as 'Faversham' and 'Arden'. Unless otherwise stated, all online sources cited were accessed on 1 July 2020.
3. *The Tragedy of Master Arden of Faversham*, ed. M. L. Wine (London: Methuen, 1973), p. xlv. All further references are to this edition and are given in the main text.
4. The play was listed there as 'The tragedie of Arden of Feuersham & blackwill' and licensed for publication by John Aylmer, Bishop of London: see Shakespeare Documented, https://shakespearedocumented.folger.edu/exhibition/document/stationers-register-entry-arden-faversham.
5. See Christa Jansohn, 'Ludwig Tieck as the Champion of Shakespeare's Apocrypha in Germany', *Cahiers Élisabéthains* 48 (1995), 45–51; and Peter Kirwan, *Shakespeare and the Idea of Apocrypha: Negotiating the Boundaries of the Dramatic Canon* (Cambridge University Press, 2015), pp. 45, 146–52.
6. Anonymous and William Shakespeare, *The Tragedy of M. Arden of Faversham; or, The Tragedy of Arden of FeYou Shame*, ed. Terri Bourus and Gary Taylor, in Gary Taylor et al. (eds), *The New Oxford Shakespeare: The Complete Works*, vol. I, *Modern Critical Edition* (Oxford University Press, 2016), pp. 117–87. On the question of authorship see *The New Oxford Shakespeare: Authorship Companion*, ed. Gary Taylor and Gabriel Egan (Oxford University Press, 2017), pp. 123–45, 151–93, 488–90; Gary Taylor, 'Shakespeare, *Arden*

of Faversham, and Four Forgotten Playwrights', *Review of English Studies*, n.s., 71.302 (2020), 867–95: https://doi.org/10.1093/res/hgaa005; and Thomas Kyd, *Arden of Faversham*, ed. Darren Freebury-Jones, in Brian Vickers (ed.), *The Collected Works of Thomas Kyd* (Woodbridge: Boydell & Brewer, forthcoming).

7. According to the *OED*, 'petit or petty treason' means 'treason against a subject; spec. the murder of one to whom the murderer owes allegiance, as of a master by his servant, a husband by his wife, etc.' See also Betty S. Travitsky, 'Husband-Murder and Petty Treason in English Renaissance Tragedy', *Renaissance Drama*, n.s., 21 (1990), 171–98, (176); Frances E. Dolan, *Dangerous Familiars: Representations of Domestic Crime in England, 1550–1700* (Ithaca, NY and London: Cornell University Press, 1994); and Dianne Berg, '"'Tis fearful sleeping in a serpent's bed": *Arden of Faversham* and the Threat of the Petty Traitor', in Larissa Tracy (ed.), *Treason: Medieval and Early Modern Adultery, Betrayal, and Shame* (Leiden: Brill, 2019), pp. 340–54.

8. Joy Wiltenburg, *Disorderly Women and Female Power in the Street Literature of Early Modern England and Germany* (Charlottesville: University Press of Virginia, 1992), p. 214.

9. Emma Whipday, '"Marrow prying neighbours": Staging Domestic Space and Neighbourhood Surveillance in *Arden of Faversham*', *Cahiers Élisabéthains: A Biannual Journal of English Renaissance Studies* 88.1 (2015), 95–110: https://journals.sagepub .com/doi/10.7227/CE.88.1.7; see also Catherine Richardson, 'Arden of Faversham', in *Domestic Life and Domestic Tragedy in Early Modern England: The Material Life of the Household* (Manchester University Press, 2006), pp. 104–27.

10. The play bears a sensational title that unmistakably reflects the moralising nature of the play. The full title reads: '*The Lamentable and Trve Tragedie of M. Arden of Feversham in Kent.* / Who was most wickedly murdered, by the meanes of his disloyall and wanton wyfe, who for the loue she bare to one Mosbie, hyred two desperat ruffins Blackwill and Shakbag, to kill him. / Wherin is shewed the great malice and discimulation of a wicked woman, the unsatiable desire of filthie lust and the shamefull end of all murderers' (*Arden of Faversham*, ed. Wine, facsimile, p. 2).

11. The excerpt from Holinshed is reproduced in *Arden of Faversham*, ed. Wine, pp. 148–59.

12. Annabel M. Patterson, *Reading Holinshed's Chronicles* (University of Chicago Press, 1994), pp. 42, 44.

13. Additional examples are given in Lena Cowen Orlin, 'Familial Transgressions, Societal Transition on the Elizabethan Stage', in Carole Levin and Karen Robertson (eds), *Sexuality and Politics in Renaissance Drama* (Lewiston, ID: Mellen Press, 1991), pp. 27–55 (pp. 29–30). See also Catherine Belsey, 'Alice Arden's Crime', *Renaissance Drama*, n.s., 13 (1982), 83–102.

14. Quoted from Kathleen M. Davies, 'Continuity and Change in Literary Advice on Marriage', in R. B. Outhwaite (ed.), *Marriage and Society: Studies in the Social History of Marriage* (London: Europa, 1981), pp. 58–80 (p. 63). See also Sk. B., *Counsel to the Husband; To the Wife Instruction*: 'A familie may bee compared vnto a commonwealth: wherein there are diuers societies and degrees, reciprocally relating, and mutually depending one vpon another. The highest degree or societie is between the husband and the wife; and this is as the first wheel of a clocke, that turneth about all the rest in

order. The next societie, is betweene the Parents and the children. The third betweene the seruants one with another, and towards all other superiors in the familie.' Quoted in Lena Cowen Orlin, 'Man's House as His Castle in Arden of Faversham', *Medieval & Renaissance Drama in England* 2 (1985), 57–89 (64).

15. Henry Smith, *A Preparative to Mariage* (1591), quoted in Lena Cowen Orlin, *Elizabethan Households: An Anthology* (Washington, DC: Folger Shakespeare Library, 1995), p. 40.

16. See Geoffrey Bullough (ed.), *Narrative and Dramatic Sources of Shakespeare* (London: Routledge & Kegan Paul, 1977), vol. I, p. 107; and *The Taming of the Shrew*, V.ii.160–9: 'Such duty as the subject owes the prince, / Even such a woman oweth to her husband, / And when she is froward, peevish, sullen, sour, / And not obedient to his honest will, / What is she but a foul contending rebel / And graceless traitor to her loving lord? / I am ashamed that women are so simple / To offer war where they should kneel for peace, / Or seek for rule, supremacy, and sway / When they are bound to serve, love, and obey.'

17. See Frank Whigham, 'Hunger and Pain in *Arden of Faversham*', in *Seizures of the Will in Early Modern English Drama* (Cambridge University Press, 1996), pp. 63–120 (pp. 78–9).

18. John M. Breen, 'The Carnival Body in *Arden of Faversham*', *Cahiers Élisabéthains: Late Medieval and Renaissance English Studies* 45 (1994), 13–21 (14).

19. Plutarch is quoted from the Arden edition of William Shakespeare, *Julius Caesar*, ed. T. S. Dorsch (London: Methuen, 1952), p. 148. A different interpretation is given in Eugene P. Walz, 'Arden of Faversham as a Tragic Satire', *Massachusetts Studies in English* 4 (1973), 23–41, (38): 'Murder is equated to a game to be viewed with more amusement than horror.'

20. On this, see *Arden of Faversham*, ed. Wine, p. 124 n. 237; referring to Symonds, Wine sees a possible parallel to *Macbeth*, II.ii.52–3: 'Infirm of purpose! / Give me the daggers'.

21. See Maik Hamburger, 'Shakespeare auf den Bühnen der DDR in der Spielzeit 1987/88', *Shakespeare Jahrbuch* 125 (1989), 155–67 (164).

22. Quoted from Lena Cowen Orlin, *Private Matters and Public Culture in Post-Reformation England* (Ithaca, NY: Cornell University Press, 1994), p. 16.

23. Arthur Vincent (ed.), *Lives of Twelve Bad Women: Illustrations and Reviews of Feminine Turpitude set forth by Impartial Hands* (Boston: L. C. Page, 1897), pp. 32–46 (p. 33).

24. The source is not given and so only the informed reader will recognise the context. The quotation is from *The Orphan; Or, The Unhappy Marriage. A Tragedy* (London, 1680), where Castalio cries out, at the end of the third act (lines 581–6): 'What mighty ills have not been done by women? / Who wast betrayed the Capitol? A Woman! / Who lost Mark Antony the world? A Woman! / Who was the cause of a long ten years' war, / And laid at last old Troy in ashes? A Woman! / Destructive, damnable, deceitful Woman.'

25. For example in *Sir Gawain and the Green Knight*, IV, line 2414. For this, see Alcuin Blamires (ed.), *Woman Defamed and Woman Defended: An Anthology of Medieval Texts* (Oxford: Clarendon Press, 1992).

26. Wiltenburg, *Disorderly Women*, p. 214.

CRITICAL REFLECTIONS AND FURTHER STUDY

GENRE AND HISTORY, THE PRIVATE AND THE PUBLIC

As early as 1983 Alexander Leggat, in a stimulating essay, wrote of *Arden*: 'The play's fascination stems from the way it keeps us guessing about the kind of play it is; is it a reporting of the facts, a slice of life – or are the facts consciously shaped to give a significant pattern?' ('*Arden of Faversham*', p. 122; see Further Reading). The play is commonly described as a 'domestic tragedy' and perhaps the most important study for considering it from this perspective is Lena Cowen Orlin's *Private Matters and Public Culture in Post-Reformation England* (see my essay, note 24). Orlin argues that domestic tragedies were 'radical' plays, identifying fault lines in patriarchal ideology, conflicts between political and economic interests in the household, gendered competitions for domestic control, and fissures in received ideals of friendship and marriage. Domestic tragedies thus offered a very different view of private life to those found in sermons, state-sponsored homilies and household advice books.

However, the question of which genre the play belongs to is still open to debate and, of course, a matter of how one interprets the text and/or conceives a stage production. Might it best be approached as a romance, where the audience sympathises with Alice in a stifling marriage, or as a moral treatise, showing the proper punishment for adultery? Or is it actually the first detective story (the footprints in the snow, the instruments of the crime, etc.)? Is it tragic, as it claims, or are the comic elements (the repeated failures of the villains) enough to cancel that out? Is it a history play (based on Holinshed's *Chronicles*, 1577, 1587)? Of course, there is no definitive answer to any of these questions, but they are useful ways of approaching different facets of the play and of considering how the play relates to its contexts and its place in the evolution of drama at this time (for example, in the transition between the moral 'tragedies' of the previous generation and Shakespeare's work).

RECEPTION: STAGE HISTORY AND ADAPTATIONS

For the history of the play's reception, it is worth noting that even as early as the nineteenth century there were numerous translations and adaptations, and the play has often been performed on the stage. Some stage productions are discussed in the editions cited in my essay (see notes 4 and 7); in addition, numerous reviews of individual productions can be found online, for example, of the production at the Swan Theatre in Stratford-upon-Avon in 2014 (directed by Polly Findlay for the Royal Shakespeare Company).

The musical world has also shown an interest in the play. For example, the 1966 opera *Arden muß sterben: Eine Oper vom Tod des reichen Arden von Faversham in 2 Akten* (Libretto: Erich Fried) by the British composer Alexander Goehr (b. 1932) had its premiere on 5 March 1967 at the Hamburg State Opera (where it occasioned vehement protests from the audience), followed by the British premiere (*Arden Must Die: An Opera on the Death of the Wealthy Arden of Faversham in Two Acts [seven scenes]*; English translation by Geoffrey Skelton) at Sadler's Wells Theatre, London, on 17 April 1971. The well-known Austrian left-winger, poet and important Shakespeare translator Erich Fried (1921–88) not only gave the text a mischievous, satirical intertextual level by inserting a large number of literary quotations; he also supercharged it with contemporary political references. Although everybody in this opera wants to murder the wealthy exploiter Arden, his neighbour Mrs Bradshaw (a new character introduced into the action by Fried) ostentatiously reminds us of the fellow travellers of the Nazi régime when she claims that 'I always was against it'. Goehr described *Arden Must Die* as a 'political opera about ourselves and the way we behave in the crises in which we find ourselves' (Programme, Hamburg State Opera 1966/7, p. 75). Its intellectual appeal lies primarily in the ambiguity of its black humour and it has much in common with the theatre of Bertolt Brecht. Goehr's blending of twelve-tone music (dodecaphony) with simple triad harmony, atonality with simple tonality, is musically reminiscent of Schönberg's atonality and Messiaen's school of exotic rhythm, as well as the techniques of early medieval harmony. Since *Arden muß sterben* was also performed in England and in English, a comparison is rewarding, especially since the English production transfers the action to the late nineteenth century whereas the German production deliberately dispenses with any specific reference to period.

FURTHER READING

Arden of Faversham, ed. Catherine Richardson, Arden Early Modern Drama (London: Bloomsbury, 2022)

Goehr, Alexander (comp.), *Arden Must Die, an Opera ... in Two Acts*, with libretto by Erich Fried, 1966, first performed 1967 by Hamburg State Opera: BBC Films 1967, www.loganartsmanagement.com/alexander-goehr-videos.html (in two parts)

Goehr, Alexander, 'Alexander Goehr – Stageworks / Opera and Music Theatre', www.fcqv .org/Goehr/Arden%20Must%20Die/Arden%20Must%20Die.html

Belsey, Catherine, *The Subject of Tragedy: Identity and Difference in Renaissance Drama* (London: Methuen, 1985)

Christensen, Ann C., 'Housekeeping and Forlorn Travel in *Arden of Faversham*', in her *Separation Scenes: Domestic Drama in Early Modern England* (Lincoln: University of Nebraska Press, 2017), pp. 49–84

Floyd-Wilson, Mary, '*Arden of Faversham*: Tragic Action at a Distance', in Emma Smith and Garrett A. Sullivan Jr (eds), *The Cambridge Companion to English Renaissance Tragedy* (Cambridge University Press, 2010), pp. 188–99

Helgerson, Richard, *Adulterous Alliances: Home, State, and History in Early Modern European Drama and Painting* (University of Chicago Press, 2000)

Helgerson, Richard, 'Murder in Faversham: Holinshed's Impertinent History', in Donald R. Kelley and David Harris Sacks (eds), *The Historical Imagination in Early Modern Britain* (Cambridge University Press, 1997), pp. 133–58

Leggat, Alexander, '*Arden of Faversham*', in Stanley Wells (ed.), *Shakespeare Survey* 36 (Cambridge: Cambridge University Press, 1983), pp. 121–33: DOI:10.1017/CCOL0521256364

Jansohn, Christa, 'From Private to Public Evil: Or from the Wicked Woman in Arden of Faversham to Alexander Goehr's Opera Arden Must Die', *Actes des Congrès de la Société Française Shakespeare* 15 (1997), 59–76: https://doi.org/10.4000/shakespeare.1143

King, Ros, '*Arden of Faversham*: The Moral of History and the Thrill of Performance', in Thomas Betteridge and Greg Walker (eds), *The Oxford Handbook of Tudor Drama* (Oxford University Press, 2018), pp. 1–19: DOI: 10.1093/oxfordhb/9780199566471.013.0038

Orlin, Lena Cowen (ed.), *The Renaissance: A Sourcebook* (Houndmills: Palgrave Macmillan, 2009)

'A Little Touch of Harry in the Night': Mysteries of Kingship and the Stage in Shakespeare's *The Life of King Henry the Fifth*

INA HABERMANN

Abstract

This essay focuses on *Henry V* in order to refine our understanding of Shakespeare's distinctive contribution to the history play in the 1590s. In particular, I argue that Shakespeare enlists the imaginative powers of the audience to bring history to life, and that, to this end, he parallels the mystery of successful performance with the mysticism surrounding kingship. Just as the natural body of the king is transformed into the mystical body of the monarch, the stage action expands into historical events of epic proportions. This is predicated on the joint emphasis on play, performance and theatricality, which may have been suggested by the former Prince Hal's preference for games and gambles. The player thus plays a king who plays dangerous games. And if it is potentially treasonous to impersonate royalty on stage, the audience must take at least part of the blame, as history comes to life in their imagination. The result is dynamic, and even though the ultimate trajectory of the play may be an exploration, or even a celebration, of English history and national identity, its emotional centre is the playhouse, so that its political impact depends on performance.

Prologue

It is generally accepted that the genre of the political history play came into its own in the 1590s and that Shakespeare's central cycle of history plays – particularly his two 'tetralogies' covering English history from the reign of Richard II to the usurper Richard III's death at the Battle of Bosworth in 1485 – played a leading role in its development.[1] In Shakespeare criticism, the importance of the histories was enhanced when the emphasis shifted from the 'character criticism' of the early twentieth century to political readings in the 1940s with work by Lily Campbell and E. M. W. Tillyard.[2] Tillyard famously argued that Shakespeare's histories should be seen as a dramatisation of the 'Tudor myth' and an endorsement of a particular concept of order, both in nature and society, which this influential critic had already explained in his book *The Elizabethan World Picture* (1943).[3]

While Robert Ornstein argued in 1972 that Shakespeare's work presented an aesthetic transcendence of political alliances,[4] the focus shifted back to politics in the 1980s and 1990s with the prevalent critical paradigms of New Historicism, Cultural Materialism and Gender Studies. Critics agreed that Tillyard's notion of Shakespeare celebrating the Tudor myth was much too facile and that the histories dramatise power struggles and negotiate the rules of the social world at the time when they were staged. There was less agreement, however, about the political views which the plays could be thought to express and in how far they reflect Shakespeare's own views. Simplifying the issues, one could say that American New Historicist critics such as Stephen Greenblatt emphasise the *containment* of social and political conflict in Elizabethan drama,[5] while British Cultural Materialists such as Jonathan Dollimore and Alan Sinfield emphasise the element of *subversion* in the plays.[6] As to Shakespeare's own views, they remain elusive.

One example of subversion in *Henry V* is the famous 'four-captains scene' (III. iii), which takes place at the beginning of King Henry's campaign in France, during the siege of the city of Harfleur. In this scene the Welsh captain Llewelyn, the Englishman Gower, the Irishman Mac Muiris and the Scotsman Jamey, testifying to the heterogeneous nature of the 'English' forces, embark on a dispute about the nation.[7] When Llewelyn begins, 'Captain Mac Muiris, I think, look you, under your correction, there is not many of your nation –' (III.iii.52f.), the Irishman furiously cuts in 'Of my nation? What ish my nation? Ish a villain and a basterd and a knave and a rascal? What ish my nation? Who talks of my nation?' (III.iii.54ff.). Mac Muiris's outburst is disconcerting and ambivalent: presumably, he expects a denigration of Ireland which he tries to forestall, not considering himself as a person of a different nation in the first place *and* finding it provoking that this should be suggested by a Welshman. This dispute foregrounds the political situation around 1599: Wales had long been colonised, with the English kings now even tracing their roots back to Wales (cf. *Henry V*, IV.vii.88–9), and a union with Scotland was looking likely because of the possible accession of James VI of Scotland to the English throne after Elizabeth's death. The continuing attempt to colonise Ireland, however, was at a particularly critical juncture as there had been a major Irish uprising against the English from the mid 1590s led by Hugh O'Neill, the Earl of Tyrone, and this had come to a head in 1599 when Elizabeth sent out a large force to try to suppress the insurrection, though this was only finally achieved in 1603. Many political and postcolonial readings of *Henry V* have foregrounded this scene, which acknowledges the presence of different nations in the English army,[8] emphasising conflict but leaving the matter curiously unresolved, with the question 'What ish my nation?' hanging in the air. In terms of seamless state propaganda, members of an army should not be seen quarrelling about political and military issues in the thick of the action.

As to the question of containment, Richard Helgerson offers an interesting variant of the argument that shifts the emphasis to the role of the theatre: he sees the histories project as a conscious move on the part of the Chamberlain's and later the King's Men to enhance their status as artists, leaving behind the less respectable elements of Elizabethan public theatre. The histories should thus be read as an expression of Shakespeare's upward mobility, written 'to secure for himself and his fellows a position that would no longer require such strategies'.[9] The history of the plays' reception endorses this argument according to Helgerson, since the histories 'have remained a paradigmatic expression of Anglo-British national self-understanding'.[10] Finally, Jean Howard and Phyllis Rackin supplement the debates about national identity with an important feminist reading of the histories, showing how a feminine dynastic logic, emphasised in the First Tetralogy with such figures as Margaret of Anjou, is contrasted with, and superseded by, an idea of the nation as a homosocial 'imagined community', most clearly expressed in *Henry V* with its evocation of the 'band of brothers' (IV.iii.60).[11] Even though critics over the decades have made a convincing case for the complexity of *Henry V*, the play has often been used for propaganda purposes, celebrating the astonishing English victory over the French at Agincourt in 1415 as an early example of English prowess and superiority (see, e.g., the wartime film still in Figure 7.1). I focus on this play in order to

Figure 7.1 Laurence Olivier in a publicity image for the 1944 film version of *Henry V.*

refine our understanding of Shakespeare's distinctive contribution to the genre. In particular, I argue that Shakespeare enlists the imaginative powers of the audience to bring history to life, and that, to this end, he parallels the mystery of successful performance with the aura and the mysticism surrounding kingship. Infused with spirituality, the natural body of the king is transformed into the mystical body of the monarch, even as the narrowly circumscribed stage action is expanded into historical events of epic proportions, with the playhouse as their emotional centre. The link for this instance of amplification is provided by the joint emphasis on play, performance and theatricality, which may have been suggested, beyond the general importance of theatricality in early modern culture, by the former Prince Hal's preference for games and gambles. The player thus plays a king who plays, as a deadly serious form of tennis match unfolds in the theatre of war.

Bringing History to Life

The very first words of *Henry V* highlight Shakespeare's artistic approach to the staging of history. The Prologue begins with an address to the muse: a conventional gesture in poetry, which is then rendered in such a unique and powerful way that it appears fresh and new.

> O for a muse of fire, that would ascend
> The brightest heaven of invention:
> A kingdom for a stage, princes to act,
> And monarchs to behold the swelling scene.
> Then should the warlike Harry, like himself,
> Assume the port of Mars, and at his heels,
> Leashed in like hounds, should famine, sword, and fire
> Crouch for employment. But pardon, gentles all,
> The flat, unraisèd spirits that hath dared
> On this unworthy scaffold to bring forth
> So great an object. Can this cock-pit hold
> The vasty fields of France? Or may we cram
> Within this wooden O the very casques
> That did affright the air at Azincourt? (Prologue, 1–14)

The subject of the play is nonchalantly introduced – this show will be about King Henry V's victory at Agincourt – but while the Prologue proceeds ostensibly to deplore the shortcomings of the stage, it becomes increasingly evident that the players will do ample justice to the royal action and the epic scale of the matter. Crucially, they enlist audience members to combine their imaginative forces to make this a success.[12] Although Shakespeare sometimes stays very close to the chronicles from which he drew his historical information, such as *Holinshed's Chronicles of England, Scotland and Ireland*, he strategically condenses events to make them more dramatic, glorifying certain figures and exaggerating the evils of others. For dramatic effect, the playwright compresses the historical series of military campaigns to one large battle, the battle of Agincourt, also considerably shortening the time between the battle and the peace treaty with France and the betrothal to the French princess. Every element that might diminish the wonder of the victory is left out – for example, issues of military technology emphasised in Holinshed, such as the English archers' superiority to the French, who fought on horseback.

In order to effect the shifts of time and space which fly in the face of any classic idea of the dramatic unities of time, place and action, an epic element in the form of a Chorus is introduced to address the audience, summarise, explain and comment on events, and, most importantly, to ensure and sustain the audience's active engagement in the drama. Cunningly, the theatre's limitations are repeatedly foregrounded only to be transcended. The Chorus's evocation of a muse of fire throws into relief the shortcomings of the stage: 'pardon, gentles all, / The flat unraisèd spirits that hath dared / On this unworthy scaffold to bring forth / So great an object' (Prologue, 8–11). Yet the following (rhetorical) question offers a challenge: 'Can this cock-pit hold / The vasty fields of France?' The short and narrow vowels of 'cock-pit' are followed by the long-drawn-out 'hold the vasty fields of France'. The representation of spaciousness insinuated by Shakespeare's neologism 'vasty' suggests that the answer to this question is 'Yes, it can!' But it will only work if the audience plays its part, letting the players work on its 'imaginary forces':

> Suppose within the girdle of these walls
> Are now confined two mighty monarchies,
> Whose high uprearèd and abutting fronts
> The perilous Narrow Ocean parts asunder.
> Piece out our imperfections with your thoughts:
> Into a thousand parts divide one man,
> And make imaginary püissance.
> Think when we talk of horses, that you see them,
> Printing their proud hoofs i'th' receiving earth;
> For 'tis your thoughts that now must deck our kings ... (Prologue, 19–28)

This passage is particularly effective because it combines *energeia*, the dynamic evocation of movement, and *enargeia*, placing vivid images in front of the mind's eye, for example in the sublime image of a dangerously narrow sea trying desperately, as it were, to keep two huge cliffs from crashing into each other. Fired by the dramatic language, the imagination of the audience, flatteringly addressed as 'gentles all', needs to supply what is missing in the theatre. In order to allow the audience's imagination full play, an extensive service is provided: 'to France shall we convey you safe, / And bring you back, charming the Narrow Seas / To give you gentle pass' (II.0.37–9). Throughout the play the Chorus exhorts the audience to 'Suppose that you have seen' (III.0.3): 'Play with your fancies' (III.0.7), 'Hear the shrill whistle' (III.0.9), 'behold the threaden sails' (III.0.10), 'Follow, follow!' (III.0.17), 'Work, work your thoughts' (III.0.25), 'entertain conjecture' (IV.0.1), 'Heave him [the king] away upon your wingèd thoughts' (V.0.8), 'behold, / In the quick forge and working-house of thought' (V.0.22–3), and, finally, 'In your fair minds let this acceptance take' (Epilogue, 14). This potent mixture of imperatives, lively images and flattery invites, or even forces, the audience to participate in the project of bringing alive English history. It incites the audience to do what the players do: to play a dangerous game, thus inviting complicity, and putting part of the blame for a successful and potentially treasonous evocation of royalty on the audience. The First Player impersonates the king himself, a fascinating figure at once omnipresent and elusive – all one can have, as the Chorus remarks, is 'a little touch of Harry in the night' (IV.0.47).

Formally, the histories contain elements of comedy and tragedy, and for the depiction of monarchs, especially in the earlier work, Shakespeare draws on the so-called *de casibus* tragedy – the story of the rise and fall of mighty men such as King Richard III, as they are borne up on the 'wheel of Fortune' and hurled down again. Far from just serving an antiquarian purpose, the plays present narratives of history which have a contemporary application. This is epitomised by an episode towards the end of Elizabeth's reign: on the eve of the Earl of Essex's attempt at rebellion in 1601, members of his entourage ordered a performance of *Richard II* which stages the deposition and murder of a king, and Queen Elizabeth is reported later to have remarked to her historian William Lambarde: 'I am Richard II, know ye not that?'[13] Incidentally, she was not; Essex, who, unusually for the history plays, gets a direct and favourable mention in *Henry V* (V.0.30–4), failed in his rebellion and was executed. Perhaps the queen and her advisors had learnt some lessons from history – and from drama.

According to Holinshed, the queen also told Parliament in 1586 that '[w]e princes are set on stages in the sight and view of all the world dulie observed'.[14] This idea, drawing on the concept of the *teatrum mundi*, the notion that all the world is a stage, suggests a reason why the theatre proved the perfect medium for an exploration of English history, and, by extension, of contemporary politics. There is an emphasis on theatricality in the early modern period, on the display of power and on self-fashioning,[15] which made the theatre a privileged site for inquiries into the nature of society and the mechanisms of power.[16] One reason for the importance of visibility and display lies in the medieval notion of kingship according to which the king has two bodies, a mortal, biological *body natural* and an immortal *body politic*.[17] The king derives his power from God, and his body has to be displayed in splendour in order literally to embody kingship as an institution in the body politic. In *Henry V* Shakespeare explores this dual nature of kingship. On the one hand, he makes much of the mysticism surrounding the figure of the king, carefully establishing the special aura of the monarch from the beginning – the presence of the Bishops who rhetorically prepare the ground for a completely reformed character, the solemn atmosphere, the weighty affairs of state, Prince Hal's newly acquired dignity, his conspicuous use of measured language and the *pluralis majestatis*. To drive this home, the Bishop of Canterbury gives an account of Prince Hal's spiritual transformation:

> The breath no sooner left his father's body
> But that his wildness, mortified in him,
> Seemed to die too. Yea, at that very moment
> Consideration like an angel came
> And whipped th'offending Adam out of him.
> Leaving his body as a paradise
> T'envelop and contain celestial spirits. (I.i.26–32)

God's grace confers majesty. On the other hand, it is pointed out in the play that the king is just a man. This is a rhetorical exercise in *argumentum in utramque partem* (debating two sides of an issue), often used in early modern plays due to its dramatic potential, and, from this perspective, we can see the structural necessity of the 'disguised ruler' scene in the fourth act where the king walks through his camp unrecognised on the eve of the decisive battle, listening to opinions that nobody could openly express to him. Ironically, the king himself presents the argument that the king is only human, like himself. 'His ceremonies laid by, in his nakedness he appears but a man, and though his affections are higher mounted than ours, yet when they stoop, they stoop with the like wing' (IV.i.99–101). In *Henry V* Shakespeare cunningly parallels this debate about kingship with the issue of representation in drama: as God breathes the holy spirit into the king, transforming him in the process, so the audience must breathe life into the characters on stage to make them real with the help of the imagination. The Prologue's exhortations promote a kind of chiastic entanglement between spectators and players: even as spectators commit imaginary treason by taking the actor for the king, treason becomes topical on stage, and even as spectators are invited to play, they feel the danger of the game that unfolds in their presence.

Harry's Game

The king in particular is a player with a propensity for dangerous play. This is how Shakespeare deals with what Katharine Eisaman Maus has described as a kind of dramatic Midas problem: 'how to interest an audience in a man who has, or wins, everything – whose life seems an unbroken series of successes'.[18] In order to create suspense, there is an emphasis on the odds and the challenges which make the success of the French campaign unlikely. Unity is repeatedly evoked on the level of rhetoric while it is dramatically deconstructed. Before Henry departs for France, he unmasks three aristocratic traitors belonging to his closest circle; troops have to be left at home in order to prevent the Scots from raiding England in the king's absence; Henry's former companions from his irresponsible Eastcheap days (and nights) are shown as very reluctant soldiers, one of them even being executed for looting; and, as we have seen with regard to the 'four-captains scene', the forces are made up of ethnically heterogeneous and quarrelling factions. When the common soldiers are given an opportunity to voice their fears on the eve of the battle of Agincourt, the king, in disguise, enters into a dispute with the soldier Williams, who reasons that the king is responsible for the fate and the soul of every soldier he leads into battle. This is a moment of insecurity and potentially eroding loyalty which can hardly be blotted out entirely by the king's subsequent rousing rhetoric and the joyful account of victory against the odds. Moreover, conquest and violent domination are sexualised and figured as rape, as in the 'half-achievèd Harfleur' (III.iii.77), in a way that could well be seen to qualify the charm of Henry's wooing as he courts the French princess Katherine.

All this, also recalling the initial debate about the rightfulness of the cause, casts doubt on the campaign and makes the king a profoundly ambivalent figure. Norman Rabkin has suggested that *Henry V* can be seen as a picture puzzle: viewed one way, showing Henry as a radiant, positive, gallant and charming figure; viewed the other way, showing Henry as a cold, calculating and brutal representative of a violent power politics.[19] Indeed, there is evidence for both views in the play. Henry is a mild, graceful and god-fearing king with high moral standards who carefully ponders his decisions, explains them eloquently, stands by his men and treats them as brothers, who does not ask anything of others he would not be prepared to give himself and who displays considerable charm and humour when trying to turn a politically necessary marriage into a love match. Henry is also a cold-blooded and brutal Machiavellian politician and warlord who does not hesitate to execute an old friend and who uses his rhetorical skill to utter blood-curdling threats, to reject all responsibility for involving his men in a dangerous campaign, and to tease or torture people, such as his future wife or the soldier Williams, with the games he plays before submitting them to his will, like a cat playing with a mouse.

This picture-puzzle quality is not only created through a succession of contradictory elements, as when Henry's threats to Harfleur (III.iii.70–113) are followed by the order to 'Use mercy to them all' (III.iii.123), but also through a dramatisation which invites alternative interpretations. For example, it is possible to see the Harfleur speech as the desperate bluff of someone who would never have done, and could never have done, what he threatened to do. Similarly, the order to kill all captured French soldiers could be seen as a necessary act of self-preservation in the face of a renewed attack. Unlike Richard III, who recalls the rather talkative medieval vice figure, or Hamlet, who is often seen to embody an equally talkative modern subjectivity, the king does not tell the audience what he thinks. While Rabkin's reading makes sense, I agree with Joel Altman, who criticises Rabkin's suggestion of the picture puzzle as too static and focused on a binary opposition. Altman argues that, rather than just showing both sides of one coin, as it were, Shakespeare finds an innovative way to dramatise the relationship between the player/king and the audience/people and that the emotional energy thus created can be channelled into aggression towards the enemy. Instead of looking on passively, pondering a Janus-faced character, the audience is drawn into the vortex of Henry's personality and the dynamics of his campaign.[20]

At the beginning of the drama, the French Dauphin taunts Henry by sending him tennis balls. Far from rejecting the game metaphor, the king promises that the matter will become serious once he starts playing:

When we have matched our rackets to these balls,
We will in France, by God's grace, play a set
Shall strike his father's crown into the hazard.
Tell him he hath made a match with such a wrangler
That all the courts of France will be disturbed
With chases.

...

And tell the pleasant Prince this mock of his
Hath turned his balls to gunstones, and his soul
Shall stand sore chargèd for the wasteful vengeance
That shall fly with them ... (I.ii.261–6 and 281–4)

The Dauphin has served, and Henry will return cannon balls. Throughout the play, there are instances of the king's taste for playing. Rather than dealing with the three traitors in a straightforward manner, he plays around, finally handing them dispatches which turn out to contain their death sentence. Before the battle, he gets into a quarrel with soldier Williams, exchanging gloves with him by way of a challenge. When he passes the glove on to create confusion, the audience gets a glimpse of the old Prince Hal, possibly recalling his pranks in Eastcheap, lately seen in *Henry IV*. The problem is that once the game is translated into the register of sovereign power, there is no level playing field. Moving on from 'glove plot' to 'love plot', Henry playfully woos the French Princess Katherine, who, there is no doubt about it, will have to marry him anyway. So here is Shakespeare's solution to the 'Midas-problem' identified by Maus: Henry is unpredictable – dangerous and attractive, courageous and subtle, both mature and childish, and, importantly, both human and divine, so that the focus is not on the fact that his forces won the battle of Agincourt, which most people in the audience can be expected to know, but on the way things are played out. This is Harry's game, and the winner is William Shakespeare.

One main element of the king's attractiveness is his rhetorical skill. This is emphasised in the very first scene, as the bishops plan their machinations and the Archbishop of Canterbury says:

> [W]hen he speaks,
> The air, a chartered libertine, is still,
> And the mute wonder lurketh in men's ears
> To steal his sweet and honeyed sentences:
> So that the art and practic part of life
> Must be the mistress to this theoric. (I.i.48–53)

Through his speech, Canterbury suggests, the king achieves a felicitous marriage between thinking and doing, between *vita contemplativa* and *vita activa*. His rhetoric is thus effective; it is a kind of action rather than just verbiage. In the play, this successful rhetoric takes various forms: there are a number of memorable closing couplets, such as 'Therefore let every man now task his thought, / That this fair action may on foot be brought' (I.ii.309–10), along with retorts such as 'tell the Dauphin / His jest will savour but of shallow wit / When thousands weep more than did laugh at it' (I.ii.294–6). Syntax is stretched here, so that the king can punch his monosyllables into the air with perfect emphasis and economy. Beyond this, there are some public speeches, the most famous one probably the St Crispin's Day speech, which is a triumph of blank verse often savoured out of context:

> We few, we happy few, we band of brothers.
> For he today that sheds his blood with me
> Shall be my brother; be he ne'er so vile,
> This day shall gentle his condition.
> And gentlemen in England now abed
> Shall think themselves accursed they were not here,
> And hold their manhoods cheap whiles any speaks
> That fought with us upon Saint Crispin's day. (IV.iii.60–7)

This is the famous evocation of an 'imagined community' of the nation, promising upward mobility and eternal fame, 'in their flowing cups freshly remembered' (IV.iii.55), to those about to fight (Figure 7.2). Again, there is an element of play, since Henry effectively asks his soldiers to take a wager on their lives. If they 'outliv[e] this day and com[e] safe home' (IV.iii.41), they will be able to tell how they were on familiar terms with noblemen, and with their sovereign. The small number of fighters is rather an advantage, since it makes victory more heroic, and cowards should depart, as Henry says, since '[w]e would not die in that man's company /

Figure 7.2 Agincourt battle scene in a 1962 production of Shakespeare's *Henry V* by the National Youth Theatre at Sadler's Wells.

That fears his fellowship to die with us' (IV.iii.38–9). Regardless of what Henry V really said before the battle of Agincourt, Shakespeare's dramatisation hits home, since there have always been those who have risked their lives for golden words.

It is one major aspect of Shakespeare's achievement that he creates a character of such ambivalence and complexity that he remains perennially interesting, despite the 'Midas-problem'. The scope of the play with its concomitant entertainment potential is extremely wide: it offers rousing and sometimes dazzling rhetoric, intimate access to affairs of state, low comedy in the scenes with Pistol and Llewelyn, as well as romance, featuring a victorious hero returning from the fight to woo a beautiful princess. At the same time the play ponders complex political issues such as the question of the subjection of Ireland or the Archbishop's explanation of the Salic Law (I.ii.33–95) touching rules of royal succession, which were topical in view of the fact that the queen was old and without issue. Where would the royal spirit go once it had left her body? In *Henry V*, Shakespeare turns the lack of formal conventions for history plays to good account. Through a structural integration of reflections on dramatic art with the issue of successful kingship and the skilful deployment of the Chorus, which supplies continuity and orientation and mediates between the staged events and the audience, Shakespeare introduces variety and complexity without dissipating the energy required in a play that deals with historical action on the grand scale.

In this encounter between history and drama the theatre emerges triumphant, since historical material is subjected to the needs and dynamics of the stage without a conspicuous loss of verisimilitude. Or in other words, theatre writes history. Shakespeare managed to create a play which gained a secure place within cultural memory, dramatically forging an 'imagined community' of the nation. The ultimate trajectory may thus be an exploration, or even a celebration of English history and identity, but the emotional centre is the playhouse. Much depends, therefore, on how the play is staged. It can descend into jingoism, but handled with care, it can also expand into a theatrical interrogation of power and violence, sending audiences home pondering the possible justification for war as well as its horrors. To finish with Henry's timely words of caution to the over-subtle Archbishop: '[T]ake heed how you impawn our person, / How you awake our sleeping sword of war' (I.ii.21–2).

NOTES

1. There used to be ten histories attributed to Shakespeare, including *The Life and Death of King John* (c. 1594–6), a kind of prologue covering the earliest period with events from around the year 1200, and *The Life of Henry the Eighth* (1612–13), written later during the reign of King James I in collaboration with John Fletcher. Subsequently, the collaborative *Edward III*, staged around 1592 and printed anonymously in 1596, was added to the Shakespeare canon. See Eric Sams (ed.), *Shakespeare's* Edward III: *An Early Play Restored to the Canon* (New Haven and London: Yale University Press, 1996). For a helpful introduction to the histories see, e.g., Warren Chernaik, *The Cambridge Introducion to Shakespeare's History Plays* (Cambridge University Press, 2007).
2. Lily B. Campbell, *Shakespeare's 'Histories': Mirrors of Elizabethan Policy* (San Marino: Huntington Library, 1947); E. M. W. Tillyard, *Shakespeare's History Plays* (London: Chatto & Windus, 1944).
3. E. M. W. Tillyard, *The Elizabethan World Picture* (London: Chatto & Windus, 1943).
4. Robert Ornstein, *A Kingdom for a Stage: The Achievement of Shakespeare's History Plays* (Cambridge, MA: Harvard University Press, 1972).
5. Stephen Greenblatt, 'Invisible Bullets', in *Shakespearean Negotiations: The Circulation of Social Energy in Renaissance England* (Oxford: Clarendon Press, 1988), pp. 21–65.
6. Jonathan Dollimore and Alan Sinfield, 'History and Ideology: The Instance of *Henry V*', in John Drakakis (ed.), *Alternative Shakespeares* (London: Routledge, 1985), pp. 210–31. For a summary of the debate see Louis Montrose, *The Purpose of Playing: Shakespeare and the Cultural Politics of the Elizabethan Theatre* (University of Chicago Press, 1996), pp. 8–12.
7. William Shakespeare, *Henry V*, ed. Gary Taylor et al., New Oxford Shakespeare (Oxford University Press, 2016); subsequent references are incorporated in the main text.

8. E.g. David Cairns and Shaun Richards, *Writing Ireland: Colonialism, Nationalism and Culture* (Manchester University Press, 1988); Graham Holderness, '"What ish my nation" – Shakespeare and National Identities', *Textual Practice* 5 (1991), 74–93; David J. Baker, '"Wildehirissheman": Colonialist Representation in *Henry V*', *English Literary Renaissance* 22 (1992), 37–61; Andrew Murphy, 'Ireland as Foreign and Familiar in Shakespeare's Histories', in Ton Hoenselaars (ed.), *Shakespeare's History Plays: Performance, Translation and Adaptation in Britain and Abroad* (Cambridge University Press, 2004), pp. 42–59.

9. Richard Helgerson, 'Staging Exclusion', in *Forms of Nationhood: The Elizabethan Writing of England* (University of Chicago Press, 1992), pp. 193–245 (p. 199).

10. Ibid., p. 204.

11. Jean E. Howard and Phyllis Rackin, *Engendering a Nation: A Feminist Account of Shakespeare's English Histories* (London: Routledge, 1997). For the notion of 'imagined community' see Benedict Anderson, *Imagined Communities: Reflections on the Origin and Spread of Nationalism* (London: Verso, 1983). For the concept of the homosocial, see Eve Kosofsky Sedgewick, *Between Men: English Literature and Male Homosocial Desire* (New York: Columbia University Press, 1985).

12. Pamela Mason also elaborates on this in '*Henry V*: "the quick forge and working house of thought"', in Michael Hattaway (ed.), *The Cambridge Companion to Shakespeare's History Plays* (Cambridge University Press, 2002), pp. 177–92.

13. See Jason Scott-Warren, 'Was Elizabeth I Richard II? The Authenticity of Lambarde's "Conversation"', *Review of English Studies* 64 (2012), 208–30.

14. 'A Report of Hir Majesties most gratious answer, delivered by hir selfe verballie … in hir chamber of presence at Richmond, the twelfe daie of November 1586', in *Holinshed's Chronicles of England, Scotland, and Ireland*, 6 vols (1808; New York: AMS Press, 1965), vol. IV, p. 934.

15. See Stephen Greenblatt, *Renaissance Self-Fashioning from More to Shakespeare* (University of Chicago Press, 1980).

16. See Montrose, *Purpose of Playing*.

17. See Ernst Kantorowicz, *The King's Two Bodies: A Study of Mediaeval Political Theology* (Princeton University Press, 1957).

18. Katharine Eisaman Maus, '*Henry V*', in Stephen Greenblatt et al. (eds), *The Norton Shakespeare* (New York: W. W. Norton, 1997), pp. 1445–53 (p. 1452).

19. Norman Rabkin, 'Rabbits, Ducks and Henry V', *Shakespeare Quarterly* 28 (1977), 279–96.

20. Joel Altman, '"Vile participation": The Amplification of Violence in the Theatre of *Henry V*', *Shakespeare Quarterly* 42 (1991), 1–32.

CRITICAL REFLECTIONS AND FURTHER STUDY

In my essay on *Henry V* as a prime example of Shakespeare's dramatic achievement in the history plays, I argue that there are scenes in the play that undermine an uncritically patriotic and jingoistic reading. This is true with respect to the version of the play printed in the Folio edition of Shakespeare's works that was posthumously published by colleagues in 1623 – an almost unprecedented honour, given that plays were not treated as works of 'Literature' worth preserving beyond their life on the stage, and evidence that Shakespeare had a high reputation as a dramatist in his own time. His colleague Ben Jonson, who also furnished a dedication for the Folio edition, is usually seen as the first playwright to publish his own *Works* in 1616. Like many plays by Shakespeare, however, *Henry V* exists in various versions: it was first printed in an unauthorised Quarto edition in 1600, which was reprinted in 1602 and 1619. In this version, which may have been put together from memory by actors, many of the more critical, violent or subversive scenes are missing. Moreover, the play was not often performed in Shakespeare's lifetime – since dating through internal reference in this case is quite easy, we know that it was first performed in the summer of 1599, and there is evidence of a court performance in 1605. In view of this, it is important to realise how little we know about what contemporary audiences actually heard and saw, and that the texts of early modern drama are notoriously unstable.

Much effort has consequently been put into the study of textual variants as well as of early modern theatre as an artistic, economic and social enterprise, including such issues as censorship, gender, authorship and the practice of dramatic collaboration. These are rewarding themes for further study, for which an ideal first port of call is often a recent critical edition. There are many to choose from: the Arden Shakespeare published by Bloomsbury, now developing a fourth series, emphasises textual variants and editorial issues in their main editions, supplementing this with separate editions suitable for performance. This editorial work is very substantial; for example, just the authoritative three-text edition of *Hamlet* published in 2016 runs to almost seven hundred pages. Cambridge University Press in turn publishes a series entitled Shakespeare in Production that is focused on the stage history of the plays while the Oxford Shakespeare offers a critical take on the Shakespeare canon. For an excellent overview of Shakespeare's contribution to the history play as a genre, I recommend *The Cambridge Companion to Shakespeare's History Plays*, edited by Michael Hattaway (2006). Linked to the question of canonicity, Shakespearean afterlives also offer a fascinating field of study. Emma Depledge shows, for example, how it happened that Shakespeare was established as a key author in the late seventeenth century in her *Shakespeare's Rise to Cultural Prominence* (Cambridge University Press, 2018).

While Lukas Erne and others have made – or revived – a case for a 'literary' Shakespeare whose work asks to be read (Lukas Erne, *Shakespeare as Literary Dramatist* (Cambridge University Press, 2013)), the plays' principal purpose was of course to be performed, and there are many productions of Shakespeare's plays, including film versions, that offer a rich, and continually evolving field of study. Works such as William B. Worthen's *Shakespeare and the Authority of*

Performance (Cambridge University Press, 1997) register, and promote, a turn to 'performance criticism' in the late twentieth century that rejects the notion of performance as an ephemeral addition to a sacrosanct text in favour of taking each production seriously as an actualisation of a text that functions like a score in need of interpretation and embodiment. Just as Shakespeare's plays were topical when he wrote them, lending themselves to contemporary application, they were subsequently made to answer the needs of audiences and performers and must now speak to today's audiences if they are to remain relevant. From this dynamic, 'progressive' point of view, performances with a strong period flavour would be seen as intrinsically conservative expressions of 'bardolatry', i.e., the worship of Shakespeare as a canonised author served up in aspic.

Undeniably, looking at the history of performances of *Henry V*, the play was most frequently used as a vehicle for national pride and jingoism at crucial moments in British history; a practice that only changed around the middle of the twentieth century, when John Barton and Peter Hall staged the play in 1964 at the Royal Shakespeare Theatre in Stratford as an anti-war drama. This focus on national identity is of course also a reason why the play was never as successful abroad as it was in Britain. One of the most radical productions in the critical vein was directed by Michael Bogdanov for the English Shakespeare Company in 1986. In an interview with the *Sun* newspaper, Bogdanov commented: 'Imperialism encourages jingoism. So the Falklands. So Agincourt. "Fuck the Frogs"' (*King Henry V*, Shakespeare in Production, ed. Emma Smith (Cambridge University Press, 2002), p. 73). Recently, the Royal Shakespeare Company appears to have reverted to the earlier practice of national celebration. The latest production of *Henry V* in Stratford, directed by Gregory Doran, was staged in 2015 to mark the 600th anniversary of the battle of Agincourt, and was then transferred to the Barbican Theatre in London as part of 'King and Country: Shakespeare's Great Cycle of Kings' to mark the 400th anniversary of Shakespeare's death in 2016. Strong on period flavour and weak on politics, this may well be the production for the age of Brexit. For the study of film, *The Cambridge Companion to Shakespeare on Film* (2007), edited by Russell Jackson, offers an excellent point of departure, discussing the practice and politics of adaptation as well as individual examples. While the study of textual variants and the culture of the early modern theatre takes us back to the past, to Shakespeare's London around 1600, the trajectory of performance criticism is the present, and the future: such are the wide horizons, the challenges and the joys of the study of early modern drama.

8 Poems and Contexts: The Case of Henry Vaughan

ROBERT WILCHER

Abstract

When Henry Vaughan's collection of religious lyrics, *Silex Scintillans* (1650 and 1655), was slowly recovered from oblivion during the first half of the nineteenth century, it was initially absorbed into public consciousness as part of the tradition of devotional poetry associated with George Herbert's much more widely known volume, *The Temple* (1633). It was also accommodated to nineteenth-century taste by reading it selectively in the contexts of Romantic nature poetry and the tradition of Christian mysticism. Gradually, other contexts were brought into play, but reluctance to admit the significance of the political situation in Vaughan's part of South Wales for the meaning and value of his poetry continued until the later decades of the twentieth century. Even though it contains a vivid evocation of the horrors of civil war, 'The Constellation' was commonly interpreted as an expression of Vaughan's belief in the harmony between God and the world of Nature. Once the political element was recognised as central to the poem's strategy, however, various details were opened up to reinterpretation. Two more examples, 'The Proffer' and 'The Seed growing secretly', are analysed to demonstrate not only that Vaughan's poetic enterprise was deeply implicated in the predicament of loyal supporters of church and king in Breconshire under the Puritan Commonwealth, but also that no single context is enough to unlock all the nuances of his complex poetic art.

I

Unlike George Herbert's *The Temple*, which went through thirteen editions between 1633 and 1709, Henry Vaughan's collection of devotional lyrics, *Silex Scintillans*, first published in 1650 and augmented in 1655, was not reprinted for nearly two hundred years (Figure 8.1). Herbert's poetry was not published again until 1799, but from then on there were regular editions throughout the nineteenth century.[1] By contrast, Henry Vaughan emerged from eighteenth-century oblivion very slowly. Four of his devotional lyrics saw the light of day in 1819 in Thomas

Figure 8.1 Frontispiece to the first edition of Henry Vaughan's *Silex Scintillans* (1650). Vaughan styled himself 'Silurist' in reference to the ancient British Silures associated with his home region of south-east Wales and the border country.

Campbell's *Specimens of the British Poets* and a few more had made their way into collections of religious verse by the time *Silex Scintillans* was reprinted in 1847. There were further editions of the religious poems during the nineteenth century, but Vaughan's secular poetry did not become widely available until E. K. Chambers edited the complete poems for the Muses' Library in 1896.[2]

These different publication histories had important consequences for the ways in which the two poets were assimilated into Victorian literary consciousness.

In spite of changing poetic and intellectual fashions, *The Temple* became established during the nineteenth century as a benchmark for later devotional verse. Vaughan's work, by contrast, was gradually popularised in small selections from *Silex Scintillans* edited by Anglican clergymen. For example, he was represented by six poems in the Revd John Mitford's *Sacred Specimens, Selected from the Early English Poets* (1827) and the Revd Richard Cattermole's *Sacred Poetry of the Seventeenth Century* (1836) offered a total of thirteen, including four of Mitford's choices. Furthermore, the first modern editor of *Silex Scintillans*, H. F. Lyte, was a member of the clergy, as was the Revd Alexander Grosart, editor of the first complete works; and Henry Beeching, who supplied a critical introduction for the first volume of the Muses' Library edition, was a canon of the Church of England. This meant that Vaughan was initially presented to the reading public as a writer of reassuringly devotional and didactic poems, some of which were doctored to make them suitable for consumption in the drawing rooms of pious households. Both Campbell and Cattermole printed only the first eighteen lines of 'The Rainbow', highlighting the 'Covenant ... 'twixt *All* and *One*' symbolised by this natural phenomenon and omitting subsequent references to 'blood & drunkeness' and the daughters of Lot, who 'lay with their sire' while Sodom burned.[3] 'Christs Nativity' was shorn of its second section by Mitford and Cattermole, so that the joyful celebration of 'the Birth-day of thy King' stands alone in their anthologies, without the concluding complaint that the Puritan authorities have abolished such red-letter days as Good Friday and Christmas from the liturgical calendar: 'Alas, my God! Thy birth now here / Must not be numbred in the year.'[4] Cattermole was typical of nineteenth-century readers in framing his judgement on this 'truly "sacred" poet' by invoking a familiar touchstone: 'there is much in Vaughan not unworthy of George Herbert.'[5]

II

Other poems that were given early exposure, and so helped to shape the contexts in which Vaughan's poetry would be processed critically, appealed to the nineteenth-century passion for nature. One of the four examples thought worthy of public attention by Campbell consisted of the first two stanzas of 'The Timber', which – cut adrift from the rest of the poem – satisfy the requirements of a Romantic sensibility:

> Sure thou didst flourish once! and many Springs,
> Many bright mornings, much dew, many showers
> Past ore thy head: many light *Hearts* and *Wings*
> Which now are dead, lodg'd in thy living bowers.

And still a new succession sings and flies;
Fresh Groves grow up, and their green branches shoot
Towards the old and still enduring skies,
While the low *Violet* thrives at their root.[6]

The twelve stanzas he omitted, however, are in a very different vein of moralistic commentary about sin and remorse. Several of the other poems in Cattermole's selection – notably 'The Shower', 'The Dawning' and 'Unprofitablenes' – contain elements that later critics would adduce as evidence of Vaughan's empathy with the processes and creatures of the natural world. And another of his choices – 'The Retreate' – was the only poem by Vaughan to find a place in the first edition of Francis Palgrave's *The Golden Treasury* (1863), successive editions of which did much to define popular taste in poetry. It was this poem, with its supposed influence on Wordsworth's view of childhood in the *Immortality Ode*, that became the major exhibit in attempts to identify Vaughan as a forerunner of the great Romantic poet and so establish another context within which to make sense of his work. Indeed, the subsequent history of Vaughan criticism can be seen as a quest for alternative or additional contexts that might help to elucidate the character and purpose of his literary activity. Later lines of investigation into the sources of his poetic inspiration and practice include the tradition of Christian mysticism, alchemy and the Hermetic philosophy pursued by his twin brother Thomas Vaughan, Counter-Reformation methods of meditation, the Jesuit-inspired emblem books of the seventeenth century, biblical allusion and typology, the 'vitalist' moment of reaction against Baconian materialism and Cartesian dualism in the 1650s, and the bardic tradition in ancient Welsh poetry.[7]

III

As a means of illustrating how the interpretation of a poem may be limited or opened up by the contextual information that is brought into play, the rest of this essay will concentrate on one particular context – the political situation in south Wales between 1648 and 1655, the years during which the poems collected in *Silex Scintillans* were being composed. It was a long time before this perspective was accepted into the critical discourse about Vaughan. Louise Guiney, one of Vaughan's earliest champions, expressed regret that 'his holiest raptures are continually deflected by the transient intrusion of questions of the day'.[8] F. E. Hutchinson, whose biography of Vaughan included a chapter on 'The Puritan Régime', was also reluctant to allow the political dimension of Vaughan's work to disturb established ways of approaching it and preferred to base 'a just assessment of the poetic value of *Silex Scintillans*' on 'those poems which are unspoiled by topical allusions' and 'independent of time and place and circumstance'.[9] Indeed, until the later decades of the twentieth century the public context of Vaughan's religious poetry was ignored entirely or lamented as an unwelcome intrusion. For example, one mid-century critic insisted that his poems were in no way 'concerned with the political aspects of the great controversy' and that the only significance of the Civil Wars for his poetry was that they 'deepened his religious life and helped him to withdraw into himself to communicate with Nature and the God of Nature'.[10] Another interpreted the contrast between 'the ordered motions of the stars' and 'the social chaos of his times' in 'The Constellation' as an expression of Vaughan's belief that 'Nature remained in harmony with Heaven' whatever 'man' might do to spoil 'the divinely-ordained pattern of being'.[11] The phrase 'social chaos' scarcely does justice, however, to the stanzas that contain his most vivid description of the religious and political conflict that tore his world apart:

> But here Commission'd by a black self-wil,
>   The sons the father kil,
> The Children Chase the mother, and would heal
>   The wounds they give, by crying, zeale.
>
> Then Cast her bloud, and tears upon thy book
>   Where they for fashion look,
> And like that Lamb which had the Dragons voice,
>   Seem mild, but are known by their noise.
>
> Thus by our lusts disorder'd into wars
>   Our guides prove wandring stars,
> Which for these mists, and black days were reserv'd,
>   What time we from our first love swerv'd.[12]

As late as 1981 there was a complaint that these lines about the Civil Wars 'violate the pattern of the poem' by moving its focus from humankind in general to the contemporary manifestation of the 'lusts' of 'Englishmen'.[13] Even this disapproving glance at the historical context is not specific enough, however, since Vaughan was reflecting the 'exceptionally' harsh rule of local Puritan officials in Wales, so that *Silex Scintillans* can be justly described as exhibiting 'the form and pressure of that particular experience in that particular place'.[14]

By the later decades of the twentieth century the significance of the historical context for both the interpretation and the evaluation of *Silex Scintillans* had begun to receive attention. In 1972 James Simmonds was insisting that 'the distractions of the state during the 1640s and 1650s' were among Vaughan's 'abiding' preoccupations not only in the secular satires but also in 'the sacred poems themselves'. This allowed him to assert that 'the central theme' of 'The Constellation' was the 'satiric attack' on the results of Puritan fanaticism, for which Vaughan's 'personal response to Nature' in the opening contemplation of 'the order and obedience of the stars' was merely the preliminary foil.[15] Once the poem has been situated in its contemporary context, it becomes evident that 'here' in the first of the civil war stanzas not only means 'on earth' (as opposed to the stars in heaven) but also refers to the poet's precise location in south Wales. Then various images in that stanza can be seen to have specific referents: the generic 'father' is also Charles I, executed in January 1649 a few months before the poem was written, and the 'mother' is the Church of England – the 'deare Mother' of George Herbert's 'The British Church', who speaks for herself in Vaughan's poem of the same title, lamenting over her 'ravish'd looks / Slain flock, and pillag'd fleeces'.[16] Those who consult God's holy book merely 'for fashion' and are now leading the state astray into 'mists, and black days' can be identified by the military connotations of 'Commission'd' and the negative word 'zeale' (commonly used in anti-Puritan satire) as the revolutionary faction in charge of the New Model Army and the Westminster Parliament. In the last three stanzas of the poem Vaughan once more invokes the 'obedience' of the constellations, but now as a model for a future political state – 'that we may move / In order, peace, and love' and become 'an humble, holy nation' – and prays that the Church (in her alternative personification as the 'spouse' of Christ) may appear once more in the 'perfect, and pure dress' that harks back to the 'fine aspect in fit aray' of Herbert's 'deare Mother'.

It was not long before *Silex Scintillans* as a whole was being reinterpreted as a personal and political response to the destruction of the Church of England, the defeat and trial of the king, and the wholesale expulsion of Welsh Anglican clergy – twenty-five in Breconshire alone – in the wake of the Act for the Better Propagation of the Gospel in Wales passed by Parliament in March 1650. One article traced a journey from 'hopelessness' via a call for 'the revival of spirits' among royalists to 'a programme of patient watchfulness' sustained by the expectation that Christ would soon return to redeem the earth or Charles II to restore the monarchy and Church of England.[17] Another attributed the 'uneasy dynamic between the two parts of *Silex Scintillans*' to the strategy of adapting the 'isolated, contemplative self' constructed in the 1650 poems to serve the more political purpose of the 1655 volume in a campaign of 'active Welsh resistance to Parliamentary rule during the early 1650s'.[18]

IV

To demonstrate in more detail how the interpretation of a Vaughan poem can be largely determined by the context in which it is read, whether that is a literary or hermeneutical tradition or a set of historical circumstances, I shall examine two poems that offer different degrees of purchase for the reader in search of political meanings. 'The Proffer' is the fifth of the items added to the 1655 *Silex Scintillans*. It follows two poems on the Ascension, which look forward to the return of Christ to 'judge this world' and 'rebuild man'; the untitled elegy 'They are all gone into the world of light', which envisions the beloved dead 'walking in an Air of glory' and prays for the resumption of the poet's spirit from 'this world of thrall'; and 'White Sunday', a meditation on the significance of Pentecost, which mocks the claim to divine inspiration made by itinerant preachers in Wales known as the 'new lights' and closes with a plea to be refined by God's 'fire' from the 'common' ignominy represented by '*Balaams* hire' (an allusion to an Old Testament figure who was offered a bribe to betray his people).[19] With its celebration of church feast days outlawed by Parliament and its exposure of Puritan hypocrisy, this sequence of four poems launches Vaughan's poetic campaign against the oppressors of his church and community.[20] In 'The Proffer', his anger and bitterness break out in a 'tour de force' of 'verbal power' that 'slides between irony and invective'.[21] It begins with a diatribe against the 'black Parasites', the 'flyes of hell / That buz in every ear, and blow on souls / Until they smell / And rot'.[22] In the second of the opening three stanzas Vaughan mimics the argument of those who seek to persuade him to collaborate with the persecutors of royalists and Anglicans, as Balaam was tempted to curse Israel. Before 'harder weather' sets in, he is advised to extract honey like the bees, with the veiled threat that those who 'do not so, too late repent'.

In a book published in 1962, R. A. Durr analysed 'The Proffer' at some length in support of his project of rescuing Vaughan from the false contexts of 'early nineteenth-century poets of nature' and the 'occult and esoteric' ideas of the Hermetic tradition by placing him 'among some of his spiritual brethren' in the long line of Christian mystics.[23] Ignoring the contemporary context provided by Vaughan himself, with its climactic reference to '*Balaams* hire', Durr read it as a poem about 'the pilgrimage of man' taking place in 'the country of the mind', where 'the World's partisans' tempt the 'regenerate heart' with a 'demonic proffer'.[24] Since the context he insists upon is that of Meister Eckhart, Walter Hilton and St John of the Cross, this critic misses Vaughan's glance back at the elegy in the next phase of the poem, in which he turns from the objects of his contempt to a defence of his own steadfast resistance. Though 'sick and spent', he will never 'consent' to their 'poys'nous' offers, but keeps his 'longing eyes' fixed on 'those skies' – the elegy's 'world of light' – where the 'souls and spirits' of his brother William and other royalist dead now 'shine in white (like stars) and rest'. As Vaughan's self-righteous indignation gathers pace, references to 'my Crown' and 'your Commonwealth' make its political causes hard to ignore:

> Shall my short hour, my inch,
>   My one poor sand,
> And crum of life, now ready to disband

> Revolt and flinch,
> And having born the burthen all the day,
>   Now cast at night my Crown away?
>
>   No, No; I am not he,
>   Go seek elsewhere.
>   I skill not your fine tinsel, and false hair,
>   Your Sorcery
>   And smooth seducements: I'le not stuff my story
>   With your Commonwealth and glory.

Durr passes over these stanzas, however, with the remark that these 'men of worldly power' want him to 'quit the way and join their ranks' because they are 'ill at ease about him … and even vaguely envious of the quiet nature of his faith'.[25] The insistent denial at the start of the second of them, the scornful dismissal of the tawdry glitter and hypocrisy of their self-assumed 'glory' in the images of 'tinsel' and 'false hair', and the hissing alliteration of the penultimate line hardly constitute a 'quiet' acceptance of his situation. Indeed, behind his determination not to 'revolt' (as his political antagonists have rebelled against everything symbolised by a 'Crown') lies his defiance of those who have destroyed the monarchy. He has suffered the consequences of defeat and oppression for too long to risk forfeiting an immortal crown now that his sick body is 'ready to disband' and his 'story' is almost completed as 'night' draws near.[26]

In the poem's next stanza Vaughan uses one of Christ's parables to warn those in contemporary Wales who have sown 'tares' among the wheat – scattering 'death / Amongst the quick' – of the consequences of their actions: 'But when thy Master comes, they'l finde and see / There's a reward for them and thee.' The shift from the first to the second person singular – from 'I am not he' to 'thy Master' – has the effect of detaching the poet from the speaker, so that the reward awaiting 'them and thee' becomes part of the universal system of damnation and salvation that is the point of the parable, identifying the 'Master' as Christ and placing an ironic gloss on the word 'reward': 'The Sonne of man shall send forth his Angels, and they shall gather out of his kingdome all things that offend … And shall cast them into a furnace of fire' (Matthew 13:41–2). The coming of the 'Master' to judge and punish, refine and save, is the burden of 'Ascension-Day' and 'White Sunday' in the group of poems that culminates in 'The Proffer'. Given the contemporary implications of 'Crown' and 'Commonwealth', however, the threat may also glance at the return of the exiled Charles II.

Finally, Vaughan turns his eyes directly upon himself – but a self now projected as a representative of royalist and Anglican loyalty – with three instructions: 'Then keep the antient way! / Spit out their phlegm / And fill thy brest with home.' For Durr, who reads the poem exclusively as a Christian pilgrimage, the 'antient way' is the way of 'retreat' from 'the world's crass foolishness', which must be voided from 'the heart' before the soul can breathe the 'pure, wholesome air' of the heavenly 'home' that is its destination.[27] But in the political context established by the preceding sequence and highlighted within the poem itself, the 'antient way' is that of monarchy rather than a new-fangled 'Commonwealth' and of the liturgy of the Book of Common Prayer rather than extemporary utterances by pretenders to inspiration, who boast access to the 'fire' of Pentecost 'each day'.[28] And the strikingly visceral image of spitting out 'their phlegm' seems to imply more than merely cleansing the heart from what Durr terms 'the noxious influence' of worldly temptation. The self-awareness signalled by the change of pronouns has permitted Vaughan to recognise the danger involved in the vehemence of his verbal assault on his enemies. As Post observes, in giving way to the 'all-too-human impulse to indulge too fervently in the language of overkill', he has adopted the corrupted discourse of those he despises.[29] 'Spit out their phlegm' is the phrase with which he 'clears his throat' of such linguistic contamination and frees himself and his sympathetic readers to contemplate with serenity the 'dream' of 'home' that ends the poem:

> A calm, bright day!
> A Land of flowers and spices! the word given,
> *If these be fair, O what is Heaven!*

The purpose of this exercise in comparison has not been to reject out of hand 'the archetypal, mythic dimension' of 'The Proffer' embraced by Durr nor to insist exclusively upon its 'topical dimension', but to amplify Simmonds's verdict that the two readings 'are not in conflict', because 'neither is adequate without the other'. This is, indeed, not a 'central fact' of this poem alone: it is 'characteristic' of Vaughan's sacred verse that he 'perceives and interprets historical circumstances ... in terms of the archetypal patterns of Christian myth'.[30]

V

This characteristic can be further illustrated by another poem from part 2 of *Silex Scintillans*, in which the political element is less overt. It is based on Christ's image of the kingdom of heaven as a seed that grows into a plant after lying hidden in the earth, bears fruit, and in due course is harvested (Matthew 4:26–9). The speaker laments in 'The Seed growing secretly' that the absence of 'dew' (a standard symbol for God's grace, described in the poem as the 'souls bright food') causes 'somthing' which he once possessed to 'fret and wrangle, pine and waste' like a weeping child. He begs God to once more 'feed that life, which makes him blow / And spred and open to thy will', before apostrophising the

'Dear, secret *Greenness*! nurst below / Tempests and windes, and winter-nights' and contrasting it with those he had dismissed as 'this worlds friends' in the first line of the poem:

Let glory be their bait, whose mindes
Are all too high for a low Cell:
Though Hawks can prey through storms and winds,
The poor Bee in her hive must dwel.

Glory, the Crouds cheap tinsel still
To what most takes them, is a drudge;
And they too oft take good for ill,
And thriving vice for vertue judge.

The poem ends by encouraging the 'seed' to quietly fulfil the purpose for which it was created:

Then bless thy secret growth, nor catch
At noise, but thrive unseen and dumb;
Keep clean, bear fruit, earn life and watch,
Till the white winged Reapers come![31]

It is no surprise that Durr interprets the seed as 'the Spirit of Christ' and cites Augustine and St Bernard on the roles of love and humility in bringing it to fruition in the human soul.[32] Seelig follows another well-trodden path in interpreting the seed as an 'image of the soul disciplined to the Christian life, leading a kind of hidden existence that shows no outward sign of success but is nevertheless under God's protection'.[33] Others, however, have picked up clues to a more topical current of meaning running beneath the devotional surface. John Wall sees a particular significance behind the remark in the first stanza that the friends of this world might 'quit' their worship of glory and gold 'and learn to kneel', if they would open their eyes to what even 'some poor man may often feel'. He points out that the Puritans had forbidden communicants to kneel when they received the Eucharist, so that the poet is regretting 'the loss of the availability of Anglican worship' for his generation.[34] The mysterious 'somthing' that the speaker had 'long ago' learned 'to suck, and sip, and taste' may then be interpreted as the liturgy he had imbibed as a child growing up in the Church of England. Once the reader has been alerted to this set of coded meanings, other details fall into place. The 'wranglers' who defile the house of God with their 'noise' in George Herbert's 'The Familie', identified as Puritans by Summers and Pebworth in an influential article, may be alluded to in the wording of Vaughan's poem: 'fret and wrangle', 'nor catch / At noise'.[35] And the 'secret *Greenness*' that survives underground symbolises the Anglican community waiting out the 'winter-nights' of Puritan dominance. While these 'storms and winds' last, loyal members of the outlawed church refuse to take the 'bait' of worldly 'glory' and like the 'poor Bee' in its 'low Cell' prefer a life of quiet privacy. Vaughan had already used the image of 'fine tinsel' in 'The Proffer' to scoff at the 'cheap' glory accorded to 'thriving vice' by the easily dazzled crowd. The injunction to 'bear fruit, earn life and watch' in the final stanza is interpreted by Wall as 'part of a larger context in which the experience of watching for the return of the master is defined as a positive, growing experience' for the church.[36] The two main contexts in which the poem can be read – the spiritual life of the individual and the topical predicament of the Church of England – are neatly brought together by Helen Wilcox: 'The poet longs for the moment when he and the church will be able to "spread and open" to God's will'; and at the end, he asks 'for a blessing on the "secret growth" of the seed – the soul, the church – since it is a glorious thing to "thrive unseen and dumb"'.[37]

VI

Towards the end of the preface to the augmented *Silex Scintillans*, Henry Vaughan made it clear that the religious and political realities of contemporary life in Breconshire were as important a context for his poetry as *The Temple*, the Bible, Christian mysticism and the Hermetic tradition in which Thomas Vaughan was labouring; and furthermore, that the products of his own pen were far more than a homage to Herbert, an aid to devotion or a personal record of his spiritual pilgrimage. Dated from Newton by Usk on 30 September 1654, only nine months after Oliver Cromwell had been declared Protector by the Instrument of Government of 16 December 1653, the Welsh poet's double-edged words, as so often, hold a subversive political message for knowing readers: 'I have begged leave to communicate this my poor *Talent* to the *Church*, under the *protection* and *conduct* of her *glorious Head*: who (if he will vouchsafe to *own* it, and *go along* with it) can make it as useful now in the *publick*, as it hath been to me in *private*.'[38] The struggle of loyal members of the outlawed Church of England under its exiled head, the son of the executed Charles I, is elided with the experience of the Universal Church under its divine head, Jesus Christ, as it moves towards the consummation of history, when the 'white winged Reapers come'. Contemporary readers who were alert to the overlapping contexts of *Silex Scintillans* would have been encouraged to persevere in their journey towards the 'order, peace, and love' of a restored monarchy prayed for in 'The Constellation' and towards the heavenly 'home' dreamed of at the end of 'The Proffer'.

NOTES

1. For significant editions of Herbert's poems between 1806 and 1905 see the introduction to F. E. Hutchinson (ed.), *The Works of George Herbert* (Oxford: Clarendon Press, 1941), pp. lxv–lxvii.

2. The secular verse was included in Grosart's Fuller Worthies' Library edition of the complete poetry and prose in 1871, but this was issued in a limited number of copies. For the gradual recovery of Vaughan's texts during the nineteenth century see 'A History of Henry Vaughan Scholarship and Criticism' in Donald R. Dickson, Alan Rudrum and Robert Wilcher (eds), *The Works of Henry Vaughan*, 3 vols (Oxford University Press, 2018), pp. li–liv. All quotations from Vaughan's work are from this edition, cited as *Works*, the three volumes of which are continuously paginated.

3. *Works*, pp. 597–8.

4. *Works*, pp. 105–7.

5. *Sacred Poetry of the Seventeenth Century*, 2 vols (New York: Burt Franklin, 1836; rpt 1969), vol. II, p. 317.

6. *Works*, p. 583.

7. Details of all these contexts for reading Vaughan can be found in 'A History of Henry Vaughan Scholarship and Criticism', in *Works*, pp. lviii–lxxxvi.

8. Louise Imogen Guiney, 'Milton and Vaughan', *Quarterly Review* 220 (1914), 353–64 (354).

9. F. E. Hutchinson, *Henry Vaughan: A Life and Interpretation* (Oxford: Clarendon Press, 1947), pp. 165–6.

10. Itrat Husain, *The Mystical Element in the Metaphysical Poets of the Seventeenth Century* (Edinburgh: Oliver & Boyd, 1948), pp. 202, 196.

11. M. M. Mahood, *Poetry and Humanism* (London: Jonathan Cape, 1950), p. 291.

12. *Works*, p. 136.

13. Sharon Cadman Seelig, *The Shadow of Eternity: Belief and Structure in Herbert, Vaughan and Traherne* (Lexington: University Press of Kentucky, 1981), p. 61.

14. M. Wynn Thomas, '"No Englishman": Wales's Henry Vaughan', *Swansea Review* 15 (1995), 1–19 (7).

15. James Simmonds, *Masques of God: Form and Theme in the Poetry of Henry Vaughan* (University of Pittsburgh Press, 1972), pp. 85–6, 101.

16. *Works*, pp. 71–2. For Herbert's 'The British Church' see *The English Poems of George Herbert*, ed. Helen Wilcox (Cambridge University Press, 2007), pp. 390–1.

17. Robert Wilcher, '"Then keep the ancient way!": A Study of Henry Vaughan's *Silex Scintillans*', *Durham University Journal*, n.s., 45 (1983), 11–24 (15, 17, 22).

18. Janet E. Halley, 'Versions of the Self and the Politics of Privacy in *Silex Scintillans*', *George Herbert Journal* 7 (1983–4), 51–71 (62, 58, 60).

19. *Works*, pp. 565–70.

20. Vaughan had already taken a public stand against the new order in church and state in the prose works *The Mount of Olives* (1652) and *Flores Solitudinis* (1654).

21. Jonathan F. S. Post, *Henry Vaughan: The Unfolding Vision* (Princeton University Press, 1982), pp. 181, 183.

22. For 'The Proffer', see *Works*, pp. 571–2.

23. R. A. Durr, *On the Mystical Poetry of Henry Vaughan* (Cambridge, MA: Harvard University Press, 1962), pp. xi–xii.

24. Ibid., pp. 101–3.

25. Ibid., p. 108.

26. Vaughan mentions in the preface to the 1655 *Silex Scintillans* that he has been '*nigh unto death*' and is 'still at no great distance from it' (*Works*, p. 559).

27. Durr, *Mystical Poetry of Vaughan*, p. 110.

28. See 'White Sunday', *Works*, p. 569.

29. *Unfolding Vision*, pp. 184–5.

30. Simmonds, *Masques of God*, p. 106.

31. *Works*, pp. 598–9.

32. Durr, *Mystical Poetry of Vaughan*, pp. 41–2.

33. Seelig, *Shadow of Eternity*, p. 83.

34. John N. Wall, *Transformations of the Word: Spenser, Herbert, Vaughan* (Athens: University of Georgia Press, 1988), p. 355.

35. See Claude J. Summers and Ted-Larry Pebworth, 'The Politics of *The Temple*: "The British Church" and "The Familie"', *George Herbert Journal* 8 (1984), 1–15.

36. Wall, *Transformations of the Word*, p. 355.

37. Helen Wilcox, '"Then bless thy secret growth": Henry Vaughan and the Church', in Elizabeth Siberry and Robert Wilcher (eds), *Henry Vaughan and the Usk Valley* (Little Logaston, Almeley, Herts: Logaston Press, 2016), pp. 43–60 (54–5).

38. *Works*, p. 558.

CRITICAL REFLECTIONS AND FURTHER STUDY

BACKGROUND

I came to the task of writing an essay for the early modern section of a volume devoted to the study of literature in context at the end of ten years or so of concentrated work on Henry Vaughan. When I retired from my university post, I had begun to draw together into a book the articles on Vaughan I had published intermittently since the 1970s during a teaching career in which his poetry had figured in several of my seminar courses and lectures. This project was interrupted by my recruitment as a joint editor of a new complete works of Vaughan to replace the standard edition that was first published in 1914. One of my contributions to this enterprise was a survey of Vaughan scholarship and criticism over the past two hundred years, since the rediscovery of his poetry in the early nineteenth century. I found that the best way to create some sort of order out of this mass of material was to deal in separate sections with the development of different approaches to his work that had come into prominence at different times in response to new information and changing critical fashions. For example, a whole new area of inquiry into Vaughan's ideas and imagery had been opened up by the publication in 1919 of the works of his twin brother, Thomas Vaughan, the alchemist and hermetic philosopher, and of the body of occult writings known as the *Hermetica* in 1924–6. In effect, what I ended up recording was the establishment of a succession of contexts in which to make sense of the poetry that Vaughan produced during his relatively brief period of literary activity between 1640 and 1657. These dates are significant because they cover the years of civil war and interregnum, during which the religious and political systems in which Vaughan had grown to adulthood were turned upside down. Furthermore, one of the ways I had encouraged students to read Vaughan was as a royalist counterpart to John Milton in the war of words that accompanied the conflict between king and Parliament and the Puritan experiments of commonwealth and protectorate. The religio-political context of the augmented *Silex Scintillans* of 1655, therefore, presented itself as the obvious choice to illustrate Vaughan's practice.

METHOD

When I eventually resumed work on my book, the experience of editing the poems helped determine its organisation into a series of chapters that placed Vaughan in a variety of contexts (topographical, intellectual, literary, religious, political), each of which provided the key to a different aspect of his literary inspiration and practice. This in turn informed the method I adopted for this essay. I understood that the purpose of the exercise was to demonstrate the significance of context for the close reading of a text, so I selected one poem that engaged directly with Vaughan's predicament as a defeated royalist during the 1650s and another which concealed its political implications beneath a more oblique mode of expression. I realised, however, the need for some preliminary explanation of the curious consequences of the way Vaughan's poetry had been mediated to the reading public by his early editors and critics. Concentration on the devotional lyrics in *Silex Scintillans*, disregard of the secular poems and verse translations (many of which dealt with experiences of the civil war decade), and a reluctance to engage with the topical elements in the religious poems themselves meant that an important dimension of Vaughan's historical context and poetic character was neglected for many years in interpreting and evaluating his poetry. 'The Constellation' from the 1650 *Silex Scintillans* provided a good example of how readers primed to read Vaughan as an otherworldly disciple of George Herbert coped with the intrusion of unwelcome realities from contemporary life into what was taken to be primarily a meditation on the harmony between the divine and natural worlds; and of how the interpretation of the text changed in emphasis when the political context was given its due weight in deciphering Vaughan's poetic strategy.

'The Proffer' and 'The Seed growing secretly' gave me opportunities to contrast in more detail how the context in which a poem is situated can produce radically different interpretations. The point of foregrounding the partisan contempt and indignation at the heart of the first example and teasing out the subversive subtext of the second, however, was not simply to displace devotional readings in favour of political ones, but to illustrate that an adequate critical engagement with Vaughan's poetry needs to recognise the range of contexts that converged in its making. Both poems weave their messages of hope and encouragement for defeated royalists and loyal members of the outlawed church from a variety of materials drawn from the processes of nature (rot caused by blowflies; green shoots germinating beneath the soil); from Herbert's *The Temple* ('The British Church' and 'The Familie'); from two of Christ's parables and the New Testament doctrine of the return of the 'Master' to judge the world; and from the traditional trope of the Christian pilgrimage traced by Durr and Seelig (cited in notes 23 and 13 of my essay). Pettet's pioneering study of *Silex Scintillans* in 1960 (see Further Reading) had confirmed the critical importance of four major sources of Vaughan's poetic imagery and symbolism: the Bible, Herbert's poetry, Hermetic philosophy, and the Book of Nature. The eventual assimilation by Vaughan critics of the historical facts about the severity of the Puritan regime imposed on South Wales added another layer to the contextual complexity of *Silex Scintillans*. The challenge then faced by readers and professional commentators alike – a challenge which is still central to the ongoing critical endeavour – was to explicate the poetic uses that were made of images and ideas derived from so many disparate contexts, often in the text of a single poem.

An important advance was made by Wall's investigation into Vaughan's poetic response to the banning of the Church of England's liturgy (see my essay, note 34); and Noel Thomas and Philip West explored different aspects of Vaughan's use of the Bible as a poetic and political resource in his literary campaign against the opponents of the 'ancient way' (see Further Reading). The following suggestions for further reading indicate other issues brought to light once Vaughan's historical context was accepted as one of the main factors in the development of his poetic methods during the dark days of the 1650s.

FURTHER READING

Forey, Madeleine, 'Poetry as Apocalypse: Henry Vaughan's *Silex Scintillans*', *Seventeenth Century* 11 (1996), 161–86

Marklew, Naomi, '*Silex Scintillans*: Henry Vaughan's Interregnum Elegy', *Scintilla* 17 (2013), 36–51

Pettet, E. C., *Of Paradise and Light: A Study of Vaughan's Silex Scintillans* (Cambridge University Press, 1960)

Rudrum, Alan, 'Resistance, Collaboration and Silence: Henry Vaughan and Breconshire Royalism', in *The English Civil Wars in the Literary Imagination*, ed. Claude J. Summers and Ted-Larry Pebworth (Columbia: University of Missouri Press, 1999), pp. 102–18

Thomas, M. Wynn, '"In Occidentem & Tenebras": Putting Henry Vaughan on the Map of Wales', *Scintilla* 2 (1998), 7–25

Thomas, Noel Kennedy, *Henry Vaughan: Poet of Revelation* (Worthing: Churchman, 1986)

Thomas, Peter, 'The Language of Light: Henry Vaughan and the Puritans', *Scintilla* 3 (1999), 9–29

Watson, Graeme J., 'The Temple in "The Night": Henry Vaughan and the Collapse of the Established Church', *Modern Philology* 84 (1986), 144–61

West, Philip, *Henry Vaughan's Silex Scintillans: Scripture Uses* (Oxford University Press, 2001)

Wilcher, Robert, *Keeping the Ancient Way: Aspects of the Life and Work of Henry Vaughan* (Liverpool University Press, 2021)

PART III
The Restoration and Eighteenth Century, 1660–1780

- -

INTRODUCTORY NOTE

In the first essay here, Lee Morrissey stages a lively and expert critical debate on
questions of literary periodisation and context-based criticism which are of obvious
relevance to the whole of this volume. Acknowledging some of the problems with
conventional periodisation raised by critics in recent times, Morrissey nevertheless
makes a clear case for the value of historically informed reading, especially for this,
his own period of specialism, which, he points out, had a very particular investment
in marking time. Morrissey illustrates his argument with a wide range of textual
examples and his essay comes to a resolving focus in an adroit extended reading
of Gray's *Elegy Written in a Country Church Yard*. The theoretical argument of the
essay draws especially on New Historicism and, among other things, Morrissey here
provides a valuable overview of a literary-critical approach that informs several of the
discussions in this collection (see, especially, Essay 15).

Aphra Behn's novel *Oroonoko*, the subject of the next essay by Oddvar Holmesland,
has claims to be the very first novel in English – as well as the first colonial novel –
and it has offered rich potential to critics for historicised readings. Not least in this
respect has been its potential for generating debate around the new genre's precise
position in relation to concepts of fact and fiction, history and storytelling, realism
and romance. In his carefully poised and precisely argued study of Behn's novel,
Holmesland focuses on notions of truth-telling and representation in order to revisit
and reinvigorate this debate while also exploring the novel's conflicted ethics of
imperialism and its potential to be read as Christian allegory. Drawing on religious,
scientific, ideological and colonial contexts of the seventeenth century, Holmesland's

finely textured essay gradually elaborates a view of the novel as offering several levels of metaphorical complexity and not a little textual ambiguity in its representations of the New World and its native peoples as well as of the enslaved Africans and the title figure, Oroonoko. The colonial context explored here naturally relates this essay to the ones in Part VIII on postcolonial literature. The essay there on Guyanese-born Grace Nichols by Izabel Brandão includes a section on Nichols's first volume of poetry, *i is a long memoried woman*, which tells the story of the slave-trade journey from Africa to the Caribbean and might be seen as an interesting intertext for *Oroonoko* for their shared backgrounds in the Guianas.

Along with the rise of the novel, the eighteenth century saw the advent and rapid growth in the publication of journals, magazines and reviews in Britain. In the final essay in this section, Richard Jones engages with this context of periodical print culture and explores some of the ways in which it influenced – and was influenced by – fiction writing during this period. Jones presents an engrossing account of one early journal, the *British Magazine*, and its publication of what appears to be the first ever novel to be published serially, *The Life and Adventures of Sir Launcelot Greaves*. The magazine and the novel were both the work of the same indefatigable Scottish writer, Tobias Smollett, and Jones discusses in detail how Smollett's two projects effectively sustained and promoted one another, developing in close interaction and influencing each other in both formal and thematic ways. In paying close attention to serial publication, Jones's essay clearly anticipates aspects of Essay 19 by Dillane.

Readers who would like to enrich their engagement with the essays in this section would find Lee Morrissey's chapter in *English Literature in Context* particularly rewarding for its general overview of the development of literary forms and institutions in this period (pp. 218–36), and, especially, for its own short reading of *Oroonoko* (pp. 252–4) and its short account of the transatlantic slave trade and eighteenth-century slave narratives by Phyllis Wheatley, Olaudah Equiano and others (pp. 245–7). Equiano's *Interesting Narrative* (1789) is one of the most important of these narratives and further information on him and on later developments relating to the slave trade can be found in Peter Kitson's chapter in *English Literature in Context* (especially pp. 291, 330–3).

9 Periodising in Context: The Case of the Restoration and Eighteenth Century

LEE MORRISSEY

Abstract

Questions of literary periodisation and related questions of context have been hotly debated in recent years, especially in relation to the discourses of New Historicism, and this essay engages critically with such questions with specific reference to the 'period' we usually refer to as 'The Restoration and Eighteenth Century'. While acknowledging some of the problems and limitations of canonical literary periodisation, the essay will suggest how a distinctive set of historical pressures make contextualisation particularly important to an understanding of the drama, fiction and poetry published after 1660 and up to the Romantic era. It will suggest, for example, the difficulties of reading Dryden out of context, and how the very novel-ty and contemporaneity of the emergent novel, as exemplified by Richardson's epistolary fiction, epitomises the period's preoccupation with time. Indeed, one might say that the eighteenth century is decidedly a *period* period because of its signal interest in marking time, and this will be one of the main lines of discussion here.

At the same time, attention needs to be paid to influences and continuities across periods, both from the past and into the future. The Restoration depends on an interregnum, so knowing the earlier period matters too; similarly, the novel emerges in part from the medieval romance, so knowing even earlier periods also matters; and our knowledge of later developments of eighteenth-century legacies, such as the realist novel for example, retroactively informs our understanding of the original developments. In this spirit, a rereading of Gray's *Elegy Written in a Country Church Yard* – 'yet once more' (to quote 'mute inglorious Milton') – will be offered here as a metaphor for literary history seen as a set of buried possibilities ready for rediscovery and reimagining.

In 2004, as one of the original contributors to *English Literature in Context* (2008), I was invited to Cambridge for editorial meetings on how to organise the book. I flew over from the United States, and, when I landed, the English press – print, television and online – was buzzing with excitement about a football player on the English national team, only eighteen years old, who had just had two breakout games in the 2004 UEFA Championship. In two consecutive matches this new star of the international scene had scored two goals: two against Switzerland in a 3–0 victory for England and two against Croatia, whom England beat 4–2. Over time, he became the top goal scorer for Manchester United and the second-highest scorer in the history of the Premier League. As you may already recognise, the teenage sensation was Wayne Rooney. That those early contributor discussions overlapped with Wayne Rooney's entry into top-flight international football is merely a coincidence, of course, but that coincidence helpfully raises contextual questions about *English Literature in Context*. Some readers will remember Rooney's 2004 exploits, the rest of his remarkable career, and maybe the occasional scandal, too. Other, younger readers might know about Wayne Rooney, maybe from seeing him play later in his career, or from the many highlight videos that circulate online. In the future that authors all hope their work will have, though, Wayne Rooney could be as obscure a reference as any explained in *English Literature in Context*. In a sense, then, Rooney's career also represents a simple way of considering time periods, the topic of this essay.

Since those editorial meetings – or, since Wayne Rooney's Euro 2004 performance – context itself has become a topic of increasing debate within literary studies. In *The Limits of Critique*, Rita Felski, for example, argues that 'Context stinks!'[1] Of course, contextualising work has many positive motivations, including a recognition that reading comprehension can increase with contextual information. But Felski's understandable concern is that a kind of micro-history has dominated literary studies, resituating works back into the time period from which they emerged. Contextualising risks turning literary studies into a branch of history and creating the impression that literary works are to be understood only in the time of their production. Why a work might matter now is either not established, or is linked to the value of the events of its originary time period. However, the very frame of 'The Restoration and Eighteenth Century' requires contextualisation, as 'The Restoration' refers to the 1660 return of the Stuarts to the monarchy after a decade. To understand the Restoration, one must grapple with why the king was killed in 1649. Because knowing the earlier period matters too, The Restoration and Eighteenth Century thus also highlights another topic that has become increasingly contentious since 2004: time periods and periodisation. With the past tense in the title of his 2013 book, *Why Literary Periods Mattered*, Ted Underwood consigns literary periods to the past, seeing them as an attribute of a recognisable historical period, the one in which periodising mattered. For Underwood, periods are – or, *were* – tautological. 'Substituting discontinuous contrast for explanation', literary periods provide their own ready-made answers: *this* material is different because it is part of *this* period.[2]

The Restoration nonetheless brings with it a distinctive set of historical pressures that make contextualisation particularly important to an understanding of the drama, fiction and poetry published after 1660. Poetry in the period is deeply informed by its contemporary context. The first decades of this period were dominated by John Dryden, whose standing hinged in part on his ability to write topical, evaluative English poetry informed by classical precedents. Some of Dryden's topical work was written for the stage, reopened in 1660 by Charles II eighteen years after it had been closed due to anti-theatrical religious objections. For the first time on English stages, Charles also allowed women to act in the reopened theatres – a double revolution: theatres, with actresses. The result was a new public negotiation of gender roles. As the prominence of theatre began to fade relative to the rise of the novel, this pattern of contextual referentiality continued, as plots of novels often enacted politically pointed and elaborate allegorical representations of then current events. The same point proceeds in the other direction: eighteenth-century developments in English literature – especially the advent of copyright, the growth of literary criticism and the flourishing of the novel – affect subsequent literary history and the reception of earlier literature.

In the same way that literary critical attention to periods can be contextualised, contextualising literature can also be periodised. For many, literary study is attractive not because of its various historical time periods but, rather, for the pleasures of reading and writing. Analysis and study follow from the initial enjoyment. In our reading, we might land on a critical problem and take a historical approach to answering it (e.g., where did novels come from?). What Cleanth Brooks influentially calls 'the well-wrought urn' (1947) offers a way of thinking about writing, a way which sees good writing as transcending mere questions of history and of biographical concerns. The urn in the museum, thrown millennia earlier by an anonymous artisan, offered its own proof of overcoming history while apparently obviating knowing about the artist. However, for generations educated in the second half of the twentieth century that debate over good writing had been occurring, regrettably, in something of a vacuum. The urn, placed on a pedestal, also seems deracinated and detached from the sources of its power – the civilisation which produced it, and its use in everyday life. Brooks's interest in paradox, but not in biography, survives into early post-structuralism, which continues to depersonalise texts and, by emphasising 'play' and '*aporias*', performs readings that would have been familiar to the New Critics decades earlier, despite the great intergenerational tensions between the two approaches.

By the late 1970s and early 1980s, influenced in part by Foucault's 'archaeological' approach, literary critics such as Edward Said, Stephen Greenblatt, Catherine Gallagher and others highlight relationships between the literary work and its historical contexts. When Stephen Greenblatt opens his 1988 book *Shakespearean Negotiations* by claiming, 'I begin with a desire to speak with the dead', the sentence represents the apotheosis of such contextualising interest in historical periods.[3] Under the pressure of this cultural materialism, the well-wrought urn is metaphorically reunited with the poorly wrought urns, the shards in the archaeological site, and even the very clay from which pottery is created. In *Practising New Historicism*, Greenblatt and Gallagher described their 'most consistent commitment: a commitment to particularity' (p. 19). Context offers a repository of particulars. In addition to increased comprehension, the particularity of context counters the generalities regarding beautiful forms and good writing found in the earlier New Criticism. Particularity also brings the maker of the urn back into the picture; the artwork is a made object, again. How it is made, and by whom, and with what supports are all back in the contextual conversation of particulars. Literary studies shifts from abstracted aesthetic and moral reflections to explanatory historical considerations, with political value informed by contexts. In its attention to historical particulars, New Historicism adopted a narrative stylistic convention of the anecdote, or short story, often placed at the beginning of an essay and used to establish a particular historical focus – as illustrated above by my story about Wayne Rooney and the Cambridge editorial meetings.

With the concept of 'the political unconscious', described in his 1981 book of that title, Fredric Jameson articulated a powerful method for reading narratives contextually. After opening with 'Always historicize!', Jameson offers a detailed vision of how history and literary narratives intersect, formally.[4] Jameson describes three ways of understanding the historical causality embedded in narratives: 'mechanical', on the model of billiard balls hitting each other, of actions and reactions; 'expressive', on the model of a synecdoche, in which a part represents the whole; and, finally, 'structural', in which invisible causes are considered to be immanent in their effects. Jameson rejects the first, mechanical, billiard-ball approach (itself a kind of contextual method), because it misunderstands the shaping and selecting that go into creating narratives – not every billiard ball is included; a pattern is created instead. The second, according to which an 'inner essence' (p. 24) is expressed in the typical work, is related, Jameson claims, to 'the category of a historical "period"' (p. 27). Jameson rejects this option, too, as 'fatally reductive' (p. 27), because it, like the New Critics' well-wrought urn, underestimates the tensions in the work. Ultimately, then, Jameson advocates the structural approach, which understands narrative as 'the imaginary resolution of a real contradiction' (p. 77). For Jameson, narratives invent solutions to contests ultimately between overlapping 'modes of production' (p. 97). In the structural, the billiard balls are converted into an economic conflict, and the synecdoche, the narrative, expresses a desire for an ideologically shaped resolution of the period's forces. In part, Jameson offers a theory of popular culture: the popularity of a narrative, that is, a novel (or, later, films and TV shows, etc.) depends on its unconscious political resonance, how it connects to 'the political unconscious'.

The Political Unconscious, New Historicism's most sophisticated method for contextual interpretations of narrative forms, has explanatory power. It can be replicated, and, bridging back to earlier modes of literary analysis such as those of

Northrop Frye and the New Critics (but also as far back as Dante, too), it confident-ly presumes the sufficiency of the text, though, unlike the New Critics', Jameson's text holds conflictual energies. However, in its focus on the narrative's imaginary resolution of those conflictual forces, Jameson's remarkable approach remains, like the novel genre itself, largely synchronic: a narrative, for him, always reveals pressures contemporary with the time of its publication. The modes of production may have histories, as indeed might the literary forms themselves, but the contex-tual focus continues nonetheless to be on the period.

This synchronic presumption is pervasive, and informs Michel Foucault's work in the 1960s, so influential for the New Historicist generation of the 1970s and 1980s. Foucault's archaeological metaphor implies layers, which he calls 'epis-temes' and 'discursive formations'. Although Foucault was interested in a 'suspen-sion of all the accepted unities', his process lent itself to the existing periods, and the contrasts which periodisation facilitates.[5] Some argue that Foucault does not explain the leaps between epistemes, that he just describes the epistemes instead, but I would like to make the related point that he offers what Jameson might call 'expressive' portraits of periods instead. Still, Foucault's archaeological metaphor can be read against the grain, though, in a way that returns us yet again to the well-wrought urn. For all the ostensible differences between the layers in an ar-cheological site, the materials are often the same. Pottery, for example, recurs. The forms might change – from, say, high-quality tiles, arranged in mimetic patterns, to cheap tobacco pipes – but fired clay represents a continuity across the layers, or the different periods. Urns are also made of a substance that survives.

A defining literary development of the Restoration and Eighteenth Century con-tributed to this kind of contextualised reading: the novel. One might say that the eighteenth century is decidedly a *period-focused* period because of its signal inter-est in marking time. As noted by Mikhail Bakhtin in his essay 'Forms of Time and of the Chronotope in the Novel', during the eighteenth century 'the problem of time in literature was posed with particular intensity, a period when precisely a new feeling for time was beginning to awake'.[6] This 'rising chronometric culture' existed not only in literature.[7] In science and technology, too, there was a new attention to measuring time. A competition was instituted, for example, with prizes funded by Parliament, to find a clock that could keep time even on board ships, rocked though they are by waves that undermine the traditional pendulum clock. Such minute attention to the passage of time directs attention to the present. The novel partic-ipates in and affects changing representations of time – as an imagined now of simultaneity. Although early English novels are often given the subtitle of 'history', the stories they tell usually do not go back far in time; they focus on the details of the lives of their protagonists, largely contemporary with the time of publication.

Just a few decades before the early English novels, Shakespeare wrote plays os-tensibly exploring the lives of English kings and other historical characters from centuries earlier. By the eighteenth century, by contrast, literature exhibits an increasing contemporaneity. The novel, like the dialectic between the shipboard clock and Greenwich, tries to represent the present, with a deep commitment to how things are faring precisely now. In Samuel Richardson's *Pamela* and *Clarissa,* the novels' epistle – or epistolary – form, consisting of letters the characters are writing to each other, highlights how the novel can 'write to the moment', to quote one character's helpful formulation in *Clarissa*.[8] The genre's very name, in English anyway, indicates its immediacy, its newness and connection to the present. The novel is so focused on now that later developments in the novel, which situate their stories in an imagined past, have their own double names – for example, the late eighteenth-century 'Gothic novel', and the 'historical novel' of the early nineteenth. Perhaps such contemporary referentiality is one way of understanding the silly, punning title of Henry Carey's 1734 play, *The Tragedy of Chrononhotonthologos* – that is, as a theatrical parody of the period's obsessive attention to the period.

Although it is not a much discussed feature of his work, Francophone Algerian philosopher Jacques Derrida, implicitly in conversation with Foucault, actively develops a theory of history, and of time, across his career, often by disputing periodised history. In *Of Grammatology* (1967), for example, Derrida argues 'one does not leave the epoch whose closure one can outline'.[9] Some of what we see in any period is a consequence, maybe even a benefit, of earlier times, and comes to us across many periods, surviving over a *longue durée*. Derrida describes the resulting mix as 'the radical and necessary *heterogeneity* of an inheritance'.[10] Because materials and forms persist across periods, the question for a full contextualisation is not only how the work signified to its contemporaries but also how the author reworked what was already available. To some extent, everyone is born into the past, into what is already extant in the present. As Derrida puts it, there is 'disjointure in the very presence of the present, this sort of non-contemporaneity of present time with itself' (p. 25). Reading literature in context, then, necessitates both synchronic and diachronic approaches; contextual readings speak to the author's present, which includes its existing conditions/influences from the past. At the same time, though, the work's reception, its afterlife, so to speak, forms another context, often long after the arrival of the work itself. For Derrida, then, 'a masterpiece always moves ... in the manner of a ghost', haunting later generations (p. 18).

With writers and readers alike suffused with sometimes overlapping pasts, context is variable, ultimately. Not solely the context of origin, nor of existing materials, context is also informed by subsequent developments. In a 1997 essay, 'A Theory of Resonance', Wai Chee Dimock argues that 'no preposition is more important to a synchronic historicism than the reassuring *in*'.[11] That is, Dimock implies, contextualising scholars feel most secure when they operate in the period of their specialism. Of course, as she notes, 'capturing a literary text only in its pastness, cannot say why this text might still matter in the present'. If a text matters not only in its past, that is, its former present, but *because* of its relationship to its times, there might not be a need to read it today. If, though, the past is present, then and now, the text might still have the 'resonance' she is theorising. Dimock argues that 'the "immortality" of literature must be understood ... as the continual emergence of interpretive contexts, which ... give way to an ongoing sequence that looks almost infinite'.[12] The reception of a work is also part of its context, as much, sometimes more, than its relationship to the time of its drafting, writing, or publication. The readers' later present, the author's future, can reconfigure the past, the author's present.

The title of Ranulf Higden's fourteenth-century chronicle, *Polychronicon*, per-haps too literally translated, means 'image of many times', but the point applies to many literary works. Like the urn whose magnetic field is forever frozen at the time of its firing, literature is, in part, an image of the times in which it is created. Like the urn, though, literature is also made of materials older than the time of its shaping, and it carries those older materials forward. And, finally, like the urn on the pedestal, carrying history but no longer water, the later context can reshape the meaning of the otherwise unchanged work. During the eighteenth century, as decades of presentist prose fictions (novels) accumulated, the idea of history itself shifts, becoming something with more chronological depth; as people become more aware of the accumulating passage of a newly measured time, history itself also acquires more density, an archaeological density.

Thomas Gray's *Elegy Written in a Country Church Yard* (1749–51), published at the midpoint of the eighteenth century, synthesises many of these periodising themes while also allowing for a presence of the past at odds with the typical novel. The poem begins with a diurnal, chronometric reference: 'The Curfew tolls the knell of parting day'.[13] The poem's sonorous first three words mark the passage of time – a bell rings in the arrival of evening, and the end of another day. The narrative of the poem begins in the resonance of its own opening image. But that strikingly present tone is simultaneously antiquated, a centuries-old way of meas-uring time, not, as they could in the eighteenth century, by the minute, but as the medieval world did, by the movement of the sun. The resonant clang with which the poem opens is also the fading echo of an older experience of time. The poem's present feels like the church's past. 'The plowman homeward plods his weary way' (3) suggests the immemorial experience of plowmen through the centuries. The poem's very premise – a narrator, exploring a church cemetery at evening – plays with the relationship between past and present. The church and gravestones, pres-ences from the past, are still, nonetheless, in the present.

The antiquity of the setting is emphasised in the 1753 edition, which featured engravings by Richard Bentley, including a rendering of the poem's initial letter, a capital 'T', on top of which an owl is perched, wings outstretched, and behind which Bentley placed an iconic ruined church (Figure 9.1). That edition places

Figure 9.1 First page of Gray's *Elegy Written in a Country Church Yard*, 1753 edition, with Richard Bentley's engravings.

readers in the position of the narrator, looking at a country churchyard, at the dusky moment its nocturnal residents emerge. The ancient, ruined church, surrounded by the headstones of the graves, apparently offers the opportunity to ruminate on history, represented by the buried 'rude Forefathers of the hamlet', as the narrator calls them (16). Then, in the negative, the narrator imagines the many things these former residents no longer do: for example, 'no more the blazing hearth shall burn' (11); 'no children run to lisp their sire's return' (23). In such negations, such descriptions of absence, the narrator makes the deceased villagers present again. With brief descriptions of harvesting, plowing and farming, a litany of their former activities, recurrent aspects of agricultural life, the narrator imagines their daily lives back into existence. These early stanzas offer a view of the period in which the church was an active part of an active community, and the narrator sketches the cyclical, seasonal context of their lives. The poem, an elegy, is also pastoral, suggesting English agrarian life in context.

As a pastoral elegy, the poem invokes Milton's 'Lycidas', a pastoral elegy from more than a century before. By the eighth stanza the poem also becomes an allegory: abstract concepts such as 'Ambition', 'Grandeur' and 'Memory' become actors in the poem, possibly mocking the 'the short and simple annals of the poor' (29, 31, 38, 32). Actually, they become the narrator's antagonists, the opposition against which the narrator is directing his poem, those who would, he thinks, judge harshly the lives in 'this neglected spot' (45). The narrator delivers this representation as a critique to signal a contest of values, between ones the narrator imagines held by the people around the country churchyard and those possibly held by the poem's metropolitan, contemporary readers. Invoking the 'storied urn' (41) decades before 'Ode on a Grecian Urn', so influential for the New Critics, the narrator displays neither the confidence of Keats's poem nor the polish implied by Brooks's formalism; instead the narrator despairs at art's limitations, its inability to bring the dead of the churchyard back to life. The poem turns essayistic, and the narrator accounts for the condition of the rural poor, who might have achieved more if it were not for the fact that 'Knowledge to their eyes her ample page / Rich with the spoils of time did n'er unroll' (49–50). Why they might not have access to knowledge is not stated, although English history offers a set of familiar possibilities: the Protestant conviction that Catholics were kept uneducated by the Catholic Church, which would have built the ancient country church; the English class system whose 'public' schools were for the privileged only; and, relatedly, the rich and powerful landowners who were combining ancient smaller, often communal holdings and enclosing them in new, larger, privatised estates.

Ultimately, the narrator decides that the denizens of this country churchyard had the advantage of living at a remove from power as it operates in London. While a 'village-Hampden' might have stood up to 'the little Tyrant of his fields', it could also be that 'some mute inglorious Milton' or 'Some Cromwell guiltless of his country's blood' lie buried, anonymously, in this churchyard (57–60). With the names Hampden, Milton and Cromwell, three opponents of Charles I, the narrator invokes the Civil Wars, which, although a century earlier, hover over the Restoration and eighteenth century. In praising those buried in the churchyard as guiltless, the narrator implies perhaps a Royalist or a constitutionalist politics, opposed to the actions of those who participated in the execution of Charles and the Interregnum prior to the Restoration. These country folk were, fortunately, 'forbad to wade through slaughter to a throne', spared the contests of the previous century, as far as the narrator is concerned (67). Moreover, perhaps England would have been more stable if these villagers, or the attitudes the narrator attributes to them, had a larger role in political life. The manuscript version of the poem has 'Cato', 'Tully' and 'Caesar' where Hampden, Milton and Cromwell are in the published version. This allegorical pastoral elegy, informed by classical precedents, and initially comparing anonymous English dead to ancient Romans, instead compares the rural and the urban, the country and London, and a peaceful agricultural setting in the eighteenth century with a bloodily politicised one in the seventeenth.

These poor people, the narrator contends, deserve and receive memorials, headstones, with 'their name, their years, spelt by th' unletter'd muse' (81). Here, the 'rude' from earlier in the poem picks up the suggestion of illiteracy, and another reason why knowledge was not unrolled 'to their eyes' (49). For John Guillory, Gray's *Elegy* narrates a 'transition to vernacular literacy'.[14] The poem concludes with the narrator imagining 'some hoary-headed Swain' telling a visitor to 'Approach and read (for thou can'st read) the lay, / Grav'd on the stone', directing visitor and reader alike to 'The Epitaph' presumably etched on a stone in the country churchyard. In three stanzas of rhyming quatrains, the village mason records 'A Youth to Fortune and to Fame unknown' (118), representative, in his way, of the village overall. The poem takes on a democratising tone, defending the unappreciated worth of the unknown rural poor and questioning the focus on the famous great men of history, doing so, in part, with a phrase translated from Petrarch's *Sonnets*. Such a 'frail memorial' (78), for them, 'the place of fame and elegy supply' (82). The dead in the imagined country churchyard do not become famous, but they do receive their elegy, a poem, set in a church cemetery which includes within it a poem engraved in stone.

In the fourth stanza of a poem which nearly concludes with an invitation to 'read … the stone', the narrator leads the reader from the herd, to the landscape, to the tower, and then down to the ground in front of the church, 'where heaves the turf in many a mouldering heap' (16). The turn in the poem to the place in which 'the rude Forefathers of the hamlet sleep' depends upon the narrator's noticing the continued surface effects of earth disturbed long ago. In short, it requires archaeological attention. The narrator's focus for much of the poem is underground; the verse operates like a ground-penetrating radar, showing readers what lies beneath. Archaeology, Foucault's metaphor which informs contextualising, periodising work, shapes Gray's *Elegy*, and Thomas Gray's experience, as well. In 1740, while in Naples, Gray visited one of the most important Roman-era archaeological discoveries of his lifetime, Herculaneum, a city buried by Vesuvius in 79 CE, and rediscovered just two years prior to Gray's arrival. In a letter home, Gray describes being lowered into the newly reopened underground spaces, and touching architectural elements undisturbed for the preceding sixteen hundred years: 'the wood and beams remain so perfect that you may see the grain', but 'burnt to a coal, and dropping into dust upon the least touch'.[15] Underground, Gray came into contact with Roman life as it was lived, including even its ancient, friable wooden timbers unusually extant because of a fluke in how Vesuvius hit Herculaneum. Of course, in touching it, Gray destroys some of it.

Gray's *Elegy*, described by John Guillory as 'a cento of quotable quotations' (p. 92), participates in a Restoration and Eighteenth Century constitution of literature – as vernacular (and thus more accessible than the Greek and Latin classics), and as drama, fiction and poetry, (and thus not as, say, sermons and histories). It contributes to a narrowing of the word 'literature', away from the sense of any text involving letters, and toward 'literature' understood as the 'literary', an increasingly self-referential field. Concern about that self-referentiality – refracted by a reading of modernism – informed New Historicist contextualising, and the attention to realisms that has followed. Contextualising Gray's *Elegy* just in its own period, to the extent that this is possible, requires knowing something about the classics, about Renaissance European literature, about John Milton, about the Reformation commitment to vernacular literacy, about English political history of the seventeenth century, about archaeology, about engraving and typefaces, and probably more as well. The poem would go on to create its own contexts, too, as can be seen, for example, in the Gothic novels, in Wordsworth's 'Tintern Abbey' and in the work of Thomas Hardy, who finds the title of one of his novels, *Far from the Madding Crowd* (1874), in Gray's *Elegy*. Gray also appears in the poetry of Seamus Heaney, a poet also attuned to digging into what the earth holds and might produce.

With so many prospective influences, Gray's *Elegy* probably makes reading in context look extremely demanding. One must think about time in more than one direction, and one must be – or become! – interdisciplinary, in order to gain a fuller sense of the period(s). However, a contextual interpretation is a construal, just a reading, an intervention in time, and thus a creation in its own right, even if maybe a kind of recreation. It might be that imagination is all that is needed for contextualising. 'Imagination' – so important to eighteenth-century English literature, from a series of essays in Addison and Steele's periodical, *The Spectator*, to Mark Akenside's four-part poem on *The Pleasures of the Imagination* (1744; rev. 1757) – had been relatively subterranean in twentieth-century literary studies until, in a published set of 1962 radio lectures, *The Educated Imagination*, Northrop Frye made the term central to his literary critical and pedagogical project, though the term then faded somewhat, in part because of its associations with the idealised aesthetics of mid-century criticism such as Frye's. However, imagination comes to matter again strongly in Jameson's *Political Unconscious* because it is seen to help resolve real contradictions and to produce sustaining illusions (which therefore provide the basis for further critique). By locating the work of the imagination in ideology, such criticism makes the literary work secondary to the work of ideology, which arrives anonymously and *ex nihilo* to give closure to popular narratives. Since 1981, when Jameson published that book in a geopolitically bi-polar world, ideology has metastasised, to the detriment of imagination. Who shapes ideology, then, and can imagination be revived to highlight and change it?

Ultimately, polychronic contextualised readings matter for imagining new possibilities, maybe new ideological possibilities, if only by reminding ourselves that things have been different, and could be again. I have focused, then, on Gray's churchyard because it offers a metaphor for (literary) history imagined as a set of buried possibilities ready for rediscovery and reimagining. In 1993, for example, John Guillory saw Gray's *Elegy* as 'bourgeois', and complained that 'we cannot imagine [the narrator] condescending to teach the peasantry to read', even as Guillory recognises that Gray's *Elegy* 'rapidly established itself in the school system as a perfect poem for introducing schoolchildren to the study of English literature' (pp. 118, 102, 86). A few decades later the critical context for the poem has changed. As I write this in 2020, the world is seeing mass graves dug for unknown victims of the Covid-19 pandemic, and the *Elegy*'s lines, 'e'en these bones from insult to protect / Some frail memorial' take on a new resonance. Hundreds of thousands of people who have died in the last few months of a new disease deserve that memorial. Meanwhile, at the same time, in the UK, the US, and elsewhere, existing memorials, from the past into which we are born, are being defaced, toppled and removed as part of the Black Lives Matter movement. Most of those monuments gave 'a throne' to men who had 'shut the gates of mercy on mankind', if not to all mankind, then to large numbers of racially defined parts of it (17–18). Today, that is, we are living through a redefinition of merit, and the dynamic is similar to that in Gray's *Elegy*; be it victims of the pandemic or centuries of racist inequities, 'their lot forbad' (65).

In 2004, when I landed in England and saw the celebrations of a young Wayne Rooney's success, it was a different era, a different period, in many ways – from easy international air travel to the terms of literary study. However, as I reread my contribution to *English Literature in Context*, I am relieved to see continued resonances from that earlier period, for example in the paragraphs on slavery and slave narratives, and on colonial developments in India and in the novel. I am also delighted that the editor had the foresight to insist on relatively long periods, such as 'The Renaissance' or 'The Restoration and Eighteenth Century', and was able to set them in a cross-period conversation with each other. Both periods *and* persistence over time: English Literature in context need not mean English Literature in its periods.

NOTES

1. Rita Felski, *The Limits of Critique* (University of Chicago Press, 2015), p. 151.
2. Ted Underwood, *Why Literary Periods Mattered: Historical Contrast and the Prestige of English Studies* (Stanford University Press, 2013), p, 133.
3. Stephen Jay Greenblatt, *Shakespearean Negotiations: The Circulation of Social Energy in Renaissance England* (Berkeley: University of California Press, 1988), p. 1.
4. Fredric Jameson, *The Political Unconscious: Narrative as a Socially Symbolic Act* (Ithaca, NY: Cornell University Press, 1981), p. 9; subsequent references are incorporated in the main text.
5. Michel Foucault, *The Archaeology of Knowledge & the Discourse on Language* (New York: Pantheon, 1972), p. 28.
6. Mikhail Bakhtin, 'Forms of Time and of the Chronotope in the Novel: Notes Toward a Historical Poetics', in *The Dialogic Imagination*, ed. Michael Holquist, trans. Caryl Emerson and Michael Holquist (Austin: University of Texas Press, 1981), pp. 84–258 (p. 228).
7. Amit S. Yahav, *Feeling Time: Duration, the Novel, and Eighteenth-Century Sensibility* (Philadelphia: University of Pennsylvania Press, 2018), p. 7.
8. Samuel Richardson, *Clarissa, or the History of a Young Lady* (New York: Penguin, 1985), p. 721.
9. Jacques Derrida, *Of Grammatology*, trans. Gayatri Chakraborty Spivak, corrected edn (Baltimore: Johns Hopkins University Press, 1997), p. 12.
10. Jacques Derrida, *Specters of Marx: The State of the Debt, the Work of Mourning, & the New International* (New York: Routledge, 1994), p. 16; subsequent references are incorporated in the main text.
11. Wai Chee Dimock, 'A Theory of Resonance', *PMLA* 112.5 (1997), 1060–71 (1061).
12. Ibid., 1061.
13. Thomas Gray, 'Elegy Written in a Country Church Yard', in *Gray and Collins: Poetical Works*, ed. Austin Lane Poole (Oxford University Press, 1970), line 1; subsequent line references are incorporated in the main text.
14. John Guillory, *Cultural Capital: The Problem of Literary Canon Formation* (University of Chicago Press, 1993), p. 118; subsequent references are incorporated in the main text.
15. Gray to Mrs. Gray, [14] June 1740, *Correspondence of Thomas Gray*, ed. Paget Toynbee and Leonard Whibley, 3 vols (Oxford: Clarendon Press, 1936), vol. I, p. 164.

CRITICAL REFLECTIONS AND FURTHER STUDY

Much of my scholarship has been contextual. In addition to *English Literature in Context*, I have also contributed to *Samuel Johnson in Context* and to a collection on *Historicizing Theory*. My first monograph, *From the Temple to the Castle*, narrated an 'architectural history of British Literature' from John Milton to Horace Walpole (and beyond). In my second monograph, *The Constitution of Literature*, I contextualised the emergence of early English literary criticism, from Dryden to Johnson, in relation to debates about literacy and democracy in the wake of the English Civil Wars.

More recently, though, I have argued against an abstract periodisation of Milton's work as 'modern' and have come to think that historically oriented literary criticism is operating in a new, more complicated context today. In short, the past seems more contested now than it was in the early 2000s. Today, all sides are focused on the past, splintering it into heritage, tradition, memory and history. This contest over the past forms a vital new context for literary scholarship (and can provide a useful focus for further discussion of the issues raised in my essay), but only if we acknowledge it, accept that contexts are plural and variable, think critically about accepted overarching terms such as 'modern', and respond as directly as we can.

In my essay I reflect on methods, and sketch a history of how, in my experience, periodising and contextualising came to dominate literary study. My early relationship to literature was entirely studious. What I knew about literature, I learned at school; I was not going to learn about it at home. As a secondary school student I became interested first in criticism, in how to read well. One folksy teacher began with what he called 'the first rule of criticism: always give the author the benefit of the doubt', which still seems like good advice, especially to young readers. Another, in my fourth and final year, had written his dissertation under the direction of Northrop Frye ('Norrie'), and as a result insisted that there was a method for criticism, Frye's 1957 *Anatomy of Criticism*. By the time I was entering my second undergraduate year I had become an independent reader, and decided to study English literature, but I worried that literature formed a limit, that there should be more to literature than reading literature. So I also studied philosophy in order to acquire some familiarity with the work of leading figures of deconstruction and post-structuralism such as Foucault and Derrida, and, thereby, some continuation of the attention to method I had experienced in secondary school. After a 'Senior Thesis' on Michel Foucault's *Order of Things* (1966) and Thomas Pynchon's *V.* (1963) (in which I read the 'V.' in a Foucauldian way, as representing Language, Labour and Life, respectively), I took a gap year. As an undergraduate, I could never have predicted specialising in Restoration and Eighteenth Century English Literature. However, my reading of Pynchon had me wondering where 'the novel' came from, and led me, during my year off, to Sterne's *Tristram Shandy* and Richardson's *Clarissa* – to eighteenth-century novels. (I also read Jameson's *Political Unconscious* for the first time that year.)

Early in my post-graduate education a professor arrived for our seminar on Milton with an armful of copies of the *New York Times*, enough for everyone in the room. She distributed them, and together we learned from them about the wartime journalism of Paul de Man, a professor at Yale who had passed away a few years earlier, and who, during the Second World War, had written for a Nazi-affiliated newspaper in his native Belgium. Because it combined a deep

attention to method, to historical context, and to what was clearly a massive shift
in literary criticism unfolding in real time around those of my generation, that
day introduced me to formal post-graduate literary study. I struggled as a student
that year, adjusting not only to graduate school and life in America's largest
city but also to arriving in a department opposed to deconstruction, a movement
which struck some members of faculty as anti-Enlightenment and others as anti-
historicist. Realising that I would need to know more about literature in context, I
applied to MA programmes in history, and, accepted as a part-time student at the
same university, the rest was, as they say, history, literally. My first class meeting
in the History department mirrored the earlier Milton seminar. A senior member
of the history faculty, a major presence, was the guest lecturer for that first day.
He began by pointing at the nearby building that is home to the departments of
English, romance languages and philosophy, and thundering: 'There is a cancer
eating at the heart of history, and its name is deconstruction!' Uniquely, I had
just acquired a degree in that building, and I knew he was pointing in the wrong
direction, as the office holders over there shared precisely his own concerns.

Today, decades later, I still wonder who in that maelstrom was right. And I
worry anew about the unresolved tension between those buildings, the conflict
of the faculties. On that campus, where the faculty members in fact more or
less agreed, it was simply an unfortunate misunderstanding, but the larger
issue about the place of deconstruction (and of post-modernism and post-
structuralism) within literary studies remained. Besides, it was also in part a
misunderstanding both of Derrida (whose biographical context and interest in
the Enlightenment went largely unrecognised) and of formalism (which *can*
offer access to history, even if it hadn't done so for the New Critics). Derrida
is right about the value of play, and that structures require it; moreover, there
continue to be many false binaries which deconstruct upon inspection. But with
so much in play now, creating the impression that there is no ground of truth,
I am also sympathetic to the historian's concern for veracity. Plato would have
told him not to search after truth in the work of poets, but I have come to prefer
Aristotle's claim that history tells us what happened, once, whereas poetry tells
what it is likely to happen, again, giving literature a prophetic power tied to
pattern and probability. And imagination. History suggests it is going to become
very important again.

FURTHER READING

Benjamin, Walter, 'Theses on the Philosophy of History', in *Illuminations: Essays and Re-
     flections*, ed. Hannah Arendt (New York: Schocken, 1969), pp. 253–64
Butt, John, *The Augustan Age* (London: Hutchinson's University Library, 1950)
Easthope, Antony, *Literary into Cultural Studies* (London: Routledge, 1991)

Foucault, Michel, *The Order of Things: An Archaeology of the Human Sciences* (New York: Vintage, 1973)

Gallagher, Catherine, and Stephen Greenblatt, *Practicing New Historicism* (University of Chicago Press, 2000)

Hutcheon, Linda, and Mario J. Valdés (eds), *Rethinking Literary History: A Dialogue on Theory* (New York: Oxford University Press, 2002)

Nussbaum, Felicity A., and Laura Brown, *The New 18th Century: Theory, Politics, English Literature* (London: Methuen, 1987)

Sherman, Stuart, *Telling Time: Clocks, Diaries, and English Diurnal Form, 1660–1785* (University of Chicago Press, 1996)

Sobel, Dava, *Longitude: The True Story of a Lone Genius who Solved the Greatest Scientific Problem of His Time* (New York: Penguin, 1995)

10 Truth-Telling and the Representation of the Surinam 'Indians' in Aphra Behn's *Oroonoko*

ODDVAR HOLMESLAND

Abstract

The Native Americans of Surinam in *Oroonoko, or the Royal Slave* (1688) have generally been regarded as a marginal group with whom the English colonists seek to maintain friendly relations for trading purposes, though Behn situates them in a paradisaical, natural world. Idealisation and commercial interest curiously seem not quite to correspond. Representations of the commodified African slaves are similarly divided, for among them is a royal specimen whose 'greatness of soul', 'true honour' and 'absolute generosity' make him seem an expatriate from a world above. One wonders what idealised connection Behn may envisage between Oroonoko and the Surinamese. Idealising interpretations of the royal slave have mostly been in terms of aristocratic ideology and romance literature. Yet the romance has variously been taken to serve the royal cause against progressive change, as well as to glorify the colonial enterprise.[1] It is, however, after all not so certain that Behn employs romance and aristocratic virtues mainly towards a political statement. Such a political, realist approach has problems accounting for certain idealising narrative analogies.

For instance, the Surinamese captains remain ethnically remote, unlike the African prince, yet their heroism and honourableness suggest some mysterious non-European affinity with him. Further, their nobility does not hierarchically distance them from the rest of their community, as the royal African stands apart from his fellow slaves, and from the ignoble English councillors. There is a sense in which the American New World represents a utopian vision contrasted to the divided world that has enslaved Oroonoko. Significantly, the portrayals of both the Surinamese and Oroonoko are couched in terms of Christian allegory. A dialectic emerges by which, in the contradictory tradition of travel narratives, an idealising quest for a new order in the New World vies with imperialist motives. It is a dialectic that can best be examined against the background of scientific, religious and ideological transition taking place in England in the seventeenth century.

This essay explores how, in Aphra Behn's *Oroonoko* (1688), Christian allegory interweaves with romance in linking the Surinamese and the royal slave. There is a significant idealising dimension counterpointing one that subserves an empirically oriented political mode. The American New World 'represented to me [the narrator] an absolute idea of the first state of innocence, before Man knew how to sin', where, unaffected by religion or any other institutional divisions or 'inventions of Man', the Surinamese but follow 'virtuous' nature.[2] Behn (Figure 10.1) makes unmistakable allusions to Montaigne's image of the noble savage in 'Of Cannibals', with its borrowed motifs of the golden age and the Garden of Eden, idealising the world as a universal organism. She in this way signals a narrative search in *Oroonoko* for a lost, ethically better world. Though romance interacts with realism to produce signs of pro-colonialism as well as anti-colonialism, there is also an idealising quest for a new order in the New World. Such a reading offers a dialectical corrective to the current scholarly focus on political readings.

The resilience of romance and idealising Christian allegory in Behn's account indicates what Michael McKeon calls 'an epistemological crisis, a major cultural transition in attitudes toward how to tell the truth in narrative'.[3] Empiricism was taking over as the normative mode of truth-telling, and Behn engaged in translations from the early Enlightenment writer Fontenelle, whose works on science suggest the kind of questioning of Christian concepts that became fashionable during the Restoration. She also admired the materialist theories in Lucretius' *De rerum natura*, translated by her friend Thomas Creech. In her letter to Lord Maitland

Figure 10.1 Portrait of Aphra Behn by Sir Peter Lely, *c.* 1670.

prefacing *Oroonoko*, Behn promises that she will differentiate 'true story' from 'anything that seems Romantic' (p. 5). Her empiricist stance and her notion of truth still do not quite match. The disunity reflects the distortive effects to traditional conceptions of the relation of things to an overarching connectedness. Restoration England, like Restoration literature, became the meeting place for contradictory sentiments, longings and genres. Absolutism was giving way, though the return of Charles II in 1660, after the divisions wrought by civil war, was a political event with providential overtones. Panegyrics of welcome to the restored king were written: Dryden's *Astraea Redux* (1660), Cowley's 'Restoration Ode' (1660). Yet a sybaritic court culture soon started to set an example for the rest of the nation, the chief proponent being Charles himself. It became difficult to maintain a worshipful tone in the poetry of love when libertinism was the norm at court. Charles's licentiousness made it ever harder to sustain the myth of the divinity of kings. One of the dazzling members of his circle, John Wilmot, Earl of Rochester, lampooned the inglorious king: 'Nor are his high desires above his strength: / His scepter and his prick are of a length'.[4] Behn, a friend of Rochester's, followed up his irreverent tone in her narrative poem *A Voyage to the Isle of Love* (1684). Here she registers the gap left by spiritual authority gone decadent: '*the King resigns, / The Robe and Crown he wore*'. He has fallen from his height; he who should be the divinely ordained sovereign of his people has become a slave – of desire, which '*Conquers where, and whom it list, / The* Cottager *and* Prince'.[5] Behn's lines here mark a striking contrast to the portrayal of the noble Oroonoko and of the sublime love between him and Imoinda.

These images of a lapse from honour need to be taken into account in analysing Behn's realist encounter with idealising discourse. The doubt she sows about the true stature of royalty does not prevent signs of her royalist loyalty. Oroonoko does express regret over the 'deplorable death of our great monarch' – Charles I (p. 11), in whom he may see himself, and analogies may also be drawn from the royal slave to James II as a likely future victim of Parliament's progressive actions involving the Glorious Revolution of 1688.[6] Behn's ethical critique is, still, not reserved solely for the classes of merchants and slave traders. The political allegorising cannot fully contain the images of the morally fallen monarch she presents elsewhere, and whom she possibly camouflages here as Oroonoko's ignoble grandfather, the Coramantien king. Coveting Imoinda for himself, he sends her the royal veil, but his royal authority fails to confine her in his seraglio. He reaches his low point when out of spite he has her exported to Surinam to be sold into slavery, letting his grandson believe she is dead. We follow a narrative structure involving romance combined with Christian allegory that includes royalty among its targets. The Coramantien king's misdeed, and his withering power (he is too frail to consummate his conquest), with echoes of the myth of the ailing Fisher King, become symbolic of a fallen world that requires an allegorico-romantic saviour. The loss of

Imoinda takes the young lover through symbolic death – lying as though 'buried for two days' – to a Christlike resurrection, for when total disintegration by an invincible foe is imminent, the noble warrior rises 'like some divine power descended to save his country from destruction', and he 'inspire[s]' the hearts of his people with a 'new order' (p. 31). Yet in the world that is, a treacherous English sea captain next fetters Oroonoko and ships him off to Surinam to be sold as a slave. In Surinam, however, he is reunited with Imoinda, as if she too were miraculously resurrected. And yet, this fallen world remains one of confinement. In the end, he is tortured to death, but stands morally upright, 'fixed like a rock' (p. 72) before his persecutors. It takes but a small leap of the imagination to associate the 'new order' with the paradisaical order of the Surinamese.

Behn here targets the 'fallen' values of colonial culture, but equally the royal 'fall' that sets Oroonoko's tragedy in motion. It is consequently difficult to read a firm political stand into Behn's ethical critique. She may be exposing her political vacillation, but there is also a level at which she incorporates political ambiguities into another concern: the retracing of a version of the Renaissance commonplace of 'life as theatre', involving discrepancies between public role and the truth of the inner self. Oroonoko's grandfather is king, but reveals his inner pettiness. The sea captain possesses mere outward marks of nobility, 'so that he seemed rather never to have been bred out of a court' (p. 33). His implied comparison with the royal slave – who 'in all points addressed himself as if his education had been in some European court' (p. 11) – is sarcastic, and his treacherous personality has more in common with the Coramantien king. Court culture and colonial culture are in this way brought together for scrutiny. Oroonoko had naively believed that white men of Christian countries live as they teach, but unmasks how they 'prefer the bare name of religion and, without virtue or morality, think that sufficient' (p. 14), assuming a merely nominal Christian stature. There is an inversion of Oroonoko's mistaking the sea captain's noble appearance for his true self. With biblical overtones, the English councillors fail to see through to Oroonoko's inner nobility – 'his misfortune was to fall in an obscure world' (p. 40) – though his inner worth is all he has left, having been deprived of title and position.[7] Behn's voyage to the New World carries the sense of a lapse of unity between the inward and outward, which might be retrieved in a more natural order.

Her exploration of worth in the New World feeds on traditional idealising discourses, but as approached by a questioning, empirically motivated narrator. In her concern to unmask empty form in the image of a restored inner–outer correspondence, she imposes her rational outlook on allegorico-romance conventions while in a sense also invoking them. From her 'eye-witness' (p. 6) point of view, Behn's narrator typifies a Protestant age in which the visible was increasingly referred to as a criterion for validating spiritual versions of truth. Such thinking later led Daniel Defoe to state that 'We can Form no Idea of any Thing that we know not and have not seen, but in the Form of something that we have seen'.[8] And yet, though new, progressive ideas liberated minds and invigorated quests for authenticity, they unsettled 'truths' handed down by feudalism and romance literature. The New World became a rendezvous for unstable as well as contradictory conceptions and motivations to be explored and resolved – not without a sense of loss of concord with some truth associated with the order of nature. In this complex situation, empiricism in *Oroonoko* serves to expose the deceptiveness of outer form, but falls short of defining how to rectify that lost concord.

The empiricist outlook places Behn's narrator as a spectator who, paradoxically, invokes a compensatory pastoral order – an innocent, stable Surinamese community living in unspoilt 'natural' harmony. Her New World idealism is still not in clear opposition to the imperialist discourse, but is, as often in the period, assimilated into it, and so keeps the spectator at an idealising distance. *Oroonoko*, in this respect, fits into a longer early modern legacy of travel narratives. Sir Walter Ralegh's *Discoverie of Guiana* (1596) seems to have been a specific influence on *Oroonoko*, recounting Ralegh's explorations of a kingdom near the Orinoco. He marvels at the unequalled idyll which 'hath yet her maidenhead, never sacked, turned, nor wrought', though he cannot resist an appeal to the 'Lady of Ladies to possesse it'.[9] The narrator of *Oroonoko* shares in this colonialising spirit when lamenting what 'his late Majesty of sacred memory' had 'lost by losing that part of America' to the Dutch (pp. 47, 57) (Figure 10.2). Yet encounter with the New World could also stir a sense in the Europeans of being non-comprehending outsiders to a truer order of nature.

The eyewitness position helps Behn dismantle established concepts that restrict opened vision, but with a remaining sense that all understanding is limited. Her empiricist method does not sufficiently serve her wider concern to recover some state of truth mysteriously associated with the Surinamese and Oroonoko. Conceiving of them in allegorico-romantic fashion, she attempts to validate these discourses through observation; or, one could say her method, of the kind McKeon calls 'naive empiricism',[10] attempts too much, and she resorts to Christian allegory and romance in order to make sense of her observations. Beyond her eyewitness range, she has to rely on her protagonist's story of himself as a prince in Coramantien, but the meaning she derives from it – involving prodigious adventures and matchless grandeur – surpasses the social particularities in which she tries to anchor it. The aspect of Christian allegory added to romance equivocates between individual history and overarching pattern. Idealising discourse is only one aspect of the attempted truth-telling, for experience teaches the narrator and her fellow English to fear Oroonoko's and the Surinamese capacity for brutality – a capacity the English also betray themselves. The complexity of truth-telling shows in terms of contrary narrative perspectives that add up to an implied irony: Behn's narrator trying to understand the otherness of Oroonoko and the Surinamese, and

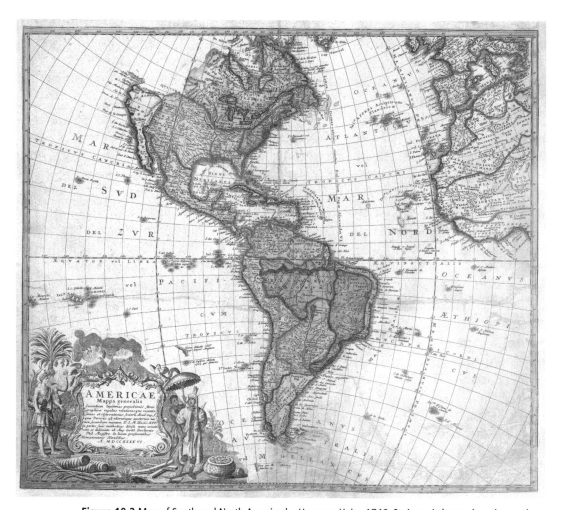

Figure 10.2 Map of South and North America by Homann Heirs, 1746. Surinam is located on the north coast of South America a little to the east of where the chain of Caribbean islands curves down to the coast; it is neighboured to the west by Guyana (formerly British Guiana). Although this historical map makes seeing detail difficult, it has the advantage of clearly showing the relative positions of Europe, West Africa and the New World, and therefore of the triangular slave-trade routes.

Oroonoko, in turn, acting as the non-comprehending explorer of the otherness of the English. There is a level at which Behn distributes contrary perspectives across her narrative, seeking to understand what bars truthful vision – and access to the Surinamese state of 'tranquillity' (p. 8).

It might be objected to this concern with Christian allegorising that neither the Surinamese nor Oroonoko live by faith, nor does Oroonoko die for it.[11] Behn's conception of true ennoblement can still not be dissociated from a Christian frame of reference. She regards the English through an African who is estranged from a clericalism that breeds mere pretence. Her truth-telling is in search of an order in which individuals freely share a code rooted in virtuous nature – somehow accounting for the Surinamese state of 'tranquillity'. This point is brought into relief through the many lapses from such an ideal. The young prince first follows his faith in a higher ethical order when breaking with the Coramantien willingness to 'pay a most absolute resignation to the monarch' (p. 14). Such unquestioning submission comes across as slavelike when viewed against the episode in which Oroonoko, wanting to stir an insurrection to gain freedom, reproaches his uninspired fellow slaves for acquiescing in slavery. They first refuse to venture, but then, swayed by his powerful rhetoric, they 'bowed and kissed his feet ... and with one accord vowed to follow him to death' (p. 59). Their motivation is dubious. Rather than demand their subjection, Oroonoko appealed to their honour as free souls, and that they should not 'leave that better part of themselves to perish' (p. 59). This becomes clear when the slaves soon abandon Oroonoko, leaving him only the brave Tuscan and his 'heroic Imoinda' to fight the pursuing mob. Oroonoko later gives voice to the irony in 'endeavouring to make those free who were by nature slaves, poor, wretched rogues, fit to be used as Christians' tools, dogs treacherous and cowardly fit for such masters' (pp. 61-2). Behn portrays him as a moral and spiritual leader appealing to an inward sense of purpose, and she grants the common multitude no constancy compared to the lone knight of epic or romance. There is a telling parallel in her play *The Widow Ranter*, in which the character General Bacon confronts a mob of planters easily swayed by those who appear most in power. To the Council's promise of a reward for capturing Bacon dead or alive, the mob chants in unison: 'let's fall on *Bacon* – let's fall on *Bacon*, hay ... Ay, ay, hang *Bacon*, hang *Bacon*'. But when Bacon, alone, faces the councillors and the crowd, their fickle loyalty shifts: 'A *Bacon*, a *Bacon*, a *Bacon*'.[12] Bacon and the native American king Cavernio equally find themselves surrounded by limited minds. The two are ethnically apart, but they make a bond according to chivalric ideals. As in romance, battle is the test of worth, and the play presents flickering images of the encounter between the English and the natives – most of whom in this case act like the slaves in *Oroonoko*. The king is in pursuit of escaping natives across the stage, crying 'turn, turn, ye fugitive Slaves, and face the Enemy'.[13] In her preface to *The Second Part of the Rover*, Behn equally denominates the white populace 'the unconsidering Rest' and berates England for having 'reduc'd all the Noble, Brave and Honest, to the Obedience of the ill-gotten Power, and worse-acted Greatness of the Rabble'.[14]

Returning to *Oroonoko*: though the situation concerns physical liberation, and ambiguously addresses the abolition issue, it also involves an idealised natural order sustained by an inner state. The royal slave tells the other slaves they have 'lost the divine quality of men' and exist in spiritual subservience to a confining system; *that* in itself is slavelike, and not for 'human souls' (pp. 57–8). By implication, this is also the enslaved spiritual state of the English, most of whom suffer from partial vision. They are outsiders to honour within. The enslaved Africans flee from combat for fear of being physically wounded, but they are, at a different level, evading the steadfastness it takes to spiritually free themselves from slavishness. This is in contrast to Oroonoko. His self-mutilation when finally surrounded by the English reveals a symbolic consanguinity with the Surinamese captains who, by self-inflicted scarring, prove their inner quality. Behn's narrator witnesses the 'formidable wounds and scars, or rather dismemberings', and infers ''tis by a passive valour they show and prove their activity', meaning 'their souls were very humane and noble' (pp. 55–6). Their unflinching calm under self-torture symbolises how contrary, self-enslaving forces must be withstood to activate humanity's noble potential. The Surinamese captains, by their noble souls, act as leaders and inspirers of their community, inducing a state of 'tranquillity' in a world of division. It is a role that Behn intends for Oroonoko, but under less promising conditions.

There are analogies between the Surinamese captains' 'passive valour' and Oroonoko passively awaiting his pursuers in the end, and then calmly smoking his pipe while being hacked to death. Oroonoko is like George Eagles in John Foxe's *Book of Martyrs*, who remains 'steadfast and constant' under torture, being finally, like Oroonoko, quartered and the quarters sent to different parts of the country.[15] Behn draws on European narrative models of martyrdom to align Oroonoko's stoic response to pain with the Surinamese ideal. However, she extends it to a native African ideal too. By association, Imoinda also demonstrates the inner constancy of a martyr through her 'heroic' (p. 67) self-sacrifice. Vincent Brown explains that 'according to Africans' prevailing beliefs, the spirits of executed rebels, at least those who were born in Africa, probably returned to Africa'.[16] Such faith sustains Imoinda's martyrdom – she will be rewarded by being 'sent in her own country (for that's their notion of the next world)' (p. 68). When knowledge of slave executions in the Caribbean spread in Britain, Brown notes, they were 'understood according to the same conventions used to describe the passion of Jesus Christ and the political executions of later martyrs'.[17] This would have been Behn's understanding after her visit to Surinam.

These analogies between European, Surinamese and African virtues of composure under pain indicate the conglomerate metaphorical levels in Behn's narrative, and the difficulty of unifying them in a politically motivated realist mode. Barbara Foley, for instance, finds that Oroonoko's 'majestic demeanor through his dismemberment' lacks verisimilitude because he is too like a 'typical Restoration nobleman' and therefore an unconvincing 'African analogue to James II'. Had Behn asserted that Oroonoko simply 'exemplifies the cardinal virtues of monarchy', Foley maintains, she could more effectively have spoken against the 'cruelties of slavery and the injustices presumably done to the Stuarts'.[18] Yet the extension of 'majestic demeanor' to both Imoinda and the Surinamese captains adds a metaphorical dimension beyond such an imputed intention. Oroonoko believes in 'honour [as] the first principle in nature that was to be obeyed', including 'all the acts of virtue, compassion, charity, love, justice, and reason' (pp. 58–9), and this faith equips him with stoic composure under pain. He is of the same grain as Imoinda and the Surinamese captains – a mysterious connection still to be fully understood by Behn exploring the New World. Imoinda triumphs over slavery through death. Oroonoko explicitly associates such heroism with inward as much as physical release – a capacity to bear suffering and 'find a glory and fortitude in oppression'. By further associating true honour with a 'divine quality of men' (p. 57), Behn rhetorically draws on cardinal virtues encompassing martyrology and the faith, hope and *caritas* of St Paul's Christian doctrine (1 Corinthians 13, AV). Honour in such classic Christian terms safeguards against slavishness, which is in Oroonoko's mind when accusing his fellow Africans of being 'by nature slaves' (p. 62). His message pertains to a metaphorical level that complicates abolitionist or anti-colonial readings. Physical freedom from slavery may not liberate minds from slavishness. Deputy Governor Byam and the local councillors are ironic proof of that.

Behn's narrator, like her fellow English in the colony, lacks understanding of Surinamese living, though it fascinates her. The Surinamese are to her as mysterious as their land: 'a continent whose vast extent was never yet known' (p. 47). An explorer of the unknown, she construes it in the discourse of a pastoral retreat suggestive of humankind's first state, with connotations of a Platonic sphere of essence. Here 'there is no novelty', and so 'no curiosity' (p. 8); justice and virtue exist to her as in an unchanging state of perfection. She makes gestures towards bringing Plato's world of Ideas down to the validating level of the senses, unconcealed by appearances or English pretence, so that 'all you can see, you see at once, and every moment see' (p. 8). Such seeing is still wishful thinking, and she puts her trust in a noble mediator, Oroonoko, who may communicate with the Surinamese through affinity, and who strikes 'an awe and reverence even in those that knew not his quality'. On an excursion into the Surinamese interior, his 'native beauty' (p. 10) forges transethnic bonds and a 'good understanding between the Indians and the English' (p. 56).

The narrator's perspective remains limited, however; she and the other English are still to understand how to 'see', for they let their utilitarian view of the Surinamese world dominate. There is a level at which the narrator imaging exotic objects of trade in an allegorically tinged setting marks her as an uninitiated seeker of inside vision. She marvels at the curiosities and 'little rarities, as marmosets … of a marvellous and delicate shape … little parakeetoes, great parrots, macaws, and a thousand other birds and beasts of wonderful and surprising forms, shapes, and colours … also some rare flies, of amazing forms and colours … all of various excellencies, such as art cannot imitate' (pp. 6–7). Ramesh Mallipeddi is partly right when taking this prodigious vision to be a mere catalogue of exotic objects, 'wonderful qua commodities', denoting England's ideological shift to an imperial trading power. He notes 'the narrator's ecstatic description' of this unknown natural life, yet concludes that the 'descriptive detail here is pleasurable' chiefly because it attaches to 'exotic commodities' to be displayed in England as commercial spectacle.[19] There are signs here of what Laura Brown interprets as 'Behn's enumeration of these goods', a 'proliferate listing' which would 'express the period's fascination with imperialist accumulation'.[20] To Katherine Acheson, the Surinamese themselves are depicted in a 'naturalistic tableau', with a sense of inspectional distance between perceiver and object.[21]

The image of the natives in their natural environment admittedly has a scopic quality, but seeing the Surinamese scene only in terms of exotic objects for commerce and display is to miss the English distance from an original state, which the narrator only vaguely apprehends. Yet it is there to be explored. Gabrielle Starr has a point when proposing that Behn writes in the Epicurean tradition, according to which the true form of the world is only accessible to the imagination (Epicurean *phantasia*) that 'perceives form because it is made of the forms it perceives'.[22] Or in Cicero's view: it takes beauty on the inside to see 'beauty, loveliness, harmony in the visible world; and Nature and Reason, extending the analogy of this from the world of sense to the world of spirit, find that beauty, consistency, order are far more to be maintained in thought and deed'.[23] Behn's narrator seeks such a correlation between inner and outer forms (an ideal that became a commonplace in the Renaissance), and so to partake of the Surinamese 'tranquillity' – a stark contrast to the situation in the English-dominated dystopian colony. The colonists' way of seeing makes them outsiders; they catalogue a natural state that to them is new and strange, selecting only appearances of full knowledge. It was as a remedy for such a condition that Francis Bacon launched his programme for the renewal of learning, in order to regain the 'pure light of natural knowledge', a fullness of insight presumed to have lapsed since the original state of perfection.[24] The Surinamese world lures the divided narrator with its image of fullness.

Oroonoko thus begins by establishing the estrangement of the Europeans from natural knowledge. Behn's narrator contemplates the Surinamese as having 'all that is called beauty'. The body decorations they share with Imoinda and Oroonoko suggest their affinity, for they have faces 'painted in little specks or flowers here and there', Imoinda is 'carved in fine flowers and birds all over her body', and Oroonoko is 'carved with a little flower or bird at the sides of the temples' (pp. 7, 44). The narrator invokes *phantasia* in terms of an Aristotelian desire for the mind to mediate anything not actually present to the senses with a mental image,[25] and the image takes on biblical overtones from Genesis and *Paradise Lost*, Book IV, showing the Surinamese as sublime forms in the bounty of the Creation. Particulars, composed of beads of many colours, the Surinamese exquisitely 'weave into aprons' that 'they wear just before 'em, as Adam and Eve did the fig leaves'; otherwise they are 'unadorned, so like our first parents before the Fall'. Paradise beckons with the prospect that 'one lives forever among 'em' (p. 7). This idealising vision sheds light on Oroonoko's complaint that the other slaves have 'lost the divine quality of men' – ennobled 'human souls' perceiving particulars with shimmerings of 'eternity' (pp. 57–8). With the Surinamese, the narrator feels she is close to knowledge. The English, relying on Oroonoko's mediating nobility, even begin to imitate Surinamese grace: 'With these people ... we live in perfect tranquillity' (p. 9).

Behn's dedicatory epistle to Lord Maitland and his wife prepares for the Surinamese items and attributes being associated with God's plenitude. The Maitlands, like the Surinamese, are seen to embody life's 'flowing plenty', so that their 'tranquil lives are an image of the new made and beautiful pair in paradise' (pp. 4–5). This idealising of the Maitlands in association with the Surinamese further contradicts a mere mercantile value given the Surinamese. The narrator explains that they 'caress 'em as friends' because they are 'very useful to us ... nor dare we do other, their numbers so far surpassing ours in that continent' (p. 9), but the amity cannot be reduced to 'pragmatic necessity' and the masking of 'hostility and fear'.[26] Wonder and fascination underlie their calculated pose. From their place in the 'fallen' world, divided by power, they seek a vital connection they have lost. They revere the Surinamese for the knowledge they hope to regain, but they cannot bear too much strangeness.

For all the idealising of Surinamese primitivism, however, Behn does not deem regression to it a European solution. Her hero is too advanced in wit and learning to be identified with the 'tranquillity they possess by ignorance' (p. 8). He has been taught 'morals, language, and science' (p. 11), and his wide education separates him from the Surinamese. And yet, the fact that his faculties are so exquisitely proportioned mimics their tranquil grace, suggestive of his kinship with them. Oroonoko has grown from his origins, but his naturalness is integral to his learning. His knowledge still has a flaw in common with the Surinamese. With allusions to Genesis 3, remedy requires a fall into knowledge of good and evil in the world beyond the Surinamese Arcady. The idyll of the Surinamese is after all not inviolate. Their lack of realist awareness exposes them to outside treachery and corruption. Behn's idealism carries a grain of irony when she notes how gullible the Surinamese are: 'it were not difficult to establish any unknown or extravagant religion among them, and to impose any notions or fictions upon 'em' (p. 54). Irony analogously adheres to Oroonoko who, in Coramantien, falls prey to the English sea captain's duplicity. The prince had naively believed the Englishman to be as honourable as himself, but his honour is only on the outside. He is similarly deceived by the deputy governor, a 'fawning, fair-tongued fellow' who 'made use of all his art of talking and dissembling', persuading him to finally yield himself in exchange for honourable treatment (pp. 60–1). Oroonoko, like the Surinamese, needs to widen his knowledge of a world that has fallen from the ideal.

From Oroonoko's perspective of honour, the 'new and strange' to be explored is paradoxically what the English have made of the world. For the colonists, however, perceiving the Surinamese world as the 'new and strange' is a symptom of their 'ignorance' – the negative of the positive 'ignorance' of the Surinamese, dividing the English off from 'tranquillity'. These divided perspectives on the ideal and the real continue to inform truth-telling in the story. The narrator's idealised impression of Oroonoko as having 'nothing of barbarity in his nature' (p. 11) reveals, perhaps, her limited understanding. After his killing of Imoinda to prevent her falling into the merciless hands of the English, she thinks him 'brave and just' when she has heard his reasons, but she makes no secret of how 'horrid it at first appeared to us all' (p. 67). Her uncertainty makes her collude with the English to spy on him to find out if he is planning an uprising, and she chooses to be absent during his trial. The English also fall out of the 'perfect tranquillity and good understanding' (p. 9) they have courted with the Surinamese, and the Surinamese similarly show signs of realist awakening. Having lived in a stable and unchanging way, the balance of their world has been disrupted and they fall into dispute with the colonists and attack them, largely because of the Dutch, 'who used 'em not so civilly as the English' (p. 52). All parties strive to sort appearance from truth, the ideal from the real, and vice versa.

Behn's attempt at truth-telling tussles with ideological ambivalence, multiple voices and positionings. Reliance on realism reveals limitations of belief in individual, rational apprehension of truth. One may trace in the narrative an aspiration to compensate for this impasse. In Bacon's phrase, man 'being a spirit newly inclosed in a body of earth, he was fittest to be allured with appetite of light and liberty of knowledge'.[27] Exploring how to restore natural vision, Behn leans on the royal slave figuring as the Surinamese's enlightened, increasingly self-conscious heir. In the final analysis, he is more like a paradigm than an embodiment of the high potential of a human order. His impact is mainly to reveal the shortcomings of the contemporary world. When, at the end, the narrator expresses hope that her pen will 'make his glorious name to survive to all ages' (p. 73), her canonisation of him has a touch of self-parody. It leaves her, along with the other English, as an outsider to an ethical order embodied by Oroonoko and the Surinamese.

NOTES

1. See Lee Morrissey's contextual account of the dynamics of truth-telling and questions of genre in his 'Reading' of *Oroonoko*, in Paul Poplawski (ed.), *English Literature in Context*, 2nd edn (Cambridge University Press, 2017), pp. 252–4.
2. Aphra Behn, *Oroonoko and Other Writings*, ed. Paul Salzman (Oxford University Press, 1994), p. 8; subsequent page references are given in the main text.
3. Michael McKeon, *The Origins of the English Novel, 1600–1740*, 15th anniversary edn (Baltimore: Johns Hopkins University Press, 2002), p. 20.

4. John Wilmot, Earl of Rochester, 'A Satyr on Charles II', in *The Complete Poems of John Wilmot, Earl of Rochester*, ed. David M. Vieth (New Haven, CT: Yale University Press, 1968), p. 60, lines 10–11.

5. Aphra Behn, *A Voyage to the Isle of Love*, in *The Works of Aphra Behn*, ed. Janet Todd, 7 vols (London: Pickering, 1992), vol. I, p. 105, lines 139–42.

6. Lee Morrissey, 'Transplanting English Plantations in Aphra Behn's *Oroonoko*', *Global South* 2 (2016), 13.

7. Behn explores a reality marked by what McKeon calls a 'crisis of status inconsistency' – in an age in which the English 'learned to question the tacit presumption that worth follows birth, separating out merit or virtue as independent variables'. Scepticism about traditional authority accompanies an 'early modern secularisation crisis' with a concomitant 'early modern division of knowledge' (*Origins of the English Novel*, pp. xxii, xxiv, xxvi).

8. Daniel Defoe, 'A Vision of the Angelick World', in *Serious Reflections during the Life and Surprising Adventures of Robinson Crusoe: With His Vision of the Angelick World* (London: W. Taylor, 1720), p. 46.

9. Walter Ralegh, *Sir Walter Ralegh's Discoverie of Guiana*, ed. Joyce Lorimer, Hakluyt Society, 3rd series, 15 (Burlington, VT: Ashgate, 2006), p. 221.

10. McKeon, *Origins of the English Novel*, p. 21.

11. Cynthia Richards argues that Behn 'systematically strips Oroonoko of any higher calling' ('Interrogating *Oroonoko*: Torture in a New World and a New Fiction of Power', *Eighteenth-Century Fiction* 4 (2013), 647–76 (654)); and Anita Pacheco views Behn as eager to 'overturn the existing religious order', and Oroonoko as 'guided by honor' as a wholly 'social and secular principle' associated with 'genteel status' and 'the ruling class' ('"Little Religion" but "Admirable Morals": Christianity and Honor in Aphra Behn's *Oroonoko*', *Modern Philology* 2 (2013), 253–80 (278, 259, 266)).

12. Aphra Behn, *The Widow Ranter*, III.ii, in *Aphra Behn: Five Plays*, ed. Maureen Duffy (London: Methuen, 1993), pp. 260–1.

13. Ibid., IV.ii (p. 267).

14. Aphra Behn, *The Second Part of the Rover*, in *Works*, ed. Todd, vol. VI, p. 228.

15. John Foxe, *Foxe's Book of Martyrs: Select Narratives*, ed. John N. King (Oxford University Press, 2009), pp. 235–6.

16. Vincent Brown, *The Reaper's Garden: Death and Power in the World of Atlantic Slavery*, new edn (Cambridge, MA: Harvard University Press, 2010), p. 152.

17. Ibid., p. 154.

18. Barbara Foley, *Telling the Truth: The Theory and Practice of Documentary Fiction* (Ithaca, NY: Cornell University Press, 1986), p. 117.

19. Ramesh Mallipeddi, 'Spectacle, Spectatorship, and Sympathy in Aphra Behn's *Oroonoko*', *Eighteenth-Century Studies* 4 (2012), 475–96 (478–9).

20. Laura Brown, *Ends of Empire: Women and Ideology in Early Eighteenth-Century English Literature* (Ithaca, NY: Cornell University Press, 1993), p. 43.

21. Katherine Acheson, *Visual Rhetoric and Early Modern English Literature* (Farnham: Ashgate, 2013), p. 150.

22. Gabrielle Starr, 'Cavendish, Aesthetics, and the Anti-Platonic Line', *Eighteenth-Century Studies* 3 (2006), 295–308 (300).

23. Marcus Tullius Cicero, *De Officiis*, trans. Walter Miller, ed. Jeffrey Henderson, Loeb Classical Library (1913; Cambridge, MA: Harvard University Press, 2001), Book I, section 4.14.

24. Francis Bacon, *Valerius Terminus: Of the Interpretation of Nature* (1603), chapter 1, ed. Gisela Engel, Project Gutenberg Literary Archive Foundation, 2002: www.gutenberg.org/files/3290/3290-h/3290-h.html (accessed 29 June 2020).

25. See Franco F. Orsucci, *Changing Mind: Transitions in Natural and Artificial Environments* (London: World Scientific Publishing, 2002), p. 82.

26. Mallipeddi, 'Spectacle, Spectatorship', 479.

27. Bacon, *Valerius Terminus*, chapter 1.

CRITICAL REFLECTIONS AND FURTHER STUDY

This essay hinges on a central structural question: does colonial commerce encroach on the paradisaical world of the Surinamese, or should one rather read the juxtaposition in terms of a separation, or 'fall', from ideals? There is trading contact between the English and the Surinamese, and one could view the unexplored paradise in line with contemporary travel narratives idealising bountiful, virgin land as a treasure for conquest. The Surinamese could thus be grouped together with the enslaved prince and fellow African slaves as subjects of colonial commerce. However, a different focus is possible: with its biblical allusions, the Surinamese world posits an ethical antithesis to the English. The story of the noble African slave similarly follows a Christian allegorical structure. This indicates some affinity between the Surinamese and Oroonoko that makes them stand apart from the English, and possibly also from the other enslaved Africans. It may in addition be significant that the Surinamese, unlike the Africans, have not 'fallen' into slavery. This could mean that the royal slave, at some metaphorical level, is not enslaved either.

What has been outlined here is a narrative of metaphorical complexity. From the political point of view, one may wonder if Behn reveals her imperialist frame of mind or her aristocratic critique of a commodifying progressive culture. She might, in an abolitionist spirit, portray Oroonoko as a victim of slavery for largely ethical reasons. If we pursue the ethical link between Oroonoko and the Surinamese, however, another interpretative level opens up: Oroonoko's enslavers are in a sense more 'enslaved' than him – by their distance from Oroonoko and the Surinamese world, and, implicitly, by their lack of truthful ethical vision. Could one, by way of comparison, also view Oroonoko's fellow slaves as being, not only physically, but also mentally and spiritually enslaved?

How one leans here has ramifications for the interpretation of the story as a whole. Behn on the first few pages presents Oroonoko as a paragon of truth and nobility. He falls victim to false honour and deceptiveness: shown first by the Coramantien king, then by the English sea captain, and finally by the glib tongue of the English deputy governor. By contrast, Oroonoko's noble appearance and demeanour reflect his inner quality – as in the world of the Surinamese, where no posing exists, but where 'all you can see, you see at once' (p. 8) – or, at least, that is how the narrator wishes to imagine it. There could be some irony in the fact that it is such incongruity between outwardness and inwardness in others that strips the prince of his formal position, so that he only retains the inward quality that the Coramantien king, the English sea captain and the English councillors lack. Oroonoko's tragic story could then be seen to follow a Christian allegorical structure: a 'fall' into betrayal and symbolic crucifixion in a world separated from the unfallen order in the New World. To Oroonoko, the English would be separated because they deceptively 'prefer the bare name of religion' (p. 14). His fellow slaves would betray their slavishness by too willingly relinquishing their free souls to the false truth of power.

This approach to *Oroonoko* – as representing a divided world in need of a restored ethical standard – has to contend with much textual intricacy and ambiguity. The heterogeneity may not only reflect Behn's political vacillation, nor just the problem of handling diverse genres in a contradictory age. It is worth considering if Behn also makes contradictoriness part of a defamiliarising strategy. She shifts the setting away from England to a world 'new and strange' (p. 6), which enables her to dismantle established conceptions of worth. Seeking to unmask hollow claims to honour and power, she imposes her empiricist point of view on allegorico-romance conventions, while also in a sense invoking ideals associated with them. Further, she views her world from contrary perspectives: the narrator trying to understand the otherness of Oroonoko and the Surinamese, and Oroonoko, in turn, acting as the estranged examiner of the otherness of the English. She even makes her Europeanised royal African an anticipator of the Enlightenment, his knowledge of science and Christian ethics conveniently equipping him as a sceptical and discriminating scrutiniser of character.

It takes close reading to discern how multiple metaphorical levels in Behn's narrative yield tentative, dialectical solutions. Many would argue that Behn's basic royalism shines through, but that does not mean she holds individual royals to be immune to ethical lapses. Fighting slavishness, moreover, is not the same as fighting slavery. By bringing Oroonoko close to the yet uncharted land of the Surinamese, Behn may be seen to explore the New World in search of healing virtues for a progressive, yet divided, Restoration world. She may be seen to look for some vital connection that has been lost.

FURTHER READING

Aravamudan, Srinivas, *Tropicopolitans: Colonialism and Agency, 1688–1804* (Durham, NC: Duke University Press, 1999). Suggests that Oroonoko's chivalric qualities subject him to 'pethood'.

Brown, Laura, *Ends of Empire: Women and Ideology in Early Eighteenth-Century English Literature* (Ithaca, NY: Cornell University Press, 1993). Argues that features of romance remove the royal slave's otherness, and so produce a site of colonial critique.

Holmesland, Oddvar, *Utopian Negotiation: Aphra Behn and Margaret Cavendish* (Syracuse University Press, 2013). Explores Behn's search for mediating solutions in an ideologically contradictory world.

Hughes, Derek, 'Race, Gender, and Scholarly Practice: Aphra Behn's *Oroonoko*', *Essays in Criticism* 1 (2002), 1–22. Finds the idea of racial otherness to be absent in Behn's writing.

Renen, Denys van, 'Reimagining Royalism in Aphra Behn's America', *Studies in English Literature, 1500–1900* 3 (2013), 499–521. Suggests that native Surinam represents royalist values that might rejuvenate England.

Ross, Deborah, '*Oroonoko*: A Pastoral History', in *The Excellence of Falsehood: Romance, Realism, and Women's Contribution to the Novel* (Lexington: University Press of Kentucky, 1991), pp. 16–38. On how Behn mixes realism and romance to make *Oroonoko* seem true.

Shakespeare, William, *The Tempest* (first performed 1611). Interesting analogies may be found between Behn's portrayal of the Surinamese and Shakespeare's treatment of his island: see, for example, Gonzalo's speech on travellers' tales in Act III, scene iii.

Sussman, Charlotte, 'The Other Problem with Women: Reproduction and Slave Culture in Aphra Behn's *Oroonoko*', in Heidi Hutner (ed.), *Rereading Aphra Behn: History, Theory, and Criticism* (Charlottesville: University Press of Virginia, 1993), pp. 212–33. Suggests that Behn's use of romance deflects ideological or political critique.

Todd, Janet, *The Sign of Angellica: Women, Writing, and Fiction, 1660–1800* (New York: Columbia University Press, 1989). Discusses Behn as a supporter of Charles II.

11 'The Pamphlet on the Table': *The Life and Adventures of Sir Launcelot Greaves*

RICHARD J. JONES

Abstract

This essay explores how a work of fiction appeared in a magazine and how the work of a magazine appeared in a fiction. The fiction is *The Life and Adventures of Sir Launcelot Greaves* (1760–1) by the eighteenth-century Scottish writer, Tobias Smollett. The magazine is one of his periodical projects, *The British Magazine*, which ran for eight years from 1760. In part, then, the essay is interested in foregrounding and backgrounding these two contexts: it is interested in how fiction was created in the expanding print culture of the mid eighteenth century; it also suggests how that same print culture was supported by a fiction.

The essay is intended to complement approaches to Smollett which see him working for the most part as a novelist. In the eighteenth century, Smollett was best known as a historian, critic and translator; he worked tirelessly on vast publishing projects, often issued in instalments. The essay first establishes this context – the culture of periodical writing that marked the Enlightenment period – and then provides a short reading of *Launcelot Greaves* as part of it. Informing this reading is Smollett's interest in Miguel de Cervantes's great work *Don Quixote* (1605 and 1615); this might be thought of as providing another context for understanding the ambitions of Smollett's writing. The essay therefore raises questions about the kind of work in which Smollett was engaged – and perhaps the kind of stories we tell ourselves about what writing is and what it does.

Over a period of two years, from around January 1760 to December 1761, the Scottish writer Tobias Smollett (1721–71) could be found working on a prose narrative: *The Life and Adventures of Sir Launcelot Greaves*. Despite this extended time frame (and the short length of the completed text), it has often been seen as one of his most careless and rushed works. Walter Scott, for example, later described Smollett as residing in the Scottish borders and writing piecemeal: 'when post-time drew near, he used to retire for half an hour, to prepare the necessary quantity of copy, as it is technically called in the printing-house, which he never gave himself the trouble to correct, or even read over'.[1] Scott's erroneous account, which has been seen as damaging the reputation of Smollett's work, has nevertheless inspired many attempts to reclaim the latter as a 'significant achievement' – in other words, to present it as deserving of a place in the history of the novel.[2] In such a history, Smollett is perhaps best known for *The Adventures of Roderick Random* (his first novel, published in 1748) and *The Expedition of Humphry Clinker* (his last novel, published in 1771). Placing *Launcelot Greaves* in this context, however – or, indeed, trying to fit Smollett's other writing into it – does not really help us to understand Smollett's significant achievements. Instead, in this essay, I want to consider Smollett's writing as part of a different history, one that can be glimpsed in Scott's anecdote about the 'post-time' and the 'printing-house'. This is the history of 'communication at a distance': the proliferation of print and other forms of mediation in the mid eighteenth century that gave rise to the event we know as the Enlightenment.[3] In this history, *Launcelot Greaves* is not so much a novel as an example of periodical writing. I want therefore to explore its relationship to the *British Magazine* – the periodical, owned by Smollett, in which the narrative was first published in instalments. In exploring this relationship, my interest is not just in the way *Launcelot Greaves* appears in the periodical, but also in the way the periodical appears in *Launcelot Greaves* – or, to put this slightly differently, how the narrative opens up a space for the *British Magazine* itself.

An article in the *Public Ledger*, published about a month after the first number of the *British Magazine*, suggests some of the ways that *Launcelot Greaves* was (literally and metaphorically) bound up with the writing of a periodical. The article purports to be a letter describing 'a WOWWOW in the country' (a 'Wowwow', we are told, is 'a confused heap of people of all denominations, assembled at a public house to read the newspapers').[4] After some discussion of events relating to the 'present war', the author of the letter describes how 'we should certainly have had a war at the *Wow-wow*, had not an Oxford scholar, led there by curiosity, pulled a new magazine from his pocket':

> He then read the adventures of Sir Launcelot Greaves to the entire satisfaction of the audience, which being finished, he threw the pamphlet on the table: that piece, gentlemen, says he, is written in the very spirit and manner of Cervantes, there is great knowledge of human nature, and evident marks of the master in almost every sentence; and from the plan, the humour, and the execution, I can venture to say that it dropt from the pen of ingenious Dr. ——. Every one was pleased with the performance, and I was particularly gratified in hearing all the sensible part of the company give orders for the British magazine.

The article is designed to promote the publication of Smollett's new magazine; however, it is notable that it does so by drawing attention to 'the adventures of Sir Launcelot Greaves'. Curiously, the situation that is described here (a gathering at a public house) resembles the scene which opens the first few instalments of *Launcelot Greaves*: characters gather for conversation in a 'little public house on the side of the highway'.[5] It is as if the narrative of *Launcelot Greaves* provides a setting for things that are otherwise outside it: 'the pamphlet on the table', for example, is the *British Magazine* (containing the narrative of *Launcelot Greaves*) but it is also part of the fiction of the 'Wowwow', a fiction into which the character of Launcelot Greaves might, at any moment, step. For readers of the *Public Ledger*, the *British Magazine* is both inside and outside a fiction. In this respect, the whole work might be said to be written in the 'very spirit and manner of Cervantes', and I shall consider Cervantes's influence on Smollett's writing later in the essay.

A Monthly Repository

The *British Magazine or Monthly Repository for Gentlemen & Ladies* began publication on 1 January 1760. In February, a copy of a royal licence was printed on its cover. Unlike the licences for other magazines (for which the bookseller usually owned copyright), this was designed to protect Smollett's interests as author and editor. Taking its text from Smollett's letter of petition, the licence describes his 'great Labour and Expence in writing Original Pieces himself, and engaging learned and ingenious Gentlemen to write other Original Pieces'.[6] Despite the involvement of numerous 'gentlemen', and the reprinting of the work of numerous others, it makes sense to read the *British Magazine* through the royal licence – that is, as an expression of Smollett's own particular kind of creative labour. A few years earlier, in 1756, Smollett had co-founded the *Critical Review*, a review journal which aimed to present the 'Progress or Annals of LITERATURE and the LIBERAL ARTS' through 'a succinct and faithful Detail of all the Performances on the Subjects of Theology, Metaphysics, Physics, Medicine, Mathematics, History, and the Belles Lettres; which shall occasionally appear at Home or Abroad' (as well as accounts of art and architecture).[7] In his proposals for the *British Magazine*, Smollett described the aims of his new 'set of gentlemen' in a similar way: 'they resolve to exert all their faculties, in ransacking the stores of amusement, collecting the flowers of genius, cropping the buds of improvement in learning, arts, and sciences, and uniting pleasure with instruction, so as to exhibit their work a delightful repository for every species of literary entertainment'.[8] Smollett continued to contribute to the *Critical Review* as he worked on the *British Magazine* – and, in fact, many of the 'gentlemen' involved in the project, including the co-founder of the *Critical Review*, the printer Archibald Hamilton, were the same. To this work of compilation, Smollett also brought an interest in narrative. As he started work on the *British Magazine*, his *A Complete History of England, from the Descent of Julius Caesar, to the Treaty of Aix la Chapelle. Containing the Transactions of One Thousand Eight Hundred and*

Three Years (originally published in four quarto volumes in 1757–8) was coming to the end of its highly successful publication in weekly instalments (from March 1758 to April 1760); in May 1760, Smollett was to start the weekly publication of its continuation: *Continuation of the Complete History of England* (1760–5), which eventually brought his historical narrative up to date. On the cover of the first number of the *British Magazine*, Smollett advertised how 'The Adventures of Sir Launcelot Greaves, and the History of Canada, will be continued through the successive Numbers ... until the Designs of both shall be compleated'.[9] This drew attention to one of the innovations of the *British Magazine* – the publication of an extended work of original prose fiction, published in instalments (following the approach of his popular *Complete History*)[10] – but it also highlighted one of the risks of periodical writing. Although Smollett might have been relatively confident that he would complete the design of *Launcelot Greaves*, his experience of writing 'continuations' of the *Complete History of England* would have told him that a history of Canada was never going to end. Smollett's 'great labour' on the *British Magazine* might best be understood as managing this relationship between continuation and completion, between the magazine's various parts and what it might be seen to offer as a whole (Figure 11.1).

Smollett began the *British Magazine* with a dedication to William Pitt (1708–78). In 1757, Smollett had started his *Complete History* in the same way, at that time appealing to what he called Pitt's 'permanent qualities: qualities that exist independent of favour or of faction'.[11] In 1757, Pitt had been on the ascendant, joining forces with the duke of Newcastle (1693–1768) to lead the country during what became the Seven Years War; by 1760 Pitt was enjoying widespread popularity after a series of military victories. Smollett's dedication, however, tempers lavish praise with some well-timed 'buts': 'We admire that resolution and conduct which you have so conspicuously exerted, amidst the tempests of war and the turmoils of government', he says, 'but we wish to see you adorned with the garlands of peace ... '; 'War, at best, is but a necessary evil', he writes (in a subtle rephrasing of the popular view of the 'just and necessary war' (p. 13), as proclaimed by Launcelot in the February instalment of *Launcelot Greaves*), 'but peace is the gentle calm, in which the virtues of benevolence are happily displayed; in which those arts which polish and benefit mankind will lift their heads, and flourish under your protection'.[12] For Smollett, the *British Magazine* is offered as a way 'to collect and keep alive the scattered seeds of literary improvement; until the genial warmth of your [Pitt's] patronage shall invigorate the bloom, and call them forth to a more perfect vegetation' – or, we might say, until Pitt comes to his senses and brings the Continental war to an end. In this respect, the *British Magazine* is presented as a repository for learning in a time of war; it is also an argument for peace. With this in mind, we might revisit the 'Wowwow' described in the *Public Ledger* upon the publication of the *British Magazine*. At the public house, the confused heap of

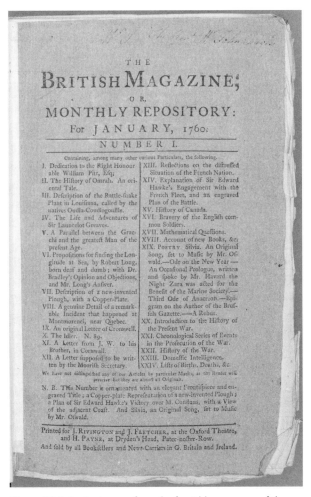

Figure 11.1 Contents page from the front blue wrapper of the
first number of the *British Magazine* (January 1760).

people are themselves on the edge of war; it is the reading of *Launcelot Greaves* that brings 'general satisfaction' to everyone. Notably, the Oxford scholar who throws the pamphlet on the table refers to *Launcelot Greaves* as 'that piece' – a mundane phrase which, in this context, is unusually resonant. *Launcelot Greaves* is, of course, a piece in the *British Magazine* (one of the 'Original Pieces' that the royal licence was designed to protect), but it also invokes a *peace* of a different kind (one that also needs government protection). We might say that the 'pamphlet on the table', tossed down with a flourish at the end of a public reading, is itself an offer of such a piece/peace.

By focusing on the wrappers of the magazine, its royal licence, title and dedication, I am considering what Gérard Genette has called the 'paratext' – that is, features that enable the *British Magazine* to be received as a magazine (or book) and understood in a certain way.[13] Another example of the paratext is the engraving in the first collected volume of the *British Magazine* which shows 'Genius … pouring down Flowers' which are collected by 'Taste' and made into a garland for 'Literature'. Appropriately enough, Literature, in the form of a gentleman, is seen sitting in the porch of the Temple of Taste, reading the *British Magazine*.[14] The image of the *British Magazine* as a pamphlet on the table of a public house during a 'Wowwow' is – as I have meant to suggest – a similar allegorical and paratextual image. One question arising from the 'Wowwow' is whether the pamphlet on the table is the paratext for *Launcelot Greaves* (as a piece within the *British Magazine*) or whether *Launcelot Greaves* itself forms part of the paratext for the magazine. Certainly, the whole point of the description of the 'Wowwow' was to promote the *British Magazine* by way of *Launcelot Greaves*; the physical position of the story (in the first year, usually the leading article of the magazine) can be considered as paratext. Furthermore, as already noted, the (fictional) setting of the 'Wowwow' coincides with the opening chapters of *Launcelot Greaves*, in which characters gather to converse and relate stories at a public house. The impression that *Launcelot Greaves* creates a setting for reading the *British Magazine* is strengthened by the temporal effects of its publication in instalments. At the end of the first chapter, for example, the conversation in the public house is 'suspended by a violent knocking at the door' (p. 9). The reader is told to 'wait with patience' for an explanation; meanwhile 'a personage of great importance' is 'forced to remain some time at the door'. In fact, this personage (no less, it turns out, than Launcelot himself) is kept at the door for a whole month – plenty of time, we might say, for those inside to read the rest of the magazine. A similar joke can be found in Laurence Sterne's *The Life and Opinions of Tristram Shandy*, which was published in long (mostly two-volume) instalments from December 1759 (just before the first issue of the *British Magazine*) to 1767: in this work, Mrs Shandy was to be kept peering through a keyhole for about two years.[15] For Smollett, two years turned out to be about the length of time that he could keep Launcelot engaged in his adventures. The text of his story thus offered the readers of the *British Magazine* an ongoing sense of completion or coherence; as we shall see, it also provided a ground or setting for how its pieces might be read.

The Life and Adventures of Sir Launcelot Greaves

In the second chapter of *Launcelot Greaves* (published in the second number of the *British Magazine*), we are told that the 'hero of these adventures makes his first appearance on the stage of action' (p. 9). He does so in two ways: first, he steps through the door of the public house (outside of which he had arrived, as we have noted, a month previously); he also appears in an accompanying engraving – what is usually referred to as the first example of an illustration in a serial work of fiction.[16] Curiously, the two appearances are somewhat different: in the text, Launcelot is an 'apparition' stepping into the public house and addressing himself to the spectators that had gathered there (Fillet, a surgeon; Captain Crowe and his nephew, Tom Clarke, an attorney; Ferret, referred to as a 'shew-man or a conjurer' (p. 14); as well as the landlady and Dolly, her daughter); in the illustration, however, Launcelot is a knight on horseback, accompanied by his squire, Timothy Crabshaw. Taken together, this double appearance signals the way in which the story of *Launcelot Greaves* engages with its own telling. Shortly after Launcelot's appearance, Ferret comments:

> What! (said Ferret) you set up for a modern Don Quixote? – The scheme is rather too stale and extravagant. – What was an humorous romance, and well-timed satire in Spain, near two hundred years ago, will make but a sorry jest, and appear equally insipid and absurd, when really acted from affectation, at this time a-day, in a country like England. (p. 15)

Ferret might as well be one of the readers of the *British Magazine*, reacting to the presence of the illustration; he establishes a form of metafictional commentary upon the whole work. Launcelot defends himself (and, to some extent, Smollett's writing of the story) by observing that he has not been 'visited by that spirit of lunacy so admirably displayed in the fictitious character exhibited by the inimitable Cervantes' (p. 15). Launcelot's view is that he is neither fictitious nor mad; nevertheless, he is clearly both. Although some critics have used this scene to suggest that Smollett is not following in Cervantes's footsteps, J. A. G. Ardila reflects that Launcelot's 'words and gestures attest to his very insanity' – an insanity Cervantes used to uncover darker social and political realities.[17] Even though Launcelot has not mistaken the 'public house for a magnificent castle' (as Don Quixote was known to have done (p. 15)), as the story unfolds – first as an interpolated tale told by Clarke at the public house and then (from the sixth instalment) as a series of adventures along the 'great northern road' (p. 3) – the way the events double up as literary imitations and fictional recreations would have become clear. Like Don Quixote, Launcelot takes a squire (the farmer Timothy Crabshaw) and idealises his lost love (Aurelia Darnel); in an inspired moment on horseback, he also begins 'to think himself some hero of romance' (p. 119). Launcelot later gives up the role of 'knight-errant' for that of a 'plain English gentleman' (p. 150), but he continues to find himself in a series of quixotic adventures with an ambiguous relationship to reality – that is, to the people and events in a world outside (his) fiction.

For the reader of the *British Magazine*, the story of *Launcelot Greaves* presents an image of their relationship to the text (especially if they happen to be taking part in a 'Wowwow'). Launcelot and Ferret comment on the kind of story they are part of; Clarke's tale is interrupted and we might say 'reviewed' ('Ferret interrupted the narrator by observing that the said Greaves was common nuisance' (p. 41)). Smollett's own intertitles, prefacing each instalment of the narrative, similarly offer editorial comment (the third chapter is seemingly one '*Which the reader, on perusal, may wish were chapter the last*' (p. 20)). Smollett creates a similar metafictional situation later in the story when, after Launcelot is imprisoned in a madhouse, Crowe and Clarke attempt to locate him by placing an advertisement 'in the daily papers' (p. 183). The text of the advertisement, like the text of Aurelia's reprinted letters (pp. 108, 124) – or even the way that Ferret seems to be quoting from *Yorick's Meditations upon Various ... Subjects* (1760) a couple of months after it was reviewed in the *Critical Review*[18] – remind the reader that they are also inside an issue of a miscellaneous magazine. The discourses at work in the text – for example, the predominance of legal and medical language – might be recognised as examples of the editing and reprinting of other texts (such as Giles Jacob's *A New Law-Dictionary* (1729) and William Battie's *Treatise on Madness* (1758))[19] as well as having a connection to voices and articles in the wider magazine (as an example, we might consider how the third chapter of *Launcelot Greaves* is followed by a letter from a reader about 'leasehold tenures').[20] In a similar way, the two illustrations that accompanied the publication of the story (the second showing Launcelot's presence at a county election in chapter 9) not only disclose the pictorial qualities of Smollett's writing – the reader is presented with a textual version of William Hogarth's *Four Prints of an Election* (1755–8) – but also suggest the wider practice of illustration at work in the magazine. The engraver of the illustrations for *Launcelot Greaves*, Anthony Walker, also provided an illustration of 'a People of America called the Natches' for the March 1760 issue; other articles were frequently illustrated.

This brief account of *Launcelot Greaves* is intended to suggest that it is as much made up of pieces (as much a 'repository for every species of literary entertainment') as the magazine that surrounds it. The collection of voices in the narrative reaches its noisiest in the madhouse. On his first night here, Launcelot's 'ears were all at once saluted with a noise from the next room', beginning 'Bring up the artillery – let Brutandorf's brigade advance' (p. 175). A second voice soon joins in: 'Assuredly, (cried another from a different quarter) he that thinks to be saved by works is in a state of utter reprobation' (p. 176). We are then told:

> This dialogue operated like a train upon many other inhabitants of the place: one swore he was within three vibrations of finding the longitude, when this noise confounded his calculation: a second, in broken English, complained he vas distorped in the moment of de proshection – a third, in the character of his holiness, denounced interdiction, excommunication, and anathemas; ... A fourth began to hollow in all the vociferation of a fox-hunter in the chace; and in an instant the whole house was in an uproar ... (p. 176)

The uproar of the madhouse is an extreme version of other uproars within the text. Examples of this include the mixing of discourses (to those already mentioned, we might add Crowe's seafaring words) and the county election, which begins with

Launcelot being similarly 'disturbed by such a variety of noises, as might have discomposed the brain of the firmest texture' (p. 67); we might also note the general 'agreeable medley of mirth and sadness, sense and absurdity' which Smollett hopes, in an editorial intertitle, readers will enjoy (p. 121). In the madhouse, order is achieved by 'the sound of one cabalistical word, which was no other than *waistcoat*' (p. 176). In the magazine, Smollett is similarly tasked with keeping the piece/peace. To this end, Smollett interrupts his story ('that the reader may have time to breathe and digest what he has already heard' (p. 41)) and notifies 'those who have favoured us with their Correspondence' that he is in the process of selecting and arranging their 'original Pieces'.[21] He might also be said to make use of a 'cabalistical' word. In the issue for April 1760, readers were presented with a rebus, the answer to which (provided in the next issue) was a fragmentary composition of Launcelot's name:

> Our Knights were accustom'd to combat with *Lance*,
> But what *Lot* they might share, was still subject to chance:
> The Coachman does *Ge* to his horses exclaim,
> And *R*, from its jar, we the dog-letter name.
> You'll find, if you stand there, rain fall from the *Eaves*:
> This, all put together, forms *Launcelot Greaves*.[22]

The notion that 'Launcelot Greaves' somehow gives order to discordant elements reflects Smollett's frequently cited theorising about the novel form. In his dedication to *The Adventures of Ferdinand Count Fathom* (1753), Smollett describes a novel as a 'large diffused picture, comprehending the characters of life, disposed in different groupes' in which a 'principal personage' serves to 'attract the attention' and 'unite the incidents'.[23] In the diffused picture of *Launcelot Greaves*, or even among the 'confused heap of readers' at the 'Wowwow', which it incorporates, the figure of the knight emerges when it is 'all put together'; similarly, in the repository of the magazine, the narrative itself provides its own cabalistical utterance, quietening the unruly voices. After all, Smollett eventually manages to bring two years of instalments to end in harmony – the noise (which, pointedly, Aurelia is 'uninfected by the rage for' (p. 193)) resolves into a 'rustic epithalamium' (p. 197) – even if it might have required some brusque editorial interventions along the way (such as when Smollett decides to tell the reader that Miss Meadows is Aurelia all along (pp. 108–9)).

A Principal Personage

In the second part of Cervantes's *El Ingenioso hidalgo don Quixote de la mancha* (published in 1615, ten years after the first), Don Quixote visits a print shop and comes across a book containing the story of his adventures.[24] This moment has fascinated many readers, including Jorge Luis Borges, who saw it as joining 'the world of the reader and the world of the book'. Borges locates his fascination and unease in the implication that 'if the characters in a story can be readers or spectators, then we, their readers or spectators, can be fictitious'.[25] Although Launcelot does not (quite) come across the book in which his story has been written, he is nevertheless led to reflect on some of his own fictional qualities. We might say, following Borges, that if Launcelot can be part of the world of the reader, then we, as his readers, can be just as fictitious. We see this idea at work in accounts of Smollett's involvement in periodical writing. In *The Battle of the Reviews*, a satirical pamphlet published in 1760, describing a war between the critics at the *Monthly Review* and *Critical Review*, Smollett is cast in the role of 'Sawney Mac Smallhead'. At the end of one of the battles, he is captured – an event which results in the setting up of the *British Magazine*: '*Sawney* ever since has left off the Trade of Reviewing, thinking, Cobler like, he should make both Ends meet better by laying up all the loose Hints that occur to him in a Sort of Repository, which he is now compiling and digesting in Conjunction with his old Crony *Timothy Crabshaw*'.[26] For the writer of *The Battle of the Reviews*, Smollett is a kind of Launcelot Greaves (alongside the printer Archibald Hamilton as Timothy Crabshaw); the disputes between the two review periodicals, and, indeed, the cobbling together of articles in the *British Magazine*, are part of his quixotic adventures. The pamphlet thus uncovers more unrest behind the publication of *Launcelot Greaves* – but it also discloses a story which can make sense of it. In this respect, Smollett can be seen as the principal personage of a fiction which holds a 'large diffused picture' together.

Smollett might well have regarded himself as such a Cervantean figure. At the end of November 1760, in an event that almost seems to have been predicted by *The Battle of the Reviews*, Smollett was imprisoned in the King's Bench Prison for libel.[27] Smollett is likely to have written parts of *Launcelot Greaves* and conducted work on the *British Magazine* during his three months of imprisonment – certainly, the account of the King's Bench in chapters 20 and 21 of *Launcelot Greaves* (published in July and August 1761) is influenced by his experience. In prison, Smollett could not have avoided the idea that he was following in Cervantes's footsteps. He had already spent many years working on a translation of *Don Quixote* (published in 1755); notably, Smollett had inserted a footnote to comment on the 'strong presumption, that the first part of Don Quixote was actually written in a jail'.[28] Some of the wider practices of the *British Magazine* – such as the mixing of fiction and topical issues, as well as its grand aims and royal licence – might be seen as Smollett's ongoing response to Cervantes's writing. The author of the account of the 'Wowwow' saw Smollett's writing in this way. Similarly, a couple of years earlier, in another pamphlet, commenting on the beginnings of the *Critical Review*, the physician and political writer John Shebbeare (1709–88) addressed Smollett: 'Then, like a true Champion, the Knight of *La Mancha*, you arrive to rescue the Charms of Literature from the avaritious Hands of the hireling Necromancers in the *Monthly Review*. What an Advantage it is in a Critic to have transcribed Don *Quixote*, tho' it may prove a great *Loss* to the Bookseller who *hired* him.'[29] In *The Battle of the Reviews*, Shebbeare is credited with the capture of Sawney Mac Smallhead. He is also present in *Launcelot Greaves* in the shape of Ferret (whose character is developed in chapter 10). Notably, Shebbeare's comparison of Smollett with the 'Knight of *La Mancha*' resembles Ferret's initial outburst upon meeting Launcelot at the public house ('What! ... you set up for a modern Don Quixote?'). This perhaps hints at the way that Smollett is able to come face to face with his own fictionality: as the 'principal personage', emerging out of the voices of the *British Magazine*, Smollett might be said, like Launcelot, to have donned his armour ('greaves' is a term for a piece of armour (p. 129)) and ridden out 'in preservation of the peace' (p. 16).

Conclusion

In *Launcelot Greaves*, Smollett tried something new. Interestingly, the *Journal encyclopédique*, which summarised and translated parts of *Launcelot Greaves* for its readers in France, perceived the need to explain its method: 'Cet ouvrage n'est point achevé', it observed, 'chaque mois, les Auteurs du *Magasin Britannique* en donnent un chapître' ('This work is not complete: each month, the authors of the *British Magazine* provide one chapter').[30] Although some magazines began to experiment with serialising original works of fiction, it was not until the nineteenth century that the practice became established.[31] Describing *Launcelot Greaves* this way, however, risks separating it, as a form, from the writing of the *British Magazine*. When the *Journal encyclopédique* reprinted summaries of its instalments, they disrupted the temporal effects; similarly, when *Launcelot Greaves* was published as two volumes in 1762, its qualities as periodical writing were obscured (and, noticeably, it didn't sell very well).[32] To read *Launcelot Greaves* as a novel only is to miss the extended noise, 'Wowwow' or 'repository' of which it was a piece (and in which it aspired to be the peace).

To read *Launcelot Greaves* outside the *British Magazine* is also to miss the *British Magazine* in *Launcelot Greaves* – that is, the way the fiction provided a ground for the work of the magazine. We started by noting Walter Scott's anecdote, which presented Smollett as hurriedly writing copy before post-time. Scott probably made that story up – but, as we have seen, Smollett would not have had a problem with being fictitious. The journey of his 'necessary quantity of copy' out into the world is the very image of the Knight of La Mancha, adventuring along the Great North Road.

NOTES

1. Walter Scott, 'Prefatory Memoir to Smollett', *Ballantyne's Novelists' Library*, vol. II, *The Novels of Tobias Smollett* (London: Hurst, Robinson, 1821), reprinted in Lionel Kelly (ed.), *Tobias Smollett: The Critical Heritage* (London: Routledge & Kegan Paul, 1987), p. 354.

2. Jerry C. Beasley, *Tobias Smollett: Novelist* (Athens: University of Georgia Press, 1998), p. 158.

3. Clifford Siskin and William Warner (eds), *This is Enlightenment* (University of Chicago Press, 2010), pp. 10–12.

4. *The Public Ledger, Or, Daily Register of Commerce and Intelligence*, vol. 1, no. 31, 16 February 1760, p. [1].

5. Tobias Smollett, *The Life and Adventures of Sir Launcelot Greaves* (1760–1), ed. Robert Folkenflik and Barbara Laning Fitzpatrick (Athens: University of Georgia Press, 2002), p. 3; subsequent page references are given in the main text.

6. A copy of the *British Magazine* for February 1760 in its original blue wrappers is available in the Bodleian Library (Vet. a5. d.782). For the text of the licence and Smollett's letter of petition, see Albert Smith, 'Sir Launcelot Greaves: A Bibliographical Survey of Eighteenth-Century Editions', *Library* 5.32 (1977), 214–37 (216–17).

7. *Public Advertiser*, no. 6599, 19 December 1755, p. [4].

8. This was printed on the blue wrappers for February 1760; see Smith, 'Bibliographical Survey', 218–19.

9. Ibid., 215.

10. On Smollett's innovations, see Robert D. Mayo, *The English Novel in the Magazines: 1740–1815* (Evanston, IL: Northwestern University Press, 1962), p. 277.

11. Tobias Smollett, *A Complete History of England*, 1st edn, 4 vols (London, 1757–8), vol. I, pp. [i–ii].

12. *The British Magazine or Monthly Repository for Gentlemen & Ladies* 1 (1760), [ii].

13. Gérard Genette, *Seuils*, 1987; trans. Jane E. Lewin as *Paratexts: Thresholds of Interpretation* (Cambridge University Press, 1997), pp. 1–3.

14. An account of the frontispiece can be found on the inside front wrapper of the first number; see Smith, 'Bibliographical Survey', 220–1.

15. Thomas Keymer, *Sterne, the Moderns and the Novel* (Oxford University Press, 2002), p. 132.

16. See Robert Folkenflik's introduction to Smollett, *Launcelot Greaves*, pp. xliv–xlviii.

17. J. A. G. Ardila, 'Tobias Smollett, Don Quixote and the Emergence of the English Novel', in J. A. G. Ardila (ed.), *The Cervantean Heritage: Reception and Influence of Cervantes in Britain* (London: MHRA and Maney Publishing, 2009), pp. 151–65 (p. 158).

18. For details see James G. Basker, *Tobias Smollett: Critic and Journalist* (Newark: University of Delaware Press, 1988), p. 259.

19. See Roger A. Hambridge, 'Smollett's Legalese: Giles Jacob's *New Law-Dictionary* and Sir Launcelot Greaves', *Revue des Langues Vivantes* 44 (1978), 37–44; cf. Smollett, *Launcelot Greaves*, pp. 6–7, 92–3, 177.

20. *British Magazine* 1 (1760), 134.

21. Ibid., 212 [editorial note].

22. Ibid., 268; the original puzzle is in the previous number, at page 216.

23. Tobias Smollett, *The Adventures of Ferdinand Count Fathom* (1753), ed. J. C. Beasley and O. M. Brack Jr (Athens: University of Georgia Press, 1988), p. 4.

24. For Smollett's translation of this episode (which occurs in chapter 61), see M. de Cervantes Saavedra, *The History and Adventures of the Renowned Don Quixote*, trans. Tobias Smollett (1755), ed. C. Battestin and O. M. Brack Jr (Athens: University of Georgia Press, 2003), pp. 691–3. In chapter 59 Don Quixote overhears some discussion of the book at an inn; see pp. 670–1.

25. Jorge Luis Borges, 'Partial Enchantments of the Quixote' (1949), in *Other Inquisitions 1937–1952*, trans. Ruth L. C. Simms (Austin: University of Texas Press, 1964), pp. 43–6 (pp. 44, 46).

26. *The Battle of the Reviews* (London, n.d. [1760]), pp. 149–51.

27. See Lewis Mansfield Knapp, *Tobias Smollett: Doctor of Men and Manners* (Princeton University Press, 1949), pp. 230–7.

28. Cervantes, *Don Quixote*, p. 21.

29. John Shebbeare, *The Occasional Critic, or the Decrees of the Scotch Tribunal in the Critical Review Rejudged: etc.* (London, 1757), p. 9.

30. *Journal encyclopédique* 4.3 (15 June 1761), 101.

31. Basker, *Critic and Journalist*, pp. 208–9; cf. Mayo, *English Novel in the Magazines*, pp. 273–4, 286–7.

32. Smith, 'Bibliographical Survey', 231–2.

CRITICAL REFLECTIONS AND FURTHER STUDY

What is this essay about? For me, it is partly about the stories we tell ourselves. In researching Smollett's work, I became interested in the way that he was sometimes presented as a Don Quixote figure – and intrigued by the possibility that he might have seen himself that way, given his translation of Cervantes's work and the chivalrous language he used to describe his periodical projects. I was reminded of Jorge Luis Borges's short story 'Pierre Menard, Author of the *Quixote*' (see Further Reading), about a writer whose ambition was 'to produce a number of pages which coincided – word for word and line for line – with those of Miguel de Cervantes' (p. 37). Might Smollett be best understood as a kind of Pierre Menard? Were there moments in his life of writing when he thought that he had succeeded in coinciding line for line, so to speak, with the work of someone else?

This is an interesting question to ask of Smollett because much of his writing proceeds through quotation. The essay mentions his *Complete History of England*, which, we might say, involved the task of 'coinciding' with other histories by Paul de Rapin (1661–1725) and David Hume (1711–76); his periodical works, including the *British Magazine*, were another kind of 'repository' of quotations, extracts and 'Original pieces'. The works of his that have been called novels might also suggest some of the ways in which Smollett was attempting to reproduce – not copy – other people's words. We might think of his insertion of the 'Memoirs of a Lady of Quality' into *The Adventures of Peregrine Pickle* (1751) or the way *The Expedition of Humphry Clinker* (1771) is assembled from the words of his characters (in epistolary form) and snippets from his historical research. Smollett's relationship to other texts raises a question about the kind of writing in which he was engaged – and the kind of stories we tell ourselves about what writing is and what it does. (Smollett's novels and translations are available in critical editions from Georgia University Press; his historical writing is included in Eighteenth Century Collections Online (Gale); the *British Magazine* is part of the British Periodicals database (ProQuest).)

In this essay, I was less interested in Smollett's place in a history of the novel than in exploring a broader notion of a history of writing. Behind this idea is the work of Clifford Siskin and William Warner. In *This is Enlightenment* (see my essay, note 3), they locate the Enlightenment as an event in a history of mediation: it is conceived as an effect of 'proliferating mediations' (p. 11), the interrelated practices of writing, reading and print in the eighteenth century. In this respect, the *British Magazine* provides the very image of the Enlightenment: a repository of mediations which is itself part of the surrounding proliferation. In the essay, I wanted to explore how *Launcelot Greaves* might be read as part of this context; however, I also became interested in how the narrative discloses a myth that seems to support it. Another way of putting this is to say that Cervantes helped to create the idea of a shared enterprise or, in Benedict Anderson's phrase, an 'imagined community' (see Further Reading). Yet another way (and one that informs the essay) is to consider *Launcelot Greaves* as the poetic ground for the work of the *British Magazine*. This notion derives from Heidegger's idea that art opens up (or reveals) the world – a world that can then be examined – but, in the essay, it is explored tangentially through the idea of paratext. Paratextual elements, according to Genette in *Paratexts* (see my essay, note 13), surround and extend a text in order 'to ensure the text's presence in the world'. They include 'an author's name, a title, a preface, illustrations' but also 'practices and discourses' beyond the text itself. For this reason, Genette refers to 'paratexts', somewhat ambiguously, as 'thresholds of interpretation' (pp. 1–2). In a book about contexts, then, it seems relevant to consider what comes into focus when reading *Launcelot Greaves* in the *British Magazine*: the magazine, its parts, a narrative or Smollett himself.

There are other contexts that might be explored further. Charlotte Lennox (1730–1804) established her periodical, *The Lady's Museum* (1760–1), just as Smollett began to publish the *British Magazine*. Notably, it had been preceded by her novel, *The Female Quixote, or The Adventures of Arabella* (1752) – and the magazine was described as being by 'the author of the Female Quixote'. Mayo, in *The English Novel in the Magazines* (see my essay, note 10), considers the 'withdrawal' of Smollett and Lennox from 'magazine writing', along with that of Oliver Goldsmith (1728–74), who had attempted his own weekly magazine, *The Bee*, in 1759, as a 'portentous sign of the fate of miscellanies and miscellany fiction for the next half century' (p. 274). Even so, there is a question as to how far the work of these writers should be distinguished from the work of the magazines. Finally, the influence of Cervantes might be considered more broadly: a key figure in this regard is Henry Fielding (1707–54), from whom Smollett took some hints about the 'Art of dividing'. Smollett was clearly interested in the notion that, as Fielding put it in *Joseph Andrews* (1742), 'those little Spaces between our Chapters may be looked upon as an Inn or Resting-Place, where he [the reader] may stop and take a Glass, or any other Refreshment, as it pleases him' (see 'Of Divisions in Authors' in Book II, chapter 1); he was probably also influenced by Fielding's play *Don Quixote in England* (1734).

FURTHER READING

Anderson, Benedict, *Imagined Communities: Reflections on the Origin and Spread of Nationalism*, rev. edn (New York: Verso, 2006)

Borges, Jorge Luis, 'Pierre Menard, Author of the Quixote' (1941), in *Fictions*, trans. Andrew Hurley (London: Penguin, 2000), pp. 33–47

Brack, Jr., O. M. (ed.), *Tobias Smollett, Scotland's first novelist: New Essays in Memory of Paul-Gabriel Boucé* (Newark: University of Delaware Press, 2007)

Heidegger, Martin, 'The origin of the work of art' (1971), in *Poetry, Language, Thought*, trans. Albert Hofstadter (New York: Harper Perennial, 2013), pp. 15–86

Powell, Manushag N., *Performing Authorship in Eighteenth-Century English Periodicals* (Lewisburg, PA: Bucknell University Press, 2012)

Wiles, R. M. *Serial Publication in England before 1750* (Cambridge University Press, 1957)

PART IV
The Romantic Period, 1780–1832

INTRODUCTORY NOTE

As Holmesland's essay on Aphra Behn has already perhaps shown, Britain's colonial history over five centuries is an inescapable background context for much of English literature, even if it is not until the twentieth century that we see the sustained 'writing back' to empire that is generally referred to as postcolonial literature. Britain's long involvement in India and the east has produced a particularly rich and complex pattern of literary interrelations between the two cultures, and Daniel Sanjiv Roberts's multifaceted essay here demonstrates this very clearly in relation to a variety of writers and different genres within the Romantic period. Oriental themes became hugely popular in Britain at this time, as Roberts explains, and these were therefore fully exploited by writers like Byron, Southey and Moore; but there were also English literary developments in India itself as scholars like Charles Wilkins and William Jones of the Asiatick Society began translating Indian material, thus making it available for further creative adaptation in English. This might refer us back again to preceding essays which discuss contexts of translation and their intercultural ramifications, but it directs us forwards too, to postcolonial writing from India and diasporic Indian writing in English, represented in this volume by Joel Kuortti's essay on Salman Rushdie, who has, of course, been a particularly prominent figure in forging a distinctively Indian voice and identity within contemporary English literature (see Essay 30). Some introductory historical background to Britain's involvement in India in this period can be found in chapters 4 and 8 of *English Literature in Context* (see especially pp. 326–30, 652–5) and Peter Kitson's short reading, in the former chapter, of Byron's *The Giaour* is also of direct relevance.

Questions of historical context become even more complicated than they already are in themselves when we come to consider them in relation to historical fiction.

Here we are immediately faced by at least two defining time coordinates – the time of writing (and/or publication) and the time of the historical setting of the fiction. With historical fiction from the past, we add the further contexts of our own time, through which we negotiate our understanding of the original dialogue between the text and its earlier contexts. But Fiona Price's essay on Romantic historical fiction in this section steers us expertly through some of these complications by staging an instructive novelistic 'debate' between Walter Scott and Jane Porter on key aspects of historical fiction and its development in the period. Through this debate and her analysis of the two main novels in question, Scott's *Waverley* and Porter's *The Scottish Chiefs*, Price systematically draws out a number of leading issues of the time, touching on matters of politics, nationhood, heroism, and aesthetics, thus providing a clear contextual picture of the Romantic period itself, while also reflecting on the historiography of the historical novel.

Addressing the very material context of the literary marketplace, Katie Halsey, in her essay, discusses the publishing context in which Jane Austen worked and precisely how that context may have influenced the development of her novel *Northanger Abbey* in the time between its conception at the end of the 1790s and its first publication in 1817. Halsey traces the changing nature of the literary marketplace in this period in some lively detail and evokes a rich sense of the many intertextual influences on Austen which are then creatively and comically woven into the fabric of her mock-Gothic novel. Halsey's essay – along with its Critical Reflections section – provides an important point of reference in the chain of essays in this volume which consider the material contexts of print culture and the production and circulation of books. Benedict Anderson, in his seminal work *Imagined Communities* (1983), provocatively reminds us that the advent of printing and book publishing in Europe was also one of the earliest manifestations of industrial-style capitalist enterprise based on the mass production of a commodity (London: Verso, 2016, pp. 33–4). It is sobering to think of the books we cherish, often precisely for their non-materialistic creativity and idealism, as being material commodities sold for profit. But, as Halsey notes by reference to W. H. Auden's 'Letter to Lord Byron', Jane Austen was never blind to all this and was nothing if not frank about 'the economic basis of society'. There is, then, some irony in the fact that Jane Austen now appears on the Bank of England's ten-pound note, given that this was the sum involved in Austen's first unsuccessful attempt at publication (as Halsey's essay relates). The note was introduced in 2017 to commemorate the 200th anniversary of Austen's death and, in addition to her picture, the small copper foil image at the right-hand corner, beside the '£10', has an open book displaying Austen's initials. (A further irony is that the words chosen to accompany Austen's image – 'I declare after all there is no enjoyment like reading!' – were, in their original context, carefully *calculated* words, with a view to financial gain, and uttered by that decidedly half-hearted reader Caroline Bingley in *Pride and Prejudice*.)

The fact that John Keats had a background of training in medicine provides the starting point for Paul Wright's subtly elaborated study of Keats's poetry in the context of scientific, medical and metaphysical debates about the body, mind and soul during the Romantic era. Wright draws together an impressive array of material – including scientific sources from earlier in the eighteenth century and a telling perspective from the twentieth-century Anglo-Welsh poet Dannie Abse – to construct a many-sided and finely balanced argument. Reviewing Keats's reputation as a poet of sensation and looking closely at his ode 'To Psyche' in particular, Wright carefully considers how Keats was influenced by his medical training and how he negotiated the scientific and medical materialism of the age within his vitalist-inflected poetry. The essay draws on the theories of Michel Foucault, among others, and provides an excellent model of New Historicist reading, an approach which Wright discusses further in his Critical Reflections and Further Study section. This theoretical aspect of the essay links it back to Lee Morrissey's essay in particular (Essay 9), while its scientific and philosophical themes naturally lead us into the following essay by Jordan Kistler (Essay 16).

12 'Transported into Asiatic Scenes': Romanticism and the Orient

DANIEL SANJIV ROBERTS

Abstract

As Britain extended its eastern empire through the Romantic period, the orient became imaginatively closer to Britons. As knowledge of eastern texts and geographies, as well as material objects and substances (such as fabrics, porcelain, tea and opium), were transported between east and west, these significant developments were registered in a variety of genres and styles, reflecting divergent political attitudes and aesthetic reactions. This essay selectively analyses early translations and imitations of classical eastern literatures by orientalists of the Asiatick Society; eastern poetry by William Jones and Lord Byron; metropolitan responses to material cultures associated with the orient by magazine essayists such as Charles Lamb and Thomas De Quincey; and early writings by eastern travellers to the west. These exemplify the diversity and extent of Romantic-period literary responses to the orient. From the charmingly domesticated to the grotesquely alien, the orient could generate widely disparate reactions in which relations of political power were inevitably embedded.

Writing in 1813 to fellow poet Thomas Moore, Lord Byron suggested a new 'poetical policy' that his friend would be wise to follow. 'Stick to the East,' he advised, quoting the authority of the exiled literary intellectual Madame de Staël, who had imparted this wisdom to him. 'The North, South, and West, have all been exhausted,' he explained, 'but from the East, we have nothing but [Robert Southey's] unsaleables.'[1] Byron's advice was spot on. The consequence of his advice, Moore's long oriental poem *Lalla Rookh* (1817), set in a lavishly detailed seventeenth-century Mughal India, proved to be one of the most successful poetic ventures of the era, attracting the unprecedented sum of £3,000 as an advance from his publisher Longman, and duly running into dozens of editions and adaptations in the decades to follow.[2] Byron himself went on to achieve remarkable success in a series of 'Turkish Tales' published between 1813 and 1814, though in his preface to *The Corsair* (1814) – which was dedicated to Moore and sold 10,000 copies on its first day – he effectively handed over the mantle to his friend whose scholarly abilities and national sympathies (as an Irishman) rendered him in Byron's view uniquely suited to the role of Britain's oriental poet.[3] Byron's suggestion here that earlier modes of poetry had been 'exhausted', and that it was 'the East' that held the best promise for the future, mirrored the qualified optimism with which Britain could look on its expanding commerce and empire in the east, even as it contemplated its losses in the aftermath of the American and French revolutions and in the context of its long and damaging war with France from the 1790s.

Yet Byron's canny advice to Moore can be misleading in some respects to modern readers. Far from reflecting a new trend, Moore's turn to the east relied on a wealth of scholarship that had preceded Byron in earlier decades of the Romantic period, and which Moore in particular would access massively in the hundreds of footnotes added to his highly allusive though inventive poetic recreation of Mughal India during the reign of Aurangzeb.[4] And Byron's sneering comment regarding his arch-enemy 'Southey's unsaleables' conceals the fairly respectable sales of Southey's major oriental poems, *Thalaba* (1801) and *The Curse of Kehama* (1810), each of which had run to several editions, even if they never quite enjoyed the immediate success of Byron's and Moore's oriental poems.[5] Oriental poetry was not new in the period and it had enjoyed significant success even before Byron's and Moore's astonishingly popular interventions. Moreover, their turn to the east was not purely a poetic phenomenon but rather a wider cultural and political development reflecting Britain's pride in an empire on which it was boasted the sun would never set.[6] More precisely, Byron's jibe reveals a locus of poetic capital in which the poets were rivally invested though with differing political and cultural significances attached to their respective commitments. In other words, while Southey on the one hand and Byron and Moore on the other could all be recognised as oriental poets, each of them displayed different strategies whereby they mined and represented the richness and strangeness of these eastern worlds to their readers. Moreover, Byron was ranging himself with Moore against the kind of fantastic and grotesque versions of the east that he believed Southey had represented in his poetical works, in particular in his recently published *The Curse of Kehama* (1810). In short, if the east was 'up for grabs' to literary writers in Britain, then it could imply different styles and poetical registers as well as cultural and political attitudes for any of them.

A basic premise of this essay is that Britain's rapid development of commercial and colonial interests in the east inevitably impacted on the literature and culture of the period. Earlier stereotypical views of the orient associated with splendour, despotism and libidinous excess (as portrayed in the *Arabian Nights* that had circulated in English translations from the early eighteenth century)[7] were overwritten – though not necessarily expunged – by detailed linguistic, geographical and historical researches conducted by the numerous officials, antiquarians and amateur scholars who encountered and studied the east in their different ways as

Britain extended its territories overseas. These innovative forms of knowledge, which generated a multiplicity of impressions regarding eastern politics, societies and cultures, were registered and transformed in the literary realm by writers who sought to advance, contest or merely profit from the growing public interest in the area. Correspondingly, this essay will seek to contextualise and to examine a range of literary texts with a view to demonstrating the diverse nature of literary responses provoked by the now multifarious aspects of the orient. Commencing with an analysis of early orientalist scholarship embodied in Charles Wilkins's preface to his 1785 translation of the *Bhagavad Geeta* – itself an episode from the great Indian epic *Mahabharata* – and Sir William Jones's first 'Anniversary Discourse' (Kolkata, 1788) delivered to the newly formed Asiatick Society of Bengal and reprinted in London, I will indicate the growth from the 1790s of a distinctly Europeanised sphere of intellectual enquiry accompanied by far-reaching networks of power and communication. These researches set influential parameters for a new understanding of the entirety of Asia based on the Indocentric perspectives of Wilkins, Jones and others of the Asiatick Society.

Turning from scholarly orientalism – the discipline of studying the east which emerged during this period[8] – to poetry, I will also offer readings of Jones's 'The Enchanted Fruit; or the Hindu Wife' (1787) and Byron's 'The Giaour' (1813) – the first of his 'Turkish Tales' – to consider specifically the challenges mounted by orientalism to notions of gender and sexuality via scientific, mythological and popular understandings of eastern customs. Prose literature will be represented by Thomas De Quincey's *Confessions of an English Opium-Eater* (1821) and Charles Lamb's essay, 'Old China' (1823), both published in the *London Magazine*. These examples of personal essays and life writings vividly exhibit the impact that material cultures associated with the east, from Turkey to China, had on metropolitan sensibilities and ideas of aesthetics. Though played out in widely differing registers denoting Gothic horror and/or comforting forms of domesticity, both works respond to substances and objects from the east – opium and porcelain tea sets – that were widely circulated, albeit denoting very different leisure and class distinctions among their British users. Finally, I will look at travel writings by eastern writers such as Abu Taleb Khan and Dean Mahomet to consider the extent to which such writers were able to 'write back' (to use the phrase coined by Salman Rushdie)[9] across the shifting and uneven lines of power and communication that were being drawn during this period between east and west.

The transformation of the East India Company (EIC), first chartered as a trading corporation in 1600, into a ruling enterprise in India from 1757 following the battle of Plassey (Pilashi in India) was marked by aggressive warfare, political intrigue and plunder. These tactics, resulting in massive famines in the region of Bengal by 1770, were largely, at least in their initial stages, greeted by the British public with increasing consternation and horror.[10] Company officials returning to Britain

Figure 12.1 Published at the time of the trial, for corruption, of Warren Hastings, former governor general of India, Gillray's satirical cartoon depicts Hastings on a commode-cum-throne, handing out money to leading members of the British establishment (with King George III shown in the bottom left corner helping himself).

with vast sums of money were dubbed 'nabobs' (a corruption of the Hindustani *nawab* or 'royal highness') and were satirised in cartoons and in print culture as in Samuel Foote's popular satirical play *The Nabob* (1772) (Figure 12.1). Amid these scandalous allegations of rapaciousness and corruption, Prime Minister William Pitt's EIC Act of 1784 sought to establish governance on a firmer footing and to legitimise Company rule in India in relation to the extant Mughal empire perceived to be in decline.[11] This is the context in which some of the earliest English literary responses to Asia, including translations of Indian classical literature, began to emerge from the imperial centre of Calcutta (now Kolkata) in the 1780s, to much acclaim in Britain and indeed across Europe. The orientalist and EIC official Charles Wilkins's prose translation of the *Bhagavad Geeta*, an episode from the great Indian epic of the *Mahabharata*, appeared in 1785, prefaced by a letter from

Governor General Warren Hastings to the director of the EIC, Nathaniel Smith, followed by Wilkins's dedication of the work to Hastings and a 'Translator's Preface'. This elaborate paratextual apparatus frames the *Geeta* (to which it is now widely referred) for English readers, introducing the hitherto unknown Hindu scriptures as literary and cultural artefacts which could be brought into conformity with European aesthetic norms, even as Indian societies were adapting to British rule led by the Company.

The *Geeta*, representing a dialogue between one of the Pandava brothers, Arjuna, and his charioteer, the god Krishna, over the morality of waging war against one's own brethren, chimes conveniently with emerging Protestant views of Britain's imperial destiny in its recommendation of *dharma* (translated by Wilkins as 'duty') as appropriate to the calling of a *kshatriya* (or 'warrior'). Wilkins's translation renders the classical Sanskrit text of the *Geeta* into deliberately archaic English prose recalling the sublimity of the King James version of the Bible:

> KRĔĔSHNĂ. Those who having placed their minds in me, serve me with constant
> zeal, and are endued with steady faith, are esteemed the best devoted. They too
> who, delighting in the welfare of all nature, serve me in my incorruptible, ineffable,
> and invisible form; omnipresent, incomprehensible, standing on high, fixed and
> immoveable, with subdued passions and understandings, the same in all things, shall
> also come to me.[12]

Krishna's emphasis on the ineffability of God and on 'faith' as the highest mark of the devotee's duty appears to suggest, as Wilkins claimed, an underlying continuity between Christian and Hindu theologies, a suggestion that would be taken further by his colleague and successor, William Jones, soon to be regarded as the foremost (British) Sanskrit scholar of his age. Wilkins's preface positions the work as a reward for the confidence enjoyed by the British government, and by Hastings in particular, among the learned Brahmins, the custodians of the textual traditions of Hinduism:

> The *Brāhmăns* esteem this work to contain all the grand mysteries of their religion; and
> so careful are they to conceal it from the knowledge of those of a different persuasion
> ... that the Translator might have sought in vain for assistance, had not the liberal
> treatment they have of late years experienced from the mildness of our government,
> the tolerating principles of our faith, and, above all, the personal attention paid to
> the learned men of their order by him under whose auspicious administration they
> have so long enjoyed ... the blessings of internal peace, ... at length happily created in
> their breasts a confidence in his countrymen sufficient to remove almost every jealous
> prejudice from their minds. (pp. 23–4)

Wilkins's translation is thus premised upon the 'mildness' of British government in India, on Christian ideas of tolerance, and on Hastings's enlightened cultivation of Brahminical support for his administration. His work purports to penetrate the 'mysteries' of Hinduism hitherto zealously protected by the Brahmins from western knowledge. Such claims conceal beneath their surface however the complicitous nature of British rule with social hierarchies of caste and learning even as British religious tolerance is subtly contrasted with the 'jealous prejudice' of the Brahmins that Hastings has largely overcome. As Hastings put it more explicitly in his letter to Nathaniel Smith published with Wilkins's prefatory materials to the *Geeta*, all such knowledge, including that of Indian literature and culture, was useful in creating a bond of sympathy between Indians and their rulers: 'it lessens the weight of the chain by which the natives are held in subjection; and it imprints on the hearts of our own countrymen the sense and obligation of benevolence' (p. 13).

Hastings's programme of mediating Indian literature and knowledge towards a conciliatory and sympathetic rapprochement between Britain and its fast-expanding territories in the east was given major institutional impetus by the foundation of the Asiatick Society in 1784 with the newly arrived Sir William Jones as its first president. Jones's inaugural address on that occasion, later to be published in the opening volume of *Asiatick Researches*, the journal of the society published in Calcutta and reprinted in London, is often regarded as a foundational text of orientalism, the study of the east that became increasingly fashionable and important in the period, which has become a key area of postcolonial scrutiny in the wake of Edward Said's influential critique of the phenomenon.[13] Jones, who had been appointed as a judge in the supreme court at Fortwilliam, in Calcutta, had already acquired a significant literary reputation as a Persian scholar and translator, and was well placed to lead the society. Recounting his voyage to his learned audience in Calcutta, Jones recalled his pleasure at discovering his location one evening when 'India lay before us, and Persia on our left, while a breeze from Arabia blew nearly on our stern'.[14] Invoking the glories of imperial Rome, Jones describes his position as being 'in the midst of … an amphitheatre' (ix). 'The vast regions of *Asia*' appeared to him as 'the nurse of sciences, the inventress of delightful and useful arts, the scene of glorious actions, fertile in the productions of human genius, abounding in natural wonders, and infinitely diversified in the forms of religion and government, in the laws, manners, customs, and languages, as well as in the features and complexions, of men' (ix–x). These would be the object of the 'learned investigations' of the Asiatick Society as Jones envisaged it, bounded only 'by the geographical limits of *Asia*' (xi).

As we have seen, Jones's vision of Asian knowledge fortifying European intellectual growth went hand in hand with the emergence of Britain's bases of political power in the region. While the Asiatick Society continued to be active throughout the Romantic period, stimulating a variety of orientalist researches that were influential on literary writers, Jones's death in 1794, and the emergence of a powerful evangelical influence in the EIC, particularly with the appointment of Charles Grant to its court of directors in 1805, spelt a significant change in policy towards native religions and customs even as Britain consolidated its power massively over portions of Asia. Moreover, as the east was studied in ever-increasing detail by the orientalists it grew more and more liable to differentiation. Such changes in attitudes and nuances of difference may be gleaned from a comparison of the above-mentioned poems by Jones and Byron, which offer contrasting images of eastern sexuality that could be challenging to western readers. Jones's 'The Enchanted Fruit; or, The Hindu Wife: An Antediluvian Tale Written in the Province of Bahar' provides in its full title an indication of its mythological origins from an era prior to the biblical flood while drawing attention simultaneously to the poet's position as a modern commentator on the action, writing his poem in 'the Province of Bahar' (now the state of Bihar adjoining West Bengal on the eastern side of India). The elaborate footnotes explain details of Indian mythology drawn from the *Mahabharata* alongside modern and botanical details of Indian flowers and fruits, while the poem itself is written in elegant mock-heroic tetrameters familiar to eighteenth-century English readers. The central character of the 'Hindu wife' is based on that of Draupadi, the female protagonist of the *Mahabharata*, married to the five Pandava brothers. The polyandrous aspect of this marriage, shocking no doubt to western notions of propriety, is explained firstly with reference to Hindu mythology, in which she remains a sanctified, even divine figure, but also, secondly, and in a modern context, with reference to Linnaean botany:

For *India* once, as now cold *Tibet*,
A groupe unusual might exhibit,
Of sev'ral husbands, free from strife,
Link'd fairly to a single wife!
Thus Botanists, with eyes acute
To see prolifick dust minute,
Taught by their learned northern Brahmen
To class by *pistil* and by *stamen*,
Produce from nature's rich dominion
Flow'rs *Polyandrian Monogynian*,
Where embryon blossoms, fruits, and leaves
Twenty prepare, and ONE receives.[15]

Far from presenting the polyandrous marriage in the mythological story in a judgemental way, Jones presents it as fully in keeping with natural phenomena as observed scientifically. The poem ends on a playful note with Britannia's mock-heroic defence of British women from the scandalous implication that they might be reputed less virtuous than '*Indian* dames', who, despite their 'sooty hue', are associated with 'primeval' virtue (lines 497–520). Jones's depiction of Draupadi recalls, selectively, early positive stereotypes of Indian women as faithful and

IMMOLATION OF A HINDOO WIDOW UPON HER HUSBAND'S FUNERAL PILE.

Figure 12.2 Engraving of a Hindu widow committing sati, 1815. The artist depicts the Indians as superstitious and deluded, while the English soldiers on the left are indifferent. Evangelical lobbying promoted an interventionist attitude on the part of the East India Company, which led to sati being outlawed by Governor-General William Bentinck in 1829.

virtuous, even to the point of immolating themselves on their husbands' funeral pyres in the performance of *sati* (Figure 12.2).[16] Britannia's defeat of the monstrous figure of '*Scandal*' in this complex interracial and intercultural competition enables British women to be judged impartially, offering a concluding placatory gesture to British readers who might be offended by the apparent sexual improprieties and invidious comparisons contained in Jones's poetic parable.

If Jones's 'antediluvian tale' presents a surprisingly feisty and unconventional view of the Hindu wife, Draupadi, Byron's 'tale' in 'The Giaour' of a female slave Leila who falls in love with a Venetian Christian and is cast into the sea by her jealous husband, Hassan, provides, contrastingly, a passive and suffering image of the eastern woman, silenced and 'disappeared' for her crime. As Byron's 'Advertisement' explains, the action of the poem is set in the Ionian islands off the Grecian coast under the last vestiges of Venetian rule. This was a period of considerable political turmoil in the region, bringing Byron's political sympathies for Greece (geographically, on the verge of the orient, and under Ottoman rule at the time) to the fore. In the poem, the Christian 'Giaour' (from the pejorative Turkish-Muslim term for 'infidel') who pursues Hassan displays a vengeful spirit remarkably akin to his adversary's, making them doppelgängers more than opposites. The fragmentary narrative employs a variety of voices and tonal shifts typical of the Byronic style established in *Childe Harold's Pilgrimage*, which had begun to appear from 1812. Grecian heroism symbolised by the battle of Thermopylae is celebrated as a thing of the past:

> Shrine of the mighty! can it be,
> That this is all remains of thee?
> Approach thou craven crouching slave –
> Say, is not this Thermopylae?[17]

Byron's lament over Greece's lost spirit of independence mirrors Leila's melancholic fate at the hands of the men who once possessed and loved her, and there seems little to choose between the masculinities of the Christian and Muslim antagonists. In their respective poems, Jones and Byron, both politically liberal Whigs, produce extremely different versions of the orient. Though both include feminised versions of the east, the former offers a challenging depiction of womanhood (albeit set in a distant, mythological, past) while the latter represents a silenced and stereotypical image of femininity indicative of modern Greece. In keeping with their politics, however, both writers envision the orient as glorious in its past and in need of liberation from Mughal/Ottoman rule in decline; while Jones as a servant of the East India Company could envisage such a prospect with optimism, Byron as a supporter of Greek resistance (he would later join their independence movement in 1823) was less sanguine. Though both resist commonly held ideas of alterity or otherness in their depictions of oriental religions, Jones's (and Wilkins's) depiction of Hinduism sought to establish continuities with Christianity in a manner that might conciliate British sympathy, while Byron writes with an ironic scepticism that portrays orthodox Christianity and Islam as equally liable to bigotry and superstition.

Turning from poetry to prose, my two examples of magazine writing from the 1820s illustrate the impact of material culture – specifically, the circulation of substances and objects that were imported from the east – on literature and reading audiences of the period. As Britain's imperial reach was extended in the early nineteenth century it remained in competition with other European imperial powers, while China continued to repulse its attempts to establish favourable trading relations along Indian lines. Furthermore, Chinese exports to Britain in the form of tea and porcelain (its other name 'china' literally repeating its origin) created trade imbalances that were inimical to British interests. These imbalances would be contested by local manufactures (such as Wedgewood's pottery from the late eighteenth century) and by an aggressive policy of opium production in British India for Chinese markets leading to the first 'opium war' of 1839–42. Though largely successful in consolidating its power in the east during the Romantic period, the British empire was by no means perfectly secure in its possessions and in the advantages of trade that it sought. De Quincey's and Lamb's writings in the *London Magazine* suggest varied metropolitan responses to the circulation of eastern goods in Britain in this wider and more ambivalent context of imperial trade and international relations.

De Quincey's evocative autobiographical account of his progressive development of opium dependency describes a widespread cultural practice of opium-taking that was still little understood in his time.[18] While opium was an integral part of the medical pharmacopoeia in the early nineteenth century and was used for a variety of ailments from cough syrups to sleeping potions, its use as a recreational drug was less widely acknowledged. Its importation from the east (in particular Turkey) led to stereotypical descriptions of the Turkish as lazy and indolent on account of habitual use of the drug. The title of De Quincey's work emphasises the Englishness of the opium-eater in contradistinction to his oriental counterparts who are described in aggressively racist terms as being 'absurd enough to sit, like so many equestrian statues, on logs of wood as stupid as themselves'.[19] On the other hand, De Quincey presents himself as a cultured Englishman whose use of opium only enhanced his pleasure in music and in meditative pursuits. This representation of opium as a stimulant, as Nigel Leask has shown, was integral to the medical argument known as Brunonianism (from the physiological theory of the Edinburgh surgeon John Brown, who proposed it) which De Quincey supported against the medical consensus of his time.[20] According to Leask's important argument, the chemical agency of opium in De Quincey's *Confessions* could be read as a materialistic response to the idealistic Romantic theory of imagination as developed by his older contemporaries (and idols), Wordsworth and (especially) Coleridge.

The racial implications of opium as a drug of eastern origin form an undercurrent to the work, revealing itself in the opium-eater's well-marked racist attitudes to Turkish opium-eaters and to the enigmatic figure of a 'Malay' who, he claimed, had visited him at his cottage in the Lake District, and to whom he gave a large dose of opium, presuming the Malay's familiarity with the drug. Such racial undertones haunt the work and are disclosed in the terrifying nightmares which he describes in the latter portion of his work under the section titled 'The Pains of Opium':

> The Malay has been a fearful enemy for months. I have been every night, through his means, transported into Asiatic scenes. I know not whether others share in my feelings on this point; but I have often thought that if I were compelled to forgo England, and to live in China ... I should go mad ... Southern Asia, in general, is the seat of awful images and associations ... The mere antiquity of Asiatic things, of their institutions, histories, modes of faith, &c. is so impressive, that to me the vast age of the race and name overpowers the sense of youth in the individual.[21]

Here, De Quincey's knowledge of the 'antiquity of Asiatic things ... institutions, histories, modes of faith' is clearly derived from the work of orientalists such as William Jones and his successors at the Asiatick Society; yet, such knowledge is, for him, overwritten by deeply racist attitudes. De Quincey's evangelical upbringing (his mother was a member of the Clapham sect which included Hannah More) clearly contributes to the horror and loathing he feels for what he describes as 'the ancient, monumental, cruel, and elaborate religions of Indostan, &c.',[22] which were the focus of aggressive evangelical propaganda in support of missionary conversions in the colonies. Fleeing from the horrors of his oriental dreams, De Quincey finds even the interior domestic spaces of British homes no longer a refuge for his nerve-wracked sensibility. The British taste for chinoiserie and oriental motifs carved into furniture ensured that even these spaces were prone to reiterate his worst nightmares: 'All the feet of the tables, sophas, &c. soon became instinct with life: the abominable head of the crocodile, and his leering eyes, looked out at me, multiplied into a thousand repetitions: and I stood loathing and fascinated'.[23]

Despite the horror and repugnance registered in De Quincey's *Confessions*, chinoiserie clearly remained a fashionable aspect of British material culture, most memorably visible in the designer John Nash's major extension of the Brighton Pavilion between 1815 and 1822. Charles Lamb's essay 'Old China', published in the *London Magazine* in 1823, celebrates the ubiquity of Chinese porcelain which had so entered the fabric of British social life through the custom of tea drinking that its aesthetic appeal appeared almost inevitable. Though the narrator of Lamb's essay, Elia, could 'call to mind the first play, and the first exhibition' he had witnessed, yet he was 'not conscious of a time when china jars and saucers were introduced into [his] imagination'.[24] Responding obviously to De Quincey's *Confessions* (itself a response to Lamb's 1813 essay 'Confessions of a Drunkard'), Lamb's Elia replies with whimsical humour to De Quincey's abhorrence for such objects: 'I had no repugnance then – why should I now have? – to those little, lawless, azure-tinctured grotesques, that under the notion of men and women, float about, uncircumscribed by any element, in that world before perspective – a china tea-cup'.[25] The spatially disorienting aspects of De Quincey's nightmare visions are transformed in Elia's comic perspective to the 'lawless' and free-floating human figures on the teacup, their admitted grotesqueness ameliorated by domestic familiarity and miniaturisation of scale. Yet Elia's whimsical take on De Quincey's opium-induced nightmare visions need not be taken as conclusive evidence of Lamb's own racial attitudes. In an earlier Elian essay, 'A Dissertation upon Roast Pig' (1822), Lamb reproduces the more familiar stereotypes of oriental cultures obdurately resistant to change. Elia's comic portrayal of the ancient Chinese obtusely discovering the joys of roast pork through the accident of a swineherd burning his house down – a circumstance that requires further destruction of their own houses for the Chinese to continue enjoying roast pork – reiterates the virulence of earlier oriental stereotypes while drawing upon Lamb's familiarity with orientalist scholarship and his own experience of working for the India House of the EIC in London.[26]

Aside from the ubiquity of eastern goods and styles in the consumer landscape of Britain, the Romantic period witnessed a significant reverse flow of travellers from eastern countries. Many of these, like De Quincey's Malay, worked in the global shipping trade and would have frequented the port cities and towns of Britain. While very few such travellers left their own impressions of Britain, the Romantic period witnessed a number of fictional, often satirical, accounts of such perspectives, from Oliver Goldsmith's character of the Chinese philosopher Lien Chi Altangi in *The Citizen of the World* (published 1760–1) to Elizabeth Hamilton's Rajah Zaarmilla in *Translation of the Letters of a Hindoo Rajah* (1796). Such accounts, though rewarding, are yet ventriloquised versions of eastern perspectives. More authentically, though, the period also witnessed some of the earliest eastern travellers to leave their own accounts of Britain or of their countries of origin for western readers. Mirza Abu Taleb Khan, employed by the EIC, travelled from Calcutta to London via Dublin in 1799, and left a vivid account of Britain which was translated from Persian by the Irish orientalist Charles Stewart in 1810. His insights into British high society and the sights and entertainments of London are remarkable for their observance of British customs and manners from a privileged though undeniably alien point of view. Countering English stereotypes of the Irish he finds them charming and hospitable, though the poverty he encounters in Britain's oldest colony is disconcerting as he finds peasantry in Ireland far poorer than in India. His admiring comments on English technologies and manufacture are accompanied by surprise at their coldness to personal appeals for charity:

> English charity does not consist in giving a small sum of money to a beggar, or a poor poet, or a starving musician. These persons they have a great aversion to; and should one of them follow a coach for miles, he would lose his labour, and not be able to soften the hearts of those seated therein. But their charities are of a public nature; for in every parish there is a house built for the poor, where they may reside, and receive a daily allowance of food.[27]

Institutionalised forms of charity in England, he suggests, were displacing sympathetic responses to the poor.

In Ireland, Taleb Khan encountered Dean Mahomet, a migrant from Bihar who had settled in Cork and had published what is now regarded as the first work in English by an Indian author. Mahomet's travel reminiscences, published in Cork in 1794 and detailing his absorption as a subaltern into the EIC's army (in which he served under his patron Captain Baker), provided for Irish readers a favourable account of the Company's growth in India, and may have contributed to the EIC's drive for recruitment in Ireland. Mahomet's description of his arrival in Ireland in his *Travels*, however, while registering his astonishment at the extremely different scenery he encountered here from those he had known in India, strikes a far more conservative note expressing his deference to and absorption in British culture:

> I found the face of every thing about me so contrasted to those *striking scenes* in India, which we are wont to survey with a kind of sublime delight, that I felt some timid inclination, even in the consciousness of incapacity, to describe the manners of my countrymen, who, I am proud to think, have still more of the innocence of our ancestors, than some of the boasting philosophers of Europe.[28]

Mahomet's view of the picturesque landscapes of Ireland which he contrasts to the sublimity of Indian scenery repeats a well-worn aesthetic trope of European travel accounts, while he deferentially contrasts the innocence of Indians with the sophistication of western culture though carried to excess by arrogant European philosophers (i.e., those tainted by political radicalism in British conservative political thinking of the 1790s). His comfortably conservative viewpoint following his marriage and acceptance into British society offers a contrast to the sharper and more unsettling perspectives of his compatriot Taleb Khan.

To conclude, this brief and selective reading reveals that despite thriving upon and generating a series of stereotypical tropes, the 'orient' throughout the Romantic period was a variable, constantly evolving and highly contested phenomenon. While early engagements with Romantic orientalism such as the still influential account proposed by Edward Said in 1978 stressed the predictability and consistency of the stereotypical aspects of orientalism, later scholarship has demonstrated the extraordinarily diverse significances attached to orientalism in the period. British involvements with the east varied from learned engagements with its knowledge culture as disseminated by the orientalists to consumerist absorption of its material products and experiential exposure to its locations. The idea of the orient was increasingly subjected to newer forms of categorisation and differentiation, and could be mediated and transmitted through ever-increasing varieties of genre, print culture and technologies of reproduction. And, though not yet 'postcolonial' in the full sense of the term, eastern cultures began to 'write back' to the west in the period through the accounts of travellers and migrants to the west.

NOTES

1. Leslie Marchand (ed.), *Byron's Letters and Journals*, 12 vols (London: John Murray, 1973–82), vol. III, p. 101.
2. Ronan Kelly, *Bard of Erin: The Life of Thomas Moore* (London: Penguin, 2008), pp. 277–306.
3. Lord Byron, *The Corsair, a Tale* (London: John Murray, 1814), pp. v–xi.
4. Daniel Sanjiv Roberts, 'Moore's Oriental Artifice: Mughal History, Irish Antiquarianism, and Romance in *Lalla Rookh*', in Sarah McCleave and Brian G. Caraher (eds), *Thomas*

Moore and Romantic Inspiration: Poetry, Music, and Politics (New York: Routledge, 2018), pp. 185–96.

5. Lynda Pratt (gen. ed.), *Robert Southey: Poetical Works 1793–1810*, 5 vols (London: Pickering & Chatto, 2004), vol. I, pp. xxi–xxvii; vol. III, pp. xxvii–xxviii; vol. IV, pp. xviii–xix.

6. This term, earlier used of the Spanish empire, began to be used of the British empire during the course of the Romantic period. It was evidently first used in English by the Irish statesman and colonial administrator George Macartney in 1773, though later commonly attributed to John Wilson. See George Macartney, *An Account of Ireland* (London, 1773), p. 55; and John Wilson, 'Noctes Ambrosianae No. 42', *Blackwood's Edinburgh Magazine* 25 (April 1829), 527.

7. Robert L. Mack (ed.), *Arabian Nights' Entertainments* (Oxford University Press, 2009), pp. 9–20.

8. The *Oxford English Dictionary* records the use of 'orientalist' in the sense of 'An expert in or student of oriental languages, history, culture, etc.' from 1723, citing an example from William Jones in 1771.

9. Salman Rushdie, 'The Empire Writes Back with a Vengeance', *Times*, 3 July 1982, p. 8.

10. Andrew Rudd, *Sympathy and India in British Literature, 1770–1830* (Houndmills: Palgrave Macmillan, 2011), pp. 12–13.

11. Nicholas B. Dirks, *The Scandal of Empire: India and the Creation of Imperial Britain* (Cambridge, MA: Harvard University Press, 2008), p. 10.

12. Charles Wilkins, *The Bhăgvăt-Gēētā, or Dialogues of Krĕĕshnă and Ărjŏŏn* (London: C. Nourse, 1785), p. 98; subsequent references are given in the main text.

13. Edward W. Said, *Orientalism* (London: Routledge & Kegan Paul, 1978).

14. William Jones, 'A Discourse on the Institution of a Society for Inquiring into the History, Civil and Natural, the Antiquities, Arts, Sciences, and Literature of Asia', *Asiatic Researches* 1 (1806), ix–xvi (ix); all subsequent references are given in the main text. My quotations are from the fifth London edition; the first edition was published in Kolkata in 1789.

15. Michael J. Franklin (ed.), *Sir William Jones: Selected Poetical and Prose Works* (Cardiff: University of Wales Press, 1995), p. 83 (lines 61–72); subsequent references are given in the main text.

16. Kate Teltscher, *India Inscribed: European and British Writing on India, 1600–1800* (New Delhi: Oxford University Press, 1995), p. 51.

17. Alan Richardson (ed.), *Three Oriental Tales* (Boston: Houghton Mifflin, 2002), p. 185, lines 106–9.

18. Barry Milligan, *Pleasures and Pains: Opium and the Orient in Nineteenth-Century British Culture* (Charlottesville: University of Virginia Press, 1995).

19. Grevel Lindop (gen. ed.), *The Works of Thomas De Quincey*, 21 vols (London: Pickering & Chatto, 2000–3), vol. II, p. 47.

20. Nigel Leask, *British Romantic Writers and the East: Anxieties of Empire* (Cambridge University Press, 1993), pp. 175–9.

21. De Quincey, *Works*, vol. II, p. 70.

22. Ibid., p. 70.

23. Ibid., p. 71.

24. *The Complete Works and Letters of Charles Lamb* (New York: Modern Library, 1963), p. 217.
25. Ibid.
26. Peter Kitson, *Forging Romantic China: Sino-British Cultural Exchange 1770–1840* (Cambridge University Press, 2013), pp. 169–74.
27. Daniel O'Quinn (ed.), *The Travels of Mirza Abu Taleb Khan* (Peterborough, Ontario: Broadview Press, 2009), pp. 155–6.
28. Michael H. Fisher (ed.), *The Travels of Dean Mahomet: An Eighteenth-Century Journey through India* (Berkeley: University of California Press, 1997), p. 34.

CRITICAL REFLECTIONS AND FURTHER STUDY

My essay can perhaps be best understood as a tussle with Edward Said's influential theory of orientalism, which I both admire and seek to refute. In *Orientalism* (1978), Edward Said argued powerfully for a recognition of the scholarly discourse of orientalism as the means 'by which European culture was able to manage – and even produce – the Orient politically, sociologically, militarily, ideologically, scientifically, and imaginatively during the post-Enlightenment period' (p. 3). While my essay develops Said's important insight – derived from Michel Foucault – into the relationship between knowledge formation and political power, my thinking departs from his work in several major respects. Firstly, while Said regards the orient as a consistent form of denigration, resulting in 'the idea of European identity as a superior one in comparison with all the non-European peoples and cultures' (p. 7), Jones and other orientalists, as we have seen, were very prepared to depict the ancient civilisations of the east as being in advance of European societies during certain eras, and in some respects. Such favourable comparisons, however, were largely located in earlier (classical) periods, and in imaginative and artistic endeavours, rather than scientific and utilitarian ones. Secondly, while Said reads the orient as the opposite of, and the negation of, European values, we may note the recognition of several similarities and cross-currents between eastern and western thinking (so constructed) emerging in this period, especially with regards to ideas of religion among the early orientalists who were keen to adopt a syncretic approach to other cultures. Their thinking emphasised similarities and even potential congruence between Christian and Hindu religious beliefs, though set firmly in an ('antediluvian') era prior to western and biblical histories. This tolerant phase of orientalism which suited the commercial aims of the East India Company in its early phase was superseded however by a more aggressive, interventionist approach to other cultures, and it was always subjected to imperialist prerogatives. And, finally, while Said insists fundamentally on seeing the orient as a mirrored inversion of western fantasies, 'a battery of desires, regressions, investments, and projections' (p. 8), my analysis seeks to show an empirically detailed, diverse and changing picture of Asia emerging from orientalism, even though its key assumptions were inevitably Eurocentric.

Accordingly, my essay emphasises change, variety and contestation in the discursive practices of orientalism, rather than adopting a 'one size fits all' approach to the topic. Furthermore, I should emphasise my obligation to numerous scholars from the 1990s whose scholarship informs my readings, often tacitly, though I have sought to acknowledge any direct or obvious connections. Nigel Leask's emphasis in his book *British Romantic Writers and the East* on the 'anxious' nature of imperial engagement, and his emphasis on the materialist aspects of this engagement within metropolitan contexts; Mary Louise Pratt's idea of 'transculturation' within what she termed 'contact zones' (in this case, late eighteenth-century Bengal; see Further Reading) where western cultures interacted with eastern ones in highly asymmetrical relationships of power; and the beginnings, within the Romantic period, of reverse flows of imperialism through the globalising forces of travel and migration – these comprise some of the major ideas I have developed through my readings. Though I have sought to include several genres and styles to illustrate the variety of Romantic-period 'orientalisms' (as James Watt usefully disaggregates the term through his use of the plural in the title of his excellent recent book; see Further Reading), there have been significant areas left untouched. Centring my account on Asia and particularly India, which emerged as Britain's 'jewel in the crown' during the period, other eastern locations, including the Middle East, which Jones included in his delineation of Asia, have been largely passed over. In terms of genre, I have avoided, for reasons of space, discussion of drama and fictional works which include a great variety of material, from the highly imaginative worlds of fabular traditions and *Arabian Nights* imitations to realistic and historical novels such as Elizabeth Hamilton's *Translations of the Letters of a Hindoo Rajah* (1796) and Sydney Owenson's *The Missionary: An Indian Tale* (1811). Ros Ballaster and Srinivas Aravamudan offer important readings of the liberatory possibilities of oriental fiction (see Further Reading). Ballaster's work in particular pays attention to the fabular traditions of oriental fiction, arguing against the common criticism that they were escapist in tendency, and suggesting instead that they offered a transformative and 'moving' experience of 'imaginary projection into the psyche and culture of an other' (p. 8). Last, but not least, Daniel O'Quinn provides a valuable insight into theatrical and oratorical productions that shaped the public imagination of colonial sexuality in the face of government attempts to curb such representations (see Further Reading).

Despite the plethora of excellent recent criticism, Romantic orientalism is still an exciting and developing field. The following reading list suggests only a small selection of new work in the area; much more remains to be discovered.

FURTHER READING

Aravamudan, Srinivas, *Enlightenment Orientalism: Resisting the Rise of the Novel* (University of Chicago Press, 2012)

Barrell, John, *The Infection of Thomas De Quincey: A Psychopathology of Imperialism* (New Haven, CT: Yale University Press, 1991)

Ballaster, Ros, *Fabulous Orients: Fictions of the East in England, 1662–1785* (Oxford University Press, 2005)

Butler, Marilyn, 'Orientalism', in David Pirie (ed.), *The Penguin History of English Literature: The Romantic Period* (London: Penguin, 1994), pp. 63–81

Festa, Lynn, *Sentimental Figures of Empire in Eighteenth-Century Britain and France* (Baltimore: Johns Hopkins University Press, 2006)

Hamilton, Elizabeth, *Translation of Letters of a Hindoo Rajah*, ed. Pamela Perkins and Shannon Russell (Peterborough, Ontario: Broadview Press, 1999)

Makdisi, Saree, *Romantic Imperialism: Universal Empire and the Culture of Modernity* (Cambridge University Press, 1988)

O'Quinn, Daniel, *Staging Governance: Theatrical Imperialism in London, 1770–1800* (Baltimore: Johns Hopkins University Press, 2005)

Owenson, Syndey, *The Missionary: An Indian Tale*, ed. Julia Wright (Peterborough, Ontario: Broadview Press, 2002)

Pratt, Mary Louise, *Imperial Eyes: Travel Writing and Transculturation* (London: Routledge, 1992)

Rajan, Balachandra, *Under Western Eyes: India from Milton to Macaulay* (Durham, NC: Duke University Press, 1999)

Watt, James, *British Orientalisms, 1759–1835* (Cambridge University Press, 2019)

White, Daniel J., *From Little London to Little Bengal: Religion, Print and Modernity in Early British India, 1793–1835* (Baltimore: Johns Hopkins University Press, 2013)

13 Historical Fiction in the Romantic Period: Jane Porter, Walter Scott and the Sublime Hero

FIONA PRICE

Abstract

Until recently, it was often assumed that Walter Scott was the first historical novelist. Moreover, it was accepted that, in writing a new form of fiction, Scott had chosen to make his heroes, caught up in large-scale historical events, relatively ineffectual. Yet when the work of the historical novelists (often women) who worked before and alongside Scott is taken into account, it becomes apparent that Scott's decision regarding his heroes is a manoeuvre within a wider debate regarding the nature of heroism. Placing Scott's heroes within a wider context, this essay examines how the Romantic historical novel first moderates, then reduces and reinvents the sublime figure of the heroic leader. My reading examines how, in *The Scottish Chiefs* (1810), Jane Porter invented a new model of sublime Christian heroism that could be extended beyond the upper ranks. It interrogates how Scott responded to Porter by minimising the potentially subversive elements of this paradigm, and it reveals how Jane Porter, in *The Pastor's Fireside* (1817), proposed a form of heroic re-education. For these historical novelists, the difficulty, ultimately, was to imagine a variety of patriotic heroism that would safely function in commercial, peacetime Britain.

Although contemporary critics have increasingly questioned this view, Walter Scott was traditionally seen as the first historical novelist. Further, it was accepted that, in writing a new form of fiction, Scott had chosen to make his heroes, caught up in large-scale historical events, relatively powerless. The ineffectual nature of Scott's heroes was almost proverbial. In her introduction to *Waverley* (1814), Kathryn Sutherland comments on how Waverley 'drifts' into his position within the Hanoverian army. The heroes of historical fiction, she insists, 'can never alter events'.[1] Yet when the work of the historical novelists (often women) who worked before and alongside Scott is taken into account, it becomes apparent that Scott's approach is part of a wider debate regarding the nature of heroism. In the 1790s, while radical writers like Charlotte Smith were suspicious of courtly and chivalric models of power, more conservative commentators like Clara Reeve and Jane West attempted to rehabilitate the knightly heroes of historical romance. Their attempts were not always convincing. Nonetheless, during and after the Napoleonic Wars, it was not sufficient to say, in the words of the writer Elizabeth Hamilton, that 'hero' was only another term for 'pest'.[2]

Placing Scott's heroes within a wider context, this essay examines how the Romantic historical novel first moderates, then minimises, and finally reinvents the sublime figure of the heroic leader. My discussion explores how, in *The Scottish Chiefs* (1810), Jane Porter invented a new model of sublime Christian heroism that could be extended beyond the upper ranks. It interrogates how Scott responded to Porter by minimising the potentially subversive elements of this paradigm, and it reveals how Jane Porter, in *The Pastor's Fireside* (1817), proposed a form of re-education that would allow a moderated form of heroism to persist and flourish within the British Isles. For these historical novelists, the difficulty was to imagine a variety of patriotic heroism that could function safely in modern, commercial, peacetime Britain. This process would involve the domestication and internalisation of the Romantic sublime.

The celebration of the kind of heroism shown in romance is seen at its plainest in the historical fiction of Clara Reeve. Reeve identified with her father, an Old Whig – that is to say, she believed in a balance of power between the monarchy, the aristocracy and the people. After a brief moment of excitement about the potential of the French Revolution (presumably because it would bring an end to royal absolutism), she felt the need to defend aristocratic influence. Best known for her 1785 critical work *The Progress of Romance*, in which she celebrates the heroic romance's 'lofty' and 'elevated' potential,[3] in 1793 Reeve published *The Memoirs of Roger de Clarendon*. Set in the reign of King Richard II, this narrative follows the template for romance fiction set out in *The Progress* but its preface also warns against 'the new philosophy of the present day' which 'avows a levelling principle'.[4] For Reeve, the discourse of knightly endeavour serves a pedagogic function in preventing such radical egalitarianism. This kind of celebration of chivalric heroism is an essentially conservative manoeuvre, protecting the status quo.

Reeve believed the need for such a corrective was urgent. As Charlotte Smith had discussed in *Desmond* (1792), in France the National Assembly had abolished titles. As well as arguing in support of their position (using historical evidence), Smith's novel critiqued chivalric heroism and romance. For Smith and other radicals (notably William Godwin), the code of chivalry and the models of military heroism that evolved from it were problematic. According to Reeve, however, such radical attitudes had generated 'many attempts … of late years to build fictitious stories upon historical names and characters[,] to falsify historical facts and characters' (p. xx). Reeve's *Memoirs* is a reply to such radical suspicions of romance. Yet although Reeve, by implication, asserts the factuality of her own novel, she also admits that she herself has 'taken some liberties' with her characters (p. xxi). Her historical heroes serve an equally partisan purpose.

This debate about chivalric romance – and the kind of heroism it promoted – gradually became complicated by the equally contested discourse of the Romantic sublime. Considering the sublime of ambition, in *A Philosophical Enquiry* (1757), Edmund Burke had proposed: 'whatever, either on good or upon bad grounds, tends to raise a man in his own opinion, produces a sort of swelling and triumph, that is extremely grateful to the human mind; and this swelling is never more perceived ... than when without danger we are conversant with terrible objects'.[5] This 'triumph', which Burke implies is sublime, seems unmerciful and, in its 'swelling', determinedly masculine. Two years later, in his *Essay on Taste* (1759), Alexander Gerard made the connection to heroism even more directly, remarking that 'the most imperfect and uncultivated taste is sensible of a sublimity in heroism'.[6] But it was only after the publication of Edmund Burke's *Reflections on the Late Revolution in France* (1790) that such assertions about the sublime became heavily politicised. Commentators, notably Mary Wollstonecraft, directed attention to the way Burke marshalled the sublime and the beautiful to reinforce his political arguments. The sublime was used to glorify tradition and to deny the need for (and even the possibility of) political change in Britain. As a result, and particularly following the rise of Napoleon Buonaparte in the first decade of the nineteenth century, the heroic sublime became problematised.

In 1809 Elizabeth Hamilton, novelist, essayist, educationalist and an aesthetician of considerable talent, wrote to Joanna Baillie about heroic ambition. Hamilton argues that the hero is a 'pest to society' because 'his delight in the deep play of war and desolation, must arise from the excitements in which the selfish principle is most predominant. The stake for which he throws is the power of identifying with self millions of human beings'.[7] For Hamilton, heroism as commonly defined is a reflection of the most extreme capitalist and imperialist forms of speculation. Any aesthetic that celebrates it and thus encourages those passions subtly inculcates those political values. Burke's 'swelling' heroic sublime is recast as an addictive urge to expand the self. In her own historical work, *Memoirs of the Life of Agrippina, Wife of Germanicus* (1804), Hamilton searched for a more moral or Christian form of heroism. Her endeavours are echoed – with, however, a greater emphasis upon desire – by Jane Porter in *The Scottish Chiefs*.

Set in the late thirteenth and early fourteenth centuries, Jane Porter's *The Scottish Chiefs* depicts William Wallace's role during the First War of Scottish Independence (1296–1328) to present a defensive Christian mode of heroism. Her vision of the heroic proved contentious. According to James Hogg, although Scott praised *The Scottish Chiefs*, he also complained that 'the character of Wallace' had been 'frittered away to that of a fine gentleman', a phrase that implies Wallace's character is insufficiently feudal, insufficiently masculine and perhaps excessively modern.[8]

In a review of Joanna Baillie's *Metrical Legends* (1821), Thomas Carlyle complained that Wallace 'has become the prey of novelists and poetasters. They have made him into a sentimental philosopher, woe-begone lover, a mere carpet knight'.[9] Carlyle's use of the term 'philosopher' (a term that had, in the 1790s, carried negative associations of radicalism) suggests some political prejudice lurks behind all this invective. Porter, however, was no radical. Admittedly, in the novel, Wallace leads the rebellion because the Scottish aristocracy have failed to contest English supremacy. But Porter neutralises any radical charge contained in this indictment by having Wallace repeatedly assert his adherence to the established social order. That order, though, needs to be underpinned by a strong morality. More specifically, the newly compassionate, Christian hero must preserve not just his country but the domestic and the familial environment. If, as Porter believed, a consciousness of history and its heroes could create and strengthen a contemporary patriotic community, it was important to fashion a more admirable variety of heroism.

While the political division between the English and the Scots (or, more accurately, between England and Scotland) drives the plot of *The Scottish Chiefs*, it is not, Porter indicates, the most significant division. The true driver of political difference is, she insists, moral difference, and there the real split is between, on the one hand, the self-interested and corrupt and, on the other, the self-sacrificing and honourable. In distinguishing between these individuals, their attitude to the domestic is an important indicator. Representative of the more supine and selfish part of the Scottish nobility, Joanna Mar (the young second wife of the Earl of Mar) claims to wish to protect her husband from the consequences of Wallace's insurrection against the English. However, advancement and her own personal desires, not her husband's safety, are her true motivators. Later, when Wallace becomes the focus of both her ambitions and her desires, she begins, temporarily, to support the Scottish cause, only ultimately to betray it. The wrong attitude towards the country and towards the family go hand in hand.

Wallace, in contrast, has had his attitude corrected. At the beginning of the novel when Scotland is in a state of vassalage to England, he remains in domestic seclusion with his wife, Marion, at Ellerslie. After her death at the hands of the English, Wallace calls upon the dispossessed Scottish peasantry: 'I come in the name of all you hold dear, of your lives, your liberties, and of the wives of your bosoms, and the children in their arms!'[10] The fight for country is also the fight for family. Yet the sight of the Scottish women and their children also precipitates one of Wallace's many moments of sentimental introspection. 'My wife, my unborn babe, they both must bleed for Scotland!' he exclaims, 'And the sacrifice shall not be yielded in vain' (p. 195). Marion and his child have had to die to jolt him into action. The family should not become inward-looking, selfish or detached. When these negative qualities adhere to it, it becomes vulnerable. Protection of one's own family can only be achieved by the protection of everyone's family.

The sacrifice (of the immediate family in favour of the ideal and the deferred family) is styled by Porter as both Christian and sublime. In large part, Wallace, whose 'sacrifice' has in fact been forced upon him, becomes a figure for these values. Kidnapped by Aymer de Valence, Helen, the Earl of Mar's daughter, is rescued by an unnamed knight (Wallace) whose 'beaming eyes were full of patriotic ardor' while 'his fine countenance, composed into a heavenly calmness by the sublime sentiments of unselfed bravery which occupied his soul, made him appear to her not as a man, but as a god' (p. 160). Wallace's rescue of Helen from potential rape reinforces the connection between the protection of women, the safety of family and the preservation of country. Protective heroism is sublime – and it is not solely a masculine trait. Just as Wallace determines to remain celibate for the sake of Scotland, so Helen also makes an ongoing sacrifice in accepting her love for Wallace will remain unfulfilled.

Given the amount of passionate energy this model of heroism demands, restraint is necessary. The desire to protect the lover or child, Porter emphasises, can quickly become a desire for vengeance. Worse still, just as patriotism becomes extended and generalised beyond the original family, the desire for vengeance can also become general, directed against a whole nation. When Heselrigge stabs Marion, Wallace is marked by 'ferocity', and claims 'vengeance' (p. 87). But after Heselrigge dies, Wallace vows to 'divide self from [his] heart' (p. 92). And when his men shout, 'So fall the enemies of Sir William Wallace!' Wallace insists, 'Rather so fall the enemies of Scotland' (p. 92). Similarly, and in still more obviously pedagogic fashion, Wallace corrects the bloodthirsty Kirkpatrick. Kirkpatrick is about to kill the corrupt Aymer de Valence, who is trying to escape – but Wallace listens to de Valence's pleas for mercy. When de Valence immediately uses his momentary freedom to treacherously stab Wallace, Kirkpatrick impatiently remarks: 'You treated him as a man ... but now you find he is a wild beast!' But Wallace argues that 'humanity', 'honour' and policy are all on his side (p. 213). The youthful Edwin is present and as such is instructed. Porter's own pedagogic purpose is as clear as Wallace's.

Porter indicates that literature (and by implication the historical novel) is key to this educational process. Fired by enthusiasm for Wallace's cause, Helen, for example, passionately urges her stepmother to support the uprising: 'Besides, ... look at our country:– God's gift of freedom is stamped upon it.– Our mountains are his seal' (p. 105). For Helen, the sublime features of the landscape underpin and reinforce Porter's model of Christian heroism. But Lady Mar disapproves: 'I rue the day in which I complied with the entreaties of Sir Richard Maitland, and permitted you and your sister to remain at Thirlestane, to imbibe the ideas of his romantic kinsman, the wizard of Ercildown' (she refers to Thomas de Ercildown or Thomas the Rhymer (fl. *c.* 1220–98)) (p. 107). To Joanna's disgust, poetry and prophecy inspire Helen's patriotism and ensure her understanding of Scotland not just as a land of heroes but also as a heroic land. The Bible (the importance of which Porter emphasises in the preface), poetry and the novel all construct the heroic relationship to the nation. The Romantic period is characterised by a deistic urge to trace God's presence in the natural world. Porter's cultural texts transform this urge into an injunction to read the landscape as a divine call to patriotism.

Jane Porter's pedadogic model of sublime Christian heroism did not go unchallenged. In *Waverley*, Scott critiques the notion of heroism and undercuts the kind of heroic impulses Porter encourages. Until recently, however, Scott's own account of the origins of *Waverley* effectively precluded the idea that Scott was influenced by or responding to Porter. In the 1829 general preface to the Waverley Novels, Scott states that he began the novel in 1806 but put it aside after the first seven chapters, only rediscovering it while searching for fishing tackle in an old writing desk (pp. 386–7). In this account the bulk of the novel was written after October 1813. Peter Garside, however, dismantles this narrative (Porter herself was to claim in the 1831 preface to her novel *Thaddeus of Warsaw* (1803) that Scott adopted 'the style or class of novel of which "Thaddeus of Warsaw" was the first').[11] Garside's account opens the way for a more dialogic reading of the two novelists – and when *Waverley* is read as a response to *The Scottish Chiefs* the results are interesting. In choosing to concentrate on the First War of Scottish Independence rather than on English history, Porter departed from the ancient constitutionalism that preoccupied novelists like Reeve. The idea that Anglo-Saxon England had certain freedoms under the law which the Normans curtailed or, as Reeve hints, modified, was put aside. But in substituting Wallace for King Alfred and creating a narrative where freedom was enshrined not in constitutional law but in the very countryside, Porter also reopened the matter of Scotland's place within the Union. Porter's aim had not been to encourage Scottish nationalism but rather to inspire the patriotism of the small nation, particularly in the context of Napoleonic imperialism. Nonetheless, her subject matter was potentially contentious. Particularly by 1814 (when the Napoleonic Wars were drawing to a close), Porter's model of a sublimely inspired patriotic citizenry was no longer either desirable or practicable. By setting *Waverley* at the time of the 1745 Jacobite rising, Scott indicates the dangers of the kind of mass heroism envisaged by Porter, its potential to produce internecine strife (Figure 13.1). Wary not just about troublesome national but also political passions, Scott satirises the idea of the hero, hints at the dangers of an educational model based on desire and reverses Porter's suggestions about the erotics of patriotism.

Scott's reduction of heroism begins in the first 'introductory' chapter of *Waverley* with his discussion of his hero's name. His claim that he has 'like a maiden knight with his white shield, assumed for [his] hero, WAVERLEY, an uncontaminated name' is somewhat disingenuous (p. 3). As Peter Garside notes, both Charlotte Smith and Jane West had had characters (albeit emphatically not heroes) of the

Figure 13.1 'Houghton dying in the arms of Edward', an engraving from Sir Walter Scott's *Waverley*, the 1826 *Oeuvres completes* edition. Edward Waverley tries to aid his dying follower Houghton, who urges him not to fight for the Stuart cause. The heroic ideal is compromised, leading to internecine strife, misunderstanding and bloodshed.

same name.[12] However, Garside does not draw any conclusions from that regarding the novel's stance on heroism and the political debates on the subject. The Waverly of Charlotte Smith's radical novel *Desmond* (1792) had been indecisive and weak, a symbol of the self-indulgence of the upper classes. In contrast, the Waverly in Jane West's conservative historical novel of the English Civil Wars and Commonwealth, *The Loyalists* (1812), was a political turncoat, wrongly abandoning his loyalty to King Charles I and currying favour with Oliver Cromwell. Oddly enough considering that he is a hero, Scott's Waverley inherits a mixture of these propensities, but they are softened and made more sympathetic. Waverley has a habit of following 'the bent of his own mind' (p. 14) that can make him, like Smith's Waverly, appear inconsistent; he is also swayed by his immediate sympathies so that he appears (like West's character) politically malleable. Yet he is also likeable, hapless and a victim of historical circumstance. Bringing together both conservative and radical political anxieties, the name condenses previous debates about the dangers of heroism. As such, Waverley seems to represent an invitation to political compromise, an invitation to put aside the quarrel not only between England and Scotland but, far more tellingly, between radical and conservative narratives of history and heroism.

The heroic narrative is reduced, sapped of political energy, but typically Scott disguises the manoeuvre. His opening discussion of his choice of title seems to be concerned with literary genre rather than political party. But as he repeatedly uses the words 'hero' and 'heroine', associating them with historical, Gothic and sentimental fiction, he continues to weaken the very idea of 'heroism' (pp. 3–4). It is possible, Scott reminds his readers, to have 'a hero from the Barouche-Club or the Four-in-hand': Waverley is one fictional hero among the many that Scott's readers have encountered and his title will perhaps prove a matter of literary convention rather than a signifier of actual virtue (p. 4). Scott's insistence on 'hero' as a term of novelistic criticism is an act of litotes. Porter had envisaged a mass heroism; Scott replies with a mass of worthless literary heroes. This is 'levelling' of a far more conservative type than Reeve had decried.

Writing in chapter 3 about 'the education of our hero', Scott similarly subjects Porter's pedagogic model to a kind of ironic reduction of litotes (p. 12). Wilful, unrestrained and imaginative, Edward seeks instruction 'only ... so long as it afforded him amusement' and the knowledge he seeks is via 'Shakespeare and Milton', 'the earlier dramatic authors', historical chronicles and 'romantic fiction', including that of 'Spenser' and 'Drayton' (pp. 14, 15). This kind of education is similar to Scott's own as he describes it in the general preface to the Waverley Novels. It is also familiar in its suspicion of romance, preparing the reader for a certain quixotism on Waverley's part. What is more unusual is Scott's waspish attack on modern educational methods only shortly before. 'The history of England,' his narrator complains, 'is now reduced to a game at cards, the problems of mathematics to puzzles and riddles' (*Waverley*, p. 14). Whether these methods impart knowledge or not, Scott fears that the pupil will be attracted to the form rather than the content and will always seek the delights of mystery and chance, never accepting the burden of pleasureless diligence. In this account, desire is suspect as a means of education. Porter's educational impulse and the kind of literature that instructed Helen Mar are both gently negated by Scott, even though, of course, he is himself still engaged in teaching.

If Wallace is in the position of tutor, Waverley remains in that of pupil. Nonetheless, desire plays a part in his education. Porter had used her female figures to construct a choice – between Joanna's drive to political and erotic satisfaction, on the one hand, and Helen's unselfish patriotism and deferred desire on the other; between the private family and the public good. Forced to abandon private family life and wedded to the nation, Wallace effectively chooses neither. Awaiting execution by King Edward II, he marries Helen, but the marriage remains unconsummated. With his heroines, Rosa Bradwardine and Flora MacIvor, Scott rewrites that choice. It is a critical commonplace that Scott draws on the stadial history of the Scottish Enlightenment – a form which sees historical development in terms of stages. Absent in *The Scottish Chiefs* (although present in Porter's earlier novel, *Thaddeus of Warsaw*), this form of history enables Scott to imply that the choice between Flora, representative of the Jacobites and of some form of public heroism, and Rosa, associated with Hanoverian Britain, is obvious and ultimately inevitable. The clanship ties of Jacobitism that inspire Flora belong to the past; the private and domestic loyalties of Rosa represent modernity. By using stadial history, Scott historicises Porter's moral and erotic choices. In having to choose Rosa (Flora is actually unavailable, dedicated, like Helen and Wallace, to the cause), Waverley selects the option that is both peaceful and domestic. The unheroic path of private fulfilment that Porter finds inadequate becomes, in Scott's novel, the correct solution for the nation. The ordinary is what the Hanoverian nation requires.

But this historicisation of the heroic is not enough for Scott. Flora is not the equivalent of Helen. Rather, as Scott's treatment of his heroines' performances makes clear, Flora has the artifice of Joanna. Flora sings an 'uncommon Highland air, which had been a battle-song in former ages', but even as Scott has her evoke the heroic sublime he implies it is illusory (*Waverley*, p. 118). Although the place where she sings an inspirational ballad has sublime qualities ('The borders of this romantic reservoir corresponded in beauty; but it was beauty of a stern and commanding cast'), it is in fact only 'as if' it were 'in the act of expanding into grandeur'; the words 'beauty' and 'romantic' are predominant (p. 117). Further, Flora has not only chosen the place in order to manipulate Waverley's political and sexual desire; she has also shaped its (almost) sublime appearance by arranging the scene beforehand. Conversely, Rosa sings a song of witchery but supplies a historical context that dispels the aura of enchantment and replaces it with Enlightenment rationality. Porter's interpretation of heroism and her reading of the landscape are undercut.

Jane Porter responds by insisting on the validity of the model of Christian heroism for contemporary Britain (Figure 13.2). Her next novel, *The Pastor's Fireside*, is set some eleven years after the Jacobite uprising of 1715 and explores and forecloses the possibility of further unrest in the 1720s. In hinting that these years saw the effective end of the Jacobite threat in Britain (at the end of the novel the Jacobite Duke of Wharton repents), Porter is not merely mimicking the preoccupations of Scott's novel; rather, she is replying to them. She proposes an alternative form of education that will generate a more austere form of self-denying heroism. This heroism, she insists, will not endanger the nation through promoting internal strife (as Scott had hinted) but will instead protect it from external threats. First, Porter presents a number of behavioural models for her protagonist and reader

Figure 13.2 Jane Porter depicted as a canonness by George Henry Harlow, 1810. The cross was purportedly sent to Porter by the abbess of the order of St John of Jerusalem. The image reinforces Porter's message of Christian heroism.

to assess. These models correspond to the sublime and the beautiful. On the one hand, there is the Jacobite Duke of Wharton, an attractive genius but an untrustworthy source of temptation to the hero, Louis. His female counterpart is the more moral Cornelia, who, after the duke's reformation, becomes his bride. On the other is Ferdinand d'Osorio, who is attracted to Cornelia's sister, Alice, because of her 'endearing, timid nature' and her 'beautiful' eyes.[13] Yet Alice enters into a secret engagement with Ferdinand that destroys her health, while Ferdinand has already formed illicit ties with a woman who appeared to have Alice's qualities but who was actually ambitious and deceitful. The Jacobitism that is associated by Scott with a certain glamorous heroism represents the wrong path. However, attraction to the beautiful, to, in other words, a reimagined, more flawed Rosa Bradwardine, is no guarantee of harmony either.

After modelling these inadequate extremes, *The Pastor's Fireside* concentrates on sketching a third alternative. Educated by his uncle at Lindesfarne but the son of the statesman Baron de Ripperda, Louis must learn the nature of true heroism. Having, like Waverley, followed his own educational bent, Louis admires 'the magic painting of Homer, Tasso and Spenser' and 'dwells with delight on the chivalric characters of Froissart' and on the illustrious 'Condés and Montmorencies of the one country, and the Talbots and Percys of the other' (pp. 31, 22). However, neither the heroism of romance nor historical heroism prove adequate guides (p. 22). When the Jacobite Duke of Wharton tries to tempt Louis to his side, he exposes him to what Porter calls an 'enchanted mist' of intellectual play and libertine pleasure. Louis is temporarily caught off-guard. Although he had admired the portraits of 'Circe, Armida, and Adessa', he had imagined that these beautiful temptresses were only the product of 'the poet's genius' and believed that in actuality: 'Vice must be as odious in outward shape as loathsome within' (p. 31). 'Real life' destroys this illusion; vice can be seductive. In this account, it is not that romance is inaccurate but that it offers no preparation, no defence. It leaves Louis's youthful idealism intact. He is saved from desire's feverish clutches only by the 'cooling freshness' of the ocean waves and the memory of 'holy Lindesfarne' (p. 31). Returning to the island against Wharton's wishes, Louis is instructed that self-denial and the avoidance of temptation are the most desirable characteristics – and the lesson is given by the Pastor of Lindesfarne.

This more austerely heroic, Christian message is reinforced when Louis, thirsty for adventure, goes to serve his Spanish father on the Continent. Instead of fighting in the 'Spanish army' to 'compel' the Emperor Charles to fulfil his 'broken treaties', as he had imagined, Louis finds himself copying manuscripts 'day after day', 'voluminous' works in unreadable 'Turkish characters' (pp. 89, 94). International politics involve hardship, subterfuge and obscurity: Louis must realise that military intervention is not the only way 'of forcing sovereigns to do their duties' (p. 89). Further, these more obscure, indirect methods must be supported by Christianity, rather than the search for personal gain or glory, as the fate of Louis' father demonstrates. Despite his heroic and successful efforts on behalf of Spain, the baron falls out of favour. Filled with personal resentment, he is about to change his faith and fight for the Emperor of Morocco against the Spanish but he is reconverted to Christianity on his deathbed by Louis. With these details, Porter makes a point about the need for Christian unity. Ripperda is Catholic. Thus, while the pastor's Protestantism offers the true variety of heroism, Porter makes the troubling argument that Christian unity against other faiths and political powers is more important than sectarianism.

In addition, although, as the *Critical Review* complains, 'at least three of the four volumes refer merely to transactions at the courts of Germany and Spain', the novel implicitly argues that Britain, taken as a whole, has the kind of landscape necessary to sustain the proper mode of Christian heroism.[14] Initially, as Louis falls under the spell of the 'extraordinary' Duke of Wharton, Wharton and Louis explore 'the caverned recesses of the Loch, its fir-clad islands, and mountains of desolate sublimity' (p. 19). As the adjective 'desolate' implies, the Jacobite sublime (or the sublime of Scottish independence as in *The Scottish Chiefs*) is no longer adequate. Instead, Lindesfarne, and by extension the British Isles, are surrounded by 'the terrible roaring of the waves, bursting and foaming against the rocks, and rushing, with the rumbling of thunder' (p. 43). Louis rides through these 'raging billows' to escape Wharton's temptations and to return home to his uncle, the pastor (p. 44). The sublime surrounds the island (and, by implication, Britain). Further, on that island stands the rectory which incorporates the 'very arch' which 'little more than a century before ... had mantled the abbot's hearth in the good monastery of Lindesfarne' (p. 7). In fact, Lindesfarne Priory was closed in 1537 during Henry VIII's dissolution of the monasteries (although the buildings remained). However, the arch's incorporation in the pastor's home suggests a modernity that nonetheless contains the sublime of antiquity. It also indicates that Britain (though Protestant) has a religion capacious enough to include its Catholic past. When, at the end of the novel, the Duke of Wharton is forgiven, marries the sublime Cornelia and settles in Hanoverian Britain, the point is underlined. Britain is the peaceful home of Christian heroes, containing a historic, spiritual sublime and surrounded by the sublime sea. Challenges to British well-being will in future come from outside. Hence Britons need a form of Christian heroism that will allow them to face the obscure and involved world of Continental politics.

In his 1841 book *On Heroes, Hero-worship and the Heroic in History*, Thomas Carlyle would once more assert the value of heroism to historical discourse; his work develops the Great Man theory of history. But for the Romantics, writing in the aftermath of the French Revolution, the matter was one of debate. Although radical writers like Charlotte Smith and William Godwin interrogated the values of chivalric romance, more conservative writers like Clara Reeve celebrated its potential to portray the nobility of the feudal past and to educate its readers in an aristocratic mode of heroism. Yet, after the politicisation of Edmund Burke's aesthetics and, more specifically, with the rise of Napoleon, the developing connection between the heroic, the feudal and the sublime created unease. For Jane Porter, the note was too triumphal. In *The Scottish Chiefs* she continues to celebrate heroism but it is moderated, modernised and redefined into a form of Christian sentiment, primarily defensive and available to the masses.

In *Waverley*, Scott reduces the heroic impulse, suggesting that it represents a danger to Britain's internal stability. Later Waverley novels continue this trend. Responding to the unrest of Peterloo, where troops attacked a meeting of those demanding parliamentary reform, Scott's 1819 novel *Ivanhoe*, for example, contains a plethora of imperfect heroes, effectively muting any celebratory note. And in Scott's 1826 novel of the English Commonwealth, *Woodstock*, the political and the heroic seem almost entirely separate. Despite his conservatism, in the end Scott arguably goes even further in his critique of heroism than the radical novelists who had initially expressed doubt. While they attacked chivalric heroism to critique the aristocracy, Scott instead indicates that heroism is a redundant quality in a conservative vision of peacetime Britain. Jane Porter found Scott's act of litotes, his reduction of the heroic, unsatisfactory. Turning, as Scott had done, to the recent history of Jacobitism, in *The Pastor's Fireside* Porter argues that a Christian form of heroism is compatible with peace at home. Her representation of other religions as potentially dangerous is disturbing but it is not the main focus of her attention. Rather, Porter seeks to retain a moderated form of patriotic heroism, a heroism that for much of the time will be internal and invisible but will emerge in response to external threats. The Romantic historical novel celebrates and then minimises the heroic before ultimately shaping an alternative form of internalised, enclosed heroism suitable for peacetime Britain. The Romantic sublime is contained but remains available to re-emerge in Victorian imperial fictions of muscular Christianity.

NOTES

1. Walter Scott, *Waverley; Or, 'tis Sixty Years Since*, ed. Claire Lamont, with an introduction by Kathryn Sutherland (Oxford University Press, 1986), pp. viii, x; subsequent references are given in the main text.
2. Elizabeth Benger, *Memoirs of the Late Mrs Elizabeth Hamilton*, 2 vols (London: Longman, 1818), vol. II, p. 108.
3. Clara Reeve, *The Progress of Romance, through Times, Countries, and Manners*, 2 vols (Colchester: for the author by Keymer; [London]: Robinson, 1785), vol. I, p. 111.
4. Clara Reeve, *Memoirs of Sir Roger de Clarendon, the Natural Son of Edward Prince of Wales, Commonly Called the Black Prince*, 3 vols (London: Hookham & Carpenter, 1793), vol. I, p. xvi; subsequent references are incorporated in the main text.
5. Edmund Burke, *A Philosophical Enquiry into the Origin of Our Ideas of the Sublime and the Beautiful* (1757), 2nd edn (1759), ed. James T. Boulton (Oxford: Blackwell, 1987), pp. 44–5.
6. Alexander Gerard, *An Essay on Taste* (1759), 3rd edn (1780), introd. Walter J. Hipple (Delmar, NY: Scholars' Facsimiles, 1963), p. 15.
7. Benger, *Memoirs*, vol. II, p. 108.
8. James Hogg, *The Domestic Manners of Sir Walter Scott*, ed. J. E. H. Thomson (Stirling, 1909), pp. 111–12.
9. Thomas Carlyle, *New Edinburgh Review* 1 (October 1821), 402–3.
10. Jane Porter, *The Scottish Chiefs, A Romance* (1810), ed. Fiona Price (Peterborough, Ontario: Broadview Press, 2007), p. 89; subsequent references are incorporated in the main text.
11. Peter Garside, 'Popular Fiction and National Tale: Hidden Origins of Scott's *Waverley*', *Nineteenth-Century Literature* 46 (1991), 30–53 (33); Jane Porter, *Thaddeus of Warsaw* (London: Colburn & Bentley; Edinburgh: Bell & Bradfute; Dublin: Cumming,1831), p. vi.
12. Garside, 'Popular Fiction,' 39; Peter Garside, 'Walter Scott and the "Common" Novel, 1808–1819', *Romantic Textualities: Literature and Print Culture, 1780–1840* 3 (September 1999): www.romtext.org.uk/articles/cc03_n02/ (accessed 4 August 2020).
13. Jane Porter, *The Pastor's Fireside* (London: Routledge, 1856), pp. 43, 8; subsequent references are incorporated in the main text.
14. 'Art. IX. *The Pastor's Fire-side, a Novel in Four Volumes*. By Miss Jane Porter', *Critical Review* 5.2 (February 1816), 173–86 (174).

CRITICAL REFLECTIONS AND FURTHER STUDIES

The Romantic historical novel is concerned with nationhood, patriotism, monarchy and government, issues of considerable contemporary importance. It is an experimental space that allows history to be rewritten and facilitates the introduction of new voices into the historical narrative, transforming our understanding of the nation. Yet it is also, at first sight, daunting. The reader needs not only the usual knowledge of the literary work's context but also some familiarity with the historical moment in which the novel is set. But, after all, the task need not be too onerous. Literary context should be provided by the period course on which the text is encountered; historical context, initially, by brief consultation of a relevant encyclopaedia entry. A certain 'negative capability' is desirable. Only the dullest form of criticism of the historical novel concerns itself with spotting errors and deviations from the historical record – it is what these discrepancies mean and the issues they raise that are far more interesting, and this work need only be undertaken after the novel has been thoroughly read. But while an irritable reaching after historical fact is not advantageous, the reader should also be aware that this kind of fiction is often only too persuasive. This effect is particularly noticeable when reading Walter Scott. As Murray Pittock comments in 'Scott as Historiographer', the idea of history as progress found in Scott's novels is one to which it is easy to 'surrender' (p. 146).

What can be helpful is to understand the particular approach to historical writing (historiography) that the writer is taking. Much Romantic historical fiction (particularly Scott's Waverley Novels) draws upon the ideas of stadial history (also referred to as conjectural or philosophical history) associated with Scottish historians like Adam Ferguson. The stadial historian, as I mention in my essay, sees historical development in terms of stages – the primitive, the feudal and the commercial – and in each stage the mode of government, the laws and form of trade all correspond. The problem for the stadial historian is the moment of transition between these stages. Here the historical novel comes into its own: it is by concentrating on such moments of change that Scott generates the sense of history taking place. Another important way of thinking about history in the eighteenth and early nineteenth centuries is ancient constitutionalism (as outlined by Colin Kidd; see Further Reading): if the writer is concerned with the idea of an ancient constitution, with freedoms held in Anglo-Saxon times, whether these freedoms are eroded by or in continuity with Norman rule, she is drawing upon this approach. Third, historical novelists often draw upon antiquarianism, an interest in the material objects and traces of history. This approach and its wider cultural significance in the eighteenth century are discussed in detail by Rosemary Sweet. Sometimes novelists use all three methods, as Scott does in *Ivanhoe* (1819), for example.

At the same time as eighteenth-century history writing was generically experimental (as Mark Salber Philips discusses), there was also a dissatisfaction with historical discourse. One of the most famous critiques of history comes from Catherine Morland in Jane Austen's *Northanger Abbey* who finds it 'odd that it should be so dull, for a great deal of it must be invention' and who famously comments that part of the dullness is because 'the men' are 'all so good for nothing' with 'hardly any women at all' (p. 108). Historical novels (like Sophia Lee's *The Recess* (1783–5)) try to fill these gaps with the voices of the missing, albeit that those voices are often fictional (Lee's novel focuses on the fictitious illegitimate twin daughters of Mary Queen of Scots).

Generic experimentation within the form of the historical novel contributes to the broader eighteenth-century experimentation with history. Although much Romantic historical fiction has been neglected by critics, the genre's overlap with other forms of fiction provides an entry point. The treatment of desire and patriotism in *The Scottish Chiefs* that I have discussed here, for instance, owes something to the eighteenth-century sentimental novel. It is well worth tracing attitudes to sentiment and feeling in Romantic historical fiction and, in particular, asking where such fiction directs our sympathies. Similarly, the Gothic plays a key role in much historical fiction. Considering the use of Gothic tropes often reveals who is oppressing whom. Historical fiction is also closely related to the national tale (and here Katie Trumpener's work provides invaluable background). The marriages of the national tale and dynastic alliances of historical fiction have much in common: Porter defers the marriage of her hero and heroine because union between Scotland and England is undesirable; Scott allows Waverley, in making the right sexual choice, to support the peaceful union of two nations. Finally, historical fiction explores the core concepts of Romantic aesthetics. This exploration occurs not least because the sublime and the beautiful are fundamentally concerned with power (often naturalising its expression) – and power is a central preoccupation of historical fiction.

FURTHER READING

Austen, Jane, *Northanger Abbey* and *Persuasion*, vol. v in R. W. Chapman (ed.), *The Novels of Jane Austen*, 3rd edn, 5 vols (Oxford University Press, 1932–4). See the discussion of history writing in *Northanger Abbey*, p. 108.

Kidd, Colin, *British Identities before Nationalism: Ethnicity and Nationhood in the Atlantic World, 1600–1800* (Cambridge University Press, 1999)

Philips, Mark Salber, *Society and Sentiment: Genres of Historical Writing in Britain, 1740–1820* (Princeton University Press, 2000)

Pittock, Murray G. H., 'Scott as Historiographer: The Case of Waverley', in J. H. Alexander and David Hewitt (eds), *Scott in Carnival* (Aberdeen: Association for Scottish Literary Studies, 1993)

Price, Fiona, *Reinventing Liberty: Nation, Commerce and the Historical Novel from Walpole to Scott* (Edinburgh University Press, 2016)

Price, Fiona, 'Resisting "The Spirit of Innovation": Jane Porter and the Other Historical Novel', *Modern Language Review* 101.3 (2006), 638–52

Robertson, Fiona, *Legitimate Histories: Scott, Gothic and the Authorities of Fiction* (Oxford: Clarendon Press, 1994)

Stevens, Anne H. 'Tales of Other Times: A Survey of British Historical Fiction 1770–1812', *Cardiff Corvey: Reading the Romantic Text* 7 (December 2001): www.cf.ac.uk/encap/corvey/articles/cc07_n03.html (accessed 3 September 2019)

Sweet, Rosemary, *Antiquaries: The Discovery of the Past in Eighteenth-Century Britain* (London: Continuum, 2004)

Trumpener, Katie, *Bardic Nationalism: The Romantic Novel and the British Empire* (Princeton University Press, 1997)

14 Jane Austen and Her Publishers: *Northanger Abbey* and the Publishing Context of the Early Nineteenth Century

KATIE HALSEY

Abstract

In this essay, I consider the publication context of *Northanger Abbey*, focusing in particular on the pressures exerted by the literary marketplace, and Austen's alertness to it, on that novel. Beginning with a discussion of Austen's interactions with the two publishing firms which failed to publish her works, Cadell & Davies and Crosby & Co., I then consider the changes in places, manners, books and opinions that occurred between the novel's first conception in 1798–9 and its final publication in December of 1817. Placing *Northanger Abbey*'s literary allusions and general intertextuality in the context of the changes in the literary marketplace through the three decades of its production, I suggest that some of the novel's tonal oddities, and its relative unpopularity with contemporary readers and reviewers are a direct result of Benjamin Crosby's decision not to publish the novel then known as 'Susan' in 1803.

In the 'Author's Advertisement' to *Northanger Abbey*, Jane Austen noted ruefully that the work had been sold for publication in 1803 but that the publisher had 'proceeded no farther' in the business. The thirteen years that had then passed, Austen worried, might have made some parts of the work 'comparatively obsolete' since 'during that period, places, manners, books and opinions have undergone considerable changes'.[1] In this essay, I will consider the pressures exerted by the literary marketplace, and Austen's alertness to it, on *Northanger Abbey*. In so doing I will suggest that the complicated composition and publication history of *Northanger Abbey* may go some way to explaining the novel's relative lack of popularity with contemporary readers and reviewers, as well as some of its oddities of tone.

I will begin with a brief description of Jane Austen's interactions with her 'non-publishers', as Anthony Mandal describes them in his excellent *Jane Austen and the Popular Novel: The Determined Author* (2007). Austen began her career as a professional author with two publishing failures, and it is my contention that these two failures coloured her impressions of the literary marketplace in important ways. In 1797, her father, George Austen, offered the novel *First Impressions* (later to become *Pride and Prejudice*) to the publisher Cadell & Davies, presumably on Jane Austen's behalf. He described it as 'a Manuscript Novel, comprised in three Vols. about the length of Miss Burney's Evelina'.[2] It was rejected, sight unseen, and no reason was given. Cadell & Davies were a big-name publisher, 'the highest aristocracy of the Trade', as Theodore Basterman puts it, and in approaching them, George Austen demonstrated both a remarkable confidence in his daughter's abilities and a total failure to understand the dynamics of the publishing market.[3] Cadell & Davies did publish novels – and had been very successful in promoting novels by eminent authors such as Frances Burney, Dr John Moore, Ann Radcliffe and Charlotte Smith – but they very rarely invested in unknown authors, and fiction 'formed only a minor part of their literary investment'.[4] It was perhaps not surprising that they showed no interest in the manuscript of a novel recommended to them by an obscure Hampshire clergyman. It is also possible that the mention of Frances Burney's *Evelina* (1778) backfired. By 1797 the reference to an already old-fashioned epistolary novel could hardly have been a selling point for a firm that prided itself on its forward-looking business model.

The Austens learned their lesson from Cadell & Davies, and in 1803, when Austen approached Crosby & Co., this time through her brother Henry's man of business, William Seymour, she had learned enough to offer her novel 'Susan' (later *Northanger Abbey*) to a publisher whose main business was in novels, and in particular in the kind of novels that sold well to circulating libraries. As Mandal points out, Crosby was 'the fourth most prolific publisher of novels during the 1800s, and, despite ceasing operation in 1814, the seventh during the 1810s'. He describes Crosby's output as 'consisting typically of sentimental romances and Gothic tales especially during the 1790s and late 1800s'.[5] Crosby was, in fact, the ideal publisher for the novel that would become *Northanger Abbey*.

However, although Jane Austen sold 'Susan' to Crosby in the spring of 1803 for the price of £10, for reasons unknown he never brought it out, despite having advertised it. Six years later, in April of 1809, Austen wrote to Crosby, using the pseudonym 'Mrs Ashton Dennis', and signing herself 'M.A.D.' She asked why the novel had never appeared in print, 'tho an early publication was stipulated for at the time of Sale'. Offering to supply another copy of the manuscript if the original had been lost, she told Crosby that if he did not respond, she would feel herself 'at liberty to secure the publication of my work, by applying elsewhere'.[6] Richard Crosby (either the younger brother or son of Benjamin Crosby, the senior partner) replied three days later acknowledging that his firm had bought a novel named 'Susan' and paid £10 for it, but claiming that 'there was not any time stipulated for its publication, neither are we bound to publish it'. He added, 'should you or anyone else [publish it] we shall take proceedings to stop the sale', and he offered her the manuscript back 'for the same as we paid for it' (*Letters*, p. 175).[7]

There the matter rested – perhaps because Austen could not at that time command the £10 needed to buy the manuscript back – until the spring of 1816, when

Henry Austen bought back the manuscript of 'Susan' for his sister. She revised it, giving it the new title of 'Catherine', probably because another novel called *Susan* had been published in 1809. She intended then to offer it for publication, but she was concurrently working on the first draft of *Persuasion* and already beginning to feel the effects of the illness that would eventually kill her in July of 1817. She was, in addition, dealing with the consequences of the failure of her brother Henry's bank. Henry – or one of his representatives – usually acted as her agent in negotiations with publishers, and it is probable that he was simply too occupied with this crisis in his own affairs to spare the time to offer the manuscript to another publisher. Or it is also possible that while revising the text and writing the 'Author's Advertisement' Austen experienced a crisis of confidence in the work, and decided not to publish it. Whatever may be the case, she wrote to her niece Fanny Knight in March of 1817 that 'Miss Catherine is put upon the Shelve for the present, and I do not know that she will ever come out' (*Letters*, p. 333). *Northanger Abbey* was finally published posthumously, by John Murray (who had also published Austen's *Emma* in 1816 and a second edition of *Mansfield Park* the previous year), in December of 1817. It appeared as a four-volume set with *Persuasion*, with a 'Biographical Notice' by Henry Austen attached, and a publication date of 1818 on the title page.

A number of previous critics have suggested that Crosby failed to publish 'Susan' because to publish such a parody would potentially have soured the market for 'true' Gothic fictions and thus spoiled sales of his other works.[8] This seems improbable, given that so many Gothic parodies already existed (as we shall see), and despite critics' and reviewers' regular denigration of the genre, sales of Gothic novels in fact remained fairly robust until at least the 1810s. Mandal argues convincingly that the reason for the non-publication of 'Susan' was, instead, Crosby's financial difficulties, brought about by the acrimonious dissolution of his partnership with another publisher, J. F. Hughes. He suggests that the £10 paid for 'Susan' may have seemed a 'fair sacrifice' when set against the £150 or so that it would have cost to produce 'at a troublesome time'.[9] Nonetheless, Crosby's failure to publish 'Susan' in 1803 clearly affected Austen's confidence in the work, reflected in the tone of the advertisement, and I would argue that it was also responsible for some of the novel's slight oddities of tone, discussed further below.

Northanger Abbey was first drafted between August of 1798 and the winter of 1798/9, and revised in 1803.[10] In many ways, Austen was right to feel uneasy about the changes in 'places, manners, books and opinions' that had taken place during the years between the conception and the 1816 revision of her work. I will return to 'books', as the central theme of this essay, shortly, but let us begin with considering why she might have felt anxious about 'places'. Austen's novel is set firmly and solidly in Bath, making use of real street names and recognisable geographical features, such as the Pump Rooms and Assembly Rooms, Beechen Hill,

Brock Street and Milsom Street. Bath was a town that, in 1797, when Austen first visited it, remained a popular resort for the genteel classes, although its star had first begun to wane in the 1780s. But by 1816 it had been almost totally eclipsed by Brighton, where the Prince Regent's Royal Pavilion acted as the unofficial court of the Regency. As both Janine Barchas and Jocelyn Harris have argued, Jane Austen followed royal scandals with interest, and commented, both directly and allusively, on the Prince Regent's actions in her novels and letters.[11] Under these circumstances, it would have been impossible for her to miss the growing importance of Brighton in his life, and thus in the fashionable life of the nation. In addition to her knowledge of the Prince Regent's affairs, Austen had a keen sense of the levels of competition between resort towns, as shown in her last, unfinished, novel, *Sanditon*, and her eye for the fine gradations of geographical fashion is also a hallmark of *Persuasion*, where the differences between Camden Place and Westgate Buildings are so snobbishly articulated by Sir Walter Elliot. To someone so alert to the resonances of place, the shifts in fashion that had made Bath the preserve of elderly invalids, rather than dashing young heroes, might well have led her to feel that even her most naive of heroines would have preferred a visit to Brighton.

'Opinions' – by which I think Austen means primarily political opinions – had shifted drastically from the 1790s. The early 1790s were remarkable for freedom of opinion, in many regards. In that decade, a number of respectable writers supported the political movements that emerged to urge parliamentary reform. Some of these movements were organised and supported mainly by skilled craftsmen and labourers; others were formed by intellectuals and political elites. They pursued political objectives drawn directly from French Revolutionary examples, and wanted to replace royal and aristocratic rule with representative government based on ideas of the inalienable rights of man. Radical political opinion was discussed and debated everywhere in this turbulent decade, including in respectable Tory families like Jane Austen's own.[12] But from about 1795 onwards, the government of William Pitt the Younger enacted a series of increasingly repressive legislative acts that curtailed freedoms of speech, movement and assembly. From 1794, radical leaders could be arrested without trial, for example, and in 1795 further laws were enacted that redefined the law of treason and made it almost impossible to hold public meetings in support of parliamentary reform. Pitt's attempts to repress support for reform succeeded, at least on the surface. Britain was at war with France from 1793 to 1815, with one brief intermission in 1802–3, for the Peace of Amiens. Throughout the remainder of the wars with France, support among all ranks in society for what was increasingly seen as a patriotic war enhanced the government's popularity, and radical political opinions were widely considered to be pro-French and hence treasonable. Disaffected radicals were thus driven underground, and radical opinions were no longer debated at Tory dinner tables.

Not unrelated to the changes in political opinion outlined above, Jane Austen was right to perceive a substantial change in public 'manners'. Between 1797 and 1816 the manners of the court of George III had given way to those of his son, the Prince Regent. The extended war with France, the influence of anti-Jacobin, anti-slavery and evangelical forces in both politics and literature, as well as the changes in fashion attendant on all of these, had given a new flavour to manners, both public and private. So public taste in 'places', 'opinions' and 'manners' had indeed shifted, and Austen, acutely attuned to the nuances of the literary market-place, and determined to gain both 'praise' and 'pewter' for her books, was too astute not to have both realised this and worried about the effects it might have on the reception of her book (*Letters*, p. 287).[13]

With regards to 'books', of all her novels, *Northanger Abbey* is the most overtly intertextual, presenting a lengthy and sustained parody of the Gothic genre, and explicitly naming the books that had been most popular in the late 1790s. Of the seven 'horrid' novels recommended by Isabella Thorpe, for example, all are published between 1794 and 1798. Catherine Morland's beloved *Mysteries of Udolpho* was published in 1794, and the vogue for Radcliffe's works belongs squarely to the 1790s. By the early 1800s, so many writers had jumped on the Gothic bandwagon that literary reviewers rejected Gothic novels almost out of hand, and parodies of the genre that mocked its sensationalist tropes were popular as early as the latter 1790s. Key parodies of that period include William Beckford's *Modern Novel Writing* (1796) and *Azemia* (1797), F. C. Patrick's *More Ghosts!* (1798) and *The New Monk* (1798) by one 'R. S.', a hilarious rewriting of John Thorpe's favourite novel, M. G. Lewis's Gothic shocker *The Monk* (1796), that sets it within the context of 1790s Methodism. Another source of opinion about the Gothic at that time was the periodical culture of review, in which so many critics parodied Gothic fictions in order to make their point that this was a moribund, highly repetitive genre. The many 'recipes for writing a novel' in contemporary reviews (and echoed in Jane Austen's own 'Plan of a Novel') are a trope that suggests that the composition of Gothic was a rote and formulaic activity not unlike the baking of a cake.[14] Mary Alcock's 1799 poem 'A Receipt [*sic*] for Writing a Novel' (1799) makes the same point. The poem begins:

Would you a favrite novel make,
Try hard your readers heart to break
For who is pleasd, if not tormented?
(Novels for that were first invented.)
Gainst nature, reason, sense, combine
To carry on your bold design,
And those ingredients I shall mention,
Compounded with your own invention,
Im sure will answer my intention.

Alcock continues by recommending 'a copious share' of 'horror', 'Hysteric fits at least a score', as well as 'fainting fits', 'duels', 'sighs and groans', storms, ghosts and carriage accidents, as well as many other familiar Gothic 'terrors'.[15]

In 1798–9, then, Austen's parody must have seemed fresh and amusing (as well as bang on trend), but even by 1803, when she sold 'Susan' to Crosby & Co., Gothic parodies might have begun to seem an outworn theme. However, the high point of parodies of the Gothic was in fact the period between the sale of 'Susan' and the publication of *Northanger Abbey*. The popularity of Eaton Stannard Barrett's *The Heroine; or, Adventures of a Fair Romance Reader*, published in 1813, with further editions in 1814 and 1815, in particular, might have given Austen pause for thought. Jane Austen had read *The Heroine* in 1814, when it first came out, writing to Cassandra that it was 'a delightful burlesque, particularly on the Radcliffe style', and that it had 'diverted me exceedingly' (*Letters*, pp. 255–6). As the title suggests, Barrett's novel follows the adventures of a female protagonist who reads too many novels. The 'heroine' of the title, Cherry Wilkinson, imagines herself to be living in a world of Gothic horrors, and makes a series of faulty judgements based on this misperception. The similarities with the basic plot structure of *Northanger Abbey* are too obvious to miss, and I think it highly likely that Austen had *The Heroine* in mind in 1816. It also seems probable that the first pages of *Northanger Abbey*, with their almost over-elaborately arch and ironic insistence on the disjunction between Catherine Morland's self-perception as 'an heroine' and her actual character and situation, were rewritten in that period, and owe something to her awareness of Barrett's work. This is a moment where we can perceive Jane Austen's anxieties that her own work might seem too close to Barrett's (*Northanger Abbey*, p. 5ff.).[16]

For all the legitimate concerns about opinions, manners and places articulated in Austen's preface, then, it is the worry about books that seems to me the most essential. The novels of Austen's youth permeate – indeed saturate – *Northanger Abbey*, but by the end of 1817, when the work was first introduced to the public, many of these were deeply unfashionable or, perhaps worse, forgotten. And because *Northanger Abbey* engages so intensely with those works – and assumes a deep and comfortable familiarity with them on the part of the reader – it is entirely understandable that Austen would have worried that readers without that familiarity might not have known what to make of her novel. For the remainder of this essay, then, I will focus in more depth on the novel's intertextual aspects.

Northanger Abbey explicitly names seventeen works, and quotes directly from six others.[17] There are also two important discussions of the relative values of particular genres (novels and history), and more general allusions – both ironic, as in the case of *The Heroine*, discussed above, and serious – to a number of well-known works of literature dispersed throughout the novel. In every case, Austen's deployment of the work of literature serves to tell us something about the characters involved in the discussion of that work, or about the narrative voice's opinion of the work. Austen's use of books, in other words, functions as a kind of shorthand, evoking the reputation of the book in the service of her plot or character development. The cultural resonances of the books thus deployed are therefore clearly vital to our understanding of what is going on in *Northanger Abbey*.

This strategy is encapsulated in a lovely comic scene between Catherine Morland and her would-be lover, John Thorpe. Catherine begins by asking if Thorpe has ever read *Udolpho*. The scene continues:

> 'Udolpho! Oh, Lord! Not I; I never read novels; I have something else to do.'
>
> Catherine, humbled and ashamed, was going to apologize for her question, but he prevented her by saying, 'Novels are all so full of nonsense and stuff; there has not been a tolerably decent one come out since Tom Jones, except the Monk; I read that t'other day; but as for all the others, they are the stupidest things in creation.'
>
> 'I think you must like Udolpho, if you were to read it; it is so very interesting.'
>
> 'Not I, faith! No, if I read any, it shall be Mrs. Radcliff's; her novels are amusing enough; they are worth reading; some fun and nature in *them*.'
>
> 'Udolpho was written by Mrs. Radcliff,' said Catherine, with some hesitation, from the fear of mortifying him.
>
> 'No sure; was it? Aye, I remember, so it was. I was thinking of that other stupid book, written by that woman they make such a fuss about, she who married the French emigrant.'
>
> 'I suppose you mean Camilla?'
>
> 'Yes, that's the book; such unnatural stuff! – An old man playing at see-saw! I took up the first volume once and looked it over, but I soon found it would not do.'
>
> (*Northanger Abbey*, p. 43; the misspelling of Radcliffe here is as given)

The literary works mentioned here are Ann Radcliffe's *The Mysteries of Udolpho* (1794), Henry Fielding's *Tom Jones* (1749), Matthew Lewis's *The Monk* (1796) and Frances Burney's *Camilla* (1796), and the key point to note is that John Thorpe exposes his ignorance, poor taste and stupidity with every line. When he fails to recognise *Udolpho* as a work by Ann Radcliffe while simultaneously praising her books, it suggests that he has never read a book by 'the great enchantress', knowing her only by reputation.[18] This clearly makes him unsuitable as a mate for Catherine, whose adoration of the author has been made abundantly clear. Moreover, his liking for *Tom Jones* and *The Monk*, both works with a reputation for libertinism, reveals his moral shadiness. His failure to appreciate *Camilla*, a work which the narrative voice describes, only two chapters earlier, as being one 'in which the greatest powers of the mind are displayed, in which the most thorough knowledge of human nature, the happiest delineation of its varieties, the liveliest effusions of wit and humour are conveyed to the world in the best chosen language', speaks for itself (*Northanger Abbey*, p. 31). In this case, fully to understand the ways in which the allusions work, it is necessary to know that *The Monk* is a work of violent horror, including mob violence, ghostly nuns, murder, sorcery and incest. A huge popular success on first publication, it was scathingly reviewed by S. T. Coleridge in the *Critical Review*, in which he described it as 'a poison for youth, and a provocative for the debauchee'.[19] It was, he said, a novel 'which if a parent saw in the hands of a son or daughter he might reasonably turn pale'.[20] *Camilla*, on the other hand, was a critically respected and morally unexceptionable work of domestic fiction by an author whom even those commentators who disliked novels on principle could recommend. Published by the reputable Cadell & Davies (Austen's first rejecters), *Camilla* was one of the foremost novels of the 1790s. John Thorpe's rejection of *Camilla*'s domestic realism as 'unnatural' is decidedly ironic when read alongside his preference for a work of Gothic horror whose very mode depends on the genuinely 'unnatural' – ghosts, incest and sorcery. When Thorpe is described, a couple of sentences later, as 'the discerning and unprejudiced reader of *Camilla*' (p. 44), the reader has no trouble in recognising the scathing irony of this description, and rejecting Thorpe accordingly. It takes Catherine, whose experience of the world is so very limited, a little longer to take John Thorpe's measure, but the reader is, from this moment on, never in doubt of his essential badness (see Figure 14.1).

It is a mark of Austen's brilliance as a writer that the strategy works perfectly well to demarcate character, even if one knows nothing about any of the texts discussed – but it is also a moment of tonal oddity, where the time lag between *Northanger Abbey*'s composition and publication is most obvious. To a reader of 1818, Catherine's obsession with *The Mysteries of Udolpho*, and Thorpe's with *The Monk* (as well as Isabella's with the seven 'horrid' novels of the 1790s), would have seemed somewhat odd. While it is entirely probable that the old-fashioned Mrs Morland's favourite novel could remain *Sir Charles Grandison*, published in 1753 (an old-fashioned book for an old-fashioned mother), it seems much less probable that the fashionable young people of the novel would still have been discussing works that had been *the* novels of twenty years earlier. Since the anonymous publication of Sir Walter Scott's *Waverley* in 1814, the hot topic in the literary world had been its authorship – and the publication of five further 'Waverley' novels (*Guy Mannering* (1815), *The Antiquary* (1816), *Tales of My Landlord* (1816), *Rob Roy* (1818) and the second series of *Tales of My Landlord* (1818)) in quick succession between 1814 and 1818 had made the historical novel the fashionable subgenre of the Regency period, entirely displacing the Gothic. But to have revised *Northanger Abbey* accordingly, in 1816, would have been completely impossible. Although it is relatively easy to imagine a dialogue between Catherine and Isabella where they breathlessly debate the identity of the 'Wizard of the North' in place of their conversation about the seven 'horrid' novels, so much of both the novel's comedy and indeed its very structure depends on its parody

Figure 14.1 James Gillray's *Tales of Wonder* (London, 1802) is an excellent example of a satire, this time in visual form, on readers of the Gothic genre. Those who look closely will observe that the book these readers are poring over is none other than *The Monk*. Gillray's caricature demonstrates a popular perception of readers of Gothic novels, commenting satirically on their total absorption in the text, as well as ironically on Lewis's attempt to capitalise on the sensationalism of the mode.

of Gothic atmosphere and Gothic tropes that a further revision to take account of altered literary trends is unimaginable. Austen was wise not to attempt it, but such moments in *Northanger Abbey* give credence to the concerns articulated in the 'Author's Advertisement'.

Another example of Austen's strategy of using books as a shorthand to delineate character and compatibility is visible in Catherine's interactions with Henry Tilney, and these demonstrate the same slight time lag problem. Where John Thorpe clearly despises good literature, and will not take the trouble to read novels that do not immediately appeal to his thirst for the vulgar and sensational, Henry Tilney has read, as he says, 'hundreds and hundreds' of them (p. 108). Earlier in the same chapter, he tells Catherine that 'the person, be it gentleman or lady, who has not pleasure in a good novel, must be intolerably stupid. I have read all of Mrs. Radcliffe's works, and most of them with great pleasure' (pp. 107–8). He goes on to tell Catherine, 'Do not imagine that you can cope with me in knowledge of Julias and Louisas', and backs up his claim with an appropriate simile, drawn from *The Mysteries of Udolpho* itself (p. 108).[21] Henry's deep and affectionate knowledge of 'Mrs. Radcliffe's works' – the books that Catherine loves – bodes well for them as a couple. However, it also marks him, in 1818, as a very unfashionable young man (which Henry clearly is not meant to be). Here, Henry Tilney refers to a long tradition of sentimental and Gothic novels with which readers of the 1790s and early 1800s would have been familiar, but readers of 1818 would have felt were rather dated. While Julia and Louisa remained popular names for heroines into the Regency period (Austen herself uses both names, in *Mansfield Park* and *Persuasion* respectively, and, indeed, an anonymous novel entitled *Julia of Ardenfield* was published in 1816), the sentimental novels in which such heroines belonged were primarily fashionable between the 1740s and the 1790s. By 1818 tastes had shifted, and the success of anti-Jacobin novels and conduct books, such as Hannah More's *Strictures on the Modern System of Female Education* (1798), which equated liking for sentimental novels with dangerous pro-French radical ideas, had produced some quite different associations for the readers of the Regency period. Expressing a liking for sentimental novels in 1798, or even in 1803, was fairly unexceptionable, even to respectable Tory families. But, by 1818, to do so was to align oneself strongly and conclusively with the revolutionary political thinking of the 1790s.

These (among many other) intertextual traces of Crosby's decision in 1803 not to publish the novel then known as 'Susan' thus mark *Northanger Abbey* in ways that only an understanding of the publishing trends of the three decades of its composition and publication can really illuminate. With such an understanding, we can imagine ourselves back into the mindset of a contemporary reader or reviewer, and begin to understand why it was so much less popular than her other novels. Criticisms of *Northanger Abbey* as uneven, erratic or rough, for example, owe much to the disjointed nature of its composition, while the responses of readers such as Maria Edgeworth and Henry Crabb Robinson, who found the novel disappointing in comparison to Austen's other mature works, become more explicable to modern readers, for whom the nuances of literary reputation in the period are now largely lost. It is impossible to know whether, had she lived, Austen would have consigned 'Miss Catherine' permanently 'to the Shelve', or whether she would eventually have risked its publication, as her brother did. The success of later negotiations with publishers who did value her works – Thomas Egerton and John Murray – must surely have taken the sting off her earlier failures with Cadell & Davies and Crosby & Co., and encouraged her to believe that her books were indeed worth both 'praise' and 'pewter'. The sales of Austen's books in the past two hundred years have certainly proven Egerton and Murray right, and Cadell and Crosby wrong.

NOTES

1. Jane Austen, *Northanger Abbey*, ed. Barbara M. Benedict and Deirdre Le Faye (1818; Cambridge University Press, 2006), p. 1.

2. George Holbert Tucker, *History of Jane Austen's Family* (Stroud: Sutton, 1998) (first published 1983 as *A Goodly Heritage*), p. 34.

3. *The Publishing Firm of Cadell & Davies: Select Correspondence and Accounts 1793–1836*, ed. Theodore Besterman (Oxford University Press/Humphrey Milford, 1938), p. viii.

4. Anthony Mandal, *Jane Austen and the Popular Novel: The Determined Author* (Houndmills: Palgrave Macmillan, 2007), p. 59.

5. Ibid., pp. 66, 67.

6. *Jane Austen's Letters*, ed. Deirdre Le Faye, 3rd edn (Oxford University Press, 1995), p. 174; subsequent references are given in the main text.

7. For a much fuller discussion of Austen's interactions with Crosby & Co. see A. A. Mandal, 'Making Austen MAD: Benjamin Crosby and the Non-Publication of *Susan*', *Review of English Studies*, n.s., 57.231 (2006), 507–25.

8. See, e.g., Jane Aiken Hodge, *Only a Novel: The Double Life of Jane Austen* (London: Coward, McCann & Geoghegan, 1972), p. 85; Park Honan, *Jane Austen: Her Life* (1987; London: Ballantine Books, 1997), p. 384; and Deirdre Le Faye, *Jane Austen: A Family Record*, 2nd edn (Cambridge University Press, 2004), p. 144.

9. Mandal, *Austen and the Popular Novel*, p. 71.

10. While attempts have been made to date the composition to as early as 1794 (C. S. Emden, 'The Composition of *Northanger Abbey*', *Review of English Studies* 19.75 (1968), 279–87), I am here following the chronology established by Deirdre Le Faye on the basis of Cassandra Austen's memorandum of the dates of composition of her sister's novels. Cassandra dated the work as 1798–9, and Le Faye narrows this further to between August 1798 and June 1799 (see *Family Record*, pp. xxii–xxix).

11. Janine Barchas, *Matters of Fact in Jane Austen: History, Location, and Celebrity* (Baltimore: Johns Hopkins University Press, 2013); Jocelyn Harris, *Satire, Celebrity and Politics in Jane Austen* (Lewisburg, PA: Bucknell University Press, 2017).

12. See Peter Knox-Shaw, *Jane Austen and the Enlightenment* (Cambridge University Press, 2004) for further discussion of the extent to which the Austen family enjoyed debating controversial issues in the 1790s.

13. It is worth noting that many writers and critics have remarked on Jane Austen's 'keen interest in money' (E. J. Clery, *Jane Austen: The Banker's Sister* (London: Biteback, 2017)). Most famous of these is perhaps W. H. Auden, who wrote, in 'Letter to Lord Byron', first published in 1937 in his (and Louis MacNeice's) *Letters from Iceland* (London: Faber & Faber), that, compared to her, James Joyce was 'innocent as grass' and that it was 'uncomfortable to see / An English spinster of the middle-class / Describe the amorous effects of "brass", / Reveal so frankly and with such sobriety / The economic basis of society' (p. 21).

14. Jane Austen's 'Plan of a Novel, according to hints from various quarters' is a hilarious pastiche of advice given to Austen from various friends, correspondents and family members about how she might improve her novels. The original manuscript is in the Pierpont Morgan Library in New York. It is reproduced in Jane Austen, *Later Manuscripts*, ed. Janet Todd and Linda Bree (Cambridge University Press, 2008), pp. 226–9.

The editors date 'Plan of a Novel' tentatively to between November 1815 and April 1816. It is likely, therefore, to be contemporaneous with the period when Austen was revising *Northanger Abbey* for the last time.

15. Mary Alcock, 'A Receipt for Writing a Novel' (1799), in *Eighteenth-Century Women Poets: An Oxford Anthology*, ed. Roger Lonsdale (Oxford University Press, 1989), p. 466.

16. Gothic parodies of the period in addition to *Northanger Abbey* and *The Heroine* include Bellin de La Liborlière's *La Nuit anglaise* (1799), which was translated into English by Matthew Lewis's sister as *The Hero* in 1817, Thomas Love Peacock's *Nightmare Abbey* (1818) and the 'Norman' cantos of Byron's *Don Juan* (published slightly later than our period, in 1823).

17. Austen names Maria Edgeworth's *Belinda* (1801), Frances Burney's *Cecilia* (1782) and *Camilla* (1796), Matthew Lewis's *The Monk* (1796), Henry Fielding's *Tom Jones* (1749), 'The Hare and Many Friends', published in John Gay's *Fables* (1727–38), Ann Radcliffe's *The Mysteries of Udolpho* (1794) and *The Italian* (1797), Henry Mackenzie's *The Mirror* (1779–80), Eliza Parsons's *The Castle of Wolfenbach* (1793) and *The Mysterious Warning* (1796), Peter Teuthold's *The Necromancer; or, The Tale of the Black Forest* (1794), Regina Maria Roche's *Clermont* (1798), Samuel Richardson's *Sir Charles Grandison* (1753), Eleanor Sleath's *The Orphan of the Rhine* (1798), Peter Will's *The Horrid Mysteries: A Story: From the German of the Marquis of Grosse* (1796) and *The Spectator*. She quotes from Thomas Gray's 'Elegy in a Country Churchyard' (1751), James Thompson's *The Seasons* (1730), Alexander Pope's 'Elegy to the Memory of an Unfortunate Lady' (1717) and William Shakespeare's *Measure for Measure* (1603), *Othello* (1603) and *Twelfth Night* (1601–2).

18. See Robert Miles, *Ann Radcliffe: The Great Enchantress* (Manchester University Press, 1995) for a discussion of Radcliffe's astonishing contemporary popularity.

19. S. T. Coleridge, 'Review of Matthew G. Lewis, *The Monk*', *Critical Review* (February 1797), 194–200 (197).

20. Ibid.

21. As Barbara Benedict and Deirdre Le Faye point out, 'within the previous twenty years, these names had appeared in such titles as *Julia, a Novel*; *Julia Benson*; *Julia de Gramont*; *Julia de Roubigné, Julia de Saint Pierre*; *Julia Stanley*; *Louisa, a Novel*; *Louisa, a Sentimental Novel*; *Louisa Forrester*; *Louisa Matthews*; *Louisa, or the Cottage on the Moor*; *Louisa, or, the Reward of an Affectionate Daughter*; *Louisa Wharton*' (*Northanger Abbey*, p. 330). In addition to these titles, one might add the heroines of such novels as Jane West's *A Gossip's Story* (1796) (Louisa Dudley) and Ann Radcliffe's own *A Sicilian Romance* (1790) (Julia Mazzini).

CRITICAL REFLECTIONS AND FURTHER STUDY

Northanger Abbey is the Cinderella of Jane Austen's novels. Not only does it regularly come last in lists of her most loved novels today (*Pride and Prejudice* pretty much always tops the list), but from the time of its publication it was much less popular than her other novels with both readers and critics. Henry Crabb Robinson, for example, found on reading *Northanger Abbey* and *Persuasion* in 1842, that 'these two novels have sadly reduced my estimation of Miss Austen. They are little more than galleries of disagreeables and the would-be heroes and heroines are scarcely out of the class of insignificants' (*Henry Crabb Robinson on Books and their Writers*, ed. Edith J. Morley, 3 vols (London: J. M. Dent, 1938), vol. II, p. 625).

I have thought, over many years of teaching the novel, that much that previous generations of critics found baffling, inexplicable or dislikeable in *Northanger Abbey* may be explained by the novel's complicated composition and publication history (which I explain in the essay). In taking this stance, I am positioning myself in a critical field usually described as book history. Book history has been a recognised academic discipline since the 1980s. While it draws on disciplinary perspectives as diverse as philology and social history, the central purpose of book-historical scholarship is to demonstrate that the material qualities of the book, as an object rather than as a disembodied 'text', are key to our understanding of that work. Thus the production, circulation and reception of books as material objects become central to our understanding of what the book contains, as well as the cultural work it does. In focusing on the ways in which *Northanger Abbey* came into being within the publishing contexts of its various stages of creation, then, we immediately enter the world of scholarship dealing with production. Fully to understand the novel, though, we would also need to think about the ways it circulated (how it was bought and sold, lent and borrowed; the number of editions it went into and what those editions looked like – were they expensive quartos, cheap duodecimos, illustrated or not, and so on), and how it was received (what critics and readers thought of it, how it influenced contemporary and later writers, and whether it eventually stood the test of time). But it is vital to emphasise that these elements of book-historical scholarship are not separate but instead intimately connected.

Those involved in the publication and circulation of books (publishers, booksellers, librarians, papermakers, printers, binders) are also readers. As Simon Eliot suggests,

> the way books are read, who reads which books, determines the intellectual and cultural context in which the next generation of books will be read, indeed significantly influences the views and techniques of those who will write the next generation of books. The reading of books thus represents a very complex feedback loop which partly determines the way in which text is written, manufactured, sold, bought, borrowed – and read. (Simon Eliot, The Reading Experience Database 1450–1945 (subtitled 'Or, what are we to do about the history of reading?'), The Open University, www.open.ac.uk/Arts/RED/redback.htm)

Robert Darnton famously represented this 'feedback loop' in diagrammatic form in his articulation of a 'communications circuit', first published in his landmark article 'What is the History of Books?', *Daedalus* 111.3 (1982), 65–83

(Figure 14.2). I would strongly advise anyone interested in book history to become familiar with this diagram, in which Darnton identified the various agents involved in the life cycle of a book, as well as the work of successive scholars who have considered and reconceptualised the communications circuit for the digital age.

There are, of course, many ways to approach Jane Austen's work, and there is no one right way to do it. In your wider reading, you will come across excellent work by feminist, historicist, Marxist, deconstructionist, reader-response, formalist, structuralist, and psychoanalytic critics, to name only a few, and all will shed light on different aspects of the books. But if you are interested in a book-historical approach, I would suggest considering the questions that follow in the final paragraph, as well as familiarising yourself with a few key works of book-historical scholarship, such as Robert Darnton's article. Following up on my essay's focus on production, you might like to try to identify the various agents involved in the communications circuit of *Northanger Abbey*, for example, or to think about the ways in which it both challenges and works within prevailing ideas of what a novel was, or should be. Anthony Mandal's *Jane Austen and the Popular Novel* (2007), on which I draw above (see my essay, note 4), is an invaluable starting point to introduce you to the literary marketplace of the period 1790–1820. *The Oxford History of the Novel in English*, volume II, *English and British Fiction 1750–1820*, edited by Peter Garside and Karen O'Brien (Oxford University Press, 2015) and Matthew Grenby's *The Anti-Jacobin Novel* (Cambridge University Press, 2001) will also provide valuable further context.

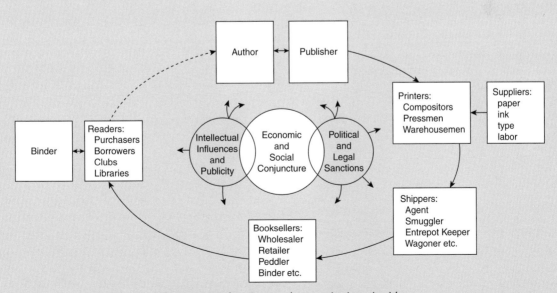

Figure 14.2 Robert Darnton, 'communications circuit'.

A series of further questions are also well worth following up. First, what were the material conditions of publication of *Northanger Abbey*, and indeed all of Austen's novels? What did they cost? What did they look like? What was the intended market for them? Were they bought by circulating and subscription libraries, and were they borrowed from them if so? I highly recommend David Gilson's *Bibliography of Jane Austen* (Delaware: Oak Knoll Press, 1997) and the Centre for Textual and Intertextual Research's excellent database British Fiction 1800–1829 (www.british-fiction.cf.ac.uk) as well as the database Books and Borrowing: An Analysis of Scottish Borrowers' Registers, 1750–1850 (https:// borrowing.stir.ac.uk) as a starting point for these enquiries. Next, you might like to consider how the novels were received and read. Brian Southam's two-volume *Jane Austen: The Critical Heritage* (London: Routledge, 1968) is a valuable entry point to the reception by reviewers, while my own *Jane Austen and Her Readers, 1786–1945* (London: Anthem, 2012) suggests some ways of thinking about how other readers responded to Jane Austen and what that might tell us about her novels; and the Reading Experience Database 1450–1945 (www.open.ac.uk/Arts/ reading/UK) will allow you to find out how ordinary readers responded to Austen across a long time period.

15 'O for a Life of Sensations' or 'the Internal and External Parts': Keats and Medical Materialism

PAUL WRIGHT

Abstract

By analysing key poems and particularly his use of the mythological figure of Psyche in the ode 'To Psyche' (1819), the least known of his odes, this essay considers John Keats (1795–1821), perhaps *the* poet-physician of the Romantic period, in the light of the vitalist versus materialist debates in medicine in the eighteenth and nineteenth centuries. It begins by exploring ways in which responses to Michel Foucault's notion of the confident clinical gaze and its accompanying surgical touch (as developed in the teaching hospitals in Revolutionary France and also by medical practitioners like William Lawrence and Charles Bell in England around the turn of the nineteenth century) might be traced in Dannie Abse's twentieth-century poem 'In the Theatre' (1972) and William Wordsworth's poetry and thought, before coming to a close focus on Keats. It outlines anxieties about the state, nature and disputed existence of the soul triggered within this wider medical debate, particularly in discussions of the nervous system, of the nature of sensation, and of what has become known as the mind–body problem; and it reads the poems as part of this debate. Referring to his medical notebooks and well-known statements in his letters, it re-examines the idea of Keats as a poet of sensation. It uses recent scholarship which seeks to revise our understanding of Keats specifically, and Romanticism in general, by drawing upon contemporaneous medical and scientific debates and highlighting the centrality of his medical training to possible understandings of Keats.

In the spirit of truth-finding and empirical experimentation which marked much of the medical enquiry at the turn of the nineteenth century, the twentieth-century poet-physician Dannie Abse (1923–2014) records a 'true incident' which took place in a hospital in Cardiff in 1938. Abse's older brother was a 'dresser', the junior doctor assisting the surgeon (often by clearing up after operations), and he reported this story to Abse as a child. In 'In the Theatre' (1972), the surgeon Lambert Rogers is attempting to operate on a brain tumour under local anaesthetic:

[M]ore brain mashed because of the probe's braille path;
Lambert Rogers desperate, fingering still

...

Then, suddenly, the cracked record in the brain,
a ventriloquist voice that cried, 'You sod,
leave my soul alone, leave my soul alone,'—
the patient's dummy lips moving to that refrain,
the patient's eyes too wide.[1]

The unease captured here does much to challenge the idea of the confident physician identified by the French philosopher and historian of ideas Michel Foucault (1926–84) as marking the birth of the 'modern' world in the clinical practice in the teaching hospitals of post-Revolutionary France at the turn of the nineteenth century. Foucault argues that 'Modern medicine has fixed its own date of birth as beginning in the last years of the eighteenth century ... it identifies the origin of its positivity with a return ... to the modest level of the perceived ... A new alliance was forged between words and things, enabling one *to see* and *to say*'.[2] He further characterises this in terms of a 'positivity' in which the 'observing gaze' of the clinician 'refrains from intervening'; his '[o]bservation leav[ing] things as they are' (pp. xii, 107). There is an echo in Abse's 'fingering' brain surgeon of Foucault's observation of the 'metaphor[s] of "touch" by which doctors will ceaselessly define their glance' (p. 122); however, Lambert Rogers's destructive 'desperate fingering' and pointed lack of sight or insight in his 'probe's braille path', juxtaposed with the patient's own 'eyes too wide', is clearly of a different order.

For Foucault's clinician, there is, at least in theory, no such anxiety. His confidence goes beyond observing and, apparently, unproblematically rendering that observation in language – he suggests that 'the great myth of a pure gaze would be a pure language' (p. 114) – to possessing a gaze which makes the body and any diseases knowable, graspable and ultimately treatable. For Abse, the surgeon's well-intentioned but blundering actions are in a sense unspeakable: the poem ends not with the assertions of the clinician but with the troubling immaterial voice of the patient and with silence. Abse's surgeon is transgressive, destructive and sacrilegious in his attack upon the soul as much as the brain.

A similar anxiety was also strongly held by those opposed to certain kinds of scientific and medical advance at the turn of the nineteenth century, which they too saw as the encroachment of materialism upon the possibilities of the transcendent. The Romantic poet William Wordsworth (1770–1850) visited Paris in the 1790s and was familiar with advances in science in general and medicine in particular. His description of a physician in 'A Poet's Epitaph' (1800) might be compared to the description of the surgeon in 'In the Theatre'. Wordsworth dismisses a version of Foucault's clinician, in language similar to that used by Abse:

he is 'one all eyes ... a fingering slave / One that would peep and botanize / Upon his mother's grave' in his search for the Cartesian 'pin-point' location of the 'soul'.[3]

For both Abse and Wordsworth the physician is engaged in an act of transgression; his 'probing' and 'peeping', embodied in the action of his 'fingers', assault the spiritual fabric of what it is to be human. Directly, and shockingly in Lambert Rogers's case, dismissively in Wordsworth's, the attack is upon the 'soul'. Such an attack – as critics with an interest in the significance of medicine to literature in general and Romanticism in particular have pointed out[4] – is a fundamental element of the medical practice noted by Foucault in the French clinic or teaching hospital, and part of a controversy in English teaching hospitals from the second half of the eighteenth century.[5]

Alan Richardson rightly warns against too simplistic an account of this vitalist versus materialist debate. He notes the material 'biological account' of the brain-mind and nervous system, championed by a range of scientists and medical practitioners in the second half of the eighteenth century, including the anatomist John Hunter (1728–93), reputedly an early sponsor of the practice of body-snatching for the purposes of medical research; Robert Whytt (1714–66), a pioneer of studies of the nervous system; Joseph Priestley (1733–1804), the polymath, and ardent supporter of the French Revolution; and Erasmus Darwin (1731–1802), the grandfather of Charles Darwin, and himself a poet-physician. This view, of course, is challenged by Wordsworth in his choice of the word 'botanize' to account for his near grave-robbing physician, who, in 'The Epitaph to a Poet', 'would peep and botanize / Upon his mother's grave' (19–20). Richardson argues that the pro- or anti-soul camps did not form 'coherent movement[s]' (pp. 5ff.). However, even accepting this, there clearly was considerable debate over the question as to whether the dualism underpinning post-Cartesian thought was – as, for example, Joseph Priestley suggests in his *Disquisitions Relating to Matter and Spirit* (1777) – 'a vulgar hypothesis'. Arguing against such a 'hypothesis', Priestley suggests that '[the] powers of sensation and perception, and thought, as belonging to man have never been found but in conjunction with a certain organized system of matter; and therefore that these powers necessarily exist in and depend upon such a system'.[6]

Abse's poem sees the soul as a 'cracked record in the brain', giving it a physical reality, and as 'a ventriloquist voice', suggesting that it is a kind of pseudo-presence or, perhaps, even a trick. Here, Priestley could be read as suggesting that higher human functions are, as it were, a matter of matter alone; but phrases like 'in conjunction with' and 'depend upon' do not necessarily preclude the possibility that the principle of life could be, as John Hunter argues in 'On the Vitalist Principle' (1786), 'something superadded' to an 'organized system of matter'.[7] Such possibilities were rejected by radical materialists at the turn of the nineteenth century: most (in)famously by the pro-revolutionary political radical John Thelwall (1764–1834) in his 'Essay towards a Definition of Animal Vitality' (1793), a direct challenge to Hunter; and by William Lawrence (1783–1867), the professor of anatomy and physiology at the Royal College of Surgeons. Echoing Priestley, Lawrence claims, in his *Lectures on Physiology, Zoology and the Natural History of Man* (1819), that 'Life ... is merely ... the state of the animal structure. It includes the notions which are obvious to common observation. It denotes what is apparent to our senses; and cannot be applied to the offspring of metaphysical subtlety, or immaterial abstractions without obscuring what is clear and intelligible.'[8]

Unlike Lambert Rogers, Lawrence was, as Marilyn Butler and others have noted, 'a household name';[9] his radical, anti-religious, stridently materialist views at the beginning of the nineteenth century were publicly criticised as mounting what Alan Richardson characterises as real 'challenges' not only to the scientific but also to the 'social order' (p. 2). Such views could be characterised as pre-Darwinian but adaptionist, in that Lawrence held that all living entities, including human beings, could only be products of physically determined processes.[10] He was attacked most notably by John Abernethy (1764–1831), professor of medicine at the Royal College of Surgeons, and his former teacher, who in his own lectures found evidence both for what we would call intelligent design and for an 'immaterial' soul. Lawrence later recanted his views, withdrawing his early publications; Priestley and Thelwall were attacked for theirs. Priestley's house and laboratory in Birmingham, then a centre for radical scientific experimentation, were burned down by an anti-revolutionary mob that rioted for three days in July 1791. The cry of Rogers's patient – 'leave my soul alone' – was something of a social if not a medical consensus in the late eighteenth and early nineteenth centuries.

More acceptable, perhaps, at the time were medical theorists and practitioners who were committed to the view of the body and brain as, in Priestley's phrase, 'organised matter', but who nonetheless made space for the soul. For example, seeking to understand how different body parts respond to pain when sometimes not directly under threat, Robert Whytt argued in the 1760s that 'the mind is only affected thro' the intervention of the optic and auditory nerves'; and that it could no longer be considered to control or direct experience alone, but was part of a larger system in which 'nerves are endued with feeling, and ... there is a general sympathy ... through the whole system; so there is a particular and very remarkable consent between various parts of the body'.[11] Whytt's 'something superadded', the 'sentient principal', was to be found throughout the body. Anticipating Abernethy, and the intrusive 'probing' of Abse's brain surgeon, he concludes, using the same appeal to reason and empirical method as radical materialists, that

> If the human frame is considered as a mere CORPOREAL system which derives all its power from matter ... it may be concluded that the IMMENSE UNIVERSE is destitute of any higher principal: but if, as we have endeavoured to shew ... our ... bodies ... are to be referred to the active power of an IMMATERIAL principal; how much more necessary must it be to acknowledge ... an INCORPOREAL NATURE everywhere and always present. (pp. 391–2)

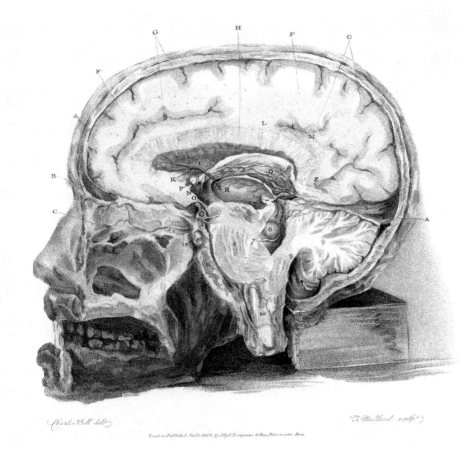

Figure 15.1 Engraving of the brain, from *The Anatomy of the Brain, Explained in a Series of Engravings*, by Charles Bell (1802).

Similarly, at the turn of the nineteenth century, Charles Bell – noted for the palsy named after him and for discovering the difference between sensory nerves and motor nerves in the spinal cord – could demonstrate, in his privately published but influential *Idea of a New Anatomy of the Brain* (1811), the emerging awareness of the complexity of human physiology and the brain in particular (Figure 15.1). He argues that '[all] ideas originate in the brain';[12] but, as a devoutly religious Anglican, he equally maintains a clear sense of dualism, distancing himself from the perceived radicalism of Lawrence's materialism. Bell remarks: 'They would have it that I am in search of the seat of the soul ... I mean only to investigate the structure of the brain as we examine ... the eye and the ear' (p. 3). He also echoes Whytt's sense of what we, again, might call intelligent design, but his language suggests an ambivalence about the claims of any transcendent or totalising systems. He writes: 'The mind was placed in a body not merely suited to its residence but in circumstances to be moved by the materials around it; and the capacities of the mind, and the powers of the organs, which are a medium betwixt the mind and the external world, have an original constitution framed in relation to the qualities of things' (p. 8).

Here, there is the same kind of 'positivity' found by Foucault in French Revolutionary clinical practice. Yet, the passive voice is at best ambiguous: the 'mind' being 'placed' and the 'constitution' being 'framed' suggests the assumed agency typical of pre-Darwinian adaptionist arguments, like those of William Paley (1743–1805), who famously argued in his *Natural Theology* (1802) that a designer was necessary to explain the complexity and variety in the world, just as a watchmaker was required to explain the existence of a watch, and the variety in the number of possible watches. However, unlike Whytt's proto-pantheistic 'higher principal', no actual agent seems to be assumed by Bell.

Picking up on this debate about intelligent design, and the wider possibility that 'literature might be considered in [the Romantic] period as a form of scientific practice', Noel Jackson finds in the language used by Whytt, Bell and other medical theorists and practitioners at the turn of the nineteenth century an echo of the Wordsworthian claim that the mind and the external world are in some way necessarily 'fitted' to one another.[13] Wordsworth writes in the 'Prospectus' to his unfinished and unpublished work *The Recluse*, of which only one part, *The Excursion* (1814), was published during his lifetime:

> My voice proclaims
> How exquisitely the individual Mind
> (And the progressive powers perhaps no less
> Of the whole species) to the external World
> Is fitted:—and how exquisitely, too,
> Theme this but little heard of among Men,
> The external World is fitted to the Mind. (lines 62–8)[14]

While this clearly was Bell's view, it is interesting to note that he was one of the first theorists to follow through on the logic of his supposition that all 'ideas originate in the brain' (p. 34) and to explore the well-reported phenomenon of phantom limbs and other pseudo-impressions in terms of brain and nerve based physiology; enquiries which might suggest a more complex, and ultimately more troubling, relation 'betwixt the mind and the external world' than can easily be accommodated by adaptionist accounts of perception. Bell notes that following a 'blow to the head', 'the ears will ring and the eye flashes light while there is neither sound nor light present' (p. 11) and more provocatively, and with a sense of transgression not dissimilar to Abse's possibly phantom soul, that 'exquisite sensations' can still be felt from the head of a penis completely destroyed by cancer!

Wordsworth's own sense of the adaptionist view that the world and the senses were 'fitted' to and for each other, was often under similar stress. He could equally record a profound anxiety about the reliability of sensory perception, the relationship, in Bell's phrase, between 'betwixt the mind and the external world'. He captures the subtleties and contradictions at play most graphically. Against this backdrop of philosophical, if not directly medical, ideas, he grew up with a sense of doubt as to the nature of things. He writes in the 'Fenwick note' to the 'Immortality' ode (1804) that, as a child 'I was often unable to think of external things as having external existence ... Many times while going to school have I grasped at a wall or a tree to recall myself from the abyss of idealism to the reality' (*Poetical Works*, vol. IV, lines 463–4).

Here, it is the fear that external things may have no external existence, and cannot be guaranteed simply by sight of them, that concerns the child Wordsworth, and the man, as it would many of the Romantics. The solution of the child is essentially childlike, a kind of clutching for an epistemological teddy bear: to grab hold of something is again to experience it. Touch becomes the guarantee of truth just as it does, rather less urgently, for Foucault's clinician in his understanding of gaze as touch. Yet, as Bell's research into the phenomenon of the phantom limb and other pseudo-sensations begins to suggest, to touch or feel something, to grab 'a wall or a tree', ultimately proves little. And, something of this uncertainty may be apparent in Wordsworth's phrasing: 'to grasp at' suggests wishful thinking as much as it does certainty.

Bell's *New Anatomy* was used by Astley Cooper (1768–1841), professor at Guys teaching hospital, as a source for his anatomy lectures to students in 1815–16. As is well known, one of his pupils, and indeed one he singled out by arranging a dresser's post for him, not unlike the role taken by Abse's brother, was, perhaps, *the* poet-physician of the Romantic period: John Keats (1795–1821). Keats entered Guys, then part of the Borough Hospitals, on 2 October 1815 after a five-year apothecary's apprenticeship; and his first published poem, the sonnet 'O Solitude', appeared in the liberal journal the *Examiner* the following May. Although his career plans vied with poetry for his attention – by April 1816, when he should have been concentrating on his forthcoming exams, he had taken to writing poetry during lectures and imitating the fashions set by the already famous poet Lord Byron (1788–1824) – in July 1816 Keats passed his examination and qualified to practise as an apothecary. Since the passing of the Apothecaries Act in 1815, which greatly increased the demands on a would-be practitioner, this was no mean feat. Keats was expected to attend lectures and hospital 'walks', and to show detailed knowledge of current medical theory and practice, including anatomy. After a long summer vacation, he returned to London to continue his studies in order to further qualify as a surgeon, which, naturally, involved attending surgery. The reality of this experience was captured by a contemporary, who wrote:

> The pupils packed in like herrings in a barrel, but not so quiet. There was a continual calling of heads, heads to those about the table whose heads interfered with sightseers.

I have often known even the floors so crowded that the surgeon could not operate till it had been partially cleared ... I was quickly upset, had to leave the theatre, and not infrequently fainted.[15]

Beyond the colourful nature of medical students' experience, which would include cooking breakfast in the corner of the operating theatre, this account gives some idea of their proximity to bodies and their role as 'sightseers' – the seeing of sights recalling both Foucault's sense of the clinician's 'gaze' and Wordsworth's 'all eyes' physician. Indeed, a version of the clinical method that concerns Foucault, with its insistence on observing the diseased and healthy body, was being practised in the English teaching hospitals, like Guys, from the 1770s. For Keats, this proximity was heightened in his role as a dresser for the infamous surgeon, William 'Mad Billy' Lucas.

Criticism in the last twenty years or so, by Hermione de Almeida, Nicholas Roe and others,[16] has done much to establish the importance of the medical context to Keats's work in terms of its imagery, themes and historical context. Although he never completely relinquished thoughts of a medical career and saw poetry itself as potentially a kind of medicine, it is interesting to note that Keats is reported to have abandoned surgery in circumstances not dissimilar to Abse's poem. His friend Charles Brown reported: '"My last operation" he told me "was the opening of a man's temporal artery. I did it with the utmost nicety but, considering what passed through my mind at the time, my dexterity seemed a miracle and I never took up the lancet again."'[17] De Almeida suggests, rightly, that this should be viewed not as the fragile Keats of literary myth, manifesting an understandable 'distaste for seeing gore and blood', but as 'reflect[ing] an anxiety for life' (p. 326n.).[18] This anxiety might best be understood in relation to the vitalist–materialist debate sketched here.

The latest materialist understanding of sensation at the time, derived directly from Bell and indirectly from Whytt and Priestley, is recorded thus in Keats's notes on Cooper's lectures: 'Sensation – it is an impression made on the Extremities of the Nerves conveyed to the Brain. This is proved by the effects of dividing a Nerve ... Volition is the contrary of Sensation it proceeds from the internal to external parts.'[19] This observation provides an interesting context for the poet who was torn between a 'life of Sensation ... [and] thought', as he notes famously in his letters;[20] and for the critical tradition of a one-sided reading of this carefully poised wish, which tends to see him as an escapist writer: for example, Matthew Arnold's dangerously sensuous Keats, F. R. Leavis's anxiety over Keats's perceived vulgarity, John Jones's unworked eroticism, and Marjorie Levinson's sense of Keats's shameful sensualism.[21] In this regard, it is worth noting that Levinson's reading, relying as it does on a sense of educational deficit, echoes the view of medical students in general held by the contemporary churchman Thomas Rennell

(1754–1840), who saw William Lawrence and radical materialist medicine as corrupters of the innocent young. Rennell writes in 1817:

> By far the larger part of those who look upon Mr. Lawrence for instruction ... have no education at all. At the age of fourteen ... they rapidly contract the range of their intellect ... Forgetting then the existence of a first cause ... the more accurately they observe the more surely they puzzle and perplex their understandings; till at last their embarrassments conclude in a state of general scepticism ...[22]

Like the voice in Abse's poem, Rennell is concerned with preserving both a 'first cause' and the soul from 'probing' materialist attack. He attacks the 'general scepticism' which in a medical as well as a broader sense might question the Wordsworthian 'fit' between thought, imagination, perception and experience; or between, in Keats's phrase, 'internal and external parts'.

In his recent study of the relationship between science, sensation and Romantic poetry, Noel Jackson argues that Keats, like Wordsworth, is able 'to sustain a balance' between 'ideation and perception' (p. 169). I want to suggest, here, that there is in Keats's absorption of much of the scientific debate about sensory perception, rather than any 'balance', a sense of unease not dissimilar to that noted by Abse in his own accounts of how 'internal and external parts' might relate. In the context of the materialist debate, it is no coincidence that this unease can be seen in Keats's treatment of the figure Psyche, or the soul, from Greek mythology.

The well-known story of Psyche falling in love with Eros (Love) is invoked in the early poem 'I Stood Tip-Toe upon a little hill' (1816) in an ambiguous way which suggests an interest beyond the merely erotic. The following might be said to be typical of the sensual Keats:

> So felt he, who first told, how Psyche went
> On the smooth wind to the realm of wonderment;
> What Psyche felt, and Love, when their full lips
> First touch'd; what amorous, and fondling nips
> They gave each other's cheeks (lines 41–5)[23]

The physical existence of Psyche and the personified Love/Eros is stressed here – 'their full lips', their 'amorous fondling nips' – as is, recalling Foucault's dominant medical trope, their ability to touch. Their presence to the voyeuristic poet and reader is secured through erotic acts of near violence: bites are perhaps the most urgent form of touching. Yet, this presence is undercut by the fact that the poem admits that it is a retelling of a story which has already been 'told'. This kind of distancing occurs more harshly in Keats's later engagement with the worlds of myth and legend, in, for example, *The Eve of St Agnes* (1820), which is famously seen by critics as either an indulgence in the sensual or an exposure of the very impossibility of such an indulgence,[24] and in the pursuit of the goddess in the long poem *Endymion* (1818).

A similar stance is taken by the poetic voice of 'Sleep and Poetry', which was completed around the same time as 'I Stood Tip-Toe', in the second half of 1816, when Keats was training to be a surgeon. In a frequently quoted passage, often seen as predictive of his desire to move beyond the mytho-erotic to the world of 'Pains and troubles' of his experience of practising medicine and necessary to form a 'soul' (*Letters*, vol. II, p. 103), Keats writes:

> First the realm I'll pass
> Of Flora, and old Pan ...
> Catch the white-handed nymph in shady places,
> To woo sweet kisses from averted faces –
> Play with their fingers, touch their shoulders white
> Into a pretty shrinking with a bite
> As hard as lips can make it; till agreed,
> A lovely tale of human life we'll read. (lines 101–10)

Here, again, the poet's ability to connect with the external world may be read parodically in its overemphasised physicality; it might be seen as a sort of exposure of the concerns expressed in the apparent confidence of a clinician's touch, or Bell's sense that 'the mind' could equally confidently know and experience 'the quality of things'. Here, the poet will 'catch' the nymphs, 'play with their fingers'. Touch is, again, a means not so much to prove that the external 'realm' has substance, but to test that assumption to breaking point. Echoing the 'fondling nips' of Eros and Psyche, the poet will even 'bite' the nymphs to prove their existence.

In his account of much of the scientific material sketched here, Alan Richardson highlights this passage. He sees it at one and the same time as 'harmless' and, in language which unwittingly echoes many of the anxieties of the sensualist readings of Keats, as an 'erotic combat which may verge too nearly on the sadistic for some' (p. 140). This reading, it seems to me, misses the sense of uncertainty about the nature of sensory experience. Using a word which might again bring Abse's brain surgeon to mind, Roe identifies the 'disconcert[ing]' nature of Keats's erotic poetry,[25] and what might equally be seen as a lack of 'balance' – a lack of balance of which Keats would have been fully aware from his own understanding of the science of the mind at the time.

This sense of uncertainty is made most apparent in Keats's last treatment of the Psyche story in the ode of that name, written in 1819 and the least considered of the sequence of odes on which his reputation as a poet, perhaps, rests. The poem is first recorded in the long journal letter to his brother, George, in which he speculates about how a soul might be 'made' (*Letters*, vol. II, pp. 102–3); and it contains a description of a 'working brain' (line 60) which has long been linked directly to Keats's medical training.[26] By the end of the poem the poet-priest promises:

> I will be thy priest, and build a fane
> In some untrodden region of my mind,
> Where branched thoughts, new grown with pleasant pain,
> Instead of pines shall murmur in the wind (lines 50–3)

But, unlike earlier versions of the myth in Keats, he has no direct access to the goddess. He doesn't even catch a voyeuristic glimpse of her; she is in a sense even less than the pseudo-presence of Bell's phantom limb or Abse's 'ventriloquist voice' soul. In a phrase which might suggest the vitalist spark of life, the poet finally vows to keep '[a] bright torch and a casement ope at night / To let the warm Love in!' (lines 66–7).

Anne K. Mellor sees in this conclusion an invitation to restage the embrace that is gazed upon at the opening of the poem, beyond its frame.[27] Yet, if we see the poet-priest here as standing in for Cupid – who, as Keats knew from *Lempriere's Classical Dictionary*, his favoured source for mythological material, made 'a place of bliss'[28] for Psyche – then there is a sense in which the personification of 'Love' here refers *not* to Cupid himself but to Psyche, or the soul. This, then, is to repeat the scene of so many of Keats's erotic encounters: an erotic location is sustained only in the poet's mind, or more dangerously and appropriately for Keats's awareness of emerging materialist accounts of consciousness, the poet's brain; and, more indirectly, it is an act of wishful volition on the part of a hopeful observer. Yet, of course, as with so many of these encounters, despite the open window, and the open vowelled 'ope', sounding the hope within the poetic or imaginative act, here, as with the phantom limb, beyond the confines of the poet's own imaginative 'sanctuary', Psyche may not be there. Unlike the confident physician, or the vitalist who is sure of a transcendent underpinning to sensory perception, the poet cannot finally guarantee the existence of the soul. But, despite the force of the materialist argument that, as Lawrence put it, 'an immortal and spiritual being' was not to be found 'amid the blood and filth of the dissecting room' (p. 8) or operating theatre, Keats's poet still looks out, not with the sense of shock of Abse's brain surgeon, but in hope.

NOTES

1. Dannie Abse, 'In the Theatre', in *Funland and Other Poems 1967–72*, reprinted in *Collected Poems 1948–1976* (London: Hutchinson, 1976), pp. 160–1.
2. Michel Foucault, *The Birth of the Clinic*, trans. A. M. Sheridan Smith (London: Tavistock,1973), p. xii; subsequent references are incorporated within the main text.
3. 'A Poet's Epitaph', lines 17–25, in *The Lyrical Ballads*, ed. Derek Roper (Plymouth: Northcote House, 1987), p. 221. The Cartesian view was developed by the French philosopher-scientist René Descartes (1596–1650), who argued that there are two kinds of experience, the mental and the physical, which both exist in a dualistic account of

what it is to be a conscious individual. In his *The Passions of the Soul* (1649) he argued that the pineal gland at the base of the brain was the seat of the soul.

4. Roy Porter, 'Medical Science and Human Science in the Enlightenment', in Christopher Fox, Roy Porter and Robert Wokler (eds), *Inventing Human Science* (Berkeley: University of California Press, 1995), pp. 53–87; Sharon Ruston, *Shelley and Vitality* (Houndmills: Palgrave Macmillan, 2005); Noel Jackson, *Science and Sensation in Romantic Poetry* (Cambridge University Press, 2008); Alan Richardson, *British Romanticism and the Science of the Mind* (Cambridge University Press, 2001) (subsequent references to Richardson are incorporated in the main text).

5. See, e.g., Hermione De Almeida, *Romantic Medicine and John Keats* (Oxford University Press, 1991), pp. 5ff.

6. Joseph Priestley, *Disquisitions Relating to Matter and Spirit* (London: Johnson, 1777), pp. xxxviii, 26.

7. *The Works of John Hunter*, ed. J. F. Palmer, 4 vols (London: Longman, 1835), vol. I, pp. 221–3.

8. William Lawrence, *Lectures on Physiology, Zoology and the Natural History of Man* (London: Callow, 1819), p. 39.

9. See editor Marilyn Butler's introduction and 'Appendix C' to *Frankenstein: The 1818 Text* (Oxford University Press, 1993), pp. ix–li, 229–51.

10. For a discussion of William Lawrence's ideas see K. D. Wells, 'Sir William Lawrence (1783–1867): A Study of Pre-Darwinian Ideas on Heredity and Variation', *Journal of the History of Biology* 4 (1971), 319–61.

11. *The Works of Robert Whytt* (Edinburgh: Balfour, Auld & Smellie, 1768), pp. 493, 152.

12. Charles Bell, *Idea of a New Anatomy of the Brain* (1811; London: Dawson, 1966), p. 34.

13. See Jackson, *Science and Sensation*, p. 8ff.; and, for a similar view, Richardson, *British Romanticism*, p. 15ff.

14. Wordsworth, *Poetical Works*, ed. E. de Selincourt and H. Darbishire, 5 vols (Oxford University Press, 1940–9), vol. V, p. 5; subsequent references to the *Poetical Works* are incorporated within the main text.

15. From William Hale-White, *Keats as Doctor and Patient* (Oxford University Press, 1934), p. 14.

16. De Almeida, *Romantic Medicine and Keats*; Nicholas Roe, *John Keats and the Culture of Dissent* (Oxford: Clarendon Press, 1997); Nicholas Roe (ed.), *Keats and the Medical Imagination* (Cham: Palgrave, 2017).

17. H. E. Rollins (ed.), *The Keats Circle*, 2 vols (Cambridge, MA: Harvard University Press, 1948), vol. II, p. 56.

18. The idea of Keats as a fragile other-worldly figure, or as someone with little interest in or knowledge of the world, principally concerned with escaping into his imagination, was begun by Percy Shelley's poem *Adonais: An Elegy on the Death of John Keats* (1821) and perpetuated by much criticism and commentary in the nineteenth and twentieth centuries. A useful summary and exploration of the different critical readings of Keats is provided by Jack Stillinger's 'The "Story" of Keats', in Susan Wolfson (ed.), *The Cambridge Companion to Keats* (Cambridge University Press, 2001), pp. 246–60.

19. *John Keats's Anatomical and Physiological Notebook*, ed. M. B. Forman (Oxford University Press, 1934), pp. 55–6. For the latest work on the relationship between these notes and his work see Hrileena Ghosh, *John Keats' Medical Notebook: Text, Context, and Poems* (Liverpool University Press, 2020).

20. H. E. Rollins (ed.), *The Letters of John Keats*, 2 vols (Cambridge, MA: Harvard University Press, 1958), vol. I, p. 185; subsequent references are incorporated within the main text.

21. For readings of Keats as a poet of sensation in a non-medical sense see, e.g., Matthew Arnold, *'Keats'*, in *Essays in Criticism* (London: Macmillan, 1888); F. R. Leavis, *'Keats'*, in *Revaluation* (London: Chatto, 1936); John Jones, *John Keats and the Dream of Truth* (London: Chatto, 1969); and Marjorie Levinson, *Keats' Life of Allegory* (Oxford: Basil Blackwell, 1988).

22. *British Critic* (n.s.) 8 (July 1817), 64–5.

23. All quotations from Keats's poems are taken from *John Keats: Complete Poems*, ed. Jack Stillinger (Cambridge, MA: Harvard University Press, 1982). References are provided by line number as the texts of the poems are widely available.

24. Stuart Sperry's *Keats the Poet* (Princeton University Press, 1994) summarises the sensualist/ironist debate over *The Eve of St Agnes*, pp. 198ff. Levinson's *Keats' Life of Allegory* provides a sustained reading of Keats's eroticism and masturbatory imagination but does so in terms of kinds of social and educational exclusion or lack that locating him against medico-empiricist debates does much to correct.

25. Citing John Bayley's 'The Vulgar and Heroic in "Bad Poetry"', Roe's *Keats and the Culture of Dissent* discusses the 'Sleep and Poetry' passage in relation to its social rather than epistemological significance (p. 16ff).

26. See, e.g., Donald Goellnicht, *The Poet Physician: Keats and Medical Science* (University of Pittsburgh Press, 1984), pp. 135–9.

27. Anne K. Mellor, *English Romantic Irony* (Cambridge, MA: Harvard University Press, 1980), pp. 80ff.

28. See *Lempriere's Classical Dictionary* (1788; London: Braken Books, 1984), p. 567.

CRITICAL REFLECTIONS AND FURTHER STUDY

My essay springs from an interest in the life of John Keats and is concerned with research that sees his medical training as centrally significant. Many biographies of Keats are available, but I would particularly recommend the one by Andrew Motion listed in Further Reading. In that list, I have also provided some introductory critical reading on the other two poets discussed, Wordsworth and Abse, along with a collection of essays on connections between science and modern poetry edited by John Holmes.

My essay is influenced by a particular approach to literary study, New Historicism. It is not any longer particularly 'new', having originated in the 1980s, but the term was coined by Stephen Greenblatt, whose book *Renaissance Self-Fashioning* (1980) is usually seen as its first incarnation (although, of course, all approaches to literature have complex origins and antecedents). It is an approach which has proved particularly fruitful in studies of the literature of the Renaissance and Romantic periods.

Chapter 9 of Peter Barry's *Beginning Theory* (2002) offers a good overview of New Historicism along with chapters on a full range of literary theories, many of which are used elsewhere in this volume. Barry summarises 'What New Historicists do', linking the practice to many of these other theories:

1. They juxtapose literary and non-literary texts, reading the former in the light of the latter.
2. They try thereby to 'defamiliarise' the canonical literary text, detaching it from the accumulated weight of previous literary scholarship and seeing it as if new.
3. They focus attention (within both text and co-text) on issues of State power and how it is maintained, on patriarchal structures and their perpetuation, and on the process of colonisation, with its accompanying 'mindset'.
4. They make use, in doing so, of aspects of a post-structuralist outlook, especially [Jacques] Derrida's notion that every facet of reality is textualized, and [Michel] Foucault's idea of social structures as determined by dominant 'discursive practices'. (p. 179)

It is point 4 which might be said to differentiate the approach from other ways of using historical material to help 'explain' a literary text.

You might want to take these points and ask some questions about my essay. Is it helpful or even legitimate to compare Keats's poems to the range of non-literary texts? Do you find convincing the reading of 'To Psyche' as in some sense a poem about medical theories of sensation and the mind–brain problem? Do you think that Keats is knowingly ironic about much of his material? Do you prefer less 'defamiliarising' readings concerned more with the immediate formal, mythic and aesthetic qualities of the poems? And to what extent do you accept that 'every facet of reality is textualized'? (Here Barry is referring to Derrida's (in)famous claim usually translated as 'There is nothing outside of the text' (*Of Grammatology*, p. 158) but perhaps better understood, although not easy to understand, as 'there is no outside-the-text').

In Keats this debate about what can be read into a poem might be best exemplified by competing readings of his ode 'To Autumn' (1819). You might usefully contrast readings of it by Roe (*Keats and the Culture of Dissent*, pp. 253–67; see my essay, note 16) and Helen Vendler in chapter 7 of *The Odes of John Keats*. Similarly with Wordsworth, you might want to read 'Tintern Abbey' (1798) and come to your own views before considering the readings offered, for example, by Marjorie Levinson in *Wordsworth's Great Period Poems* and the counterblast by Thomas McFarland in *Intensity and Achievement* which accuses Levinson, and by inference New Historicism as a whole, of 'a Herculean headlock to force us toward [an] interpretation' (p. 6). Do you think that these poems are being 'seen anew' or being distorted by juxtaposing them with such historical materials?

Many critics question the methods of New Historicism. Some argue, like Harold Bloom, that in prioritising the text's relation to history, it ignores the 'aesthetic ... autonomy of imaginative literature' (*The Western Canon*, p. 10). Others argue that in limiting itself to historicity – that is, to a concern with the ways in which history is, and can only be, represented in multiple and often competing historical documents and accounts (Derrida's texts), rather than in any sense known for certain – it denies the reality of what Terry Eagleton, in *Literary Theory*, calls 'the truths of history' (p. 208).

Foucault looms large in my essay in the ways that Barry suggests. The claim underlying my argument is that the 'discursive practice' of the idea of the clinician, as he defines it, fundamentally shaped medical practice at the time and continues to do so (see the introduction to *The Foucault Reader*). It becomes, for Foucault an 'episteme': a form of words which determines the nature of what we can know (see 'Truth and Power' in *The Foucault Reader*, pp. 51–75). You might like to reflect upon how medicine and science more generally are culturally constructed. My essay and this reflection were written during governmental and public health responses to the Covid 19 crisis of early 2020. Although not explicitly part of my essay's interest in the 'gaze', it seems appropriate to end by pointing out that Foucault is particularly interested, as New Historicist readings of Keats often suggest he was, in the idea of (government) control by observation (see 'Panopticism', *The Foucault Reader*, pp. 206–213, and also Roe).

FURTHER READING

Archard, Cary, *Dannie Abse: A Sourcebook* (Bridgend: Seren, 2010)

Barry, Peter, *Beginning Theory* (Manchester University Press, 2009)

Bloom, Harold, *The Western Canon* (New York: Harcourt, Brace, 1994)

Derrida, Jacques, *Of Grammatology*, trans. Gayatri Spivak (Baltimore: Johns Hopkins University Press, 1987), pp.157–64.

Christopher Norris's *Derrida* (London: Fontana, 1987) is a useful introduction to Derrida.

Eagleton, Terry, *Literary Theory: An Introduction (Anniversary Edition)* (Oxford: Blackwell, 2008)

Foucault, Michel, *The Foucault Reader*, ed. Paul Rainbow (London: Penguin, 1991)

Gill, Stephen (ed.), *The Cambridge Companion to Wordsworth* (Cambridge University Press, 2003)

Greenblatt, Stephen, *Renaissance Self-Fashioning*, new ed. (University of Chicago Press, 2005)

Holmes, John (ed.), *Science and Modern Poetry: New Directions* (Liverpool University Press, 2012)

Levinson, Marjorie, *Wordsworth's Great Period Poems: Four Essays* (Cambridge University Press, 1986)

McFarland, Thomas, *William Wordsworth: Intensity and Achievement* (Oxford: Clarendon Press, 1992)

Motion, Andrew, *Keats* (London: Faber & Faber, 1997)

Vendler, Helen, *The Odes of John Keats* (Cambridge, MA: Harvard University Press, 1983)

Vesser, H. Aram (ed.), *The New Historicism* (London: Routledge, 1989). In addition to the readings of Keats which are New Historicist in nature cited in my essay, this provides discussions of the theory and its application.

PART V
The Victorian Age, 1832–1901

INTRODUCTORY NOTE

Moving onwards from Paul Wright's essay into the Victorian era, we see, among other things, vitalism continuing to vie with materialism in Jordan Kistler's wonderfully engaging survey of scientific influences in the poetry of the period. The essay bristles with illuminating insights into the many ways in which poets responded in their work to a range of debates and discoveries in the different sciences. This was the age of Lyell and Darwin, marked by much anxious and impassioned discussion of evolutionary theory and its many ramifications, not least in the field of religious belief, and Kistler revisits this whole issue in a fresh and entertaining way. She draws closely on a variety of texts to illustrate her argument and discusses works by both familiar and less familiar authors.

Maria Frawley introduces a new type of contextual focus in her intensive study of Charlotte Brontë's *Villette* from within a life-writing perspective – or rather from the double perspective offered by the novel itself and by Elizabeth Gaskell's biography of Brontë which, along with Brontë's letters, Frawley uses as a sort of dialogic echo chamber for her analysis of how the novel, in exploring Lucy Snowe's affective world, follows the contours of Brontë's own inner emotional landscape. Drawing judiciously on recent scholarship in this broad field, Frawley develops her own critically sophisticated model of life writing to account for what she suggests may be 'the nineteenth-century novel's most sustained study of a character's interiority'. Loneliness and the fear of being forgotten are identified as major affective elements in the novel, along with a countervailing desire to affirm the enduring value of love. In the course of her analysis of the novel, in which Lucy Snowe is constantly shown to be self-consciously narrating her own 'book of life', Frawley identifies a 'rhetoric of writing' as being an essential feature of Brontë's quest to understand the complexities of the self. In this rhetoric, Frawley suggests, the practice of writing itself becomes both the means to self-realisation and an 'indelible' legacy of enduring love. This stress on *writing*, on textuality, might be seen subtly to recalibrate the meaning of the phrase 'life writing' and once more to put in question the distinction between texts and contexts, literature and life.

In addition to the growth in the circulation of scientific ideas, the Victorian era also saw an increase in the circulation of paper money and the eventual dominance of a cash economy or 'cash nexus' in society. The representational challenges and opportunities this development presented for realist fiction provide the main focus for Ben Moore's essay as he explores representations of money in selected novels by Dickens and Gissing and considers how their fiction reflected a world being reshaped by money and political economy. Moore draws partly on a Marxist analysis and partly on post-structuralist theories to outline some of the paradoxes involved in trying to represent something that is itself already a representation, with no inherent value or meaning of its own outside the socioeconomic system of signification in which it functions: like language and literature, the essay explains, money is a system of signs. But if this sounds rather abstract, it yields a substantial harvest in practical interpretative insights as Moore picks out some fascinating chains of fictional significance generated by the circulation of money in the novels he discusses. It is made plain, too, that Dickens and Gissing certainly shared Jane Austen's clear-eyed understanding of the economic bases of society (noted in Halsey's earlier essay on Austen).

Richard Jones's essay in Part III considered how the serial publication of a novel in the eighteenth century affected its composition and reception, and what sort of practical and promotional interaction there was between fiction and serial. In this section, Fionnuala Dillane takes up this broad topic in the context of Victorian print culture, analysing in detail the complex characteristics of the serial as a product of industrial modernity and looking in particular at the dynamics of reader reception of serial fiction through a close textual focus on Sheridan Le Fanu's Gothic vampire story *Carmilla*. Dillane also takes the story (in both senses) forwards to the present day to consider contemporary technological iterations of serial mediation, again using *Carmilla* as her case-study text as it has been adapted for television, film and Web vlog series across different media platforms. The scope and sophistication of Dillane's discussion, which, among other things, includes attention to questions of spatiality, temporality and the literary marketplace, make her essay especially rich with potential for dialogue with the other essays in this collection. Indeed, Dillane's overall sense of how fluidly and flexibly texts and contexts relate to one another in serial mediation speaks directly to the defining spirit of this volume.

The serial in which *Carmilla* was originally published was, as Dillane tells us, an early champion of European aestheticism and was called *The Dark Blue*; and it is perhaps not accidental that the later flagship periodical of avant-garde aestheticism in the 1890s was also colour-styled, as the *Yellow Book*. This influential journal was particularly important – aesthetically, ideologically and economically – in offering an outlet for women's writing and was part of a general growth in opportunities for magazine publication which facilitated a *fin-de-siècle* breakthrough for women writers into the previously male-dominated literary sphere. Reflecting on this development, Sue Asbee's discussion in this section's final essay considers women's *literal* entrance into the public literary sphere (and their greater access to public places generally at this time) and what this meant for their sense of identity. The public literary sphere is here represented especially by the iconic British Museum reading room, which became a centre at this time for the 'New Women' writers on whom Asbee mainly focuses. As she says, along with the other more general social freedoms women were gradually acquiring, women could now for the first time 'take their seats in the reading room as intellectual equals to men'. Women's greater access to public places like this came with both challenges and opportunities in negotiating new versions of identity in public space and Asbee illuminatingly explores how New Women writers variously represented these challenges and opportunities in their fiction and poetry and in a range of moods and styles. Asbee especially teases out the gender politics of the texts she discusses, along with how they test new relations between public places and private spaces. Her initial staging of the discussion in the British Museum reading room is an intentional reference to Virginia Woolf's feminist critique in her essay *A Room of One's Own*, and this makes a clear link between this essay and Judith Paltin's essay on the latter text in Part VI; and both essays have evident continuities with Catherine Riley's discussion of women in publishing in Essay 25.

16 Poetry and Science in the Victorian Period

JORDAN KISTLER

Abstract

In the nineteenth century many poets viewed their craft as analogous to science, employing similar methods to reach similar conclusions. Victorian poets engaged with science on a number of different levels: they wrote about scientific ideas, employed scientific methods like empirical observation and induction, and sought to verify scientific truths. They also were keenly aware of what poetry could offer that science did not: an insight into human nature and moral truths. In response to scientific theories that upended accepted beliefs about the world and humanity's place within it – geological uniformitarianism, evolution and natural selection, sexual selection and the coming heat death of the universe – poets like Alfred Tennyson, George Meredith, Constance Naden and May Kendall conducted poetic experiments in human nature, testing the impact of groundbreaking scientific theories on human society and behaviour. In so doing, they advocate for productive exchange between science and poetry, but also champion poetry's unique remit.

In her seminal work, *Darwin's Plots* (1983), Gillian Beer demonstrates the 'two-way traffic' between nineteenth-century literature and science. Writers did not simply react to scientific ideas; rather, there was an exchange of 'not only *ideas* but metaphors, myths, and narrative patterns' between scientists and non-scientists.[1] Beer explores the way scientists employed literary language (e.g., metaphors) and narrative structures (the *Bildungsroman*, the multi-plot novel) in order to communicate their theories to a wide reading public. Since *Darwin's Plots*, the study of nineteenth-century literature and science has grown exponentially, providing us with a number of different approaches to this topic.

Many critics focus on similarities between science and poetry in either methods or conclusions. John Holmes identifies correspondence in the *methods* of poetry and science, particularly empiricism (close observation of the world) and induction (theorising based on those observations), pointing to their shared 'aspiration to establishing truth through unprejudiced and scrupulous observation'.[2] Yet, as Holmes demonstrates, these similar methods could be used to different ends, achieving results that 'are complementary to, not identical with, those of science itself'.[3] For example, art could employ observation and induction in order to reveal moral, rather than material, truth.[4] In contrast, Clare Stainthorp examines the way poetry and science might offer different methods to reach similar *conclusions*. She points specifically to Constance Naden's search for synthesis between poetry and science, disciplines Naden thought of as 'synonymous', because they sought the same universal truths.[5] Michelle Geric similarly notes the nineteenth-century belief that 'truths were capable of surfacing in different forms of writing'.[6] In this view, poetry and science are different ways of discovering truth applicable to both disciplines.

Beyond disciplinary similarities, critics like Gregory Tate point to the 'cultural authority' invested in poetry in the nineteenth century.[7] This authority allowed poets to scrutinise new scientific theories, uncover their potential ideological biases, and 'test out [their] fitness', as Michelle Geric argues.[8] This essay will follow Tate and Geric in positioning poetry as a form of experiment, 'in the broad sense implied by John Hershel's definition of experiment, in his 1830 *Preliminary Discourse on the Study of Natural Philosophy*, as an "active observation" of nature, in which "we cross-examine our witness", which allows "us to make up our minds"'.[9] The poets considered here can be seen to 'cross-examine' scientific theory, testing its validity and analysing its potential cultural and societal impact.

Each of the theories covered in this essay – geological uniformitarianism, evolution, sexual selection and thermodynamics – revolutionised Victorian science and Victorian society. They were met by a wide spectrum of emotional responses: from outrage and fear to acceptance and celebration. The writers included here treat their poems as laboratories in which they can, under controlled conditions, apply new scientific theories to the human population and analyse the results. In doing so, they often pushed further than the scientists themselves were willing to go (Charles Lyell and Charles Darwin were famously reluctant to discuss their theories in relation to humankind). As Geric argues, poets writing about science helped to disseminate these ideas to a wider audience, but also gave it 'cultural meaning' and 'helped explain [science] to itself'.[10]

Geology and Uniformitarianism

In 1830 Charles Lyell published the first volume of *The Principles of Geology*, which set out to prove that '*no causes whatever* have from the earliest time to which we can look back, to the present, ever acted, but those *now acting*; and that they never acted with different degrees of energy from that which they now exert'.[11] That is, the topography of the earth (e.g., mountains and canyons) can be explained by forces witnessed in the present day. This may not seem controversial, but it flew in the face of accepted orthodoxy, which said that the earth had been shaped through periods of violent change happening at accelerated rates unlike anything observed in the present day, a theory known as catastrophism. Catastrophism was a comforting idea, as these periods of geological violence were the result of far different conditions than those of the nineteenth century, believed to be a period of stability.

In contrast, Lyell's theory of uniformitarianism suggested that geological change was an ongoing process, happening all around us. This was unsettling to Victorian society for a number of reasons. Uniformitarianism contended that the changes observed in the geologic record were not only capable of occurring again, but were in the *process* of occurring already. This included the extinction of species, which scientists like Georges Cuvier had previously speculated happened en masse during periods of violent geological change. Thus, in the stability of the nineteenth century, life on earth was safe. Uniformitarianism, in contrast, revealed the possibility of the extinction of modern life forms – including humankind.

Further unsettling for his audience was the fact that Lyell's theory of change via gradual and consistent processes like erosion, glacial advance and regular flooding necessitated a 'vast extension of the temporal framework within which understanding of geological processes was to be established'.[12] Lyell's theory required a time frame of many millions of years to be feasible, an idea which challenged both religious and scientific beliefs about the age of the earth. This was an amount of time that Charles Darwin would later insist 'the mind cannot possibly grasp'.[13] The incomprehensibility of deep time had the effect of estranging humanity from the history of the earth; it was impossible to reconstruct that amount of time into an intelligible narrative. Deep time also radically decentred humanity within that history. The relatively recent appearance of humans within the geologic record revealed that the world had existed for aeons *before* humankind, challenging the prevailing belief that the earth existed for the special use *of* humankind.

Alfred Tennyson is perhaps the most famous poet to have grappled with these ideas. Critics have long noted the influence of geology on Tennyson's verse, particularly *In Memoriam A.H.H.* (1850).[14] They often point to sections LV and LVI, in which Tennyson laments the cruelty of nature – 'red in tooth and claw' (LVI, 15) – and the brutality of extinction – 'From scarped cliff and quarried stone / She cries, "A thousand types are gone: / I care for nothing, all shall go"' (LVI, 2–4) – to suggest that Tennyson was deeply anxious about the new scientific theories of his age. In contrast, Michelle Geric argues that 'Tennyson had an enduring interest in geology ... [his] poetics specifically and consistently engaged with geological patterns of thinking, theories and ideas in and around geological time and the reading of fossil remains'.[15] Tennyson does what, in *Principles*, Lyell would not do: he applies uniformitarianism to humankind and examines the consequences. Geric argues that Tennyson uses poetry to 'test out the fitness of geological concepts, processes, and patterns of change', and thus his poems can be read as 'experiments in a uniformitarian poetics'.[16] *In Memoriam* does not just document Tennyson's anxieties; it works through them, charting his progress from anxiety to acceptance to actually drawing comfort from uniformitarianism.

In Memoriam enacts the conflict between catastrophism and uniformitarianism on the scale of the individual. Arthur Henry Hallam's death (the subject of the poem) is a catastrophe in Tennyson's life, a resolute break between Tennyson and Hallam and between past happiness and present sorrow. This is evident in the recurring reference to 'The path by which we twain did go' (XXII, 1), which 'bore thee where I could not see / Nor follow, though I walk in haste' (17–18). However, it is change, not death, that Tennyson fears. Tennyson never doubts that Hallam's spirit lives on in the afterlife; he worries that Hallam will forget him or become unrecognisable to him 'beyond the second birth of Death' (XLV, 16). It is the 'Eternal process moving on' (LXXXII, 5), which 'put our lives so far apart' (15), that he fears. Hallam's death is thus cast as a sudden, violent change which reshapes him into something so different it is practically unrecognisable. This is catastrophism.

Yet, the poem formally resists catastrophism. *In Memoriam* is fragmented into 133 parts of varying length, but the continuity of the poem's unchanging quatrains undermines that fragmentation. No changes in structure or rhyme mark the beginning or end of each section, just as Lyellian time has 'no discernible beginning or end'.[17] Tennyson's 'uniformitarian poetics' can be defined by continuity of form and repetition which enacts gradual change, as in the recurring events that mark the passage of time (Christmas and the anniversary of Hallam's death). This is further evident in the repetition of certain images, like a hand reaching out across time. Thus, the 'hand that can be clasped no more' (VII, 5) becomes a touch that exists only in the imagination, 'the dead man touched me from the past' (XCV, 34), and finally transforms into a moment of near palpable contact at the end of the poem, which reassures Tennyson that no final break has occurred between him and Hallam: 'I take the pressure of thine hand' (CXIX, 12). In contrast to the endless, purposeless repetition through time that some feared was revealed by uniformitarianism, Tennyson offers gradual change that leads to positive progression.

Positive progression is reflected in the poem's shift from catastrophism to uniformitarianism. In section CXVIII, Tennyson finds comfort in the continuity between past, present and future offered by uniformitarianism. 'Contemplate all this work of Time', the first line commands. The vastness of deep time combats the fragmentation of the fossil record and the frightening finality of extinction charted in sections LV and LVI. The earth now seems to offer reassuring continuity between stages of change, links that scientists can trace back through the depths of time. In this section, as Lyell demonstrated in the geologic record, 'time subsumes the greatest changes'.[18]

The poem concludes on hills that 'flow / From form to form' (CXXIII, 5–6), the verb 'flow' signalling the gradualism of uniformitarianism rather than the violent change of catastrophism. Like those hills, in the epilogue Tennyson finds that he too has been remade and changed over the course of the poem – '[the years] went and came,

/ Remade the blood and changed the frame' (10–11) – and has 'grown / To something greater than before' (19–20). Unlike at the start of the poem, here change is positive. Hallam has changed, but Tennyson is changing too, and he finds comfort in the idea that he will eventually arrive at Hallam's level. As Geric notes, uniformitarianism offers Tennyson 'a stable vision of an earth responding to measured, regular laws'.[19]

Evolution and Natural Selection

Though Lyell resisted the idea, his conception of deep time helped to pave the way for Charles Darwin's theory of evolution. Of course, the theory of evolution – the transmutation of species over time – did not begin with Darwin in 1859. It had been actively debated by the scientific community since the late eighteenth century, and was widespread in the public consciousness since the publication of Robert Chambers's *Vestiges of the Natural History of Creation* (1844). Nevertheless, Darwin's *On the Origin of Species* (1859) was still a watershed moment in the history of science because of his theory of natural selection. Previous accounts of evolution left room for a Creator – a higher power guiding progressive development. Natural selection, which posited random mutation and the 'struggle for survival' as the means of change, did not. As Peter J. Bowler notes, in Darwin's theory 'Nature was a scene of constant death and endless selfish struggle, hardly the sort of progress one would expect a benevolent God to establish'.[20] Darwinian evolution was not teleological – that is, moving towards a predetermined end or goal. Darwin's theory revealed that no life form is 'more' or 'better' evolved than any other, an idea which unsettled the deeply hierarchical Victorian society.

Though Darwin deliberately avoided discussing the origins of humankind, his readers inevitably extended his theory to themselves. The result was widespread outrage from the public, the church and even other scientists, and the topic would become the regular butt of satirical humour in the popular press of the period (Figure 16.1). Darwin was famously opposed by the leading naturalist of his day, Richard Owen, who argued that the newly discovered hippocampus in the human brain gave indisputable proof that man was not descended from apelike primates. Owen did not dispute evolution itself, but offered a counter-theory that maintained the possibility of a guiding Creator and the special status of humankind. It was the idea that humanity was not distinct from animals that truly shocked Victorian society.

Poets wrestled with this idea in a variety of ways. The Romantic poetic tradition had positioned the poet *in* nature but not *of* nature. Nature could soothe the Romantic poets and reflect their emotions, but on the whole they still stood apart from and above it. Post-Darwin, many poets sought to explore a humankind that was *of* nature, experimenting with the emotional and psychological outcome of such a scenario. For some, this could be positive. As John Holmes notes, 'The realisation

Figure 16.1 'Man is but a worm': cartoon by Edward Linley Sambourne in the *Punch Almanack* for 1882, published 6 December 1881.

that we are animals ourselves, not merely taxonomically but by nature, is another of the blows that Darwinism has struck at humanity's self-image. But it also changes fundamentally how we think about other animals, as we recognise that they are our kin and that they too are conscious creatures.'[21] The Bible told humankind that the natural world was *for* us, while Darwin insisted that the natural world *is* us.

For many, this led to a new ecological sensibility which sought to reckon with the often negative impact mankind has on the natural world. Yet others recognised the harshness of Darwinian nature and worried about the application of natural law to humankind – a concern fully warranted by the rise of social Darwinism in the second half of the nineteenth century, which used natural selection and competition to justify free markets, unlivable wages and a lack of social welfare.[22]

Much of the evolutionary poetry of the second half of the century responds to social Darwinism, testing the potential result of a humanity that is not just subject to but revels in the laws of nature. One such poem is George Meredith's *Modern Love* (1862). Sonnet 30, which begins 'What are we first? First, animals; and next / Intelligences at a leap' (1–2),[23] considers the impact of Darwinism on love and courtship. As Holmes argues, 'Since Darwin, sex has been at the very heart of biology ... natural selection only operates at all because of the variations between organisms thrown up during the process of reproduction.'[24] *Modern Love*, which charts a husband's and wife's infidelity, positions sex as a matter of instinct, yet viscerally confronts readers with the emotional impact of treating it as such: the sequence ends with the wife's suicide.

In sonnet 30, the speaker initially suggests that 'Love' can unite 'Intelligence and instinct' (8), the higher moral sentiments of man entwined with sexual instinct. However, this ideal is undermined by the fact that the sonnet is addressed to the husband's mistress, who is only ever a distraction from his wife's infidelity. Instead of love, it is cruelty that the sonnet explores. Nature is cruel, the poem argues, and makes humans cruel. The sonnet ends:

> Then if we study Nature, we are wise.
> Thus do the few who live but with the day:
> The scientific animals are they.–
> Lady, this is my sonnet to your eyes. (lines 13–16)

The shock of the ironic final line makes Meredith's point: to treat ourselves as mere 'scientific animals' certainly destroys romance, but perhaps even further destroys what is good about humanity – love, friendship, community. Meredith, in the end, argues that we must recognise that human intelligence and morality are also the product of evolution and thus rise above mere 'instinct'.

Sexual Selection

The ideas that Meredith explores in *Modern Love* were brought even further to the fore after the publication of Darwin's *Descent of Man* in 1871. Though Darwin discussed 'sexual selection' briefly in the *Origin*, it was in the second and third parts of *Descent* that he laid out the whole of this theory and its specific application to humanity. Sexual selection explains the differences in males and females of the same species in secondary sexual characteristics (those beyond reproductive organs). These can be traits that either aid competition between members of the same sex for access to the opposite sex, or aid in attracting members of the opposite sex; so, for instance, the antlers of a stag or the tail of a peacock.

Sexual selection introduces the intriguing notion of *choice* into evolution. Darwin compares sexual selection to artificial selection (such as when humans engineer a new breed of dog or orchid), writing, '[j]ust as man can give beauty, according to his standard of taste, to his male poultry ... so it appears that female birds in a state of nature, have by a long selection of the more attractive males, added to their beauty or other attractive qualities'.[25] In the animal kingdom, males, not females, needed to be beautiful to be desirable. It is *she* who chooses *him*. This emphasis on the power of female choice, especially in a society in which middle- and upper-class women often had their partners selected for them, seemed to some Victorians quite revolutionary.

The history of science typically portrays Darwin challenging Victorian beliefs, but in many ways Darwin's work actually reinforced existing gender ideologies. Darwin insisted that sexual selection – the necessity of males competing for female partners – explained the superiority of men in strength, intelligence and creativity:

> The chief distinction in the intellectual powers of the two sexes is shewn by man's attaining to a higher eminence, in whatever he takes up, than can woman – whether requiring deep thought, reason, or imagination, or merely the use of the senses and hands ... if men are capable of a decided pre-eminence over women in many subjects, the average of mental power in man must be above that of woman.[26]

Thus, a theory that superficially seemed to grant women agency and power was instead used to reinforce the dominant gender ideology of the age, rebranding a social construct as a biological reality.

In the above passage, Darwin simply restates the principle of biological essentialism, the commonly held belief that character and aptitude are determined by biology.[27] In the Victorian age, sexual difference was viewed as a binary opposition; this led to the widespread belief that the sexes were naturally complementary, destined for (allegedly) equal but opposite paths in life. Thus, woman's reproductive function was taken to mean she was suited for care work but not intellectual or creative endeavours. These ideas were inscribed in the popular imagination by Coventry Patmore in his enormously popular poem *The Angel in the House* (1854–62). The poem, which presents a slightly fictionalised version of Patmore's courtship of his first wife, is an exercise in benevolent sexism. Through praise of her 'natural' qualities, the speaker reinforces the belief that his future wife is destined for nothing more than marriage, motherhood and unending support of his creative practice. The poem portrays men and women as complementary opposites, like 'North and

South / And sun and moon'.[28] Through words like 'instinct' and 'impulse', Patmore presents women as *biologically* modest, virtuous, maternal, and self-sacrificing, allowing men to be naturally (and blamelessly) immoral and selfish. This lead to Patmore's assertion – in what is probably the most quoted passage of this poem – that 'Man must be pleased; but him to please / Is woman's pleasure'.[29]

The Angel in the House is an excellent example of Beer's 'two-way' traffic between science and culture. Patmore didn't invent the ideal of womanhood his poem celebrates; rather, he gave an existing ideology a catchy name. The ideal of the naturally self-sacrificing woman was, in part, drawn from scientific studies of the late eighteenth and early nineteenth centuries.[30] As Mary Poovey shows, however, these ideas didn't begin in science but in society; scientists studied the body in order to justify existing social hierarchies.[31] Patmore's poem then further verified the 'reality' of biological essentialism through its mixture of scientific, religious and literary discourses, which seemed to demonstrate that these ideas were transhistorical and cross-disciplinary. The commercial and cultural success of *The Angel in the House* gave further weight to essentialism, and ensured its widespread cultural currency at the time Darwin was writing the *Descent* and attempting to explain sexual difference. Science and culture reinforce one another.

Yet, scientific discourse can be invoked to support very conflicting ideologies. Writers turned to Darwin to justify misogyny *and* to support calls for women's rights. Constance Naden, who studied science at Mason College (later the University of Birmingham), responds to this tension in 'Evolutional Erotics' (1887).[32] This set of four poems 'interrogate[s] the triangulated relationship between science, poetry and British Victorian gender-based expectations', Andrea Tange argues.[33] 'Evolutional Erotics' tests Darwin's hypothesis that men are more intelligent than women in order to secure a mate by exploring the benefits of a scientific mind on courtship.

The speaker of 'Scientific Wooing' attempts to turn his scientific education to seduction, with lines like, 'Oh for a spectroscope to show / That in thy gentle eyes doth glow / Love's vapour, pure and incandescent!' (58–60). The humorous tone of the poem undermines the speaker's certainty in his romantic tactics. Thus, when he confidently asks 'can I fail to please / If with similitudes like these / I lure the maid to sweet communion?' (61–3), the reader is poised to answer with a resounding 'Yes!' However, these poems do not just repeat Meredith's insistence that viewing humanity as 'scientific animals' is unromantic. Rather, Naden uses her 'scientific' speakers to reveal the *intellectual* failings of these supposedly superior men. They fail to understand human nature, demonstrating significant gaps in their scientific educations, including the burgeoning late-Victorian fields of psychology and anthropology. They also demonstrate an insufficient understanding of the fields from whose lexicon they borrow. Thus, 'Scientific Wooing' ends with a confident '*Quod erat demonstrandum!*', a phrase traditionally placed at the end of a mathematical proof, meaning 'thus it has been demonstrated'. But the speaker has not yet attempted his scientific wooing, and thus all that has been 'demonstrated' is speculation and fantasy. He has determined the outcome before the experiment and believes a hypothesis is the same as a proof, which is simply bad science.

Tange argues that Naden gives us four very unsuited couples in 'Evolutional Erotics' in order to argue for the *biological necessity* of equality of the sexes: '[Naden] turns on its head the Victorian use of natural selection to essentialize an inferior "feminine" intellect by suggesting that if human intellectual progress depends on evolution, then only unions of like minds can succeed'.[34] Furthermore, the female choice so tantalisingly offered by Darwin's theory is reinstated in this sequence as the women rightly reject pompous men convinced of their own superiority. In this way, Naden suggests that it is not Darwin's *theory* that is wrong but the ideological interpretation of it that was used to naturalise women's inferior place in society. Rescued from that ideology, sexual selection could be the basis of what Marion Thain calls 'science-based feminism'.[35]

Thermodynamics and the End of the World

While Naden suggests that evolution could lead to social progress, the idea of progress of any form was brought up short at the close of the century by the idea of the end of the world. Victorian physics demonstrated that while energy is constant (the first law of thermodynamics), it is also subject to entropy, or transformation from a useful to a non-useful form (the second law of thermodynamics). Thus, William Thomson, Lord Kelvin, explained that while energy converted into heat is not 'annihilated', it is 'lost to man irrecoverably'.[36] Formulated in the 1850s, the second law of thermodynamics states that 'although mechanical energy is *indestructible*, there is a universal tendency to its dissipation, which produces gradual augmentation and diffusion of heat, cessation of motion, and exhaustion of potential energy through the material universe. The result would inevitably be a state of universal rest and death'.[37] Thomson explained that the sun's supply of energy 'is not inexhaustible'. Eventually it will run out of fuel. Victorian theories about what would follow varied; we know now that the sun will first expand into a red giant, and then will contract, shrinking to a white dwarf barely bigger than earth. The red giant may engulf earth in a fiery death, or may stop short of our planet, leaving it to turn to a planet of ice after the sun cools and contracts.

Though the coming heat death of the universe was identified in the 1850s, it was not until the end of the nineteenth century that the idea caught the public's attention.[38] Decadent literature of the 1880s and 1890s reflects the pessimism and even nihilism generated by the idea of the end of the world; its writers trace the impact of entropy on individuals, societies, empires and worlds, creating a body of literature obsessed with decline and death.

Not every writer responded with negativity, however. Like Naden, May Kendall used humour to engage with science, as in her poem 'Taking Long Views' (1887), which discusses theories of the coming destruction of the earth.[39] As Lee Behlman argues, the humour of so-called 'light verse' offers 'a philosophic position of detachment from and acceptance of life's suffering'.[40] 'Taking Long Views' reflects both acceptance and detachment: the poem accepts the coming end of the universe, but it suggests that it is absurd to fixate on something that won't happen for billions of years. Kendall, like Tennyson, turns to deep time as a source of comfort. Where Tennyson derived comfort from the permanence of the immortal soul, Kendall finds it in humanity's impermanence.

The first stanza of Kendall's poem mirrors that of Coleridge's 'Rime of the Ancient Mariner' (first published in 1798). Coleridge's 'wedding guest' is accosted by 'an ancient Mariner' with 'long beard and glittering eye' (1–3) and Kendall's speaker is confronted by a man whose 'locks were wild, and wild his eyes' (1–2). Both men have tales of ice, fire and doom to relate. This glance back to the Romantic period allows Kendall to take a 'long view' of the impact nineteenth-century science had on the conception of the individual and his or her place in the world. Romantic poetry centres on the individual and a nature which reflects his subjective experiences. In the 'Rime' the natural world responds to the actions of the Mariner; becalmed seas and violent storms are punishments for his sins, while favourable winds represent absolution. The events of the 'Rime' happen *to* the Mariner, while the questioner in Kendall's poem worries about events that will happen 'aeons' after his death, demanding to know 'shall we wander into space / Or fall into the sun?' (7–8). Kendall's poem draws attention to the newly realised insignificance of humanity within the scale of planetary time.

Kendall pokes fun at the decadent preoccupation with the eventual fate of the universe; after all, as her speaker says: 'However dark / The destiny the aeons bear, / *You* won't be here the wreck to mark' (57–9). Yet, it is this very fact that the questioner objects to, responding:

> *That* causes my despair.
> I want to know what will take place,
>   I want to see what will be done,
> *Oh, shall we wander into space*
>   *Or fall into the sun?* (lines 60–4)

It is his own absence from this planetary drama that distresses him. Humanity was used to thinking of itself as the centre of the universe, but here the questioner realises that not only will he personally never know the answer to this question, but no human will be able to 'see what will be done'; the earth will be uninhabitable long before either fate befalls it. Within the history of the earth, humanity is only a footnote.

In her tongue-in-cheek humour, Kendall turns this terrifying insignificance around, offering it as a source of comfort. While uniformitarianism, evolution and thermodynamics revealed the vast changes that had happened, were happening and will happen to the earth and its inhabitants, individuals are protected by their own transience. Nothing changes too drastically within the short life span of a human. As Holmes argues, 'the implication [of Kendall's poem] ... is that too great an obsession with science, or too much investment in it, can be debilitating'.[41] The questioner's anxieties – which define much of the literature of the 1880s and 1890s – are 'both crippling and ridiculous'.[42] It is absurd to worry *how* the world will end when you are sure *that* it will end; equally, it is absurd to worry about something that will happen long after humanity's extinction. Kendall thus offers a 'philosophic position of detachment' as the only reasonable or sane response to the science of the day.

Conclusion

In 'The Line of Beauty' (1881), Arthur O'Shaughnessy imagines the end of the world:

When mountains crumble and rivers all run dry,
  When every flower has fallen and summer fails
  To come again, when the sun's splendour pales,
And earth with lagging footsteps seems well-nigh
Spent in her annual circuit through the sky,[43]

In this bleak future landscape, he wonders, 'What is eternal? What escapes decay?' (9). The second law of thermodynamics says that nothing escapes decay. But O'Shaughnessy responds: 'a certain faultless, matchless, deathless line' (10) – the line of beauty. A scientist and a poet, O'Shaughnessy contrasts the material world that science explains with a metaphysical world understood only through art. He invokes Plato's Theory of Forms, the belief in immaterial essences, like Beauty, that exist beyond the material world, to insist that while science can tell us the eventual fate of the physical universe, it cannot speak to what exists beyond it.

Each of the poets we have considered similarly expresses faith in abstract concepts which transcend natural law: Tennyson's belief in the eternal soul; Meredith's insistence that we have evolved to be more than 'scientific animals'; Naden's hopes for a more equal future; Kendall's optimism in the face of the end of the world. Like O'Shaughnessy, they suggest that science's remit stops at the material world, while art extends beyond into the immaterial, the eternal, the moral. It is for this reason that they advocate for exchange between the arts and the sciences; both are needed to make sense of the world. These poets remind us that humanity is subject to, but not bound by, natural laws.

NOTES

1. Gillian Beer, *Darwin's Plots: Evolutionary Narrative in Darwin, George Eliot and Nineteenth-Century Fiction*, 2nd edn (Cambridge University Press, 2000), p. 7.
2. John Holmes, *The Pre-Raphaelites and Science* (New Haven and London: Yale University Press, 2018), p. 10.
3. Ibid., p. 33.
4. Ibid., p. 38.
5. Clare Stainthorp, *Constance Naden: Scientist, Philosopher, Poet* (Oxford: Peter Lang, 2019), pp. 2, 14.
6. Michelle Geric, *Tennyson and Geology: Poetry and Poetics* (London: Palgrave Macmillan, 2017), p. 8.
7. Gregory Tate, *Nineteenth-Century Poetry and the Physical Sciences: Poetical Matter* (Cham: Palgrave Macmillan, 2020), p. 68.
8. Geric, *Tennyson and Geology*, p. 6.
9. Tate, *Nineteenth-Century Poetry*, p. 3.
10. Geric, *Tennyson and Geology*, p. 6.
11. Lyell writing to Roderick Murchison, quoted ibid., p. 81.
12. Peter Dear, 'Darwin and Deep Time: Temporal Scales and the Naturalist's Imagination', *History of Science* 54 (2016), 3–18 (3).
13. Charles Darwin, *On the Origin of Species*, ed. Gillian Beer (Oxford University Press, 2008), p. 354.
14. Alfred Tennyson, 'In Memoriam A.H.H.', in Thomas J. Collins and Vivienne J. Rundle (eds), *The Broadview Anthology of Victorian Poetry and Poetic Theory* (Peterborough, Ontario: Broadview Press, 2005), pp. 204–53; subsequent references to section and line are incorporated in the main text.
15. Geric, *Tennyson and Geology*, p. 2.
16. Ibid., pp. 6, 13.
17. Ibid., p. 117.
18. Ibid., p. 137.
19. Ibid., p. 92.
20. Peter J. Bowler, *Monkey Trials & Gorilla Sermons* (Cambridge, MA: Harvard University Press, 2007), p. 91.
21. John Holmes, *Darwin's Bards: British and American Poetry in the Age of Evolution* (Edinburgh University Press, 2009), p. xiii.
22. See Mike Hawkins, *Social Darwinism in European and American Thought, 1860–1945: Nature as Model and Nature as Threat* (Cambridge University Press, 1997).
23. George Meredith, 'Modern Love', in Collins and Rundle (eds), *Broadview Anthology of Victorian Poetry*, pp. 793–805; subsequent references to lines are incorporated in the main text.
24. Holmes, *Darwin's Bards*, p. 185.
25. Charles Darwin, *The Descent of Man, and Selection in Relation to Sex*, 2nd edn (London: John Murray, 1874), p. 211.
26. Ibid., p. 564.
27. Cynthia Eagle Russett, *Sexual Science: The Victorian Construction of Womanhood* (Cambridge, MA: Harvard University Press, 1989), p. 6.

28. Coventry Patmore, *The Angel in the House*, 4th edn (London and Cambridge: Macmillan, 1866), p. 23.

29. Ibid., p. 48.

30. Mary Poovey, *Uneven Developments: The Ideological Work of Gender in Mid-Victorian England* (University of Chicago Press, 1988), p. 6.

31. Ibid.

32. Constance Naden, *A Modern Apostle; The Elixer of Life; The Story of Clarice; and other poems* (London: Kegan Paul, 1887), pp. 135–47; subsequent references to lines are incorporated in the main text.

33. Andrea Kaston Tange, 'Constance Naden and the Erotics of Evolution: Mating the Woman of Letters with the Man of Science', *Nineteenth-Century Literature* 61 (2006), 200–40 (203).

34. Ibid., 238.

35. Marion Thain, '"Scientific Wooing": Constance Naden's Marriage of Science and Poetry', *Victorian Poetry* 41 (2003), 151–69 (161).

36. William Thomson, 'On the Dynamical Theory of Heat', *Transactions of the Royal Society of Edinburgh* 20 (1853), 261–88 (271).

37. William Thomson, 'On the Age of the Sun's Heat', *Macmillan's Magazine* 5 (1862), 388–93 (388).

38. Ted Underwood, *The Work of the Sun: Literature, Science, and Political Economy, 1760–1860* (New York: Palgrave Macmillan, 2005), p. 179.

39. May Kendall, *Dreams to Sell* (London: Longmans, Green, 1887), pp. 20–2.

40. Lee Behlman, 'The Case of Light Verse or *vers de société*', *Victorian Poetry* 56 (2018), 477–91 (478).

41. John Holmes, '"The Lay of the Trilobite": Rereading May Kendall', *19: Interdisciplinary Studies in the Long Nineteenth Century* 11 (2010), 1–15 (7).

42. Ibid., 6.

43. Arthur O'Shaugnessy, *Songs of a Worker* (London: Chatto & Windus, 1881), p. 106, lines 1–5; subsequent references are incorporated in the main text.

CRITICAL REFLECTIONS AND FURTHER STUDY

I began this essay as you should begin any research project: by doing some general reading. One thing that students sometimes get wrong is that they limit their secondary reading to a very narrow field, for instance only reading essays on the specific author they plan to write about. Better practice is to identify the 'big ideas' you wish to engage with and read general works on that topic. So, for my essay, I explored a range of works on Victorian poetry and science. I was already familiar with the foundational works in this field: Lionel Stevenson, *Darwin among the Poets* (1932; New York: Russell & Russell, 1963); Tess Cosslett, *The 'Scientific Movement' and Victorian Literature* (Brighton: Harvester Press, 1982); Gillian Beer, *Darwin's Plots* (1983; see my essay, note 1); George Levine (ed.), *One Culture: Essays in Science and Literature* (Madison: University of Wisconsin Press, 1987); Mary Midgley, *Science and Poetry* (London: Routledge,

2001); and John Holmes's *Darwin's Bards* (2009; see my essay, note 21). However, there were some recent publications I had not yet had the opportunity to read, including the works by Gregory Tate, Michelle Geric and John Holmes, that underpin much of my essay (see my essay, notes 2, 6 and 7). John Holmes's *The Pre-Raphaelites and Science* (2018) is a good example of the necessity of reading widely; my essay barely touches on the poets known as the 'Pre-Raphaelites', yet Holmes's book has an argument that ranges far beyond that movement. Geric, too, superficially seems like she might have quite a narrow topic – *Tennyson and Geology* – but her introduction offers a compelling analysis of the broader relationship between poetry and science in the nineteenth century.

NARROWING DOWN THE TOPIC

Having brushed up on the recent contributions to the field, I began to think about how to shape my own essay. The nature of the topic seemed to demand a fairly broad overview of the period as I knew I wanted to address several different scientific theories to develop my theme. Looking back on Victorian science, it is tempting to focus only on Charles Darwin. His is the name that everyone knows and, crucially, he was 'right'. As the section of my essay on sexual selection shows, however, Darwin was not free from the biases of his society and nor was he entirely correct in his ideas. For instance, he did not know about genes and genetics, which are central to our modern understanding of evolution. When we think about the history of ideas, we need to look past what was 'right' in order to understand what was widespread or popular. It is essential to engage with science of the past on its own terms, and to attempt to reconstruct how it was understood during that period. Peter J. Bowler's work provides important insight into how to go about this: see, for example, his *Evolution: The History of an Idea* (University of California Press, 1983) and *The Non-Darwinian Revolution* (Baltimore: Johns Hopkins University Press, 1988). Similarly, in choosing my poets, I wanted to include those like Coventry Patmore who were enormously popular during their time, but little read now. The canonical texts that we study today were not always the most read in their own historical moment.

There are any number of groundbreaking scientific ideas I could have covered in this essay, but I wanted to focus on those which fundamentally shifted how the average person viewed the world and their place within it. It is hard, sometimes, to put ourselves in the mindset of someone in the past, but it is worth trying to think about how you would react to something that completely upended your understanding of the world in the way that deep time, extinction, evolution, and heat death did in the nineteenth century. It might be akin to discovering that aliens exist and they had, in fact, been visiting earth for millennia. Some people would feel vindicated, while many others would be terrified. Our belief in our 'special status' in the universe would be overthrown. How would this affect how we understand our selves? The chapter entitled 'Humanity's Place in Nature' in Holmes's *Darwin's Bards* is a good starting place to think about these ideas.

SHAPING THE ARGUMENT

I began my essay with Gillian Beer's assertion of the 'two-way traffic' between literature and science in the Victorian era. This is important to me, because too often when we talk about the relationship between the arts and the sciences, it is suggested that art's role is to communicate science to the masses (ignoring the fact that sci-comm, or science communications, already exists). This suggests that literature is the 'handmaiden' to science – that is, subservient to science. Instead, whenever you approach an interdisciplinary or cross-disciplinary topic, like this one, try to think about them as equal participants in the exchange. What does poetry gain from science? What does science gain from poetry? What can poetry do that science can't, and vice versa? These questions helped to shape my argument.

As I state, nineteenth-century scientists often were unwilling to apply their theories to humanity, for fear of religious backlash. But as geologists, biologists and physicists, they were also unable to speak to human psychology, to theology and to ethics. Here, the arts are needed. It is this contention that forms the backbone of my argument: that poetry is an experiment in human nature, and thus can test the application of scientific theory to humanity.

QUESTIONS FOR FURTHER STUDY

There are many other Victorian poets who engage with science: you might consider Robert Browning, Matthew Arnold, Mathilde Blind, A. C. Swinburne, Agnes Marie Robinson, Thomas Hardy or Gerard Manley Hopkins, among many others. In looking at any one of these poets, ask yourself:

1. Does the poem engage with science on the level of theory, method, or conclusions reached?
2. Can the poem be read as an experiment (e.g., does it have a hypothesis which it 'tests' in a controlled way)?
3. What 'truth' does the poem seem to be seeking or asserting? Is it a material or a moral one?
4. What kind of 'two-way traffic' is evident? What does the poem do or offer that science cannot?

17 'In Characters of Tint Indelible': Life Writing and Legacy in Charlotte Brontë's *Villette*

MARIA FRAWLEY

Abstract

A life writing focus enables dimensions of Charlotte Brontë's ambitious and multifaceted exploration of the self in *Villette*, too easily overlooked when the novel is reductively categorised as autobiographical, to come into view. Although Brontë clearly drew on a range of actual experiences and real persons for *Villette*, her final novel demonstrates the extent to which her wide-ranging interest in complexities of self-understanding, self-presentation and concepts of personhood expand the remit of her fiction. Reading *Villette* alongside correspondence written by Charlotte Brontë reveals just how central feeling and emotion were to Brontë's understanding of the truth claims of a work of art. This essay identifies loneliness and the corollary fear of being forgotten as linchpin emotions experienced by Charlotte Brontë (particularly at the time she drafted *Villette*) and vividly represented in her heroine Lucy Snowe's narrative as she constructs what she refers to as a 'book of life'. For both, letters function as life-sustaining 'tokens' of remembrance, tools with which to manage loneliness and counter the perceived threat of being forgotten. This emphasis in *Villette* is amplified through Brontë's nuanced use of a rhetoric of writing more generally, which she invokes both to convey experiences of deeply knowing and being known by another and to anchor and make permanent the memories used to structure her narrative. She writes, in other words, 'in characters of tint indelible', as an expression of love, the emotion that Brontë herself posited as impervious to decay and a guarantor of immortality. Elizabeth Gaskell's *The Life of Charlotte Brontë*, relying heavily as it does on Brontë's letters, extends an understanding of the relationship between life writing and legacy so richly examined in *Villette*.

Charlotte Brontë's *Villette* (1853) might well be the nineteenth-century novel's most sustained study of a character's interiority (Figure 17.1).[1] Part of Brontë's achievement is to develop her heroine Lucy Snowe's inner world not only through passages of intense self-examination but in moments when Lucy's attention is drawn away from herself. Consider, for example, chapter 23, 'Vashti', the subject

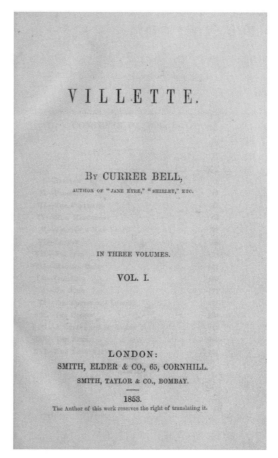

Figure 17.1 Charlotte Brontë, published under the name of Currer Bell, title page of vol. I of *Villette*, 1853.

of much critical attention.[2] In this chapter Lucy describes a theatrical performance depicting the famous figure from the Book of Esther, a beautiful woman banished for her refusal to follow the king's orders to appear at his banquet. The episode was based on Brontë's experience of the performances of the famous French actress Elisa Félix, known as 'Rachel'.[3] Lucy Snowe has a strong response to the actress and describes the spectacle as 'low, horrible, immoral' (p. 299). She then eagerly searches the face of her companion, 'Dr John', to ascertain his response, which she describes as a 'branding judgment'. The episode concludes with Lucy's telling comment that the night 'was already marked in [her] book of life, not with white, but with a deep-red cross' (p. 301). She continues, 'But I had not done with it yet; and other memoranda were destined to be set down in characters of tint indelible'.

The passage is one of many in the novel that showcase the extent to which Lucy Snowe draws on the rhetoric and practice of writing to secure her memories and render them permanent. Such passages foreground the textual nature of her narrative, what she refers to here as her 'book of life', while also signalling just how plagued Lucy is by a fear of being forgotten. Throughout *Villette*, Lucy recounts incidents and events in her life, and her narration is often laden with the emotional response the situations elicited. Yet she also on occasion, as in the passage referring to her 'book of life', steps back to remind readers that she was even then, in the immediacy of a particular moment, compiling a register of sorts, one that she presumably draws on much later to construct her narrative. If some events from her past were to be forever lost to memory, others were 'set down in characters of tint indelible' and made permanent.

I want to use this multivalent episode, and specifically Lucy Snowe's reference to her 'book of life', as a starting point from which to consider *Villette* through the lens of life writing. My invocation of 'life writing', as opposed to 'autobiography' or even 'autobiographical fiction', is deliberate. The wider and more flexible lens of 'life writing' – made possible by scholarship that has burgeoned in the past few decades – broadens the range of novelistic components that can be marshalled for study as constituting an autobiographical agenda; and it invites more robust recognition of the multivalent interplay of genres and narrative modes that may be deployed by the life writer in a given text. Commenting that 'Victorian life-writings do a great deal more than narrate lives or describe selves', Trev Lynn Broughton contends,

> Life-writers intervened in and helped to shape contemporaneous debates about the meaning and constitution of self-hood; they posed questions about the nature of individualism and individuality; they explored the cultural uses of publicity, privacy, intimacy, and sociability; they investigated the production and commodification of identity; they sometimes even experimented with ideas of an embodied self.[4]

Villette could profitably be studied from the vantage point of any one of these objectives, so multifaceted is its investigation of Lucy Snowe's sense of self. 'Lucy Snowe is not one but several selves', Anna Gibson has written.[5] Depending on her situation or mood, Brontë's narrator might describe herself as a 'wan spectacle' (p. 39), a 'fugitive' (p. 134) or a 'mere looker-on at life' (p. 162). She frequently emphasises her felt erasure from the world, describing herself at one point as 'living my own life in my own still, shadow-world' (p. 134) and at another as 'a mere shadowy spot on a field of light' (p. 150). Lucy at times invokes the third person to speak of and to herself, sometimes in an act of overt self-regulation (e.g., 'Well done, Lucy Snowe, cried I to myself' (p. 387)) and sometimes in a mock-testimonial stance: 'I, Lucy Snowe, plead guiltless of that curse, an overheated and discursive imagination', she writes by way of contrasting herself to the young Paulina (Polly) Home (p. 11). She often engages in what she describes as 'deep argument[s] with [herself] on life and its chances, on destiny and her decrees' (p. 286). She is keenly attentive to how others see her. An older woman (Miss Marchmont) asks her to be her 'chaplain' (p. 45); a younger woman (Polly) calls her 'Spartan girl' (p. 494). She writes that she 'seemed to hold two lives—the life of thought, and that of reality' (p. 86). Her relationship to her readers is just as varied and unstable: she is a self-proclaimed 'faithful narrator' (p. 228) as well as a 'partial eulogist' (p. 229). She toys with readers from early on, inviting them at one point to picture her sailing peacefully beneath the sunshine and then abruptly writing: 'Cancel the whole of that, if you please, reader—or rather let it stand, and draw then a moral—an alliterative, text-hand copy—*Day-dreams are delusions of the demon*' (p. 62). At one critical juncture, Lucy refers to the story she is writing as a 'heretic narrative' (p. 186). In these moments, one senses Charlotte Brontë moving beyond the customary remit of autobiographical fiction to a far more wide-ranging approach to narrative as a tool for investigating the complexities of self-understanding, self-presentation and personhood.

Despite the range and ambition of the study of selfhood evident in *Villette*, Brontë's personal life story has long exerted a powerful hold on its interpretation. Tom Winnifrith, surveying Brontë biography from its beginnings, blames Elizabeth Gaskell's biography, *The Life of Charlotte Brontë*, published in 1855. Gaskell's text 'probably encouraged readers to see the novels as autobiographical, a vision damaging to biography and criticism', Winnifrith concludes.[6] As Sue Lonoff has written, Charlotte Brontë 'seems to have pieced every scrap of her experience into the fabric of her fiction. Characters, episodes, methods of instruction, allusions to her readings and to cultural events gave her matter for all four of her novels'.[7] Co-editors of the Modern Library edition of *Villette*, A. S. Byatt and Ignês Sodré, echo legions of Brontë biographers and critics when they begin their introduction by describing it as 'Charlotte Brontë's last, strongly autobiographical novel' (p. xiiv). Since its publication, Brontë's readers have been keen to identify autobiographical elements in the novel, shaped as it was by her experiences in the early 1840s as a student in Brussels, Belgium, at the Pensionnat Héger and particularly by her relationship while there to Constantin Héger, a married man and powerful intellectual influence.[8] Moreover, the arc covered by Lucy Snowe's narrative – it begins with her girlhood and ends late in life – combined with the first-person narration imbue the novel with an autobiographical flavour even without a reader's knowledge of Charlotte Brontë's lived experiences. Just as in *Jane Eyre*, subtitled 'An Autobiography', Brontë drew on the tropes and structure of fictional autobiography, as well as on her own experiences, when she wrote *Villette*.

Yet to frame the novel as autobiographical risks being reductive, particularly when the autobiographical is understood to reference the factually accurate. Just as Lucy Snowe manipulates and thwarts her readers' expectations, so Charlotte Brontë deliberately stymies readers intent on extracting from her last novel much 'data' about her actual experiences abroad, or her real relationship with Monsieur Héger, or any other tangible facet of her life. What *Villette* instead provides is evidence that a 'book of life' is a necessarily kaleidoscopic enterprise, where immediacy and the retrospective commingle, where different modes of narration and temporalities can and must be drawn on to accurately convey (or, conversely, to withhold) experience and emotion; and where the author not only reflects but also constructs an understanding of personhood and a sense of self, rendering that self obliquely, but, as Brontë put it, 'in characters of tint indelible'.

Through its multifaceted representation of Lucy Snowe's mind, *Villette* reveals the complicated but essential relationship between life writing and affect, the emotional dimensions of lived experience and the vexed functions of memory as a conduit for emotional experience. Consider by way of illustration the moment from chapter 12 when Lucy writes, 'Oh, my childhood! I had feelings: passive as I lived, little as I spoke, cold as I looked, when I thought of past days, I could feel. About the present, it was better to be stoical; about the future—such a future as mine—to be dead. And in catalepsy and a dead trance, I studiously held the quick of my nature' (p. 124). Lucy experiences the present as besieged and overtaken by both experienced past and anticipated future; it is rendered inert in the process. Brontë conveys not only the fluidity of Lucy's experience of time but also the intersubjective dimensions of her sense of self – the deliberate ways she wrestles with an awareness of how others see her. This preoccupation surfaces forcefully in *Villette*'s early episodes, and it manifests itself throughout Lucy's later time in the city of Villette, where she is viewed and judged as an English woman, a Protestant. At one point Lucy reflects, 'What contradictory attributes of character we sometimes find ascribed to us, according to the eye with which we are viewed' (p. 348). Brontë also registers well in the passage from chapter 12 the emotional stakes of her narrator's attempts at stoic self-control, holding 'the quick of [her] nature' at bay. In this and kindred moments in *Villette*, readers grasp a dimension of its autobiographical status not linked to a specific event but rather to its author's disposition and fraught emotional state.

Villette, drafted after Charlotte Brontë's siblings had died and during a period in which she lived alone in Haworth with her nearly blind father, is at its most autobiographical when she represents Lucy's profound loneliness, her anxieties about her isolation and her fears for her future. Elizabeth Gaskell includes a revealing excerpt of a letter written to a Brussels schoolmate in April of 1852, while Brontë was working on *Villette*: 'I struggled through the winter, and the early part of the spring, with great difficulty ... It cannot be denied that the solitude of my position fearfully aggravated its other evils. Some long stormy days and nights there were, when I felt such a craving for support and companionship as I cannot express'.[9] A letter to her close friend Ellen Nussey, written in August of that same year, goes further in exposing the depths her despair. To Nussey she wrote: 'I am silent because I have literally *nothing to say*. I might indeed repeat over and over again that my life is a pale blank and often a very weary burden—and that the Future sometimes appals me—but what end could be answered by such repetition except to weary you and enervate myself?'[10] Brontë draws on multiple meanings of *appals* here: that which incites horror and despair, but also growing pale, whitening, and thereby rendering something – in this case her life – blank. Applying the word to her sense of her own Future (capitalising the 'F' as if to magnify its threat), Brontë's affective kinship to her literary creation, Lucy Snowe, is indubitable.[11]

Other portions of Charlotte Brontë's correspondence confirm that she understood the truthfulness of *Villette* not as a matter of its exactitude in depicting situations or persons but instead as a matter of tone, with tone understood as an emotion. Feeling (and its inevitable counterpart in Brontë's writing, the repression of feeling), she suggests, lies at the heart of the writing enterprise, both Lucy Snowe's and her own. In correspondence with publisher William Smith Williams when her novel was nearly finished, she anticipates her readers' responses in just these terms and articulates her position in rhetoric remarkably like Lucy Snowe's description of the 'tints indelible' with which she recorded events in her life. Brontë writes: 'Still – I fear they must be satisfied with what is offered: my palette affords no brighter tints – were I to attempt to deepen the reds or burnish the yellows – I should but botch. Unless I am mistaken – the emotion of the book will be found to be kept throughout in tolerable subjection' (*Life of Charlotte Brontë*, p. 485). Brontë fuses life and fiction; the soft colours of the 'palette' with which she 'paints' refer to her limited life experiences, living a largely reclusive and, as she sees it, monochromatic life in Haworth. Many of *Villette*'s readers would disagree with her contention that its emotion is 'kept throughout in tolerable subjection' – the novel is, like much of its author's correspondence, a treasure trove of its heroine's affective life, where emotions are anticipated, experienced, represented, thought about and managed with varying degrees of success. Of the emotions that occupy positions of prominence in *Villette,* most have a negative valence – loneliness, estrangement and anxiety, a gamut that runs from despair at one end to what Brontë describes as 'flatness of spirits' at the other (*Life of Charlotte Brontë*, p. 274).

While nearly every episode of *Villette* touches in some way on Lucy Snowe's sense of seclusion and isolation from others, the chapter that follows on from the episode with Vashti exposes an important feature of her response to that loneliness. Chapter 24 begins:

> Those who live in retirement, whose lives have fallen amid the seclusion of schools
> or of other walled-in and guarded dwellings, are liable to be suddenly and for a
> long while dropped out of the memory of their friends, the denizens of a freer world.
> Unaccountably ... there falls a stilly pause, a wordless silence, a long blank of oblivion.
> Unbroken always is this blank; alike entire and unexplained. The letter, the message,
> once frequent, are cut off; the visit, formerly periodical, ceases to occur; the book,
> paper, or other token that indicated remembrance, comes no more. (p. 308)

Lucy goes on to hypothesise about the life of the hermit, one who, she imagines, struggles to endure 'weeks of an inward winter', and she compares herself to a dormouse, forced to wall itself in when coldness arrives, not knowing if its 'snow-sepulchre' will one day open, if it will survive the long months of cold (p. 309). The chapter's opening commentary underscores the extent to which Lucy believes herself at this particular juncture to have been 'dropped out of the memory' of her small set of friends, leaving her – as she experiences it – alone within 'a stilly pause, a wordless silence, a long blank of oblivion' not unlike the 'pale blank' that Brontë wrote of to Ellen Nussey when describing her life in Haworth. As importantly, Lucy relies on textual signs to counter that isolation, to know and feel that she has not been forgotten.

Crucially, letters function as 'tokens', less to remind her of others than to comfort herself with the feeling of having been remembered. Time itself is likened, in Lucy's imagination, to paper on which her life is imprinted, if she is to know herself to exist. The seven weeks of her 'stilly pause' are thus described 'as bare as seven sheets of blank paper: no word was written on one of them; not a visit, not a token' (p. 309). As the chapter unfolds, Lucy becomes increasingly honest about the depths of despair caused by her solitude, writing 'I underwent in those seven weeks bitter fears and pains, strange inward trials, miserable defections of hope, intolerable encroachments of despair' (p. 310). Again, she posits a need for textual evidence in the form of a letter to put an end to her misery, the misery of thinking herself forgotten: 'The letter—the well-beloved letter—would not come; and it was all of sweetness in life I had to look for' (p. 310). She incessantly rereads five letters previously sent to her by Dr John to bide her time and manage her depression, although she admits that they eventually lose 'all sap and significance' and that she becomes 'as thin as a shadow' (p. 311), the last phrase offering a haunting indication of the fragility of her sense of self.

The extracts of letters that Elizabeth Gaskell wove into her biography make clear that Charlotte Brontë, like Lucy Snowe, relied on correspondence sent to her Haworth home to maintain her emotional equilibrium (Figure 17.2). Her appeals to friends for letters are tinged with desperation even before her sisters died. 'You must write to me,' she implored Mary Taylor in 1845. 'If you knew how welcome your letters are, you would write very often. Your letters, and the French newspapers, are the only messengers that come to me from the outer world beyond our moors ... ' (*Life of Charlotte Brontë*, p. 549). Corresponding with Ellen Nussey late in 1846, Brontë writes of her 'haunting terror lest you should imagine I forget you – that my regard cools with absence' (*Life of Charlotte Brontë*, p. 310). 'It is not in my nature to forget your nature,' she continues, her word choice suggestive of the way forgetting was linked in her mind to potent feelings about being truly or deeply known. When Nussey had to back out of an engagement to visit

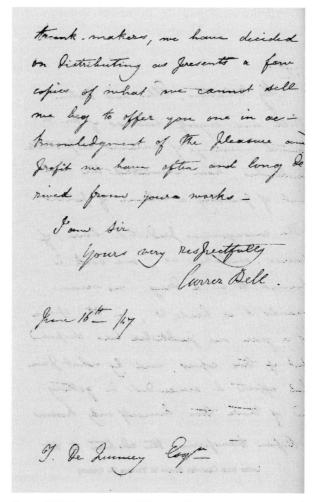

Figure 17.2 Charlotte Brontë, letter to Thomas De Quincey, signed with the pen name Currer Bell, 17 June 1847.

at Haworth, Brontë sent a terse note in return, writing of her 'cruel chill of disappointment' (*Life of Charlotte Brontë*, p. 315).

This particular dimension of Charlotte Brontë's affective life was not disconnected from her professional life. In her biography, Elizabeth Gaskell takes note of Brontë's attentiveness to reviews – they were not just of professional interest, but satisfied her need for notice and prompted opportunities for further correspondence. At one point Gaskell quotes Brontë as having written to a friend, 'The reappearance of the *Athenaeum* is very acceptable, not merely for its own sake ... but because as a weekly token of the remembrance of friends, it cheers and gives pleasure' (*Life of Charlotte Brontë*, p. 423). If Brontë's experience of isolation produced fears of being forgotten, those emotions mingled with anxiety about how much she wanted literary notice and fame. Shortly after publishing *Shirley*, Brontë wrote to the critic George Henry Lewes that 'out of obscurity I came, to obscurity I can easily return' (*Life of Charlotte Brontë*, p. 386). In the gap of time between finishing *Shirley* and beginning *Villette*, she wrote to William Smith Williams: 'You inquire after *Currer Bell*. It seems to me that the absence of his name from your list of announcements will leave no blank' (*Life of Charlotte Brontë*, p. 461). Writing several months later to Ellen Nussey, she again invokes the 'obscurity' of her status and situation: '[t]he most profound obscurity is infinitely preferable to vulgar notoriety' (*Letters*, p. 105). Such claims are belied by Lucy Snowe, who eschews 'the eating rust of obscurity' (p. 52), not wanting to 'moulder' there 'for the rest of [her] life' (p. 87).

Whatever her comfort level with obscurity, the emotion that Charlotte Brontë betrays in her letters about her own need for correspondence, whether personal or professional, helps one better appreciate the significance when, nearing the end of *Villette*, Lucy tells her readers that she steadily received letters from Paul Emanuel after he had departed:

> By every vessel he wrote; he wrote as he gave and as he loved, in full-handed, full-hearted plenitude. He wrote because he liked to write; he did not abridge, because he cared not to abridge. He sat down, he took pen and paper, because he loved Lucy and had much to say to her; because he was faithful and thoughtful, because he was tender and true ... his letters were real food that nourished, living water that refreshed. (pp. 571–2)

The repetition and emphasis of the passage is striking ('he wrote', 'he did not abridge', 'he took pen and paper'), and her word choices accrue meaning in light of what her readers have learned along the way about the value of letters as 'tokens of remembrance' and signs of her very existence. The frequency of Paul's letter writing affirms her importance to him; the spirit in which she understands the letters to have been written deeply satisfy her, so much so that she likens them to the most basic necessities of life – food and water. The letters sustain her; they enable her to experience herself as alive.

The whole of *Villette* – Lucy Snowe's 'book of life' – might be similarly understood as an act of self-preservation. In light of the emotional weight that letters have as 'tokens' that preserve memory, her narrative ensures that she herself will not be forgotten, consigned to the 'eating rust' of obscurity or to a 'long blank of oblivion'. Chapter 31 depicts how Lucy approaches life writing. The chapter features her again seeking to identify 'an object in life' while simultaneously acknowledging that, as a Christian, she believes 'this life is not all; neither the beginning nor the end' (p. 419). She then concludes:

> It is right to look our life-accounts bravely in the face now and then, and settle them honestly. And he is a poor self-swindler who lies to himself while he reckons the items,

and sets down under the head happiness that which is misery. Call anguish–anguish, and despair–despair; write both down in strong characters with resolute pen: you will the better pay your debt to Doom. Falsify; insert 'privilege' where you should have written 'pain'; and see if your mighty creditor will allow the fraud to pass, or accept the coin with which you would cheat him. Offer to the strongest–if the darkest angel of God's host–water, when he has asked blood–will he take it? Not a whole pale sea for one red drop. I settled another account. (pp. 419–20)

A rhetoric of writing infuses this sermon-like speech, which is directed to her self as well as her imagined readers. Her invocation of the term 'life-accounts' to frame her thoughts is worth highlighting, connoting both a written narrative of events and situations but also an evidentiary document, a record that consigns what has been recorded (her life story) to permanency. Notably, Lucy's emphasis is on emotions as the proper content for her 'life-account', and she counsels herself to record her anguish and despair. 'Write both down in strong characters with resolute pen' suggests the discipline and punishment of a self-imposed exercise; 'I settled another account' reinforces a resolute acceptance of what God has been meted out. The language is reminiscent of the 'deep red cross' that Lucy used in her record of the evening she saw 'Vashti' perform.

Lucy's urge to record her emotions, making them 'indelible', dovetails with the novel's relentless examination of experiences of being remembered or forgotten. Early on, when she seeks out the counsel of an old family servant as to her plans for work after Miss Marchmont has died, she notes, 'Me she had forgotten. I was changed, too, though not I fear, for the better. I made no attempt to recall myself to her memory; why should I?' (p. 48). Later, when Dr John returns Lucy to the *pensionnat* after an extended recuperation from illness at his mother's home, he senses her fear and promises her, 'We will not forget you' (p. 264). Such moments anticipate two more consequential episodes of Lucy's subsequent experiences, the first when she feels herself condemned to have to 'forget' Dr John (and to bury his letters) and the second when she understands herself to be commanded by Madame Beck and her co-conspirators to 'forget' Paul Emanuel, even in advance of his planned departure ('Forget him?' she writes. 'Ah! They took a safe plan to make me forget him–the wiseheads! They showed me how good he was' (p. 461)). Moreover, Monsieur Paul keenly understands this dimension of her personality, as the conversation taking place soon after he has learned of his impending need to travel reveals:

'Petite sœur,' said he: 'how long could you remember me if we were separated?'

'That, monsieur, I can never tell, because I do not know how long it will be before I shall cease to remember everything earthly.' (p. 444)

Lucy's determination not to forget Paul, or to be forgotten by him, is a function of having come to deeply know him and to experience herself as truly known by him. Ignês Sodré, in the introduction to *Villette*, is spot on in her assessment that 'Lucy—like Jane Eyre before her—wants to be profoundly known' (p. xxxi). Here again Brontë's interest in expanding the remit of autobiographical fiction to explore foundational matters of selfhood comes into view. *Villette* explores in a multitude of ways Lucy Snowe's experience of *not* being understood by, or fully known to, others. In many ways she strategically resists being known, as, for example, when she takes care that Madame Beck, rifling through her belongings, does not see that she is seen. On one such occasion, Lucy explains:

> The searcher might have turned and caught me; there would have been nothing
> for it then but a scene, and she and I would have had to come all at once, with
> a sudden clash, to a thorough knowledge of each other: down would have gone
> conventionalities, away—swept disguises, and *I* should have looked into her eyes,
> and *she* into mine—we should have known that we could work together no more, and
> parted in this life for ever. (p. 135)

At a much later juncture in the story, Paulina comments to Lucy on her impenetrability: 'Lucy, I wonder if anybody will ever comprehend you altogether?' she asks (p. 494). Lucy conveys her gradual realisation of her love for Paul Emanuel with a rhetoric that fuses writing with being known. After the conversation with Père Silas ignites her deep awareness of Paul's character, she admits to wanting to read his countenance, confident that it would offer 'a page more lucid, more interesting than ever' (p. 462). She experiences a 'longing to trace in it the imprint of that primitive devotedness, the signs of that half-knightly, half-saintly chivalry which the priest's narrative imputed to his nature' (p. 462).

Such passages of course build to the novel's highly emotional climax, just before Paul departs for his voyage to the West Indies. Prior to his seeming disappearance during what would have been his last few days in Villette, Lucy has experienced love, writing that 'the mutual understanding was settling and fixing; feelings of union and hope made themselves profoundly felt in the heart' (p. 512). Instructed by a note to wait for him for a leave-taking, she waits for hours and eventually days, enduring suspense – the 'corroding pain of long attent' (p. 555) – as well as the unsettling after-effects of having been given a sleep-inducing drug on the momentous night of the fete. Tellingly, Brontë shifts from a clearly retrospective narration of this time (chapter 61 begins, 'Must I, ere I close, render some account of that Freedom and Renovation which I won on the fête night?' (p. 554)) to a narrative technique intended to convey the anxiety she experiences in its immediacy: 'Shall I yet see him before he goes? Will he bear me in mind? Does he purpose to come? Will this day—will the next hour bring him?' (pp. 554–5). When they finally meet, Lucy confesses: 'It kills me to be forgotten ... I was crushed with the possibility, growing to certainty, that you would depart without saying farewell.'[12] It is a deeply moving moment of emotional expression and release, using precisely the terms her narrative has taught us to understand and appreciate. Not only has Paul *not* forgotten Lucy, he has been absorbed in creating a future for her in the shape of a schoolroom she can call her own. ('Ah! You said I had forgotten you all these weary days', he teases her (p. 563)). The famously ambiguous ending of *Villette* that follows offers only to readers with 'sunny imaginations' the hope that Paul does not himself die in the storm that wreaks so much destruction on his eventual return from three years in the West Indies, but the language of the novel's final two lines, focused on the long lives of Lucy's nemeses (Madame Beck, Père Silas and Madame Walravens) and concluding with a simple 'Farewell', instruct us otherwise (p. 573).

This ending, of course, instantiates the philosophy of life that Lucy has proffered in *Villette*, one that sees human happiness as meted out only to some, those 'guided from a soft cradle to a calm and late grave', for whom 'no excessive suffering penetrates their lot, and no tempestuous blackness overcasts their journey' (p. 506). These are, in her imagination, 'Nature's elect', people 'blessed' by God, she tells us in a chapter entitled 'Sunshine'. However, 'It is not so for all', the chapter that follows begins (chapter 38, 'Clouds'), and Lucy clearly believes her lot to be cast with this group of 'sufferer[s]', 'pilgrims' and 'brother mourners' (p. 508).

Reading *Villette* as a kaleidoscopic exercise in life writing nevertheless prompts us to grapple with other dimensions of the novel's concluding episodes. Just after Paul presents Lucy with her new school room in Faubourg Clotilde, she writes, 'And what did I say to M. Paul Emanuel?' and explains:

> Certain junctures of our lives must always be difficult of recall to memory. Certain points, crises, certain feelings, joys, griefs, and amazements, when reviewed, must strike us as things wildered and whirling, dim as a wheel fast spun.
>
> I can no more remember the thoughts or the words of the ten minutes succeeding this disclosure than I can retrace the experience of my earliest year of life: and yet the first thing distinct to me is the consciousness that I was speaking very fast, repeating over and over again:–
>
> 'Did you do this, M. Paul? Is this your house? Did you furnish it? Did you get these papers printed? Do you mean me? Am I the directress? Is there another Lucy Snowe?' (pp. 562–3)

Comparing the lost memory of her 'wildered and whirling' emotions to her earliest year of life, Lucy provides a compelling way to rethink what she has or hasn't forgotten. She implies that moments seemingly lost to memory might still be deeply consequential, even formative – lost to consciousness but not to one's subconscious. Asking a series of questions that conclude with 'Do you mean me?' and 'Is there another Lucy Snowe?', Brontë accentuates the centrality of this moment – Paul's gift of a schoolroom and a new home, a new identity – to the self-acceptance and self-fulfilment she comes to with him. She deems herself 'the steward of his property' and determines 'to render a good account', her chosen rhetoric linking this new dimension of her life to her status as the writer of a 'life-account'. Moreover, as already noted, Paul's years away are marked by continued attentiveness and remembrance ('By every vessel he wrote' (p. 571)). Lucy Snowe does not share the content of these letters with her readers, but her narrative has enabled us to recognise their worth as life-sustaining documents, ones written in 'characters of tint indelible', impervious to the elapse of time.

Paul's letters, like the schoolroom at Faubourg Clotilde, are thus a legacy, and of this legacy Lucy tells us: 'And was I grateful? God knows! I believe that scarce a living being so remembered, so sustained, dealt with in kind so constant, honourable and noble, could be otherwise grateful to the death' (p. 572). Describing herself as 'so remembered, so sustained', Lucy distills Paul Emanuel's acts down to the most essential, most vital, components of what Lucy Snowe needed to live on.

Coda

And live on she did. Although *Villette* does not identify Lucy Snowe's age, a passing reference along the way to her white hair and the fact of her living long enough to tell her readers about the lifespans of her enemies enables readers to understand that she, too, lived a full life. Not so Charlotte Brontë, who died on 4 April 1855, just shy of her thirty-ninth birthday. Brontë's death came a mere two years and two months after *Villette* was published and was soon followed by calls for a biography. Brontë's father, her husband (Arthur Nicholls) and Ellen Nussey shared a concern for her legacy, and Elizabeth Gaskell was commissioned for the task both to ensure that Brontë's name be cleared of charges of coarseness and unfemininity levied in some unfavourable reviews and to shape her legacy more generally. Linda Peterson has shown the extent to which Gaskell's biography drew not only on Brontë's correspondence but also on an obituary that the journalist Harriet Martineau had written for the *London Daily News* very shortly after Brontë's death and that emphasised her compromised constitution, supposed morbid sensitivity and secluded life.[13] Describing the 'dreary wilds' and 'forlorn house' in which Brontë had lived, Martineau concluded, 'in such a living sepulcher her mind could not [but] prey on itself; and how it did suffer, we see in the more painful portions of her last novel – *Villette*'.[14]

Harriet Martineau was thus one of the first to assume an autobiographical understanding of *Villette*, and she could not have chosen more resonant language, positing Brontë's home as a 'living sepulcher', an incubator for her mind and artistry. The phrase calls to mind the 'snow sepulchre' that Lucy Snowe once imagined for herself and arguably haunts the entirety of Gaskell's biography, which did so much to shape Brontë's afterlife. Much of Gaskell's biography is, of course, comprised of Brontë's own letters, a feature that enhances its complicated association with *Villette*. Gaskell told her publisher that Brontë's 'language, where it can be used, is so powerful and *living*, that it would be a shame not to express everything that can be, in her own words'.[15] Her characterisation of Brontë's language as 'living' implies that the biography, like Keats's Grecian urn, would preserve its emotional vitality for posterity. Of her biography's *raison d'être*, she explained that she wanted to ensure her readers would appreciate the emotional foundations of the whole family's fiction, how their writing 'was wrung out of them by the living recollection of the long agony they suffered' (*Life of Charlotte Brontë*, p. 334). The idea of 'living recollection', like Martineau's 'living sepulcher', of course recalls rhetoric that percolates through the letters (where Brontë writes of feeling 'buried' in her remote home) and throughout *Villette*, collapsing the distinction between fiction and life writing in representing Charlotte Brontë's lasting legacy.

Brontë herself yearned for a legacy that would ensure that she, and those she loved, would not be forgotten. Shortly after reading a posthumous review of *Wuthering Heights* she wrote to William Smith Williams:

> There must be a heaven or we must despair—for life seems bitter, brief—blank. To me—these two have left in their memories a noble legacy. Were I quite solitary in the world—bereft even of Papa—there is something in the past I can love intensely and honour deeply—and it is something which cannot change—which cannot decay—which immortality guarantees from corruption. (*Letters*, p. 138)

'Bitter, brief—blank': the language is Lucy Snowe's as much as it is Charlotte Brontë's. While Brontë tended to her sisters' legacies in tangible ways (by, for example, writing the 'Biographical Note' to preface a second edition of *Wuthering Heights* and ensuring that errors on Anne's gravestone were corrected), her comments here reveal once more how deeply the amalgam of ideas and emotions probed in *Villette* were her own. In the end, they articulate, as did Charlotte Brontë's last novel, the most essential purpose of life writing: to create a legacy, written 'in characters of tint indelible' and impervious to change, as an expression of love.

NOTES

1. Charlotte Brontë, *Villette*, ed. A. S. Byatt and Ignês Sodré, notes by Deborah Lutz (New York: Modern Library, 2001); subsequent references to page numbers are incorporated in the main text.
2. For some representative discussion of 'Vashti' in *Villette*, see Rachel Brownstein, 'Arnold and Brontë on Rachel', *Browning Institute Studies* 13 (1985), 1–24, or, more recently, Patsy Stoneman's '*Villette*', in *Charlotte Brontë* (Liverpool University Press / Northcote House, 2013), pp. 63–78.

3. In her edition of Charlotte Brontë's letters, editor Margaret Smith confirms that Élisa Félix (1820–58) was Brontë's model for Vashti and notes, 'Charlotte saw her in *Adrienne Lecouvreur* by Scribe and Legouvé at the St James's Theatre on 7 June and in Corneille's *Horace* (*Les Horaces*) on 21 June' of 1851 (*Charlotte Bronte: Selected Letters* (Oxford University Press, 2007), p. 192 n. 4).

4. Trev Lynn Broughton, 'Life Writing', in Dennis Denisoff and Talia Schaffer (eds), *The Routledge Companion to Victorian Literature* (New York and London: Routledge, 2020), pp. 69–82 (p. 69).

5. Anna Gibson, 'Charlotte Brontë's First Person', *Narrative* 25.2 (May 2017), 203–26 (214).

6. Tom Winnifrith, 'Brontë Biography: A Survey of a Genre', in Marianne Thormählen (ed.), *The Brontës in Context* (Cambridge University Press, 2012), pp. 169–74 (p. 169).

7. In her introduction to *The Belgian Essays*, editor Sue Lonoff writes, 'No one who knew Heger (including his son Paul) could mistake the source of *Villette*'s Paul Emanuel' (*The Belgian Essays: A Critical Edition* (New Haven, CT: Yale University Press, 1996), pp. xxi–lvxxvi (p. lxix)).

8. Ibid., p. lvi.

9. Elizabeth Gaskell, *The Life of Charlotte Brontë* (1855), ed. Alan Shelston (Harmondsworth: Penguin, 1975), p. 474. References to this biography will hereafter be cited in the main text.

10. Charlotte Brontë, *Selected Letters*, ed. Margaret Smith (Oxford University Press, 2010), p. 207, emphasis Brontë's.

11. Lucy Snowe's name, of course, amplifies her association with Brontë's sense of the future as 'appalling'. Writing to W. S. Williams in November of 1852, she asked that her heroine's last name be changed from 'Frost' to 'Snowe', explaining, 'A *cold* name she must have—partly—perhaps—on the *lucus a non lucendo*—principle—partly on that fitness of things—for she has about her an external coldness' (*Letters*, p. 210).

12. Karen Lawrence begins her study 'The Cypher: Disclosure and Reticence in *Villette*' with this moment in the novel, but argues that throughout much of the novel Lucy Snowe 'cultivates the oblivion she here resists' (Barbara Timm Gates (ed.), *Critical Essays on Charlotte Brontë* (Boston: G. K. Hall, 1990), pp. 306–19 (p. 306)).

13. Linda Peterson, 'Triangulation, Desire, and Discontent in *The Life of Charlotte Brontë*', *Studies in English Literature 1500–1900* 47.4 (2007), 901–20.

14. Juliet Barker quotes from the obituary in *The Brontës* (New York: St Martin's Press, 1994), p. 776.

15. Gaskell's comment is recorded by Arthur Pollard in 'Mrs. Gaskell's The Life of Charlotte Brontë, with an Appendix on Some New Gaskell Letters', *Bulletin of the John Rylands Library* (1965), 453–88 (459).

CRITICAL REFLECTIONS AND FURTHER STUDY

'Life Writing' might strike one as little more than an umbrella term designed to gather for study genres of personal writing (or writing about persons) usually seen as distinct from one another but recognised for their kinship (e.g., autobiography and biography) or for being distant cousins of these two major expressions of life writing (diaries, letters, obituaries, public tributes, and even epitaphs spring to mind). But scholarly study of life writing, particularly over the past few decades, has blossomed as a result of its broader and more inclusive lens, its vitality and usefulness amply evident in scholarly work featured in journals such as *Life Writing* and *a/b: Auto/Biography Studies* (see Further Reading). Its multipronged focus has enabled scholars to explore the interplay between genres and narrative modes within texts, and it has been considerably enriched by adjacent fields of study concerned with notions of selfhood – history, psychology and cognitive science, and philosophy, among others.

Despite proving such a generative category of criticism, scholarly study of life writing continues to rely on existing understandings of its subgenres, their histories and their conventions. Laura Marcus points out that life writing was a 'familiar appellation in the eighteenth century', used alongside 'biography' (p. 148) and hence shaping the understanding of the autobiographies that emerged in the nineteenth century. Alison Booth explores nineteenth-century life writing via its varieties, including the popular 'life-and-letters' approach taken by many of the period's biographers. Philip Davis similarly approaches the era's life writing through its manifestation in subgenres – autobiography, biography and travel narratives especially. Tim Peltason, considering 'life writing' as a category of Victorian studies, contends that it

> includes by courtesy those novels and poems that pose as truthful documents or that are known to have borrowed much of their matter from the life stories of their authors. But it is defined and anchored by the avowedly biographical and autobiographical narratives that make distinctly different truth claims – for all the powers of imagination that were required in their construction – and that thus offer to the contemporary reader distinct pleasures in reading and distinct forms of access to that familiar and deeply entangled Victorian couple, Letters and Lives. (p. 370)

My study of *Villette* is as indebted to the robust and wide-ranging approaches to 'life writing' produced in the past few decades as it is intrigued by the challenges of categorisation and the problems of 'truth claims' that seem especially to plague fictional autobiographies, as is the case with Brontë's novels. If, as I argue in my essay, an autobiographical frame of reference limits critical appreciation of a literary work when it over-imposes expectations of the verifiable, I ask what happens when we foreground instead an author's representation of emotional experiences. While I explore *Villette* primarily through Charlotte Brontë's and Lucy Snowe's response to loneliness and the related fear of being forgotten, many critics have found equally enlightening avenues to expand our understanding of the novel's status as a fictional autobiography or to showcase the extent to which Brontë was influenced by and contributed to her culture's investigation of the self. Leila May is one among many to foreground the explanatory power of Brontë's dualism, derived from Cartesian metaphysics. In contrast, Sally Shuttleworth influentially argued that *Villette* reveals an emerging materialist understanding of selfhood, an understanding built on and taken in new directions by Anna Gibson (cited in my essay, note 5) in her exploration of Brontë's use of first-person narrative techniques. Other studies of *Villette*, while not overtly invoking life writing as a critical lens, identify narrative techniques that shed crucial light on Brontë's understanding of the challenges of representing emotional experience in narrative. Emily W. Heady, to cite just one example, explores the fascinating ways that Brontë's use of Gothic and realist modes inform and complicate her understanding of 'the authority of inner life' (p. 341).

The preoccupation with 'the authority of inner life' that these and other scholars locate in her fiction manifested itself from the start in her correspondence, the body of personal writing that all of Brontë's biographers have depended upon to construct histories of her life experiences and understandings of her mindset. In this regard, it is impossible to overestimate the influence of Elizabeth Gaskell's *The Life of Charlotte Brontë* (1855), which drew so heavily on Brontë's letters, and Gaskell's biography itself, too, deserves deep study as a complicated exercise in life writing. Deirdre D'Albertis ('Bookmaking', 21, 22) in fact locates models for Gaskell's critique of Brontë's 'subjective morbidity' in Thomas Carlyle's essays and his *Life of Sterling*, observations that remind us that the flowering of life writing in the nineteenth century, a flowering that includes both *Villette* and *The Life of Charlotte Brontë*, was predicated on a vast 'root system' that drew for its sustenance on the myriad forms of writing in which people examined themselves and each other.

FURTHER READING

a/b: Auto/Biography Studies, journal of the Autobiography Society (Abingdon: Taylor & Francis. 1985–)

Booth, Alison, 'Life Writing', in Joanna Shattock (ed.), *The Cambridge Companion to English Literature, 1830–1914* (Cambridge University Press, 2010), pp. 50–70

Carlisle, Janice, 'The Face in the Mirror: *Villette* and the Conventions of Autobiography', in Barbara Timm Gates (ed.), *Critical Essays on Charlotte Brontë* (Boston: G. K. Hall, 1990), pp. 264–86

D'Albertis, Deirdre, '"Bookmaking out of the Remains of the Dead": Elizabeth Gaskell's *The Life of Charlotte Brontë*', *Victorian Studies* 39.1 (1995), 1–31

Davis, Philip, 'Lives and Thoughts', in Philip Davis (ed.), *The Oxford English Literary History*, vol. viii, *1830–1880: The Victorians* (Oxford University Press, 2002), pp. 404–55

Gilbert, Sandra, and Susan Gubar, 'The Buried Life of Lucy Snowe,' in *The Madwoman in the Attic: The Woman Writer and the Nineteenth-Century Literary Imagination* (New Haven, CT: Yale University Press, 1979), pp. 399–440

Heady, Emily W., '"Must I Render an Account?": Genre and Self-Narration in Charlotte Brontë's *Villette*', *Journal of Narrative Theory* 36.3 (2006), 341–64

Helms, Gabriele, 'The Coincidence of Biography and Autobiography: Elizabeth Gaskell's *The Life of Charlotte Brontë*', *Biography* 18.4 (1995), 339–59

Hughes, John, 'The Affective World of Charlotte Brontë's *Villette*', *Studies in English Literature, 1500–1900* 40.4 (2000), 711–26

Life Writing (Abingdon: Taylor & Francis, 2004–)

Marcus, Laura, 'Life Writing', in Dermot Cavanagh et al. (eds), *The Edinburgh Introduction to Studying English Literature* (Edinburgh University Press, 2014), pp. 148–57

Peltason, Timothy, 'Life Writing', in Herbert Tucker (ed.), *A Companion to Victorian Literature and Culture* (Malden, MA: Wiley-Blackwell, 1999), pp. 356–72

Shuttleworth, Sally, *Charlotte Brontë and Victorian Psychology* (Cambridge University Press, 2009)

Stoneman, Patsy, '"Such a Life …": Elizabeth Gaskell and Charlotte Brontë', *Brontë Studies* 41.3 (2016), 193–204

18 Money, Narrative and Representation from Dickens to Gissing

BEN MOORE

Abstract

Beginning with *Great Expectations*, this essay explores the relationship between money and representation in nineteenth-century literature through two major Victorian novelists: Charles Dickens and George Gissing. It argues that money is both ubiquitous and complex in their writing, and that it simultaneously provokes and resists attempts at literary representation. Money is first shown to be central to the complex of guilt and desire that drives *Great Expectations*. The discussion then turns to Mr Merdle and Mr Lorry, bankers who appear in Dickens's novels *Little Dorrit* and *A Tale of Two Cities* respectively. They are read as representing two different sides of money, the public/fantastical and the private/intimate, which cannot be effectively combined in a single character. The final part of the essay considers Gissing's response to Dickens, arguing that Gissing attempts, in novels such as *The Nether World* and *The Odd Women*, to correct what he saw as Dickens's incomplete realism through a renewed focus on the harsh realities of economic life. The limited horizons of Gissing's characters are so overwhelming, however, that they dominate his narrative vision, meaning the very attention to money that is supposed to make Gissing's fiction more realistic also restricts the representative range of his writing.

When Mr Jaggers tells Pip of his 'great expectations', in Dickens's novel of that name, the first monetary outlay he recommends concerns Pip's appearance: "'First," said Mr. Jaggers, "you should have some new clothes to come [to London] in, and they should not be working clothes. Say this day week. You'll want some money. Shall I leave you twenty guineas?"'[1] As Jaggers is aware, the most pressing priority for a newly minted gentleman like Pip is to present himself appropriately. His clothes must from now on not be *working* clothes; that is, they must represent for all to see his status as a person living off unearned income, rather than under the necessity of hard labour. The line between Pip the gentleman and Joe Gargery the blacksmith is already being drawn. It is reiterated in the 'change' which passes over the shopkeeper Mr Trabb when he hears that Pip has come into a 'handsome property' (p. 150). As Trabb's inspection reveals, Pip is not only beginning to signify a higher social class, but to embody money itself: 'Mr. Trabb measured and calculated me, in the parlour, as if I were an estate and he the finest species of surveyor' (p. 152). If in the eighteenth century, under what Raymond Williams calls 'agrarian capitalism', which developed out of the post-feudal period, wealth was still primarily measured in terms of land, then in the nineteenth century it is now Pip himself who has become an 'estate', surveyed greedily by Trabb.[2] The symbolic shift here is away from a society in which wealth was first and foremost a function of agricultural produce and land rents, and towards a society increasingly dominated by what Pip's London acquaintance Mr Wemmick refers to as 'portable property' (p. 201). In such a society, all objects – and even people – come to be valued in monetary terms.

Not only in *Great Expectations* (1860–1) but across the nineteenth-century novel, the free-floating capacities of money in its guise as portable property – and hence easily transferable, for instance, from Magwitch's labour as a sheep farmer in Australia to Pip's lodgings in London – open up a new range of narrative possibilities. Money in Dickens, as in Elizabeth Gaskell, George Eliot, W. M. Thackeray, Anthony Trollope and many others, is frequently at the centre of the narrative. It is gifted, inherited, disputed, swindled, invented, married into, forged, invested, seized, and even sometimes earned. But although the modern portability of money enables the radical reinvention of Pip's identity, and helps generate the narrative drive of *Great Expectations*, this portability also frequently blocks or obscures narrative connections. It is the modern abstraction of money, the separation from material origins that Marx termed the fetishism of the commodity, which allows Pip to assume that Miss Havisham rather than Magwitch is his mysterious benefactor. In doing so, he chooses the non-labouring middle classes over working-class criminality, and hence the fantasy that money is the modern form of a fairy-tale godmother's magic; a replacement for work rather than the product of it.

If Pip chooses to believe that, to use David Copperfield's words, he is going to be the 'hero of my own life',[3] then Magwitch has other plans. Pip's attempt to represent his life as a narrative he can control – 'I want to be a gentleman', he tells Biddy in chapter 17 (p. 127) – is enabled by money, but it is also money that allows Magwitch to perpetrate the novel's great act of misrepresentation, which is eventually overturned by his return: 'I've made a gentleman on you! It's me what has done it!' he triumphantly informs Pip in chapter 39 (p. 319). This link between money and misrepresentation is obliquely recognised in chapter 28, when Pip describes himself as a 'self-swindler' for inventing reasons not to stay at Joe's house, the truth being that Pip is ashamed of his old friend: 'That I should innocently take a bad half-crown of somebody else's manufacture, is reasonable enough; but that I should knowingly reckon the spurious coin of my own make, as good money!' (p. 225). Pip the narrator, looking back on his life, not only demonstrates his former capacity for self-delusion but also the inextricability of morality and economic thinking in the nineteenth century.[4]

As Michal Ginsburg argues in a classic article, Pip's life is framed by two worlds: the world of guilt represented by Magwitch, the criminal whose escape he aids, and the world of desire represented by Miss Havisham's house, and in particular Estella, whom he encounters there. Pip's misinterpretation of the source of his great expectations reveals 'the wish to see desire as totally independent of guilt, and the lesson Pip learns is that such a separation is impossible'.[5] This desire to cleanse desire of guilt leads to what Ginsburg calls misinterpretation, or what I am calling misrepresentation: the failure to picture the world as it really is and to figure forth the interpersonal connections that touch upon us. At the risk of over-generalising, we might say that the aspiration of the nineteenth-century realist novel as a genre is to open up these interpersonal connections to the reader, even if they remain obscured for the protagonists, and hence to render transparent an increasingly obscure and complex world.[6]

The relationship Ginsburg identifies between the worlds of guilt and desire can be rearticulated in terms of money. As Friedrich Nietzsche observes in *The Genealogy of Morals* (1887), guilt and debt are linked conceptually and, in the German words *Schuld* ('guilt') and *Schulden* ('debt'), etymologically. 'The feeling of "ought", of personal obligation', Nietzsche argues, has 'its origin in the oldest and most original personal relationship that there is, the relationship between buyer and seller, creditor and owner'.[7] In this alternative to the Freudian primal scene, it is economic exchange that is at the origin of both guilt and moral duty. Appropriately enough, the beginning of *Great Expectations* can be read as depicting just such an exchange, in which Pip trades the right to keep his 'heart and liver' safe from Magwitch for 'a file' and 'wittles' (p. 5), which he must in turn steal from his sister's pantry and Joe's forge.

On the other hand, money is also a medium of desire. As Karl Marx puts it in his *1844 Manuscripts*:

> If I long for a particular dish or want to take the mail-coach because I am not strong enough to go by foot, money fetches me the dish and the mail-coach: that is, it converts my wishes from something in the realm of imagination, translates them from their meditated, imagined or desired existence into their *sensuous, actual* existence – from imagination to life, from imagined being into real being.[8]

Money has a transformative power here. It is a philosopher's stone that translates desires into reality. Indeed, according to the title of a book by James Buchan, money is 'frozen desire'.[9] In Pip's case, he desires money mainly because he desires Estella, whose name, meaning 'star', indicates both her beauty and her inaccessibility. Their first encounter is tellingly presented as an exploitative financial encounter, as they play the card game 'beggar my neighbour' (p. 60). 'Beggar him' Miss Havisham orders Estella (p. 60); a command that gives voice to the cold-hearted cynicism of unfettered free-market capitalism. Estella represents money too, then, especially the side of money which provokes desire and promises to satisfy it (Satis House, we might recall, is where she is encountered). Or at least, she is presented in this way by Miss Havisham, who at one dinner puts 'some of the most beautiful jewels from her dressing-table into Estella's hair, and about her bosom and arms', creating 'rich flushes of glitter and colour' (p. 243) that draw a reaction even from Mr Jaggers. Yet Estella's glittering appearance, like Pip's expectations, conceals an origin in debt and guilt: her father and mother are both criminals, and she was given into Mr Jaggers's care as a form of payment for his legal representation (p. 413). She is in effect both cleansed and corrupted by Miss Havisham's money, as Pip is by Magwitch's.

Part of the complexity and indeterminacy of money in *Great Expectations*, and in nineteenth-century literature more widely, is due to the fact that money at this time was not only one thing. As John Vernon has argued, even though Bank of England banknotes became legal tender in 1833, and investment capital was becoming ever more mobile, 'The nineteenth century is characterized not so much by the conquest of paper money as by the long-drawn-out transition, extending back to the previous century, from older forms of wealth to paper. Many still thought of gold as the only real money and land as the only stable and secure form of wealth.'[10] What money really *was* was not obvious, even if its influence was everywhere. Gold, paper and land all laid a claim to representing the soul of money (to which list we might add labour in the work of Karl Marx).

Commentators such as Thomas Carlyle recognised this confusion. In *Chartism* (1839), he deplored 'these complicated times, with Cash Payment as the sole nexus between man and man', insisting that 'Cash is a great miracle; yet it has not all power in Heaven, nor even on Earth'.[11] Later in the century, just a few years after *Great Expectations*, John Ruskin's lecture 'Work', given to a Working Men's Institute at Camberwell in 1865, attacked not only the popular obsession with making money but also the meaninglessness of this activity: 'Ask a great money-maker what he wants to do with his money – he never knows. He doesn't want to do anything with it. He gets it only that he *may* get it. "What will you make of what you have got?" you ask. "Well, I'll get more," he says, just as at cricket you get more runs.'[12] Money here has become wholly self-referential. It has done away with any connection to the production of goods, and instead exists entirely in a world of its own creation. This self-sufficient world is the hallmark of capitalism, Marx argues, and it produces mystification. The existence of the commodities that money is exchanged for gradually recedes from view, until money appears to gain a life of its own, in which it 'comes out of circulation, enters into it again, preserves and multiplies itself within its circuit, comes back out of it with expanded bulk, and begins the same round ever afresh'.[13] For Marx, this marks the transition from money to capital. Growing and developing like the hero of a *Bildungsroman*, money in its guise as capital is no longer a background feature of narrative but the main protagonist. As Kurt Heinzelmann argues, it is possible to read Marx's *Capital* (1867–83) as one of the great three-volume novels of the nineteenth century, with its own plot and characters. In this case, the word 'capital' is no longer a dry economic description but, in the manner of *Jane Eyre* or *David Copperfield*, the name of the central character, now the hero of its own story.[14]

Since money in the Victorian period has come to appear as the 'sole nexus' of interpersonal connection and to have a self-sufficient life of its own, as well as remaining indeterminate in its material form, then representing it and its effects is simultaneously necessary and challenging. How should we think about such fundamental features of narrative fiction as representation, character and reality in a world dominated by the cash nexus? And conversely, how might narrative fiction help us understand a world that is being reshaped by money and political economy? A number of broadly post-structuralist critics and thinkers who addressed these questions in the seventies, eighties and nineties, including Marc Shell, Jean-Joseph Goux and Jacques Derrida, pointed to the relationship between money and language as a key part of the answer. Both money and language are systems of signification that allow us to interact with the world around us, and both are as capable of generating distance and disjunction as they are of enabling interpersonal connection. As Shell points out, the medium of writing, which 'seems to confer belief in fiduciary money (banknotes) and in scriptural money (created by the process of bookkeeping) also seems to confer it in literature'.[15] Paper money and literature are both representations in writing that require an act of faith on the part of the reader, seller or customer; a 'willing suspension of disbelief', to use Coleridge's phrase from 1817.[16]

Fredric Jameson, in his commentary on volume one of Marx's *Capital*, has argued that representation is a problem for both literary theory and economics.[17] He notes that in the case of a system as vast and complex as modern capitalism, 'every representation is partial'.[18] Our conclusion, however, should not be that 'since it is unrepresentable, capitalism is ineffable and a kind of mystery beyond language or thought', rather 'one must redouble one's efforts to express the inexpressible in this respect'.[19] If Marx's work represents one attempt to represent the complex world of capitalism within language, I want in the following pages to suggest that both Dickens and George Gissing experimented with ways of expressing the inexpressible life of money, and its intimate connections with human life under nineteenth-century capitalism, in their literary writing.

In the case of Dickens, the depictions of bankers in his novels can be productively read as representing different sides of money's multifaceted nature. This becomes clear if we examine two bankers in two books that followed one another in the 1850s: Mr Merdle in *Little Dorrit* (1855–7) and Mr Lorry in *A Tale of Two Cities* (1859). Taken together, Merdle and Lorry capture money's distance and its intimacy, its simultaneous resistance to interpretation and role as a mediator and enabler of social life. Tellingly, these opposing elements cannot be contained within one individual, but are split across different characters and texts.

Mr Merdle's name, as Mr Dorrit tells us, is 'the name of the age'.[20] The narrator agrees, commenting that 'The famous name of Merdle became, every day, more famous in the land' (p. 581). The reason for this is simple: 'All people knew (or thought they knew) that he had made himself immensely rich; and, for that reason alone, prostrated themselves before him, more degradedly and less excusably than the darkest savage creeps out of his hole in the ground to propitiate, in some log or reptile, the Deity of his benighted soul' (p. 581). Merdle represents money – and that alone is enough for people to idolise him. He is figured as an embodiment of Mammon, wealth that provokes a false and debased form of worship, as indicated by the colonialist description of prostration by 'darkest savages'. Merdle is elsewhere described as a 'Midas without the ears, who turned all he touched to gold' (p. 265), making him a magically alchemical figure who transmutes the desire (of himself and others) for gold into the real thing. What he works in is not precisely clear, but he is 'in everything good, from banking to building' (p. 265). As the plot proceeds, Merdle's Bank gains more and more prominence, until its precipitate collapse in chapter 26 of Book II, when it becomes clear that 'the Bank was broken, the other model structures of straw had taken fire and were turned to smoke' (p. 743). Rather than Midas, Merdle here proves to be a Rumpelstiltskin in reverse, spinning gold back into straw. In that fairy tale, it is the discovery of Rumpelstiltskin's true name that spells his doom, and, indeed, attentiveness to Merdle's name might have revealed the truth to those who were taken in by his fraudulent enterprises.[21] As Katerina Kitsi-Mitakou points out, Mr Merdle's name has 'scatological echoes' – it suggests the French *merde* – anticipating Freud's idea that money is 'the symbolic equivalent of excrement', which for the child is both desired and detested.[22] Wealth is also contaminated and contaminating elsewhere in Dickens, as in the famous dust-mounds (which may contain human waste among their other rubbish) in *Our Mutual Friend* (1864–5). More prosaically, the word 'Merdle' suggests the English 'muddle', hinting at the confusion and uncertainty behind the facade of the banker's apparent success.

Mr Merdle therefore stands for the fantastical side of money, its alchemical transformation of base things into gold, but also for the deceptions of financial capitalism, such as the railway manias and mining speculations that were a recurrent feature of Victorian Britain.[23] He is also, like money, both a catalyst for narrative movement (it is the collapse of his bank that sends Arthur Clennam to the Marshalsea, inaugurating the final section of the novel) and resistant to effective representation. He is a 'reserved man' with a 'somewhat uneasy expression about his coat-cuffs as if they were in his confidence, and had reasons for being anxious to hide his hands' (p. 266). Even the features of his body withdraw from view here, his clothes becoming complicit in the concealment.

The name of Mr Jarvis Lorry in *A Tale of Two Cities* is equally suggestive. As the *Oxford English Dictionary* shows, the word 'lorry' was in use from at least 1838 to describe a wagon or truck, especially on the railway. Mr Lorry's name is therefore anachronistic for a novel set in the late eighteenth century (the story opens in 1775), but it signals an association with movement, travel and connection. This is evident in his first appearance, when he is not only travelling to Paris from London on business but is involved in an exchange of messages (including the enigmatic phrase 'RECALLED TO LIFE').[24] Though Lorry is a reluctant traveller, his movements between France and London, and those of other bank employees, are emphasised. A waiter in Dover remarks, 'We have oftentimes the honour to entertain your gentlemen in their travelling backwards and forwards betwixt London and Paris, sir. A vast deal of travelling, sir, in Tellson and Company's House' (p. 21). Like the flows of capital which normally pass back and forth between Britain and France, Mr Lorry helps to make connections between countries and between people. He also pulls the narrative thread of the novel forward by reconnecting the Manette family, and by linking Dr Manette's past to his present. In addition he represents the ability of money to operate anonymously, to conceal its origins, and to insulate the wealthy from whatever is unpleasant. When Mr Stryver announces his intention to propose to Lucie Manette, Lorry advises against it, but offers to act as a go-between, 'committing you in no way, representing you in no way' (p. 152), but still testing the acceptability of the proposal. It also falls to Lorry, in this novel preoccupied with secrets, to keep the secret of Doctor Manette's relapse into mental sickness following Lucie's wedding: 'Two things at once impressed themselves on Mr Lorry, as important above all others; the first, that this must be kept secret from Lucie; the second, that it must be kept secret from all who knew him' (p. 203). Lorry is thus both messenger and protector for the Manette family, representing the intimate closeness of money, the opposite of the public but distant face presented by Mr Merdle.

The name of the bank Lorry works for – Tellson's – also implies a relationship between fiction and finance. As Deirdre Lynch explains, in the context of Daniel Defoe's interest in money, in the eighteenth century 'stories and money alike were things that (along with ships' cargoes and tradepeople's stock) required *telling*'.[25] To tell is to count, and to make account of, as well as to narrate. Telling is not neutral in Dickens's novel, but must take place in the right way. Miss Pross (another of Lucie Manette's protectors) admonishes Mr Lorry on their first meeting: 'couldn't you tell her what you had to tell her, without frightening her to death? ... Do you call *that* being a Banker?' (p. 30). A telling can also be a threat and an accusation, in which case we might gloss the name as 'tells on' rather than 'Tell's son'. This is evident of Madame Defarge, who keeps account in her knitting of the wrongs done by the French aristocracy, which must be paid in blood. Speaking of the 'earthquake' that is to come, Madame Defarge prophesises to her husband: 'I tell thee ... that although it is a long time on the road, it is on the road and coming. I tell thee that it never retreats, and never stops. I tell thee that it is always advancing' (p. 185). Madame Defarge 'tells' in the sense of listing or counting, but also anticipates the balancing of ledgers that will take place later in the novel, as Darnay's family sins 'tell' against him when he is put on trial.

While Madame Defarge's 'telling' drives the narrative towards a future revolution, Tellson's Bank itself is by contrast marked by stasis and decay. It is an 'old-fashioned place' (p. 55) – always an important word in Dickens – and proud of its inconvenience. Its banknotes have 'a musty odour, as if they were fast decomposing into rags again' (p. 56). John McLenan's original illustration of Tellson's Bank reflects this status, depicting it as dark and prison-like, its entrance sunken below street level (Figure 18.1) For David Trotter, the bank poses 'an unmistakeable threat to the circulations upon which the health and the wealth of Britain depend', and which according to him Dickens consistently sought to promote in his writing.[26] But although the bank building itself resists circulation, its employees pass repeatedly between London and Paris, so that it both generates and disrupts flows of capital, just as its representative Mr Lorry by turns promotes and restricts flows of information.

As a pair, Merdle and Lorry can help us to triangulate the representative capacities of money in Dickens's writing. Merdle is the public face of money, which is both distant and fantastical, and which seems disconnected from material origins and authentic social relations. On the other hand, Lorry is the intimate, private face of money, which is personal, friendly and comfortable – old-fashioned even – and which promotes social connections while also providing social protection. These different and even contradictory functions are separated across two very dissimilar characters, both of whom are nonetheless bankers in novels of the 1850s.

One of the most significant nineteenth-century commentators on Dickens was George Gissing, and it is to him that I turn for the final part of this essay. Gissing commented that Dickens wrote 'with an eye fixed steadily upon the publisher's sale-room', even altering his plots in response to declining sales.[27] Yet Gissing also found an 'essential truth' in Dickens's statement that 'No man ... attaches less importance to the possession of money, or less disparagement to the want of it, than I do'.[28] It was not money itself Dickens valued, Gissing argues, but what money *represented*: the 'stimulus of praise', indicating approval from and personal connection with his readers. This made him a new kind of writer for a new age. Unlike Walter Scott in the early part of the century, who wrote for money but maintained creative independence, for Dickens the rises and falls of the marketplace helped shape his literary practice. Gissing takes this marketisation a step further, writing the definitive novel of the new commercial

Figure 18.1 Tellson's Bank in *A Tale of Two Cities* by Charles Dickens: chapter headnote illustration by John McLenan from *All the Year Round*, 28 May 1859.

writer in *New Grub Street* (1891), where, as one critic puts it, literature is 'not a profession, but a trade'.[29]

Gissing also seeks, in texts such as *The Nether World* (1889) and *The Odd Women* (1893), to shift the representational role of money away from Dickens's supposedly idealising tendencies towards an increased realism. Yet, paradoxically, the desperate need for money that dominates these novels ends up reinforcing money's symbolic power, even as it becomes drained of the magically transformative properties Dickens had assigned to it.

Dickens was a 'Realist', says Gissing, but his characters do not precisely imitate life.[30] Rather, he created individuals 'to become once and for ever representative of their time'.[31] This is a form of representation which is typological and allegorical rather than productive of uniqueness. It is particularly appropriate to money, since money itself had become allegorical by Dickens's time, always representing someone or something beyond itself; even though, as we have seen, who or what was represented was often obscure, fragmented or multiple. Despite applauding Dickens's representative realism, Gissing contends that his writing is at times too divorced from social realities. He gives the example of Lizzie Hexam in *Our Mutual Friend*, a poor and uneducated girl who unconvincingly 'uses language and expresses sentiment which would do credit to a lady in whatever position'.[32] Gissing aimed to insert some of this missing reality back into Dickens's world, correcting his 'avoidance of the disagreeable' by attending non-idealistically to the suffering of everyday life.[33]

Often such suffering is tied to money, or the absence of it. As Simon James observes, 'The subject of money preoccupies Gissing more than it does any other novelist in English literature', putting him at the head of a crowded field.[34] Money and its lack are in Gissing 'usually the medium of the world's incursions into the vulnerable self, which fails to reach its potential'.[35] We can see this in *The Nether World*, a partial rewriting of *Great Expectations*, when Sidney Kirkwood tells his wife: 'Lives may be wasted – worse, far worse than wasted – just because there is no money. At this moment a whole world of men and women is in pain and sorrow – because they have no money. How often have we said that? The world is made so; everything has to be bought with money.'[36] There is no prospect here of the world being altered. In a manner typical of the naturalism of Émile Zola or Thomas Hardy, the driving forces of the world cannot be shaped by individual characters – even in the ambiguous manner of a Magwitch – but instead impose relentlessly upon them. The need for money impinges on human potential to such an extent that it is inimical to life, which becomes 'worse than wasted'.

In emphasising the intense pressure that economic forces had brought to bear upon the bodies and private spaces of nineteenth-century British life, Gissing raises a set of concerns which have interested critics such as Gail Houston, Mary Poovey and Catherine Gallagher in recent decades. In Gissing's case, the focus is on figures like Sidney, who exist on the narrow border between respectability and poverty. 'The budget, the budget!' exclaims Gissing's narrator, focalising Sidney: 'Always so many things perforce cut out; always such cruel pressure of things that *could* not be cut out'.[37] The self-representational capacity of these characters is reduced to such narrow proportions that their existence becomes a matter of accounting for smaller and smaller fragments of both money and sustenance. This is evident in the name and actions of the character Pennyloaf, who expends 'her few pence daily on whatever happened to tempt her in a shop, when meal-time came round'; and in the reduction of Sidney's interests to 'nothing but the cares of his family, the cost of house and food and firing'.[38]

In *The Odd Women*, this shrinking of horizons is symbolised by the London room rented by the two unemployed Madden sisters, who share a single bed and a table measuring 'three feet by one and a half'.[39] The 'close atmosphere' of the room draws in upon them along with their financial prospects: even the barely sustainable prospect of supporting life on 'fourpence' a day means only that they are '*independent* for another six months'.[40] Nonetheless, this marginal independence still gives Virginia an 'obvious thrill', because it means freedom from work.[41] Virginia and her sister Alice are among the 'odd women' of the book's title, without a husband or (now in their thirties and with failing health) any realistic prospect of acquiring one. Such odd women, as the New Woman figure Rhoda Nunn explains, cannot be accounted for: 'do you know that there are half a million more women than men in this happy country of ours? … So many *odd* women – no making a pair with them. The pessimists call them useless, lost, futile lives'.[42] With no husband to support them, unless they have wealthy families or inherited capital these women are forced to work to survive. If this is shocking, it is because Gissing's interest is fundamentally in middle-class women, who had been portrayed for decades as necessary guardians of the domestic sphere by commentators like John Ruskin (Figure 18.2). By contrast, working-class women had laboured outside the home throughout the nineteenth-century, as novels like Gaskell's *Mary Barton* (1848) demonstrate. Such women typically faced even worse prospects and lower pay than Gissing's characters, who manage to retain at least the appearance of gentility.

Indeed, despite its challenges, financial independence outside marriage offers middle-class women their greatest chance of self-realisation in Gissing, as it will a few decades later for Virginia Woolf in *A Room of One's Own* (1929).[43] Rhoda Nunn refuses marriage or 'free union' with Everard Barfoot, on the basis that either will compromise her freedom and principles.[44] The paradox is that the necessity of working for money, which risks complete subjection to it, must be embraced by women in this period in order to gain the chance of self-determination. This is the opposite of Dr Madden's declaration in the opening chapter that 'women, old or young, should never have to think about money'.[45] To be removed from cares about money, however, is to be helpless in all matters money touches, and for Gissing that is a wide field indeed.

Gissing's attempt to inject reality into Dickens by dwelling on the harsh economic realities of lower-middle-class lives also leads to a problem of representation. In order to accurately represent these lives he must focus on money as obsessively

Figure 18.2 A middle-class housewife counts her savings: engraving from the 1880s.

as his characters, yet this extreme focus drains his writing of representational range. As James observes, 'Gissing's characters are rendered unable to represent themselves and their surroundings without the right sum of money that would make such self-expression possible', and this 'poverty of imagination' is replicated in his own narrative practice.[46] This is the case because money is itself an abstract and reduced form of life, as Marx, Carlyle and Ruskin had all recognised. In Gissing, it is as if Pip has been replaced as narrator by Mr Trabb, so that the only perspective we have is the shopkeeper's measuring and calculating gaze. Even though money in Gissing no longer produces the magical reversals in fortune it did in Dickens, this does not mean the representational limitations Gissing found in Dickens's writing are overcome. Rather, they are replaced by constant financial calculation, which becomes the overarching horizon that determines all meanings and shapes all relationships, leaving no room for heroes (even deluded ones) – or for fairy tales.

NOTES

1. Charles Dickens, *Great Expectations* (London: Penguin, 2003), pp. 138, 141; subsequent references are incorporated in the main text.

2. Raymond Williams, *The Country and the City* (Oxford University Press, 1973), p. 60.

3. Charles Dickens, *David Copperfield* (Oxford University Press, 1997), p. 1.

4. On this topic see Geoffrey Searle, *Morality and the Market in Victorian Britain* (Oxford: Clarendon Press, 1998) and, more recently, Elaine Hadley, Audrey Jaffe and Sarah Winter (eds), *From Political Economy to Economics through Nineteenth-Century Literature: Reclaiming the Social* (Cham: Palgrave, 2019).

5. Michal Peled Ginsburg, 'Dickens and the Uncanny: Repression and Displacement in *Great Expectations*', *Dickens Studies Annual* 13 (1984), 115–24 (121).

6. On realism and transparency see Peter Brooks, *Realist Vision* (New Haven, CT: Yale University Press, 2005).

7. Friedrich Nietzsche, *The Genealogy of Morals*, trans. Horace Samuel (1913; Mineola, NY: Dover, 2003), pp. 44–5.

8. Karl Marx, *Economic and Political Manuscripts of 1844* (published posthumously in 1932), Marx–Engels Archive, www.marxists.org/archive/marx/works/1844/manuscripts/power.htm.

9. James Buchan, *Frozen Desire: An Inquiry into the Meaning of Money* (London: Picador, 1997).

10. John Vernon, *Money and Fiction: Literary Realism in the Nineteenth and Early Twentieth Centuries* (Ithaca, NY: Cornell University Press, 1984), p. 33.

11. Thomas Carlyle, *Chartism*, 2nd edn (London: James Fraser, 1840), p. 66.

12. John Ruskin, *The Crown of Wild Olive: Three Lectures on Work, Traffic, War* (New York: Bay View Publishing, 1902), p. 42.

13. Karl Marx, *Capital: An Abridged Edition*, ed. David McLellan (Oxford University Press, 1995), p. 99.

14. Kurt Heinzelmann, *The Economics of the Imagination* (Amherst: University of Massachusetts Press, 1980), pp. 181–2.

15. Marc Shell, *Money, Language and Thought: Literary and Philosophic Economies from the Medieval to the Modern Era* (Baltimore: Johns Hopkins University Press, 1993), p. 7.

16. Samuel Taylor Coleridge, *Biographica Literaria*, vol. II (Oxford: Clarendon Press, 1907), p. 6.

17. Fredric Jameson, *Representing Capital: A Commentary on Volume One* (London: Verso, 2011), p. 4.

18. Ibid., p. 6.

19. Ibid., p. 7.

20. Charles Dickens, *Little Dorrit* (London: Penguin, 2003), p. 508; subsequent references are incorporated in the main text.

21. On Dickens and fairy tales see Harry Stone, *Dickens and the Invisible World* (Bloomington: Indiana University Press, 1979).

22. Katerina Kitsi-Mitakou, '"A Little Life among the Multitude of Lesser Deaths": Productive Life Cycles in *Little Dorrit*', in Valerie Kennedy and Katerina Kitsi-Mitakou (eds), *Liminal Dickens: Rites of Passage in His Work* (Newcastle upon Tyne: Cambridge Scholars, 2016), p. 148.

23. Railway mania reached its height in 1846, when 9,500 miles of new routes were proposed. Of mining, Jim Silver notes that 'Gold Coast mining shares became the rage on the London and Paris stock exchanges' in the 1880s, with seven companies registered in 1881 and eleven in 1882, many of which failed (' The Failure of European Mining Companies in the Nineteenth-Century Gold Coast', *Journal of African History* 22.4 (1981), 511–29 (513)). See also Tamara Wagner, *Financial Speculation in Victorian Fiction: Plotting Money and the Novel Genre, 1815–1901* (Columbus: Ohio State University Press, 2010), where Mr Merdle is discussed on p. 104.

24. Charles Dickens, *A Tale of Two Cities* (London: Penguin, 2003), p. 12; subsequent references are incorporated in the main text.

25. Deirdre Lynch, 'Money and Character in Defoe's Fiction', in John Richetti (ed.), *The Cambridge Companion to Daniel Defoe* (Cambridge University Press, 2008), pp. 84–101 (p. 84).

26. David Trotter, *Circulation: Defoe, Dickens, and the Economies of the Novel* (London: Macmillan, 1988), p. 107.

27. George Gissing, *Charles Dickens: A Critical Study* (New York: Dodd, Mead, 1898), p. 86.

28. Ibid., p. 90.

29. Paul Delaney, *Literature, Money and the Market: From Trollope to Amis* (Basingstoke: Palgrave, 2002), p. 51.

30. Gissing, *Dickens*, p. 94.

31. Ibid., p. 95.

32. Ibid., p. 96.

33. Ibid., p. 99. But see Jeremy Tambling's argument that Gissing's writing includes a kind of impressionism or idealism (*Going Astray: Dickens and London* (Harlow: Pearson, 2009), p. 267).

34. Simon James, *Unsettled Accounts: Money and Narrative in the Novels of George Gissing* (London: Anthem Press, 2003), p. 1.

35. Ibid., p. 30.

36. George Gissing, *The Nether World* (Oxford University Press, 2008), p. 377.

37. Ibid., p. 372.

38. Ibid., pp. 266, 374.

39. George Gissing, *The Odd Women* (Oxford University Press, 2000), p. 17.

40. Ibid., pp. 20, 19.

41. Ibid., p. 19.

42. Ibid., p. 44.

43. On this connection, see Delaney, *Literature, Money*, pp. 49–64.

44. Gissing, *Odd Women*, p. 206.

45. Ibid., p. 6.

46. James, *Unsettled Accounts*, p. 32.

CRITICAL REFLECTIONS AND FURTHER STUDY

This essay has asked you to think about money and literature – especially nineteenth-century literature – as deeply interconnected. But when does this relationship begin? Is there really something special in this respect about the Victorian period? Eminent Victorians such as Carlyle, Ruskin, J. S. Mill and Marx (an honorary Victorian, since he lived longer in London than anywhere else) certainly seemed to think so. A deeper history of money and western literature might look back as far as the *Odyssey* and the *Iliad*, where there is gold and silver, but no money. This is not the case in the Bible, which in the New Testament condemns money-lending, and introduces the figure of Mammon as a false god, an idea Dickens reactivates in his portrayal of Mr Merdle.

Somewhat more recently, but still well before Dickens and Gissing, William Shakespeare produced one of the great literary depictions of money-lending in *The Merchant of Venice* (*Timon of Athens* also dwells on gold, and is quoted by Marx in the *1844 Manuscripts*). Shakespeare's Shylock might remind us of the long-standing association between Jews and banking, especially in relation to the charging of interest on borrowed money, long condemned by Christianity as 'usury'. An important question not considered in my essay is how far literature has contributed to or challenged anti-Semitic depictions of Jews as lovers of money. Dickens's most famous Jewish character is Fagin in *Oliver Twist* (1837–9), who secretly collects portable property stolen by his young accomplices, but Dickens would also later create the benevolent Riah in *Our Mutual Friend* as a response to criticism of Fagin by Mrs Davis, a Jewish acquaintance.

What about the eighteenth century? In the essay I mention Daniel Defoe, probably the first truly economic novelist in English (and arguably the first British novelist of any description, in which case the English novel's 'primal scene' is one of economic calculation). Robinson Crusoe is one of the great accountants in fiction, as are Defoe's Moll Flanders and Roxana, who make little distinction between marriage, prostitution and investment in their pursuit of financial success. Sarah Comyn's recent literary study of 'Homo Economicus' (economic man) takes the eighteenth century as its starting point, beginning with the political economist Adam Smith and the novelist Henry Fielding.

Another starting point for thinking about money in the nineteenth century is the Bank Restriction Act of 1797, which lasted until 1821. Prompted by a financial crisis caused by the Napoleonic Wars, this government act cancelled the requirement of the Bank of England to convert banknotes into gold. For the first time in Britain, paper money was divided from the supposedly real value of gold. The gap between the material worthlessness of paper and the value it represented became more apparent than ever before. During this time, Percy Shelley famously condemns paper money as the 'ghost of gold' in *The Mask of Anarchy* (1819). Yet in 1816, Britain also introduced an official 'Gold Standard' that tied its coinage to a specific quantity of gold, beginning a system that would last for over a hundred years. This helped create the virtual absence of inflation that allowed people like Miss Havisham to live comfortably off the interest on investments, without doing any work at all. The important cultural and literary legacies of this period have been traced by Matthew Rowlinson and Alexander Dick, among others.

Also not discussed in the essay, but deserving of consideration, is the legacy of the transatlantic slave trade, which literally equated human bodies with money. Dickens wrote his first pieces of fiction around the time slavery was being abolished in most of the British empire in 1833–4, but its influence lasted much longer. Ian Baucom has argued that the violent conjunction of the slave trade and finance capital that came out of the eighteenth century continued to shape philosophy and literature throughout the nineteenth, and even influenced twentieth-century literary theory. In a US context, Michael Germana has made the argument that many literary authors of the nineteenth and early twentieth centuries, including Harriet Beecher Stowe and Ralph Ellison, drew analogies between American money and race relations, so that racial and monetary values are negotiated simultaneously in their writing.

Readers of this essay might also like to think about what assumptions it relies upon, and to consider whether these are convincing or should be challenged. Does it, for instance, repeat the weakness it accuses Gissing of by reading too extensively through the lens of money? Is the reading of Merdle and Lorry as two sides of money useful, or are there better ways to read their roles within Dickens's novels? Finally, on a more constructive note, are there any concepts or conceptual tools here that can be utilised in your own work? What, to use a monetary metaphor, might be melted down and recoined elsewhere?

FURTHER READING

Baucom, Ian, *Specters of the Atlantic: Finance Capital, Slavery and the History of Philosophy* (Durham, NC: Duke University Press, 2005)

Comyn, Sarah, *Political Economy and the Novel: A Literary History of 'Homo Economicus'* (Cham: Palgrave, 2018)

Derrida, Jacques, *Given Time: I. Counterfeit Money*, trans. Peggy Kamuf (University of Chicago Press, 1992)

Dick, Alexander, *Romanticism and the Gold Standard: Money, Literature, and Economic Debate in Britain 1790–1830* (London: Palgrave, 2013)

Gallagher, Catherine, *The Body Economic: Life, Death, and Sensation in Political Economy and the Victorian Novel* (Princeton University Press, 2006)

Germana, Michael, *Standards of Value: Money, Race, and Literature in America* (University of Iowa Press, 2009)

Goux, Jean-Joseph, *The Coiners of Language*, trans. Jennifer Curtis Gage (Norman: University of Oklahoma Press, 1994)

Houston, Gail, *From Dickens to Dracula: Gothic, Economics, and Victorian Fiction* (Cambridge University Press, 2005)

Poovey, Mary, *Genres of the Credit Economy: Mediating Value in Eighteenth- and Nineteenth-Century Britain* (University of Chicago Press, 2008)

Rowlinson, Matthew, *Real Money and Romanticism* (Cambridge University Press, 2010)

Smith, Grahame, *Dickens, Money and Society* (Berkeley, CA: University of California Press, 1968)

19 | Reading and Remediating Nineteenth-Century Serial Fiction: Closing Down and Opening Up Sheridan Le Fanu's *Carmilla*

FIONNUALA DILLANE

Abstract

This essay explores the economic, temporal, spatial and aesthetic dynamics of Victorian serial fiction. The serial is positioned as a product of industrial modernity, created and consumed to the pulse of modernity's differentiated temporal rhythms (including regulated time, forward propulsion, heightened anticipation, and reflective pause). It is considered as an 'information object' that draws meaning from the material context in which it was typically situated so the importance of spatial reading is emphasised along with attention to the temporal. I draw out some of these issues in the second part of the essay through a critical reading of Sheridan Le Fanu's Gothic vampire story, *Carmilla*, published in four instalments from December 1871 to March 1872 in the short-lived monthly magazine the *Dark Blue*. I suggest that the original publication format underscores the serial's inherent potential for mutability and adaptability, much like the 'vampire' Carmilla who gives her name to Le Fanu's ambiguous story. Carmilla's rich afterlife across various media formats in the twenty-first century demonstrates both the serial's ongoingness and its reiterative embeddedness in its various historical and technological moments.

Introduction

Serial fiction is fiction (novels, novellas or short stories) published at regular intervals (daily, weekly or monthly) in either individual 'parts' or in magazines or newspapers. By the middle decades of the nineteenth century most fiction reading was done serially. Writing serially, publishing serially and reading serially provided opportunities and challenges for writers, publishers and readers. I will draw out some of these issues in the second part of this essay through a critical reading of Sheridan Le Fanu's Gothic vampire story, *Carmilla*, published in the *Dark Blue* from December 1871 to March 1872.[1] I suggest that the original publication format underscores the serial's inherent potential for mutability, adaptability and ongoingness, much like the 'vampire' Carmilla who gives her name to Le Fanu's intriguingly ambiguous story. Carmilla's rich afterlife in various media formats in the twentieth and twenty-first centuries reminds us that serialisation is both a 'transhistorical and transmedial process'.[2]

The gaps produced by publication in serial instalments invite a different type of transactional arrangement between writer and reader than those that are at play when reading a novel with the complete text in hand. Serial reading is an affective gamble as readers wait for the next part and speculate about what will happen to the characters to whom they have been introduced in scenarios that could play out in many different ways. And though all good storytellers strive to engage readers with the 'what if?' and 'what next?', serial instalments widen the speculative gap as the desire to drive to the end is not in the hands of the reader but in the control of the writer, the editor and the daily, weekly or monthly publication schedules. As Peter Brooks has emphasised, the increasingly mechanised nineteenth-century press that pulsated to the rhythms of industrial modernity and capitalist modes of production and distribution supported, sustained and spread the serial fiction boom, stoking consumer desire to maximise profits through anticipation and withholding.[3]

Since readers never knew in advance how many 'parts' there would be to the serial story, each instalment created its own proliferating possibilities as the narrative unfolded over time and repeatedly deferred gratification. The monthly or weekly 'breaks' typically served to heighten gossip and conjecture, and, if the story was sufficiently compelling, the serial both arrested attention and expanded interest with that systole–diastole rhythm pulsing through the feeling reader. Nicholas Dames, turning his attention to such feeling readers, asks: 'What transpired in mind and body as reading occurred? ... What quality of attention do certain texts or genres demand and receive? What rates of consumption and comprehension are normative for given genres? How does the mind make sense of elongated narrative forms? How does the eye traverse different texts differently?'[4] Book historians, critics interested in the imbrication of the feeling of reading with the physiology of the brain and the body, theorists of affect, scholars of the 'cognitive turn' in literary studies, and cultural studies specialists interested in the economics of industrial modernity will all take different approaches to answering these questions. Dames's questions have a particular charge when considering serial fiction forms, especially those serial parts that are surrounded by other texts and genres in miscellaneous magazines and newspapers. Dames, alert to the various ways in which the Victorian 'novel' took shape, argues that 'the novel of the nineteenth century trained a reader able to consume texts at an ever faster rate, with a rhythmic alternation of heightened attention and distracted inattention locking onto ever smaller units of comprehension' and concludes, in line with arguments shared by theorists of the serial form, that 'the Victorian novel was a training ground for industrialised consciousness, not a refuge from it'.[5] This claim is even more apt for the serial reader.

This open-ended potential of the serial is recapitulated in the economics of the form, which ensured that remediations also proliferated. The more successful weekly or monthly serials in parts were repackaged as three-volume novels or story collections either for purchase or for loan through circulating libraries. Cheaper one-volume editions followed once the sales of the more expensive book formats were deemed exhausted. All iterations strived to maximise profit margins for the publisher, the writer or the imitator. That bestselling serial writer of lurid mystery serials, G. W. M. Reynolds, swiftly capitalised on the success of Dickens's *Pickwick Papers* (serialised from April 1836 in nineteen parts over twenty months) with his imitative *Pickwick Abroad*, serialised in the *Monthly Magazine* between 1837 and 1838, notoriously overlapping with later instalments of Dickens's *Pickwick*, which he shamelessly copied.

Twenty-first-century inheritors of nineteenth-century serial formats – including the long-form television series and the box set, and the release of full series or weekly instalments on paid platforms such as Netflix, Now TV and Amazon Prime – have inherited these temporal, commercial, aesthetic and physiological rhythms. Such serial forms are ever more speeded up in our current transmedial contexts, which are increasingly crowded with distractions across the distributing and competing media platforms that have multiplied over the past ten years. The 2014–16 free-to-view Web series *Carmilla*, which takes the form of a one-shot camera vlog, not only testifies to the vibrant afterlife of Le Fanu's work but also to the importance of the relationships between narrative seriality and historical context.[6] It demonstrates how mode and moment matter, but also how we need to think relationally to understand the serial's plasticity – to follow it across its transmedial repurposing as a way of understanding how technological (and in this case digital) infrastructures allow for new serial possibilities. The vlog is supplemented by a Twitter feed that fills in the narrative and strives to hold and tease its audience between instalments and between each season. The production team used its own YouTube channel (the Canadian-based KindaTV), with actors, predominantly Natasha Negovanlis, who plays Carmilla, providing short interviews and audience Q & A to maintain its fan base both between the seasons and after the complete series concluded, by which time it had secured over seventy million views in total. A spin-off film, *The Carmilla Movie* (dir. Spencer Maybee), followed in 2017 and negotiations are ongoing for a mainstream television series.[7] In 2020 Le Fanu's *Carmilla* was read by Negovanlis and Elise Bauman, who played the main narrator, Laura, in sixteen separate 7–10-minute videos presented each day between 19 August and 3 September, bringing the 'original' text to their mostly teen and early twenties audience – again, in serial format with intertextual asides from Bauman and Negovanlis further connecting Le Fanu's *Dark Blue* story to their Web series script.[8] These multiplying outputs remind us that serial fiction conceived by a single author finds its readers through a media ecology that has a determining role in shaping and sustaining the 'story'. The 'many hands' mode of nineteenth-century periodical and book production, for instance, which includes editorial and reader input into an evolving serial story (with parts appearing in print before the writer has finished the work), demands that we consider nineteenth-century serial and part publication in terms that relate it to other media art forms that readily acknowledge the tension and cooperation between the 'auteur/director' and the produced 'work'.

Serial Investments: Time, Space, Economics and Affects

Serialisation was a feature of literary production well before the nineteenth century, but crucial economic, cultural and political factors saw the form's growth from the 1830s onwards, when it moved from being an often derided form of working-class popular literature played for cheap thrills to the mode through which, by the 1860s, the most celebrated novelists of the period found fame and their way into the middle-class home. Key external factors that shaped the increasing dominance of serial fiction production included the repeal of 'taxes on knowledge', on news and on advertising for instance, which made newsprint production cheaper. Advances in technologies facilitated paper production, processing and printing at faster, more efficient rates. The railway system meant a more effective cross-island and Continental flow of consumer goods. Each unit part selling for a penny or tuppence or a shilling, meant that the cost of consumption was spread over weeks, months or years, in contrast to the prohibitively expensive standard three-volume novel (which at 31s 6d was accessible to most readers only through subscription libraries). The affordability and anticipation mechanisms of the serial encouraged emotional and financial investment through ownership, as Feltes puts it, 'prolonging while measuring months of shared intimacy'.[9]

Thus a significant majority of original novels that were published as books in the nineteenth century, as Graham Law has shown, 'appeared previously in monthly or weekly instalments'.[10] From mid-century, new literary miscellanies, such as *Household Words* (1850–9), *All the Year Round* (1859), *Once a Week* (1859), *Macmillan's Magazine* (1859), the *Cornhill* (1860) and *Temple Bar* (1860), established audiences in multiples of thousands by serialising fiction. Deborah Wynne has drawn out the particular symbiotic relationship between the rise of the family magazine and serialised sensation fiction from 1859, starting with the dramatic success of Wilkie Collins's *The Woman in White* that appeared in parts in Charles Dickens's weekly, *All the Year Round* (November 1859–August 1860).[11] Sensation fiction's focus on murder, bigamy, female transgression and duplicity was distinguished from earlier incarnations of crime fiction, such as the hugely popular 'Penny Bloods' serials like G. W. M. Reynold's *Mysteries of London* (published in parts in 1844–8). These serials were dominated by graphic violence and nefarious incidents among the working classes. Sensation fiction controversially relocated serial criminality within the 'domestic space of the property-owning classes'[12] and within the pages of monthly miscellanies priced for and pitched to the middle classes. As Deborah Wynne observes, 'the process of serialization itself ... worked to heighten the impact and influence of the genre'.[13] What better way to draw out the suspense of a bigamy plot than to break off the narrative at a cliffhanger moment and make your readers wait a month for the big reveal?

As scholars of periodical culture have demonstrated of that ubiquitous first mass media mode, the newspaper or magazine, time is a key coalescing concept for an understanding of nineteenth-century seriality.[14] Serial fiction production turns around time: the timing of delivery of the author's and illustrator's copy to the editor and to the printers to meet the advertised deadlines for release; the timing of the story's next major plot climax; the timing of remediation in volume form to maximise profits while interest in the product is at a peak; the timing of the wait or delay in between parts that increases anticipation or reflection (or, if badly judged, leads to distraction and disengagement). Writers and publishers calculating how to retain their readers had to be mindful of how to play that gap. Serial writing required particular aesthetic effects and created a range of contradictory affects because the aim was to keep the reader sufficiently interested not just to keep reading in the moment but also to come back. Viewers of serial dramas on streaming platforms will be familiar with the techniques of 'curtain and climax'[15] as well as the need for a 'hook' from the outset and recapitulation on the return to the next instalment – especially if there has been a month-long delay, as there was between instalments of Le Fanu's *Carmilla*.

The tension between a sense of the reader's freedom to speculate and the crafted fictional web into which the skilled writer entraps the same reader is just one of the multiple contradictions that play out in serial fiction. These 'Curtains and Climax' dimensions that characterise sensational fiction in particular can be contrasted with what Hughes and Lund identify as slow unfolding narrative such as characterises the work of Elizabeth Gaskell, for example, with its steady accumulation of detail and character development that builds an alternative temporal pattern.[16] In this latter rhythm, the pause between parts provides readers with time to ruminate, reflect, reread. A key question then is that asked by Damkjær of weekly and monthly serial narratives: 'Did the structure of interruption in fact form part of their representational power?'[17]

Other important aspects of the serial's representational power are the significance of the relationship between the serial part and the material that surrounded it in the magazine or newspaper in which it first appeared, and the role of the brand name of the publication title (such as *Dark Blue, Household Words, Blackwood's Edinburgh Magazine*) in shaping responses to the serial story. Daniel Blanchard, in the interests of drawing out the significance of such original publication formats, has argued thus for the importance of attending to the serial part and, if published in a periodical, the magazine in which the serial is published, as 'information objects': 'Documents reflect the historical contexts of their creation, and in doing so, become information objects. The serial novel is a type of information object, but due to re-editioning, reversioning, and digitization, most readers have lost touch with its historical significance.'[18] Undoubtedly, we need to consider where the serial part first appeared and how that original publication format adds information to our object of study, how the narrative's affects are potentially otherwise charged than those at play in volume or book format. Reading the serial serially in a magazine or newspaper, for instance, allows for rich intertextual engagement across and between the different genres that appear on the pages before and after and around the serial instalment. William McCormack describes this process as reading 'laterally' or, to use Linda Hughes's term, reading 'sideways'.[19] Both conceptual approaches address the magazine or newspaper in spatial terms. Such sideways or lateral reading is a form of intertextual reading: such as Wynne's analysis of how Dickens purposefully surrounded Wilkie Collins's *Woman in White* with non-fiction articles, poems and short stories that would reinforce the main themes of Collins's sensational story: 'crime, danger and "nervousness"'.[20]

The dominance of the 'novel' or book edition in literary culture has obscured the dynamics of serial writing and serial reading. The more ephemeral serial part has been papered over in ways that make invisible some of the key strategies, tempos and contexts of serial writing. However, it is equally important not to reify the original publication context: such 'fixing' moves would run counter to the serial's ambient potential, closing down interpretations by indexing meaning too rigidly to the periodical in which the work was published or the texts surrounding it through which it may have been read. Such caution is needed because, at times, there was not one 'original' publication context but many, as the practice of syndication, especially from the 1870s onwards, demonstrates. The same narrative appeared serially and synchronously in multiple newspapers that each 'packaged' their purchased story in different frames, surrounded by different material that informed the ways it could be read.[21] This practice warns us to be alert to which version, which platform and which reading context we are talking about when we make claims about the interdependence and intertextual relevance of text and illustration, the serial part and other genres surrounding it, and the 'fit' of the part for the magazine in which it appears. It also reminds us again of the messiness of serial texts, of their endemic 'unruliness', to use Mark Turner's potent descriptor.[22]

Figure 19.1 Illustration for chapter 14 of Sheridan Le Fanu's *Carmilla* in its final instalment in the *Dark Blue* in 1872.

Carmilla's 'Ambiguous Alternations'

This 'unruliness' makes reading serially, or studying the serial, challenging. In this last section, I want to draw together some of these historical, theoretical and aesthetic aspects of the serial form through a reading of Sheridan Le Fanu's four-part serial, *Carmilla* (Figure 19.1). In the final paragraph of that story we are told of the 'ambiguous alternations' that define the narrator's feelings for the eponymous character, vampire or lover, who has transformed the narrator's life: 'to this hour the image of Carmilla returns to memory with ambiguous alternations – sometimes the playful, languid, beautiful girl; sometimes the writhing fiend I saw in the ruined church; and often from a reverie I have started, fancying I heard the light step of Carmilla at the drawing room door' (p. 319).

'Playful, languid beautiful girl' or 'writhing fiend', the 'ambiguous alternations' of Le Fanu's serial ramify from the opening chapter well before we meet Carmilla with her disruptive many-sidedness. Midway through the *Dark Blue*'s December number in 1871, following a conservative article on active Christianity, an opinion piece on why English sculpture is unsuccessful and two clichéd sonnets on rapturous prayer, we are launched into a first-person narrative that thrives on disorientation and unruliness. The narrator lives in a remote part of Styria, an Austrian province on the Hungarian border. The household is small: an English father with two governesses, one Swiss and one French, who, between them, speak in English, French and German to varying degrees of fluency – so a veritable 'Babel' (p. 245), we are told. Addressing us in perfect English and 'bearing an English name' (which is not given to us until chapter 8 in the third of the four monthly instalments), our first-person narrator has 'never seen' England and is not gendered until nine paragraphs into the story. Her age is indeterminate – somewhere in her late twenties but recounting an experience when she was nineteen. And, to add to our confusion as readers, the narrative is apparently addressed to an English woman: the 'nearest inhabited village', we are told, is 'about seven of *your* English miles to the left' (p. 243, emphasis added). 'Ambiguous alternations' are seeded from the outset: spatial, national, linguistic, gendered. We never find out the identity of the mysterious 'you' to whom the story is addressed. She remains a more spectral presence than the apparently undead Carmilla.[23]

Readers of the serial were caught in a similar state of confusion about what to feel about this unfolding story in this strangely uneven miscellany, the *Dark Blue*. A reviewer in *Lloyd's Illustrated Paper* in February 1872, reacting to the first three parts of the story, tells us it is 'made up of indescribable *vague* horrors that prompt the nervous person to glance uneasily from side to side as he reads'.[24] Those indescribable vague horrors could derive from a range of potential unsettlements on which the serial narrative thrives: these relate to form, context and content and collectively establish a sense of uncertainty and therefore the potential that *anything* could happen. The intense, sexualised friendship that is established between the hitherto sheltered Laura and the mysterious beautiful Carmilla is likely to have horrified our male reviewer as much as the suggestion that Carmilla might be a vampire. Carmilla may have twice pierced the breast of Laura, having penetrated her bedroom or her dreams, once when she was around six years old and again in the narrated time of this story. There are many maybes. The vampire, part animal, part human, neither fully dead nor fully alive, is an unnerving in-between 'thing'. Carmilla may be depicted as a vampire because same-sex desire in 1871 was culturally and socially invisible, an abhorrent, unspeakable 'thing' that required representation that emphasised the predatory and aberrant.[25] The second instalment in January 1872 ends with a recollection by Laura that ratchets up the affective tension and irresolution in terms that sustain the tonal ambiguity of a piece already full of hedging phrases ('I saw or fancied I saw'), contradictions and oxymorons (Figure 19.2). Is Laura asleep or awake? Conscious or in the realm of the unconscious? Is it pitch dark or is it light? Is she a victim of a vicious predatory attack or is she struggling with repressed desire?

I had a dream that night that was the beginning of a very strange agony.

I cannot call it a nightmare, for I was quite conscious of being asleep.

But I was equally conscious of being in my room, and lying in bed, precisely as I actually was. I saw, or fancied I saw, the room and its furniture just as I had seen it last, except that it was very dark, and I saw something moving round the foot of the bed, which at first I could not accurately distinguish. But I soon saw that it was a sooty-black animal that resembled a monstrous cat. It appeared to me about four or five feet long for it measured fully the length of the hearthrug as it passed over it; and it continued to-ing and fro-ing with the lithe, sinister restlessness of a beast in a cage. I could not cry out, although as you may suppose, I was terrified. Its pace was growing faster, and the room rapidly darker and darker, and at length so dark that I could no longer see anything of it but its eyes. I felt it spring lightly on the bed. The two broad eyes approached my face, and suddenly I felt a stinging pain as if two large needles darted, an inch or two apart, deep into my breast. I waked with a scream. The room was lighted by the candle that burnt there all through the night, and I saw a female figure standing at the foot of the bed, a little at the right side. It was in a dark loose dress, and its hair was down and covered its shoulders. A block of stone could not have been more still. There was not the slightest stir of respiration. As I stared at it, the figure appeared to have changed its place, and was now nearer the door; then, close to it, the door opened, and it passed out. (p. 278)

Figure 19.2 Illustration for Laura's 'nightmare' in the January 1872 instalment of the *Dark Blue*.

Nina Auerbach, writing in 1995, makes the point that Carmilla, 'one of the few fully self-accepting homosexuals in Victorian literature or any literature', is all body.[26] Unlike Dracula, she notes, she has no monstrous or sexually ambivalent presence. There are no fangs, no mesmerism or dematerialising through walls or locked doors. Critics, however, are divided in reading the coding of this homoerotic story: is it a panicked reaction to aberrant sexuality, not just, or not even, lesbianism, but the social-political shift that was seeing more women move out of the domestic space and into the public sphere, challenging dominant patriarchal ideologies? Or is it a radically sympathetic story of the perverse damage such patriarchal ideologies inflict on women?[27] This is how the Gothic serial, thematically unsettling, contextually confusing, tonally vague, gains its traction: it operates on that liminal space between the real and the supernatural, the conscious and dream state, the framed (within the *Dark Blue*) and the unframed, since we do not know when it will end.

Since the republication of the story in Le Fanu's story collection *In a Glass Darkly* (1872), little attention has been paid to the original context. Anne Maria Jones is an exception in this regard: she offers a valuable reading of the story in the context of the *Dark Blue*'s promotion of European aestheticism.[28] Founded in March 1871 by Oxford graduate John C. Freund, who named the shilling monthly after his university's colours, it was a miscellany that led each week with an instalment from a long-running serial. Freund published essays by his mother, Amelia Lewis, which were inflected by her interest in women's issues. These included pieces that, though marked by conservative ideas of femininity, emphasised the need for better education for women. These articles alone offer rich intertextual resonances with Le Fanu's work, which so often foregrounds gender and sexuality. The cover of the *Dark Blue* featured three figures, two of whom are distinctly female, and the third gendered more ambiguously. The two women are figured in the classical style on the steps of a portico and are reading books; one is fully arrested by whatever she is reading while the other looks directly at her viewer in defiant mode, her bare feet exposed and sensual figure emphasised under her flowing robe. That clash between the cover and the magazine's more conservative content is reinforced in the juxtaposition we find inside of reactionary imperialist and racist politics with what Anne Maria Jones has summarised as its 'aesthetically radical, cosmopolitan, even transgressive' pieces on European literature, including essays on radical French writers such as Theophile Gautier. Also included is art, poetry and fiction by A. G. Swinburne, D. G. Rossetti, William Rossetti and William Morris, with many of these works, along with some by less well-known (and less accomplished) writers, carrying the characteristic erotic charge and sensual dynamics that marked both the mid-century Pre-Raphaelite movement and the French Symbolists.[29] Jones acknowledges that 'Truly, the content in *Dark Blue* is a bit of a hodgepodge', but productively suggests that 'we can read the journal's eclecticism not as a sign of its failure but rather as an opportunity to explore the unusual juxtapositions – strange bedfellows, as it were – and thus see new facets of each contribution'.[30] Though she does not address serial forms, the approach aligns with considerations of the serial as positively unruly. She draws out important resonances in Le Fanu's work by reading across the magazine, focusing on three main threads: synaesthesia, translation and sexual dissidence.

There are other possible sideways readings. There was a consistent presence of articles promoting the purpose and rightfulness of England's imperialist mission. These politics were reinforced by travel pieces (fictional and non-fictional) on Ireland, China and India, for instance, that did little to conceal endemic racism and the degradation of the foreign other. Such reactionary keynotes are amplified by articles on the value of the army and police force, some of which appear in the same issues as Le Fanu's serial. Interpretations of *Carmilla* that situate the text in relation to Anglo-Irish Protestant anxieties in a politically unstable Ireland, including the threat of Fenianism, colonial legacies and British colonial policy during the Irish famine in the mid 1840s, have not yet addressed the contending frequencies of its surrounding anti-Irish and other racist material in the *Dark Blue* that could offer new dimensions to the 'Irishing of *Carmilla*'.[31]

Carmilla concludes with such an excessive representation of the forces of patriarchal authority gathering to execute the vampiric/lesbian other (there are two generals, a baron, two medical doctors, a priest and a woodman, with his axe, just to be absolutely sure) that we could interpret this ending, reading and thinking laterally, as either a serial reinforcing of the conservative tones of the magazine or as an ironic undercutting of its masculinist imperialism (axes and all!). *Carmilla* has a stake driven through her heart and she is beheaded, burned and her ashes are scattered in a nearby river according to the 'copy of the Report of the Imperial Commission' (p. 316). But importantly, Laura, our witness throughout this narrative, cannot verify this final scene. Into the gap, we might envisage the possibility that Carmilla was not a vampire but a victim of homophobic retribution, or that Laura still lives and might indeed turn up again at Laura's door, as she imagines in the final line of the story. Speculation persists, and I want to conclude with two examples of how subsequent remediations take different approaches to the serial's open-endedness.

In a Glass Darkly (1872) was published in three volumes, with *Carmilla* placed as the last story in the third volume. This first remediation has come to dominate critical readings in ways that regularly overlook the openness of the serial version. For example, Kathleen Costello-Sullivan's critical edition of *Carmilla* uses the original text from the *Dark Blue*, but nonetheless includes Le Fanu's interpolated 'prologue' that appears for the first time in *In A Glass Darkly* because 'it has come to be considered a relevant part of most critical readings of the text'.[32] Carmilla is the last of five 'case histories' purportedly gathered by the fictional Dr Hesselius, whom we meet first in Le Fanu's 'Green Tea' (first published in 1869 in Dickens's *All the Year Round*). That story begins with an account by Hesselius's personal secretary and editor of his posthumous papers, asserting his master's expert qualifications and attesting to the authenticity of the strange narrative that follows, which is recounted by Hesselius. The four subsequent first-person narratives in the 1872 volume are framed in each instance by an editorial intervention from Hesselius's private secretary. Le Fanu critics have parsed the ambiguous and ironic dynamics of these 'frames' but few note the original context, despite the fact that, in a drastic and transformative way, this interpolated prologue restricts and limits the serial story's interpretative openness by having the narrator of the prologue tell us that Laura has died.

As noted above, readers of the story in the *Dark Blue* had no framing context for the narrative other than the fact that they might recognise Le Fanu's brand of Gothic and so anticipate something of the strangeness of the story in seeing his name in the table of contents. Or perhaps they were accustomed to the disruptive aestheticism or more conservative gendered discourses that featured in the journal. One thing of which we are more sure is that Laura is alive or at least 'undead' at the end of Le Fanu's serial story. The prologue that closes off this possibility in the 1872 edition is a fixing interpretive gesture that undercuts the fluidity that pervades the serial text and both Laura's and Carmilla's ambiguous alternations.

In marked contrast, *Carmilla* the Web series refuses that 'relevant part of critical readings of the text', the Hesselius framing prologue, to instead emphasise continuity and speculative potential. It entirely ignores the 1872 remediation that has become the critical standard and returns to the original text in terms that both playfully and seriously tease out Laura's conflicting attitude towards Carmilla. Crucially, that conflict is not rooted in repression of her own lesbian desires. Laura and the mostly female cast that feature in this 126-episode continuation and extension of Le Fanu's text are entirely comfortable in their respective LGBTQI identities. Laura's struggle, rather, is with the fact that Carmilla is a vampire, the original Carmilla Karnstein from Le Fanu's original story. Set in a fictional Silas University (in a nod to Le Fanu's novel *Uncle Silas*), the series draws out some of the deliberate narrative opacities of Le Fanu's Gothic tale and invents around them rather than closing them down. Carmilla is presented as a victim of her mother's thirst for power and revenge and, over three seasons, Carmilla, Laura and a cast of characters loosely based on Le Fanu's minor figures prevent her mother from ending the world. Vampire hunters are 'jocks' with wounded egos; the controlling and threatening masculine ideologies of the original story are reinterpreted as neoliberal university politics and the threat of the masculine recast as the threat of campus rape. The casual racism of the original story, which includes the unreliable governess's account of a 'hideous black woman' (p. 257) who never emerges from the carriage in which Carmilla arrives at Laura's schloss, is challenged in this version. The woman is given a fully embodied presence as Carmilla's black sister, a powerful, stylish, witty and decidedly cosmopolitan vampire, older than Carmilla, affectionate, and ever more predatory, but though she talks about killing young students on campus, she never does. She appears in the second series along with two other actors of colour in response to criticism of the first series' all-white cast. Such responsiveness to audience feedback replicates the nineteenth-century patterns that saw writers such as Dickens amend and adjust serial parts in response to dips in audience engagement (evident in poor sales) or to reader or reviewer criticism. Though *Carmilla* the Web series plays out across a range of digital formats and interprets Le Fanu's story to reflect a twenty-first-century multicultural, gender-fluid Canada and to capture a digitally engaged teen to early twenties audience, there are aspects of the serial fiction process that transcend time, place and platform.

When the fourth monthly instalment of Le Fanu's *Carmilla* appeared in the March 1872 issue of the *Dark Blue*, there was no reason for readers not to suppose that the very open-ended final paragraph, cited above, might mean that Laura would return to the pages of the magazine, and that perhaps Carmilla might too: the revenant back again. *Carmilla* the Web series is not so much an adaptation of Le Fanu's story than an extension, continuation and interpretation of this original suggestiveness. Through it, we come to understand that Carmilla is not executed at the end of Le Fanu's story. So not only does this version not kill off Laura, it allows Carmilla to live too. And on the story goes.

NOTES

1. Part 1 of *Carmilla* appeared in the December 1871 number of *Dark Blue*; parts 2–4 followed in January, February and March 1872. See the Hathi Trust digital library, https://catalog.hathitrust.org/Record/010308459 (accessed 1 October 2020). Subsequent references to Le Fanu's story are from Sheridan Le Fanu, *In a Glass Darkly*, ed. Robert Tracy (Oxford University Press, 1999), and are incorporated within the main text.

2. Christopher Lindner, foreword to Rob Allen and Thijs van den Berg (eds), *Serialization in Popular Culture* (New York: Routledge, 2014), pp. ix–xi (p. x).

3. Peter Brooks, *Reading for the Plot: Design and Intention in Narrative* (Cambridge, MA: Harvard University Press, 1984), p. 170.

4. Nicholas Dames, *The Physiology of the Novel: Reading, Neural Science and the Form of Victorian Fiction* (Oxford University Press, 2007), p. 6.

5. Ibid., p. 7.

6. For the three series of *Carmilla* (dir. Spencer Maybee, 2014–16), season zero and additional Web content, see YouTube, www.youtube.com/c/KindaTV/playlists?view=50&sort=dd&shelf_id=8 (accessed 1 October 2020).

7. The year 2019 saw the release of another film version, *Carmilla*, written and directed by Emily Harris. Unlike *The Carmilla Movie*, which follows on from the final part of the

Web series, this later film is an adaptation of Le Fanu's story. It emphasises both the romantic and homoerotic charge of the original as well as its horror elements.

8. For *Carmilla the Novella* see YouTube, www.youtube.com/playlist?list=PLbvYWjK-FvS5pVBdVs8-eL6oBgsHRuR3cu (accessed 1 October 2020).

9. N. N. Feltes, *Modes of Production of Victorian Novels* (University of Chicago Press, 1986), p. 14. The prices cited refer to pre-decimal British currency, where the abbreviation 'd' (L. *denarius*) stood for 'penny' or 'pence' and where there were twelve pennies in one shilling and twenty shillings in one pound.

10. Graham Law, *Serializing Fiction in the Victorian Press* (Houndmills: Palgrave Macmillan, 2001), p. 13.

11. Deborah Wynne, *The Sensation Novel and the Victorian Family Magazine* (Houndmills: Palgrave Macmillan, 2001), pp. 38–54.

12. Ibid., p. 4.

13. Ibid., p. 3.

14. See, e.g., Margaret Beetham, 'Time: Periodicals and the Time of the Now', *Victorian Periodicals Review* 48.3 (2015), 323–42; Maria Damkjær, *Time, Domesticity and Print Culture in Nineteenth-Century Britain* (Houndmills: Palgrave Macmillan, 2016); and Mark W. Turner, 'Periodical Time in the Nineteenth Century', *Media History* 8.2 (2002), 183–96.

15. Walter C. Philips, *Dickens, Reade, and Collins, Sensation Novelists: A Study in the Conditions and Theories of Novel Writing in Victorian England* (New York: Columbia University Press, 1919), p. 86.

16. Linda K. Hughes and Michael Lund, *Victorian Publishing and Mrs Gaskell's Work* (Charlottesville: University Press of Virginia, 1999); see also their seminal work on serial rhythms, *The Victorian Serial* (Charlottesville: University Press of Virginia, 1991).

17. Damkjær, *Time*, p. 2.

18. Daniel W. Blanchard, 'Charles Dickens' *David Copperfield* as an Information Object: A Case Study of Serial Literature in the Victorian World of Documents', *Serials Librarian* 77.1 (2019), 15–22 (15).

19. W. J. McCormack, '"Never Put your Name to an Anonymous Letter": Serial Reading in the *Dublin University Magazine*, 1861 to 1869', *Yearbook of English Studies* 26 (1996), 100–15 (115); Linda K. Hughes, 'SIDEWAYS! Navigating the Material(ity) of Print Culture', *Victorian Periodicals Review* 47.1 (2014), 1–30.

20. Wynne, *Sensational Novel*, pp. 38–59 (p. 38).

21. Law, *Serializing Fiction*.

22. Mark Turner, 'The Unruliness of Serials in the Nineteenth Century (and in the Digital Age)', in Rob Allen and Thijs van den Berg (eds), *Serialization in Popular Culture* (New York: Routledge, 2014), pp. 11–32 (p. 20).

23. On fixing assumptions about this woman, see Richard Haslam, 'Theory, Empiricism and "Providential Hermeutics": Reading and Misreading Sheridan Le Fanu's *Carmilla* and "Schalken the Painter"', *Papers on Language and Literature* 47.4 (2011), 339–62.

24. Anonymous, 'Magazines', *Lloyds Illustrated London Newspaper*, 11 February 1872, p. 5, emphasis added.

25. Jarleth Killeen, 'An Irish Carmilla', in Sheridan Le Fanu, *Carmilla: A Critical Edition*, ed. Kathleen Costello-Sullivan (Syracuse University Press, 2013), pp. 121–32 (p. 124).

26. Nina Auerbach, *Our Vampires, Ourselves* (University of Chicago Press, 1995), pp. 41, 45.

27. See, e.g., Elizabeth Signoretti, 'Repossessing the Body: Transgressive Desire in "Carmilla" and *Dracula*', *Criticism* 38.4 (1996), 602–32.

28. Anna Maria Jones, 'On the Publication of *Dark Blue*, 1871–7', 2015, Britain, Representation and Nineteenth-Century History (BRANCH), ed. Dino Franco Felluga, an extension of Romanticism and Victorianism on the Net: www.branchcollective.org/?ps_articles=anna-maria-jones-on-the-publication-of-dark-blue-1871-73 (accessed 1 May 2020).

29. Ibid.

30. Ibid.

31. Killeen, 'An Irish Carmilla', p. 124. See also the consideration of the Irish and serial dimensions to 'Carmilla' in Sheridan Le Fanu, *In A Glass Darkly*, ed. Elizabeth Tilley (Ontario: Broadview, 2018).

32. Kathleen Costello-Sullivan, 'Notes on the Text', in Le Fanu, *Carmilla*, ed. Costello-Sullivan, pp. 10–12 (p. 11).

CRITICAL REFLECTIONS AND FURTHER STUDY

The *Dark Blue* is a marginal magazine when considered among the vast swathes of print that created the vibrant literary market in nineteenth-century Britain. It folded by its fifth issue because of financial difficulties, yet it remains present to us in the twenty-first century because some of its writers, such as the Rossettis, Swinburne and Le Fanu, continue to be significant presences in histories of art, in literature and in popular culture. Presumably, these are the factors that determined why it was selected for digitisation, free to view, by the Hathi Trust. That decision is certainly the reason why the magazine is an accessible part of our cultural history when so many other newspapers and magazines are lost or buried in what Patrick Leary has memorably called the offline penumbra. And there is wide recognition too of the online penumbra: digitised material that remains inaccessible behind paywalls or institutional subscriptions.

These questions of accessibility and lack of accessibility demand that we are mindful of the gaps in the archive and are cautious of assumptions reached about serial fiction or the press based mainly on the well-known magazines (*All the Year Round, Cornhill*) and well-known writers (Dickens, Collins, Gaskell), writers whom we study because they *are* studied. As pioneering work by Andrew Hobbs among others has shown (see Further Reading), regional newspapers carried vast amounts of serial fiction, much of which continues to go unread, many of those serials never having made it into book format. Reading laterally, Matthew Rubery has reminded us of the cross-influence of newspaper modes on the development of plot and characterisation in serial fiction, and the Victorian novel more broadly, that only comes to light if we do not privilege the 'novel'. Much serial fiction from the past remains unstudied and quite often unattributed in newspapers, especially in English language newspapers from across the former British empire. This is a gap and a challenge. Groundbreaking large-scale distant reading projects such as Katherine Bode's work on Australian newspapers, which has yielded a digital scholarly edition of 9, 200 works of serialised fiction, offer new directions on how we might begin to understand both the scale and the cultural significance of wider print media ecology, while remaining alert to the instabilities and necessary contingencies of our conclusions when working across such scales. And though there are illuminating studies of the instructive and didactic dimension to serial reading that engaged and shaped readers of the temperance press, for instance, or the religious press, or the radical press, there is still much more to read.

How do we do such reading and what are the effects (and affects) of reading digitally? While acknowledging the ongoing expansion of the digital archive, with more and more nineteenth-century runs of journals coming online, media historians have pointed out the limitations of replacing the material archive with digital text. There are basic affective losses, such as the feel of the paper that can indicate its cost and durability; the absence of the advertising wrappings in which the monthly magazine was packaged; the advertising encountered before the journal's first page and after its last (some of which has been included in the digitised version of *Dark Blue*). It can also be difficult to get a sense of the dimensions of the page. All of these paratextual details help to code the information object, and tell us something about the economics, affects and cultural status of the individual instalment or the magazine run, as periodical scholars such as Laurel Brake and James Mussell have shown. Having each issue follow the next by the mere click of a mouse also closes the temporal gap that so defined initial serial encounters. Can we read serially if the serial is all there already?

But Mussell has reminded us too that it is not that encountering such material in digital format robs it of its affective potential, rather it encodes a new set of affective experiences, new distractions for the eye, new tools to focus on and with which to enlarge an image or to read intertextually in ways unavailable to non-digital readers. Digital platforms can create new 'lateral' pathways, new 'sideways' reading through word search functions, for example. So a word search of 'vampire' within a run of a magazine could present you with a diachronic snapshot of the frequency peaks in 'vampire mentions' in the journal and direct you to the fiction, articles or poems that included 'vampires', all in the space of seconds. Or you might focus on one month in one year across a number of journals and do a synchronic search on the same topic, all the time keeping in mind that word searches do not produce 100 per cent accuracy and there are, of course, all the works that remain unknown in the penumbra.

Images are also a crucial part of how serial stories are told. Projects such as the Illustrated Image Analytics project at North Carolina State University led by Paul Fyfe is exploring ways of mapping illustrations across these digitised nineteenth-century print media, which, in conjunction with work by the many scholars of illustrations in serial fiction, might allow us to provide new and enriched comparative readings of how the serial illustration 'thickens' the plot of less well-known serials, to use the concept (and title) of Leighton and Surridge's work on the Victorian illustrated serial fiction.

So, as well as close reading and careful reading of context, we might embrace the messiness of the serial text by reading somewhat more 'messily' and indiscriminately ourselves, to see what hooks us, to push beyond the entrenched canons, to compare the various forms of miscellany and seriality for their different textures, layout and rhythms – features we only perceive when considered relationally. And in so doing we might strive for more nuanced approaches to what we call the serial, the miscellany, the series, as Turner suggests. Such approaches, I hope, might provide not fixing definitions, but a differentiated constellation of affects.

FURTHER READING

Bode, Katherine, *A World of Fiction: Digital Collections and the Future of Literary History* (Ann Arbor: University of Michigan Press, 2018)

Brake, Laurel, 'Half Full *and* Half Empty', *Journal of Victorian Culture* 17.2 (2012), 222–9

Hobbs, Andrew, *A Fleet Street in Every Town: The Provincial Press in England, 1855–1900* (Cambridge: Open Book Publishers, 2018): DOI: 10.11647/OBP.0152

Leary, Patrick, 'Googling the Victorians', *Journal of Victorian Culture* 10.1 (2005), 72–86

Leighton, Mary Elizabeth and Lisa Surridge, *The Plot Thickens: Illustrated Victorian Serial Fiction from Dickens to Du Maurier* (Athens: Ohio University Press, 2019)

Mussell, James, *The Nineteenth-Century Press in the Digital Age* (Houndmills: Palgrave Macmillan, 2012)

Nineteenth-Century Newspaper Analytics project, North Carolina State University: https://ncna.dh.chass.ncsu.edu/imageanalytics/ (accessed 20 October 2020)

Pettitt, Clare, *Serial Forms: The Unfinished Project of Modernity* 1815–1848 (Oxford University Press, 2020)

Rubery, Matthew, *The Novelty of Newspapers: Victorian Fiction after the Invention of the News* (Oxford University Press, 2009)

Turner, Mark W., 'Companions, Supplements, and the Proliferation of Print in the 1830s', *Victorian Periodicals Review* 43.2 (2010), 119–32

20 Public Places, Private Spaces in *Fin-de-Siècle* British Women's Writing

SUE ASBEE

Abstract

Focusing on the nineteenth-century *fin de siècle*, this essay analyses ways in which different versions of women's identity are constructed and performed in public places. The British Museum reading room was a centre for 'New Women' writers such as Amy Levy, Edith Nesbit, Dollie Radford and John Oliver Hobbes (Pearl Richards) to read, research, meet and exchange ideas. In their short stories and poems the museum functions as a space for solitary contemplation, chance encounters, or a place to perform. Through their narrators, Nesbit in 'Miss Lorrimore's Career' and Ella D'Arcy in 'The Smile' imagine their sex from the point of view of the male gaze, while Amy Levy's poem 'To Lallie' suggests gender boundaries are fluid and ambiguous. Same-sex attraction is much less playfully explored in Charlotte Mew's short story 'Passed'. In the last decades of the nineteenth century London's streets afforded liberated women the freedom to walk unaccompanied. 'Passed' explores that freedom. The female narrator's independence, her confidence to own the streets at night, leads to an encounter – in this 'glorious and guilty city' – with death, desire and prostitution. Language proves barely adequate and strains to convey the experience.

While the women writers discussed here were as different from each other as any collection of individuals could be, they had one thing in common: they were no longer confined to the home. They had the freedom to walk the streets or catch an omnibus unaccompanied, to visit exhibits in the British Museum or to take their seats in the reading room as intellectual equals to men. In the last decades of the nineteenth century the city environment offered opportunities for transient meetings and chance encounters. Street life featured in the lives as well as in the poems and short stories that these 'New Women' writers – including, among others, Dollie Radford (1858–1920) Amy Levy (1861–89), Netta Syrett (1865–1943), Ella D'Arcy (1857–1937), Edith Nesbit (1858–1924), Charlotte Mew (1869–1928) and John Oliver Hobbes (1867–1906) – produced.[1] Capturing the sense of excitement of the times in her biography of Charlotte Mew, Penelope Fitzgerald says these women felt they were 'on the crest of the wave that was sweeping away Victorian tradition'.[2] Significantly her image also implies the risk, uncertainty and responsibilities which come with freedom and independence. If Hobbes presents a staged meeting played out in the galleries of the British Museum – the protagonist more interested in being observed than observing – a walk through London's streets is psychologically threatening for Charlotte Mew's narrator when a chance meeting forces her to confront unacknowledged aspects of her own sexuality and identity.

It was imperative that many New Women, Radford, Nesbit and Mew among them, earned a living from writing. They sold their work to journals and magazines and all but Levy, who died in 1889, contributed poems or short stories to John Lane's avant-garde *Yellow Book* periodical, edited by Henry Harland and illustrated by Aubrey Beardsley (Figure 20.1) Ella D'Arcy was Harland's assistant editor and, as a consequence, she became friends with Syrett and Mew. Socialism also brought some of them together: Nesbit and her husband were founder members of the Fabian Society, Dollie Radford and her husband members of the Socialist League. They and others like them – Eleanor Marx, Olive Schreiner, Annie Besant – regularly worked in the British Museum reading room. Women had never been excluded, even if they had not been actively encouraged, but, by the late nineteenth century, culturally and politically engaged women were regularly reading, researching, exchanging ideas, writing and socialising there. Amy Levy describes the reading room as the headquarters of 'the great business' of book and article-making.[3]

Correspondence in contemporary newspapers testifies to women's presence turning the reading room into a contested space, but the author of 'Ladies in Libraries' presents a balanced, though comically jaundiced, view: 'To tell the truth, the Museum Reading Room is not the place for a fastidious scholar. Only a robust genius can stand it. The place gives most people a headache; the society coughs, grunts, and clears its throat in a marvellous variety of strange sounds'. But he goes on to say, 'ladies are not really much to be blamed. Many of them are just as serious readers, and as industrious and quiet grubbers in the past, as any man can be'. Tellingly he adds, 'There may be men who cannot work when a woman is near them, but women do not seem nearly so much disturbed by the neighbourhood of men.'[4] Imagining a middle-class male perspective, Ruth Hoberman suggests that the presence of women must have seemed complicit in the 'dissolution of the public sphere – as their mere presence blurred public/private boundaries and as they profited from the expanding market for their writing'.[5]

The British Museum with the reading room at its centre had evolved and expanded during the nineteenth century; it was a complex that functioned '"as a set of cultural technologies concerned to organise a voluntarily self-regulating citizenry" *who survey each other* as well as whatever is on display' (Figure 20.2).[6]

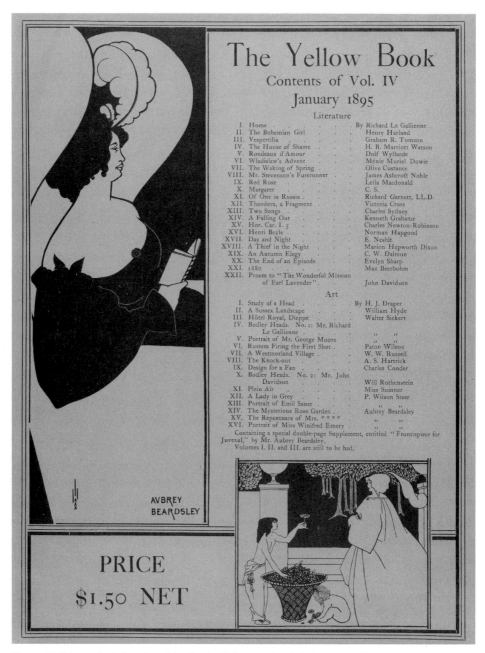

Figure 20.1 Poster by Aubrey Beardsley for the *Yellow Book*, vol. IV, January 1895.

As the author of 'Ladies in Libraries' implied, the idea of surveying each other was as applicable in the reading room as it was to displays in the exhibition galleries. Edith Nesbit (Mrs Bland) met and engaged in a dalliance with George Bernard Shaw there – in his view she 'looked every inch an advanced woman'.[7] Her light-hearted short story 'Miss Lorrimore's Career' (1894), told from the point of view of a (rather limited) male gaze on 'the beauty of the Museum', may have been inspired by their association:

> No one would have suspected that she was an author and a member of the Women's Rights Association, or that she had a 'career', or that she made a living by journalism. She did not look at all that sort of person. She wore Liberty gowns it is true, and queer floppy silken hats; but they became her, as the green leaves become the rose.[8]

In the opening paragraphs the narrator is forced to revise his stereotyped image of the new breed of women who study political economy as he observes Delia Lorrimore in the reading room. She 'filled that round torture chamber with all the splendour of sunshine and summer' and though she enters 'demurely', yet 'every man within eye-reach looked up as she entered' (p. 313). Economic pressures compel Delia and her brother – orphans – to earn a living from literature and journalism. Nesbit's own writing supported her unconventional household, which included her husband Hubert Bland's complex extramarital relationship and children, as well as their own children. In her companion poems, 'The Husband of Today' and 'The Wife of All Ages', the wife wonders, 'Why should one rule be fit for me to follow / When there exists a different law for you?' – hence, perhaps, her pursuit of George Bernard Shaw, of which more later. In her dress and her attitudes, Nesbit transformed the place 'into a stage for her self-presentation as a "new woman"'.[9] While Nesbit appears to have been fully conscious of the impact of her own physical presence, the lovely fictional Delia Lorrimore is not. Against all the expectations of the male readers in the reading room, she is competent and perfectly capable of writing her own request slips for books; she never drops them, knows her way around the reference library, and finds the *Encyclopaedia Britannica* on her very first day – all, disappointingly (for the men), without male assistance (p. 314). Her presence next to him renders the narrator incapable of work, while she, 'on the contrary, was diligent, even, as it seemed to me', he says, 'to excess' (p. 313).

Nesbit's story gently mocks her own (and her husband's) political beliefs through the male narrator's limited point of view: Delia's publications keep 'the domestic pot boiling' while her brother 'was a member of the Fabian Society and other extraordinary bodies, but otherwise respectable enough'; he is often 'off somewhere lecturing on "The theory of Value" or "Wood Pavement Under Democracy"' (p. 315). Delia is affronted by the narrator's first marriage proposal – 'You ask me to give up all my work, my career, my chance of fame, my independence, my life, in fact, and you offer me in exchange –' (p. 316) – but fails to blaze a trail for independent womanhood because of her penchant for reading novels: 'I cannot resist them. I took to them as people take to gambling or drink. As long as there's a novel, I can't work ... At first I used to get a little work done; but it has gone from bad to worse, and now I'm a slave of it' (p. 318). Disappointingly, she accepts a second marriage proposal, declaring, 'I don't want independence. I want you' (p. 320).

Figure 20.2 Engraving of the Reading Room of the British Museum, by Walter Thornbury, 1897.

The British Museum reading room was also where Dollie Radford met her husband, Ernest. Members of the Socialist League, their circle included William Morris, Olive Schreiner, H. G. Wells and D. H. Lawrence. When Ernest suffered the first of several mental breakdowns and was institutionalised, Radford, like Nesbit, needed income from writing to help support herself and their three children.[10] 'To the Caryatid *in the Elgin Room – British Museum*' is one of the poems in her *Songs and Other Verses* (1895). Whether the voice of the poem is her own or that of a persona, the address to the exhibit is so focused and intent that it might have been spoken in a confessional as in a public gallery:

> So long ago, and day by day,
> I came to learn from you, to pray,
> You did not hear, you did not know
> The thing I craved, so long ago.
>
> The days were always days of spring,
> Hope laid her hand on everything,
> And in your golden room, on me,
> She rested it most lovingly.[11]

A caryatid is a load-bearing pillar in female form supporting the weight of a roof or beam on a flat head. The architectural function is important for appreciating the mass of metaphorical weight Radford's caryatid carries – and it has specificity. Originally one of six caryatids from the Parthenon in Athens, it was 'acquired' by Lord Elgin and then purchased for the British Museum along with other marbles in 1816. Representing two and a half thousand years of history, the displaced object is no longer functional but simply an exhibit. Radford's contemporary Violet Paget, known as Vernon Lee (1856–1935), argued (as Hoberman explains) that 'part of the pleasure of responding to art involves recognising that … the art object is in fact a projection of one's own imagination'.[12] This poem echoes that sense in that the exhibit exerts a powerful influence over the viewer's private history.

With the vast wealth of images and statuary representing women in the British Museum this nameless marble makes an interesting choice. Radford's speaker responds only to the caryatid's burden-bearing reason for existence. Both she and it are divorced from context – of family, home or history. Alone and unobserved in the apparently deserted gallery she recalls her own 'long ago' when she first began visiting 'day by day'. Her 'long years' and her prayers 'long since dead and cold' are measured implicitly against the caryatid's millennia. She confers it with wisdom and endurance: '[I] prayed to stand, in strength as you … With dauntless mien and steadfast gaze'. Inevitably her patient prayer is rejected: 'You were too wise to grant it me'. Her emotional life is simplified in six stanzas as the hope of youth is unfulfilled in age: from days of 'sun and showers' to the present 'tired years', 'dead and cold'. The famous public place becomes a space for private contemplation.

Several of Radford's poems are London-based. The speaker of 'Nobody in Town' for example observes the bustle of Regent Street with detachment, 'the ceaseless foam / Of traffic breaking at my feet', 'the airless alleys, in the heat' and the men and women who meet 'With tired eyes, and settled frown'.[13] The title and refrain, 'That there is nobody in town', apparently deliberately excludes this unfortunate working population, until the final lines puncture the privileged voice of ennui by recasting the refrain: 'Ah world beneath the sky's blue dome, / In flannels white, and spotless gown, / Ah would that such a day might come, / When there was nobody in town.'

John Oliver Hobbes's sharp, witty comedies are about 'Society', the kind of upper-class, aristocratic families Radford's social conscience imagines levelled in a hope for a more equal future. In Hobbes's *Some Emotions and a Moral* (1891), the museum's galleries provide a stage for young – but newly widowed – Cynthia Cargill to exhibit herself, observed rather than observing. Hobbes's characters own no interior lives or private spaces, all is surface and display.[14] Cynthia flouts convention by remaining in London after her husband's funeral instead of retiring to the country for a period of mourning, scandalising her sister's sense of propriety – 'You always want to do the most improper thing you can think of' – a comment which neatly identifies the social self-awareness of her class. But Cynthia claims she will 'take up some kind of study, and – and try to be a little serious' (p. 223). Privately this is not what she has in mind at all. The museum represents so many opportunities that several reasons for Cynthia's frequent visits are suggested: her mother-in-law fears worship of pagan gods; her aunt says it is merely a 'fancy'; her sister an affection, while Cynthia herself 'said it was a rest'. While her ability to please herself and her sense of independence are evident, Cynthia is neither an aesthetic nor a 'new' woman, just a woman with an eye for self-display. Dressed in deep mourning, she wanders alone through the long galleries of the museum 'like some uneasy spirit'. 'Her unusual height and grace, her deep mourning, and what her maid called "her way of putting on her clothes", attracted considerable attention from the intelligent public, who were scattered in thin groups through the various rooms' (p. 224). This is performance with intent: to meet her former lover, Godfrey, the impecunious son of an Egyptologist, known to spend each day at the museum. Artfully she exploits the theatrical possibilities of the exhibition space; in the three years since they last met both have been unsatisfactorily married. Ignoring their surroundings, they are captivated by each other once more. Cynthia says if their meeting was on the stage, slow music would aid the awkwardness of their situation. In its absence they start blindly down the nearest gallery, but fail to find the museum's newly acquired mummy, the ostensible pretext for taking this turning. The galleries present an impressive location for the superficiality and artifice of emotions; the narrator comments, 'As an actress she was dangerously good: her art was more convincing than the average woman's nature' (p. 225).

The impressive entrance to the British Museum is vital for Amy Levy's poem 'To Lallie *(Outside the British Museum)*' (1884), as the grandeur of the location is juxtaposed with the disappointing outcome of an authentic chance encounter.[15] The speaker's desire is kindled on sight as 'Up those Museum steps you came, / And straight away all my blood was flame, / O Lallie, Lallie!' The use of the pet name implies an intimacy and a history between the two. Melvyn New, reading this as a personal poem, despite the (apparently) male speaker, suggests that Lallie is Violet Paget.[16] Whether Paget (Vernon Lee) is indeed Lallie is less significant than the gender ambiguities New's suggestion raises. The speaker's memories – buying Lallie strawberries and rowing a boat – suggest a male voice, but only if we think in cultural gender stereotypes. Kate Flint suggests that the hat-raising,

> ostensibly suggesting a male speaker – seems an attempt on the part of a lesbian poet to hide her own emotional response behind a sartorial gesture: woman-authored poetry addressing women was often reviewed as though the speaker had adopted a male voice; by the same token ... a woman-identified reader could easily practice queer reading, aligning herself with a heterosexual male poetic speaker.[17]

Lallie and 'a friend, my friend ... A meagre dame, in peacock blue / Apparelled quaintly' walk up the steps and meet the speaker. S/he 'bowed and smiled and raised my hat; / You nodded – faintly'. Lallie fails to respond, her 'nonchalant small nod' is ambiguous, suggesting no recollection or (more likely) deliberate rejection. New comments on the effect of Levy's rhyming of 'pathetic' with 'aesthetic' (in the lines a 'funny joke, / Yet half pathetic' and 'I think you patronised the sect / They call "aesthetic"'), citing Swinburne, the Rossettis, Walter Pater, Wilde and Beardsley as part of the 1880s aesthetic movement, adding that Levy and Violet Paget are among their number. But he also notes Levy's 'self-deprecating' tone and the way in which the speaker excludes him/herself from aestheticism.

The poem designates the British Museum as a fashionable meeting place for members of the avant-garde with the leisure and the intellectual and educational confidence to go beyond the steps outside to the galleries within, as Lallie and her companion

> passed inside
> To where the marble gods abide:
> Hermes, Apollo,
>
> Sweet Aphrodite, Pan; and where,
> For aye reclined, a headless fair
> Beats all fairs hollow ...

But the poem suggests that the speaker, despite apparently having the leisure to meet Lallie in the first place and take her boating, and despite displaying poetic wit and skill, still finds him/her self excluded from the British Museum club, and thus from what remains a private space of friendship associated with the public spaces described in the poem. The museum steps – and the 'Outside' of the subtitle – endorse this subtle exclusion at the same time as they deliver a stage-set visual image of the imposing approach to the entrance, and consequently the meeting's anticlimax and the speaker's humiliation.

In *A Sinner's Comedy* (1894), Hobbes refers to new bohemian freedoms and a relaxation of social mores between men and women. Hobbes writes, for example, 'In Jasper Street, Bloomsbury, where nature was more in vogue than respectability, a chaperone was considered an unnecessary and tedious addition to the ordinary plagues of life';[18] while in Netta Syrett's 'Fairy Gold' (1896), Hasleton, having escorted a young woman lost in St James's Park through mist and moonlight to her home in Chelsea, is surprised at her invitation to come in for tea, as she lives alone. This is socially confusing until he remembers that 'it was the dawn of the twentieth century, and ceased to marvel'.[19] In her memoir, Syrett recalled that, 'Even in the eighties, so long as a girl was working at some art, profession, or business, she was perfectly free and could go about her lawful occasions without censure – even from the censorious'.[20] On the other hand, in life rather than in fiction, George Bernard Shaw, beginning to feel that he had taken on rather more than he bargained for in his association with Edith Nesbit, recorded in his diary that having reluctantly allowed her to accompany him to his Fitzroy Square place, sent her away again on discovering that his mother was not at home. There was an 'unpleasant scene ... as I was afraid that a visit to me alone would compromise her'.[21] Free association of men and women, with its possibilities of impropriety or sexual availability evident in contemporary fiction, is revoked in Shaw's case in the interests of real-life respectability – or, perhaps, simply for the purposes of a convenient excuse.

The male gaze in Ella D'Arcy's short story 'The Smile' (1891) reminds us that 'one is called, in the city, to observe and be observed, never sure if one is actor or audience, on the stage or off it'.[22] This story of an omnibus journey quotes from Amy Levy's poem 'Ballade of an Omnibus' in its opening paragraphs, indicating the poem's popularity as well as recalling Levy herself, who committed suicide at the age of twenty-seven, two years earlier.[23] The London streets and urban environment D'Arcy's commercial traveller describes from an omnibus on a raw wet night are romanticised: 'The wood pavements that hurried away in serpentine curves behind us gleamed like looking-glass, wherein shop-lights, street-lights, the red lamps of the retiring hansom dropped reflections, long and tremulous as those of stars in a river'. The romance is rudely deflated, however, when someone steps on his toes. The diversity of omnibus travel is as evident in D'Arcy's story as it is in Levy's 'Ballade'. Levy celebrates the democracy of cheap fares, envying 'not the rich and great' who can afford carriages or hansom cabs, but intent on enjoying 'The Human tale of love and hate, / The city pageant, early and late' which 'Unfolds itself, rolls by, to be / A pleasure deep and delicate'.

D'Arcy's traveller lists the other passengers on the omnibus: the fat woman, the deprecating gentleman, the major, the elderly female with newspaper parcel, and 'the hungry-looking girl with the fiddle case'. 'The Smile' of the story's title belongs to a young woman who, before the advent of the omnibus, would not have been travelling alone and who is here the object of the narrator's romantic fantasy: 'She whom I had sought so long and so eagerly in suburban drawing rooms and at subscription dances in country towns and bar-parlours, and fashionable assembly rooms, yea! even in the columns of the matrimonial papers – and let me add, hitherto in vain' (p. 115). His vain search appears finally to have ended on public transport – or it would have been, had the narrator not fallen asleep, missed his stop, and dreamt of the glories of their conversation and her smile, which 'penetrated to the recesses of my soul' (p. 116). D'Arcy may have had Levy's rejection of the popular stereotype of a New Woman in mind: 'the female club-lounger, the *flâneuse* of St James's Street, latch-key in pocket and eye-glasses on nose', who, Levy says, 'remains a creature of the imagination'.[24] D'Arcy's female in 'The Smile' represents a different but equally imaginary romantic ideal.

Unlike the previous texts, Charlotte Mew's short story 'Passed' (1894) portrays a self-assured woman whose sanity is threatened by a chance meeting.[25] It came out in the second edition of the *Yellow Book* edited by Henry Harland, and he loved it, as 'he favoured hurrying-through-the-mean-streets stories'.[26] Mew distanced herself from the *Yellow Book* after Oscar Wilde's trial (1895), fearing that its decadent reputation might damage her own; her need to conceal her life of *genteel* poverty clearly increased the importance to her of status and propriety. It is relevant to an understanding of her work, too, to note that she and her sister Anne believed that their family had a genetic predisposition for mental illness. Together, they shared the lifelong cost of private hospitalisation for another sister, Frieda, who had been diagnosed with *dementia praecox*, and this was the same condition from which their brother Henry died. Their Gordon Street home was close to the British Museum but also only a stone's throw from the desolate urban slums Mew describes in 'Passed'. Marylebone was known for the proximity of wealthy streets hard against some of the poorest slums in London, with the recent development of New Oxford Street as a fashionable retail location largely responsible for this juxtaposition of wealth and poverty.[27]

'Passed' describes the narrator's walk on a late December afternoon as the sun sets and twilight and darkness follow. That she ventures alone beyond the affluent glass-plated shop fronts to the urban slums behind them, without a thought that this might in any way be risky, demonstrates her independence and self-confidence. The contrast between her comfortable fireside and the 'splendid cold of fierce frost' of outdoors testifies to sensuous pleasure, and what she notices and comments on as she walks suggests that she is secure in her considered opinions about art, architecture, and religion. Her confidence provides protection in an alien and threatening environment. When she walks past slum dwellings from which 'faces of diseased and dirty children leered into the street', she thinks that such 'shelters' are 'travesties ... of the grand place called home' (p. 246). But she is not upset or threatened by this forgotten underclass; she recognises poverty, but uses aesthetic appreciation as a defence against its horror, admiring instead the way the prison-like walls are transformed by the red, gold and crimson sunset.

Two significant female encounters are dealt with in a similar way. Surprisingly to her, given the nature of the neighbourhood, no men threaten or beg, but the 'poor desecrated face' of a young girl catches her attention. It prompts neither sympathy nor social conscience; instead the narrator's imagination and the dying sunlight transform the girl's reality into 'mystically pictured faces of some medieval saint'. Aesthetics come to her defence against any meaningful intrusion of slum life into her consciousness and the illusion lasts until the light fades 'when the girl demanded "who was I a-shoving of?"' (p. 246). The second encounter is with an image in a shop window. This is a 'chromo' – or chromo-lithograph – a cheaply produced colour picture of a girl at prayer with 'eyes turned upwards, presumably to heaven', leaving the viewer 'in no state to dwell on the elaborately bared breasts below'. The narrator's distaste is obvious and her comment tart: its 'pseudo-purity was sensually diverting, and consequently marketable'; that is, she is aware of the commodification of a quasi-religious icon and uses that response to shield herself from another form of commodification she would be unwilling even to own. She turns 'sickly away' from what she deems 'prostitution' (p. 247). Cultural and aesthetic sensibilities distance and protect her from her own unacknowledged visceral attraction to the bared breasts in the chromo.

Kate Flint, Patricia Pulham and C. Maxwell all discuss 'Passed' in terms of Mew's same-sex desires; Pulham points out the difficulties of writing *now* about women's sense of their own sexuality *then*. In their own time, she says, 'it had yet to be fully defined'.[28] Lesbianism was not a widely recognised term in that period, and without language or definitions how can such desire be described? Flint asks how conscious Mew herself was of the 'sexual and emotional tensions between women that lie at the heart' of 'Passed'.[29] Amy Levy and Dollie Radford often use ambiguously gendered speakers in their poems, while setting aside sewing is the only clear indication here that Mew's narrator is female. Her educated and opinionated language constructs the persona of a disinterested observer, but this disintegrates when she finds herself emotionally defenceless against her third female encounter. Within a newly built, architecturally celebrated church of 'forbidding exterior' and murky interior she finds not a fanciful medieval religious image nor a vulgar chromo, but a 'magnetism of human presence', an unnamed something huddled in the dark church: 'Here was human agony set forth in meagre lines, voiceless, but articulate to the soul. At first the forcible portrayal of it assailed me with the importunate strength of beauty. Then the Thing stretched there in the obdurate darkness grew personal and banished delight'. 'It' eventually becomes 'she' as a young woman's hand 'grasping mine, imperatively dragged me into the cold and noisy street' (p. 248). Their journey through deafening noise is an urban nightmare: 'weirdly lighted faces', 'flaring booths' and 'staggering children' succeed each other, and only the two women are silent – 'we said nothing'. From this chaos the narrator is dragged into a silent room of destitution, nevertheless dazzlingly bright, lit by lamp and candles illuminating a half-clothed woman, apparently asleep, in fact dead. Ever observant and class-conscious, the narrator recognises that 'these deserted beings must have first fronted the world from a sumptuous stage' (p. 249), but the stock Victorian tableaux of a fallen woman produces apathy, not sympathy. She finds her companion's distress 'sickening to watch' until detachment is replaced by revulsion at actual physical contact:

> I tried to raise her, and kneeling, pulled her reluctantly towards me. The proximity was distasteful. An alien presence has ever repelled me. I should have pitied the girl keenly perhaps a few more feet away ... Her heart throbbed painfully close to mine, and when I meet now in the dark streets others who have been robbed, as she has been, of their great possession, I have to remember that. (p. 249)

Aware that she should feel pity, with callous honesty she remarks, 'I reviewed the incident dispassionately, as she lay like a broken piece of mechanism in my arms' (p. 249). Nevertheless, 'My gaze was chained; it could not get free' (p. 251) and her 'realisation of the thing called Death' provokes hysterical hallucinations, a macabre dance where nightmare figures are, and are not, her own loved ones, 'as they mocked my recognition of them with soundless semblances of mirth'. In her mind her 'heart went home. The dear place was desolate' (p. 251). Further horrors in this increasingly psychotic episode feature the 'homeless house' by prison walls which she passed earlier and the image of the bare-breasted girl, and the narrator's mind is depicted as 'fast losing landmarks amid the continued quiet of the living and the awful stillness of the dead' (p. 252). Motionless throughout, 'the burden on [her] breast' continues to sleep through the narrator's emotional turmoil.

Later, refusing all entreaties to stay, she is dragged 'passionately' back into the room where the 'divine radiance' of her companion's 'young and blurred and never-to-be-forgotten face' provides 'an exquisite moment'. But the narrator resists this even as the trembling young woman holds on to her, and the woman is then cast once more as an object, not a person: 'still it clung. I thrust it off me with unnatural vigour' (p. 253). If confinement in the desolate room forces her to confront her deepest fears of death and desire, escape into the deserted street provides relief:

> A man staggering home by aid of friendly railings, set up a drunken song. At the first note I rushed towards him, pushing past him in wild departure, and on till I reached the noisome and flaring thoroughfare, a haven where sweet safety smiled. Here I breathed joy, and sped away without memory of the two lifeless beings lying alone in that chamber of desolation. (p. 254)

Penelope Fitzgerald comments: '*Passed* seems almost as overwritten as a story can be, hurrying along in distraught paragraphs, only just hanging on, for decency's sake, to its rags of English grammar'.[30] In stark contrast to that description of the story's style, once at home the narrator says that her 'account of the night was abridged and unsensational'. The familiar domestic space and her loved ones' ignorance of her experience allows her to take refuge in her family's perception of her normal everyday identity.

Four months later she walks through 'a notorious thoroughfare in the western part of this glorious and guilty city': 'The place presented to my unfamiliar eyes a remarkable sight. Brilliantly lit windows, exhibiting dazzling wares, threw into prominence the human mart' (p. 256). Goods displayed in the street's shop windows serve to highlight another aspect of what is for sale: 'the human mart' refers to the red light district and the commodification of women. Among the crowd she recognises the young woman, now dressed in dull vermilion with 'a large scarf of vehemently brilliant crimson' – thus literally and metaphorically a scarlet woman.

She is with a man, and the couple 'met my gaze with a void incorporate stare'. The narrator's last impressions as she acknowledges her part in 'the despoiled body' are of the sounds of the street, 'a laugh, mounting to a cry', clanging church bells and carriage wheels. Whether the cry is the narrator's or the girl's remains unclear. Fitzgerald suggests that 'The whole business of hurrying in desperation through a maze of mean streets is one of romance's standbys ... As to the blank encounter and the cry of despair at the end of *Passed*, not to mention the mumbling priest and the cynical seducer, they are part of the nineteenth century's unreal city'.[31] Mew's story, distanced, detached, hectic and passionate by turn and peopled by unnamed, unknown characters sums up the anonymity of the metropolis. Alex Murray's comment on Mew's contemporary, the decadent Arthur Symons, could be describing 'Passed' when he says, 'A poetry that could capture London would need to dissolve the public and the private, projecting the fleeting, amorous encounters of the bedroom onto the anonymous experience of the city'.[32]

In the last decades of the nineteenth century educated and independent (though not necessarily secure or content) women writers like Charlotte Mew and the others discussed here found countless opportunities in London's public places, streets and transport to explore a range of new freedoms in their writing. Aware that in the city they were always on display and observed by others, in their poetry and fiction they in turn analyse and observe their own complex reactions to the new situations they find themselves in, situations created by a changing society and changing social roles, and including their relationships with men – and with each other.

NOTES

1. E. Nesbit was the professional name of Edith Bland, now best remembered for her children's stories. Several other of the writers discussed in this essay also published under different names: Ella D'Arcy as Gilbert Page, and Pearl Richards as John Oliver Hobbes. Henceforth in this essay I use the names by which the writers are best known, hence Nesbit and Hobbes, but D'Arcy.
2. Penelope Fitzgerald, *Charlotte Mew and Her Friends* (1984) (London: Fourth Estate, 2014), p. 59.
3. Amy Levy, 'Readers at the British Museum' (1889) cited in Susan David Bernstein, 'Radical Readers at the British Museum: Eleanor Marx, Clementina Black, Amy Levy', *Nineteenth-Century Gender Studies* 3.2 (2007): www.ncgsjournal.com/issue32/bernstein.html (accessed 2 February 2022).
4. 'Ladies in Libraries', *Saturday Review* 62, 14 August 1886, p. 213.
5. Ruth Hoberman, 'Women in the British Museum Reading Room during the Late-Nineteenth and Early-Twentieth Centuries: From Quasi- to Counterpublic', *Feminist Studies* 28 (2002), 489–512 (502).

6. Ibid., 492, emphasis added.

7. Ibid., 504.

8. 'Miss Lorrimore's Career' appeared in *Sylvia's Journal* (February 1894), 27–31. Like some of the other texts discussed, it is not easily available in original form so I have used Jane Spirit et al. (eds), *The Women Aesthetes: British Writers, 1870–1900*, 3 vols (London: Pickering & Chatto, 2013); Levy's 'To Lallie (on the steps of the British Museum)' comes from vol. II, *1880s and 1890s*, and all the others are from Sue Asbee (ed.), vol. III, *Yellow Book Writers*. Subsequent references are given in the main text.

9. Hoberman, 'Women', 504.

10. Ruth Livesey, 'Dollie Radford and the Ethical Aesthetics of *Fin-de-Siècle* Poetry', *Victorian Literature and Culture* 34 (2006), 495–517: https://doi.org/10.1017/S1060150306051291.

11. Asbee (ed.), *Yellow Book Writers*, p. 296.

12. Ruth Hoberman, 'In Quest of a Museal Aura: Turn of the Century Narratives about Museum-Displayed Objects', *Victorian Literature and Culture* 31.2 (2003), 467–82 (475).

13. Asbee (ed.), *Yellow Book Writers*, p. 301.

14. Ibid., p. 177.

15. Spirit (ed.), *Women Aesthetes*, p. 114.

16. Melvyn New, *The Complete Novels and Selected Writings of Amy Levy* (Gainesville: University Press of Florida, 1993). Thanks to my colleague Jane Spirit for discussion by correspondence of Levy's poem.

17. Kate Flint, 'The "Hour of the Pink Twilight": Lesbian Poetics and Queer Encounters on the *Fin-de-Siècle* Street', *Victorian Studies* 51 (2009), 687–712 (693).

18. John Hobbes, 'A Sinner's Comedy', in Asbee (ed.), *Yellow Book Writers*, pp. 137–75 (p. 141).

19. Netta Syrett, 'Fairy Gold', in Asbee (ed.), *Yellow Book Writers*, pp. 325–45 (p. 329).

20. Netta Syrett, *The Sheltering Tree* (London: Geoffrey Bles, 1939), p. 90.

21. J. Briggs, *Edith Nesbit: A Woman of Passion* (London: Hutchinson, 1987), p. 88.

22. Ella D'Arcy, 'The Smile', in Asbee (ed.), *Yellow Book Writers*, pp. 113–16; Alex Murray, *Landscapes of Decadence: Literature and Place at the Fin de Siècle* (Cambridge University Press, 2016), p. 81.

23. Amy Levy, *A London Plane and Other Verses* (London: T. Fisher Unwin, 1889), pp. 21–2.

24. Quoted in Flint, '"Hour of the Pink Twilight"', 536.

25. Charlotte Mew, 'Passed', in Asbee (ed.), *Yellow Book Writers*, pp. 241–57.

26. Fitzgerald, *Mew and Her Friends*, p. 57.

27. Kate Henderson, 'Mobility and Modern Consciousness in George Egerton's and Charlotte Mew's *Yellow Book* Stories', *Literature in Transition, 1880–1920* 54.2 (2011), 185–211 (198).

28. C. Maxwell and P. Pulham (eds), *Vernon Lee, Decadence, Ethics, Aesthetics* (Houndmills: Palgrave Macmillan, 2006), p. 5.

29. Flint, '"Hour of the Pink Twilight"', 705.

30. Fitzgerald, *Mew and Her Friends*, p. 56.

31. Ibid.

32. Murray, *Landscapes of Decadence*, p. 77.

CRITICAL REFLECTIONS AND FURTHER STUDY

My essay introduces poems and short stories by Amy Levy, Dollie Radford, E. Nesbit, John Oliver Hobbes, Ella D'Arcy and Charlotte Mew. Apart from Nesbit, now remembered mainly for her children's books, their names are likely to be unfamiliar, but that was not the case at the end of the nineteenth century. Talia Shaffer's *The Forgotten Female Aesthetes* (2000) has ensured that they and other women like them continue to be subjects of ongoing research. Shaffer discusses inherent tensions within the complex term 'female aesthetes', so – given space constraints – I have avoided using it in my essay and have relied on the label 'New Women' as a means of focusing on women's independence. However, Shaffer's book is an indispensable first port of call for further study of *fin-de-siècle* women's writing.

Why were these writers 'forgotten'? Dollie Radford's first volume of poems has the self-deprecating title *A Light Load* (1891); almost inevitably, contemporary male critics saw little in her work beyond charming verses. W. B. Yeats, joint founder of the exclusively male Rhymers' Club (1891–4), thought her poems 'fine' but concluded that, although genuine and thoughtful, they are 'all trifling' (*Letters to Katherine Tynan*, ed. R. McHugh (Dublin: Clonmore & Reynolds, 1953, p. 124); Radford's husband, Ernest, was also a member of the Rhymers' Club). Shaffer suggests that if women like Radford 'were writing in a pretty style, readers might not notice what they were actually describing' (p. 5); this presents interesting lines of enquiry. In what ways might a 'pretty' verse reveal deeper, darker – or simply different – preoccupations from the ones that are immediately apparent? Paying attention to point of view in Amy Levy's poems (including the one I discuss) reveals a playfulness to ideas about gender boundaries and same-sex desire, but is this attitude found elsewhere in other women's writing? How does the narrative voice in Charlotte Mew's 'Passed' compare with this sort of playfulness, and what are the results of that story's chance encounters on her sense of identity and mental stability? What are the effects of the masculine point of view some of these writers adopt, and if you detect androgynous voices, what might they reveal or conceal? In the essay 'The "Hour of Pink Twilight"' (cited in my essay, note 17), Kate Flint asks questions that help to explore ideas on this subject. 'What if,' she asks, 'at this moment in history, she did not quite possess a vocabulary, a readily available conceptual framework, through which to recognise, name, understand – or even necessarily welcome these feelings?' (p. 690). Flint also warns about the 'dangers of emotional identification involved in literary and social history – of projecting backwards, from some tacitly superior vantage point, our assumption that we unquestionably know and understand how these women felt' (p. 690).

Virginia Woolf's *A Room of One's Own* (1929) was in my mind as I wrote the section on the British Museum and its reading room. Woolf's second chapter is set in the reading room as her persona sets about a search for 'the essential oil of truth' about women. The description of the experience bears little resemblance to that of the previous generation of women writers who researched and networked there thirty or forty years earlier, and indeed, although Woolf asserts that 'we think back through our mothers if we are women', the mothers she cites are Charlotte Brontë, Jane Austen, George Eliot, not the more immediate earlier generation discussed here. Ruth Hoberman's essay 'Women in the British Museum Reading Room' (cited in my essay, note 5) is essential reading for exploring such apparent discrepancies. Hoberman argues that 'late-nineteenth-century, progressive, middle-class women seem to lay triumphant siege to the reading room, forming a quasi-public sphere in which they to some extent share the space, resources and media used by men' (p. 505). But by the 1920s Dorothy Richardson and Woolf 'respond quite differently, treating the room not as a source of knowledge and influence' that they can lay claim to, but instead 'a specifically male tradition from which they recoil' (p. 505).

Class-consciousness is another productive area for further study. It is implicit in every text discussed in my essay – for example, in terms of the characters' education, their need to earn a living (or not), whether they have the leisure to enjoy a winter's evening walk or whether they travel by omnibus rather than by hansom cab. Class and status are also visibly apparent in dress. There was no room to explore the representation of dress in my essay, but the importance of fashion houses and clothing to the women's writing of the period is unmistakable. It is evident, for example, on every page of John Oliver Hobbes's novellas *Some Emotions and A Moral* (1891) and *A Sinner's Comedy* (1894); Nesbit's Miss Lorrimore wears artistic floral print gowns from London's Regent Street Liberty shop, identifying herself as a modern woman, a reader of political economy. If what one wears and one's appearance defines the self, what does that say about Mew's narrator in 'Passed' who tells us nothing of herself on either score? She encounters a half-clothed woman – dead – and later the sister of that young woman, dressed in 'brilliant crimson' and 'dull vermillion'.

Jane Spirit's three-volume edition of *The Women Aesthetes: British Writers 1870–1900* (2013), cited in the essay (note 8), includes all of the texts I discuss, except for Amy Levy's 'Ballade of an Omnibus' which, like many of the others, is widely available electronically.

FURTHER READING

Ledger, Sally, *The New Woman: Fiction and Feminism at the Fin de Siècle* (Manchester University Press, 1997)

Hughes, Linda K., 'A Club of their Own: The Literary Ladies, New Women Writers and *Fin-de-Siècle* Authorship', *Victorian Literature and Culture* 35 (2007), 233–60

Parsons, Deborah, *Streetwalking the Metropolis: Women, the City and Modernity* (Oxford University Press, 2000)

Schaffer, Talia, and Kathy A. Psomiades (eds), *Women and British Aestheticism* (New Brunswick, NJ: Rutgers University Press, 1999)

Shaffer, Talia, *The Forgotten Female Aesthetes: Literary Culture in Late-Victorian England* (Charlottesville: University of Virginia Press, 2000)

Showalter, Elaine (ed.), *Daughters of Decadence: Women Writers of the Fin de Siècle* (London: Virago, 1993)

PART VI
The Twentieth Century, 1901–1939

INTRODUCTORY NOTE

The essays in this section offer innovative readings of works by three writers strongly associated with 'modernism' – D. H. Lawrence, T. S. Eliot and Virginia Woolf. Often summed up, in appropriately brash and declarative style, by Ezra Pound's famous injunction to 'Make it new!', modernism could be considered an epochal context all of its own. Even though 'modernism' was a retrospective label that only became fully established in the second half of the twentieth century and it has never really been solely a period designation, we might borrow the title phrase of Stephen Kern's seminal study *The Culture of Time and Space* (1983) to characterise it as a major cultural paradigm shift that was closely associated with the scientific, technological, philosophical and artistic developments of roughly the first half of the twentieth century. As mentioned earlier, this whole volume tends to circle around questions of time and space, and these concepts certainly feature prominently here in the essays by Anna Budziak and Stefania Michelucci. Taking an anthropological perspective, the latter presents a sophisticated exploration of the spatial dynamics of Lawrence's modernist classic, *Women in Love*, subtly suggesting how this novel, largely written during the First World War, almost literally maps out the structure of feeling of a culture in crisis – although perhaps the orientational metaphor of a map is rather misleading here, in that what is depicted in the psychology of Lawrence's characters is, as Michelucci suggests, more a matter of modernist *disorientation*. Identity is commonly associated with ideas of rootedness and a stable sense of belonging, to 'home', community and place. Michelucci's discussion of *Women in Love* skilfully throws into relief Lawrence's modernist reconfiguration of identity as something at least as much to do with movement and travel, with a certain degree of rootlessness or nomadism. What her discussion suggests, in fact, is that the process of exploring and negotiating identity is a type of dialogue between 'home' and 'away' and that identity and relationality develop through various forms of movement or mobility. In this, Michelucci's essay reflects a 'turn' towards the study of mobilities within the humanities in recent years (as represented, for example, by Palgrave Macmillan's recent book series, Studies in Mobilities, Literature and Culture, edited by Lynne Pearce and colleagues). T. S. Eliot's search for orientation in the modern world was related more to time than to space and, in typically paradoxical modernist style, he might be said to have made it new by making it old, and Budziak teases out this paradox in her essay through an absorbingly forensic investigation into the significance of Eliot's use of a classical epigraph for his 1930 poem *Marina*. The epigraph, from Seneca, mediated through the lenses of both Renaissance and modernist classicism, and inflecting Eliot's intertextual dialogue with Shakespeare's *Pericles*, thus becomes the occasion for a time-tunnelling contextualisation of a poem that Budziak also sets in relation to its contemporary concerns. The third essay in this section, by Judith Paltin, provides a cleverly double-focused feminist reading of Virginia Woolf's feminist classic *A Room of One's Own*, effectively reading the essay both with and against the grain. Following Woolf's overarching critique of women's historical exclusion from spheres of literary-cultural authority, Paltin nevertheless cautions against too uncritical an acceptance of the views filtered through the consciousness of Beton, the fictional figure Woolf creates to illustrate her argument. In what is, in part, a stylistic study of Woolf's technique in this work, Paltin suggests a sort of second-level critique operating in the way that Woolf lures the reader into a false sense of complacency about Beton that risks missing the extent to which her views are already compromised by the male discourses she seeks to challenge. Woolf's essay as framed by Paltin's essay usefully reminds us that a powerfully determining context for literature is the institution of literary criticism and there are many pertinent connections to be made in this respect with other essays in this volume – in particular, with Essays 5, 11, 12, 14, 20 and 25.

21 | D. H. Lawrence's *Women in Love*: An Anthropological Reading

STEFANIA MICHELUCCI

Abstract

This essay analyses D. H. Lawrence's *Women in Love* (1920) in the light of recent theoretical debates about concepts of time, space and location. Drawing extensively on anthropology, as far as the relationships between culture and nature, power and place are concerned, the essay highlights the experimental nature of *Women in Love* and combines a close reading with critical suggestions based on semiotics, sociology and recent research in human geography and environmentalism.

    Following introductory comments on the categories of space and place and representation in European modernism, the essay examines the spatial correlatives of the psychological traumas and thematic oppositions underlying *Women in Love*. What emerges is, on the one hand, the opposition between inside and outside, which will be explored in their various implications, and, on the other, the great theme of the quest, defined in the novel as a recovery of primitive roots and alternative ways of being. Attention then shifts to the crisis of home, read as an expression of modernist disorientation, and to the use of places of threshold – liminal, borderline, known and unknown, familiar and unfamiliar – as they contribute to the formation of the characters.

Space and Place

Most artistic revolutions of the twentieth century involved a reflection on space and new methods of conceptualising and utilising it (Figure 21.1). The so-called crisis of representation considered space a central issue, not only in the visual arts but also in literature. Starting from the seminal essay by Joseph Frank, 'Spatial Form in Modern Literature', critical studies on spatial artistic structures in twentieth-century art and literature have not been lacking, but the category of place still needs further study.[1] Space is a physical and philosophical category while place is a cultural and anthropological category.[2] On a map, places are represented by the human marks and names inscribed upon physical space for the affirmation and differentiation of a particular

Figure 21.1 Lyubov Sergeyevna Popova, *Space-Force Construction*, 1920–1. Popova was an avant-garde Russian artist influenced by cubism and futurism and a leading figure in the Constructivist movement which particularly sought to represent the material and spatial properties of objects.

culture.[3] Every culture inscribes itself upon a certain space by selecting places and assigning them specific functions of importance to the survival of the community. A specific social group carves out and shapes its own identity mainly by differentiating its own environment from the surroundings, as Martin Heidegger suggests in 'Art and Space' discussing the concept of 'clearing away'. 'Clearing-away brings forth the free, the openness for man's settling and dwelling ... clearing away is the release of places towards which the fate of dwelling man turns in the preserve of the home or in the brokenness of homelessness or in complete indifference of the two'.[4]

'Space' and 'place' also share an overlapping area on account of the primary psychological distinction between 'self' and 'not-self', between the 'I' and the surrounding world, which produces a fundamental binary opposition in the way the human mind organises space and consequently place. From the primeval opposition self–world, other binary spatial oppositions develop which play an important role in the human organisation of cultural places: in–out, near–far, finite–infinite, closed–open, static–moving, full–empty. From these, other psychological oppositions emerge: known–unknown, familiar–unfamiliar, security–threat, friend–foe, to mention just a few. The adult representation of space is not an immediate *reproduction* of the environment by the perceptive apparatus, but the result of intellectual manipulations of the spatial environment.[5]

The not-self can be the unknown, what is not humanised or culturalised (as, for example, the myth of the American frontier), but it can also be another place, outside the familiar place of being and beyond the controllable site of the community. The relationship with the not-self may vary from culture to culture, yet it is always a necessary condition for the identity of the community and the relationship of its members to the inhabited place. As Christian Norberg-Schulz underlines in his study of forms of human settlement, 'place ... unites a group of human beings, it is something which gives them a common identity and hence a basis for a fellowship or society'.[6]

Thus it becomes possible to formulate the anthropological categories of 'our places' and 'places of others' which are particularly relevant to this essay. Franco La Cecla emphasises the importance assumed by the dialectical relationship with the unknown beyond the place of the community as it enables us to consider our own place from another viewpoint, to evaluate it in relation to all of the cosmos, to discern its weaknesses and possible threats from the outside.[7] In *Tipologia della cultura*, Jurij Lotman and Boris Uspenskij discuss how the frontier, the threshold between inside and outside, known and unknown, is an essential element in the spatial metalanguage used for the description of culture. By these means, in every society and cultural system, the world of organisation and goodness and the world of disorganisation, chaos and evil are determined.[8] By constructing its own site in space, a community creates a microcosm, on the basis of which it is possible to explain and understand the rest of the world and to cohabit in a dialectical relation with it, reinforcing one's own sense of belonging to one's own place.

As noted, the predominance of spatial form in twentieth-century literature has received sustained attention. For example, Stephen Kern has offered an overall view of changing concepts of time and space found in various fields of knowledge and of their effect on the arts, while Frank's essays insist on the prevalence of the synchronic aspect over the diachronic in the avant-garde literary texts of the early 1900s.[9] The aim of this essay is to represent the *geography* of *Women in Love*, how the novel organises places to create the *field* of action for the activities of characters, and thereby to develop a system of functional relations carefully integrated into the structure of the text. Lotman and Uspenskij emphasise the distinction between unchangeable (fixed) and changeable spaces, between trespassable (or passable) places and closed boundaries, showing how the fixed elements in a literary text form the cosmogony, geography and social structure, the so-called 'field/scenario' of the hero.[10]

While the binary oppositions of space and place transfer readily from psychology and anthropology to literary discourse, one must also note that literature itself defines spaces and places. In other words, the geography (or topography) of literary works constitutes a system of meaningful relationships. Such a system can be defined as a system of *differences*, a code, a *langue*. Ferdinand de Saussure's term is apposite, considering that places are connected to one another and communicate via definite routes and accessible ways, so that it becomes possible to think of them as a communication system, a spatial *langue* which can mirror a particular world view. For Lotman and Uspenskij, 'the space of a cultural text represents the universal totality of the elements of a given culture, since it is the model of the whole'.[11] As a model of the whole, this spatial *langue* carries the conventions of a culture, but it then becomes the object of personal appropriation by the writer, turning itself into a particular textual *parole*. In turn, this *parole* constitutes a *langue* for the characters, who, shaping their cultural model upon it, then each create their own distinctive *parole* from it. Thus, we can see a double function of places in literary works relating to the interaction of *langue* and *parole*. In this light, places in *Women in Love* act as objective cultural reference points for all the characters while they are also interpreted and perceived in personal ways, individual 'readings' of places reflecting a personal semantic investment shaped by psychological or ideological factors.

In Lawrence's artistic evolution the function of places changes significantly, although the opposition between places of nature and places of culture persists throughout his work, a polarisation between the 'natural' and the 'artificial' indicative of an innovative development from the Romantic tradition. Both nature and culture are seen and represented by Lawrence as the effect of a polarity between a Darwinian and an aesthetic viewpoint. Whereas the latter leads him to highlight the poetic aspect of nature and to view culture as a means for intellectual development, the former constantly unfolds the brutal force of nature and views culture as damaging to spontaneity, as a source of artifice and corruption.[12]

Lawrence's early works, especially *The Prussian Officer and Other Stories* (1914) and the novels *The White Peacock* (1911) and *The Trespasser* (1912), reflect the yearning for escape to a world of 'refined' experience, one perceived inevitably as fragile and inauthentic and therefore destined to failure. The publication of *Sons and Lovers* (1913) sees this impasse overcome and from 1913 onwards Lawrence succeeds in turning upside down the polarity known–unknown, making the latter a positive pole, increasingly identified with what is chronologically and spatially remote. Embracing the unknown involves the exploration of an other universe, of other places, and from *Sons and Lovers* onwards most of his characters become indefatigable travellers. This engagement with an 'other, unknown' universe also applies to a central leitmotiv of Lawrence's aesthetics: the relationship between the sexes in which the greater the 'distance' between the partners, the more vital their relationship. Whereas in *The Lost Girl* (1920) the relationship with the revitalising other fails because the Midlands-born protagonist proves incapable of 'reading' and adapting to her lover's remote southern Italian village, in which she inevitably 'loses herself', in *The Rainbow* (1915) and *Women in Love* (1920) similar encounters with different environments become essential to the characters' self-fulfilment and individual growth. In the two later novels, place and experience are strictly interrelated, to the point that the characters define themselves along the chain of their movements from one place to the next.

The vital role of place is defined by Lawrence in *Studies in Classic American Literature* (1923) with his theorisation of the 'spirit of place', developing from the classical idea of a *genius loci*: 'Every continent has its own great spirit of place. Every people is polarised in some particular locality, which is home, the homeland. Different places on the face of the earth have different vital effluence, different vibration, different chemical exhalation, different polarity with different stars: call it what you like. But the spirit of place is a great reality.'[13] This sense of 'spirit of place' emerges strongly in Lawrence's late works, which are characterised by the profound tension generated by the desperate attempts of western characters to relate to other places. In *Kangaroo* (1923), *The Boy in the Bush* (1924), *The Plumed Serpent* (1926), 'The Woman Who Rode Away' (1925), 'The Princess' (1925) and *The Virgin and the Gipsy* (1930), Lawrence measures the capacity of a figure for growth by success or failure to confront a disturbing other world, whether it be the wild core of the Rocky Mountains in 'The Princess', the Chilchuis tribe in central Mexico in 'The Woman who Rode Away' or the mystery of wild nature as represented by the Australian bush in *Kangaroo*.

Women in Love: Known–Unknown

A family saga which covers several generations, *The Rainbow* (1915) and *Women in Love* (1920), originally conceived as one novel, can be seen in part as Lawrence's response to a vogue for novels with a large canvas such as naturalist masterpieces like Thomas Mann's *Buddenbrooks* (1901) or Émile Zola's earlier *Rougon-Macquart* cycle of novels (1871–93). Most importantly, however, the social and cultural transformations taking place throughout early twentieth-century Europe are the humus for the ultimately modernist evolution of Lawrence's characters, who are sometimes presented as heroes, sometimes as victims, and sometimes, especially in *Women in Love*, as both. Whereas the saga form in *The Rainbow* develops diachronically through three generations, *Women in Love* focuses synchronically on a single generation as it interweaves the experiences of *The Rainbow*'s third-generation character Ursula Brangwen with those of other characters, Gudrun, Birkin, Gerald, Hermione, Loerke. Indeed, the novel's treatment of time is highly original. Instead of events unfolding in a linear sequence as in *The Rainbow*, episodes in *Women in Love* follow one another in a seemingly casual way, as a collage of fragments. One consequence is that the novel appears almost filmically composed of detached narrative sequences, linked to one another through flashbacks and flash-forwards.

From the opening chapter of *The Rainbow* the characters never stop looking for 'a beyond', an enlargement of their horizons and expectations which appears simultaneously utopian and dystopian, like a dream with a nightmare lingering behind. Personal growth involves the exploration of the unknown, but it is depicted hand in hand with the breaking down of an 'organic' community whose members have thus far lived rooted in visceral communion with the earth. In *The Rainbow*, the rhythm of this devastating but unavoidable process quickens at an increasing pace from generation to generation, but in *Women in Love* it moves at a positively frenetic pace, as well as in scattered, apparently aimless directions, as if the characters are moving hysterically, deracinated and without purpose. The representation of the characters' development draws on two interacting perspectives, a historical one and a mythical or anthropological one. Lawrence interweaves these continuously, bringing each character symbolically into contact with the great archetypes of existence while also associating them directly with historical processes. From one generation to the next, this interaction involves a progressive widening of the characters' horizons, but also, paradoxically, a narrowing of their living spaces, which in some cases leads them to the total loss of any firm sense of belonging.

In both novels the English Midlands is the centre from which all the characters – despite their different and even contrasting personalities – attempt to distance themselves. Their urge to explore and experience new places is seen by Lawrence as an ethical drive, a vital impulse, which, from character to character, takes different forms. The drive stems chiefly from intolerance of a suffocating home environment and the constraints of middle-class provincial life, shown as inhabited by empty shadows moving mechanically, like 'subdued beast[s] in sheep's clothing',[14] or, in Gudrun's words, as 'a country in an underworld'.[15]

Despite their expectations, most characters discover that the rest of Europe is not immune from the superficiality and emptiness which, in a pandemic way, has affected all cultural centres. Not only London but also Paris and Dresden are just phantoms of themselves. Each city wears a mask of intellectual sophistication to hide an inner void, rapidly exposed on closer acquaintance. The 'large, lofty room' of the Pompadour Café, for example, a Bohemian haunt in London, turns out to be a place of haze and smoke 'repeated ad infinitum' in 'great mirrors' (p. 62). The provincials drawn there by expectations of intellectual open-mindedness end up embittered, disillusioned, even disgusted: '"I feel I could *never* see this *foul* town again–. I couldn't *bear* to come back to it",' cries Gudrun (p. 386). If London is a nightmare which fills Birkin with desperation ('"I always feel doomed when the train is running into London ... as if it were the end of the world"' (p. 61)), Paris turns out to be just a place of frivolous artists' parties. Dresden is presented even more negatively, as it is symbolically identified with Loerke, a grotesque caricature of an artist, whose activity Lawrence sees as a negation, rather than an expression, of life.[16]

Just as disappointing is the escape to the south, where the romantic myth of Italy as the paradise of exiles turns out to be an illusion: the Imperial Road leading there is not, as Birkin says at the end of *Women in Love*, "'a way out ... —It was only a way in again'" (p. 478). What he encounters resembles what he left behind; there is no escape, therefore, apart from a destructive annihilation (Gerald dying in a desert of snow) or a defeating return home.

In the characters' search for a place ethically and ideologically *other* than arid, materialistic England (the root of their existential angst), the novel at times points to the promise of radically different cultural horizons, as suggested, for instance, by the primitivism of Halliday's African statue –'Pure culture in sensation ... mindless, utterly sensual' (p. 79); or of new spatial horizons in uncontaminated corners of old rural England. However, the vital interaction between centre and margins, between known and unknown, which is anthropologically essential for the development and survival of the community, unfolds in *Women in Love* in a kind of vortex, where the traditional unknown (the city as opposed to the country, the south and the Continent as opposed to England) offers no truly vital source as a viable alternative to the centre. Therefore such a nourishing, vital place outside the community, has to be found elsewhere.[17]

'One Should Never Have a *Home*'

The demarcation apparent in *The Rainbow* between 'places of us' (where 'us' coincides with the house and its 'under places' offering a refuge from external threats) and 'places of others' (the reflection of an order imposed from above, the seat of institutions and power) breaks down in *Women in Love*.[18] In the later novel the sense of functional organisation of space is greatly diminished, suggesting a state of crisis from which, as Birkin prophetically announces, it will be possible to exit only through a rebirth. For him, this will require, first of all, the destruction of the old order, not only in England but in Europe as well.

Home is no longer seen as the place where an individual *lives*, organically belonging to an environment in a larger community, but as a mere lodging or dormitory.[19] In the 'crisis of home', not only the working-class habitations are involved (in *Women in Love* the miners' villages appear as a sinister, hostile underworld), but also those of the upper classes. The name of the Crich residence, Shortlands, suggests the reduction of liveable space in industrialised England. Its upper-class architecture ('it has form ... it has a period' (p. 48)), does not conceal the ugliness of the nearby mines, that desolate, dirty, subterranean world which constitutes its *raison d'être*, as for Wragby Hall in *Lady Chatterley's Lover*.[20] The decline of the country estates matches the inexorable process by which the characters become alienated from their places of origin. Even more than for the individuals, this process affects couples, the traditional starting point for nuclear families. They repudiate their homes of origin and, in the case of Ursula and Birkin, have no wish to create another one because that would mean rooting themselves in the old order, renouncing complete fulfilment of the self. For Birkin, this nesting instinct to avoid exposure to the external world proves a lethal germ capable of exterminating his generation: "'One should avoid this *home* instinct. It's not an instinct, it's a habit of cowardliness. One should never have a *home*'" (p. 352). For him, the 'place of us' of married life is 'anywhere'. To the lethal stability of home, he counter-proposes the fertile precariousness of homelessness: "'it isn't really a locality, though'", Birkin argues, "'It's a perfected relation between you and me'" (p. 316).

Faced with this vital but uncomfortable idea, Gudrun draws back in discomfort. Despite her self-declared restlessness, she, like Gerald, is tormented by the desire to possess a place and to be possessed by it: 'the wonderful stability of marriage. She did want it ... She suddenly conjured up a rosy room, with herself in a beautiful gown, and a handsome man in evening dress who held her in his arms in the firelight, and kissed her' (p. 376). This projection of domesticity conflicts with the character's frenetic restlessness. It corresponds more to the assumption of a role than to the intimate desire of married life in a stable home, reflecting Gudrun's indulgence in 'the rituals of her life' (p. 414), her wearing a mask to hide her inner self.[21]

The process which moves the characters from rootedness in an apparently self-sufficient home life to total uprooting, takes place in an alternation between regressive centripetal movement and progressive centrifugal movement – that is, between the tendency to absorb external space into the domestic environment and the opposite tendency to expand the self into a space free of predetermined limits. In *Women in Love* closed spaces are often projections of an individual will which absorbs the space, cutting all contact with the external world and excluding others: the house therefore becomes a place of conflict and mutual violence. Lawrence uses the parallel development of the two couples' stories to confirm, by comparison and contrast, the idea of a crisis of 'home'.

Ursula and Birkin move slowly towards mutual acceptance when each of them ceases to try to engulf the other in his/her own world, after a series of bruising conflicts which, significantly, are always more bitter when they occur indoors. This process ultimately leads them to give up the very idea of home and to choose a vagabond existence in which their residence is (as it was for Lawrence and his wife, Frieda) a perpetually changing 'anywhere'. While they are outdoors, especially in unbounded places, they achieve moments of mutual identification, or at least of closeness. Islands, metaphorical or real, feel restrictive. This is the case, for example, of the one in the pond of Willey Water, where they experience a discouraging incommunicability: "'Do let us go to the shore'", Ursula pleads, 'afraid of being any longer imprisoned on the island' (p. 131). Her reaction is not dissimilar from that of Siegmund and Helena on the Isle of Wight in *The Trespasser*, or Paul and Miriam in their unhappy experiment of wedded life in an isolated cottage in *Sons and Lovers* (chapter 11, 'The Test on Miriam').

By contrast, the most intensely intimate encounters always occur outdoors. The first moment of complete harmony between Ursula and Birkin takes place in the chapter 'Excurse', in which the two set off by car one afternoon with no destination in mind. After travelling in silence through empty lanes for a while, Ursula wonders where they are and asks, '"And where are we going?"' '"Anywhere"', Birkin replies – 'It was the answer she liked' (pp. 303–4). This exchange foreshadows the discoveries offered by their subsequent erotic encounter. The experience also marks a further step forward in their relationship, confirming their decision to open themselves to the outside world and to a new life by burning their bridges to the previous one, that is, by leaving school and home.[22]

Unlike Birkin and Ursula, Gerald and Gudrun are involved in a centripetal relationship which reflects each partner's desire to attract and enclose the other in his/her own world. Gudrun and Gerald's erotic initiation occurs in her closed bedroom, to which he brings a sense of death – symbolised by the soil on his shoes from his father's grave – and an obscure, destructive desire which he passes on to his lover: 'She was exhausted, wearied ... There was something monstrous about him, about his juxtaposition against her' (p. 346). This stolen intimacy with Gudrun (Gerald enters the cottage like a thief) results from a centripetal movement. Gerald's intention to enclose Gudrun within his own space has already been illustrated by his inviting her to Shortlands on the pretence of teaching art to his younger sister Winifred. Gudrun herself tends to transform every outdoor environment into a studio, a place in which she can exercise her own control and power, as in the hypnotic, domineering dance in front of the cattle (pp. 167–8), which is not an interaction with wild nature but an attempt to draw its energies into her own sphere and to tame them.[23] So centripetal is the relationship between Gudrun and Gerald, demanding a near total assimilation of the external, that they manage to make even the immense stretch of snow in the Tyrol into a closed place, a prison which becomes, for Gerald, a tomb.[24] Even in this environment, which at the beginning promised freedom because of its difference ('One could never feel like this in England' (p. 394)), the two experience an oppressive sense of claustrophobia. Especially in the interiors of the chalet rooms, they flare up into violent conflicts – 'finally, he might kill her' (p. 445) – linked especially to the violation of personal space which each feels he/she has suffered because of the other. Paradoxically, the conflict expands out into the ethereal, inhuman mountains, that literal and metaphorical blank space which catalyses the freezing of their intimacy and highlights their incompatibility: '"Don't try and come between it and me. Take yourself away, you are out of place—"' (p. 447).

The ice-bound mountain peaks and the Swiss valley have an opposite effect on Birkin and Ursula; it is actually the difference of the place, the unnaturalness of its whiteness, which forces them to find each other, contrasting the cold of the snow to the warmth of their love: "'I couldn't bear this cold, eternal place without you'" (p. 408). While Ursula and Birkin manage to break the deadly spell exerted by this environment ('Miracle of miracles! – this utterly silent, frozen world of the mountain-tops was not universal! ... One might go away' (p. 434)), Gudrun and Gerald succumb to it, finding themselves incapable of turning back or of escaping to salvation in another place.

Thresholds: A Conclusion

The opposition between centrifugal and centripetal movements draws attention to the category of the threshold, or line of demarcation between two different places, the crossing of which on the one hand can make the process of growth possible, but on the other entails the risk of being unable to return. Thresholds become more and more indefinite in *Women in Love*, mirroring the characters' difficulties in finding a true direction in life. Sometimes, when the goal cannot be envisaged, the road ahead may even appear to be totally blocked. This happens to Gerald, who, once he has left England, 'gets stuck' in the ethereal whiteness of the Tyrolean snow, completely incapable of identifying a new destination: 'He had lost all his sense of place' (p. 473). While the thought of return arouses a sense of repulsion in him ('he shuddered with nausea at the thought of home' (p. 460)), he perceives a sort of circle around himself which, instead of becoming wider, as the opening towards the Continent had seemed to promise, is closing tightly around him: 'he set himself to be free ... But for the first time there was a flaw in his will. Where shall I go?' (p. 445).

Ursula and Birkin avoid the debacle of Gerald because they gradually learn to cross the threshold of the other's space without trying to conquer it. They succeed in accepting the unknown space of the other, overcoming the sterile, self-destructive contradiction between ideal and real and its destructive effect on human relationships.

Ursula and Birkin's acceptance of the reality of their otherness contrasts with its rejection by Gudrun and Gerald, whose privileging of the artificial over the natural, of the empty, worldly rituals in which both of them indulge, is clearly intended to suggest the surrogate nature of their lives: 'Gerald was dressed for dinner, as usual in the evening, although he was alone ... She stood before the mirror every night for some minutes, brushing her fine dark hair. It was part of the inevitable ritual of her life' (pp. 267, 414). The vanity inherent in their individual routines produces an attraction to the void, the non-life, which Gerald feels when he meets his destiny and his frozen death in the snow: 'He only wanted ... to keep going, until it was finished' (p. 473).

Unharmonious, but dynamic, relationships in *Women in Love* are the mirror of an epoch – the one surrounding the First World War – fragmentary, chaotic, even tragic, but not without potential for renewal. The individual, the novel suggests, faces a multitude of doors, some of which will open on to a void, others of which will lead to fulfilment. On such thresholds rest the two couples at the close of *Women in Love* in a conclusion bleak in tone and intentionally devoid of a soothing ending while yet still open for the reader.[25]

NOTES

1. Joseph Frank, *The Widening Gyre: Crisis and Mastery in Modern Literature* (New Brunswick, NJ: Rutgers University Press, 1963), pp. 3–62, later expanded and furnished with responses to his critics in *The Idea of Spatial Form* (New Brunswick, NJ: Rutgers University Press, 1991).

2. According to Francesco Remotti, 'every society is made of places and bodies, that is, it consists of bodies which live, work, interact, and dwell in certain places ... every society spreads out into a space, articulates and organises itself in it, designating certain specific places in its territory which are destined to certain specific activities'. *Luoghi e corpi. Antropologia dello spazio del tempo e del potere* (*Places and Bodies: The Anthropology of Space, Time and Power*) (Turin: Bollati Boringhieri, 1993), p. 31, my translation.

3. Ibid., pp. 36–46.

4. Martin Heidegger, 'Art and Space' (1969), trans. Charles H. Seibert, *Man and World* 6 (1973), 3–8 (5).

5. John H. Flavell, 'Space, Geometry, Chance, Adolescent Reasoning, and Perception', in *The Developmental Psychology of Jean Piaget*, with a foreword by Jean Piaget (Princeton: D. Van Nostrand, 1963), pp. 327–56.

6. Christian Norberg-Schulz, *The Concept of Dwelling: On the Way to Figurative Architecture* (New York: Rizzoli, 1985), p. 9.

7. Franco La Cecla, *Perdersi: L'uomo senza ambiente* (*Getting Lost: Man without an Environment*) (Bari: Laterza, 1988), pp. 92–100.

8. Jurij M. Lotman and Boris A. Uspenskij, *Tipologia della cultura* (*The Typology of Culture*), ed. Remo Faccani and Marzio Marzaduri (Milan: Bompiani, 1987), pp. 145–81.

9. Stephen Kern, *The Culture of Time and Space 1880–1918* (Cambridge, MA: Harvard University Press, 1983); Joseph Frank, *The Idea of Spatial Form* (New Brunswick, NJ: Rutgers University Press, 1991). Interesting remarks on the subject are offered by Eric S. Rabkin, 'Spatial Form and Plot', *Critical Inquiry* 4 (1977), 253–70; William Holtz, 'Spatial Form in Modern Literature: A Reconsideration', *Critical Inquiry* 4 (1977), 271–83, Gabriel Zoran, 'Towards a Theory of Space in Narrative', *Poetics Today* 5 (1984), 309–35; and Jo A. Isaak, *The Ruin of Representation in Modernist Art and Texts* (Ann Arbor, MI: UMI Research Press, 1986). Particular attention to spatial form in the novel is given by Joseph Kestner in *The Spatiality of the Novel* (Detroit: Wayne State University Press, 1978); in Jeffrey R. Smitten and Ann Daghistany (eds), *Spatial Form in Narrative* (Ithaca, NY: Cornell University Press, 1981), furnished with an extensive bibliography; and in Ruth Ronen, 'Space in Fiction', *Poetics Today* 7 (1986), 421–38.

10. Lotman and Uspenskij, *Tipologia della cultura*, pp. 145–81.

11. Ibid., p. 154. Ferdinand de Saussure's influential distinction between the underlying system or grammar of a language, *langue*, and actual instances or utterances of the language, *parole*, derives from his *Course in General Linguistics* (first published in French in 1915).

12. See Stefania Michelucci, *Space and Place in the Works of D. H. Lawrence* (Jefferson, NC: McFarland, 2002); the present essay builds in particular on some of the ideas developed in chapter 6 of that work. See also Roger Ebbatson, *The Evolutionary Self: Hardy, Forster, Lawrence* (Brighton: Harvester Press, 1992).

13. *Studies in Classic American Literature*, ed. Ezra Greenspan, Lindeth Vasey and John Worthen (Cambridge University Press, 2003), p. 17.

14. D. H. Lawrence, *The Rainbow*, ed. Mark Kinkead-Weekes (Cambridge University Press, 1989), p. 415.

15. D. H. Lawrence, *Women in Love*, ed. David Farmer, Lindeth Vasey and John Worthen (Cambridge University Press, 1987), p. 11; citations are hereafter given in the text. Michael Bell underlines that Gudrun provides the viewpoint for a defamiliarised vision, which Lawrence clearly wishes to present as not merely hers: 'She experiences it as an unnerving, vertiginous sense of unreality, a sense of living in a completely different world'. *D. H. Lawrence: Language and Being* (Cambridge University Press, 1992), p. 102.

16. On Loerke's repulsive attraction see Joyce Carol Oates, 'Lawrence's Götterdämmerung: The Tragic Vision of *Women in Love*', in David Ellis (ed.), *D. H. Lawrence's Women in Love: A Casebook* (Oxford University Press, 2006), pp. 25–49.

17. Living in any community involves the constant need to compare one's place with the outside world, with the diversity of other places, a comparison which on the one hand jeopardises one's identity, but also saves one from isolation, paralysis and death. See Remotti, *Luoghi e corpi*, pp. 76–107.

18. For the anthropological opposition between places of us and places of others, see ibid., pp. 11–75.

19. Theories of the 'home' have seen it as the place where a person lives in harmony with the surrounding environment, rather than simply a lodging, as it tends to be in modern industrial societies. On this, see especially Gaston Bachelard, *The Poetics of Space* (1958), trans. Maria Jolas (New York: Penguin, 2014), especially the chapter 'House and Universe', where he shows how the archetypical home is closely connected to its universality, to its being, for its inhabitants, the centre of the world. Emma Corigliano, *Tempo, Spazio, Identità: No Place like Home* (Milan: Angeli, 1991); La Cecla, *Perdersi*. See also John Worthen, *D. H. Lawrence: The Early Years 1885–1912* (Cambridge University Press, 1991), pp. 29–74.

20. The ideal home should allow the inhabitants to keep intact their own identity and at the same time to draw stimulus and nourishment from the surrounding environment. See Emmanuel Levinas, 'The Dwelling', in *Totality and Infinity: An Essay on Exteriority* (1963), trans. Alphonso Lingis (Pittsburgh: Duquesne University Press, 1969), pp. 152–74; Norberg-Schulz, *Concept of Dwelling*, pp. 89–110; Remotti, *Luoghi e corpi*; and Lotman and Uspenskij, *Tipologia della cultura*. See also Stefania Michelucci, 'Capsized Classes: The Annihilation of History in *Women in Love*', in *The British Aristocracy in Popular Culture*, ed. Stefania Michelucci, Ian Duncan and Luisa Villa (Jefferson: McFarland, 2020), pp. 140–56.

21. See Erving Goffman, *The Presentation of the Self in Everyday Life* (New York: Double-day, 1959); Remotti, *Luoghi e Corpi*.

22. For Diane S. Bonds, the place of their encounter is like 'a place not to be perceived as a place, a "nowhere." In this non-place, the language of the chapter insists, they achieve a transcendent, liberating union' ('Going into the Abyss: Literarization in *Women in Love*', *Essays in Literature* 8 (1981), 189–202 (194)).

23. For Jack Stewart, Gudrun's 'characteristic mode of seeing is to enclose within a frame ... Gudrun regards others with "objective curiosity", as material for her art, just as Gerald regards men and matter as instruments of his will' ('Dialectics of Knowing in *Women in Love*', *Twentieth Century Literature* 37 (1991), 59–71 (63–5)).

24. For Bonds, Gerald's abandonment to the ecstasy of velocity in the freezing snow 'implies no life-giving release of energy, but rather moves in the direction of snow-abstract annihilation' ('Going into the Abyss', 197).

25. See Giovanni Cianci, '*Introduzione a Donne innamorate*' (Turin: Einaudi, 1995), pp. v–xxvii, and the essays by Mark Kinkead-Weekes, 'Violence in *Women in Love*', and Ginette Katz-Roy, 'The Dialogue with the Avant-Garde in *Women in Love*', in Ellis (ed.), *Women in Love: A Casebook*, pp. 221–44, 245–72.

CRITICAL REFLECTIONS AND FURTHER STUDY

From the second half of the nineteenth century contributions to scientific thought by Freud, Einstein, Darwin, Frazer and Bergson, among others, began to revise conceptions – and consequently altered literary representations – of ontological categories such as time, space, place, community and identity. This essay on *Women in Love* examines how fictional characters perceived from an anthropological perspective embody a distinctive *Weltanschauung*, as they experience, interpret and react to space and place. In different ways, all of them rebel against the norms of the community to which they belong and seek to explore new constellations of the categories mentioned above. The approach adopted can be clarified in relation to travel literature, where typically the narrator/traveller explores a different country in pursuit of understanding and representing the otherness of an unfamiliar environment. A highly relevant intertext here, in relation to my discussion of *Women in Love*, would be Lawrence's own collection of travel essays, *Twilight in Italy* (1916), the composition of which overlapped with the early evolution of the novel. My introduction to this collection in *Twilight in Italy and Other Essays*, (ed. Paul Eggert, London: Penguin, 1997, pp. xv–xlv) is also of relevance here in introducing Lawrence's fascination with foreign environments and 'places of others'.

Applied further to Lawrence, an anthropological perspective can also illuminate his later works, especially his novels, short stories and travel writing, whose settings involve far-away countries and cultures. Ironically, some of Lawrence's later fiction of the 1920s (most notably his Mexican-set novel *The Plumed Serpent* (1926)) has been criticised for embodying totalitarian tendencies, a turn to the right at odds with his predisposition to look beyond national boundaries, explore unfamiliar terrain and embrace otherness.

Anthropological criticism more generally has additional applications. It offers a fresh perspective on literary canons defined solely by national borders and strengths; it also reinforces a growing trend to study world literature unconfined by restrictive labels. From the turn of the twentieth century and following two world wars, interest in the periphery rather than in the centre has grown. Writers from former colonies, for example, have come forward ready to challenge the hierarchical categories to which they have been subjected. Recent interest in migrant literature signifies a related development. For most migrants, including artists who choose a voluntary exile and write in a language different from their mother tongue, the interaction between different places, the often contrasting organisation of space in the place of origin and that of destination, plays a vital part in their artistic output and individual growth. Central to the experience of migrants is the category of 'placelessness', also connected to the idea of identity in transit, involving frequent expressions of regret over the loss of old places and bitter disaffection with new ones. Such responses are hardly surprising; to survive, one must adapt to a new place and a new community. To what extent might it be illuminating to view some of Lawrence's works in the light of contemporary migrant literature and the critical discourses surrounding it? (See the final section of Ulla Rahbek's essay in this volume for a convenient introduction to 'conceptualising migration' through two recent novels by Mohsin Hamid and Helon Habila.)

Lawrence's close engagement with nature in his writing has been a key theme in Lawrence criticism from the very start. In recent years, moreover, he has increasingly been studied from an ecocritical perspective and seen as one of the major environmentalist writers of the twentieth century. His 'anthropological' fascination with foreign environments is usually very closely interconnected with his observations of the natural environment, and this suggests a further area of possible study in combining anthropological and ecocritical readings of his works. Drawing on his concept of the 'spirit of place' mentioned in my essay, one might, for example, consider how in his works Lawrence often explores such a spirit in some detail through a subtly blended depiction of both interpersonal social relationships and the non-human environment.

In addition to the works cited in the notes to my essay, the list that follows offers some further reading suggestions for works on the representation of space and place and for critical studies on Lawrence and *Women in Love* that draw attention, in particular, to interdisciplinary modernist experimentation.

FURTHER READING

Arai, Hidenaga, *Literature along the Lines of Flight* (Amsterdam and New York: Rodopi, 2014)

Bammer, Angelika (ed.), *Displacements: Cultural Identities in Question* (Bloomington: Indiana University Press, 1994)

Bromley, Roger, *Narratives of Forced Mobility and Displacement in Contemporary Literature and Culture* (Cham: Palgrave Macmillan, 2021). Part of a series launched in 2017: Studies in Mobilities, Literature, and Culture, ed. Marian Aguiar, Charlotte Mathieson and Lynne Pearce.

Crang, Mike, Phil Crang and Jon May, *Virtual Geographies: Bodies, Space and Relations* (London: Routledge, 1999)

Ellis, David (ed.), *D. H. Lawrence's Women in Love: A Casebook* (Oxford University Press, 2006). A collection of selected, interdisciplinary studies on *Women in Love*, by Joyce Carol Oates, John Worthen, David Parker, John B. Humma, Gerald Doherty, Jack F. Stewart, Carola M. Kaplan, Bethan Jones, Mark Kinkead-Weekes, Ginette Katz-Roy, J. B. Bullen, previously published in literary journals.

Fay, Stephen and Liam Haydon (eds), *An Analysis of Homi K. Bhabha's 'The Location of Culture'* (London: Macat Library, 2017)

Hoshi, Kumiko, *D. H. Lawrence and Pre-Einsteinian Modernist Relativity* (Newcastle upon Tyne: Cambridge Scholars, 2018)

McLuhan, Marshall, and Harley Parker, *Through the Vanishing Point: Space in Poetry and Painting* (New York: Harper & Row, 1968)

Milton, Kay (ed.), *Environmentalism and Cultural Theory: Exploring the Role of Anthropology in Environmental Discourse* (London: Routledge, 1996)

Mitchell, W. I. T. (ed.), *Landscape and Power* (University of Chicago Press, 1994)

Reid, Sue, *D. H. Lawrence, Music and Modernism* (Cham: Palgrave Macmillan, 2019)

Robertson, George, et al. (eds), *Traveller's Tales: Narratives of Home and Displacement* (London: Routledge, 1994)

Smith, Stewart, *Nietzsche and Modernism: Nihilism and Suffering in Lawrence, Kafka and Beckett* (Cham: Palgrave Macmillan, 2018)

Stewart, Jack, *The Vital Art of D. H. Lawrence: Vision and Expression* (Carbondale: Southern Illinois University Press, 1999)

Todorov, Tzvetan, *On Human Diversity: Nationalism, Racism and Exoticism in French Thought* (1989), trans. Catherine Porter (Cambridge, MA: Harvard University Press, 1993)

Widdowson, Peter (ed.), *D. H. Lawrence* (London and New York: Longman, 1992)

22 The Epigraph for T. S. Eliot's *Marina*: Classical Tradition and the Modern Era

ANNA BUDZIAK

Abstract

When preparing *Marina* for publication, T. S. Eliot decided to leave the poem's epigraph unattributed; at the same time, in his correspondence, he explained that it came from Seneca. The question, however, of why the epigraph was derived from Seneca's *Hercules Furens* – instead of from Euripides' *The Madness of Heracles*, as would have been more usual at the time – requires clarification, as does the question of why the reference to Seneca, suppressed in the published text, was stressed in Eliot's letters. Both questions are related to Eliot's sense of literary tradition and of its ancient roots. This essay suggests that Eliot's decision to omit the attribution resulted from his awareness of the decline of classics in schools and universities and it considers his predilection for Seneca in the light of reviews of classical translations in which Eliot effectively proposes a correction to the Victorian version of classical antiquity. Specifically, it reads Eliot's review of H. D.'s translations of Euripides – an unpublished review written in the year the Gallipoli campaign ended and the Battles of the Somme and Verdun were fought – as postulating the need for a new tradition and a new language to express the era's permeating sense of shock and despair. Emotions that were similar in their intensity to those he had experienced in the war years affected Eliot in the late 1920s, but now he *had* a new language through which to express them, as shown in 1930 by *Marina*. Heightened by their echoes of *Hercules Furens*, these feelings are articulated through the poetic technique which Eliot developed under the influence of scholarly treatises on the Elizabethan Seneca – a classic who, over time, also proved more congenial than Euripides to the modern literary tradition with which Eliot concerned himself as early as 1916.

Eliot once said that interpreting is instinctual, a matter of a drive to solve literary puzzles, that to interpret is 'to pounce upon a secret, to elucidate the pattern and pluck out the mystery, of a poet's work.'[1] He made this remark in his introduction to *The Wheel of Fire* (1930) by G. Wilson Knight, whose earlier work, *Myth and Miracle* (1929), had inspired his interest in two themes which would become the major motifs of *Marina*: 'the contrast of death and life'[2] and fatherhood. With its lexicon of 'singing', 'laughter' and 'hope', one of Eliot's happiest poems (although accompanied by the gloomiest epigraph), *Marina* relies on the juxtaposition of two stories. The main text rewrites the scene in which Shakespeare's Pericles, in the final act of the play of that name (1609), is reunited with his daughter, whom he thought to be dead (Figure 22.1); the epigraph – providing a horrifying contrast and a disturbing parallel – recalls the words spoken by another father, Seneca's Hercules, awakening from a fit of frenzy to see that he has murdered his own children (Figure 22.2). Still confused, he asks the questions which Eliot put above the lines of his *Marina*: '*Quis hic locus, quae regio, quae mundi plaga?*' – 'What place is this? what region? or of the world what coast?'.[3] These two scenes are connected in a manner Eliot described as a 'crisscross',[4] and which he further theorised in 'The Use of Poetry and the Use of Criticism' (1933) as the indispensable design in poetry. There he states: 'Organisation is necessary as well as "inspiration".[5] Making observations on other poets' strategies (Coleridge's imagery in *Kubla Khan* and Chapman's borrowings from *Hercules Œteus* and *Hercules Furens*), which was frequently Eliot's means of commenting on his own creativity, he adds that a poetic effect depends on the work's textual environment,

Figure 22.1 Pericles and his daughter Marina: illustration from a Victorian edition of Shakespeare's plays (London: Cassell, 1864–8).

that 'even the finest line draws its life from its context'.[6] But, while stressing here that literary context was essential, in *Marina* Eliot seems to have deliberately obscured part of the poem's literary context by leaving its epigraph unattributed. In his letters, on the other hand, he repeatedly highlighted the quoted author, openly explaining that the citation had come from Seneca. Nevertheless, he left the reasons for his choice of epigraph, and for the omission of the tragedian's name, to linger among the poem's secrets.

One possible answer to the question of why Seneca's name was removed may have been provided indirectly by Eliot when, commenting on what he perceived as the failures of his plays, he confessed that he had learnt the lesson of not revealing his sources too quickly. With reference to *The Cocktail Party* (1949) – its plot based on Euripides' *Alcestis* – he admits his resolve 'to conceal the origins so well that nobody would identify them until I pointed them out myself'.[7] He explains that, as a playwright, he strived to integrate the dramas of antiquity and modernity,[8] without erecting a barrier of classical learning between himself and his audience, that the ancient origins of the play were not to create an obstacle for the reader unfamiliar with the ancients. A similar concern – for the reader – was expressed in his letter to Knight, clarifying that the reference to *Hercules Furens* was removed 'for fear of misleading people who had not read the play itself'.[9] Eliot was aware that he could not expect the majority of his readers to understand classical allusions instantly. He knew only too well that, due to the elective system of education in American universities – a system fostered by his grandfather William Greenleaf Eliot, third chancellor of Washington University in St Louis, and by his grandfather's cousin Charles William Eliot, president of Harvard – fewer and fewer students were prepared to undertake the effort of studying Latin and Greek as optional courses. The result was a decline in classics, which led the renowned historian Samuel Eliot Morison to accuse Harvard's famous president of 'the greatest educational crime of the century against American youth – depriving him of his classical heritage'.[10] The offence, if overstated, was however redressed by T. S. Eliot, the president's cousin twice removed, who returned this heritage to American youth as a new classical tradition – a tradition created through diverse adaptations and dislocations, one of which consisted in replacing Euripides with Seneca.

Eliot was ever evasive about the reason for this shift. In a conversation with William Empson in 1959 he confided that he had intended to play a prank on 'the classical men' who would have read Euripides at school and, therefore, would fail to recognise the line from Seneca's play. But Empson doubted that the epigraph could be wholly explained through 'this little tease'.[11] Earlier on, around the time *Marina* was composed, Eliot remarked to Michael Sadler that his greater knowledge of Seneca was merely accidental.[12] Nevertheless, he had known the Roman tragedian's work since the days he spent at Smith Academy (1898–1905), where he first read Seneca together with other authors studied for their style.[13] Moreover, when appointed assistant in philosophy for the period 1913–14 at Harvard, he discussed Seneca's moral dialogues with undergraduates,[14] and returned to Seneca in the context of Elizabethan drama while teaching as an extension lecturer in Southall, west London, in 1918.[15] His two seminal texts on the Roman tragedian – an introduction to *Seneca: His Tenne Tragedies Translated into English, Edited by Thomas Newton Anno 1581* (reprinted as 'Seneca in Elizabethan Translation' in 1932) and 'Shakespeare and the Stoicism of Seneca' – were published for the first time in 1927, the year declared a turning point for Seneca's reputation in English, with the only comparable cultural watershed in *anno* 1581.[16] However, while knowledgeable about Seneca, Eliot was also thoroughly familiar with Euripides. In his second year at Harvard – with Greek antiquity constituting the 'center of gravity' of his studies – he read Euripides' *Medea*;[17] and in the 1940s, as a mature poet and playwright, he alluded in one of his plays to Euripides' *Alcestis*. Significantly, in the year his two Senecan essays appeared, Eliot, as a director of Faber & Gwyer, was seeking a reviewer for a 'critical book' on the dramatist of classical Athens – *Euripides the Idealist* by R. B. Appleton.[18] Therefore, his choice to cite from the Roman was hardly caused by his alleged lesser familiarity with the Greek. Neither was it merely a prank, given that he had written several letters to clarify the organisation of the poem as related to the source of the epigraph.[19]

The key to this decision should be sought elsewhere, possibly in Eliot's unpublished review of translations by H. D. (Hilda Doolittle) of Euripides' choruses from *Iphigeneia in Aulis*. Eliot's review is a little known prose text of 1916 but it constitutes both an anticipation of his famous 'Tradition and the Individual Talent' (1919) and a context for his notorious criticism of Gilbert Murray's rendering of Euripides (1920). In fact, as observed by Hannah Sullivan, Eliot's views on literary translation and on tradition were connected: both were regarded as processes of adjustment, and they both revealed a breach between sunny nineteenth-century Hellenism and war-torn modernity.[20]

Having first heard Murray in 1907 at Harvard, when the celebrated young scholar from Europe came to deliver a series of lectures,[21] Eliot in 1920 – a poet on the cusp of fame – attacked the classicist for his affectedly Pre-Raphaelite rendering of *Medea*. In his review of the play performed in English, Eliot praises Sybil Thorndike's impersonation of the heroine, but only to observe sardonically that her acting was powerful enough to distract the audience's attention from 'her words'[22] and thus conveniently to obscure Murray's allegedly disappointing text. He criticises Murray for using the idiom of Swinburne and William Morris,[23] and for rhetorical belatedness which, elsewhere, he describes as 'the style of fifty years ago'.[24] Significantly, condemning Murray's translation of *Medea*, Eliot does not critique the Pre-Raphaelite mannerisms per se, but only Murray's effort to emulate them – the attempt to look at the Greek through nineteenth-century binoculars instead of observing them through a modern lens. Robert Ackerman states that Eliot's attack on Murray was prompted by the need of 'the then virtually unknown avant-garde poet and critic T. S. Eliot'[25] to sanction his own poetic style. More, however, was at stake than just an individual style: the requirement for a new expressive language was significant for the whole generation – as was its corollary, the re-examination of a cultural heritage for the sake of a new tradition.

The watchword of this revisionist project is 'contemporaneity', or the relevance of the past for modern times, and the same watchword informs Eliot's review of H. D.'s translations, which expresses opinions as radical as his critique of Murray. Eliot states that antiquity, the past remaining 'foreign, but not strange',[26] must provide moderns with a mirror rather than with enchanting escapism. The ancient plays and passions, therefore, must move modern audiences deeply rather than simply offering meticulous reconstructions of an exotic past – dug out, dusted down and displayed by literary archaeologists for contemplation by experts. The past recognised as tradition must be functional rather than full of 'fetishes'.[27] Hence, though Eliot deplores the decline of classical education, he also boldly declares that 'Greek poetry' no longer stimulates the creation of 'contemporary poetry', that the Victorianised Greece has outlived its purpose. 'Greek poetry', he says, leaves him unmoved: the gravity of the Greek 'bores me stiff. The marbles of the Pantheon leave me cold'.[28] In the declaration which alludes to Walter Pater's admiration for the German classicists – and is a jab at Pater's aestheticism: 'I am neither Winckelmann nor Goethe'[29] – Eliot makes it clear that he is hardly nostalgic about nineteenth-century Hellenism and that he has already distanced himself from the Harvard aestheticism of his student days.[30] By implication, together with Pater's Winckelmann and Goethe, Pater's Euripides, 'a lover of sophisms',[31] also has to be renounced. This is because to abide by the Euripides of Pater means to accept the vision of antiquity as established through Oscar Wilde's New Hellenism, and as celebrated by Wilde's tutor John Pentland Mahaffy. It means to stand for the Euripides of late Victorians and of aesthetes[32] – the tragedian acclaimed by Wilde as 'the cor cordium [heart of hearts] of antiquity',[33] praised for his psychological subtlety, and also for his 'belatedness' as reflecting the late coming of the Victorian Decadence.[34]

By referring to the Greek dramatist, however, one declared one's stance not only in aesthetics but also on the matter of religion. Before the Great War, according to Ackerman, 'Euripides was the liberals' tragedian', frequently connected 'with rationalism, atheism, secularism, Ibsenism, pacifism, and no doubt other forms of *nefaria*'.[35] After the war, other connections were enlisted. To E. R. Dodds (in 1929), the ideas of Euripides remained in tune with the theories propounded 'by theosophists and by spiritualists, by Dr. Jung and by Dr. Freud'.[36] Thus, Euripides was transformed into an anti-clerical intuitionist of ancient Greece. In Appleton's *Euripides the Idealist* (for which Eliot had sought a reviewer), the Greek tragedian appears as a subjectivist and, above all, as a humanist for whom 'man is himself ... the center of his world'[37] – a view reflecting the Euripides of Wilde. On the face of it, the scholarly opinions differ. But there is one point at which they concur, best expressed by Appleton's optimistic conviction that Euripides' *Heracles* still teaches us to 'direct our lives according to our lights' in a human-centred world.[38] To Eliot, such confidence was untenable. He would see it as diluting the dogmas of Christianity and as characteristic of religious modernism, the nineteenth-century intellectual and spiritual movement of which he disapproved as much as of Pater's and Wilde's aestheticism.[39] For Eliot, Appleton's Euripides would be a religious modernist of antiquity.

Notably, it was the Euripides of Pater and Wilde whom Murray continued to rehabilitate (in the face of his dismissal by Wilhelm Schlegel).[40] But Murray's effort resulted in tainting Euripides with yet another, political, brush since Murray was a staunch supporter of H. H. Asquith, the Liberal prime minister (1908–16), whose government took Britain into war and was held responsible for the defeat at Gallipoli. It is significant that it was in 1916 that Eliot urged the literati to relinquish the ancient Greek pleasant mood. In his review of H. D.'s translations, he sarcastically concedes: 'Agreed: when we are tired of current affairs, current current affairs, current affairs currently current in 1916, let us go see what affairs were current in 1600.'[41] This is a pivotal sentence. The year 1916 ended with the trauma of the Somme; it overlapped with the longest battle of the First World War, the ten-month ordeal of Verdun; and its beginning coincided with the end of the Gallipoli campaign. It affected a generation, with Eliot having been gravely afflicted also in the personal sense when he lost his close friend Jean Verdenal, killed in the first days of the Gallipoli campaign. He informed Conrad Aiken of Verdenal's death in the course of a grammatically repetitive, painfully stretched-out sentence, where nearly a dozen thats force together the torturous events of the preceding six months with two scatological stanzas about King Bolo and his 'bassturd kween'.[42] This personal outburst of January 1916, both filled with pain *and* flippant, stoical with a shrug, verges on Senecan bombast but is undercut by bawdiness. A violent style for the violent times, it represents the self-defensive, and face-saving, rhetoric of the helpless.

While the new and terrifying epoch needed a startling new language – a style different from Pater's slow cadences and Swinburne's romantic effusions – it also needed a new tradition for its legitimisation. Preceding 'Tradition and the Individual Talent' by three years, Eliot's unpublished review of H. D.'s translations foreshadows ideas that would reappear in his celebrated 1919 essay: the distaste with tradition seen as a matter of literary archaeology; an aversion to imitation in literature, anticipating the essay's recommendation for poets to steal lines directly

Figure 22.2 Seneca's Hercules driven to madness. Engraving from 'Tableaux du temple des muses' (1655) by Michel de Marolles, known as the abbé de Marolles.

from their masters; and the insistence on the contemporaneity of tradition, or its relevance for present affairs. However, unlike the later essay which discusses these ideas in literary-philosophical contexts 'at the frontier of metaphysics and mysticism',[43] the review of 1916 relates them to a more immediate material context, that of the humanitarian disaster of the war. In impassioned spirit, Eliot insists that the role of tradition is not only aesthetic but also moral, in fact, compensatory: it is to 'uphold and re-establish each day the communal life we share with our new ancestors',[44] after the communal life the British had shared with their European contemporaries had been disrupted.

At its core, the dispute about translations revolved around whether the present epoch, 'current affairs currently current in 1916', could recognise its historical analogy – temporally remote, but close in terms of sensibility – in the ancient past. Indeed, by the time the exotic Hellas of the Pre-Raphaelites and aesthetes (which Murray had tried to revive) became obsolete, the need had emerged for a new poetic method and for a classic other than the Victorianised Euripides. To Eliot, the answer to this need revealed itself in 1923 when he was invited to write the introduction to a collection of late-sixteenth-century translations of Seneca's plays. Responding to Charles Whibley, who commissioned the introduction, Eliot says he intends to defend 'the merit of Seneca as a dramatist and a poet, in comparison with Euripides'.[45] But, after the introduction's four years of gestation,[46] little remained of the proposed comparison: Eliot focused on the importance of Seneca as judged on his own terms, the new classic providing a model of how to express modern sensibility.

Thus, if in 1916 Eliot was saying goodbye to Hellas, then, in 1923, he hailed ancient Rome in the figure of Seneca. This shift in interests was a culmination of a broader 'classical revival' in this period, promoted, among others, by writers like Ezra Pound and Richard Aldington, though it was a revival that was later sharply criticised by the eminent classicist Duane Reed Stuart for its frequent errors.[47] In his critique of 1941, Stuart identifies a farrago of mistakes in the classical translations of Aldington and Pound, additionally noting a lack of consistency on Eliot's part in the latter's praise for Jasper Heywood's translations, which, ironically, exhibit the same feature of verbosity that Eliot condemned in Murray.[48] Stuart also caustically observes that the *Satyricon* of Petronius, Seneca's contemporary, at one time 'leaped into notoriety along with D. H. Lawrence's *Women in Love*', thus 'becom[ing] a drugstore classic'.[49] (It also supplied the epigraph for Eliot's *The Waste Land*.) Although Eliot eventually denied having participated in the movement,[50] from 1923 he systematically read Neronian Rome into the literary tradition of the English Renaissance – with the same persistence as Pater and Wilde had shown in construing the Renaissance as shaped by ancient Greece, whether Classical or Hellenistic. While Oscar Wilde's Renaissance was Euripidean, Platonic and hermeticist, mannerist and magical (because shaped by Marsilio Ficino's translation of the Greek *Corpus Hermeticum*),[51] Eliot's Renaissance, by contrast, was increasingly Roman and to a large extent Senecan. In his 'Wanly and Chapman' (1925), he concedes that George Chapman represents a peculiar combination 'of Roman stoicism ... with the diffused hermetic and "Areopagitic" moods';[52] two years later, he asserted that the Renaissance intellectual aura (besides being Machiavellian and Montaignian) was manifestly Senecan,[53] with Seneca influencing not only tragedy (with his use of bombast and stichomythia, and his development of the closet drama and horror) but also Donne's metaphysical poetry.[54]

His two essays on Seneca, if not scholarly, were firmly embedded in a scholarly context. Eliot read, among other works, John Cunliffe's *The Influence of Seneca on Elizabethan Tragedy* (1893), which highlighted Seneca's modernity – including the cosmopolitan aspect of his work as typical of the Latin literature of the Neronian age[55] – and which he considered, 'within its limits', the most valuable of such treatises.[56] He also referred to F. L. Lucas's *Seneca and Elizabethan Tragedy* (1922), agreeing with Lucas's claim that Seneca's bombastic rhetoric and coarseness were naturally attractive to the Elizabethans (Lucas noting that Queen Elizabeth would 'swear like a fishwife'),[57] yet disagreeing with Lucas's censure of the pompous and the crude.[58] In 'Seneca in Elizabethan Translation', Eliot insists that the Elizabethans did not derive their bombast and the liking for horror from Seneca, but only saw it, their very own, as reflected in the Roman tragedy.[59] However, if Seneca's work provided a mirror for the Elizabethan era, it also reflected the sensibilities of modernism. Tellingly, in his 'Shakespeare and the Stoicism of Seneca', Eliot describes the Renaissance as 'a period of dissolution and chaos',[60] which would have also been the way to describe the period and the aftermath of the Great War. Thus, even if Eliot considered Senecan rhetorical stoicism as uncommendable posturing (Shakespeare's Othello '*cheering himself up*' and John Ford's broken-hearted Calantha wishing to 'die smiling'),[61] he would nevertheless have found it understandable in the circumstances – a rhetoric of self-consolation in the face of ultimate defeat, as Eliot realised when he wrote to Aiken in 1916, having himself only a proud posture and bawdy verse to hold on to.

Exaggerated rhetoric, Fleming and Grant observe, and a 'focus on the (all-too-modern) self-conscious display' were the reasons why Seneca was unacceptable to the eighteenth century and attractive to both the Renaissance and the twentieth century, the early modern and the modernist.[62] Self-consciousness, or introspectiveness, in Seneca's protagonists was also noted by Cunliffe,[63] of whose study Eliot spoke so highly. Eliot, however, saw Seneca's self-reflexivity as a moral rather than psychological trait – a matter of conscience rather than of consciousness – explaining, in his famous introduction to the Elizabethan Seneca, that Roman dramatic characters, rather than wading through psychological complexities, had to choose between pulls of desire and dictates of duty,[64] that they were characterised in relation to a clear-cut conflict.

Similar dramatic tension is also paramount in Eliot's poetry. It is reflected in the organisation of thought in his verse, including the ironic contradictions of his early poems, the anticlimactic juxtapositions of *The Waste Land* (1922), and the method of *Marina*, which he described as 'a crisscross' – a nearly Cubist technique of images presented simultaneously and used here, with the help of the Senecan epigraph, to express a conflict of horror and hopeful anticipation. *Marina* is organised like a picture, filled with echoes and contrasts.[65] The interrogatives from the epigraph – '*quis*' and '*quae*' – reverberate in the opening 'what' questions. But the questioning tone is quickly supplanted by the condemnatory, only to segue back into the lyrical when the image of a human face appears against the backdrop of coastal imagery. The fog-wrapped vision contrasts with the materiality of a ship. Eliot, having created resonance and dissonance, nevertheless refused to tell the reader that the questions came from Hercules and Pericles.[66]

This method of superimposition was inspired by the extensive lists of Senecan reverberations in Elizabethan plays provided in Cunliffe's and Lucas's treatises. The orderly series of corresponding English and Latin quotations gathered by the scholars embody the ideal which Eliot formulated in 1916, of English being 'enriched' through an enlivening connection with the ancient tongue.[67] Among the parallels highlighted in Lucas's study, attention is drawn to the juxtaposition of *Hercules Furens* and *Macbeth*[68] which brings together the scenes where Seneca's Hercules and Shakespeare's Lady Macbeth and her husband contemplate their guilt and their blood-stained hands.[69] Eliot, surely aware of this echo, in his epigraph for *Marina* invoked the lines spoken by Hercules earlier in the same act. But he created a pattern substantially denser than the mere parallel cited by the scholars: in *Marina* the motto from Seneca provides both an echo to the act of recognition and a contrast to the happy reunion as experienced by Shakespeare's Pericles. Thus, unsurprisingly, the anonymous *Times Literary Supplement* review of his 'Introduction' to the Elizabethan translations – with its author conceding that Eliot's work was 'both able and interesting', if inferior to scholarly treatises such as Lucas's ('the work of more heavily equipped investigators')[70] – annoyed the poet greatly. Incensed by the reviewer's remarks, Eliot dismissed Lucas's book as 'wholly useless'.[71] His frustration could be attributed to the fact that the reviewer had entirely missed the point of his 'Seneca', which was neither to repeat nor to compete with what the 'investigators' had said, but rather to discuss the relevance of their findings for the method – of crisscrosses and juxtapositions – used in modernist poetry, the type of 'organisation' deployed in *Marina*.

Eliot returned to Euripides in his later years. But it was Seneca, along with a notion of tradition nourished by a romanised Renaissance, that proved crucial to Eliot's brand of modernist rebellion against the nineteenth century and his modernist response to the horror of the war. Eliot's engagement with Elizabethan translations of Seneca also significantly influenced his poetic technique as it sought to express intense but impersonal emotion – or, rather, *transpersonal* emotion – capable of affecting the reader as much as the poet. Thus, while Eliot may have quipped that he had taken a line from Seneca to tease the 'classical men', his choice of the Roman tragedian in his epigraph to *Marina* was clearly anything but a joke.

NOTES

1. T. S. Eliot, 'Introduction to *The Wheel of Fire: Essays in Interpretation of Shakespeare's Sombre Tragedies* by G. Wilson Knight', in Ronald Schuchard et al. (eds), *The Complete Prose of T. S. Eliot: The Critical Edition*, 8 vols (Baltimore: Johns Hopkins University Press and (vols I and II only) London: Faber & Faber, 2014–19), vol. IV, ed. Jason Harding and Ronald Schuchard (2015), p. 148.

2. Eliot to Edward McKnight Kauffer, 24 July 1930, *The Letters of T. S. Eliot*, ed. John Haffenden et al. (London: Faber & Faber, 2009–), vol. V, *1930–1931*, ed. Valerie Eliot and John Haffenden (2014), p. 270.

3. *Marina* was first published in pamphlet form in 1930 as part of a Christmas series for Faber and it appears in Eliot's later collections as one of his 'Ariel Poems'. It can be found in Christopher Ricks and Jim McCue (eds), *The Poems of T. S. Eliot*, 2 vols (London: Faber & Faber, 2015), vol. I, pp. 107–8, and, as noted there (p. 776), Eliot's epigraph comes from line 1138 of *Hercules Furens* in Jasper Heywood's translation of 1561.

4. See Eliot to Michael Sadler, 9 May 1930, *Letters*, vol. V, p. 166; Eliot to Edward McKnight Kauffer, 24 July 1930, ibid., p. 270; Eliot to G. Wilson Knight, 30 October 1930, ibid., p. 368. J. P. Brockbank indicates an alternative source in 'Apollonius, Prince of Tyre', included in John Gower's *Confessio Amantis*. See his '"Pericles" and the Dream of Immortality', in Kenneth Muir (ed.), *Shakespeare Survey* 24 (Cambridge University Press, 1971), pp. 105–16 (p. 116).

5. Eliot, *Complete Prose*, vol. IV, p. 687.

6. Ibid.

7. Eliot, 'Poetry and Drama', *Complete Prose*, vol. VII, ed. Iman Javadi and Ronald Schuchard (2018), p. 601.

8. Ibid., p. 600.

9. Eliot to G. Wilson Knight, 30 October 1930, *Letters*, vol. V, p. 368.

10. Samuel Eliot Morison, *Three Centuries of Harvard: 1636–1936* (Cambridge, MA: Belknap Press, 2001), p. 390.

11. William Empson, *Argufying: Essays on Literature and Culture*, ed. John Haffenden (London: Chatto & Windus, 1987), p. 365. For Eliot's veiling of the sources of quotations and for the correlation between his concept of tradition and his use of classical authors for epigraphs, see Hannah Sullivan, 'Classics', in Jason Harding (ed.), *T. S. Eliot in Context* (Cambridge University Press, 2011), pp. 169–79 (pp. 173–4).

12. Eliot to Michael Sadler, 9 May 1930, *Letters*, vol. V, p. 166.

13. Robert Crawford, *Young Eliot: From St. Louis to The Waste Land* (London: Vintage, 2016), p. 60.

14. See Eliot, 'Philosophy A: Syllabus for an Introductory Course from the Pre-Socratics to the Renaissance', *Complete Prose*, vol. I, ed. Jewel Spears Brooker and Ronald Schuchard (2014), p. 777.

15. Ronald Schuchard, *Eliot's Dark Angel: Intersections of Life and Art* (Oxford University Press, 1999), p. 45.

16. C. J. Herington, 'Senecan Tragedy', *Arion* 5 (1966), 422–71 (170), quoted in Betine van Zyl Smit, 'Jasper Heywood's Translations of Senecan Tragedy', *Acta Classica* 55 (2012), 99–117 (98): www.jstor.org/stable/24592572?&seq=1 (accessed 10 September

2019); Katie Fleming and Teresa Grant, 'Introduction: Seneca in the English Tradition', *Canadian Review of Comparative Literature* 40.1 (2013), 7–15 (7): https://journals .library.ualberta.ca/crcl/index.php/crcl/article/view/25712 (accessed 21 March 2020).

17. Crawford, *Young Eliot*, pp. 89, 86.
18. Eliot to H. V. Routh, 2 June 1927, *Letters*, vol. III, ed. Valerie Eliot and John Haffenden (2012), p. 541.
19. See note 4 and also Eliot to John Hayward, 30 October 1930, *Letters*, vol. V, p. 369.
20. See Sullivan, 'Classics', pp. 174–5.
21. Crawford, *Young Eliot*, p. 86.
22. Eliot, 'Euripides and Professor Murray', *Complete Prose*, vol. II, ed. Anthony Cuda and Ronald Schuchard (2014), pp. 195–201 (p. 196).
23. Ibid., pp. 196–7.
24. Eliot, 'Classics in English', review of the Poets' Translation series I–VI, *Complete Prose*, vol. I, pp. 493–6 (p. 493).
25. Robert Ackerman, 'Euripides and Professor Murray', *Classical Journal* 81.4 (1986), 329–36 (329): www.jstor.org/stable/3297216 (accessed 13 September 2019).
26. Eliot, 'On a Translation of Euripides', trans. John Morgenstern, *Complete Prose*, vol. I, pp. 500–3 (p. 501).
27. Ibid., p. 502.
28. Ibid.
29. Ibid. Pater included 'Winckelmann' (1867) in *Renaissance* (1873) and paid homage to Goethe in 'Duke Carl of Rosenmold' (1887), in *Imaginary Portraits* (1887).
30. On the 'Bohemian Boston' as influencing Eliot, see James E. Miller Jr, *T. S. Eliot: The Making of an American Poet, 1888–1922* (University Park: Pennsylvania State University Press, 2005), pp. 52–61.
31. Walter Pater, 'The Bacchanals of Euripides', in *Greek Studies: A Series of Essays* (1895; Macmillan Library Edition, 1910), pp. 53–80 (p. 78): www.gutenberg.org/cache/ epub/4035/pg4035.html. The volume also contains 'Hippolytus Veiled: A Study from Euripides'.
32. Thomas Prasch, 'Clashing Greeks and Victorian Culture Wars: Euripides vs. Aristophanes in Late-Victorian Discourse', *Victorian Studies*, special issue, *Papers and Responses from the Ninth Annual Conference of the North American Victorian Studies Association*, 54.3 (2012), 464–73 (467–71): www.jstor.org/stable/10.2979/victorianstudies.54.3.464 (accessed 20 February 2020).
33. Oscar Wilde, 'Commonplace Book', in Philip E. Smith II and Michael S. Helfand (eds), *Oscar Wilde's Oxford Notebooks: A Portrait of Mind in the Making* (Oxford University Press, 1989), p. 132. On Wilde's interest in Euripides, see Kathleen Riley, 'All the Terrible Beauty of a Greek Tragedy: Wilde's "Epistola" and the Euripidean Christ', in Kathleen Riley, Alastair J. L. Blanshard and Iarla Manny (eds), *Oscar Wilde and Classical Antiquity* (Oxford University Press, 2018), pp. 175–95. On the university lampoon *Aristophanes at Oxford O.W.* (1894) ridiculing Wilde's aestheticism via a mocking representation of Euripides, see Prasch, 'Clashing Greeks', 464–7.
34. Isobel Hurst, 'Tragedy in the Dispute of Mirth: Robert Browning, George Eliot, and Wilde' and Clare L. E. Foster, 'Wilde and the Emergence of Literary Drama', in Riley et al. (eds), *Wilde and Classical Antiquity*, pp. 127–41 (pp. 126–8) and pp. 107–26 (p. 111) respectively.

35. Ackerman, 'Euripides and Professor Murray', 334.

36. E. R. Dodds, 'Euripides the Irrationalist', *Classical Review* 43.3 (1929), 97–104 (104): www.jstor.org/stable/700798 (accessed 2 March 2020).

37. R. B. Appleton, *Euripides the Idealist* (London and Toronto: J. M. Dent and New York: E. P. Dutton, 1927), p. xiii.

38. Ibid., p. 190.

39. Anna Budziak, 'Modernism and Muddle: Religious Implications of T. S. Eliot's Use of the Term', *E-rea* 15.2 (2018): http://journals.openedition.org/erea/6200 (accessed 10 September 2019).

40. See Prasch, 'Clashing Greeks', 467–71.

41. Eliot, *Complete Prose*, vol. I, p. 500.

42. Eliot to Conrad Aiken, 10 January 1916, *Letters*, vol. I, ed. Valerie Eliot and Hugh Haughton, rev. edn (2009), p. 137.

43. Eliot, *Complete Prose*, vol. I, p. 112. For a brief description of 'Tradition and the Individual Talent' as a response to war and part of the restorative effort, see Aleida Assmann, 'Exorcising the Demon of Chronology: T. S. Eliot's Reinvention of Tradition' and Jason Harding, 'Tradition and Egoism: T. S. Eliot and The Egoist', in Giovanni Cianci and Jason Harding (eds), *T. S. Eliot and the Concept of Tradition* (Cambridge University Press, 2007), pp. 13–25 (p. 23) and pp. 90–102 (p. 97) respectively.

44. Eliot, *Complete Prose*, vol. I, p. 502.

45. Eliot to Charles Whibley, 23 August 1923, *Letters*, vol. II, ed. Valerie Eliot and Hugh Haughton (2009), p. 198.

46. Eliot refers to the commission to write the introduction in several letters. See Eliot to Richard Aldington, 23 August 1923, *Letters*, vol. II, p. 191; Eliot to Leonard Woolf, late July? 1925, ibid., p. 710; Eliot to Charles Whibley, 1 November 1926, *Letters*, vol. III, p. 295; Eliot to Marguerite Caetani, 18 November 1926, ibid., p. 314; Eliot to Charles Whibley, 3 February 1927, ibid., p. 406.

47. Francis R. B. Godolphin, 'Modernistic Critics and Translators: An Unpublished Essay by Duane Reed Stuart', *Princeton University Library Chronicle* 11.4 (1950), 177–98 (178): https://doi.org/26400348.

48. Ibid., 183.

49. Ibid., 177.

50. See '"Classic Inhumanism [I]": To the Editor of *The Times Literary Supplement* (9 Aug. 1957)', *Complete Prose*, vol. VIII, ed. Jewel Spears Brooker and Ronald Schuchard (2019), pp. 176–7.

51. See Oscar Wilde, 'The Portrait of Mr. W. H.', in *Collins Complete Works of Oscar Wilde: Centenary Edition* (New York: HarperCollins, 1999), pp. 326–7. For a discussion of these connections, see Anna Budziak, *Text, Body and Indeterminacy: Doppelgänger Selves in Pater and Wilde* (Newcastle upon Tyne: Cambridge Scholars, 2008), pp. 203–4. See also Yvonne Ivory, 'Wilde's Renaissance: Poison, Passion, and Personality', *Victorian Literature and Culture* 35.2 (2007), 517–36: https:/doi.org/10.1017/S1060150307051613; and Anna Budziak, 'Oscar Wilde's Renaissance References: Neo-Platonism, Hermeticism and Mannerism', *Anglica Wratislaviensia* 53 (2015), 25–34: http://wuwr.pl/awr/article/view/190/169 (accessed 21 March 2020).

52. Eliot, *Complete Prose*, vol. II, p. 606.

53. Eliot, 'Shakespeare and the Stoicism of Seneca', in *Complete Prose*, vol. III, ed. Frances Dickey et al. (2015), pp. 245–60 (p. 249). See also Eliot, 'Toward a Definition of Metaphysical Poetry', *Complete Prose*, vol. IV, p. 718.

54. See Eliot, 'Donne and the Middle Ages', in *Complete Prose*, vol. II, p. 630; and Eliot, 'Cowley and the Transition', in *Complete Prose*, vol. II, p. 733. On Seneca's importance for Eliot as a dramatist, see Gregory A. Staley, 'T. S. Eliot's Seneca', in George W. M. Harrison (ed.), *Brill's Companion to Roman Tragedy* (Leiden: Brill, 2015), pp. 348–63.

55. John W. Cunliffe, *The Influence of Seneca on Elizabethan Tragedy* (London: Macmillan and New York: Anastatic Reprint, 1907), p. 15.

56. Eliot, 'Seneca in Elizabethan Translation', in *Complete Prose*, vol. III, pp. 195–234 (p. 204).

57. F. L. Lucas, *Seneca and Elizabethan Tragedy* (Cambridge University Press, 1922), p. 108.

58. See Eliot, 'Seneca in Elizabethan Translation', p. 196.

59. Ibid., p. 204.

60. Ibid., p. 249.

61. Ibid., p. 248; John Ford, *The Broken Heart*, V.iii.85–6, quoted in Eliot, *Complete Prose*, vol. IV, p. 479.

62. Fleming and Grant, 'Introduction: Seneca', 8.

63. Cunliffe, *Influence of Seneca*, p. 17.

64. See Eliot, 'Seneca in Elizabethan Translation', p. 199.

65. See F. R. Leavis, 'Marina', in B. C. Southam (ed.), *T. S. Eliot: Prufrock, Gerontion, Ash Wednesday and Other Shorter Poems* (London: Bloomsbury, 1978), pp. 223–5 (p. 225).

66. Steven Matthews has identified another Elizabethan echo in the questions asked by the eponymous protagonist of George Chapman's *Conspiracy and Tragedy of Charles, Duke of Byron* (1608): see 'T. S. Eliot's Chapman: "Metaphysical" Poetry and Beyond', *Journal of Modern Literature* 29.4 (2006), 22–43 (28).

67. Eliot, *Complete Prose*, vol. I, p. 494.

68. The parallel was first identified by G. E. Lessing. Lucas, *Seneca and Elizabethan Tragedy*, p. 121.

69. Ibid., pp. 121–2.

70. 'Senecan Tragedy', *Times Literary Supplement*, 9 February 1928, p. 92.

71. Eliot to Mario Praz, 21 February 1928, *Letters*, vol. IV, ed. Valerie Eliot and John Haffenden (2013), p. 55.

CRITICAL REFLECTIONS AND FURTHER STUDY

Crucial for my essay were the studies gathered in Cianci and Harding's *T. S. Eliot and the Concept of Tradition*, where, for example, Stan Smith's essay (see Further Reading) stresses the revolutionary nature of Eliot's notion of tradition, in which the past can be reconceived to serve present needs. Hannah Sullivan's overview of Eliot's attitude to the classics provided me with a further significant critical context for my discussion (see my essay, note 11). I focused on one aspect of this interest: Eliot's favouring of the ancient Roman over the ancient Greek, insofar as his preference influenced *Marina*'s epigraph. My study also greatly benefited from the recent publication of Eliot's letters, prose and newly annotated complete poems, which creates an unprecedented expansion of research resources, many of which were restricted in the past. Exploring these materials, I was intrigued by an apparent inconsistency in Eliot's attitude to the poem's epigraph: his insistence on removing the reference to Seneca while also highlighting it in his letters (only to humorously play it down in his later conversation with Empson). It was this puzzle that led me through several cultural contexts – Eliot's rebellion against Victorian Hellenism, his romanising of the Renaissance, and his immersion in scholarly treatises on the classics – which, together, seemed to offer a glimpse of an era in the epigraph.

A number of issues arose, however, which could not be approached within the scope of a short essay. In turn, they offer five points for further consideration, beginning with the relationship between the poem and its illustration and proceeding to questions of biography and style.

1. As mentioned in my essay, F. R. Leavis compared *Marina* to a picture (see my essay, note 65). The poem's pictorial aspect was also vividly captured in the illustrations for the first edition drawn by Edward McKnight Kauffer, Eliot's favourite graphic designer and one of the addressees of his letters explaining the thematic 'crisscross' of the poem and its epigraph. Kauffer's illustrations can be viewed at the British Library online at https://bit.ly/35yrPLB. To what extent could they be considered both as an interpretation of the poem and as reverse ekphrasis? (See Appendix A: Glossary of Critical Terms for a definition of this term.)

2. Referring to the poem's epigraph, J. P. Brockbank observes that the words of Seneca's Hercules have their echo in the words spoken by the wife of Apollonius, when she's awakening, in John Gower's *Confessio Amantis* (a source of Shakespeare's *Pericles*; see my essay, note 4). It should also be noted that G. Wilson Knight, whose *Myth and Miracle* Eliot read, comments on Pericles' reunion not only with his daughter but also with his wife. Consequently, the question arises of how a reading of the poem might change assuming it is not only the horrified father but also the revived wife speaking in the epigraph.

3. Biographical context – in particular, the relationship between Eliot and Emily Hale – might shed further light on the poem's nostalgic evocation of American coastal scenery and the poem's sense of happy expectation. Eliot's letters to Hale – the first one following shortly after the poem's publication – were made available to the public in January 2020 at the Princeton Library. Their content is also available through the paraphrase by Frances Dickey (*Reports from the Emily Hale Archive*, The International T. S. Eliot Society: https://tseliotsociety.wildapricot.org/news). However, the seaside imagery of the poem can be read in a different way if, for example, approached through

John Brannigan's essay '"[P]art of the nature of things" (see Further Reading), which views the littoral setting of the poem as related to problems of (mis) recognition and to modernist questioning of culturally defined borders and identities (coastlines being seen as the porous edges of cultural identities). Brannigan's emphasis is, in a sense, on physical geography while my essay focuses on history and the porous borders of culture over time. It might therefore be fruitful to consider further how questions of geographical and historical contexts intersect here.

4. In his introduction to Knight's *The Wheel of Fire* (see my essay, note 1), Eliot states that '"the greatest poetry", like the greatest prose, has doubleness' (p. 147), the effect which he also considers in essays on 'Wanley and Chapman' (1925) and 'John Marston' (1934). Eliot's technique of 'doubleness' is discussed by Steven Matthews in 'T. S. Eliot and Chapman' (see my essay, note 66). This device of doubleness, referring to the juxtapositions of the scholarly and the popular, the physical and the metaphysical, the present and the past, is one useful frame through which to approach *Marina* – and can also helpfully inform readings of *Triumphal March* (1931), the poem which immediately followed *Marina* in the 'Ariel' series.

5. In *Marina*, the sense of doubleness is evoked, among other things, by the combination of the lyrical and the menacing. Such forced marriages of discordant elements – lyricism and revulsion, eloquence and terror – characterise the work of not only Eliot but also of contemporary filmmaker Quentin Tarantino, whose protagonists fire rounds of words with the same ease as pulling a trigger. Eliot's and Tarantino's common inspiration in Seneca could be a useful starting point for bringing up to date the story of Eliot's conception of tradition through a comparative study of the two artistic languages of modernist poetry and postmodernist film.

FURTHER READING

Atkins, Douglas G., '*Marina*: "Living to Live in a World of Time beyond Me": Recovery, Perceiving, and Understanding', in *T. S. Eliot's Christmas Poems: An Essay in Writing-as-Reading and Other 'Impossible Unions'* (Houndmills: Palgrave Macmillan, 2014), pp. 72–85

Brannigan, John, '"[P]art of the Nature of Things": Towards an Archipelagic and Maritime History of Literary Modernism', in Paul Poplawski (ed.), *Back to the Twenties: Modernism Then and Now, Yearbook of English Studies* 50 (2020), 81–94

Cameron, Elspeth, 'T. S. Eliot's "Marina": An Exploration', *Queen's Quarterly* 77.2 (1970), 181–9

Cuda, Anthony J. 'Who Stood over Eliot's Shoulder?', *Modern Language Quarterly* 66.3 (2005), 329–64: https://doi.org/10.1215/00267929-66-3-329

Donoghue, Denis, 'Eliot's "Marina" and Closure', *Hudson Review* 49.3 (1996), 367–88: https://doi.org/10.2307/3852506

Griffin, Ernest, G., 'Sweeney, Becket, and the "Marina Figure" in Eliot's Modern Plays', *Modern Drama* 36.4 (1993), 569–77: https://doi.org/10.1353/mdr.1993.0051

Haughton, Hugh, 'Allusion: The Case of Shakespeare', in Jason Harding (ed.), *T. S. Eliot in Context* (Cambridge University Press, 2011), pp. 157–68

Matthews, Steven, *T. S. Eliot and Early Modern Literature* (Oxford University Press, 2013)

Ricks, Christopher, *T. S. Eliot and Prejudice* (Berkeley: University of California Press, 1988)

Smith, Stan, 'Proper Frontiers: Transgression and the Individual Talent', in Giovanni Cianci and Jason Harding (eds), *T. S. Eliot and the Concept of Tradition* (Cambridge University Press, 2007), pp. 26–40

Thomson, Stephen, 'The Adjective, My Daughter: Staging T. S. Eliot's "Marina"', in Nicola Bradbury (ed.), *The Yearbook of English Studies 2002: Children in Literature* (Cambridge: Modern Humanities Research Association, 2002), 110–26: https://doi.org/10.2307/3509051

Timmerman, John H., '"Marina": T. S. Eliot's Moment of Recognition', *Christianity and Literature* 41.4 (1992), 407–19: www.jstor.org/stable/44312098 (accessed 4 April 2020)

23 Passing as a Male Critic: Mary Beton's Coming of Age in Virginia Woolf's *A Room of One's Own*

JUDITH PALTIN

Abstract

In *A Room of One's Own* (1929), Virginia Woolf's ambitious narrative invention, Mary Beton, visits the British Museum, and censures the male anger she unearths there while prodding at an avalanche of books written by men about women.[1] Yet Woolf performs a clandestine ironisation of Beton's own criticism, for Beton colludes with male misogyny in her analysis of women writers and their alleged forfeiture of the intellectual quality she calls 'integrity'. With whose voice is this said, for example: 'It is clear that anger was tampering with the integrity of Charlotte Brönte the novelist' (p. 73)? How is it that Beton is satisfied to argue that Brönte 'had more genius … than Jane Austen', only to bring forward the record that concludes *Jane Eyre* is diminished by anger, ignorance, fear and rancour? This essay argues that with Beton's disparagement of female emotionalism and her rally behind the cultivation of integrity that produces the shape of the work 'whole and entire', Woolf suggests that Beton has adopted patriarchal aesthetic criteria; indeed, Beton betrays herself in this section of the narrative when she says that 'it is the masculine values that prevail' (p. 73). And if she has let them prevail with her, then we need, at the minimum, to stop automatically inscribing 'Woolf says' for 'Beton says'. By writing this nuanced expression of Beton's complex wrestling with critical tradition, Woolf not only brings mainstream literary criticism to the bar for its failure to extract women and their productions from misogynistic frameworks, but she works, with fictional disguise, to sophisticate the reader's understanding of the female critic's lengthy struggle with Britain's anti-feminist critical machinery, and she instructs us in how to become better critics and readers of women writers and of women in fiction.

Virginia Woolf's famous essay on women and fiction, *A Room of One's Own* (1929), offers several interesting problems for the critical reader. Nearly a century after its first publication in this form, its generic classification, its position as an influential feminist text, and its precise intention are still available for debate. The publication's paratext, just after the title page, announces, 'This essay is based upon two papers read to the Arts Society at Newnham and the Odtaa at Girton in October 1928. The papers were too long to be read in full, and have since been altered and expanded' (p. v).[2] This implies that the essay has already undergone a Frankenstein-like procedure of stitching together a variety of parts composed for other occasions and other types of presentation. That seems to violate the essential character of the essay as a genre, and perhaps to produce something new and modern out of the broken form. As most people know, the essay (named from the French word *essai*) is traditionally described as 'an attempt or endeavour', as the *Oxford English Dictionary* has it, 'on any particular subject, or branch of a subject; originally implying want of finish'. As such, the essay is one of the great established first-person forms of writing. An author typically writes an essay in their own voice, sharing their personal reflections on a subject, offering to bring the reader along on a project of intellectual discovery, which may be literary and imaginative, but categorically remains non-fictional.

However, in *A Room of One's Own*, Woolf's first-person exploration is complicated by her own disappearance during most of the essay; Woolf's narrative persona is replaced instead by the voice of a fictional construct: 'call me Mary Beton, Mary Seton, Mary Carmichael, or by any name you please', she says, as Woolf invites her to introduce herself to the reader (p. 5). To attribute this merely to Woolf moving back toward the genre she knows best, fiction, I argue, would be to underread her project. Woolf, before she cedes her voice to the new narrator, insists on the importance of her methodical fictionality; she says that, here, '"I" is only a convenient term of somebody who has no real being' (p. 4). But why invent a Mary Beton to stand in for Woolf's own 'essay' on her subject? Why is Woolf unwilling to continue to speak in her own persona? It is surprising how often readers have understood *A Room of One's Own* as an unironic feminist presentation, with Beton serving as Woolf's mere mouthpiece. I believe this risks rendering the essay possibly the least strategically versant of Woolf's published writings, by making the creation of Beton as narrator an elaborate ruse with little pay-off, and rendering the essay more overtly didactic and straightforwardly polemical than Woolf intends. Moreover, Woolf gives the reader a task: 'Lies will flow from my lips, but there may perhaps be some truth mixed up with them; it is for you to seek out this truth and to decide whether any part of it is worth keeping' (pp. 4–5). It is my object in this essay to curate this truth, if I can find it, and to try to identify the lies as well, which might not all be obvious. I wish to show that Woolf's essay is exemplary of the modernist voice, which is almost always ironic, to analyse the effectiveness of that irony, and to understand why, in this case, it is so apt to go unrecognised. I argue that, instead of writing a critical essay about 'Women and Fiction', as she was expected to do, Woolf seizes the opportunity to show, first the students of Newnham and Girton, and now us, some hard truths about the education and miseducation of a woman-identified critic. Woolf is interested in the problem of how women come to think critically about writing, a vital part of their education, because every good writer is also a strong and well-informed critic. What are the obstacles women face as they become writers and critics? What double consciousness do they develop as members of a category that is oppressed and trying to make its way within a universe of male-centric institutions and practices? How do those outside the privileged gender negotiate systems that were created to work against them? Of course, all these questions remain timely and urgent in our own moment for every disprivileged category of social identity, including racialised identities, citizenship and economic status.

The story that Woolf will show, not tell, is of her fictional narrator's development and maturation as a critic, her coming of age as a public intellectual. Mary Beton speaks almost as in a stream of consciousness, but one that has been retrospectively edited ('and then I thought …'). This editing is crucial, because it provides evidence of Beton's critical growth, and of the limit she reaches, a limit to which I believe Woolf wants us to pay careful attention. Just as Beton leaves the full flourishing of a woman writer to some future generation, Woolf demonstrates that this generation's feminist critics can also only proceed so far; as a movement, they must first build their tradition. An extended monologue such as Beton's gives the reader an opportunity to know a speaker's thoughts intimately, and sometimes to learn more about them than they mean to reveal, or perhaps more than they realise about themselves.[3] In that gap, irony may bloom. In chapter 2, Mary Beton visits the British Museum, and censures the male anger she unearths there while prodding at an avalanche of books written by men about women (Figure 23.1).[4] I maintain that Woolf performs a clandestine ironisation of Beton's own criticism, especially at this stage in Beton's development, for Beton colludes with male misogyny in her analysis of women writers and their alleged forfeiture of the intellectual quality she calls 'integrity'. Moreover, Beton's proposed remedy in the writer whose formation produces an 'androgynous mind' is a matter of concern for Woolf as it has been for generations of feminist critics who have followed Woolf. Beton's version of an idealised androgynous construct has been critiqued as more a renunciation than a reclamation of place for non-privileged writers. In sum, Woolf's aim is to explicate a feminist critical movement still under development, and to view it as an intervention in cultural life that deserves encouragement and sympathy, but always and only in a clear-sighted register.

As Beton examines Charlotte Brönte's *Jane Eyre*, she says:

One might say, I continued, laying the book down beside *Pride and Prejudice*, that the woman who wrote those pages had more genius in her than Jane Austen; but if one reads them over and marks that jerk in them, that indignation, one sees that she will never get her genius expressed whole and entire. Her books will be deformed and twisted. She will write in a rage where she should write calmly. She will write foolishly where she should write wisely. (pp. 68–9)

Figure 23.1 Drawing of the reading room in the British Museum by Fortunino Matania, from *L'Illustrazione Italiana*, 28 July 1907.

How is it that Beton is satisfied to argue that Brönte had genius, only to bring forward the record that concludes *Jane Eyre* is diminished by 'anger', 'ignorance', 'fear' and 'rancour' (p. 73)? Who has influenced Beton's model of 'genius'? Who benefits when women's anger over injustice and male contempt is suppressed? Is Beton's depiction of 'some Emily Brönte who dashed her brains out on the moor or mopped and mowed about the highways crazed with the torture that her gift had put her to' more caricature than compliment (p. 49)? With Beton's disparagement of female emotionalism and her rally behind the cultivation of an impersonal 'integrity' that produces the shape of the work 'whole and entire', Woolf may suggest that Beton has adopted patriarchal male-coded aesthetic criteria; indeed, Beton herself admits within this very discussion that 'it is the masculine values that prevail' (pp. 73–4) – and 'prevail' derives from the Latin *valēre*, meaning both to thrive and to rule over or overcome. If Beton has let them prevail with her, then we need, at the least, to stop automatically inscribing 'Woolf says' for 'Beton says'.

It arouses one's suspicions, in other words, that Beton's remarks about Charlotte Brönte sound very like the criticisms of emotionalism and defect of intellect that Beton would have read in the British Museum, as if she had mused instead that 'a man might say of Brönte'. By reiterating patriarchal-coded criticism, Beton, in effect, consciously or unconsciously, presents herself as a male critic, and solicits the establishment's approval. Is Beton independently evaluating the feminist history contained in the shape of Austen's sentence, or is it male critical tradition that prefers Austen to Brönte because Austen keeps her personality properly hidden from view and writes sentences men feel are 'the right shape' for a woman writer (p. 80)? Is Austen's genius less because her thematic subjects are relationships and domesticity? How can a member of a disprivileged gender or other non-dominant identity hope to precipitate out a free and individual educational formation as a critic from the history of canonical criticism? Woolf, in her own name, that is, as she first introduces Beton, has already put us on guard that 'one cannot hope to tell the truth'; one may infer a broad hint about how to read Beton's language with critical caution (p. 4). And after 'Mary Beton ceases to speak', Woolf makes it a point to concede Beton's 'failings and foibles' and she reiterates that 'truth is only to be had by laying together many varieties of error'; here and elsewhere she amply cues us to read warily (p. 105). I argue that Beton's cession to the distorting interpellations of contemptuous male criticism surreptitiously but strongly undermines even her famous resolution of the problem in the construction of an 'androgynous mind', which may, in the context of the whole, take on an anti-feminine implication. By writing this nuanced expression of Beton's complex wrestling with established critical tradition, and showing us how difficult Beton finds the work of disentangling her own thinking from that history, Woolf not only brings literary criticism to the bar for its failure to extract women and their productions from misogynistic frameworks, but she works in the most effective way possible (given the prejudices in play), that is, with fictional disguise, to sophisticate the reader's understanding of a female critic's lengthy struggle with Britain's anti-feminist critical machinery. *A Room of One's Own* is a brief but complex proposal for radical critical freedom and liberation. In short, by treating Beton ironically, Woolf demonstrates how to become better and freer critics and readers of women writers and of women represented in fiction.

While Beton is concerned about the emotion she discerns in texts by women writers such as *Jane Eyre*, she is not blind to the existence of male emotionalism, and she is equally willing to demonstrate that it also has distorting and debilitating effects on the male critic. Beton realises the problem it has been for the woman writer that there is a vast and pervasive male prejudice, contempt, and anger towards women. This anger puzzles her: 'It seemed absurd, I thought, turning over the evening paper, that a man with all this power should be angry. Or is anger, I wondered, somehow, the familiar, the attendant sprite on power? Rich people, for example, are often angry because they suspect that the poor want to seize their wealth' (p. 34). Beton intuits some treasure or, as we are likely to say today, privilege, which a man may fear is at risk of being seized from him, and which he has profoundly entombed in vault-like structures poised in iconic order, emblematic in Oxbridge,[5] with all its wealth, and its material control of the distribution of political and economic power (p. 9). From here the privileged male critic extracts his consciousness of superiority, the freedom and confidence that he gains by the virtue of imagining himself twice his own size in the mirror of his female relations and companions (pp. 34–6). The relative poverty of the women's colleges reassures him that *his* work is more important than the work done there.

Beton, however, aims for an Achilles heel: male anger has 'distorted and twisted' male-authored books as much as any woman's book; their ideas have become 'creased and crushed into shapes so singular' that the cultural apparatus of knowledge production, 'the splendid equipment of costly and delicate instruments which now stands on glass shelves', is farcically obsolete (pp. 9–10). Tradition's surface attractions produce a gimcrack imitation of a principled and vibrant community: 'how good life seemed, how sweet its rewards, how trivial this grudge or that grievance, how admirable friendship and the society of one's kind' (p. 11). Beton annotates the moment in the British Museum where the aura of intellectual tradition – the spirit of peace she hoped to find in the courts and quadrangles of Oxbridge – breaks down, and her deconstruction of established tradition is achieved: 'I knew that he was angry by this token. When I read what he wrote about women I thought, not of what he was saying, but of himself. When an arguer argues dispassionately he thinks only of the argument; and the reader cannot help thinking of the argument too' (p. 34). It is difficult to find any cue of insincerity in that final sentence – on Beton's part, I mean – and dispassion, mentioned so shortly here, gradually transforms into the talisman of the 'androgynous' mind that Beton trusts to protect the non-male critic against patriarchal anger and scorn. Avoidance of anger preserves one's 'integrity', an intellectual quality in *A Room of One's Own* that is connected on the one hand with an expression or 'conveying' of reality, and, on the other, with that which relieves the 'severances and oppositions in the mind', giving the critic the necessary freedom to achieve resonance as a voice (pp. 96–7). The most immediate cure for the unhappy effects of male contempt is to seize, if one can, a sum of five hundred pounds per year as a permanent release from economic dependency (Beton's was a windfall legacy, and unanticipated); it is a more difficult problem to cultivate the critical 'freedom to think', to truly cleanse the mind of the effects of centuries of scorn (pp. 38–9).

Increasing the hazard is Beton's discernment that to defy and overcome 'the world's notorious indifference' and, in the woman-identified writer's case, its critical male anger, makes a woman's attempt to write, which is to overleap a barrier, almost an act of violence (pp. 51–2). Since, as Beton says, 'mirrors are essential to all violent and heroic action', a woman must be able to find the new mirror that will energise her novel action, without sacrificing her life and psyche (p. 36). If we read the following passage as a criticism of the critic rather than as a dubious

metaphysical assertion about fiction's correspondence to the actual world, its resonant meaning shifts under our feet: 'One holds every phrase, every scene to the
light as one reads – for Nature seems, very oddly, to have provided us with an
inner light by which to judge of the novelist's integrity or disintegrity' (p. 72).
Integrity and its 'odd' 'natural' light are constructed from experience; if 'masculine values' prevail, then the woman writer's integrity may appear as disintegrity,
for she may not succeed in convincing the male reader that 'this is the truth'; his
experience is definitively other than hers. All she can attempt is to gain the skill
to write 'a man's sentence' such as Beton's careful 'The ape is too distant to be
sedulous' (p. 75). When Beton insists a woman 'may be beginning to use writing as
an art, not as a method of self-expression', she is still echoing patriarchal criticism
of female expressionism (p. 78). She is still looking for her mirror.

Beton thus sets herself the difficult problem of reconciling the harsh conditions
of the world with what she proposes as the writer's necessity for 'integrity', a resolution that achieves its ultimate formulation in the difficult aesthetic of an androgynous mind. Female poverty was the first historical barrier to the integrity of the
woman writer. Once we are fortunate enough to have gained, somehow, our five
hundred pounds per year, what is the next barrier to be overcome – the powerful
barrier Beton believes to be challenged at the moment when women are able to
keep a room of their own, with a lock on the door? A lock on the door implies the
power to refuse patriarchal demands. Intellectual integrity cannot be sustained if
one is not able to have sovereignty over one's own physical integrity. Beton sees a
tailless cat on the lawn at Oxbridge, and, in London, 'a bustling lady who had, by
some means or other, acquired a splendid fur coat and a bunch of Parma violets',
and a young couple meeting and leaving in a cab together (pp. 11, 96, 104). As
we shall see, each of these figures presents a different aspect of the complexities
of living within or without the traditions supporting the custody kept over wom-
en's bodies and autonomy through what Beton calls the fetish of chastity (p. 49).
That an old-fashioned word such as 'chastity' should become a major concern in
an essay about modern fiction may come to readers as a surprise – it did to me.
However, the surprises in a text are often where one may find the richest veins
of interpretation, or, at least, new questions inviting explication. Beton's principal concern in *A Room of One's Own* about female chastity, as an ideal, is that
it sets up continual hazards to the writing woman's integrity, and keeps women
out of official history. For the critic, it exposes the foundation of the relationship
patriarchy establishes between men and women, wherein women (and any other
disprivileged categories) are serviceable property.

The woman in the fur coat is probably a sexualised figure; it is with polite
reticence that Beton refrains from saying that some man gave her the coat and
flowers. The difficulty Beton observes is that a woman thus becomes exposed to
certain male drives: 'the instinct for possession, the rage for acquisition' (p. 38).

This woman will not be left in peace by men, 'in obedience to their instinct, which murmurs if it sees a fine woman go by, or even a dog, *Ce chien est à moi*' (p. 50). She suffers loss of status, not only if she is unchaste but even if married, for in effect and in law, through much of British history she becomes 'the slave of any boy whose parents forced a ring upon her finger' and 'the property of her husband' (p. 44). In the end, her sexualised representation may become a millstone around her neck, as 'Mr. Justice – commented in the Divorce Courts upon the Shameless-ness of Women' (p. 33).

The Manx cat which Beton saw passing alone across the grass, on the other hand, is a desexualised creature; chiefly defined by its tailless condition, it becomes a subject of laughter, for 'it is a queer animal' (p. 13). Beton expresses a camaraderie with the animal, for they both observe reality critically:

> The sight of that abrupt and truncated animal padding softly across the quadrangle changed by some fluke the emotional light for me. It was as if someone had let fall a shade. Perhaps the excellent hock was relinquishing its hold. Certainly, as I watched the Manx cat pause in the middle of the lawn as if it too questioned the universe, something seemed lacking, something seemed different. (p. 11)

To examine reality closely is a strong quality in a writer, and Woolf, returning at the end of the essay in her own voice, informs us of reality that

> whatever it touches, it fixes and makes permanent. That is what remains over when the skin of the day has been cast into the hedge; that is what is left of past time and of our loves and hates. Now the writer, as I think, has the chance to live more than other people in the presence of this reality. It is his business to find it and collect it and communicate it to the rest of us. (p. 110)

A little emotional distance, such as a desexualised animal might be presumed to possess, perhaps may enhance the discernment of whatever reality underlies perception. But something is lacking, the animal is truncated; Beton notices that 'it is strange what a difference a tail makes' (p. 13). The reception of reality's communication is interrupted by the laughter of the audience.

Beton thus arrives at motives for a man to subsume a woman either by custody or by scorn, by all the codified behaviours that construct, enclose and guard women, and, she concludes of women as 'magic' mirrors for men, 'if they were not inferior, they would cease to enlarge. That serves to explain in part the necessity that women so often are to men' (p. 36). Beton invites us to reflect on 'the value that men set upon women's chastity and its effect upon their education', this law that constrains women physically and mentally (p. 64). She cites Jane Eyre's longing from the rooftop of Thornfield for 'a power of vision which might overpass that limit' and for 'more of practical experience than I possess' (p. 68). To upset the world's expectation provides no escape from the enclosure; George Eliot, living with a married man, still 'must submit to the social convention, and be "cut off from what is called the world"' (p. 70). Beton speaks here not of one century only, but says the effect upon a woman's poetic gift of swimming against the social current remains the same in all historical eras: 'To have lived a free life in London in the sixteenth century would have meant for a woman who was poet and playwright a nervous stress and dilemma which might well have killed her. Had she survived, whatever she had written would have been twisted and deformed, issuing from a strained and morbid imagination' (p. 50). Beton logically concludes, 'That woman, then, who was born with a gift of poetry in the sixteenth century, was an unhappy woman, a woman at strife against herself. All the conditions of her life, all her own instincts, were hostile to the state of mind which is needed to set free whatever is in the brain' (pp. 50–1). This is so because, Beton asserts, 'Chastity had then, it has even now, a religious importance in a woman's life, and has so wrapped itself round with nerves and instincts that to cut it free and bring it to the light of day demands courage of the rarest' (pp. 49–50). Whether or not men have been bound at any given time or place by a similar expectation of sexual temperance, they have not been bound by the same enclosure.

Therefore, the ideal of female chastity cannot continue as the controlling context for women's creative work. Beton argues that, whether acting as a cause of laughter or as a millstone around the neck, it is one of those things likely to create a swerve in one's thought, a mind 'slightly pulled from the straight, and made to alter its clear vision in deference to external authority' (p. 74); it raises barriers to one's ability to express the reality in one's mind with integrity. It is, Beton says, sufficiently difficult for anyone to overcome the barriers to creating a work that 'comes from the mind whole and entire', for 'fiction is like a spider's web, attached ever so lightly perhaps, but still attached to life at all four corners', and when the conditions of life are inauspicious, 'the web is pulled askew, hooked up at the edge, torn in the middle' (pp. 51, 41–2). The quality of creative work is dependent on material circumstances – lack of interruptions, ample money and health – and on certain immaterial conditions, 'intellectual freedom' (p. 108). As a remedy, Beton hints at the extinction of the sexes: as 'womanhood' become less protected, she says 'that one will say, "I saw a woman today," as one used to say, "I saw an aeroplane"' (p. 40), and of men, she predicts that if woman 'begins to tell the truth, the figure in the looking-glass shrinks; his fitness for life is diminished ... Take it away and the man may die' (p. 36). The things extinguished are 'manhood' and 'womanhood', old ways of acting and perceiving gender. In searching for the mirrors that will help a woman write, and will permit a man to let her, Beton, recalling Coleridge's assertion that a great mind is androgynous, hypothesises an evolution in each sex toward the androgynous mind, such that male and female would both have a role to play in observing reality, for 'the normal and comfortable state of being is that when the two live in harmony together, spiritually cooperating' (p. 98).

Finally, Beton concludes in a utopian credo that the mind has the ability both to participate in the human current and to separate itself from people, to stand 'at an upper window looking down on them' (p. 97); in Beton's terms, it has the ability to perform both male and female qualities. The couple Beton observes meeting on a London street, who are part of the current both coming and going, are able to form their connection despite the diverging pressure of that current; she says, 'when I saw the couple get into the taxi-cab the mind felt as if, after being divided, it had come together again in a natural fusion' (pp. 97–8). This couple, then, presents a third way to deal with the peril of sexuality. Because the mind after this fusion is 'resonant', it is sensitive to reality; because it is 'porous', she says, 'it transmits emotion without impediment' (p. 98); androgynous fusion restores the transmission of affect that had been interrupted, and escapes being caught within the custodial bonds created when one is defined by a relation to chastity. What we learn from Beton's intervention is that the writer's essential task is to carry out desire, 'thinking by the body of the people' (p. 65). Beton looks for the ability to make the work take shape, not 'by the relation of stone to stone, but by the relation of human being to human being' (p. 70), in the interspace between us, where Hannah Arendt says we make the world.[6]

We can measure the carefully calibrated distance between Woolf and Beton most closely in the last section of the essay, where Woolf sums up the work. Many have overlooked the potential irony in *A Room of One's Own*, I think, because Woolf makes Beton such a sympathetic character. Beton's struggle to become an insightful and knowledgeable critic is real, and it serves Woolf's argument that women have not yet had 'a dog's chance' of being free, although the liberation has begun (p. 108). Beton took us as far as she was able, envisioning a hope of future fullness, freedom between the sexes, and peace (p. 104). However, the contemplative target in *A Room of One's Own* is not exactly the woman writer's exact position in relation to power, or men's, but the (political) action of criticism itself. What Woolf is finally after is to demonstrate a criticism that is capable of a new articulation of freedom, its gestures, movements and energies. The writer of any kind of book who understands criticism as affective interspace has the opportunity to attend to those movements and containments, and to find new language to register them. In the end, Woolf suggests that what matters is not how critics or readers define, alter or play with their sexuality and gender, but rather that they make themselves able to accompany the writer in that plunge into our specificity. Woolf concludes by leaving us two gifts: 'the power to contemplate' and 'the power to think for oneself', the fruits of that five hundred pounds per year and the lock on the door (p. 106). Finally, she leaves us a promise: that good books are always worth writing, that lifting half the human race out of poverty and into intellectual freedom will benefit everyone, and will perhaps even provide a strong antidote against the fascist version of masculinity Beton references near the end of her portion of the essay (p. 102). Perhaps the most unironic passage in the text is the one where, after Beton has disappeared, Woolf says:

> where books are concerned, it is notoriously difficult to fix labels of merit in such a way that they do not come off ... So long as you write what you wish to write, that is all that matters ... But to sacrifice a hair of the head of your vision ... in deference to some Headmaster with a silver pot in his hand or to some professor with a measuring-rod up his sleeve, is the most abject treachery, and the sacrifice of wealth and chastity which used to be said to be the greatest of human disasters, a mere flea-bite in comparison. (p. 106)

Women are both 'inheritors' and 'originators', building up their tradition after a long struggle, which is not yet complete (p. 109). Woolf is at heart a historical materialist. She says that oppression has made women unconventional, subtle, often anonymous, and, thankfully, not given to composing 'noble' sentiments. Of course, women's fiction and criticism and even women's sentences really are different from men's, because their experience and positionality in the world has been defined as categorically different, by patriarchal power. Beton concludes by observing the taxi that took the man and woman, now fused, into the 'tremendous stream', but Woolf concludes on the note of radical freedom, a common life, and equality: 'Be oneself', she orders, and 'think of things in themselves', not as convention or patriarchy dictates (p. 111). The 'real life' is a common life, after all, which is enriched and dignified by our freedom and those conditions of equality that permit women and all people to flourish and create (p. 113).

NOTES

1. Virginia Woolf, *A Room of One's Own,* gen. ed. Mark Hussey, annotated and introduced by Susan Gubar (Orlando, FL: Harcourt, 2005); subsequent references are incorporated in the main text.
2. Newnham and Girton are two historic women's colleges of the University of Cambridge, although they did not attain full status as such until 1948, two decades after Woolf's lectures. The acronym of Girton's Odtaa Society stands for 'One damn thing after another'.
3. Woolf would have known very well a category of poem which plays with this idea of an unreliable but self-revealing narrator: the dramatic monologue. See, e.g., Robert Browning's 'My Last Duchess'.
4. The British Library formed a part of the British Museum (as the British Museum Library) until 1973, when it became independent as a result of the British Library Act. *A Room of One's Own* speaks here of accessing textual materials in the museum's iconic domed Round Reading Room.
5. For the purposes of her essay, Woolf refers to 'Oxbridge' as if it were one place but this is of course the common way of referring to both Oxford and Cambridge universities.

6. Hannah Arendt writes of 'the world, which can form only in the interspaces between men in all their variety' as they discourse together. 'On Humanity in Dark Times: Thoughts about Lessing', in *Men in Dark Times* (New York: Harcourt, 1968), p. 31. See also *The Human Condition*, 2nd edn (University of Chicago Press, 1998).

CRITICAL REFLECTIONS AND FURTHER STUDY

Has Woolf's essay aged well, from our (multiple) standpoints in the twenty-first century? What should we think of *A Room of One's Own* in terms of its feminist practice, almost a hundred years later? Does it still have something to say to experts in feminist theory and gender studies, and to scholars of social justice, considering where the scholarly conversation around gender and social justice has moved over the course of a century? Most urgently, is it complicit with systemic racism and reactionary gender politics in promoting a palatable version of white feminism which only attends to the material conditions and the politics of white cis women of the middle class? Beton's selection of historical women writers is canonical and includes no writers of colour, and she explicitly argues that writers who identify as women must inhabit circles of class prestige and power, exercising (whether she acknowledges it or not) racial privilege. Because Woolf's work was deeply meaningful to many successive waves of feminist thinkers, and was often cited by them, it would be easy to burden this essay with all the sins of a pernicious 'non-racial' feminism that fails to attend to intersectional causes of oppression, and even more conspicuously fails to attend to the experience of women of colour and of trans and gender nonconforming people.

It makes sense that Woolf would centre on a logic of gender in her essay. Women's legal and professional rights had been under intense debate in Woolf's time, and she is certainly not inventing the profound, explicit misogyny she and Beton describe. It was only fourteen months before Woolf's essay was published that the United Kingdom had finally extended voting rights to all women over the age of twenty-one, the same criterion required of male voters, in the Representation of the People Act. As to the question of suffrage, the essay might at times prompt us to ask how narrowly Woolf construes the rights to gender equality. Whom would she exclude, if anyone? We have some of the same difficulties in reading Woolf on gender as we have with other modernists who write in an ironic vein using unreliable narrators, such as Joseph Conrad on race in *Heart of Darkness*, for example. To what degree should we associate Marlow's explicitly racist articulations with Conrad's views? To what degree does Woolf involve herself as a living thinker in the actual world with Beton's fictional efforts to think her way out of an oppressive gender binary? I have suggested that Beton stands at some distance from Woolf, and I am also persuaded that Woolf's attitude is fundamentally anti-normative, and that she has more sophisticated theories about gender identity and expression, fluidity, and performance than Beton does, even if Woolf's views might not align perfectly with contemporary and academic discourse around gender identity and expression. I understand Woolf not as enamoured with the idea of mental 'androgyny' forced upon everyone as an ideal, but as deploying Beton's half-attempts to think her way out of the gender binary as a means to destabilise gender categories and enlarge the possibilities for any gendered being to create their own radical freedom. When one thinks of Woolf's other exploratory works, such as *Orlando*, one can see just how much more provisional and experimental gender and its social arrangements were for Woolf than for her society at large.

In *A Room of One's Own* Woolf is interested in specifying what gender and sexuality may signal either rhetorically or philosophically to various players in her narrative. The notion Beton introduces that there may be a male-shaped sentence, or a sentence that violates that shape, is challenging to pin down definitionally, but it leads to a set of historically informed reflections on what produces style and standards of literary-critical taste under various social arrangements. A feminist approach to style would, as Woolf's does, cast doubt on the 'invisible universality' of the established norms of merit, since these are a production of patriarchal power. In short, *A Room of One's Own* forcefully brings gender to consciousness in the context of fiction and criticism, and it works on several planes simultaneously, including the inherited and the originary, to borrow Woolf's language (p. 109).

It is worth reading through a range of Woolf's essays, novels and short stories to discover the breadth of her concerns and to see that she was always thinking through the structures of imperialism, war, masculinity, racism and civil rights together. Her geographic imaginary is cosmopolitan, not chauvinistically nationalist, and her work offers a strong critically based account of the politics of reading. For example, her 1940 essay 'The Leaning Tower' (published posthumously in 1947 in *The Moment and Other Essays* (London: Hogarth Press)) attempts to think through her own positionality and the politics of her generation of writers. In *Orlando* (1928), a novel written at about the same time as *A Room of One's Own*, Woolf playfully destabilises and parodies gender categories *as* categories which are often accepted uncritically as given or 'natural'. And *Three Guineas* (1938) is an appropriate final example here as this polemic is a sort of sequel to *A Room of One's Own*, bringing to the bar what we would now call toxic masculinism for its war fever and failure to imagine the horrors it creates, and persuading women not to lean in to that culture.

FURTHER READING

Berman, Jessica Schiff (ed.), *A Companion to Virginia Woolf* (Chichester: John Wiley, 2016)

Bernstein, Susan David, *Roomscape: Women Writers in the British Museum from George Eliot to Virginia Woolf* (Edinburgh University Press, 2013)

Burns, Christy L., 'Powerful Differences: Critique and Eros in Jeanette Winterson and Virginia Woolf', *Modern Fiction Studies* 44.2 (1998), 364–92

Cuddy-Keane, Melba, *Virginia Woolf, the Intellectual, and the Public Sphere* (Cambridge University Press, 2003): https://doi.org/10.1017/CBO9780511485060

Ellmann, Maud, *The Nets of Modernism: Henry James, Virginia Woolf, James Joyce, and Sigmund Freud* (Cambridge University Press, 2010)

Felski, Rita, *The Gender of Modernity* (Cambridge, MA: Harvard University Press, 1995)

Fernald, Anne E., *Virginia Woolf: Feminism and the Reader* (New York: Palgrave Macmillan, 2006)

Henke, Suzette, and David Eberly (eds), with the assistance of Jane Lilienfeld, *Virginia Woolf and Trauma: Embodied Texts* (New York: Pace University Press, 2007)

Lee, Hermione, *Virginia Woolf* (London: Chatto & Windus, 1996)

Moran, Patricia, '"The Flaw in the Centre": Writing as Hymenal Rupture in Virginia Woolf's Work', *Tulsa Studies in Women's Literature* 17.1 (1998), 101–21

Nadel, Ira Bruce, *Virginia Woolf* (London: Reaktion Books, 2016)

Restuccia, Frances L., '"Untying the Mother Tongue": Female Difference in Virginia Woolf's *A Room of One's Own*', *Tulsa Studies in Women's Literature* 4.2 (1985), 253–64

Rooney, Ellen (ed.), *The Cambridge Companion to Feminist Literary Theory* (Cambridge University Press, 2006)

Sellers, Susan (ed.), *The Cambridge Companion to Virginia Woolf* (Cambridge University Press, 2010)

Showalter, Elaine, *A Literature of Their Own: British Women Novelists From Brönte to Lessing* (Princeton University Press, 1977)

Woolf, Virginia, *Women and Fiction: The Manuscript Versions of 'A Room of One's Own'*, ed. S. P. Rosenbaum (Oxford and Cambridge, MA: Blackwell, 1992)

PART VII
The Twentieth and Twenty-First Centuries, 1939–2020

INTRODUCTORY NOTE

Reflecting a widespread commitment among academics and teachers to make the study of literature socially relevant and socially transformative, each of the essays in this section orients its discussion very firmly towards social critique and social change. Terry Gifford presents a masterly ecocritical account of the poetry of Ted Hughes, covering almost the whole of Hughes's career and focusing in particular on his ecological vision and on his development as a 'post-pastoral' poet. Gifford grounds his discussion in several acute close readings of extracts taken from different periods in Hughes's career and he systematically introduces key concepts in contemporary ecocriticism in order to explain different phases and aspects of Hughes's development. In suggesting the increasing recognition of Hughes's contemporary relevance for ecocritical writers, he cites the example of Hughes's influence on the current Poet Laureate, Simon Armitage. In addition to their shared environmental concerns and a shared regional heritage as Yorkshire-born poets, they share an intertextual influence in the form of the alliterative medieval verse romance, *Sir Gawain and the Green Knight* (also with links to the north of England). As Gifford notes, Hughes draws on that work for his 1967 poem 'Wodwo'; and, in 2007, Simon Armitage published his own modern English translation of *Gawain*. This apparently fugitive link across the ages seems to me worth noting here for its suggestiveness in reminding us that contexts can take many different and subtle forms, including intertextual ones, and can work in mysterious ways both across long periods of time and simultaneously among contemporaries. It could be fruitful, moreover, to explore how exactly these two modern poets were influenced by the Middle English poem and how they might have been influenced by each other's interest in it. Also, how might their 'recycling' of this text be related to the essays in Part I on the medieval period, and to my comments on communications circuits in my introductory note to that part? And how might our reading of *Sir Gawain and the Green Knight* now be influenced by Terry Gifford's ecocritical reading of Ted Hughes here?

Catherine Riley's essay returns our focus to the world of publishing and print culture in its probing examination of the recent history of direct professional participation of women in British publishing and of the complex dynamics of how such participation (or non-participation) impacts upon women writers and readers, influencing what is written and published and how it is marketed and read. Riley's feminist analysis of the gender politics of the contemporary book business and literary marketplace shows that gender issues continue to play an influential role in the production and consumption of literature and, while she celebrates the many significant achievements of women in publishing over the past fifty years, there is, Riley concludes, still much to be done to ensure gender equality within this field. Riley's essay clearly chimes with aspects of Paltin's essay in the preceding part and partly also with Halsey's earlier discussion of Jane Austen's publishing experiences.

The immediately public and communal nature of drama has made it a medium particularly valued for its potential for social critique and this is clearly reflected in the concerns of the next essay by Clare Wallace, who presents a set of detailed case studies in contemporary British theatre through which she traces a 'structure of feeling' in wider society that is, she suggests, marked unmistakably by a sense of crisis, anxiety and precarity. Looking closely at an aesthetically and technically varied range of plays from the 1990s onwards, Wallace carefully analyses both ideas and methods in her chosen works and her lucid account of these conveys a helpful sense of how they might be experienced in performance. Identifying some radical approaches in contemporary theatrical technique, she also conveys a keen sense of theatre's continuing potential for radical social critique.

As the phrase 'structure of feeling' indicates, Wallace draws inspiration for her essay from the works and ideas of Raymond Williams, whose many classic studies (e.g., *Culture and Society 1780–1950* (1958), *The Long Revolution* (1961), *The Country and the City* (1973), *Keywords* (1983)) have had a permeating influence on British literary and cultural criticism over the past fifty years or so. That influence can certainly be seen in the present volume's main defining terms, for if anyone can be said to have inaugurated the study of literature in the full complexity of its contexts, then surely it was Williams, with his meticulously detailed analyses of the networks of cultural relations within which texts are embedded. But for Williams, as a Marxist critic, the point of any form of cultural critique was never just to analyse or interpret the world in various ways, but to *change* it. In clarifying the ways in which contemporary drama represents a form of cultural critique seeking to change the world, Clare Wallace's discussion carries its own socially transformative potential – and, in that, it can be seen as a fitting homage to Williams's legacy in 2021, the hundredth anniversary of his birth.

24 An Ecocritical Reading of the Poetry of Ted Hughes

TERRY GIFFORD

Abstract

This essay offers an ecocritical reading of Hughes's poetic career. First, ecocriticism is defined and the successive 'waves' of its development outlined. In contrast to Larkin's 'Movement' poetry, the case is made for Hughes's work as post-pastoral poetry that seeks to counter nostalgic idealisation of the countryside, its inhabitants and its elemental forces. Hughes's first two volumes, *The Hawk in the Rain* and *Lupercal*, satirise pastoral defences against the forces of nature, but also celebrate the 'elemental power circuit of the universe' at work in the inner life of humans, animals and landscapes. *Wodwo* then seriously extends these themes. Between critique and celebration of forces in the human and more than human worlds, the course of Hughes's poetic career was remarkably consistent, despite the variety of forms that each volume took, from the mythic narratives of *Crow* and *Cave Birds* to the shamanic verse narrative of *Gaudete*, the georgic poetry of *Moortown Diary*, the cultural organicism of *Remains of Elmet* and the redemptive achievement of *River*. The maturity of these three latter volumes deepens both language and themes. Even in *Birthday Letters*, Hughes and his late wife, Sylvia Plath, can be seen to be defined by their different responses to the natural world.

The distinctive feature of this essay is the way in which ecocritical concepts are revealing of aspects of Hughes's poetry: pastoral, post-pastoral, otherness, inhabitation, biosemiology, ecofeminism, material ecocriticism, agency, natureculture and re-enchantment. These concepts are defined in the context of specific texts. Consideration is also given to poetry written 'within hearing of children', as Hughes put it, together with reference to Hughes's poetic translation of *Tales from Ovid*. The significance of Hughes's influence upon Alice Oswald and the Poet Laureate, Simon Armitage, is emphasised as twenty-first-century poets and readers engage with the consequences of the Anthropocene.

Ted Hughes recognised that the environmental crisis is a cultural crisis. The depth of this crisis becomes clear when, as Poet Laureate in 1992, he began an article in a national Sunday newspaper with these words:

> If Earth is a casualty of modern civilisation, that is not her only problem ... Unluckily for the Earth, mankind has difficulty finding a language in which to understand her case. A language that will not only interpret the Earth's needs exactly, but will also, by sheer power of conviction, realign mankind to those needs, like an irresistible magnetic field.[1]

Several features of this discourse are characteristic of Hughes's way of thinking and writing. First is the anthropomorphism of Earth which, like us, has a problem. The puzzled figure of God in Hughes's creation stories for children makes creatures that he cannot quite get right.[2] Second is the gendering of Earth as female. Hughes had just published *Shakespeare and the Goddess of Complete Being* (1992) in which he argued that male fear of the feminine in nature was a strong theme of Shakespeare's works. Third is the belief that realignment is not only possible, but restorative of a relationship that should be as natural as the alignment in a magnetic field. Finally, there is the resolution that a language can be found that carries the force of a 'sheer power of conviction' to begin this realignment. For Hughes, this was the language of poetry and story (which include the forms of song and drama). In these few sentences in 1992 Hughes could have been describing his life's work. An ecocritical reading of it should be able to demonstrate poetry's power and magnetism in attempting to contribute to the healing of Earth's problem. Of course, Hughes knows that Earth's problem is really our problem.

In *English Literature in Context*, John Brannigan cites Greg Garrard's book *Ecocriticism* (2004) in his discussion of Alice Oswald's poem, *Dart* (2002), and it is notable that Oswald was initially hugely influenced by the poetry of Ted Hughes.[3] Ecocriticism began in the late twentieth century as a deconstruction of representations of nature, in the United States as celebratory readings of contemporary nature writing, and, independently in Britain, as a rereading of Romanticism in the light of contemporary environmental concerns. Two collections of essays were quickly compiled on both sides of the Atlantic – in America, Cheryl Glotfelty and Harold Fromm's *The Ecocriticism Reader: Landmarks in Literary Ecology* (1996) and, in the UK, Laurence Coupe's *The Green Studies Reader: From Romanticism to Ecocriticism* (2000). Following on from these starting points, ecocritics have charted several waves of development, including a second wave of self-critique,[4] to a third wave of the exploration of subfields such as environmental justice, ecofeminism, indigenous studies, biosemiology, material ecocriticism and post-pastoral theory.[5] At the same time a fourth wave of the globalisation of ecocriticism has resulted from national and regional connections of ecocriticism with local traditions.[6] The work of Ted Hughes remains a distinctively British mode of examining our connection with nature, although it is a mode that benefits from being read through the prisms of several new notions of ecocriticism which highlight key aspects of his work.

John Brannigan suggests that Philip Larkin's poem 'MCMXIV' 'appears to be nostalgic for the lost continuity of a pastoral England'.[7] Ted Hughes's first collection of poetry was immediately seen as a stark contrast to Larkin's nostalgic, slightly diffident, poetry that was associated with the Movement poets of the 1950s. Reviewing *The Hawk in the Rain* (1957), Edwin Muir, for example, said that Hughes was 'clearly a remarkable poet and seems to be quite outside the currents of his time'.[8] When Muir wrote, 'His images have an admirable violence', he was identifying a feature of Hughes's early poetry that was distinctly anti-pastoral, celebrating elemental forces in landscapes and animals while also satirising humans who were disconnected from the powerful emotions and dreams of their own inner lives. Hughes sought to counter pastoral idealisation of the countryside, its inhabitants and its elemental forces. His first two volumes satirise pastoral defences against the forces of nature, but also celebrate what he called 'the elemental power circuit of the universe' at work in the inner life of humans, animals and landscapes.[9] In the poem 'Egg-Head' from the first collection, the intellectual's head is an eggshell that filters out 'the flash / Of the sun, the bolt of the earth'. But he is also merely 'Peeping through his fingers at the world's ends, / Or at an ant's head', or at 'a leaf's otherness'.[10] Ecocriticism seeks to celebrate literature that engages with 'otherness' in nature and, in Hughes's second collection, *Lupercal* (1960), the poem 'Crow Hill' attempts to create a sense of the otherness of the forces at work in the West Yorkshire landscape of the poet's childhood, including its human and non-human inhabitants. In the first draft of this poem, farmers appeared in all three stanzas, but in the published poem their presence is reduced: 'Between the weather and the rock / Farmers make a little heat'. The poem goes on to balance forces of erosion with the vitality of life brilliantly adapted to the tough conditions. These forces of vitality and decay are referred to as a single 'What':

What humbles these hills has raised
The arrogance of blood and bone,
And thrown the hawk upon the wind
And lit the fox in the dripping ground.[11]

The otherness of 'What' is the same 'elemental power circuit' responsible for the strong verbs 'thrown' and 'lit' which emphasise adaptation to Yorkshire weather.

Ecocritics would call such adaptation 'inhabitation' or 'dwelling' which, in this poem, includes farmers, hawk and fox, all of whom are at home in the tough landscape that is the actual Crow Hill above the Calder Valley where Hughes grew up (Figure 24.1). Hughes is poetically undertaking what Jonathan Bate defines as 'dwelling with the earth': 'True inhabiting necessitates a willingness to look

Figure 24.1 The Calder Valley, West Yorkshire, birthplace of Ted Hughes.

at and listen to the world. It is a letting go of the self which brings the discovery of a deeper self.'[12] Bate could be describing here Hughes's purpose in writing the poem 'Wodwo' which gave his third collection its title (1967). In this poem Hughes recognises the difficulty of 'letting go of the self' in 'listening to the world'. In the voice of the half-human, half-animal mythical wood spirit from the Middle English poem *Sir Gawain and the Green Knight*, Hughes asks, 'What am I?': 'Do these weeds / know me and name me to each other / have they seen me before, do I fit in their world?'[13] Through the figure of the wodwo, Hughes treats, with questioning irony, the human assumption that although the weeds obviously have their own world, humans are not only part of it but at the centre of it. The poem's final line is: 'very queer but I'll go on looking'. This is the final poem in a collection that repeatedly rejects the recognisably human notion of, in the wodwo's words, 'I suppose I am the exact centre', especially in the tempting hubris of inventing a purpose for the universe.

The poem 'Pibroch' is a lament for the notion of a 'heaven', as is clear in the opening lines: 'The sea cries with its meaningless voice / Treating alike its dead and its living, / Probably bored with the appearance of heaven.'[14] 'Appearance' cleverly combines both the sense of the sea looking up and the human invention (comparatively recent in evolutionary terms) of 'heaven' in the religious sense. The sea, here, is 'without purpose, without self-deception', so 'Minute after minute, aeon after aeon, / Nothing lets up or develops. / This is neither a bad variant nor a tryout'. While evolutionary biologists might argue with 'nothing develops', it is questionable whether anything develops in terms of value, as opposed to simply changing. The poem asks the reader to consider questions about the human desire to see evolutionary 'progress' in terms of creation's 'purpose' and whether this is a 'self-deception' comparable, perhaps, to the egg-head's.

Many such human cultural defences against 'the bolt of the earth, the whelm of the sun' are tested in the collection named after its central figure, *Crow* (1970). From his own studies of indigenous cultures as a student of social anthropology in his final year at Cambridge University, Hughes was familiar with Native American folk tales about the trickster who sometimes took the form of a crow. By breaking all social conventions and getting himself into trouble, the trickster's amusing and amoral behaviour in these tales demonstrates why the conventions are needed. Similarly, Hughes's Crow emerges from blackness, in arrogance and innocence, following his appetites and instincts, in poems which combine myth, legend and the biblical creation story. Crow sets about testing to destruction, with a playfulness that turns to amazement, the constructions of western civilisation that excuse, or explain away, a direct experience of nature: pastoral idealisation ('Crow and the Birds'), Romantic self-projection ('Owl Song'), the Oedipus complex ('Revenge Fable'), scientific determinism ('Crow's Account of the Battle'), the reification of evil ('The Black Beast'), the killing of 'otherness' ('Crow's Account of St George'), a Christian God ('Crow communes') and LOVE ('Crow's First Lesson'). The persistence of these self-deceptions and their self-destructiveness is characteristically illustrated towards the end of the sequence in the short poem 'Glimpse' when Crow, despite all he has seen, attempts a pastoral lyric that begins, '"O leaves –" / The touch of a leaf's edge at his throat / Guillotined further comment'.[15] Nevertheless, Crow finds in this poem that he can continue in this Romantic vein, as Hughes playfully says, 'Through the god's head instantly substituted'. Even in the face of material reality, Crow finds that the godlike human desire for transcendence can persist, despite its ultimate self-destructiveness.

Occasionally throughout the sequence there are poems in which Crow seems to be tentatively developing an ethical sense of himself in the universe. First, he must show some signs of empathy or at least desire for connection with the otherness of nature. He tries 'just being in the same world as the sea', but it is in terms of his own feelings for the sea – ignoring it, talking to it, hating it, feeling sympathy for it – all to no avail.[16] Finally he finds that he cannot even turn his back and march away from the sea, 'As a crucified man cannot move'. The pain caused by this blow to his ego in the realisation that he will always be marching towards a sea, 'crucifies' him into immobility. In 'Crow and the Beach' he listens to 'the sea's ogreish outcry and convulsion' and, with humility this time, he is able to empathise enough to feel its pain instead of his own: 'His utmost gaping of brain in his tiny skull / Was just enough to wonder, about the sea, / What could be hurting so much?'[17] We read this now with the knowledge that Hughes was aware of global warming and the rising of sea levels.[18] But more significant for readers in 1970 was the very idea of listening and looking for the signs of hurt coming from the sea and its inhabitants – what is now called 'biosemiology'.

In notes Hughes made about his earliest experience of the moors above his house, he himself wondered about 'the rocks, the birds, the silence, the flowers, full of something wonderful, if only one could learn to interpret their sounds or their signs'.[19] In a sense the practice of biosemiology was the earliest motivation for his poetry. It is celebrated in the final poem of *Crow*, a hymn to 'Littleblood'. Here Hughes is listening to the life force that runs through the land ('eating the medical earth') and its creatures ('dancing with a gnat's feet'). It is a life force that has 'Grown so wise grown so terrible / Sucking death's mouldy tits. // Sit on my finger, sing in my ear, O littleblood'.[20] The importance of biosemiology was emphasised in one of Hughes's last works, his translations of Ovid's *Metamorphoses* in *Tales from Ovid* (1997) when he suggested that, in the Age of Gold, 'Listening deeply, man kept faith with the source'.[21]

'Deep listening' is impossible for Crow. At various points in the sequence he encounters his female creator, the goddess of nature, but cannot recognise her. The closest he comes is in 'Crow's Undersong', but all he finds are riddles of her retreat under the trappings of modern civilisation, 'with eyes wincing frightened / When she looks into wheels'.[22] The poem begins, 'She cannot come all the way', but ends, 'If there had been no hope she would not have come // And there would have been no crying in the city // (There would have been no city)'. There is still hope here for a reconciliation that might come from 'listening deeply' in the city that is both the source of human alienation from nature and representative of the capacity for human creativity.

Ecofeminist readers would note the danger of essentialism in Hughes's apparent association of the feminine with nature. But the mythic narrative of the poem sequence that followed *Crow* indicates that Hughes is attempting to reduce the male ego and the arrogance of patriarchy to bring out an innate, but resisted, male closeness to nature. In *Cave Birds* (1978) an arrogant cockerel is put on trial for the neglect of his inner nature that connects him to outer nature. In a folkloric narrative that Hughes subtitled 'an alchemical cave drama', the male figure is found guilty and made to confront his own mortality. In refusing a series of false heavens, he shows himself ready to be symbolically married to a female figure who represents both his own inner spirit and the goddess of nature.

In the moving poem 'Bride and Groom Lie Hidden for Three Days', the pair of lovers physically remake each other's bodies, part by part:

> She gives him his eyes, she found them
> Among some rubble, among some beetles
>
> He gives her her skin
> He just seemed to pull it down out of the air and lay it over her
> She weeps with fearfulness and astonishment[23]

The mutual giving is characterised by tenderness and wonder. The final lines of this poem led me to first propose the notion of the 'post-pastoral' as being clearly in the pastoral tradition, but avoiding the dangers of idealisation.[24] Hughes evokes a moment of ecstatic connectedness that manages to encompass both that between the lovers in their animality and a human sense of connection to the earth:

> So, gasping with joy, with cries of wonderment
> Like two gods of mud
> Sprawling in the dirt, but with infinite care
>
> They bring each other to perfection.[25]

That last word could so easily suggest a pastoral idealisation, but this is eclipsed by their 'sprawling in the dirt' of the earth like two gods of its materiality. Far from being transcendent they are of the earth, at one with its messy, physical, sometimes unattractive nature that can nevertheless at such moments offer 'joy' and 'wonderment'. Such moments might be transient since the force of the human desire for control of nature can reassert itself. So the cockerel is reborn as a falcon in a poem entitled 'The Risen', which ends in a question that has the inevitability of a statement: 'But when will he land / On a man's wrist'. It will have been noticed that, in 'Wodwo' and 'Littleblood' in particular, Hughes leaves out punctuation for poetic effect. The missing question mark here is another case of challenging the reader to ask why it is missing. *Cave Birds* concludes with a 'Finale' which provides the answer: 'At the end of the ritual / up comes a goblin'. No pastoral complacency is possible because in a post-pastoral text, which goes beyond (rather than 'after') pastoral, it is acknowledged that the human desire for control, mastery, purposes or protections can reassert itself.

In his critique of patriarchal arrogance and masculine control, Hughes is implicitly exploring an ecofeminism that ran deep in his thinking about the history of English literature and culture. He was to elaborate this thinking in his monumental study *Shakespeare and the Goddess of Complete Being* (1992). But by 1970 Hughes had a fully formed cultural theory of western patriarchy's responsibility for human alienation from nature, as he revealed in a review of Max Nicholson's book *The*

Environmental Revolution (1970). (This review, incidentally, was in the third issue of a new magazine called *Your Environment*, which Hughes had persuaded his friends David Ross and Daniel Weissbort to launch with him in 1969.) Hughes believed that a religious patriarchal society had encouraged the biblical rejection of a feminised Nature: 'The subtly apotheosized misogyny of Reformed Christianity is proportionate to the fanatic rejection of Nature.'[26] In his later study Hughes argued that Shakespeare was exploring, in his plays and his long poems, the tension between Puritan suppression and a deeper Marian religion that sought energy from what Hughes called 'the Goddess of Complete Being'. The sense of a need to bring modern masculinity into closer contact with the feminine in human and outer nature should inform a reading of the otherwise perplexing verse narrative of *Gaudete* (1977).

The narrative of this book, which had its origins in ideas for a film script, combines a shamanic healing journey with apparently everyday village life. Although the narrative is a farcical satire, the tone is unwaveringly serious throughout. Hughes knew from his studies of indigenous cultures at Cambridge that a shaman takes a journey in trance into the world of spirits in order to return with healing songs and stories for his community. *Gaudete* opens as the Reverend Nicholas Lumb is carried away into the spirit world to perform a healing task there. (The spirit world seems to have thought that a Church of England vicar is some kind of shaman.) In his place is a changeling Lumb has made from an oak log, who, taking a rather 'wooden' approach to the ministry of the Gospel of love, turns the Women's Institute (a rural women's organisation) into a coven to be impregnated in the hope, Lumb convinces them, of producing a messiah. The men of the parish discover what is going on, hunt Lumb down and kill him at the very moment that the spirits have decided to cancel him. The original vicar turns up in the west of Ireland, whistles up an otter and goes off, leaving behind a notebook of poems that are 'hymns and psalms to a nameless female deity'.[27]

These poems constitute an epilogue that has a quite different tone – a seriousness appropriate to personal religious encounters with the Goddess – that contrasts with the main narrative and makes an implicit critique of it. If the narrative asserts male confidence and exploitation of women, the epilogue poems strain with male inadequacy and humility in the face of a mysterious and marvellous feminised creation. Thus they inevitably also express something of the feminine in their writer that counters the victimisation of women by the wooden Lumb:

Each of us is nothing
But the fleeting warm pressure

Of your footfall
As you pace

Your cage of freedom.[28]

The epilogue poems are in the Indian tradition of *vacanas* – 'poems based on the mystical process of becoming one with a god or with a divine Creative Source'[29] – and sixty-three more of them were published in the limited edition volume entitled *Orts* (1977), which in northern dialect means 'left-overs'. This volume contains some of Hughes's most complex attempts to connect to the force of creation in direct addresses to the Goddess. Poem '41', for example, celebrates 'this planetary rawness': its

> aimless elation
> And stone-dullness
> That empties me every instant
> Pulses your fullness.[30]

The paradoxes of this ordinary yet breathtaking connection are as close as Hughes can get to feeling on the pulse the ego-emptying mystery of being alive within the 'fullness' of the universe.

From his honeymoon with the American poet Sylvia Plath in Benidorm in 1956, to the very end of his life, Hughes wrote 'within hearing of children', as he put it.[31] As this phrase implies, he was reluctant to regard his children's writing, in poetry, stories and plays, as separate from his writing for adult readers, including his central project of exploring environmental reconnection for our species. In poetry, perhaps the best example of this are the animals poems in *The Cat and the Cuckoo* (1987) (Figure 24.2), especially its opening poem 'Cat' in which the healing action of stroking a cat makes a connection with 'powers / Of the beasts who ignore / These ways of ours'. In his immensely popular story, *The Iron Man* (1968), the impulse of men to destroy the otherness of the eponymous metal man is countered by the boy, Hogarth, who finds a positive role for him suited to his individual qualities. He eats scrap metal and can withstand heat, so he is enlisted to fight, in a trial by fire, against a Space Being that is threatening the Earth. Since the Space Being can only fly and sing, it is inevitably defeated and is afterwards given the job of making 'the music of the spheres' in space. It is a story with the sort of redemptive closure that Hughes was unable to find in adult works such as *Crow* and *Cave Birds*.

A quarter of a century later, Hughes wrote *The Iron Woman* (1993) which is explicitly ecofeminist and has a polemical environmental agenda that is really only fully articulated in the book's final pages. Lucy is called by the Iron Woman to help the fish and eels in the rivers that are dying from human pollution of their waters. The Iron Woman turns all the men in the country into fish who have to be carried as quickly as possible by the women to water, where the men are made to share in the pollution-engendered pain of all riverine creatures. Lucy's father works at the Waste Factory that is contributing to the pollution and the focus of the story becomes the challenge of finding a solution to dealing with waste. From a series of shape-shifting narrative moves, an organic antidote to pollution is found in webs from the Cloud-Spider of Mess that grow over any rubbish and are

Figure 24.2 Carol Hughes, the poet's widow, at the launch in 2004 of the nature-themed Ted Hughes Poetry Trail at Stover Country Park near Newton Abbot, Devon, holding his 1987 collection *The Cat and the Cuckoo*. The trail opened in 2006.

non-toxic when mixed with water. 'But where,' Lucy asks, 'did the Cloud-Spider of Mess come from?' 'Deep, big, fright,' says the Iron Woman, and 'deep, big, change'.[32] The message is absolutely clear to readers in the twenty-first century who are now confronting the 'deep, big, frights' that are the consequences of the Anthropocene and contemplating with difficulty 'deep, big, change'.

The poetry of Hughes's mature years produced three volumes of poetry that looked in more detail at the complexities of 'deep, big, change' in environmental attitudes in practical, cultural and metaphysical modes. *Moortown Diary* (1979) contained poems documenting in georgic detail the poet's taking on personal responsibility for land and animals when, in 1972, he bought Moortown Farm, close to the Devon home in North Tawton that he had bought with Sylvia Plath ten years earlier. Seven years after Plath's suicide in 1963, Hughes married Carol Orchard and her father worked on the farm, as will be seen in the final poems of the collection. The *Moortown Diary* poems are literally unaltered diary entries that Hughes called 'improvised verses' written on the day of their inspiration.[33] In the poem 'February 17th' the poet faces the trial of dealing with a sheep whose partially born lamb is already dead. He catches the sheep, but cannot get his hand past the protruding head, so, he writes, 'I went / Two miles for the injection and a razor'.[34] The description of what the poet then had to do and its visceral consequences resulted in audience members fainting when Hughes read this poem aloud. But this is not an anti-pastoral poem countering popular images of innocent lambs. It is post-pastoral, partly because of the farmer-poet's physical fight to save the mother, taking responsibility for his relationship with nature, and partly because of the poem's final image: 'And the body lay born, beside the hacked-off head.' This is a knowing image suggesting the idea that death is born of the very earth itself. Material ecocriticism focuses upon the agency of material nature and in this poem there are several agencies at work, at several levels. At the physical level the sheep and the farmer work against – and finally with – each other, while at the elemental level of the birth push and the release of the dead lamb, the mother's life is saved by human intervention. All this is symbolised by that final image of death in life – the head on the earth.

The final six poems of *Moortown Diary* celebrate the agency of Hughes's father-in-law, Jack Orchard, who devoted his final years to this farm, working against the agency of rain and 'hedge-boughs' and fencing wire. Hughes remembers him at the end of the poem, 'A Monument', battling to erect a fence in an overgrown ditch, 'Under December downpour, mid-afternoon / Dark as twilight, using your life up'.[35] The final stanza of 'The day he died' celebrates a human life so attuned to the land that it has now been deprived of a part of its agency:

From now on the land
Will have to manage without him.
But it hesitates, in this slow realisation of light,
Childlike, too naked, in a frail sun,
With roots cut
And a great blank in its memory.

The series of reversals in this anthropomorphism is both an affirmation of a relationship between man and land, and a moving act of mourning by the poet, whose own 'slow realisation' this really is. In fact, this mourning feels as if it is, in a sense, for both of them, since it is for their 'rooted' mutual dependency.

Hughes had wanted for some time to write poems about the family members and West Yorkshire environment he had left behind in his youth. When, as a result of directing the photographer Fay Godwin to the Calder Valley in 1970, he began writing poems six years later to accompany her photographs, the poems were more about human adaptation to that bleak landscape than about family members. *Remains of Elmet* (1979), which collected photographs and poems from this project, was jointly assembled by photographer and poet together.[36] But the family poems had to wait for the second edition, entitled simply *Elmet* (1994), to be included. Ecocritics use the term 'natureculture'[37] to emphasise the closeness of human life to nature and in the poems of *Remains of Elmet* the rise and fall of cultural presences in this landscape – industry, churches, farms – in the face of topography, rock and rain, is treated as a natural flowering and decay. Nowhere is this more explicit than in 'Lumb Chimneys' about abandoned industrial chimneys which look like organic growths as they are actually overtaken by nature: 'The huge labour of leaf is simply thrown away. / Great yesterdays are left lying.'[38] Now human culture itself and its great achievements here are a part of 'the elemental power circuit of the universe' that Hughes celebrated in his earlier statement about his poetic work.

Many critics regard the collection *River* (1983) as Hughes's most personally re- demptive achievement and the poem 'That Morning' has come to represent this achievement. It was read at his memorial service in Westminster Abbey and its last lines are on Hughes's memorial stone in the abbey's Poets' Corner. Hughes had always been a fisherman since his birthplace home was very close to the Calder Canal. In *River* he expresses a personal sense of natureculture as a fisherman; but more than that his poetry offers a 're-enchantment'[39] of all aspects of the river en- vironment. This is not to ignore its pollution by a bird-watching, 'nature protector' intensive farmer in the poem, '1984 on "The Tarka Trail"', who nevertheless makes extensive use of 'Pesticides, herbicides, fungicides, the grand slam'.[40] Hughes takes a poetic gamble in listing more prosaically precise details of these pollutants be- fore addressing the reader directly:

> Now you are as loaded with data
> That cultivates his hopes, in this brief gamble
> As this river is –
> As he is too.

Hopes for wealth that are 'cultivated' by this farmer are actually produced by toxins that compromise his own health through insidiously compromised water quality. This was a local (as well as a national) issue for Hughes against which he actively campaigned with friends, unknown to the original readers of *River*.[41]

Re-enchantment of the riverine environment in *River* is more than a poetic cele- bration; it achieves an almost religious aura. Indeed, in the poem 'Salmon Eggs' Christian religious language heightens the significance of the fish's desperate jour- ney to lay its eggs and die:

> And this is the liturgy
> Of Earth's advent – harrowing, crowned – a travail
> Of raptures and rendings.[42]

In 'That Morning', Hughes is in Alaska with his son, fishing in a river where there were 'wild salmon swaying massed / As from the hand of God'.[43] Two bears arrive to swim beside them and stand, 'as on a throne / Eating pierced salmon off their talons'.[44] The bears have journeyed to eat like the kings of this wilderness, just as father and son have journeyed to experience this enchanted wilderness together. So the repetition in the final line of the poem refers to each species, living together in this magical moment they have somehow 'found' like the end of a quest:

> So we found the end of our journey.
> So we stood, alive in the river of light
> Among the creatures of light, creatures of light.

Again, the repetition of 'light' seems to carry a suggestion of 'enlightenment' as both species find their rightful place, 'alive' in nature that flows around and through them.

Hughes went on to publish, in the last year of his life, his poems addressed to Sylvia Plath in *Birthday Letters* (1998). But even in *Birthday Letters* Hughes and Plath can be seen to be defined by their different responses to the natural world, most clearly in the poem 'Epiphany' in which Hughes refuses to buy a fox cub for sale on the street in London because he knows it would test his marriage. It had been his totem animal since childhood, but he knew that Plath would strongly object to him bringing the fox home. The last line is, 'But I failed. Our marriage had failed.'[45] And Hughes's legacy of influence can be seen in the work of the current Poet Laureate, Simon Armitage, and Alice Oswald, who succeeded Armitage as Oxford Professor of Poetry. Both poets have edited selections of Hughes's work to encourage future readers to study the work of one of the most important poets of the twentieth century and an increasingly relevant poet for the twenty-first century as we now address the Anthropocene's damage to nature.[46]

NOTES

1. Ted Hughes, 'If', *Observer*, 29 November 1992, p. 31.
2. See Ted Hughes, *How the Whale Became* (London: Faber & Faber, 1963).
3. See Paul Poplawski (ed.), *English Literature in Context*, 2nd edn (Cambridge University Press, 2017), pp. 605–6; and *London Review of Books*, Bookshop interview, 7 March 2017: www.92y.org/archives/75-75-alice-oswald-ted-hughes-92y-poetry-center-director-bernard-schwartz.aspx (accessed 7 February 2022).
4. See, e.g., Dana Philips, *The Truth of Ecology* (Oxford University Press, 2003).
5. See Greg Garrard (ed.), *The Oxford Handbook of Ecocriticism* (Oxford University Press, 2014).
6. John Parham and Louise Westling (eds), *A Global History of Literature and the Environment* (Cambridge University Press, 2017).
7. Poplawski (ed.), *English Literature in Context*, p. 599.
8. Edwin Muir, 'Kinds of Poetry', *New Statesman*, 28 September 1957, p. 392.
9. Ekbert Faas, *Ted Hughes: The Unaccommodated Universe* (Santa Barbara, CA: Black Sparrow Press, 1980), p. 200.
10. Ted Hughes, *Ted Hughes: Collected Poems* (London: Faber & Faber, 2003), p. 33.
11. Ibid., p. 62.
12. Jonathan Bate, *The Song of the Earth* (London: Picador, 2000), p. 155.
13. Hughes, *Collected Poems*, p. 183.
14. Ibid., p. 179.
15. Ibid., p. 256.
16. Ibid., p. 252.
17. Ibid., p. 229.
18. Yvonne Reddick, *Ted Hughes: Environmentalist and Ecopoet* (Houndmills: Palgrave Macmillan, 2017), p. 2.

19. Ted Hughes Archive, Stuart A. Rose Library, Emory University, MSS 644, Box 115, folio 8.

20. Hughes, *Collected Poems*, p. 258.

21. Ted Hughes, *Tales from Ovid* (London: Faber & Faber, 1997), p. 8.

22. Hughes, *Collected Poems*, p. 237.

23. Ibid., p. 437.

24. Terry Gifford, 'Gods of Mud: Hughes and the Post-Pastoral', in Keith Sagar (ed.), *The Challenge of Ted Hughes* (London: Macmillan, 1994), pp. 129–41.

25. Hughes, *Collected Poems*, p. 438.

26. Ted Hughes, *Winter Pollen* (London: Faber & Faber, 1994), p. 129.

27. Ted Hughes, *Gaudete* (London: Faber & Faber 1977), p. 9.

28. Ibid., p. 195.

29. Ann Skea, 'Ted Hughes' Vacanas: The Difficulties of a Bridegroom', in Mark Wormald, Neil Roberts and Terry Gifford (eds), *Ted Hughes: Cambridge to Collected* (Houndmills: Palgrave Macmillan, 2013), p. 81.

30. Hughes, *Collected Poems*, p. 406.

31. Ted Hughes, Season Songs, BBC Radio 3, 6 September 1977.

32. Ted Hughes, *The Iron Woman* (London: Faber & Faber, 1993), p. 85.

33. Ted Hughes, *Moortown Diary* (London: Faber & Faber, 1979), p. x.

34. Hughes, *Collected Poems*, p. 519.

35. Ibid., p. 534.

36. Terry Gifford, 'Interview with Fay Godwin', *Thumbscrew* 18 (Spring 2001), 114–17.

37. Donna Haraway, *When Species Meet* (Minneapolis: University of Minnesota Press, 2008), p. 16. See also Donna Haraway, *The Companion Species Manifesto* (Chicago: Prickly Paradigm, 2003).

38. Hughes, *Collected Poems*, p. 456.

39. See Patrick Curry, *Enchantment: Wonder in Modern Life* (Edinburgh: Floris Books, 2019).

40. Hughes, *Collected Poems*, p. 843.

41. Terry Gifford, *Ted Hughes* (Abingdon: Routledge, 2009), p. 25.

42. Hughes, *Collected Poems*, p. 681.

43. Ibid., p. 663.

44. Ibid., p. 664.

45. Ibid., p. 1117.

46. Simon Armitage, *Ted Hughes: Poems Selected by Simon Armitage* (London: Faber & Faber, 2000); Alice Oswald, *A Ted Hughes Bestiary* (London: Faber & Faber, 2014).

CRITICAL REFLECTIONS AND FURTHER STUDY

Why did teachers of English literature in the UK and the USA in the early 1990s independently feel the need to invent 'ecocriticism'? In Britain, Jonathan Bate introduced his book *Romantic Ecology* (London: Routledge, 1991) as 'a preliminary sketch towards a literary ecocriticism', arguing that 'ecology has to be an attitude of mind before it can be an effective set of environmental policies' (pp. 11, 83). The growing awareness of an environmental crisis and of an urgent need for environmental policies informed by ecology sent teachers and scholars back to Wordsworth or, in the United States, to the nature writers of the present, in order to understand the 'attitude of mind' behind presentations of nature in the literature we had been studying in terms of power relations in class, race and gender. Now there was an additional dimension to those questions of ideology and its discourses – writers' attitudes towards an ecology that included the human species. Questions of what is now called 'environmental justice' concerning class, race and gender have not been displaced, but enlarged. In this essay I wanted to question Hughes's conception of ecology in each of the major books in turn in order to attempt an evolving overview of his sense of 'ecology as an attitude of mind'. It turns out that it begins in power relations between outer and inner nature and moves towards gender in order to be able to find some provisional resolution in the metaphor, and the metaphysics, of the fisherman (Hughes himself) in the river.

At the same time I wanted to introduce some key terms of ecocriticism that seemed to highlight some of Hughes's concepts. Other ecocritics might have used other terms. Other ecocritics might have asked different questions. Is the 'violence' of the early animal poems actually self-indulgently shocking? Is the early satire too melodramatic, too biting, too patronising? Is my account of 'Crow Hill' and 'Egg-Head' too neatly programmatic? Are the narrative schemes behind *Crow* and *Cave Birds* actually evident to the reader of the texts? Some readers might ask whether the Goddess of Complete Being in her various forms is feminising nature in an essentialist way that excludes the possibility of reformed masculinity? Indeed, does Hughes ultimately remain a masculinist writer? Why, for example, spend so much time on the 'wooden' Lumb's activities with the village women in the main narrative of *Gaudete*? Is it really plausible to claim that these activities are implicitly critiqued by the brief religious poems of the Epilogue? Aside from his personal activism (see Reddick, cited in note 18 of my essay), can Hughes be called an 'ecopoet', or even an environmental poet, if he is so indirect in his poetry? Does his mythic discourse end up failing to address the really urgent questions his twenty-first-century readers face?

There are at least two larger questions about Hughes's writing that are not addressed by this essay but which surely need consideration. Clearly Hughes wants to encourage in the reader a sense of wonder and awe at the powers of nature by connecting our inner nature of dreams, intuition and understanding at a symbolic level with the forces of outer nature in weather, landscapes and animals. But can this be done in a language that avoids idealising those powers? This is a challenge that faces all poets, including those of his readers who write their own poetry about the natural world. The second question follows on from the first one. Can humans really be equal 'creatures of light' among the bears and the salmon as 'creatures of light'? Hughes is seeking images for humans reconnected with nature in what ecocritics call 'natureculture'. But doesn't our culture, especially in the form of our language, separate us from outer nature in the very act of finding images for it? Can the fisherman live in nature as naturally as the bear or the fish? Isn't the very image of the hunter, the fisherman, flawed by his human activity? Doesn't his or her presence disturb the ecology of which the fisherman is trying to be part, even as a fellow hunter with bear and fish? Indeed, is it possible for a poet to find an uncompromised image for humans living sustainably in our natural home, given the evidence of the Anthropocene so far? Perhaps these are the larger questions which studying the poetry of Ted Hughes demands that we address. Would Hughes himself have approved of this? On the evidence of his poetry I believe that he would. Perhaps there is a slight admission of failure under the strong element of hope in what Hughes wrote in *Winter Pollen* (1994) about future generations of his readers, especially readers of his children's books: 'Every new child is nature's chance to correct culture's error' (p. 149).

FURTHER READING

Adamson, Joni, Mei Mei Evans and Rachael Stein (eds), *The Environmental Justice Reader: Politics, Poetics, Pedagogy* (Tucson: University of Arizona Press, 2002)

Bate, Jonathan, *Ted Hughes: The Unauthorised Life* (London: William Collins, 2015)

Buell, Lawrence, *The Future of Environmental Criticism: Environmental Crisis and Literary Imagination* (Oxford: Blackwell, 2005)

Clark, Timothy, *The Cambridge Introduction to Literature and the Environment* (Cambridge University Press, 2011)

Clark, Timothy, *The Value of Ecocriticism* (Cambridge University Press, 2019)

Gifford, Terry (ed.), *Ted Hughes in Context* (Cambridge University Press, 2018)

Kerslake, Lorraine, *The Voice of Nature in Ted Hughes's Writing for Children: Correcting Culture's Error* (Abingdon: Routledge, 2018)

Reid, Christopher (ed.), *Letters of Ted Hughes* (London: Faber & Faber, 2007)

Roberts, Neil, *Ted Hughes: A Literary Life* (Houndmills: Palgrave Macmillan, 2006)

Roberts, Neil, Mark Wormald and Terry Gifford (eds), *Ted Hughes, Nature and Culture* (Houndmills: Palgrave Macmillan, 2018)

Scigaj, Leonard M., *Ted Hughes* (Boston: Twaine, 1991)

Westling, Louise (ed.), *The Cambridge Companion to Literature and the Environment* (Cambridge University Press, 2014)

Wormald, Mark, *The Catch: Fishing for Ted Hughes* (London: Bloomsbury, 2022)

25 | Women Publishers in the Twenty-First Century: Assessing Their Impact on New Writing – and Writers

CATHERINE RILEY

Abstract

This essay examines the contemporary UK publishing scene, foregrounding women's participation in it as readers, writers and publishing professionals. As historians of feminist publishing have noted, women have always figured in the book business in numbers. At the turn of the millennium, publishing was figured by many as an industry in which women dominated, but, as the first section of this essay sets out, this situation has shifted. I show the ways that women's status in the mainstream industry has, more recently, fallen back, before turning to look at the women writers who have risen to the top of the bestseller lists in the twenty-first century, examining the ways in which they are presented and their work received. Finally I examine the reader experience, and the relationship(s) between the book consumer and the publisher, and whether there is a gendered exchange in this dynamic. In particular I look at the way the books that we read are curated by the publishing industry, and women's role within this: as editors, reviewers, retailers and recommenders of female authorship. I will demonstrate that gender continues to have a profound effect on the ways in which literature is both produced and consumed.

Women's role in the contemporary UK publishing scene is complicated. As historians of feminist publishing have noted, women have always figured in the book business in large numbers.[1] Indeed, having the power to publish was posited at the start of feminism's first wave as crucial to its success. Virginia Woolf, who co-founded the Hogarth Press with her husband Leonard in 1917, set the terms of the argument: 'to enjoy freedom, if the platitude is pardonable, we have of course to control ourselves'.[2] Following Woolf, women's absence from the mainstream publishing industry became an important issue as feminism's second wave got underway in the late 1960s and grew its momentum throughout the 1970s and early 1980s. Charlotte Bunch argued early on that 'controlling our words corresponds to controlling our bodies, our selves, our work, our lives'.[3]

The argument that publishing was central to women's empowerment led to a surge in the founding of women-run publishing houses in the 1970s and 1980s in the UK. First among these was Virago, established in 1973 by Carmen Callil, which was swiftly followed by The Women's Press, Sheba, Pandora, OnlyWomen, Stramullion, Feminist Books, Honno, Black Woman Talk, Aurora Leigh, Urban Fox Press, Scarlet and others. All had their own working methodologies (some were run as co-operatives, some along more traditional, hierarchical lines) and their own publishing priorities (they variously prioritised black women's writing, lesbian writing, separatist principles, working-class writing and so on) but together they helped reshape and diversify the mainstream publishing landscape. They proved that there was a market for women's writing while also showcasing the talents of women as editors, marketers, distributors, agents and publishers. They helped women move into the industry in numbers. And they emboldened women to accede to the very top of the profession, with many climbing to the rank of executive as feminism's second wave progressed into its third at the start of the 1990s.

In fact, there came a point by the end of that decade when it was generally accepted that publishing had evolved into a women's business, as Carmen Callil, by then a feminist publishing icon, acknowledged: 'I think they [women] run things now in a way that they never did in my day. It's fabulous. I'm happy about it.'[4] At the turn of the millennium, as literary agent and former publisher Clare Alexander pointed out, Caroline Michel was managing director of Harper Press, Amanda Ridout (who hired Michel) was managing director of HarperCollins's general division, Victoria Barnsley was chief executive officer and publisher of the UK division, and the head of HarperCollins publishing worldwide was Jane Friedman.[5]

Gender Politics and Praxis in Contemporary Publishing

Since then things have, it seems, rebounded. In 2018, following new legal requirements around pay reporting in the UK, a significant gender pay gap was revealed by figures reported to the government equalities office from Penguin Random House, Hachette UK and HarperCollins – the UK's 'big three' publishers. They showed that while women made up almost two-thirds of the workforce in these companies, on average men were being paid between 11 and 30 per cent more. It was reported that

> all three companies employ more women than men, with a split of 58% at PRH, 66% at Hachette and 64.5% at HarperCollins. But the balance was reversed at board level, with 44% of the board at PRH female, 33% at Hachette and the executive committee at HarperCollins made up of a male CEO in addition to eight men and eight women.[6]

In total, nineteen publishing companies revealed details of the disparity in pay between their male and female staff.

Industry commentator Danuta Kean, whose 2015 report 'Writing the Future' had earlier revealed a marked absence of ethnic diversity both among publishing executives and the writers they published, had also noted prior to this gender pay gap reporting that women executives were being squeezed out:

> This is not to say that women have left the boardroom completely. But, as one senior female editor notes, women such as Random House's Gail Rebuck, Penguin's Helen Fraser, Macmillan's Annette Thomas and Little, Brown's Ursula Mackenzie, who had all embodied the ideal that women publishers faced no glass ceiling, have in the last five years all been replaced by men.[7]

Kean argued that on the boards of the big publishing companies, women were taking charge of 'softer' roles such as publishing, communications, human resources or education: 'look at the magical "c-circle" of group chief executive, group chief operating officer and group chief finance officer – where the real power lies – and women are notably absent'.[8] By 2018, while women dominated mainstream publishing in terms of numbers, they had dwindled dramatically in their representation among its highest echelons.

For some in publishing, the pay gap data evidenced structural inequalities that continued to limit women's careers. Grace McCrum, rights manager across Hachette's imprints Hodder & Stoughton, Headline, John Murray and Quercus, said: 'you only need to look at the top of all major publishing houses to see that having a majority female workforce does not equate to gender equality in the boardroom. Now we have this data, it shows there are very real structural and cultural issues preventing women from progressing.'[9] In twenty-first-century Britain, and in an industry that undoubtedly welcomes women in larger numbers than many others, the gendered expectation that women will be primary caregivers – to children or to older relatives, or both – still limits their potential in the workplace, making them less able (or less willing) to take on the top jobs as the demands of balancing private and professional life are so much greater than for men. And even for those who are not caregivers, the expectation that they *might* one day become such leads to a recruitment and remuneration bias that goes against them.

Added to this, mergers have left most of British publishing in the hands of three multinational conglomerates: Hachette, Bertelsmann-owned Penguin Random House, and HarperCollins, part of Rupert Murdoch's News Corp empire. 'This has not just left fewer influential jobs for women, but has led to a change in the kind of beast who does rise to the top.'[10] Young, white, middle-class men are still seen as safe hands in an industry which, although based on the production and consumption of creativity and ideas, has never been more financially cut-throat.

There have been attempts to tackle this intrinsic bias within corporate publishing. At Hachette, a Gender Balance Network had been established the year before the pay gap data story broke. When the data was revealed, the group pledged to ensure 66 per cent of its top-paid employees were women by 2020 to match its overall gender balance, with 50 per cent of its board to be female. There is no data on whether this has been achieved, but examination of the top-ranking jobs across Hachette UK reveals that just three of the umbrella group's ten imprints are led by women. The overall UK chief executive officer is a man, David Shelley, as is his deputy Richard Kitson, as is the global CEO Arnaud Norry. So much for gender balance.

Of course, we must acknowledge the role and the influence of women in the publishing world working as editors, publicists and agents, just as much as CEOs. Shona Abhyankar, an award-winning book publicist who has worked in-house as well as within agencies for more than twenty years, puts it this way: 'it gets my goat when so few people acknowledge that there are other departments [such as publicity] who have valuable contributions to make in acquisitions meetings. I fear that many men believe the Bridget Jones analogy that all we publicists do is "fanny around with press releases". If only our jobs were that simple.'[11] Women in a huge variety of roles are working across the publishing industry in ways that are helping to make it more diverse, and more welcoming to women writers as well as to those from minority groups – in terms of both the make-up of the industry itself and the books it produces.

And happily, there are still exceptional women making themselves exceptions to the rule that has, for now, installed men in the top jobs across the UK's publishing conglomerates. For example, while almost all of the women-run publishing houses that sprang up at the start of the second wave have since shuttered their operations, Virago has endured – albeit now as an imprint within Little, Brown, itself part of the Hachette group. Lennie Goodings, who joined Virago in 1978 and ran the company as publisher for twenty-seven years until stepping aside in 2017, has long defended Virago's move under Hachette's umbrella, bringing as it did greater financial clout, further penetration into distribution networks, and more profile and power – all of which allowed Virago to continue to proudly publish writing by women. Goodings continues to argue for Virago's usefulness in a changed marketplace, as well as within the changed cultural, political and gendered paradigms of today: 'I go back to books, to the words on a page that will not be erased, so we don't forget and so we can build on the energy and successes of this time.'[12]

Also part of Little, Brown is the new 'inclusive' imprint Dialogue Books, established in 2017 by Sharmaine Lovegrove with a mission to publish writers from black, Asian and minority ethnic (BAME) backgrounds, the LGBTQ+ community, working-class writers and writers with disabilities. It was set up in response to sales data from 2016 that showed, of the thousands of titles published in the UK that year, only a tiny minority – fewer than a hundred – were by non-white British authors. In 2016's bestseller charts, just one of the top hundred titles was written by a BAME British writer (Kazuo Ishiguro). 'It is now recognised that UK publishing has failed to do justice to a diverse range of voices, and working class and BAME writers struggle to be heard within an overwhelmingly white, middle-class publishing world,' says academic and literary festival director Helen Taylor.[13]

In Dialogue's first year Lovegrove published six titles and since then the imprint has grown steadily. Virago's current publisher Sarah Savitt recognises the urgent need for the publishing industry as a whole to welcome greater diversity of all kinds: 'I see a renewed energy around publishing not just more and a greater variety of books by women but also more and a greater variety of books by other writers whose voices have been historically marginalised, whether that's writers of colour, writers with disabilities, LGBTQ+ writers and so on. It's exciting.'[14] Initiatives such as Penguin Random House UK's ongoing campaign 'Write Now' to find, mentor and publish new writers from under-represented communities are a step in the right direction. But with mainstream publishing continuing to demonstrate that it is an industry which recruits in its own image – an image that is overwhelmingly white, straight, urban and middle-class – there is an important role for smaller, independent publishers to play in enabling and encouraging all kinds of women writers and women's writing.

The failings of the larger corporations have, to some extent, been redressed by independent publishers like Serpent's Tail and Canongate, as well as other, smaller presses. Magdalene Abraha at Jacaranda Books, for example, set out plans to publish twenty BAME British writers in 2020; a bold move for such a small-scale enterprise. Kean argues that 'corporate publishing's loss has been independent publishing's gain', pointing to the work of another woman, Kate Wilson, who set up independent children's publisher Nosy Crow after leaving Hachette-owned Hodder. Kean argues:

> Wilson is among a band of women who have started independent businesses that not only allow them to better juggle professional and home commitments, but also to exercise their creativity in a way the tiers of management in global businesses do not allow. It is one of the reasons that the most interesting and innovative books coming out are from independents – whether Juliet Mabey at Oneworld with her Booker winners Marlon James and Paul Beatty, the translated fiction choices of Meike Ziervogel's Peirene Press or Miranda West's Do Books Company's publishing list.[15]

As John Thompson argues, small and/or independent publishers ('indies') are more able to follow the 'whim' or instinct of an editor than a multinational, with its tight budgeting and set algorithms for 'success'.[16] While Thompson acknowledges the marked decline in indie presses in the last twenty years, he also notes their ongoing role in building the reputations of new books and new writers. This is important for women writers in general, who are less likely than men to receive a fair share of review attention (as I will show later), but particularly so for women of colour, LGBTQ+ women, working-class women and women with disabilities, all of whom are under-represented by reviewers. Some independent publishers, such as And Other Stories, have made explicit their intention to tackle the gender imbalance in publishing. In 2018 this small indie committed itself to a Year of Publishing Women, taking up author Kamila Shamsie's call in 2015 to do just that in order to challenge the enduring biases of mainstream publishing and review traditions.

And as the Internet has come to dominate all areas of both culture and the economy, there has been a rise in online self-publishing that has allowed women writers to circumvent these biases entirely. The proportion of self-published best-sellers by women sold through the online publishing platform FicShelf is almost twice as large as in traditional publishing: 67 per cent of top-ranking titles were by women, while 61 per cent of the top hundred traditionally published titles on Amazon were written by men. As Alison Flood reports:

> 'The scale of the discrepancy shows that women writers aren't being treated equally in traditional publishing,' said the author Roz Morris. 'We're usually pigeonholed into obviously feminine genres such as chick-lit and romance, but not generally allowed to be complex artistes, to write the unusual books that break new ground. These figures show a huge vote of confidence for the writer in charge of their artistic destiny – and indicate that the literary world should take more notice of what women writers are publishing.'[17]

What Does a Successful Woman Writer Look Like?

In 2000 Joe Moran identified what he called the 'star author' phenomenon, whereby writers are made into desirable, consumable commodities to be marketed just as fiercely as the literature they produce.[18] The ways that female star authors are presented and their work received are distinct from those of male star authors. For women writers, the intersection of celebrity and consumerism is always based on the marketability of their looks. 'Hot' new authors such as Zadie Smith at the start of the millennium, and more recently Sally Rooney, are subject to scrutiny not only in regard to their writing, but also to their personal lives and their self-presentation, with this emphasis on their looks impacting upon – and often undermining – the ways their writing is interpreted (Figure 25.1).

In some ways, star authorship is a double-edged sword: while such assessment is clearly the result of the patriarchal structures still surrounding the production and reception of women's writing, it also helps establish such writing as of cultural and literary importance, if through no other measure than the sales they generate. Following her debut novel, for example, Smith has gone on to create a body of writing that has explored the themes of ethnicity, multiculturalism, femininity

Figure 25.1 Zadie Smith, Ali Smith and other shortlisted authors for the 2005 Man Booker Prize.

and feminism, making her a significant and influential writer for the twenty-first century. But in spite of this, the extent to which her literary success has been predicated on the selling of her image also serves to keep Smith as somehow less serious, less *literary*, than her male counterparts. She has described the issue herself:

> She tells me about the time she went to do a photo shoot for a magazine and found herself lost in a sprawl of make-up artists, dressers and little Prada dresses that could never have fitted her. 'I wouldn't mind it if I saw five-hour photo shoots for Martin Amis, but that doesn't happen. If you're a woman it's as if they want to reduce everything to the same denominator.' Which is? 'That you must present yourself as an attractive woman even if you're a rocket scientist. It's total arse isn't it?'[19]

It is of course ironic that this emphasis on attractiveness has been applied to Smith, who has used her body of work to expose and challenge the culturally imposed ideals of the 'perfect' body as both gendered and racialised. But it is a standard that is applied to all young women writers, from Smith to Jessie Burton to Sally Rooney – a way of keeping them in their place, returning them to the position of consumable object, sexual plaything; as corporeal rather than intellectual.

Danuta Kean notes in her Emilia Report into review coverage of women's writing that the reception of Rooney's second novel *Normal People* demonstrates vividly this tedious and sexist emphasis on the author's looks: 'in the case of Sally Rooney, only five articles out of 16 failed to mention her age – of these three were reviews. As this was her second novel, it could be argued that her age was "old news".[20] In addition, Rooney-the-writer is consistently conflated with the characters in the books she writes, as breathless reviewers emphasise the author's good looks along with those of the people she imagines in her stories. Journalist Clare Cohen perfectly encapsulates the double standard: 'I'm still smarting over the radio interviewer who asked [Rooney] whether she had conducted an affair with an older man, like one of the characters in her debut novel *Conversations with Friends*. When was the last time that anyone asked Bret Easton Ellis if he had butchered people while listening to Phil Collins?'[21]

Rooney has, with great eloquence, met the issue head-on in many interviews when asked (again and again) if her work is autobiographical – the inference being, always, that her writing cannot purely be the product of a rich and lively imagination:

> I'm always curious to know what I could possibly communicate to readers by answering this question. How would the story be different if it was or wasn't autobiographical? … Does it imbue the reading experience with some kind of increased authenticity because of its proximity to my real life? Or does it imply that rather than being the invention of a creative mind, this incident was just something that happened to me as a passive observer? In which case, is the story somehow less 'literary'?[22]

Star authorship, and its attendant focus on 'lifestyle' reportage of a writer's work, does female authors a disservice. As Lennie Goodings puts it, 'even in this new world of outspoken writers and readers it appears that not all words are equal. Something seems to happen to a novel when it has a woman's name on the spine.'[23] Part of that 'something' is an insidious and reductive aspect of the contemporary publishing industry: the commodification of the female author – especially if she is young and good looking – in ways that diminish and devalue her work.

The Female Reader's Relationship to Publishing

As Ficshelf's sales figures show, writers themselves are now seizing the power to publish in ever-greater numbers. But these figures also point to something else. As Helen Taylor notes, 'overall sales for fiction books and e-books are 63% female to 37% male' and women are, overwhelmingly, the biggest *consumers* of books: 'we are the main readers of fiction, the largest market for novels and short stories – for ourselves and for our children – and the main buyers and borrowers of fiction'.[24] This of course means that, for publishers, 'the female reader is a commercial and critical force to be reckoned with'.[25] While it might be true that men are currently dominating publishing's boardrooms, the reality remains that their target audience is predominantly female. Further, women readers are in ever-greater numbers buying the work of women writers: 'in 2018 *The Bookseller* magazine announced that female writers (including two BAME women) dominated the UK's top ten bestselling authors of literary fiction' for the previous year.[26] Only one man made the top ten.

This is an important moment for literary fiction (as distinct from commercial fiction, which has long been dominated by women writers (and readers) across most genres). It suggests that literary culture has – at the very least, and at long last – come to include the contributions of women writers, their recognition borne out by the greater financial reward and larger distribution suggested by these sales figures. Except ...

In 2019 Danuta Kean's Emilia Report set out the continuing challenges women writers face in having their work recognised, reviewed and recommended. In 'Are You Serious? The Emilia Report Into The Gender Gap For Authors', she argues that, just as Shakespeare's contemporary Emilia Bassano was undervalued and overlooked by the literary culture of her time, so today's female writers are similarly obscured:

> It may seem that the struggles of a 17th Century woman to be taken seriously as a poet are incomparable to modern women who have benefitted from three waves of feminism, 40 years of equality legislation, universal suffrage and advances in science that have freed them from the tyranny of their bodies, but, though the landscape of their lives may be different, the structures that inhibit their path to recognition and success are not.[27]

Kean conducts a qualitative comparison of the broadsheet coverage of five male and five female writers across five literary fields in 2017 and 2018: literary fiction, prize winners, debut novelists, commercial fiction and fantasy fiction. She demonstrates a 'marked bias' towards male writers, who receive 56 per cent of review coverage – 12 per cent more than their female counterparts. Within this, there are more startling details: comparing the reception of works of fantasy fiction by Neil Gaiman and Joanne Harris, Kean showed that while Gaiman received widespread coverage, Harris did not receive any coverage at all. In the commercial fiction category, author Matt Haig was mentioned twelve times by newspapers, in a mix of reviews, while Rowan Coleman got just three mentions. Within the report, Coleman also discloses that she has never been reviewed by a broadsheet, despite writing a string of bestselling novels. This chimes with how Virago's chair Lennie Goodings describes the current literary-cultural arena: 'getting published isn't the problem. What has long been the big hurdle is how women's writing is regarded. Novels by women are most often seen as books for women only, and this is just not true of novels by men.'[28]

This matters for two reasons. Firstly, it makes it harder for women to cut through the noise of a literary marketplace that churns out more than two hundred thousand new novels every year. Secondly, and perhaps more significantly, it perpetuates a public perception of literature as still somehow a male domain. Kean notes that a majority of the reviews that were focused on women also emphasised the author's personal life over their work: 'questions about family and parenthood directed to men are different in tone: there is no assumption that they are the main care-givers'.[29] Even in the moment of their work being considered as of literary value, women writers are still returned to the private, domestic sphere of non-literary life.

The consequences of this for women writers are not only symbolic, but practical, making it 'harder for them to sustain an income, and ultimately a career, as a professional writer. It goes some way to explain the 25% gap between the average earnings of men and women writers,' says Kean.[30] The Emilia Report makes a number of recommendations for tackling this ongoing bias, which was first set out in 1987 with the publication of *Reviewing the Reviews: A Woman's Place on the Book Page* by the Women in Publishing group.[31] Kean advocates for three key recommendations: that the cover designs for women's books do not undermine the credibility of their writing; that literary editors are watchful for gendered bias in their review writers' output; and that journalists and publishers alike agree a code of conduct for the process of interviewing women writers.

All of this is to say that the reception of texts, just as much as their production, is vital to the success of the female writer in the marketplace. In this context, then, the women who are behind literary prizes, book clubs, festivals and book fairs have a significant role to play in influencing the publishing industry, and impacting on who is published, who is read, and what is written. All of these events are part of the process of cultural production in which writing is afforded meaning, and value.

Let's take the Women's Prize for Fiction as an example. Catalysed by the exclusion of Margaret Atwood and Angela Carter from the 1991 Booker Prize shortlist, this prize for women writers was launched in 1996. Its founder, Kate Mosse, thought the only way to address gendered bias in prize-giving, as exemplified by Booker's omission of Carter and Atwood in 1991, was to institute a prize for which only women could be considered: 'paradoxically, the way to take gender out of the equation was for all the entrants to be women'.[32]

It is difficult to overstate the influence book prize lists have on sales, and consequently on the way books are contracted, produced and marketed. Further, literary prizes also dictate to a not inconsiderable extent what goes on to be taught and to be subsequently included in the canon of 'great' writing. The historical bias of such prizes is easily evidenced: the Booker Prize, for example, has had almost twice as many male winners as female in its fifty-year history. And it's not just about the gender of the author. In 2015 author Nicola Griffith showed that the gender of the *characters* in winning novels was also significant: twelve of the previous fifteen winners of the Booker Prize had had male protagonists.[33]

The Women's Prize for Fiction has had a significant impact on the literary prize scene, and the wider world of publishing. Just five years after its inception, women writers outnumbered men in the *Guardian*'s Fastseller list, the definitive guide to the year's hottest paperbacks, for the first time.[34] It has continued to carve out space for women to be recognised (and rewarded – it offers a very generous cash prize), free from the literary biases that always see men's writing more favourably looked upon than women's. As Goodings puts it: 'we've got rid of "poetess" and "authoress", but we still have "woman writer". You will never hear the term "man writer". He's a writer ... neutral and therefore universal and of universal appeal.'[35]

Goodings notes that literary prizes and competitions have been a useful method for promoting diversity. As well as the Women's Prize, others have been established to locate and promote writers that can challenge this construction of the 'universal' writer. First awarded in March 2017, the Jhalak Prize for books by British/British resident BAME writers has become established as an annual celebration of the achievements of BAME writers in the UK. Newer still is the Primadonna Prize for writers who have yet to be signed by a publisher, and who do not have representation by an agent. The prize is judged blind and without regard to grammar and spelling: an attempt by its organisers to sidestep entirely the standard criteria that so often serve to exclude the work of women and minority writers.

These organisers are also behind the Primadonna festival, a new literary event which has similarly set out to shake up another, significant, area of the literary industry. For all publishers, literary festivals provide vital showcases for new books and authors, bringing writers and readers together with the aim of boosting sales, raising profiles, and increasing readerships, all under the auspices of creating and sustaining a reading 'community'. Significantly, audiences at literary festivals are overwhelmingly female – which makes them an opportunity to communicate directly with women readers, outside of the gendered paradigm of the review tradition. Peculiarly, however, mainstream festivals remain skewed towards the male voice while, as Helen Taylor argues, literary festivals taken as a whole are not diverse: 'literature festivals have a certain class cachet and thus bias – more garden party than rave'.[36]

Festivals like Primadonna (and BareLit, which celebrates British writers of colour, and The Coast is Queer for LGBTQ+ authors) counter the predominance of male writers on the line-up of other events, as well as open up access to the festival experience itself. One of Primadonna's co-founders is multiple-award-winning author Kit de Waal, who spent the advance she earned from her first novel on establishing a creative writing scholarship at Birkbeck College for a working-class student and also crowdfunded *Common People*, an anthology of working-class memoirs by new and established writers. She explains: 'Primadonna is a celebration of brilliant writing by brilliant women (and men that support us) and by diverse voices, a chance for those writers who don't usually get a place at the table to have an opportunity to talk about the content of their work rather than their bra-size or lack of a bra at all.'[37]

These new festivals are providing a space for the emergence of new talent, as well as for women readers to engage with the work of a more diverse range of writers. We should not underestimate the power of the female reader in this exchange, and indeed across the publishing industry more widely. Women have long been gathering to discuss writers and their works, creating their own book club networks which Guy Pringle, who set up the book club magazine *newbooks*, has described as 'the female equivalent of freemasonry'.[38] Book clubs – from small gatherings of friends in front rooms to the corporate behemoths of Oprah, Richard and Judy, Zoe Ball and more – have launched the careers of countless novelists and have made specific books bestsellers.[39] Taylor cites, for example, Elizabeth Day's *Eat, Pray, Love* and even Hilary Mantel's *Wolf Hall* as having been discovered and made into phenomena by book club readers. It is not insignificant, either, that the 'big name' clubs are named after women.

Literary prizes, festivals and book clubs show the ways in which women can organise in order to bypass some of the persisting barriers to female authorship. The books we read are of course curated for us by those in the publishing industry, but the industry itself is greatly influenced by these (and other) aspects of the literary marketplace. That women have taken control of them means they are impacting significantly on new writing and on the opportunities available for women writers in particular, as well as for a greater diversity of writers from under-represented communities.

Publishing is certainly an industry in which women have had an enormous impact over the past fifty years, an impact made in parallel with the (at times far too slow) progress achieved by feminist politics and praxis more generally. But there is further to go. The power to publish remains, as Carmen Callil once put it, a wonderful thing. But until more women – and in particular more women of colour, LGBTQ+ women, working-class women and women with disabilities – take their place in the book business, it will continue to be limited in its understanding, exploration and celebration of the lives of minority communities. And that is a loss to all of us who read.

NOTES

1. Simone Murray, *Mixed Media: Feminist Presses and Publishing Politics* (London: Pluto Press, 2004); Catherine Riley, *The Virago Story: Assessing the Impact of a Feminist Publishing Phenomenon* (New York: Berghahn Press, 2018).
2. Virginia Woolf, *The Common Reader Second Series* (London: Hogarth Press, 1932), p. 258.
3. Charlotte Bunch, 'Feminist Journals: Writing for a Feminist Future', in J. Hartman and E. Messer-Davidow (eds), *Women in Print II: Opportunities for Women's Studies Publication in Language and Literature* (New York: Modern Language Association, 1982), p. 140.
4. Personal communication with Carmen Callil, 10 November 2004.

5. Clare Alexander, 'Are Women Now the Dominant Force in UK Publishing?', question posed in a digital dialogue on the website of *The Bookseller*, www.thebookseller.com (accessed 17 February 2003).

6. Harriet Marsden, 'A Gentleman's Profession? The Women Fighting for Gender Equality in Publishing', *The Independent*, 6 April 2018.

7. Danuta Kean, 'Are Things Getting Worse for Women in Publishing?', *Guardian*, 11 May 2017.

8. Ibid.

9. Marsden, 'Gentleman's Profession'.

10. Kean, 'Are Things'.

11. Personal communication with Shona Abhyankar, 16 April 2020.

12. Lennie Goodings, *A Bite of the Apple: A Life with Books, Writers and Virago* (Oxford University Press, 2020), p. 234.

13. Helen Taylor, *Why Women Read Fiction: The Stories of Our Lives* (Oxford University Press, 2019), p. 9.

14. Goodings, *Bite of the Apple*, p. 231; and see Sharmaine Lovegrove, 'If You Don't Have a Diverse Workforce or Product, Sooner or Later You Won't Exist', *Guardian*, 18 March 2018.

15. Kean, 'Are Things'.

16. John B. Thompson, *Merchants of Culture: The Publishing Business in the Twenty-First Century* (Cambridge: Polity, 2001).

17. Alison Flood, 'Self-Publishing Lets Women Break Book Industry's Glass Ceiling, Survey Finds', *Guardian*, 6 March 2016. See also the following articles by Flood: 'Female Writers Dominated 2017's Literary Bestsellers, Figures Show', *Guardian*, 17 January 2018; and 'Male and Female Writers' Media Coverage Reveals "Marked Bias"', *Guardian*, 18 March 2019.

18. Joe Moran, *Star Authors: Literary Celebrity in America* (London and Sterling, VA: Pluto Press, 2000).

19. Simon Hattenstone, 'White Knuckle Ride', *Guardian*, 11 December 2000.

20. Danuta Kean, 'Are You Serious? The Emilia Report into the Gender Gap for Authors' (2019), p. 5: www.eilenedavidson.com/wp-content/uploads/2019/03/The-Emilia-Report .pdf (accessed 14 April 2020).

21. Claire Cohen, 'Sally Rooney's *Normal People* is Not 'Chick Lit' – We Need to Stop Patronising Female Authors', *Telegraph*, 8 January 2019.

22. Sophie Haydock, 'Sally Rooney, 26, Reveals the Secrets of Her Shortlisted Story, Mr Salary', 2010–2022 Short Story Award, 30 March 2017: www.shortstoryaward.co.uk/news/sally-rooney-26-reveals-secrets-her-shortlisted-story-mr-salary (accessed 31 March 2020).

23. Goodings, *Bite of the Apple*, p. 236.

24. Taylor, *Why Women Read Fiction*, p. 4.

25. Ibid., p. 5.

26. Ibid., p. 231.

27. Kean, 'Are You Serious?', p. 3.

28. Goodings, *Bite of the Apple*, p. 236. Goodings's point is that novels by men are not usually seen as books for men only in this way.

29. Kean, 'Are You Serious?', p. 9.

30. Ibid.

31. London: Journeyman Press.

32. Geraldine Bedell, 'Textual Politics', *Guardian*, 6 March 2005.

33. Nicola Griffith, 'Books about Women Don't Win Big Awards: Some Data', blog post, 26 May 2015: https://nicolagriffith.com/2015/05/26/books-about-women-tend-not-to-win-awards/ (accessed 3 March 2020).

34. Fiachra Gibbons, 'Women Lead the Way in "Hottest" Books List', *Guardian*, 29 December 2001.

35. Goodings, *Bite of the Apple*, p. 237.

36. Taylor, *Why Women Read Fiction*, p. 199.

37. Kit de Waal, 'The Primadonna Festival: Yes, Not Why', *The Bookseller*, 4 April 2019.

38. Quoted in Taylor, *Why Women Read Fiction*, p. 175.

39. TV presenter and actor Oprah Winfrey started her book club in 1996 and it ran in its first incarnation until 2011: 'Oprah editions' of the seventy books it recommended amassed total sales of more than 55 million copies. The Zoe Ball Book Club launched in June 2018 and has had a similarly transformative effect on sales of books selected as recommended reads.

CRITICAL REFLECTIONS AND FURTHER STUDY

Examining women's place in the contemporary publishing scene must be set in the context of feminism's less recent history. It is important to look back at the outpouring of literature that marked the start of the 'second wave' of feminism at the end of the 1960s, as well as the theoretical formulations of women's writing which pushed back against received ideas of the canon. In addition, so much has been written about what women read – and why – that we must always consider women's role as consumers, as well as producers, of literature. Below, I reflect briefly on some of these contexts and suggest some questions for further consideration.

There is much to learn about the second wave feminist publishing phenomenon of the 1970s and 1980s. At this time, a burgeoning feminist movement was drawing away from the sexually libertarian counterculture of the 1960s which was felt to exclude women's experience. Against this backdrop, the publication of now seminal feminist texts provoked women to agitate for change. As writer Joyce Nicholson describes: 'When I read *The Female Eunuch* by Germaine Greer, I could not sleep for three nights' (*What Society Does to Girls*, p. 7). *The Female Eunuch* was followed by other works of fiction and non-fiction that set out to challenge women's position in culture. Why do you think the written word was so central to the feminist challenge to women's inequality? And how inevitable was it that women would look to own the means of producing literature as part of their battle for equality?

A raft of feminist publishers emerged on to the scene, starting with Virago in 1973 and rapidly expanding in numbers thereafter. These women-run presses produced a very wide range of books by women, for women, proving in the process that women could not only *write* brilliant literature, but they could also *produce* it. This combination of feminist theory and praxis – words and deeds – dismantled the still held belief that 'great' literature was a male domain, and that the business of books was similarly an arena for men only. What would you consider to be the challenges of this incursion into the publishing world? How easy would it have been to balance questions of profit with the principles of publishing feminist literature? And is the meaning of 'feminist literature' changed at all by considering it in the context of publishing?

Part of the challenge for women – as publishers and as writers – was that the review press had long excluded or diminished the achievements of women. During the 1980s feminist critics investigated this vital area of literary culture, and found evidence that women were systematically excluded from it. Dale Spender, for example, in *Mothers of the Novel* (see Further Reading), found that male critics in the seventeenth and eighteenth centuries had drawn parallels between female writing and prostitution in their attempts to discourage women novelists. Spender's sister, Lynne, in her book of 1983, *Intruders on the Rights of Men*, developed a theory of literary 'gatekeeping' to show that canonical inclusion was protected by reviewers and scholars whose interests were served by the texts to which they granted entry. The feminist challenge to the 'review tradition' continued with publications like Women in Publishing's *Reviewing the Reviews*, which surveyed the contemporary review press to show its bias towards men.

Such sexist review bias meant that feminist publishers were making an important intervention by creating their own literary networks and review channels as well as by prioritising women's writing for mainstream review attention. Several of them went further still, establishing lists of reprints that excavated works by women from the past, publishing them for a new audience – and so proving that women had always written, and written well. Investigate what these reprinted series were: who started them, what impact did they have, and what books did they (re)discover?

Finally, there is much to consider in terms of the reader's relationship to the publisher: how we read, why we read and what we read can be both very personal and very political (or ideological). Feminist critics have looked into women's relationship with literature, and the intimacy of exchange between writer and reader that it affords. How important do you think it is, from a reader's perspective, that women produce the books that women read? Can an author communicate political ideas through fiction, and is this an effective route to effecting real-life change? When we consume stories can we also consume – or resist – a political or ideological position?

Feminist publishers also enabled the creation of specific types of genre fiction – crime, romance and science fiction – that were distinct from mainstream versions of these kinds of stories. These texts allowed female readers to enjoy all the formulaic aspects of such literature without its sometimes problematic elements (e.g., private detective stories that were not centred around helpless female victims). These generic fiction series were money-spinners for the feminist publishers that produced them: but how true is it to say that, in the contemporary marketplace, women no longer need their 'own' versions of these kinds of stories?

FURTHER READING

Moi, Toril, *Sexual/Textual Politics: Feminist Literary Theory* (London: Routledge, 1985)

Nicholson, Joyce, *What Society Does to Girls* (London: Virago, 1977)

Pearce, Lynne, *Feminism and the Politics of Reading* (London: Edward Arnold, 1997)

Radway, Janice A., *Reading the Romance: Women, Patriarchy, and Popular Literature* (Chapel Hill and London: University of North Carolina Press, 1991)

Rowbotham, Sheila, *Hidden from History* (London: Pluto Press, 1974)

Showalter, Elaine, *A Literature of Their Own: British Women Novelists from Brontë to Lessing* (London: Virago, 1982)

Spender, Dale, *Mothers of the Novel: 100 Good Women Writers before Jane Austen* (London: Women's Press, 1986)

Spender, Lynne, *Intruders on the Rights of Men: Women's Unpublished Heritage* (London: Pandora, 1983)

Whelehan, Imelda, *The Feminist Bestseller: From 'Sex and the Single Girl' to 'Sex and the City'* (Houndmills: Palgrave Macmillan, 2005)

Women in Publishing, *Reviewing the Reviews: A Woman's Place on the Book Page* (London: Journeyman Press, 1987)

26 | Crisis and Community in Contemporary British Theatre

CLARE WALLACE

Abstract

This essay contends that since the 1990s, as the outcomes of the neoliberal turn of the previous decade became increasingly palpable, one of the most noticeable aspects of a contemporary 'structure of feeling' is an evolving sense of crisis experienced both individually and communally. The essay explores this sensibility in a sample of six plays: David Hare's *Skylight* (1995), Mark Ravenhill's *Some Explicit Polaroids* (1999), Tim Crouch's *The Author* (2009), David Greig's *The Events* (2013), Caryl Churchill's *Escaped Alone* (2016) and debbie tucker green's *ear for eye* (2018). Despite their formal and thematic diversity, these works present images of crisis that expand from local to global. *Skylight* and *Some Explicit Polaroids* gauge the mood at the end of the twentieth century in terms of social alienation and a clash of values. In contrast, *The Author* and *The Events* mine the collective itself as a paradoxical site of magnetism and ambivalence. Finally, *Escaped Alone* and *ear for eye*, through disruptions of form and language, render systemic crises tangible. Drawing together Lauren Berlant's notion of 'crisis ordinariness' with theatre's proto-communal predisposition, the essay unpacks how crisis is evident not only thematically but also in representational strategies that emphasise states of precarity.

British theatre since the mid twentieth century has boasted a robust and varied tradition of dramatic writing. A key feature of this tradition is the way playwrights have engaged with the sociopolitical conditions of their time, developing theatre as a space of debate, critique and intervention. Although various social, political and cultural phenomena have been of significance in the decades following the end of the Second World War, arguably the most fundamental transformation of modern Britain was wrought by Prime Minister Margaret Thatcher's policies in the 1980s. I will not rehearse the ways theatre in the 1980s grappled with the new market-led regime; rather, I take as a point of departure the following decade in which the outcomes of the neoliberal turn began to percolate through culture. Literary and cultural theorist Raymond Williams coined the phrase 'structures of feeling' to account for 'a particular quality of social experience and relationship, historically distinct from other particular qualities, which gives the sense of a generation or a period'.[1] My analysis of British theatre rests on the contention that, since the 1990s, one of the most salient aspects of a contemporary 'structure of feeling' is an unfolding sense of crisis of crisis expanding from local to global as we move towards the present. This is evident not only thematically but also in representational strategies that emphasise states of precarity.[2] Such concerns intersect with received notions of theatre as proto-communal and as an art form offering impressions of community for interrogation and reflection. The essay surveys these issues using a sample of six aesthetically diverse plays: David Hare's *Skylight* (1995), Mark Ravenhill's *Some Explicit Polaroids* (1999), Tim Crouch's *The Author* (2009), David Greig's *The Events* (2013), Caryl Churchill's *Escaped Alone* (2016) and debbie tucker green's *ear for eye* (2018).

Crisis, Community and Theatrical Performance

What is crisis? An exceptional event, a time, a turning point, or even an ongoing condition? Considering crisis in relation to affect and period, literary scholar Lauren Berlant argues that the impasses produced by current neoliberal realities result in a state of perpetual, ordinary crisis, a 'crisis ordinariness', that comes to be mediated culturally.[3] This chimes with cultural theorists Stuart Hall and Doreen Massey's discussion of crisis in terms of conjuncture, as 'a period during which the different social, political, economic and ideological contradictions that are at work in society come together to give it a specific and distinctive shape'.[4] One of the central forces here is neoliberalism. Economic geographer David Harvey describes neoliberalism as 'a theory of political economic practices that proposes that human well-being can best be advanced by liberating individual entrepreneurial freedoms and skills within an institutional framework characterized by strong private property rights, free markets, and free trade'.[5] It is perhaps not immediately apparent why such economic practices, with their heavy emphasis on 'freedom', should be so bound to sociocultural crisis. However as Harvey and numerous others have noted, the neoliberal policies propagated in the United States by Reagan and in Great Britain by Thatcher throughout the 1980s and in operation since then, have resulted in radical inequality – the progressive enrichment of a small minority of individuals and corporations alongside mass erosion of social cohesion and stability. As the plays discussed here illustrate, such states of pervasive precarity produce patterns of expectation and experience that can be mapped in an evolving set of aesthetic modes and concerns.

Theatre is distinct from purely literary genres in its attention to the complexities of community both in its enduring stage-as-world formulations and also in the dynamics of the collective experience of performance. Indeed, the temporary gatherings created by theatre performance are regularly tasked with shoring up ideals of community, in order to activate audiences in the world beyond. An influential example is Jill Dolan's notion of 'utopian performatives'.[6] Citing anthropologist Victor Turner's description of 'spontaneous communitas',[7] Dolan argues 'that theatre and performance create citizens and engage democracy as a participatory forum in which ideas and possibilities for social equality and justice are shared'.[8] Such a generous appraisal of the role of performance, however, is more sceptically assessed by sociologist Zygmunt Bauman, who describes the collective at such events as a merely transient 'cloakroom community'.[9]

There is a tangible tension between the utopian politics of performance espoused by Dolan, Bauman's scepticism about the effectiveness of such temporary communities, and the narratives and affective structures of crisis in specific post-1990 works of British theatre. These works, I suggest, endeavour to engage difficult questions of community and coexistence without collapsing into unambivalent bids for activation or engagement. Their reflections on the individual and communal are purposefully crafted, communicating a contemporary 'structure of feeling' through scenarios of estrangement, the performance of collectives and decontextualised scenes of systemic crisis.

Patterns of Adjustment: *Skylight* and *Some Explicit Polaroids*

Closing his critical study of mainstream British theatre between 1979 and 1993, John Bull states:

> What is clear is that without some kind of reanimation the British theatre will continue its march towards total irrelevance and yet another avenue of opposition and of debate will be lost to a perpetuation of the present parade of bland product uniformity. Social and political pressures virtually unconsidered by the contemporary theatre must eventually find a platform. There is another world ... waiting in the wings.[10]

Indeed, the 1990s was to prove a decade of transformation in many ways: from Margaret Thatcher's resignation in 1990 and the 1997 landslide victory of the rebranded New Labour Party led by Tony Blair, through to the Peace Process in Northern Ireland and policies of devolution across the UK. Despite a surge of optimism and confidence in 'Cool Britannia' after 1997, the 1990s was a decade of coming to terms with that other world Bull mentions, and with an irrevocably changed political discourse. Crucially, New Labour's pursuit of centrist policies foregrounded social inclusion but continued to consolidate and advance privatisation, globalisation and consumerism. In theatre, this coming to terms took various forms, but was perhaps most palpable among an emergent generation of playwrights who had grown up in Thatcher's Britain. Bursting with transgressive images of social disaffection and violence, their work is described by Aleks Sierz in his influential history of the period, *In-Yer-Face: British Drama Today* (2001). For Sierz, the defining quality of the new writing of the nineties was its visceral tactics of provocation. Young writers such as Sarah Kane, Mark Ravenhill and Anthony Neilson were, he argued, producing an experiential 'theatre of sensation'.[11] Though the purpose of such provocation was hotly debated, Sierz defended 'In-Yer-Face theatre' as an incisive form of modern social critique that drew on models of provocation to be found in the European avant-garde.

The two works I turn to now illustrate how drama from very separate provenances – one archetypally In-Yer-Face, the other decidedly not – depicted the end of the century in terms of social alienation and a clash of values. *Skylight* and *Some Explicit Polaroids* initially seem to have little in common.[12] David Hare is part of a late 1960s generation of left-wing alternative political dramatists who throughout the 1970s produced a string of acerbic dramatic critiques of post-war Britain. Since the 1980s Hare has become a mainstream presence, establishing himself as a voice of social conscience at the National Theatre. Mark Ravenhill erupted into 1990s theatre with a cluster of self-reflexive, provocative, sexually explicit plays that typify an In-Yer-Face aesthetic – and his theatre work has continued to develop in a wide range of ironic, satirical and experimental forms. For all their contrasts, however, there are some telling convergences in the ways *Skylight* and *Some Explicit Polaroids* transmit a structure of feeling, albeit on rather different frequencies.

Both plays are structured around the motif of hiatus and re-encounter as a means of drawing attention to 'crisis ordinariness'. *Skylight* slowly and tenderly exposes the wounds of the past with a steady focus on two former lovers, Tom and Kyra, meeting again, for the first time in three years, in the chilly confines of a small flat in north-west London. *Some Explicit Polaroids*, as its title suggests, presents a series of snapshots of life in London at century's end. The play moves rapidly between sundry scenes and vaguely defined locations largely following Nick, a former Socialist militant who has just been released from prison after fifteen years, and his efforts to adjust to a society characterised by rampant individualism, consumerism and the eradication of the past. What these structures suggest is an ambivalent sense of awakening to the impacts of the Thatcher era. In Hare's play, this is mediated through a dramatic focus on personal interactions, losses and failures, and is situated in a specific London locale; in Ravenhill's work the premise is more schematic, less invested in psychological or geographical nuance, and the resulting picture has more spiky political clarity.

Generational frictions bristle in these plays. Hare's characters span three generations: Tom, a businessman in his fifties, Kyra a schoolteacher in her early thirties and Edward, Tom's eighteen-year-old son. Tom, Kyra and, to a lesser extent, Edward are figures of different Britains: she is a middle-class, university-educated woman who has chosen to teach underprivileged children in a rough school in London; he is a self-made man who has accumulated a fortune in the restaurant trade and his son is on a gap year, working aimlessly at a casual job before starting university. Ravenhill's six characters fall into two generational blocks from more diverse social backgrounds: the older group comprises Nick, his friend Helen, now a city councillor with parliamentary ambitions, and his former antagonist Jonathan, a businessman and wealthy philanthropist; the younger group includes Nadia, a table dancer, Tim, her gay friend who is dying of AIDS, and Victor, a young Russian whom Tim met online.

Repeatedly, each play reminds us of the characters' stark differences in world view. A particularly significant feature is the younger generation's reluctance to make fixed connections with others and their acceptance of a fluidity in relationships. In the opening scene of *Skylight*, in response to Kyra's question as to whether he has a girlfriend, Edward replies: 'I don't know ... I don't like the word "girlfriend". All that stuff's finished. Relationships. Permanence. It's out of date, I think.'[13] Similarly, in *Some Explicit Polaroids*, to Nick's questions about the man who has just attacked her on the street, 'So? Ex-boyfriend? Ex-husband? / Pimp or ... ', Nadia responds 'Oooo ... Labels, labels. Simon's a friend who I shag once in a while.'[14]

The titular aperture in Hare's play is a resonant symbol of the complicated relationships the drama unfolds – the expensively constructed skylight in Tom's house affords his dying wife, Alice, a view on the outside world, but the perspective does not buy him any forgiveness or peace of mind. After a fashion, the stage itself is a skylight into Kyra's bleak world and, as with Alice's expensive room for dying, there is little solace in the view. Hare holds our gaze on the emotional wreckage among the protagonists as a metaphor for something more extensive. As Kyra and Tom catch up after three years, what emerges is an insuperable divide in values despite their continuing love for one another. Tom fondly reminisces about the mid eighties – a golden time for entrepreneurs when 'through that little opening in history you could feel the current ... running your way'.[15] When Kyra ended their affair, she separated herself from the world of comfort she once enjoyed. She tells Tom: 'I've seen the way things now are in this country. I think for thirty years I lived in a dream.'[16] Unsurprisingly, he sees her teaching job as a masochistic waste of her talents, while she sees his career as the apotheosis of empty and selfish materialism. Neither, Hare seems to suggest, is entirely wrong.

The dramatic force of awakening to new realities is more overt in Ravenhill's play. Nick's first encounters with the minutiae of everyday life set a punchy tone for the sense of disorientation in a realm of overturned values and commodification. In place of their radical student ideals, Helen can only advise 'start with the little stuff ... Bit by bit, you do what you can and you don't look for the bigger picture, you don't generalise'.[17] Nadia's friends introduce Nick to a new world of postmodern 'trash'[18] culture at its most self-indulgent. Their celebration of the inauthentic, the kitsch and the frivolous, clashes with Nick's apparently hopelessly outdated ideas and politics. The younger characters mock his concern for social justice, dismissed by Tim as outmoded, very 'nineteen eighty-four'.[19] *Some Explicit Polaroids* reflects upon society in the thrall of consumerism. Ravenhill triangulates the shallow individualism espoused by the younger generation and the exhausted oppositional politics of Nick with the views of corporate capitalist, Jonathan. Jonathan advocates an almost mystical submission to the dynamism of the market: 'you embrace the chaos ... you see the beauty of ... the way money flows, the way it moves around the world faster and faster. Every second a new opportunity, every second a new disaster. The endless beginnings, the infinite endings. And each of us swept along by the great tides and winds of the markets'.[20] When Nick and Jonathan finally meet, they acknowledge a nostalgia for the certainties of the old left–right political dichotomy. And although *Some Explicit Polaroids* ends with would-be MP Helen declaring that she 'want[s] to make [Nick] into what [he] used to be'[21] – that is, activist and angry – Ravenhill hardly suggests that this is a likely prospect.

For all their tonal and structural contrasts, Hare and Ravenhill steer a discursively realistic course through a set of positions. Dramaturgically, *Skylight* and *Some Explicit Polaroids* sit firmly within established patterns of debate drama that can be traced back to Bernard Shaw. Crisis operates at personal and social levels as a series of ongoing and unresolved debates over economic privilege, precarity, political action and the limits of individualism in a distinctly British context. Common to both plays is a sense of waning expectations that registers the impossible tension between good-life fantasies and the need to adjust 'to the structural pressures of crisis and loss'.[22]

Participation and Precarity: *The Author* and *The Events*

Within the first decades of the new century British theatre increasingly began to explore the collective itself as a paradoxical site of magnetism and ambivalence. *The Author* and *The Events*[23] are compelling examples of such shifting theatrical modes. They invite audiences to consider questions of community and responsibility by embedding crisis in their formal premises. One does so by apparently bringing the playwright into the centre of the action, the other by apparently bringing the public onstage. Tim Crouch began his career as an actor, and then around 2003 he started to write, perform and direct his own plays. Rejecting the realistic conventions of drama, he regularly asks audiences to imaginatively co-create the performance of his work. David Greig's theatre career began in the mid 1990s; a prolific writer and theatre maker, he has created over fifty formally diverse plays, translations and adaptations. Since 2016 he has also been the artistic director of the Royal Lyceum Theatre in Edinburgh.

In *Theatre in the Expanded Field*, Alan Read argues that theatre is a space where the tensions between community and immunity are continuously rehearsed and physically experienced.[24] In this regard, *The Author* has prompted a lively discussion about ethics and manipulation (Figure 26.1). Central to its affective impact is a blurring of the boundaries of the performance situation – what is fiction, what is real? To what extent are audiences supposed to participate? A reconfiguration of the safe distance of theatrical representation is already insinuated by the arrangement of space – *The Author* welcomes audiences into a space where performers and audience sit together in two facing banks of seats, there is no stage, no set, no dramatic entrances or exits. The performance situation and scene of action is the audience themselves. This is where the 'play' actually begins. Adrian, a loyal and enthusiastic patron of the Royal Court Theatre in London (home to a much celebrated form of new playwriting and a cosmopolitan cultural community), encourages other spectators to share their experiences of theatre-going, their expectations of the work they are about to see and their feelings about actors as they wait for the performance. The intimation that the audience themselves are the subject of the show is visual – when the lights come up for the play proper and they find themselves 'beautifully lit'.[25] Ameliorating these subtly destabilising arrangements, *The Author* layers non-matrixed acting[26] with the traditions of dramatic

Figure 26.1 From a performance of Tim Crouch's *The Author* at the Traverse Theatre as part of the Edinburgh Fringe Festival in 2010. The author/performer is seated in the middle of the picture, middle row.

storytelling; hence Tim Crouch performs 'Tim Crouch', a writer and director, while three other roles – two actors (Vic and Esther), one audience member (Adrian) – are presented by performers using their own names. As a result, a chief quality of the piece is the ambiguous effect of its ludic attitude to truth/illusion and the risks of the games it initiates.

The Events also blurs the stage situation, even though the ambiguities of acting and not-acting are not its driving force. The play is set in a generic community hall schematically represented by a piano, a tea urn and some plastic chairs. The audience faces an open and largely empty stage area; upstage are several rows of raked seating. As in *The Author*, the play presents a narrative performance, enacted by two characters, Claire and The Boy who are accompanied on stage by a choir (a different local choir is invited to participate in each of the performances). Claire and The Boy voice various roles in the story, but the energy of these roles is strategically offset by the presence and participation of the amateur local choir who have rehearsed only their own parts briefly before the show, and are not necessarily acquainted with the play as a whole or in detail. The choir thus provides the sounding board for the two forceful and demanding professional performances. They serve a quasi-choral role; they are at times mobilised by Claire as 'her' choir, but often just follow the performance with scripts in hand from the seating upstage, forming a duplicate audience facing the auditorium.

Both *The Author* and *The Events* debate violence in representation and as an expression of social crisis. In *The Author* the four performers deliver a collage narration about the development, performance and consequences of a provocative play by 'Tim Crouch' for the Royal Court. As gradually becomes evident, this earlier In-Yer-Face-style play centres on a graphically abusive relationship, and via that story, the processes of brutalisation, led and fostered by the playwright, become visible. While 'Tim Crouch' defends the play on aesthetic grounds, it becomes clear that his methods of research and obsession with representing 'what was happening in the real world'[27] in order to make an egotistical theatrical statement, has detrimental effects on all concerned. *The Events* is a response to the traumatic resonances of the massacre of sixty-nine people on the island of Utøya and eight in Oslo on 22 July 2011 by Norwegian far-right terrorist Anders Behring Breivik. Claire is a priest who has survived a 'mass shooting event'[28] in which many members of her multi-ethnic community choir have died. She now wrestles with the grief, trauma and injustice of the events she has survived. The Boy is a composite role; he slides between the voice of the shooter, his father, his acquaintances, Claire's partner, her doctor and so on. The socially constructive impetus of Claire's choir collides with the destructive desire of The Boy and the play surveys the fallout.

Crouch and Greig work with violence here in very different ways, but they converge in an interest in the ethical challenges of responsibility in times of precarity. Crouch does so by crafting a self-consciousness about being a member of a select, if transient, community and guiding the audience with disarming sensitivity and a friendly warmth to share the in-jokes about British theatre culture and, specifically, Royal Court traditions of provocative new writing. The encouragement to take part seems consequence-free. As Adrian gushes, 'This is the safest place in the world! ... I mean, nothing really happens in here, does it? Not really. Nothing real.'[29] *The Author* builds an unsettling feeling of collusion by linking the conventions of British theatrical provocation with voyeuristic consumption of dehumanising images and then with the shocking revelation of the playwright's weakness for internet child pornography. The juxtaposition of an artistically 'acceptable' provocation and an utterly unacceptable one produces a crisis of connectedness that electrifies the communication space the performance has so carefully constructed. What makes *The Author* both deeply difficult and strangely resonant is the way it, in Christoph Henke's words, 'opens up a precarious space for its spectators, seemingly to grant them "virtual" agency, while actually manipulating and restricting it severely.'[30] While Crouch has stated that '*The Author* is a play about responsibility, how active we are as spectators and how responsible we are for what we choose to look at',[31] it is worth also framing this work within the broader structure of feeling I have been mapping here. Crouch's subtle curation of the energies of the audience problematises violence as a stage device, but also gives rise to thorny questions of the limits of agency.

Greig also fosters a self-consciousness about community formations, splicing a panoply of contradictory responses to violent extremism to capture a sense of raw vulnerability. If Crouch makes a community through the performance situation which he then subjects to crisis, Greig probes the source of rupture and the ethical demands it makes on us. At one point, Claire asks 'What *are* you?', to which The Boy and the choir recite a long list of potential explanations from 'Europe-wide malaise', 'the product of the welfare state', 'the end point of capitalism', 'a blankness out of which emerges only darkness and a question', concluding with 'What is to be done with me?'[32] This is the central question of the play. Greig's community, like the different local choirs who participated in the various performances, is defined by polyvocality; it is perched between possibilities of tolerance and intolerance, hospitality and hostility. That sense of paradox reaches its apex during the final moments of *The Events*, when the original invitation to join in the choir first extended to The Boy, who destroys it, is repeated word for word. The choir begins to sing facing the auditorium. The repetition of the invitation, with its attendant risks and implications, is pivotal. It approaches, in Dolan's terms, a 'utopian performative',[33] defying common sense and expanding infectiously into the surge of voices that close the play, as a fragile and precarious token of inclusion.

Systems Failure: *Escaped Alone* and *ear for eye*

As noted at the start of this essay, Berlant discusses systemic crisis as 'a process embedded in the ordinary'.[34] In this last section I turn to two works that perform the expansion and intensification of 'crisis ordinariness' through disruptions of form and language – *Escaped Alone* and *ear for eye*.[35] Churchill's career as an experimental, feminist playwright began in the late 1970s. From well-known early works such as *Top Girls* through to recent plays like *Far Away*, *A Number* or *Love and Information*, Churchill has challenged audiences to scrutinise the workings of power. Increasingly over the last two decades, she has produced a sequence of searing theatrical images that bind consumer capitalism to ecological crisis. debbie tucker green (*sic*), since her debut in 2003 with the plays *born bad* and *dirty butterfly*, has become a major figure in British playwriting. Like Churchill, her work is aesthetically innovative, characterised by a poetic handling of rhythmic speech and a penetrating, uncompromising political sensibility that lays bare the operations and experiential toll of racial discrimination. Both plays offer arresting scenarios of interruption and formal instability that critically adumbrate crises at systemic levels. This is not to suggest these plays arrive at the same destination, but they share an affective urgency of connection and a simmering rage with the systems they disclose.

This appears obliquely in *Escaped Alone* (Figure 26.2). Churchill initially presents a micro-community of four older women chatting over tea in a garden setting which

Figure 26.2 From a production of *Escaped Alone* by Caryl Churchill, directed by James Macdonald at the Royal Court Theatre, Jerwood Downstairs Theatre, 2016. With Linda Bassett as Mrs Jarrett, Deborah Findlay as Sally, Kika Markham as Lena, and June Watson as Vi.

seems deliberately ordinary and suburban. The women's conversation drifts over banal worries, their everyday activities and memories. Yet, there is something in the stage image that contains a suspicion of the uncanny nagging at the fringes of their talk, belying the placid ordinariness of the scene. The dialogue is cross-hatched with half-finished statements through which a pulse of paranoia and irrational fear occasionally swells in bizarre monologues. The disturbed quality of the communal scene is further heightened by a sporadic and unexplained intervention. Each of the play's eight sections is punctuated by a surreal speech delivered by the character of Mrs Jarrett. Recited in an abstract and impersonal tone, these seem to be dispatches from a parallel universe, distant from yet impinging upon the garden setting in an ominously undefined way. By splicing the ordinary with the extraordinary, the dramatic structure of *Escaped Alone* insinuates a sense of insecurity and imminent collapse.

In *ear for eye*, form is also mobile and, blatantly, inconsistent. Constructed of three parts plus a brief epilogue, the play's different modes are jarring. The first presents a sequence of short monologues and dialogues flipping between African-American and Black British experiences of racism and resistance. The second is an elliptical debate between a self-assured Caucasian man who may be a teacher or tutor and an African-American woman who may be a student – an allusion to David Mamet's controversial 1992 drama, *Oleanna*. They seem to be reviewing case studies of gun violence, though the background of their subject remains cryptic. With increasing frustration and anger the young woman challenges the man's rationalisations of the root causes and nature of white supremacism, insisting that these are not anomalous incidents but an ignored form of organised terrorism. The third part consists of two films in which white actors/non-actors read excerpts from the Jim Crow Laws, the legislation that enforced racial segregation in the United States in the nineteenth and twentieth centuries, and from a mixture of British and French slave codes from the seventeenth century. The epilogue is a brief exchange among younger and older voices from part one.

In parts one and two, practices of interruption, blocking, repression and silencing pervade the scenes. The contorting linguistic, cognitive and even physical codes repeated here relentlessly unmask the constant requirement that black people explain and justify themselves. In the opening scene an African-American son and mother have a halting exchange about body language. The son repeatedly seeks 'acceptable' ways of moving his body or directing his gaze in order to avoid confrontation:

SON: So if I put my hands up –
MOM: a threat, threatening.
SON: Slowly?
MOM: Provocative.
SON: Showed my palms

MOM: inflammatory. Could be.
SON: ... (If I) raised my hands just to –
MOM: no
SON: to just –
MOM: no
SON: but[36]

His mother's responses reveal how each and every gesture – hands up, hands down, palms showing, palms together, hands in pockets, behind the back and so on – might be perceived as potentially aggressive, insolent, defiant or hostile 'To them'.[37] tucker green leaves the audience to intuit who 'they' might be. The absolute confinement of the black body is mimicked in the staccato nature of their conversation – the speakers barely utter more than a word or two at a time, the gaps are supplemented with bodily demonstration that is swiftly curtailed. In scene 8 an almost identical conversation is enacted among a Black British mother, father and son. It finishes with the son asking his parents: 'Then what do I ... ? What do I even – ?'[38] The absence of an answer points to the intolerable conundrum of black existence and resistance, and the pressure cooker of frustration about the absence of change or progress.

As we can see, then, formal and linguistic disjunctions crack open environments of catastrophic, systemic damage. In *Escaped Alone* the crisis-scape is obviously more phantasmagorical than in *ear for eye*. An associational logic of dread in the former maps a sense of calamity seeping into the most ordinary of situations. Mrs Jarrett's monologues are peculiarly objective accounts of exponentially increasing disasters: 'Four hundred thousand tons of rock paid for by senior executives split off the hillside to smash through the roofs, each fragment onto the designated child's head ... Survivors were now solitary and went insane at different rates'.[39] Each is a cascade of semi-futuristic descriptions of interlinked economic and environmental disasters. Such catastrophes are manifested as systemic dysfunctions, anonymously produced, with proliferating consequences. The surrealistic visions of future disaster are, as Dan Rebellato notes, emblematic of current experiences of neoliberal capitalism.[40]

In *ear for eye*, damage is also anonymously produced but is evidently part of a recognisable world of violent and mundane disenfranchisement maintained through complicity, ignorance and consensus within society at large. A wilful blindness and thinly veiled hostility radiating through part two is evident in the way the young woman is boxed in by the arrogant gaslighting language of white academia and is forced to exhaustingly reassert herself and her right to interpret the world. If parts one and two leave any doubts about the mechanisms of endemic racism, then the insertion of the filmed readings of segregationist and slave legislation serves as a brutal reminder of what is still at stake. In its ferocity and pace, *ear for eye* refuses to sweeten a bitter critique with reasonable qualifications. By making visible the underlying structures of racism that lead to the instances of police violence, institutional denial and personal revenge, it contracts the space of comfortable passive apathy, and especially white passive apathy, in the collective audience experience.

The affective response to the crisis environments in both these plays is rage. Mrs Jarrett's interjections reach an apex in her last speech, which comprises the words 'terrible rage' repeated twenty-five times. In contrast to the narrative accumulation of calamities, this monologue shudders into the repetition of adjective and noun, spoken, in the Royal Court production, with a modulating emphasis that mismatched the words' meaning. It functions as a seizure in the system, but also as an involuntary response to it. The jagged speech textures and discordant dramatic structure of *ear for eye* similarly embody a system in convulsion, that demands revulsion. Its black speakers vent their frustrations with the failure of polite protest and 'progress' that 'meanders, wanders, languishes',[41] even when they disagree on how to make change happen. The epilogue bears the vital challenge to act – as the young female speaker states 'Give me one reason to not'.[42]

Conclusion: Destabilising the Ordinary

This essay has looked at the ways 'crisis ordinariness' is perceptible as a network of themes and forms of British drama since the 1990s. As we have seen, crisis is not a singular thing but a multifaceted aspect of a contemporary structure of feeling experienced individually and collectively. States of estrangement, alienation, precarious communality, environmental destruction and systemic racial violence are among the crises these playwrights have sought to illuminate and interrogate. Above all, the plays surveyed here testify not only to British theatre's ongoing engagement with the social sphere, debating its politics and ethics, but also to the practice of community in bringing people together in a participatory forum, in a particular place and time. As the coronavirus crisis has made painfully clear, it is a practice that cannot be taken for granted.

NOTES

1. Raymond Williams, *Marxism and Literature* (Oxford University Press, 1977), p. 131.
2. For a concise definition of precarity and precariousness see Sharryn Kasmir, 'Precarity', *The Cambridge Encyclopedia of Anthropology*, 13 March 2018: http://doi.org/10.29164/18precarity.
3. Lauren Berlant, *Cruel Optimism* (Durham, NJ: Duke University Press, 2011), p. 10.
4. Stuart Hall and Doreen Massey, 'Interpreting the Crisis', *Soundings* 44 (2010), 57–71 (57).
5. David Harvey, *A Brief History of Neoliberalism* (Oxford University Press, 2005), p. 2.
6. Jill Dolan, 'Performance, Utopia, and the "Utopian Performative"', *Theatre Journal* 53.3 (2001), 455–79.

7. Victor Turner, *From Ritual to Theatre: The Human Seriousness of Play* (New York: PAJ Publications, 1982), pp. 47–8.

8. Dolan, 'Performance, Utopia', 473.

9. Zygmunt Bauman, *Liquid Modernity* (Cambridge: Polity, 2000), p. 200.

10. John Bull, *Stage Right: Crisis and Recovery in Contemporary Mainstream British Theatre* (New York: Macmillan, 1994), p. 219.

11. Aleks Sierz, *In-Yer-Face: British Drama Today* (London: Faber & Faber, 2001), p. 4.

12. David Hare, *Skylight*, in *David Hare: Plays 3* (London: Faber & Faber, 2008). First performed in the Cottesloe auditorium of the National Theatre, London, 4 May 1995. Mark Ravenhill, *Some Explicit Polaroids*, in *Mark Ravenhill: Plays 1* (London: Methuen, 2001). First performed at the Theatre Royal, Bury St Edmunds, 20 September 1999.

13. Hare, *Skylight*, p. 13.

14. Ravenhill, *Some Explicit Polaroids*, p. 247.

15. Hare, *Skylight*, p. 32.

16. Ibid., p. 71.

17. Ravenhill, *Some Explicit Polaroids*, p. 236.

18. Ibid., p. 241.

19. Ibid., p. 267.

20. Ibid., p. 293.

21. Ibid., p. 314.

22. Berlant, *Cruel Optimism*, p. 7.

23. Tim Crouch, *The Author* (London: Oberon, 2009). First performed at the Royal Court, Jerwood Theatre Upstairs, 23 September 2009. David Greig, *The Events* (London: Faber & Faber, 2013). First performed at the Traverse Theatre, Edinburgh, 4 August 2013.

24. Alan Read, *Theatre in the Expanded Field: Seven Approaches to Performance* (London: Bloomsbury, 2013), p. 196.

25. Crouch, *Author*, p. 46.

26. In 'On Acting and Not-Acting', *Drama Review* 16.1 (1972), 3–15, Michael Kirby describes an acting–not-acting spectrum ranging from the traditional impersonation of fictional characters within a dramatic frame to performances in which there is no representation of story or character and performers are, apparently, themselves. His examples of not-acting or non-matrixed performing include Happenings and work by the Living Theatre.

27. Crouch, *Author*, p. 32.

28. Greig, *Events*, p. 38.

29. Crouch, *Author*, p. 46.

30. Christoph Henke, 'Precarious Virtuality in Participatory Theatre: Tim Crouch's *The Author*', in Mireia Aragay and Martin Middeke (eds), *Of Precariousness: Vulnerabilities, Responsibilities, Communities in 21st Century British Drama and Theatre* (Berlin: De Gruyter, 2017), pp. 77–90 (p. 79).

31. Susan Mansfield, 'Interview: Tim Crouch', *Scotsman*, 21 July 2010: www.scotsman.com/news/interview-tim-crouch-theatre-director-1-820005 (accessed 29 June 2012).

32. Greig, *Events*, pp. 53–4.

33. Dolan, 'Performance, Utopia', 460.

34. Berlant, *Cruel Optimism*, pp. 10–11.

35. Caryl Churchill, *Escaped Alone* (London: Nick Hern, 2016). First performed at the Royal Court, Jerwood Theatre Downstairs, 21 January 2016. debbie tucker green, *ear for eye* (London: Nick Hern, 2018). First performed at the Royal Court, Jerwood Theatre Downstairs, 25 October 2018.

36. tucker green, *ear for eye*, p. 4.

37. Ibid., p. 5.

38. Ibid., p. 58.

39. Churchill, *Escaped Alone*, p. 8.

40. Dan Rebellato, 'Of an Apocalyptic Tone Recently Adopted in Theatre: British Drama, Violence and Writing', *Sillages Critiques* 22 (2017): https://journals.openedition.org/sillagescritiques/4798 (accessed 1 February 2018).

41. tucker green, *ear for eye*, p. 49.

42. Ibid., p. 135.

CRITICAL REFLECTIONS AND FURTHER STUDY

My treatment of the topic of contemporary British theatre is influenced by a network of interests in my own research and writing that radiate from a central concern with relationships between the aesthetic and the political. There are many possible and exciting routes into thinking about these relationships, but in the essay I have chosen to limit the focus in several ways in order to maintain a sense of coherence in the analysis. One of the most obvious decisions I made for the purposes of the essay was to discuss playwriting and specific authors. I have done so partly out of a deep, personal attachment to the rich tradition of dramatic writing in Britain especially since the 1950s and partly because of the energy and quality of the scholarship available on contemporary British playwriting. As a teacher not based in Britain, I am alert to the issue of access; published plays, unlike some forms of performance, can be read and discussed even by those who haven't had an opportunity to see them staged. This is not to insist on theatre as (mere) literature or to deny its embodied force, but is rather an appreciation of the enduring value of a published play text as a map of a possible performance, bearing with it the exhilarating potential of being imagined and staged in radically different ways. That said, it is worth noting that such a focus excludes other equally valid approaches. You might equally consider contemporary British theatre as a story of institutions and funding; you might turn to traditions of directing, acting, companies and performers; or you might focus on performance in its non-textual, devised and live-art formulations. Jen Harvie's *Staging the UK* (Manchester University Press, 2005) and Liz Tomlin's *British Theatre Companies: 1995–2014* (London: Bloomsbury, 2014) are good places to start if this is where your interests lie.

The works I have chosen are not intended as a representative overview of the range of socially engaged or political theatre practice in Britain since the 1990s. Rather, they are presented as thought-provoking attempts to find impactful, aesthetic vehicles to address political challenges and impasses and to raise questions about the nature of community and the potential of critical resistance. Kwame Kwei-Armah, Alice Birch, Tanika Gupta, Ella Hickson, Sarah Kane, Lucy Kirkwood, Andy Smith, Simon Stephens and Roy Williams are just some of the other writers who may have been included and who are certainly worth further investigation. In my discussion of the six plays, I have highlighted theme and form in a necessarily selective way, setting aside some interesting aspects of the discourses they broach: for example Mark Ravenhill's tongue-in-cheek allusions to postmodernism, or the way Tim Crouch's *The Author* seems to critique Sarah Kane's use of stage violence in her 1995 play, *Blasted*. Dan Rebellato's essay 'Of an Apocalyptic Tone Recently Adopted in Theatre' (see my essay, note 40) unpacks some of the problems of this interpretation in a particularly lucid way.

Conceptually the essay is informed by the cultural materialist premise that cultural practices are entwined with social and political conditions, participating in the production of meaning and reflecting on the nature of power whether through acceptance or resistance. I took 1980s Thatcherism as a foundation for later expressions of neoliberal capitalism. The essay is not particularly invested in mapping neoliberalism, although David Harvey's *A Brief History of Neoliberalism* (Oxford University Press, 2005) provides an excellent overview. Rather, I wanted to think about the legacies of the shift in terms of a new conjuncture, and how those legacies are felt as precariousness. To this end, I lean on Raymond Williams's phrase 'structure of feeling' to lever a discussion of crisis as a feature of post-1990s theatre.

How one defines 'crisis' is pivotal to how one responds, and among many recent books, often of a political or sociological nature, see for instance Sylvia Walby, *Crisis* (Cambridge and Malden, MA: Polity, 2015), or Zygmunt Bauman and Carlo Bordoni, *State of Crisis* (Cambridge and Malden, MA: Polity, 2014). However, I wanted a vocabulary that addressed aesthetic and cultural responses specifically. I found Lauren Berlant's book, *Cruel Optimism*, to be a productive and stimulating frame of reference that combines an interest in how the present feels with how that feeling produces new forms of narrative, genre and artistic response. Notably, Berlant does not discuss theatre, but her concepts of 'cruel optimism' and 'crisis ordinariness' are really useful tools to open up the structures of feeling we find in so much contemporary theatre work.

Theatre is pre-eminently communal. In the essay, I gesture towards some perspectives on the audience as community and the relational dimensions of plays in performance. But theatre is also very much about representation – who and what is seen – and this too is a crisis-scape. We need to be acutely aware of the patterns of silence, exclusion and racial violence that Black British playwright debbie tucker green so starkly illuminates. Now more than ever we need to hold on to Jill Dolan's aspiration that 'theatre and performance create citizens and engage democracy as a participatory forum in which ideas and possibilities for social equality and justice are shared' (p. 473).

FURTHER READING

Angelaki, Vicky, *Social and Political Theatre in 21st-Century Britain: Staging Crisis* (London: Bloomsbury, 2017)

Aragay, Mireia, and Enric Monforte (eds), *Ethical Speculations in Contemporary British Theatre* (Houndmills: Palgrave Macmillan, 2014)

D'Monte, Rebecca, and Graham Saunders (eds), *Cool Britannia? British Political Drama in the 1990s* (Houndmills: Palgrave Macmillan, 2008)

Fragkou, Marissia, *Ecologies of Precarity in Twenty-First Century Theatre: Politics, Affect, Responsibility* (London: Bloomsbury, 2019)

Goddard, Lynette, *Contemporary Black British Playwrights* (Houndmills: Palgrave Macmillan, 2015)

Harvie, Jen, *Fair Play: Art, Performance and Neoliberalism* (Houndmills: Palgrave Macmillan, 2013)

Kritzer, Amelia Howe, *Political Theatre in Post-Thatcher Britain: New Writing 1995–2005* (Houndmills: Palgrave Macmillan, 2008)

Luckhurst, Mary (ed.), *A Companion to the British and Irish Drama* (Oxford: Blackwell, 2006)

Rebellato, Dan, *Modern British Playwriting: 2000–2009* (London: Bloomsbury, 2013)

Sierz, Aleks, *Modern British Playwriting: The 1990s* (London: Bloomsbury, 2014)

Sierz, Aleks, *Rewriting the Nation: British Theatre Now* (London: Bloomsbury, 2011)

Wallace, Clare, *Suspect Cultures: Narrative, Identity & Citation in 1990s New Drama* (Prague: Litteraria Pragensia Books, 2006)

PART VIII
Postcolonial Literature in English

INTRODUCTORY NOTE

We began with an essay on an Old English poem with its immediate linguistic roots in Germanic dialects from northern Europe. We end with a focus on works written by writers from, or with roots in, Africa, the Indian subcontinent, and the Caribbean. The modern English these writers use, moreover, is rarely straightforwardly standard English and almost all of them experiment creatively with and through English to try to find a voice, and to express an identity, that can still clearly register their original cultural, linguistic and geographical roots. One of these writers, Grace Nichols, has given famous expression to this situation in her lines, from *i is a long memoried woman*: 'I have crossed an ocean / I have lost my tongue / from the root of the old one / a new one has sprung'.

   Fiona Moolla's essay on romance and romantic love in the African novel also in some ways harks back to the start of the volume and to K. S. Whetter's essay on medieval romance in particular, although, obviously, the context here is very different and the meanings of 'romance' have greatly diversified since medieval times. Moolla's choice for her case study text, Chinua Achebe's *Things Fall Apart*, is a brave one given that novel's reputation as a landmark publication in the development of the modern African novel in English and given the vast amount of commentary it has generated. However, the choice is a deliberate and strategic one, intended to draw attention to the relative neglect of questions of romantic love in mainstream African fiction and critical discourse, and Moolla certainly presents us with an unusual and original perspective on Achebe's novel. Romance elements have always existed in African fiction, of course, but, using *Things Fall Apart* as a symptomatic example, Moolla suggests how they have often remained in the shadows of other plot elements. A helpful frame for her reading is provided by brief discussion of two works by

Ghanaian writer Ama Ata Aidoo whose more prominent foregrounding of romance in her fiction presents a good contrast to Achebe – and might suggest some gender differences at play in their different genre orientations. Be that as it may, Moolla's central reading of Achebe's novel casts new light on certain narrative elements whose romantic nature has been underplayed, if not entirely neglected, by a critical tradition understandably focused primarily on the novel's anti-colonialist critique. This can be seen to touch on a longstanding debate within postcolonial studies as to the extent to which the African novel is in some ways inherently political, but Moolla's essay is oriented more towards advocating further research in romance studies as these might be applied to African fiction.

Moolla might nevertheless be said to be refocusing critical emphasis here away from the public and political realm and towards the private and the personal, or interpersonal, and this resonates with Loretta Stec's approach to Bessie Head in the next essay through 'everyday life studies'. Drawing on the ideas of Michel de Certeau and feminist thinkers influenced by these, and also taking her cue from Njabulo S. Ndebele's call for a 'rediscovery of the ordinary' in literature, Stec explores the ways in which Head's writing establishes a 'feminism of everyday life' which, though focused on the ordinary details of daily life, nevertheless represents its own form of resistance to broader social structures of oppression, inequality and injustice. Such resistance, Stec argues, is registered in the small everyday practices of caring, sharing and creativity that Head concentrates on in her writing and that 'constitute a realm of non-alienation' in which an alternative set of values can be nurtured to set against those of capitalist modernity, colonialism and patriarchy. Stec's rich and compelling interdisciplinary study focuses in particular on Head's short fiction and, appropriately, on her oral history of Serowe, the village in Botswana where she eventually settled. If we consider Head's work as a form of 'everyday-life writing', then Stec's essay might usefully be compared with Maria Frawley's life-writing approach to Charlotte Brontë in Essay 17.

Although a very different sort of writer from Bessie Head, the poet Grace Nichols could also most aptly be described as a feminist of everyday life, as Izabel Brandão's detailed study of her work demonstrates in the next essay. Brandão's ecofeminist reading sensitively surveys the characteristic themes and features of Nichols's poetry over the whole range of her career up to the present. While Brandão centres her study on gender politics, highlighting Nichols's critique of the normative stereotyping of women and her celebration of women's diversity, Brandão is fully alive to the trademark humour and non-doctrinaire nature of Nichols's poetry. Indeed, perhaps more than anything, she reveals a writer who is very firmly grounded in the ordinary everydayness of women's lives – though it would probably be more appropriate to say the *extra*ordinary everydayness of women's lives, for, as Brandão's analysis repeatedly suggests, Nichols's poetry is constantly seeking to infuse women's everyday experiences with a sense of joy and delight. This is one of her distinctive forms of 'everyday' resistance to oppressive social norms and prejudices and it is a key element in the overall 'poetics of resistance' that Brandão elucidates for us. Brandão's discussion of how Nichols's poetry addresses questions of ethnicity and identity but is not defined by them, and the points just made about her focus on the ordinary, make a relevant link with Ulla Rahbek's discussion later in this section of black British identity in the novel *Ordinary People* by Diana Evans.

Joel Kuortti, in the following essay on Salman Rushdie, presents a comprehensive account of the many diverse contexts informing the writer's work, but especially those related to the Indian subcontinent which provides the main setting for many of his best known novels, including *Midnight's Children*, *Shame* and *The Satanic Verses*. These novels, all part of Rushdie's 'India cycle', take centre stage in Kuortti's discussion. In addition to straightforwardly outlining the relevant political, religious and cultural contexts of Rushdie's fiction, however, Kuortti explores in particular the many complex ways in which Rushdie's texts *internally* dialogise their contexts. Rushdie's novels are 'deeply embedded in the contextuality of their subject matter', Kuortti explains, and they are written in a way that suggests not just a general background awareness of contexts, but a direct and explicit engagement with them (indeed, almost as though they are actual characters in the fiction), and this is what Kuortti describes as their *metacontextuality*. Clearly, then, Kuortti's essay speaks very pertinently to the central relationship between texts and contexts that informs this volume, and his analysis of Rushdie's works provides us with a wonderfully involved and involving practical illustration of the full potential complexity of that relationship.

Perhaps appropriately in a volume of many voices, the final essay, by Ulla Rahbek, skilfully sets six different contemporary literary voices in play in order to try to capture something of the evolving social and cultural context of present-day Britain, particularly as it is seen from within a postcolonial perspective. Rahbek's title registers the 'complexities' of this context and she organises her discussion of her chosen texts around three key elements: black British identity, the notion of the nation, and migration. Rahbek's choice of texts for discussion was an inspired one and, taken together, they give the essay some sort of thematic connection to almost every one of the other essays. It would take too long to list all these connections, but they include, in addition to the key elements mentioned above, questions of time and space, travel, mobility, migration and globalisation – and Rahbek's texts also contain elements of social critique which clearly reflect the 'structure of feeling' of crisis and precarity in contemporary Britain that Clare Wallace identifies in Essay 26. However, if Rahbek's choice of texts was inspired, her discussion of them is inspiring too. She ends her essay by stressing that literature, and, by implication, the *study* of literature, is a 'world-making' activity. By helping us, for example, to reconceptualise 'fundamentally human experiences' such as migration 'in inclusive and equitable ways' in the twenty-first century, the sorts of texts Rahbek introduces here, understood in their full contexts, can hopefully help us to address the crises of our times and, together, to start to make the world a better place for the future. Even as I write this, another humanitarian crisis is unfolding in Afghanistan as thousands of people flee from the war-torn country once again, and I am reminded of some thought-provoking words, of direct relevance to Rahbek's and other essays in this section, by the prominent postcolonial scholar, Paul Gilroy (from his laureate's lecture on winning the Holberg Prize): 'It is imperative to remain less interested in who or what we imagine ourselves to be than in what we can do for one another, both in today's emergency conditions and in the grimmer circumstances that surely await us' (quoted in Yohann Koshy, 'The Last Humanist: How Paul Gilroy Became the Most Vital Guide to Our Age of Crisis', *Guardian*, 5 August 2021).

The essays in this section touch on a range of issues that should be of broad interest to anyone working within mainstream postcolonial literary studies. For those new to the subject, some general background orientation to the field can be found in my chapter, 'Postcolonial Literature in English', in *English Literature in Context* (pp. 619–708). This provides an introductory overview of the 500-year history of colonialism and of the growth and development of postcolonial writing in English, and the chapter includes several short readings of texts that can be related in various ways to the longer readings provided here. It also has an extensive annotated reading list which can be used to supplement the references and further reading suggestions given in the essays and their sections of critical reflection.

Finally, in their concerns with the topics of gender, ethnicity, identity, transculturalism, migration and mobility, these essays as a group can be related to several earlier essays in the volume – for example, to the essays dealing with early colonial and postcolonial writing by Grogan, Holmesland and Roberts; the essays on gender and social identity by Asbee, Frawley, Paltin, Riley and Wallace; and the essays by Petrina and Michelucci dealing with questions of travel, space and place.

27 | Complexities and Concealments of Eros in the African Novel: Chinua Achebe's *Things Fall Apart*

F. FIONA MOOLLA

Abstract

Chinua Achebe's *Things Fall Apart* is the widely acknowledged ur-text that launched the anglophone African novel on to the international literature scene. Although this novel succeeded in challenging imperial cultural stereotypes of Africa through strategically represented Igbo characters and community, who come metonymically to figure the wider continent, it also established the trend where romantic love is relegated to the background of other more prioritised concerns. However, since eros is so significant a part of human relationships, the novel does not elide romance entirely. Instead, romantic love interludes are presented as brief counterpoints to the 'utilitarian' marriage which forms a more substantial narrative focus. The love story of the tragic hero, Okonkwo, and his second wife, Ekwefi, is at odds with social conventions which do *not* dictate that love should constitute the rationale for marriage. Economic considerations prevent Ekwefi and Okonkwo from marrying when they fall in love, but do not preclude them from marrying later when passionate desire causes Ekwefi to leave her first husband for Okonkwo. This love story, which ends in polygynous marriage, contrasts with the love-marriage plot as it has developed in Anglo-American literary history. In the western version of the love-marriage plot, which has acquired a global normativity through globalised media and culture, love is an essential condition for marriage. Because love is also culturally understood as mutually exclusive, the western love-marriage is necessarily monogamous. Achebe's first novel implicitly suggests the cultural specificity of the globally dominant love-marriage plot with its own opening up of a wider range of connections between love and marriage.

The study of love has been a fascinating topic for many thinkers in the western tradition, beginning with Plato and including, among others, Ovid, Rousseau, Nietszche, Freud and Proust. Denis de Rougemont's *Love in the Western World* (1940) was one of the first modern studies to suggest a theory of love which claimed to identify the unique specificities of love in a European context.[1] Many other interdisciplinary survey studies have followed, presenting broad approaches to love in the Anglo-American tradition,[2] with a number of works more strongly grounded in literature.[3] Defining the word 'love' is difficult since it encompasses so much. It includes the emotion felt for friends and family, and the appreciation of inanimate things and abstract ideas. This essay narrows the focus to 'romantic' love. But even the epithet 'romantic' introduces complications, especially in a historical and cross-cultural context. For some scholars, for example the anthropologists William Jankowiak and Edward Fischer, romantic love is a truly universal emotion.[4] By contrast, for the sociologist Anthony Giddens, among others, 'romantic love', as opposed to 'passionate love', originates in Europe, and achieves its full expression in the late eighteenth century.[5] One's understanding of the cross-cultural history of love finally is determined by the way one defines the term. In this essay, following the lead of Mary Evans, the word 'love' will be used to refer to 'an individual relationship which also involves a sexual relationship'.[6] The ancient Greeks delineated love more clearly, with terms existing for general charitable fellow-feeling (*agape*) and the attachment to friends (*philia*); with the word *eros* referring to the emotion of affection tied to sexual desire. In this essay, the word 'love' will be used interchangeably with 'romantic love' and 'eros'.

Even though the study of romantic love has had a long and illustrious history in western culture, the study of love, especially as it forms part of the genre of the romance novel, has suffered some prejudice. Catherine Riley notes the way the 'derogation' of romance writing as a 'low' form has been a way of 'disregarding women's writing'.[7] This has been the case even for feminist literary study where romance novels have been regarded as reinforcing oppressive and discriminatory stereotypes of women.[8] In the context of African literature, especially the study of the anglophone novel, apart from a few articles and book chapters, dedicated extended studies of romantic love do not exist.[9] Lynne Pearce, whose cultural history of love explores transformations in conceptions of love in Europe over the past five centuries, suggests in this regard that 'there is no question that a further book is waiting to be written on the complex relationship that exists between different races and cultures and romantic love in its white, Western specificity'.[10]

The work and comments of the well-known Ghanaian writer Ama Ata Aidoo represent a good case study of the tensions regarding eros in African literature. All of Aidoo's novels and plays centre on the romantic relationship, even though early in her career she expressed the view that love stories are trivial. Aidoo's initial attitude underscores the misrecognition of the importance of romantic love where, even as the author was writing love stories, she needed to deny that they were love stories, feeling obliged to highlight the political significance of her work – using a narrow definition of what constitutes the political. It is only with the publication of her second novel, *Changes: A Love Story* (1991),[11] that Aidoo acknowledges the central role that eros plays in her literary and social imagination, and this is most clearly articulated in the introduction to her edited volume, *African Love Stories*

(2006).[12] *African Love Stories* brings together romantic short fiction by seventeen established women writers from all over the continent. The fact that it is only stories by women that have been included perhaps reinforces the idea of love as 'a light concern of the ladies'. Aidoo, referring to the extensive oral traditions that exist in every region of the continent, suggests that 'Africa ... has been, and is, full of great love stories'.[13] She also lists the major African writers in whose work love plays an important but unrecognised role. Aidoo explains the inattention to love by referring to a conversation she had with an avid reader of African novels. She was told

> The only problem ... is that in the modern African novel as a love story, the love story
> is *never* revealed as such [b]ecause it is completely subsumed under 'the more important
> social and political issues' which the modern African writer (thinks she/he) has to
> deal with: incompetent leadership and their betrayal of their peoples, the antics of the
> 'lumpen militariat', ... complete economic collapse, racial tensions, outmoded traditional
> thought and practices.[14]

Aidoo's brief overview shows that love stories flourish in African literature and culture, but that their importance has not been fully acknowledged in literary critical discourse. The issues that are addressed in this essay through *Things Fall Apart*, Chinua Achebe's iconic first novel,[15] constitute the main, openly acknowledged focus of Aidoo's novel *Changes: A Love Story*. This novel tackles the question of love in relation to marriage in late twentieth-century Africa, especially the unexpected permutations of eros in its connection with both monogamous and polygynous marriages.

The connection between love and marriage is an especially interesting one. As suggested above, while the experience of romantic love may be universal, the link between love and marriage is more complex, and more culture-bound. In most cultures across history, marriage appears to be utilitarian, where it generally serves wider social, economic and political purposes.[16] In such contexts, arranged marriages, polygyny, concubinage or the adultery of European medieval courtly love are accepted and not regarded as an affront to the 'injured' party. It is only in European culture when, by around the end of the eighteenth century, love becomes the *sine qua non* of marriage, that one can no longer admit to marrying for economic or political advantage without seeming irredeemably crass. Love, from this period in European culture, becomes the only *acknowledged* foundation of marriage, but, of course, the other economic and social reasons continue to play a tacit part.[17] Through European colonialism and imperialism, ideas about love and its relationship with marriage have been exported to other parts of the world. Today, through globalisation, especially a globalised media and culture industry, a very historically and culturally specific conjunction of the relationship between love and marriage has become globally normalised.[18]

The connection between love and marriage in an African socio-anthropological context generally follows the trends observed internationally, where the love marriage is linked with becoming 'modern'.[19] Here, 'love can be used as an alternative to kinship obligation and to justify economic individualism'.[20] From a literary perspective, representations of marriage in oratures and literatures have been broadly considered by the novelist and scholar Isidore Okpewho, who finds that often creative expression complicates the reductive picture of marriage that emerges from sociology and anthropology.[21] Representations of many aspects of marriage, including gender politics, sexuality, motherhood, cross-racial marriage and questions of identity are cast in a diasporic frame by Cécile Accilien in a survey of francophone African and Caribbean novels and films.[22] This essay narrows the focus from general representations of marriage to a consideration of the love-marriage plot in novels; specifically, its variations as may be identified in Chinua Achebe's *Things Fall Apart*.

Joseph Allen Boone's analysis of the tradition of love and marriage in the Anglo-American novel establishes a helpful counterpoint.[23] Boone surveys the cultural and literary currents that feed into the establishment – by around the end of the eighteenth century in Europe – of marriage as an end point and generally assumed framework for love. These love plots are the narrative embodiment of a culturally and historically located understanding of marriage, where marriage appears to represent the individual self-fulfilment of, especially, the heroine. An important template for the love plot is the one established through the novels of Jane Austen, which is structured around the encounter of the lovers, the obstacles to their union (both objective and subjective) and their final triumphant marriage. It is this 'classic' plot structure that establishes the template for later popular romance novels. Boone argues, however, that despite the apparent harmony and mutualism of the ending of such plots, they 'deviously ... conceal under the trope of oppositional "balance" the sexual asymmetries inherent in a hierarchical order based on male dominance and female suppression'.[24] It is the implicit containment of the heroine within the marriage plot that has been another source of criticism of popular romance novels.[25] The following analysis of Achebe's *Things Fall Apart*, however, does not critique the love-marriage plot as much as show how the relationship of love and marriage displays cultural variation. The novel presents permutations of the love-marriage plot on a wider continuum of alternative apprehensions of love and marriage than are allowed by existing critiques of the love-marriage plot in Anglo-American novels and scholarship. My study suggests further that Achebe's first novel, which lays the foundation for anglophone African literature internationally, may also have set the pattern where stories about love form concealed segments of narratives so that these novels may not easily be described primarily as love stories.

Chinua Achebe (1930–2013) is one of the most well-known writers in African and world literature circles. Achebe is identified by Maya Jaggi, a leading critic within postcolonial literature, as the 'founding father of African writing in English',[26] and *Things Fall Apart* (1958), his first novel, is described by Lyn Innes, author of a number of important interventions into Achebe scholarship, as a novel that 'not only contested European narratives about Africans but also challenged traditional assumptions about the form and function of the novel' (Figure 27.1).[27] Influential African literature scholar Simon Gikandi goes so far as to suggest that Achebe is the person who 'invented African literature' because of his major impact on the literary establishment and his entry into and interruption of 'the institutions of exegesis and education'.[28] Gikandi suggests further that Achebe established the 'terms by which African literature was produced, circulated, and interpreted'.[29] Achebe's accomplishment was largely achieved through *Things Fall Apart*, first published in the iconic Heinemann African Writers series. Achebe's novel was conceived as a 'writing back to Empire' and, in particular, to the negative stereotypes of Africa as backward and barbaric, a view which seemed to be consolidated in canonical English literary works, especially Joseph Conrad's *Heart of Darkness* (1902). For Achebe, *Heart of Darkness* 'projects the image of Africa as "the other world," the antithesis of Europe and therefore of civilization, a place where man's

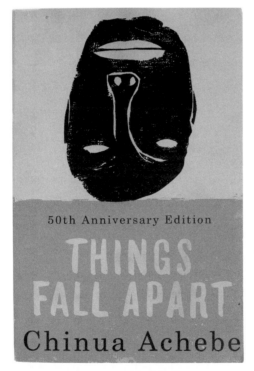

Figure 27.1 Front cover of the fiftieth anniversary edition of *Things Fall Apart*, designed by illustrator and artist Edel Rodriguez for Random House (Anchor Books/Vintage, 2008).

vaunted intelligence and refinement are finally mocked by triumphant bestiality'.[30] Using the techniques of the oral tradition, an Igbo-infused English, and a story that presents the individual human failings of its protagonist, Achebe's novel challenges stereotypes of Africa.

Things Fall Apart is also the African novel which has generated the most critical comment in the form of innumerable journal articles, book chapters and edited volumes. The scholarship on Achebe's first novel suggests clusters that centre on various themes and approaches, including the influence of key 'intertexts' (e.g. *Heart of Darkness*), issues around language and style, the significance of the epic and ancient Greek tragedy to narrative conceptualisation, concerns with gender, questions of Igbo culture and colonial encounter, and also, more recently, explorations of the impact of *Things Fall Apart* on Achebe's literary descendants. Although many of these studies, especially the ones addressing gender issues, discuss the representation of the wives of the male protagonist, the focus does not fall squarely on marriage and its relationship with romantic love, despite its importance to the project of 'writing back to empire' undertaken in the novel. This, in part, may be a consequence of the sublimation of considerations of intimate relationships in the novel itself, notwithstanding their implicit importance to the cultural intervention and challenge presented by Achebe's groundbreaking novel. In an evaluation of realist and modernist narrative modes in Achebe's writing, Gikandi notes, as an aside, Achebe's hesitation to address the significance of eros. Gikandi observes that 'One of the most salient, and perhaps unexpected, aspects of Achebe's fiction was his rejection of romance, both as love or wish fulfillment'.[31] He proceeds further: 'Tragedy, rather than romance, would become the central trope in Achebe's early works'.[32] The elision of eros from Achebe's vision is, however, beginning to be observed more popularly, possibly indirectly through the foregrounding of romantic love in the work of Chimamanda Ngozi Adichie,[33] literary descendant of the Igbo-anglophone novel originated by Achebe. Brittle Paper, an African literary blog, for example, commissioned Kiru Taye, 'Nigeria's queen of erotica', to develop the romance elements of Achebe's iconic novel by taking its hero into the bedroom. The short fiction 'Thighs Fell Apart' expands into a sizzling sex scene: the brief but important incident which sees the hero of the novel marry his second wife.[34] In the current study, however, intimations of eros in *Things Fall Apart* will be explored in connection with marriage rather than with a full-blown erotics.

Things Fall Apart tells the story of Okonkwo, a renowned wrestler, warrior and man of wealth and standing in his village. Okonkwo is, however, a tragic hero whose flaw consists in his fierce masculinity unbalanced by the feminine flexibility also prized by the Igbo. When Okonkwo unnecessarily and full of bravado himself kills a young man, who had become like a son in his family, he seems to lose the favour of his *chi*, or personal god. Thereafter he accidentally shoots another young man at the funeral of a village elder. For this offence he is banished to his mother's village, where missionaries arrive and convert his eldest son to Christianity. Okonkwo's furious response sees his son abandon his culture and family for the religion of the missionaries. When Okonkwo returns to his own village, he finds that the British colonial administration has established itself in the district. Determined to expel the colonial outsiders, Okonkwo urges war, of which, given their insight into their relative powerlessness, and the complexities of the context, the rest of the village is wary. When it becomes apparent that Okonkwo does not have the support of his community, he commits suicide, which is the worst abomination among the Igbo.

This synopsis makes it clear why *Things Fall Apart* has largely been read as a novel about Igbo anthropology, a clash of cultures, the development of a distinctive Igbo-English, and questions of gender in relation to Igbo culture and cosmogony. However, the novel allows itself to be read also as a love story, following lines that are unconventional in relation to normative expectations about love stories. The love stories which globally predominate through popular print culture like Mills & Boon and Harlequin romances, and through Hollywood movies, generally are about obstructions to the love of a young heterosexual couple, obstructions which are then removed at the end, allowing the lovers to marry. In order to bring the love stories in *Things Fall Apart* out of the shadows, one needs to widen this lens to focus on Okonkwo's relationships with his wives. In a polygynous society, which does not even recognise itself as polygynous since monogamy does not exist in the cultural imaginary, Okonkwo's relationship with his second wife, Ekwefi, stands out. It stands out since it exists against a backdrop of marriages that are collectively facilitated, and which form a functional part of social life. The narrative reveals that Ekwefi and Okonkwo had been in love when they were young, but could not marry since Okonkwo was too poor at the time to pay the bride-price. We see that the dominant romance plot which foregrounds obstacles to the union of the lovers occurs also in *Things Fall Apart*, but that it is embedded within a wider range of intimate relationships, and it is not deliberately brought to the fore. It also challenges the 'classic' romance narrative in that the lovers are both married when the obstruction of Okonkwo's low economic standing is removed, and the marriage of the lovers does not require Okonkwo to leave his first wife.

In order to illustrate the ways in which Ekwefi and Okonkwo's marriage is quite unconventional in the society described, the novel provides a normative background against which it may be considered. In terms of this background, wives throughout are presented as part of a man's wealth and standing – as are marriageable daughters. Romantic love that brings two unique but ultimately compatible individuals to union in marriage is not scripted into the culture presented – but it exists as the relationship between Ekwefi and Okonkwo illustrates. Customary expectations about marriage are conveyed through descriptions of marital negotiations and a marriage ceremony or *uri*, in which the question of the love between the bride and groom is not mentioned. However, the marriage presented is strategically framed by love relationships which point to a broader cultural conceptualisation of romantic love and marriage. Obierika is the man whose daughter is getting married. Obierika, not coincidentally, is the man who reminds Okonkwo of the legendary love of another couple just before the scene in which the marriage negotiations are entered into. The novel, in a carefully considered 'aside', refers to the death of the oldest man in a neighbouring village, for whom the funeral drums have not yet sounded since his first wife has to be buried before he can be interred. The reader is informed that, upon hearing of her husband's death by the younger wives, the elderly first wife went over to her husband's quarters, saluted him in death, and died herself shortly thereafter. Obierika comments that it was said of the elderly couple that they 'had one mind' (p. 60). Obierika adds that he remembers as a young boy there was a song about the couple's love, and that the husband 'could not do anything without telling her' (p. 60). Thus we see that in the context of the predominantly 'utilitarian' marriage, whose negotiation will be described in the next sequence of the narrative, the marital love that is foregrounded in cultural expression, in this case the song mentioned, is the love that develops in the course of matrimony rather than the love that needs to exist as a rationale to establish the marriage.

The description of the marriage negotiations presents this intimate relationship as forged between families, where the consolidation of the relationship is confirmed by the community. The bride-price is a crucial part of the negotiation between families since it is the bride's 'security' should she return to her family home if the marriage fails. Marriage is presented in the narrative thus as having an importance wider than the desires of the individuals getting married. It is presented as having broader social functions and purposes tacitly accepted by the couple getting married. However, even with the 'utilitarian' marriage represented through the wedding, and, of course, the lived experience of polygynous marriage shown throughout in Okonkwo's relationships with his wives, the narrative, nonetheless, highlights love in marriage. Unlike marriage under the conditions of modernity for which love is the foundation, *Things Fall Apart* reveals love that develops in the course of the 'utilitarian' marriage.

Likewise, the marriage ceremony itself is preceded by an incident that attests to the existence in this culture of romantic love which precedes and leads to marriage, and which endures during marriage, but with some differences compared with the 'classic' love-marriage plot. Ekwefi and Okonkwo's relationship is unusual against the backdrop outlined since it is a relationship of marriage based on individual desire; and it is a relationship precipitated by the female partner, Ekwefi. The passion between Ekwefi and Okonkwo endures into marriage and translates, given the strength of character of the lovers, into battles of will which see Okonkwo on one occasion shooting at Ekwefi in a fit of temper. But it is clear that Okonkwo has a special relationship with Ekwefi that is qualitatively different from the relationship with his other wives. Of all Okonkwo's children, he loves Ezinma, Ekwefi's daughter, best since she reminds him of her mother, especially of her mother's strength and feistiness. Okonkwo's love for Ekwefi also shows itself in his concern and care for Ekwefi despite Okonkwo's masculine swagger. In a key episode in the novel, Okonkwo has no sleep because he spends the whole night following Ekwefi, trying to protect her. Ekwefi covertly trails the priestess who comes to fetch Ezinma since the god Agbala wishes to see the girl. Ezinma is an *ogbanje* child, a child destined for cycles of death and rebirth. Okonkwo, in turn, secretly follows Ekwefi, making numerous trips until he knows she is safe. When Ekwefi becomes aware of Okonkwo's efforts to protect her and her daughter, '[t]ears of gratitude' (p. 96) fill her eyes, triggering Ekwefi's recollection of the consummation of their love:

> Two years after her marriage to Anene she could bear it no longer and she ran away
> to Okonkwo. It had been early in the morning. The moon was shining. She was going
> to the stream to fetch water. Okonkwo's house was on the way to the stream. She went
> in and knocked at his door and he came out. Even in those days he was not a man of
> many words. He just carried her into his bed and in the darkness began to feel around
> her waist for the loose end of her cloth. (p. 96)

Ekwefi's 'adultery' and subsequent marriage to Okonkwo do not appear to provoke societal censure, and her release from her first marriage appears unproblematic. This spare but strong testament of the power of eros and its differential connection with marriage in varying cultural contexts occurs immediately before the description of the wedding ceremony, acting as another counterpoint to the 'utilitarian' marriage. The significance of childbearing to marriage is shown to be paramount in the nuptial celebration scene, with reference to the hoped-for fecundity of the marriage: 'We are giving you our daughter today. She will be a good wife to you. She will bear you nine sons like the mother of our town' (p. 103). Even though romantic love in marriage, and eros as catalyst for marriage, act as corrective counterpoints to the customary 'utilitarian' marriage, the narrative nonetheless emphasises the functional aspect of marriage through the crucial importance of procreation. It is clear that Achebe 'invents' the international African novel in such a way that love stories are embedded in a narrative where more conventional political and sociocultural concerns are foregrounded. Relegating love stories to a background, requiring that they be retrieved through a focused scholarship of eros, sets the pattern for most other anglophone African novels.

  A focus on the love stories that *Things Fall Apart* allows to recede into the background throws the identified trend into relief. Through these love stories we identify instances that signify a more complex range of forms of intimate relationship, and more varied connections between love and marriage, than we find when we compare these with the modern, monogamous love-marriage plot that has come to be globally normalised, in part through romance novels. Let us return once again to Ama Ata Aidoo, who, more than any other African writer, has recognised the importance of understandings of love in a cross-cultural, rapidly transforming world. *Changes: A Love Story* allows its heroine to follow her heart without prejudice in both monogamous and polygynous marriages – only to have it broken in both. It is apt to close with the final words of Aidoo's heroine which magnify the complexities of questions of love and marriage in postcolonial Africa. Aidoo's heroine asks on behalf of contemporary African women, in particular: 'So what fashion of loving was she ever going to consider adequate?'[35]

NOTES

1. Denis de Rougemont identifies the myth of Tristan and Isolde as the archetypal western romance, where eros is intimately tied to death and the narrative drive of the romance plot is sustained by obstructions to love (*Love in the Western World* (Princeton University Press, 1983)).

2. Jose Ortega y Gasset, *On Love … Aspects of a Single Theme* (London: Jonathan Cape, 1959); Irving Singer, *The Nature of Love*, 3 vols (University of Chicago Press, 1984); Simon May, *Love: A History* (New Haven, CT: Yale University Press, 2011); Pascal Bruckner, *The Paradox of Love* (Princeton University Press, 2012); Paul A. Kottman, *Love as Human Freedom* (Stanford University Press, 2017).

3. E.g., A. O. J. Cockshutt, *Man and Woman: A Study of Love and the Novel 1740–1940* (London: Collins, 1977); Allan Bloom, *Love and Friendship* (New York: Simon & Schuster, 1993); Catherine Belsey, *Desire: Love Stories in Western Culture* (Oxford: Blackwell, 1994); Pamela Regis, *A Natural History of the Romance Novel* (Philadelphia: University of Pennsylvania Press, 2003).

4. William R. Jankowiak and Edward F. Fischer, 'A Cross-Cultural Perspective on Romantic Love', *Ethnology* 31.2 (1992), 149–55 (149–50).

5. Anthony Giddens, *The Transformation of Intimacy: Sexuality, Love and Eroticism in Modern Societies* (Cambridge: Polity, 1992), pp. 38–47.

6. Mary Evans, *Love: An Unromantic Discussion* (Cambridge: Polity, 2003), p. 1.

7. Catherine Riley, 'Romance', in Catherine Riley and Lynne Pearce, *Feminism and Women's Writing: An Introduction* (Edinburgh University Press, 2018), pp. 113–27.

8. For a discussion of these debates see Sally Goade's edited volume *Empowerment Versus Oppression: Twenty-First-Century Views of Popular Romance Novels* (Newcastle upon Tyne: Cambridge Scholars, 2007).

9. A PhD dissertation by Felicia Annin is a rare example of an extended study of romantic love in the work of a single author. 'Eros and Politics: Love and it Discontents in the Fiction of Ngũgĩ wa Thiong'o', University of the Western Cape: http://hdl.handle.net/11394/7125.

10. Lynne Pearce, *Romance Writing* (Cambridge: Polity, 2007), p. xi.

11. Ama Ata Aidoo, *Changes: A Love Story* (London: Women's Press, 1991).

12. Ama Ata Aidoo (ed.), *African Love Stories: An Anthology* (Banbury: Ayebia, 2012).

13. Ibid., p. viii.

14. Ibid., p. xi.

15. Chinua Achebe, *Things Fall Apart* (Oxford: Heinemann, 1958); subsequent references are incorporated in the main text.

16. Norman Goodman, *Marriage and the Family* (New York: HarperCollins, 1993), p. 135.

17. Transformations in ideas about love and marriage in western culture are clarified most notably in the following sociological studies: Niklas Luhmann, *Love as Passion: The Codification of Intimacy* (Cambridge: Polity, 1986); Giddens, *Transformation of Intimacy*; Ulrich Beck and Elisabeth Beck-Gernsheim *The Normal Chaos of Love* (Cambridge: Polity, 1995); and Zygmunt Baumann *Liquid Love: On the Frailty of Human Bonds* (Cambridge: Polity, 2003). Philosophical, historical and literary critical works of relevance here are Lawrence Stone, *The Family, Sex and Marriage in England 1500–1800* (London: Weidenfeld & Nicolson, 1977); Tony Tanner, *Adultery in the Novel: Contract and Transgression* (Baltimore: Johns Hopkins University Press, 1979); and Stephen Kern, *The Culture of Love: Victorians to Moderns* (Cambridge, MA: Harvard University Press, 1992).

18. These trends are broadly theorised by Elizabeth Povinelli in *The Empire of Love: Toward a Theory of Intimacy, Genealogy, and Carnality* (Durham, NJ: Duke University Press, 2006) and in the edited volume by Holly Wardlow and Jennifer S. Hirsch, *Modern Loves: The Anthropology of Romantic Courtship and Companionate Marriage* (Ann Arbor: University of Michigan Press, 2006).

19. The general trend in the African context is captured in Arthur Phillips (ed.), *Survey of African Marriage and Family Life* (Oxford University Press, 1953) and in David Parkin and David Nyamwaya (eds), *Transformations of African Marriage* (Manchester University Press, 1987).

20. Jacqueline Sarsby, *Romantic Love and Society* (Harmondsworth: Penguin, 1983), p. 3. Sarsby relies on a 1967 study by Kenneth Little and Anne Price which shows how the individual commitments of the love marriage release the couple from group obligations, but, paradoxically, also create 'new demands on the partners because of the absence of traditional support' (p. 3). The shift to the love marriage as an index of modernity and the social implications of this shift are also explored in numerous localised sociological and anthropological studies, for example, those collected in the volume, *Love in Africa*, ed. Jennifer Cole and Lynn M. Thomas (University of Chicago Press, 2009).

21. Isidore Okpewho, 'Understanding African Marriage: Towards a Convergence of Literature and Sociology', in Parkin and Nyamwaya (eds), *Transformations*, pp. 332–45.

22. Cécile Accilien, *Rethinking Marriage in Francophone African and Caribbean Literatures* (Lanham, MD: Lexington Books, 2008).

23. Joseph Allen Boone, *Tradition Counter Tradition: Love and the Form of Fiction* (University of Chicago Press, 1987). The book also analyses the counter tradition to the love-marriage plot structure as it emerges in the later nineteenth and early twentieth centuries, where women's oppression and bondage in marriage are explored in fiction.

24. Ibid., p. 33.

25. A helpful overview of the feminist critique of the marriage plot in popular romance novels, going back to Germaine Greer in the 1960s, is Pamela Regis, 'The Romance Novel and Women's Bondage', in *Natural History of the Romance Novel*, pp. 3–8.

26. Jaggi, Maya, 'Profile: Chinua Achebe – Storyteller of the Savannah', in Nana Ayebia Clarke and James Currey (eds), *Chinua Achebe: Tributes and Reflections* (Banbury: Ayebia Clarke, 2014), pp. 8–17 (p. 8).

27. Lyn Innes, 'Chinua Achebe (1930–2013): Obituary: Founding Father of African Fiction whose Novels Chronicled Nigeria's Troubled History', in Clarke and Currey (eds), *Achebe*, pp. 3–7 (p. 3).

28. Gikandi, Simon, 'Chinua Achebe and the Invention of African Culture', *Research in African Literatures* 32. 3 (2001), 3–8 (5).

29. Ibid., 5.

30. Chinua Achebe, 'An Image of Africa: Racism in Conrad's *Heart of Darkness*', *Massachusetts Review* 18.4 (1977), 782–94 (783); reprinted in Chinua Achebe, *Hopes and Impediments: Selected Essays 1965–87* (London: Heinemann, 1988), pp. 1–13.

31. Simon Gikandi, 'Between Realism and Modernism: Chinua Achebe and the Making of African Literature', in Ken Seigneurie (ed.), *A Companion to World Literature* (Hoboken, NJ: Wiley, 2019), pp. 1–10 (p. 6).

32. Ibid., p. 6.

33. In *Half of a Yellow Sun* (London: Harper Perennial, 2007), Adichie's Biafran war novel, questions of Igbo culture are highlighted, as they are in *Things Fall Apart*, in relation to colonial stereotypes, but also Igbo ethnicity as a minority identity is foregrounded in the post-independence Nigerian state. Unlike *Things Fall Apart*, where eros goes unemphasised, romantic love is set in relief by Adichie against the social background, in this case the civil war backdrop, in the relationships of the central couples, Olanna and Odenigbo, and Kainene and Richard.

34. Kiru Taye, 'Achebe's *Things Fall Apart* Fan-fiction Erotica: Thighs Fell Apart': https://brittlepaper.com/2014/02/thighs-fell-kiru-taye-fall-fan-fiction-erotica/ (accessed 11 February 2022).

35. Aidoo, *Changes*, p. 198.

CRITICAL REFLECTIONS AND FURTHER STUDY

It is clear that studying romantic love in African forms of cultural expression is a relatively open field when compared with scholarship of sexuality in African literature and culture, which is an area that has received considerable scholarly attention. Because eros has been understudied, there are not many small focused studies, nor big cultural-historical overviews that could be recommended for further study. Usually in scholarship, one refers to oneself as a dwarf standing on the shoulders of giants. In this case, there are neither many dwarves nor any giants, so one is left with the anxiety (or the excitement) of creating a field oneself. The novel selected for analysis in the preceding essay is sub-Saharan. However, if one opens up the terrain to arabophone Africa – for example, Egypt, Morocco and Libya – or to the

Horn of Africa, through Ethiopia and Somalia, the plethora of primary texts, questions and trends becomes even wider.

A number of preliminary nodes of enquiry present themselves: if one considers the early African anglophone writers of the late 1950s and 1960s, there are a number of very interesting works that suggest radically different conceptions of love, especially in its relationship with marriage. Many of these works are Nigerian since Nigeria was an early African literary 'powerhouse'. Novels that come to mind include Elechi Amadi's *The Concubine* (1966) and the early novels (*Efuru* (1966) and *Idu* (1970)) of Flora Nwapa, the first published African woman writer. These novels, and there will be others if the bookshelves are carefully scrutinised, seem to rewrite assumptions about love, marriage, monogamy and polygyny. The relative merits of love, as experienced in monogamy and polygyny, for the 'modern' African woman are examined, as noted in my essay, in Ama Ata Aidoo's *Changes: A Love Story* (1991), and transcultural conceptions of love and marriage are projected on to a world stage in many of the novels of Egyptian writer, Ahdaf Soueif. But doubtless there are many other works of fiction that explore these questions, inviting analysis through the multiple points of entry opened up by romantic love, of which the link with marriage is only one.

Ama Ata Aidoo's edited volume, *African Love Stories* (2006), also demands further attention. The volume includes short stories by Sudanese-Scottish writer Leila Aboulela and Nigerian-American celebrity writer Chimamanda Ngozi Adichie, but also short fiction by many other women writers. The approach to eros in these short stories is very varied and could certainly generate interesting observations. To return to Aboulela's and Adichie's writing more generally, both these authors introduce questions of transnationality into their narratives which seem disproportionately to revolve around romantic relationships. Aboulela's most well-known novel, *The Translator* (1999), explores the emotional conflict of a young Sudanese woman of Islamic faith, who falls in love with a Scottish professor. Here we see the possibility presented by love of drawing people together across literal borders, as well as across religious and cultural divisions. Adichie's great African romance of the twenty-first century is also a great transnational romance. *Americanah* (2013) seems to require the identity transformations effected by the diasporic experiences of the heroine in America and the hero in England in order for the obstructions to their relationship to be removed. Some male twentieth-century African writers who bring romantic love out of the shadows include the well-known British-Nigerian writer Ben Okri. Okri's novel *Dangerous Love* (1996) opens a range of intriguing questions, as does the novel *Season of Crimson Blossoms* (2015), by Hausa Nigerian writer Abubakar Adam Ibrahim.

The growth of popular romance imprints on the African continent is another area that would make for fruitful study. The Ankara imprint of Cassava Republic, a Nigerian publishing house, quite deliberately intervenes in African print culture to set romance in relief. The Ankara imprint produces slimline, handbag-sized hard copy love stories, but with the bulk of its sales generated through e-books. These are love stories set in Africa, with African characters, following the dreams and desires of modern, urban women. Cassava Republic additionally commissioned a number of established African writers, including the late Binyavanga Wainaina, to write short fictions for its online free-to-download Valentine's Day Anthology.

These nodes for further study are really just a few points of departure, as is the handful of relevant readings that follow. There are many, many more texts, authors, genres, periods and regions that, viewed through the lens of romantic love, may force a reconsideration of African literature – if you only follow your heart ...

FURTHER READING

Adejunmobi, Moradewun, 'Romance without Borders: Narrating Love, Femininity, and the Local in Contemporary Ivory Coast', in *Vernacular Palaver: Imaginations of the Local and Non-native Languages in West Africa* (Bristol: Multilingual Matters, 2004), pp. 131–63

Davis, Emily, 'Romance as Political Aesthetic in Ahdaf Soueif's *Map of Love*', *Genders* 45 (2007), n.p.

Emecheta, Buchi, 'Feminism with a Small "f"!', in Kirsten Holst Petersen (ed.), *Criticism and Ideology: Second African Writers' Conference, Stockholm, 1986* (Uppsala: Scandinavian Institute of African Studies, 1988), pp. 173–81

Moolla, F. Fiona, '"Foundational Fictions": Variations of the Marriage Plot in Flora Nwapa's Early Anglophone-Igbo Novels', in Moradewun Adejunmobi and Carli Coetzee (eds), *Routledge Handbook of African Literature* (London: Routledge, 2019), pp. 290–304

Moolla, F. Fiona, 'Love in a State of Fear: Reflections on Intimate Relations in Nuruddin Farah's Dictatorship Novels', *Journal of the African Literature Association* 10.1 (2016), 118–30

Newell, Stephanie, *Ghanaian Popular Fiction: "Thrilling Discoveries in Conjugal Life" & Other Tales* (Oxford: James Currey, 2000)

Obiechina, Emmanuel, *An African Popular Literature: A Study of Onitsha Market Pamphlets* (Cambridge University Press, 1973)

Sommer, Doris, *Foundational Fictions: The National Romances of Latin America* (Berkeley: University of California Press, 1991)

28 Bessie Head's Feminism of Everyday Life

LORETTA STEC

Abstract

Rather than address the violence and exploitation of apartheid in South Africa directly, Bessie Head forged a literary focus and style that foreground the everyday lives of ordinary people, particularly women, in her country of exile, Botswana. Her works critique not only colonialist modernity but also rigid, patriarchal village traditions that subordinate women and smother individual desires. Throughout her works, but particularly in her short stories in *Tales of Tenderness and Power* and *The Collector of Treasures*, and her oral history *Serowe: Village of the Rain Wind*, Head illustrates that everyday acts of caring, neighbourliness and creativity form an alternative system of values that resists and exceeds the established order imposed from above, whether traditional village structures or capitalist modernity. The field of 'everyday life studies' – especially the work of Michel de Certeau and numerous feminist thinkers – illuminates how Head's work performs its critiques by focusing on the micro-politics of the everyday. Head anticipated debates within literary criticism in southern Africa, as her work predates the influential call by Ndebele for a 'rediscovery of the ordinary' in literature; she is surprisingly neglected in those debates. Head's works also manifest a feminism of everyday life that prepares for contemporary discourses, for example Ahmed's *Living a Feminist Life* and the websites The Everyday Sexism Project and Everyday Feminism. Through a focus on the everyday, Head's works narrate not an explicit political revolution such as 'protest literature' might call for, but figure a more subtle method of resistance that allows ordinary people to survive (and sometimes thrive) despite multiple systems of oppression.

In her volume of oral history about Serowe, the village in Botswana where she lived for the latter part of her life, Bessie Head criticises 'white historians' for their representation of African history as a series of 'petty tribal wars'.[1] Head explains that rather than rewriting the stories of war and conquest directly,[2] 'My own work concentrated more on the everyday world'.[3] This statement summarises Head's literary project through much of her career; in novels, short stories, essays, journalism, oral history and works difficult to categorise[4] she often focused on what she called 'the endless round of ordinary village life'.[5] While other writers from the calamitous milieu of apartheid South Africa tackled racial politics and histories head-on in 'protest writing', Head critiqued the oppressive rationalist/capitalist/colonial regime of modernity by forging a literary mode that emphasised 'the everyday'. In particular, she represented the everyday tribulations and joys of women characters, and her writing manifests what numerous critics have interpreted as a feminist apprehension of everyday life[6] – even as Head distanced herself from the feminist movement. Head's writing forges worlds in which women help each other to survive, materially and emotionally, and in so doing to evade, exceed and arguably resist not only the structures of modernity manifest in the apartheid era of her youth but also the patriarchal systems of traditional village life. Contemporary cultural theorists, especially Michel de Certeau, focus on the 'everyday' as a potential site of 'silent and unacknowledged forms of resistance' that 'break through the grid of the established order'.[7] Head is among those who can be seen as optimistic about the power of everyday practices to constitute a realm of non-alienation, a space of creativity and care beyond the 'vast external disciplines' of precolonial traditions[8] under which 'the people lived without faces',[9] or the oppressive structures of capitalist modernity under apartheid.

Many critical works on Bessie Head begin with biography as particularly important to understanding her work. Bessie Amelia Emery – named after her mother – was the child of a wealthy white woman in South Africa who, after becoming pregnant by an unidentified black man, was institutionalised in a psychiatric hospital, and gave birth to her daughter there in 1937. When Head was thirteen, she learned that she was mistaken about her foster parents being her birth family, and that her biological 'mother had been insane and [her] father was "a native"'.[10] When Bessie Head was a teenager, South Africa was codifying the oppressive system of apartheid and passed legislation prohibiting marriage and sexual intimacy across racial categories through the Mixed Marriages Act (1949) and the Immorality Act (1950).[11] The news of her origins had designated her doubly illegitimate: a child born out of wedlock, and a product of parents forced to inhabit opposing racial categories.

As an adult, Head lived in major cities in South Africa – Durban, Cape Town and Johannesburg – and was subjected to the full force of the apartheid regime as a 'Coloured' woman. She wrote comparatively little about her experiences living under apartheid, summing them up in an essay in 1978: 'Our only education in South Africa, as black people, is a political one. We learn bitterly, every day, the details of oppression and exploitation.'[12] With her marriage to fellow journalist Harold Head in trouble, and their son, Howard, about to turn two, Bessie Head left South Africa on a one-way exit visa in 1964 to take up a teaching post in Bechuanaland, which would gain independence two years later and become Botswana.

She was now a stateless refugee and a single mother. Despite experiencing years of alienation from the community in Botswana, and suffering a complete breakdown in 1971,[13] Head wrote that she eventually found refuge in the village of Serowe: 'I have lived most of my life in shattered little bits. Somehow, here, the shattered bits began to grow together. There is a sense of ... wholeness in life here; a feeling of how strange and beautiful people can be – just living' (Figure 28.1).[14]

Head's aesthetic choices, to write about people 'just living' their everyday lives, not under the oppressive conditions of apartheid but in a rural village in Botswana, emerge out of the circumstances of her exile. In an oft-quoted paragraph from 'Some Notes on Novel Writing', Head explains her resistance to writing with an explicit political focus, for in South Africa 'a writer automatically feels pressured into taking a political stand of some kind or identifying with a camp. It was important to my development to choose a broader platform for my work, so I have avoided political camps and ideologies because I feel that they falsify truth.'[15] Despite a brief involvement with the Pan-Africanist Congress in 1960,[16] Head kept her distance from political organisations and ideologies. About the detriment to her writing career the extreme conditions of apartheid had caused, she declared: 'You can't think straight about anything if you're hating all the time.'[17]

Figure 28.1 Women from a village near Serowe, Botswana, collecting water, 1950.

The desire to keep distance from 'political camps and ideologies' extended to the feminist movement as well: 'Fearful of any movement's exclusionist practices and of being conceptually boxed in, she eschewed being celebrated as a feminist icon'.[18] Head remarked in a letter to Alice Walker: 'When you are truly alone and unpampered ... the question of women's lib does not even arise. You just do everything for yourself and every now and then a male buddy knocks in a nail you can't reach'.[19] Even in her erasure of the concept of 'women's lib', Head emphasises a domestic task that illustrates the labour of everyday life. The comment presumes women's independence and competence – 'you just do everything for yourself' – while admitting that on occasion one needs a little help, an arm that extends beyond one's own reach. In that sense, the everyday detail flowers into metaphor: why can't the woman reach what she needs to build or repair? Where is the ladder that would suffice? Is this a metaphor about power and/or sex? Why does she need a 'male buddy' to knock in a nail when a tall female friend might do just as well? Perhaps this is an inadvertent or sly way of Head admitting the limitations women experience in a patriarchal society. She claims: 'I am not a feminist ... in the sense that I do not view women in isolation from men';[20] she rejects separatism,[21] and illuminates an overarching patriarchal system based on binary gender categories. In the realm of feminist theories of the everyday, one finds a 'shift of everydayness to micro-politics' which challenges 'politics previously taken for granted'.[22] While Head clearly rejects the category 'feminist', her writing nevertheless offers an analysis of the micro-politics of the everyday that functions as a critique of traditional village patriarchy as well as of the oppressive and gendered structures of capitalist modernity.

The work of Michel de Certeau (and his collaborators Luce Giard and Pierre Mayol) provides an influential and relatively optimistic perspective on the power dynamics of everyday life.[23] He responds most broadly in his theories to conditions of European capitalist modernity, and argues that ordinary people are not passive consumers of the products of late capitalism, but rather, through acts of consumption, demonstrate 'subtle moments of creativity and festivity within the delicate skein of everyday life as it [is] actually experienced'.[24] While ordinary people in Europe have their lives organised by 'late capitalism', they nonetheless have the power to 'subvert the structures of power in the less visible and nonconfrontational ways that are available to them'.[25] This analytical paradigm can be extended to the fictional worlds Bessie Head creates as de Certeau also references colonialism, by arguing, for example, that the indigenous cultures colonised by the Spanish in the New World 'subverted' the colonial system 'from within'.[26] For de Certeau, 'strategies', or the dominant system of a given society, 'produce, tabulate and impose', while 'tactics', or the creative actions of ordinary people, 'use, manipulate, and divert' the system from within.[27] Bessie Head illustrates in her writing subtle moments of connection between women that take place within the overarching strategies of traditional village life, of capitalist modernity or of a mixture of both that can be seen as a deployment of 'tactics' as de Certeau defines the term.

'The Woman from America', a short, generically hybrid piece that helped to launch Head's international career, describes a woman from America who has married a man from Serowe and arrived in the village with 'the wind of freedom' swirling about her.[28] The narrator says this woman 'loves both Africa and America ... She can take what she wants from both and say: "Dammit." It is a most strenuous and difficult thing to do' (p. 36). The woman from America is characterised as heroic, and yet the narrator does not present heroic acts; rather, she emphasises the 'short notes written in a wide sprawling hand' (p. 33) that she receives from the woman regularly, notes which constitute neighbourliness and solidarity. These notes complain of domestic tasks: 'I'm all fagged out from sweeping and cleaning the yard, shaking blankets, cooking, fetching water, bathing children, and there's still the floor inside to sweep and dishes to wash and myself to bathe – it's endless!' (p. 34). The notes also give advice, discuss cooking, and describe quotidian dilemmas that form a bond with her reader – the narrator – but also with Head's reader. 'Have you an extra onion to give me until tomorrow?' begins one such note, and the ordinariness and concreteness of that 'extra onion', tied to the everyday acts of cooking and eating, manifests and symbolises 'the creative practices of daily life that rely on the logic of the "gift" rather than of exchange'[29] and thereby potentially evade the domination of either a patriarchal or a capitalist rationality.[30] The everyday notes that the women in Head's piece exchange, these bits of writing designed for sharing but not publication, nevertheless wind up being published by Bessie Head and enter the circuits of cosmopolitan print culture. 'The Woman from America' illustrates the lives of these women as within the dominant systems that structure everyday life: women are still performing the reproductive labour necessary for society to continue; as feminist political theorist Silvia Federici provocatively summarises 'the attributes of femininity are in effect work functions'.[31] Simultaneously, Head reveals that everyday life, particularly among women, has the potential to evade imposed strategies from above by creating an alternate set of relationships (neighbourly), values (gifts) and rhythms (caring, self-reflexive notes exchanged regularly) that exceed their work functions.

Head emphasised the everyday from the earliest phase of her career as a journalist.[32] During her first job as a reporter with the weekly tabloid *Golden City Post* in Cape Town, 'sordid court cases and scandalous incidents were not [her] forte at all'.[33] Her editor remembered her preferring to write 'sensitive' pieces.[34] After relocating to the *Golden City Post* office in Johannesburg, Head became acquainted with many of the writers for *Drum* magazine,[35] the publication crucial in shifting journalistic discourse about black Africans from a rhetoric of 'rural life and tribal traditions' to one of urban modernity.[36] *Drum* addressed burgeoning apartheid in the 1950s with exposés about prison conditions, farm labour, exclusion of black people from Dutch Reformed churches, as well as in hard-boiled short stories that represented life in the urban townships; the *Golden City Post* ran sensationalised stories on 'prostitution, adultery, and the behavior of "bad girls"'.[37] Bessie Head sidestepped both types of journalism to write articles and an advice column directed at young readers.[38] In her posthumously published first novel, *The Cardinals*, the protagonist Mouse similarly runs into trouble with her editor: 'She's a talented writer, but definitely not a news reporter.'[39]

Allusions to the urban life of Johannesburg do appear in some of Head's stories, most pointedly in 'Life', from *The Collector of Treasures*. The character, Life, migrates with her parents from a Botswana village to Johannesburg when she is a child. When she returns to her birth village years later, the women who would be her neighbours say 'kindly': 'we can help you to put your yard in order'.[40] And they do, fixing the walls, hoeing the ground, and making the hut habitable. However, these respectable women begin to shun Life when they realise how much of Johannesburg she has brought back to the village. In South Africa, Life had been 'a singer, beauty queen, advertising model, and prostitute' (p. 39), and it does not take her long to begin to commodify herself, and sell sex to male villagers. The independent 'beer-brewing women' begin to frequent Life's yard, with its continuous party. They remain even after Life marries Lesego, a cattle-man who reminds her of the 'Johannesburg gangsters she had associated with' (p. 41). When Lesego discovers her having sex with another man, he kills her with a knife 'he used for slaughtering cattle' (p. 45). The white judge sentences him to only five years in prison, claiming the murder was 'a crime of passion' (p. 46).

This summary outlines a lurid and sensational tale. The story foregrounds, however, the traditions and habits of village life, and the numerous ways in which the character Life is unsuited for those everyday actions. On the one hand, the narrator tells us that Life falls 'into the yawn' (p. 43) of her married life, unable to cope with 'the everyday round of village life [that] was deadly dull in its even, unbroken monotony ... drawing water, stamping corn, cooking food' (p. 43). But the narrator makes clear that the imposed grid of women's daily tasks is not Life's undoing. Rather, what she lacks 'inside herself' is the ability to be emotionally sensitive and sympathetic to other people: 'People care about each other, and all day long there was this constant traffic of people in and out of each other's lives. Someone had to be buried; sympathy and help were demanded ... there were money loans, newborn babies, sorrow, trouble, gifts' (p. 43). In the interstices of the 'deadly dull' reproductive labour of the everyday, citizens of the village, especially the women, have the opportunity to be creative in their neighbourliness and care for one another. Life simply makes and spends money, and that is not enough in the fictional world

that Bessie Head creates. The cosmopolitan narrator of the tale critiques capitalist commodification, the functioning of patriarchal power in the village, and the
legacies of colonialism personified in the white judge while praising the 'basic
strength of village life' that is care for others.[41]

Head's most famous tale, 'The Collector of Treasures', features another murder, but again foregrounds neighbourly relations as a source of strength, care
and creativity in the face of the 'grid' of patriarchal and capitalist strategies.
The story opens with the character Dikeledi being transported to prison for having killed her abusive husband by castrating him. Before the tale flashes back
to past incidents that have brought Dikeledi to this pass, the narrator provides
an overview of South African history that reads like an essay in the middle of
a short story. The three phases of this history are 'before the colonial invasion',
'the colonial era and the period of migratory mining labour to South Africa',
and the period of independence.[42] These developments lead to 'only two kinds
of men in society', the brutal and empty man, and the man who has 'the power
to create himself anew' (pp. 91–3). Garesego is the first kind of man, who drinks,
womanises and abuses his wife Dikeledi. He abandons the family, and the talented and creative Dikeledi supports her three sons for years through sewing
and other skilled work; she is the 'woman whose thatch does not leak' (p. 90).
Eventually a new family moves next door to Dikeledi, and they become enmeshed in each other's everyday lives in a 'quiet rhythm of work and friendship'
(p. 98). The everyday actions and cooperation of these neighbours are characterised in this story as idyllic.

The dramatic crisis occurs when Dikeledi does not have sufficient funds to
pay for the school fees of the oldest son, and she approaches her estranged
husband to take responsibility. Instead of offering help, Garesego returns to
Dikeledi's yard to demand she serve him, with food, a hot bath and sex, while
displaying 'no interest in the children whatsoever' (p. 102). Finding the circumstances of her abuse intolerable, Dikeledi uses 'the precision and skill of her
hard-working hands' to slice off his genitals, and she is duly convicted of man-
slaughter (p. 103). Despite the extreme disciplinary grid of the prison, Dikeledi
finds that her cellmates have committed similar crimes, and that they offer her
kindness and companionship. Again, what Head highlights is the 'daily routine'
of the prison: cell clean-up, breakfast, inspection, 'daily work' of sewing and
knitting, 'lock-up time' and the rolling out of blankets for sleep. One character
says 'it's not so bad here' and the narrator reports that 'the day passed pleas-
antly enough' (pp. 90–1). Daymond argues that the community of women in
prison is 'defensive and compensatory [and] has no future'.[43] While the prison
walls are not torn down, nor patriarchy destroyed, Daymond's interpretation
diminishes the metaphorical resonance of the community of women within
the prison. Hemmed in by the grid of pre-colonial gender hierarchy, colonial/

capitalist inequities and disenfranchisement in the world of post-independence Botswana, these women are represented as having found solace and creativity in interpersonal relationships within the cell block that are structured by everyday activities in common. Given that disciplinary grids are difficult to undo, Head provides a relatively optimistic vision of women's solidarity, outside the prison in everyday neighbourliness, and inside the prison in mutual concern during collective daily activities. The reader witnesses, rather than revolution, an imaginative space in which women can deploy tactics to subvert the prison strategy, and thereby help each other to survive.

If 'The Collector of Treasures' could be considered a species of literary realism representing post-independence conditions, despite the melodramatic castration upon which the plot hangs, then Head's short story 'The Lovers' retells a Botswana folktale and in the process critiques traditional social arrangements that persist despite colonialism and independence. The retelling of the Botswana folk tale occurs in the colonial language of English with echoes of European stories such as Aesop's 'Androcles and the Lion', as well as the story of Romeo and Juliet. 'The Lovers' tells the tale of a young man, Keaja, and young woman, Tselane, who meet unexpectedly in a cave during a rainstorm; Keaja removes a thorn from Tselane's foot. Eventually they break the very strict taboos of traditional village life, and Tselane becomes pregnant. They realise that to tell their parents about their love is to 'invite death or worse', for, in this traditional society, 'the individual was completely smothered by communal and social demands'.[44]

Once their story becomes public, the village endures 'a week of raging storms and wild irrational deliberations' (p. 99). The second wife of Tselane's father, Mma-Monosi, described as emotionally sensitive and somewhat 'precariously balanced' (p. 89), walks 'grief-stricken' to the hill to which the lovers have retreated and witnesses 'the whole drama of [their] disappearance ... re-created before her eyes'. Among 'loud groans of anguish', 'the rocks parted and a gaping hole appeared' into which the lovers sank (p. 100). While some readings of the story imply that the vision may be due to Mma-Monosi's 'hysterical' reaction to the disappearance,[45] the narrator reports that strangers to the area see the same vision. The narrator designates this fate 'horrible' (p. 100).

In her retelling of the traditional cautionary tale, Head creates a narrative that presents with ambivalence a traditional society whose structures are so rigid that there is no place for the personal love of Keaja and Tselane. The story appears to value exactly that affection missing from the marriages of both Keaja's and Tselane's parents. The story grounds its representation of the village in details of everyday life – Keaja returning from the cattle lands to bring 'gourds of milk for his family'; the rhythms of planting, hoeing, and harvesting; the visits of women to Tselane's mother's hut to receive herbal medicine; the village girls' trips to gather wood (pp. 88–94). The repetition of these activities creates 'a community [that] proceeded from day to day in peace and harmony' and yet the narrator points out that this occurs at the expense of 'personal unhappiness' being 'smothered and subdued' (p. 93). The 'laws of the ancestors' are characterised as 'vast external disciplines' riddled with 'errors', including, most importantly for Head, the subordination of women as 'an inferior form of human life'.[46] Head's retelling of the myth begins to correct traditional 'errors' in part through the everyday actions and love between Tselane and her father's second wife, Mma-Monosi, even as the structure of the mythic, heterosexual plot remains.

During their life together in Tselane's father's compound, Tselane and Mma-Monosi forge a 'free and happy relationship' and treat 'each other as equals'. In a powerfully heterosexual tale, the domestic relationship between these two women exceeds the strict and distanced relationships between married couples, and between most parents and children represented in the story. Mma-Monosi and Tselane habitually work together in the fields 'tending their crops'; Tselane shares questions and details about her life with Mma-Monosi. Even though Mma-Monosi appears to support conventional taboos – 'it is no light matter to break custom' – she makes a statement of extreme love and support for Tselane after learning of her relationship with Keaja: 'I am your friend and I will die for you. No one will injure you while I am alive' (pp. 97–9). The closeness of these two female characters built upon their everyday 'hard work' (p. 89) together illustrates that emotional closeness, warmth, support and love can survive in the easy and affectionate relationship between women despite the 'smothering' of traditional village life.

In addition to the fiction Head wrote that 'concentrated ... on the everyday world',[47] her oral history *Serowe: Village of the Rain Wind* illustrates everyday rhythms in the words of village inhabitants. This volume uses as its overarching structure a kind of 'great man history' model, dividing the phases of Botswana history via the rulers Khama the Great (1875–1923) and his son Tshekedi Khama (1926–59), and the educator and cooperative community leader Patrick van Rensburg (1963 to the volume's publication in 1981). Within that overarching structure, however, the interviews Head transcribed focus largely on the everyday lives of ordinary people: dressmaker, farmer, tanner, pot maker, cattleman, school teacher, gardener, textile weaver, etc. In this ethnographic text, Head presents a portrait of the everyday lives of villagers for nearly a century. This invaluable work not only functions as history from below but promotes social organisation that exceeds the structures of capitalist/colonial modernity that were unfolding during that century. For example, a potter, Mmatsela Ditshego, who works with a collective in Serowe, contrasts her experience with that of workers in a pottery factory in Zimbabwe: 'The people working there were limited to the job they were doing. A glazer was glazing all the time. A potter never moved away from the wheel ... I have had to learn everything, from digging out the clay to sticking on the price ticket. I think of myself as a skilled person.'[48] The grid of alienated labour oppresses the worker, but even within a system that ultimately aims to sell items created in the collective, Head highlights how everyday labour has the potential to be non-alienated, creative, skilled.

Given this long career of focusing on the everyday and its potential to exceed the disciplinary grids of village traditions as well as colonial/capitalist modernity, it is instructive to realise that Head's contribution to Southern African literature has been neglected in some of the most important critical conversations about aesthetics and politics since the 1980s. Njabulo Ndebele, South African critic and scholar, jump-started a debate in 1984 with his keynote address 'The Rediscovery of the Ordinary: Some New Writings in South Africa'.[49] This talk (along with other essays in a subsequent volume) argues that South African literature of the 1980s fits primarily within the category of 'protest literature', and as such exemplifies a literature of 'spectacle',[50] where 'subtlety is avoided' and the emphasis is on a 'spectacular contest between the powerless and the powerful'.[51] Ndebele calls for South African literature to move beyond the spectacular, and to focus instead on 'the ordinary daily lives of people' and the 'active social consciousness of most people'.[52] O'Brien, drawing in part on scholarly work by Daymond, argues that 'Head's writings stand in an exemplary relation to Ndebele's theory of black fiction, which seems to owe a lot to them'.[53] Head herself asserted in 1979: 'Literature is very functional in Southern Africa and bound inextricably to human suffering; the death of South African literature is that it is almost blinded by pain; people hardly exist beside the pain'.[54] In a manner that comports well with the type of fiction Ndebele subsequently called for, Head devoted much of her career to narrating people 'just living'.

Head's work anticipates certain contemporary feminist theories as well, and resonates with Sara Ahmed's recent volume *Living a Feminist Life*.[55] Ahmed details how everyday life is for many the sphere of subtle and not so subtle experiences of sexism, racism and violence.[56] Her volume meditates on choices one might make to live as a feminist, for 'crafting a life is political work'.[57] As we saw, Bessie Head's work does not explicitly call for or narrate a wholesale or revolutionary overturning of the systems within which we live our lives. Rather, she illustrates the systems within which we are entangled every day, and focuses on how her characters resist those systems through quotidian acts of care, compassion and creativity. Ahmed explains: 'It is not necessarily the case that ... struggles always lead to transformation (though neither does one's involvement in political movements). But to struggle against something is to chip away at something'.[58] The tactics Head's characters enact make very imperfect worlds survivable, and make a case to her readers that 'We need each other to survive; we need to be part of each other's survival ... Survival can be protest'.[59] Bessie Head's *œuvre* offers us a feminism of the everyday.

NOTES

For help with this essay, many thanks to Deborah Gussman, Sara Hackenberg, Lee Hammel and Michael McKinney.

1. Bessie Head, *Serowe: Village of the Rain Wind* (Oxford: Heinemann, 1981), p. 67.

2. The final work published during her lifetime, the historical novel *A Bewitched Crossroad* (1984), tells the story of the founding of the Bechuanaland Protectorate. Craig MacKenzie calls it 'valuable as an Afrocentric reappraisal of the history of the southern African region'. 'Bessie Head', in Paul A. Scanlon (ed.), *Dictionary of Literary Biography, vol. 225, South African Writers* (Farmington Hills, MI: Cengage Gale, 2000), pp. 205–12.

3. Head, *Serowe*, p. 67.

4. Head's most famous work, *A Question of Power* (1973), chronicles the psychological breakdown of its protagonist Elizabeth. While the plot includes everyday village activities of communal gardening, the novel is more concerned with the interior life and presents hallucinatory sequences as well as realistic passages. Her novels *When Rain Clouds Gather* (1968) and *Maru* (1971) take as their subjects the refugee experience and the oppression of the Basarwa in Botswana respectively.

5. Head, *Serowe*, p. 125.

6. M. J. Daymond, 'Inventing Gendered Traditions: The Short Stories of Bessie Head and Miriam Tlali', in M. J. Daymond (ed.), *South African Feminisms: Writing, Theory, and Criticism 1990–1994* (New York: Garland, 1996), pp. 223–39; Shiera S. el-Malik, 'Against Epistemic Totalitarianism: The Insurrectional Politics of Bessie Head', *Journal of Contemporary African Studies: Writers and Social Thought in Africa* 32 (2014), 493–505; Linda Susan Beard, 'Bessie Head's Syncretic Fictions: The Reconceptualization of Power and the Recovery of the Ordinary', *Modern Fiction Studies*, special issue, *Postcolonial African Fiction* 37.3 (1991), 575–89; Anthony O'Brien, *Against Normalization: Writing Radical Democracy in Africa* (Durham, NJ : Duke University Press, 2001).

7. Michael E. Gardiner, *Critiques of Everyday Life* (New York and London: Routledge, 2000), p. 168.

8. Bessie Head, 'The Collector of Treasures', in *The Collector of Treasures and Other Botswana Tales* (Oxford: Heinemann, 1977), pp. 87–103 (p. 92).

9. Bessie Head, 'The Deep River', in *Collector of Treasures*, pp. 1–6 (p. 1).

10. Gillian Stead Eilersen, *Bessie Head: Thunder behind Her Ears: Her Life and Writing* (Cape Town and Johannesburg: David Philip, 1995), p. 24.

11. William Beinart, *Twentieth-Century South Africa* (Oxford University Press, 2001), p. 147.

12. Bessie Head, 'Some Notes on Novel Writing', in Craig MacKenzie (ed.), *A Woman Alone: Autobiographical Writings* (Portsmouth, NH: Heinemann, 1990), p. 63.

13. Eilersen, *Bessie Head*, pp. 134–9.

14. Head, *Serowe*, p. x.

15. Head, 'Some Notes', p. 63.

16. Eilersen, *Bessie Head*, pp. 46–9.

17. Bessie Head, 'Letter from South Africa', in MacKenzie (ed.), *Woman Alone*, p. 14.

18. Stephane Robolin, *Grounds of Engagement: Apartheid-Era African American and South African Writing* (Urbana: University of Illinois Press, 2015), p. 116.

19. Quoted in Eilersen, *Bessie Head*, p. 237.

20. Ibid., p. 240.

21. Eilersen asserts that when travelling in Europe, Head 'met many women in love with each other and in her opinion they confused these emotions with the idea of women's liberation' (ibid., p. 238). Robolin says that Head 'subscribed to a very rigid, heterosexual code and was subject to flashes of homophobia', but that some of her friendships, especially with lesbians, might be seen to mitigate her 'sexual conservatism' (*Grounds of Engagement*, p. 116).

22. Simona de Simoni, '"Everyday Life": A Feminist Analysis', trans. Elisabeth Paquette, *Viewpoint Magazine* (12 February 2015): https://www.viewpointmag.com/2015/02/12/everyday-life-a-feminist-analysis/.

23. Gardiner calls de Certeau the 'least pessimistic' of the postmodern and post-structuralist theorists (*Critiques*, p. 168). Susan Fraiman lauds his 'political optimism relative to Foucault: 'Everyday Life Studies and Feminism', in Tasha Oren and Andrea Press (eds), *The Routledge Handbook of Contemporary Feminisms* (London: Routledge, 2019), pp. 113–26 (p. 120).

24. Gardiner, *Critiques*, p. 164.

25. Ibid., p. 171.

26. Michel de Certeau, *The Practice of Everyday Life*, trans. Steven F. Rendall (Berkeley: University of California Press, 1984), p. 32.

27. Ibid., p. 30.

28. Bessie Head, 'The Woman from America', reprinted in MacKenzie (ed.), *Woman Alone*, pp. 31–6 (p. 35); subsequent references are incorporated in the main text. See Eilersen, *Bessie Head*, pp. 80 and 111 for the publication history of this piece.

29. Gardiner, *Critiques*, p. 177.

30. Fraiman asserts that 'no single figure has been seen as so plainly coextensive with everyday life as a woman caught up in cycles of cooking, cleaning, and caring for her family' ('Everyday Life Studies', p. 115); she analyses at length (pp. 119–23) Luce Giard's work on cooking in Michel de Certeau, Luce Giard and Pierre Mayol, *The Practice of Everyday Life, vol. II, Living and Cooking*, trans. Timothy J. Tomasik (Minneapolis: University of Minnesota Press, 1998).

31. Quoted in Simoni, '"Everyday Life"'.

32. Barbara Green in *Feminist Periodicals and Daily Life: Women and Modernity in British Culture* (Houndmills: Palgrave Macmillan, 2017) asserts that 'the newspaper offers a signal example of sensationalizing discourse against which the everyday can be measured' (p. 13).

33. Eilersen, *Bessie Head*, p. 39.

34. Ibid.

35. Ibid., p. 42.

36. R. Neville Choonoo, 'The Sophiatown Generation: Black Literary Journalism during the 1950's', in Les Switzer (ed.), *South Africa's Alternative Press: Voices of Protest and Resistance, 1880s–1960s* (Cambridge University Press, 1997), pp. 252–65 (p. 257).

37. Ibid., p. 258.

38. Eilersen, *Bessie Head*, p. 41.

39. Bessie Head, *The Cardinals with Meditations and Stories*, ed. M. J. Daymond (Cape Town: David Philip, 1993), p. 27. In her introduction Daymond also emphasises that Head prefers 'the radiance of ordinary daily life' to sensationalised, urban news (p. viii).

40. Bessie Head, 'Life', in *The Collector of Treasures and Other Botswana Tales* (Oxford: Heinemann, 1977), pp. 37–46 (p. 38); subsequent references are incorporated in the main text.

41. Daymond makes a similar point in 'Inventing Gendered Traditions', p. 232.

42. Bessie Head, 'The Collector of Treasures', in *The Collector of Treasures and Other Botswana Tales* (Oxford: Heinemann, 1977), pp. 87–103 (pp. 91–2); subsequent references are incorporated in the main text.

43. Daymond, 'Inventing Gendered Traditions', p. 231.

44. Bessie Head, 'The Lovers', *Tales of Tenderness and Power* (Oxford: Heinemann, 1989), pp. 84–101 (pp. 97, 93); subsequent references are incorporated in the main text.

45. Sara Constantakis, 'Overview: "The Lovers"', in Sara Constantakis (ed.), *Short Stories for Students*, Gale Virtual Reference Library 33 (Farmington Hills, MI: Cengage Gale, 2011).

46. Head, 'Collector of Treasures', p. 92.

47. Head, *Serowe*, p. 67.

48. Ibid., p. 176.

49. Reprinted in Njabulo S. Ndebele, 'Rediscovery of the Ordinary', in *Rediscovery of the Ordinary: Essays on South African Literature and Culture* (Scottsville: University of Kwa-Zulu-Natal Press, 1991), pp. 31–54.

50. While Ndebele does not reference Guy Debord's *Society of the Spectacle* (1983), Dorothy Driver asserts that his theories 'bear some relation' to Debord's work, as seems quite evident. Dorothy Driver, '"On These Premises I am the Government": Njabulo Ndebele's *The Cry of Winnie Mandela* and the Reconstructions of Gender and Nation', in Maria Olaussen and Christina Angelfors (eds), *Africa Writing Europe: Opposition, Juxtaposition, Entanglement* (Amsterdam: Rodopi, 2009), pp. 1–38.

51. Ndebele, 'Rediscovery of the Ordinary', p. 38.

52. Ibid., pp. 49, 52.

53. O'Brien, *Against Normalization*, pp. 54–5, 236.

54. Bessie Head, 'Social and Political Pressures that Shape Southern African Writing', in MacKenzie (ed.), *Woman Alone*, pp. 65–72 (p. 67).

55. Sara Ahmed, *Living a Feminist Life* (Durham, NC: Duke University Press, 2017).

56. See also the Everyday Sexism Project, https://everydaysexism.com/ and the online information platform and magazine Everyday Feminism, https://everydayfeminism.com/.

57. Ahmed, *Living a Feminist Life*, p. 227.

58. Ibid., p. 214.

59. Ibid., pp. 235–7.

CRITICAL REFLECTIONS AND FURTHER STUDY

When I started to think about this essay, I considered how Bessie Head's reputation as a feminist writer – despite her resistance to the label – rested in large part on her novel *A Question of Power*, which an early critic claimed 'almost single-handedly brought about the inward turning of the African novel' (Charles Larson quoted in MacKenzie, cited in my essay, note 2). *A Question of Power* foregrounds the visionary and hallucinatory states of the protagonist Elizabeth, and puts them in counterpoint to the everyday activities of her village, in particular collective gardening, which helps her heal from her breakdown. Drawing on previous critics' insights, I began to think about how Head invests everyday activities and relationships, particularly among women, with a healing function throughout many of her works. My goal with this project became to understand Head's work within the interdisciplinary field of 'everyday life studies' more broadly. Future research might consider aspects of 'everyday life studies' that I was unable to address in this essay and, more specifically, linkages between 'everyday life studies' and postcolonial studies. The diagrammatic constellation in Figure 28.2 indicates some of the contiguous fields of this interdisciplinary area of scholarship.

The very definition of 'the everyday' and whether or how it can be represented are fundamental questions within this field. In the literary realm, Virginia Woolf in her autobiographical 'A Sketch of the Past' (see Further Reading) contrasts the 'cotton wool of daily life' (p. 72) with 'exceptional moments' (p. 71) that typically form the subject of fiction or memoir. Woolf's career was in part an attempt to develop a literary form to chronicle 'an ordinary mind on an ordinary day' (Woolf, 'Modern Fiction', p. 160), but with the aim of finding the 'pattern hid behind the cotton wool' ('Sketch', p. 73), thereby reaching meaning in life. *Modernism, Feminism and Everyday Life* by Tara Thomson investigates this literary rethinking of the everyday among early twentieth-century writers. Some posit that any attempt to represent the 'everyday' necessarily distorts what Woolf called 'cotton wool': 'the everyday eludes our grasp and investigative systems [including language] ... because intentional scrutiny transforms

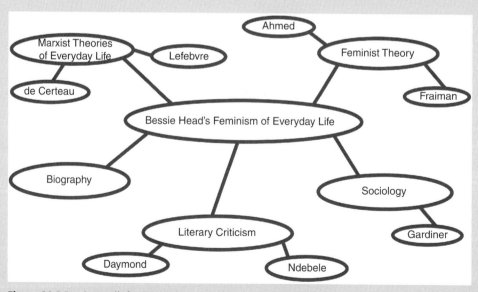

Figure 28.2 Bessie Head's feminism of everyday life: a constellation diagram.

non-event into event, inattention into some other order of awareness' (Green, *Feminist Periodicals*, p. 9; see my essay, note 32). When we shine a spotlight on elements of 'the everyday', they gain a glow which marks them out from otherwise undifferentiated experience. Thus the art of surrealism is sometimes included among modernist approaches to the everyday (see Gardiner, *Critiques of Everyday Life*, ch. 2; see essay, note 7).

Marxist theorists also approach the question of the 'everyday' and its relation to human alienation under capitalism. Henri Lefebvre's three-volume *Critique of Everyday Life* (1947, 1962 and 1981) elaborates on Marx's theory of alienation to argue that capitalist modernity in the twentieth century 'caused everyday life to degenerate' into a function of consumer society (Trebitsch, 'Introduction', p. 22). Lefebvre's critique of everyday life in modernity is twofold: 'a rejection of the inauthentic and the alienated, and an unearthing of the human which still lies buried therein' (ibid., p. 20). Michel de Certeau, who figures prominently in my reading of Bessie Head, parallels Lefebvre in articulating the spaces and acts under capitalism that evade or resist alienation and subjection. His theories outline numerous ways humans make use of the systems of capitalist modernity for their own purposes, illustrating an agency of resistance even when the system as a whole persists.

What then is the place of gender in this field of research? Green, in her rich work *Feminist Periodicals and Daily Life*, explains: 'The association of women with the mundane drudgery and routines of daily life is a central, perhaps even foundational, component of discussions of the everyday' (pp. 18–19). She points out that while Lefebvre acknowledges the importance of newspapers and the periodical press in constructing femininity (p. 11), he also succumbs to a view of women as so immersed in the everyday that 'they are incapable of understanding it' (quoted in Green, p. 19). Feminist theorists have much to say about that view, and of course understand very well the position of women in relation to 'mundane drudgery', even going so far as to perpetrate 'counterplanning from the kitchen', as one critic puts it, a 'vast storehouse of … strategies, which are by definition feminist and postcolonial' to resist capitalist and other types of exploitation (Simoni, '"Everyday Life"'; see my essay, note 22).

Within the field of postcolonial studies, anthropological and ethnographic works investigate everyday life in postcolonial situations. Examples range from Jean and John Comaroff's publications on rituals and folk belief systems in southern Africa to David Kerr's study of hip hop culture in Dar es Salaam. Many scholars in diaspora studies investigate everyday life and postcolonial identity in diasporic communities. Creative works of literature, film and the visual arts continue to provide a rich field for representations of everyday life. James Procter in 'The Postcolonial Everyday' considers the 'distaste' of postcolonial studies for the '"vulgar" world of mass consumption' and then turns his attention to a series of South Asian films set in Britain to discover a new 'English everyday life'. The field of 'everyday life studies' is vast and waiting to be more fully explored, especially by literary scholars.

FURTHER READING

Comaroff, Jean, and John Comaroff (eds), *Modernity and Its Malcontents: Ritual and Power in Postcolonial Africa* (University of Chicago Press, 1993)

Kerr, David, 'Thugs and Gangsters: Imagination and the Practice of Rapping in Dar Es Salaam', in *Suomen Antropologi* 42.2 (2017), 10–24: https://journal.fi/suomenantropoligi/article/view/65792.

Lefebvre, Henri, *Critique of Everyday Life: The One-Volume Edition*, trans. John Moore, introduction by Michael Trebitsch (London and New York: Verso, 2014)

Procter, James, 'The Postcolonial Everyday', *New Formations: A Journal of Culture/Theory/Politics* 58 (2006), 62–80

Randall, Bryony, *Modernism, Daily Time and Everyday Life* (Cambridge University Press, 2007)

Thomson, Tara, *Modernism, Feminism and Everyday Life* (London: Routledge, 2021)

Trebitsch, Michael, introduction to Lefebvre, *Critique of Everyday Life*, pp. 5–24

Woolf, Virginia, 'Modern Fiction', in Andrew McNeille (ed.), *The Essays of Virginia Woolf*, vol. IV, *1925 to 1928* (London: Hogarth Press, 1984), pp. 157–65

Woolf, Virginia, 'A Sketch of the Past', in Jeanne Schulkind (ed.), *Moments of Being* (New York: Harcourt, Brace, 1985), pp. 64–159

29 | The Gender Politics of Grace Nichols: Joy and Resistance

IZABEL F. O. BRANDÃO

Abstract

This essay offers a feminist reading of Caribbean poet Grace Nichols whose gender politics are a *sine qua non* of her poetical discourse. For her, to speak of black women does not at all imply the exclusion of other women and her poetry constantly celebrates the diversity of women's experiences and offers a cutting critique of normative gender stereotypes. Collections such as *i is a long memoried woman*, *The Fat Black Woman's Poems* and *Lazy Thoughts of a Lazy Woman* explore alternative ways of understanding the workings of gender for women and they give voice to a heroine persona who is more often than not presented as an *anti*-heroine (her anti-woman). In talking about the body and body image, for example, Nichols forthrightly challenges conventional views of fatness in order to generate perspectives that can enhance rather than harm women's self-esteem. Her images sometimes associate the body with fruits and other positive elements of nature, renewing the language of eroticism as a source of empowerment and affirmation for women. The essay highlights the fact that, although Nichols's poetry has a serious political message for contemporary readers, her characteristic use of humour nevertheless ensures that it is through a poetics of fun and joy that she resists gender stereotyping, celebrates freedom and offers hope for a world where respect for everyone is possible.

'The poet I am is the woman in me, with all her possibilities, trying to have her voice heard.' This is Grace Nichols in an interview for the *Guardian*'s Women's Page back in 1991, when she was first beginning to have her voice heard in Britain.[1] Born in the former British Guiana (now Guyana), this black woman-mother-poet now lives in Sussex, considering herself a 'world citizen' though inevitably with the legacy of the black people 'pushed' from one continent, Africa, to another, America. Rootless and free is how the poet felt in her early forties, back in the late twentieth century. How much has she changed, now that we are two decades into the twenty-first century? Ten years ago, in an unpublished personal interview, she said that 'women are still at the periphery of things in terms of power', as well oppressed in many ways: 'You only have to listen to the news to realize the constant violence committed against women and the desire to control them'.[2] Clearly, the position of women in society continues to be a pressing issue for Nichols, and her poetical discourse is still undoubtedly concerned with gender politics.

Her writing does not come from 'exaltation' nor 'deep sadness', she has said: it comes from a 'sense of loss'.[3] First she writes for herself, so as to 'have control, to make a world a little more to my liking'.[4] Then come the other women, black and white. And, in her more recent words, she says that she writes in order to create 'some fun for myself and anyone who would like to share in it'.[5] As this suggests, her intended audience is a wide and inclusive one that goes beyond any narrowly limited definitions of identity. Her subject range, too, is wide and includes, for example, a deep commitment to fighting oppression of any kind. She has, she says, 'an unconscious striving towards wholeness and freedom. I have an innate sense of horror of anything that tries to stifle or control another human being; of deliberately trying to cripple their potential'.[6] Such an emphasis on freedom is evident throughout her poetry, where Nichols creates women that 'Aaaaaahhh in spite of me ... slip free'.[7] She contests constraining western notions of beauty, which she sees as 'white, unattainable',[8] and the women in her poetry are fat, happy (or not), hairy, mocking. In fact, her notion of woman is a sort of anti-woman who subverts idealised notions of women grounded on western, white, European models.[9] But perhaps a better way of understanding Nichols's characteristic portrayal of women is to see them as in a process of renewal and rebirth, an important theme or motif developed by Nichols in her much praised first collection from 1983, *i is a long memoried woman*, which traces the experiences from Africa to the Caribbean of an archetypal enslaved black woman whose 'long' ancestral memories sustain her and ultimately give grounds for hope of a new life in a new world. Accordingly, I want to concentrate in this essay on exploring how Nichols's poetry challenges normative stereotypes and reweaves or reconfigures our notions of womanhood in order to suggest new possibilities for women in the future.

Nichols's work is always alive to the particular difficulties and injustices faced by black women and it certainly does not ignore racial issues, but it should be noted that she is wary of the expectation that, because she is black, she should write just about this feature of her identity: 'I refuse to be controlled in this way', she has said, 'I am ... no one thing'.[10] She may be black, but she is also many other things. Moreover, 'black' has to be understood as a culturally constructed category that is subject to change, redefinition and tension: it is a site of contestation.[11] As such, any discussion of black identity, or indeed any identity, inevitably has a political dimension[12] and Nichols's poetry clearly registers this. However, Nichols's poem 'Of Course When They Ask for Poems about the "Realities" of Black Women' points ironically to the dangers and constraints on creativity of being expected to write in a *programmatically* political way.[13] For her, the colour of one's skin is not the only determinant to explain the marginalisation of women in society, but, where black women are concerned, what 'they' really want, Nichols suggests, is a 'specimen', 'a little black blood' and 'validation / for the abused stereotype / already in their heads'.[14] The very same stereotype used to stigmatise black women in the first place thus becomes a stereotypical subject of its own and a type of straitjacket for writers like Nichols who, because they are black, are expected to write solely about black issues – whereas, as a poet, she needs to be free to write about anything she feels inspired by. The poem's counter-discursive emphasis is on her multiplicity as a woman and as an individual – and imagination, she argues, should have no boundaries. In any case, no poem she could write would be 'big enough / to hold the essence / of a black woman / or a white woman / or a green woman'.[15]

The (Anti-)Heroine in Search of Her Identity

i is a long memoried woman 'gave voice to the unheard, it sang the triumph of a disenfranchised slave girl. It looked back to myth and legend, to the spirit of centuries of silent black people, and it looked forward to a new birth, or rebirth'.[16] Nichols's book takes us on a psychic journey, the hero journey – or rather, the heroine journey of her anti-heroine. The story behind the collection was outlined by the poet, back in 1990, as part of a beautiful reading of the poems for BBC Radio 3:

> The whole cycle came about through a dream I had one night. I dreamed about this young African girl who was swimming from Africa to the Caribbean, and she had a garland of flowers around her when she came up as she walked along the shore, and I interpreted this dream to mean that she was to cleanse the ocean of all the pain and suffering that she knew her ancestors had gone through.[17]

As this might suggest, the poems in the cycle are effectively spun from its second poem, 'Web of Kin', where the girl from Nichols's dream tells her story of migration and blesses those who have been through the same process:

> even in dreams I will submerge myself
> swimming like one possessed
> back and forth across that course
> strewing it with sweet smelling
> flowers
> one for everyone who made the journey[18]

The collection is divided into five parts, each dealing with specific topics related to the journey. These topics range from collaborationism ('Taint'), adaptation ('I go to meet him'), oppression and violence ('Ala'), to the appropriation and sexual abuse of the enslaved black woman by the white master ('Love act'). The last part deals with the black woman regaining control of her life in the new land ('Holding my beads'), as we shall see.

The poems of part one ('The Beginning') talk about the path of black people forced from Africa to the Caribbean, and show the anguish of those arrived in the new continent looking at those still arriving. They talk about the promise of protection, of compensatory attempts to escape from reality occasioned by their severance from the cultural and spiritual grounding of traditional African rituals, as well as of the processes of violent white oppression designed to consolidate the colonisers' power and sense of superiority. They also denounce the collaboration- ism of black people in the process of slavery and colonisation.

In 'Taint' the moral corruption of the girl's kin is revealed as she describes how she was 'stolen by men / the colour of my own skin' and traded in for almost noth- ing, just a few beads and trinkets.[19] 'Daily', we hear, she has to rinse 'the taint / of treachery' from her mouth.[20] The lack of final punctuation at the end of the poem implies a continuation of the ordeal. The pain and grief depicted here are assuredly real and unquantifiable. But – without in any way minimising or under- playing what is at stake here – life and the business of living inevitably have their own demands and imperatives. It is the bitter task of those who attempt to move on from psychological, physical or sexual violence to wrestle, or try to wrestle, with some sort of adaptation – however imperfect, sketchy or provisional it may be – to the challenging matter of somehow simply carrying on. As its title signals, the poem 'I go to meet him' (from part two, 'The Vicissitudes') displays a change of attitude, and, beginning to move away from anguish, despair and longing, the girl expresses a more conciliatory resolve to get along with her 'kin', motivated by a growing desire for new relationships, for a new passion. The change emerges at the beginning of day, plentiful with 'dew / and promises' when the flowers, 'pink and red', are 'kissing'.[21] The compact and understated fourth stanza neatly translates the gathering feelings and expectations of the young girl:

I must devote
sometime to the
joy of living[22]

Typically of Nichols, there is a touch of irony here, and while the simplicity of address captures the potential for joy, the painful background memories continue to reverberate as part of Nichols's subtle 'poetics of resistance'.[23] The poem, though, thus introduces the idea that, along with that history of pain, the search for guilt- less pleasure can also – *must* also – belong to the experiences of this new land; and, significantly, the language of pleasure is elaborated through natural imagery of the locale, here sugar cane (Figure 29.1), elsewhere watery fruits (watermelon, melon and others), insinuating sensuality.[24] Such images recur in Nichols's other

Figure 29.1 Cutting sugar cane in the West Indies, 1833.

collections, as we shall see later. Here, the erect, almost ripe, sugar cane is a witness to the girl's own burgeoning arousal as, rising from her work weeding the cane, she makes eye contact with a man to whom she is obviously attracted.[25] The receptiveness to passion by the girl-turning-woman is revealed by her attentive observations of the man's gestures, his hands and lips. She nods and states simply 'I like this man': 'Tonight / I go to meet him / like a flame'.[26]

Despite this apparent freedom, sexuality is not an easy issue for Nichols. Among other things, she seeks to reflect critically on the myth of black sexual potency.[27] For Nichols, the black woman, always appropriated by the white master, became sexually insecure, while the black man lives a castration dilemma because he was led to see in the white woman a desirable though unattainable ideal.[28] The black male, Nichols suggests, is also insecure, looking to his past for excuses and conforming to the white stereotype, as she argues in her interview in the *Guardian*. The poem 'I go to meet him' clearly shows a resolved sensuality, but traces of trauma are still there.

Appropriation of the black woman by the white master is depicted in another poem, 'Love Act' (part three, 'The Sorcery'). The irony of the title is soon evident in what happens as the enslaved girl is taken to the master's house to kindle 'the thin fire in his blood',[29] disclosing some kind of sexual maladjustment between the master and his wife. The latter is happy to escape the 'love act' and the girl is forced to extend her duties from the field through to the master's bed to supply 'the fuel / that keep them all going'.[30] The complicit master and mistress are presented as parasites drawing on the girl's breasts 'like leeches'.[31] Yet deep ambiguity is present in the poem, for the enslaved woman appears, paradoxically and troublingly, to gain some advantage from the situation in becoming pregnant, as this is described as 'her triumph' through which she can 'slowly stir the hate / of poison in'.[32] The 'Sorcery' of this part of the sequence relates to its references to African witchcraft, rituals and magic, and in 'Love Act' magic and poison shroud the racial mixture between the white master and the black slave with a sense of doom. The future off-spring seems also doomed from the start to a life of enslavement, or to premature death, as the poem 'Ala' illustrates with the rebel mother who commits infanticide and 'died a painful death' to set an example for all the others.[33]

'Holding My Beads' (part five, 'The Return') closes the journey and marks the girl's repossession of her own life. In 'Sunshine' (part one, 'The Beginning'), the girl cries that her 'life has slipped out / of [her] possession',[34] but now that she is fully reinvigorated and empowered, she is ready to resume command of her life. The central image of the poem is that of a necklace whose beads represent each fragment of life that has been rewoven until the circle has been closed, and now the girl's new status is fully unveiled as a woman 'with all my lives / strung out like beads / before me'.[35] It is important to recall that the girl was traded for beads when she became enslaved. Now they belong to her and her life is again under her own control. She has achieved 'the power to be what I am / a woman / charting my own futures / a woman / holding my beads in my hand'.[36]

This final emphasis, moreover, suggests other 'realities' beyond slavery and black women only. In fact, Nichols's writing speaks of human oppression more generally, and the project of freedom for her black woman extends to all who, like her, want to hold the beads of their lives in their own hands. Indeed, for Gudrun Webhoffer, Nichols's character can be seen as an archetype of a universal kind of woman,[37] though the idea of such an archetype is far from unproblematic, and this black woman's singularity does not guarantee her plight as 'universal', for she is neither western nor white – and, as suggested earlier, the notion of blackness is not a unitary one.[38]

The (Anti-)Heroine Is, besides Being Black, Fat and Lazy

In *The Fat Black Woman's Poems* the notion of the anti-woman is clearly set: a fat woman happy about her biotype and who makes of her fat a life motto, boldly announced by the poem 'The Fat Black Woman's Motto on Her Bedroom Door':

IT'S BETTER TO DIE IN THE FLESH OF HOPE
THAN TO LIVE IN THE SLIMNESS OF DESPAIR[39]

Beyond its comic edge, this unavoidably brings to mind the numberless accounts of women who become seriously ill with anorexia nervosa or bulimia in an attempt to conform to the tyrannical norms of western models of beauty.[40] While the precise models of beauty may have changed since the 1980s, when Nichols wrote this book, there is still a huge amount of pressure on women to fit in with such models, and Nichols's subversive stance in this collection remains highly topical.

Here, with much humour and carefully calibrated mockery and sarcasm, Nichols champions an alternative image of the female body and another kind of woman.[41] In 'Invitation' the body of her black woman is shown as a discursive protest, for, after all, fat is something that contemporary western society has always condemned in women.[42] Nichols's heroine is fat and happy to be so. She sees no need to change her 'lines' and her self-esteem is exemplary: 'If my fat / was too much for me / I would have told you / I would have lost a stone / or two'.[43] This woman feels good about herself, free of tyrannical diets.[44] Hers is an invitation to pleasure. The fat woman feels her body to be appetising and inviting. The body and its parts are associated with images of fruits and sea-life that stimulate the senses. Thus, this woman who escapes the ordinary seems to be at one with herself, her sensuality is liquid, tasty, like a slice of watermelon, or like a 'purple cherry' that she places below her huge black 'seabelly'; her thighs are like twin seals, 'fat and slick'.[45] The erotic charge here suggests empowerment in the terms defined by Audre Lorde: the 'assertion of the life force of women'.[46]

One common focus of feminist ecocriticism in the study of literature by women is how images of food are portrayed,[47] and a number of Nichols's poems clearly invite this sort of attention. Though she sometimes employs food imagery as a sensory link back to her Caribbean roots (her mother's plantains, saltfish and sweet potatoes recalled in 'Like a Beacon', for instance),[48] such imagery is mostly erotic and diet-defyingly celebratory, as in the example discussed above. In particular, it calls attention to the healthy ways in which sexuality can be expressed by a woman (black or otherwise) who empowers herself through accepting her own body as it is and rejecting the models imposed by a commodified market that exploits women in contemporary society.

The 'anti-woman' conceived by Nichols is not interested in being tied down in any relationship. What she wants is pleasure, not commitment. This woman fiercely defends her freedom, even if this means dispensing with one partner and having to find another. In the poem 'The Decision', from *Lazy Thoughts of a Lazy Woman*, the first partner is dismissed. He has done everything for her, but she decides to leave him because he is 'squeamish'.[49] The next partner is more satisfactory because he, like her, searches for pleasure without the loving sensitivities that would inevitably lead to demands and dependency. The result is intense desire and search for sexual satisfaction: her new lover doesn't take her to restaurants or say he loves her but 'buries his face / in plain curiosity of her taste // And tells her how good she is O'.[50] The stripping of desire in such a candid and open way suggests that sexuality is now taken as an asset. This woman gradually distances herself from the woman – described by Nichols in her *Guardian* interview – whose sexuality is synonymous with insecurity.

Lazy Thoughts of a Lazy Woman maintains the mocking tone of *The Fat Black Woman's Poems*, but here the anti-woman focuses her attention on a different body. The space is now the domestic home, incorporating the stuff of daily life and whatever reveals not only that the woman may be different, but that her multiplicity of being is part of the female psyche despite the stereotypes. Nichols's politics of resistance has a sense of humour that is more than just funny.

'Grease', one of the first poems of the collection, shows the inverse of what is expected from a 'true' housewife: this one is neither very keen on housework nor does the kitchen appeal to her. This place where one expects at least a little cleanliness is raided by dirt. Yet, instead of presenting the situation negatively, the poet, with characteristic playfulness, finds a surprising way of looking at things differently: 'Grease steals like a lover / over the body of my oven'. This image of grease-as-a-lover may be a comical one, but as the grease spreads and takes possession of everything – the cooker's knobs, the spoon handles, the skin of the tablecloth – the sensuous suggestiveness of the conceit also comes to the fore. The ending of the poem circles back to its beginning, with its talk of love and grease, but now grease is not only 'dating' the cooker and several other things around the kitchen, it is also, we are told, 'obviously having an affair with me'.[51]

'Who was it' presents a sharp criticism of the beauty industries that ensnare women with campaigns that are heavily invested in idealised images of supposedly typical 'feminine' women. Nichols's attack is directly addressed to cosmetic companies who produce shavers for women intended to make them as smooth as dolls. In her view, women should be able to develop naturally, but instead they are pressured to remain childish, as if trapped in some kind of fairy-tale complex.

The body of Nichols's anti-woman is associated with virgin forests, before deforestation and depredation. The poem eulogises a woman's body *in natura*:

No Gillette
I will not defoliage my forests

Also, let the hairline of the bikini
Be fringed with indecency
Let 'unwanted body hair' straggle free[52]

Names of known companies – and such a strategy is crucial – are ironically modified by the poet: 'O Mary Cant / O Estee Laud / O Helena Frankinstein'.[53] The words as they are read out loud disclose the poet's intended meaning. Nichols plainly won't be bought off by any brand, neither will she conform to norms that seek to regulate the female body or to dictate what should or should not be 'out'.[54] The fact that the 'new' woman is *hairy* disrupts a norm whose idealisation is rooted in masculine culture for the sake of exploiting the female body.

Associating the body with nature here is a clear protest against the devastation of the environment too. Nichols's alignment of women with nature may carry a slight tinge of essentialism, but, if so, it is perhaps most usefully considered as a contingent form of essentialism or 'strategic essentialism', a political stance that defends nature and women against exploitation of their bodies.[55] From this perspective, Nichols's perception may even be understood as a contemporary way of reading nature and women as both being socially and culturally constructed categories. In depicting the female body as a 'natural' sanctuary that needs to be defended against the depredations of consumer society, the poem simultaneously conveys a valuable feminist ecocritical message. (Nichols's subtle blending of body and nature is often suffused by Guyanese memories, as in the section of *Fat Black Woman's Poems* entitled 'Back Home Contemplation', where, for example, she remembers being urged in childhood not to be a 'kyatta-pilla' but to 'Be a Butterfly' (p. 49); see Figure 29.2.)

The poem 'In Spite of Me' continues Nichols's quest for the acceptance of multiplicity as far as the self is concerned. Humour is still at the core of this reflection on the different personas that make up the self and on how we all tend to adapt our behaviours according to pre-established patterns in order to get along in society – a process that often forces people (mostly women) into conforming to normative stereotypes. But, along with the humour, there are notes of pessimism here too and, in particular, the poet's activist self feels denied and undermined

Figure 29.2 Copper engraving from *Metamorphosis insectorum Surinamensium* by Maria Sibylla Merian.

in her struggle for change by other selves, the other women who live within her, such as the demure 'all smiles' 'Graceful' who, despite mockery, 'just goes on being graceful'.[56]

For Nichols, the self is complex and rich in contradictions and 'Graceful' is followed by 'Indiscreet', the ordinary 'biological' woman who insists on continuing to wear 'her womb on her sleeve'.[57] This implies a critique of the myth of the 'eternal feminine' that justifies women's submission to biology. Recently, however, Stacy Alaimo has called attention to the discarding of biology by part of feminist theory as harmful to the understanding of how life works, and she calls for a sense of trans-corporeality: women – humans – are all part of nature and nature is part of us, beyond the body.[58] Considering this in relation to the poem, we might say that Nichols's understanding of women's multiplicity also implies the need to embrace biological identity traits and to leave women to decide for themselves whether or not to wear their wombs on their sleeves, in her half-playful phrase.

In spite of the poem's 'me', other women of the self keep emerging: 'Obsessional', who lives by cleaning ('head tied, cloth soaked in lemon juice, / to keep her thoughts at bay');[59] 'Dissatisfied', who, as she has no absolute answers for anything, relaxes and lazily gives up: as she can't change anything 'she won't do anything. Not even / crawl out of her dressing gown'.[60] 'Focused' perhaps reflects the poetic 'me' who wants to be left alone to 'delve' into life, 'raw, stewed down or evoked'.[61] Her last woman-self, 'Reassuring', is the one that cares for everyone and everything and, at this point, Nichols reaffirms her sense of the diversity and complexity of women. She (we) can never be just one 'self'; reality dictates otherwise.

Nichols's (Anti-)Heroine Is a Long Memoried Woman

Grace Nichols in *Passport to Here and There*, her latest collection of poetry, says that 'now that I've been living in England for much longer than I've lived in Guyana, my sense of identity, my new-world-self has grown more fluid'.[62] This suggests a sense of mature consolidation in the Caribbean poet's thinking, but her new book indicates that her creative imagination continues to spark from whatever most touches her feelings. It may be that her perception of women has changed, but what matters here is that, throughout her many collections, she has developed a uniquely rich understanding of women's psyche and experience, along with her own unique means of expressing these, and that, for her, this anti-woman who is multiple is neither black nor white, nor green: her skin colour is human. Without losing a sense of her own distinctive African-Guyanese heritage, she has thus also attained a sense of fundamental and universal personhood, a humanity and personhood which at some significant level transcends racial or ethnic differentiation.

The growing fluidity of Nichols's 'new-world-self' is perhaps most aptly captured by reference to the oracular narrative voice of her 2005 volume *Startling the Flying Fish*, for 'Cariwoma' – a blending of 'Caribbean' and 'woman' – is effectively the mother who stayed behind as the daughter migrated to the new world. In this long flowing sequence of poems, in a sense 'stitched' together both by Cariwoma and 'the bright seamstresses of flying-fish', Nichols dives into the archaic myths of several different cultures, recreating them in contemporary colours and demarcating the place of women in history especially.[63] Persephone, the ancient and the contemporary, goes on playing the naive and credulous girl; what changes here is the maternal focus, for, after all, the mother becomes a sister to her daughter who wants to escape from her origins. Demeter, the mother, will not nowadays move heaven and earth to prevent her Persephone from growing up. In her Cariwoma contemporary cloak, she comes to be an observer of the learning process, watching to see that her daughter/sister learns from her mistakes. It seems implicit in Nichols's voice that the ancestral voices were right to say what they said, but who had the nerve to listen to them? Who does? On the other hand, it is necessary to understand that the ways of speaking and of being heard nowadays are different, and Cariwoma is attuned to this, understanding the need for the young to go through their own learning experiences and hence the need to redraw the map of learning that usually separates mothers from their children. The fat black woman might just be one of these daughters/sisters that Cariwoma set free in the new wide/wild world to learn how to fend for herself and to deal with the challenges gender imposes on women's lives.[64]

NOTES

1. Grace Nichols, 'Free Verse', *Guardian*, 16 October 1991.
2. Personal communication with Grace Nichols, 4 November 2011.
3. Nichols, 'Free Verse'.
4. Ibid.
5. Personal communication with Grace Nichols, 4 November 2011.
6. Ibid.
7. Grace Nichols, *Lazy Thoughts of a Lazy Woman* (1989; London: Virago, 1994), p. 8.
8. Nichols, 'Free Verse'.
9. Izabel Brandão, 'Grace Nichols: do Fragmento à Costura do Feminino sem Culpa, ou Uma Apologia à Anti-Mulher' ('Grace Nichols: From a Fragment to a Stitching of the Guiltless Female, or an Apology to the Anti-Woman'), *Boletim do GT A Mulher na Literatura* (Natal: Federal University of Rio Grande do Norte (UFRN), 1996), pp. 148–72: https://bit.ly/3uEOQXg (accessed 14 July 2020); see also Izabel Brandão, 'Grace Nichols and the Body as a Poetics of Resistance', *Englishes* (Rome: Pagine, 2006), 71–94.
10. Nichols, 'Free Verse'.
11. See Maite Escudero, 'Race, Gender and Performance in Grace Nichols's *The Fat Black Woman's Poems*', *Journal of International Women's Studies* 1.2 (2000), 12–26 (12).

12. Stuart Hall, 'Introduction: Who Needs Identity', in Stuart Hall and Paul Dugay (eds), *Questions of Cultural Identity* (London: Sage, 1996), pp. 1–17.
13. Irony features strongly, as in this poem, mostly as counter-discourse in the sense described by Linda Hutcheon in *Irony's Edge* (London and New York: Routledge, 2005).
14. Nichols, *Lazy Thoughts*, p. 52.
15. Ibid.
16. Nichols, 'Free Verse'.
17. Grace Nichols, *i is a long memoried woman*, BBC Radio 3, 30 November 1990.
18. Nichols, *i is a long memoried woman* (London: Karnak House, 1983), p. 9.
19. Ibid., p. 18.
20. Ibid.
21. Ibid, p. 36.
22. Ibid.
23. Nichols, BBC Radio 3.
24. See Greta Gaard, 'Hiking without a Map: Reflections on Teaching Ecofeminist Literary Criticism', in Greta Gaard and Patrick D. Murphy (eds), *Ecofeminist Literary Criticism: Theory, Interpretation, Pedagogy* (Urbana: University of Illinois Press, 1998), pp. 224–48.
25. Nichols, *long memoried woman*, p. 36.
26. Ibid., p. 37.
27. Nichols, 'Free Verse'.
28. Ibid.
29. Nichols, *long memoried woman*, p. 48.
30. Ibid.
31. Ibid.
32. Ibid., p. 49.
33. Ibid., p. 24. See Izabel Brandão, 'O corpo como travessia: o canto da resistência de Grace Nichols', in Maria Conceição Monteiro and Tereza Marques de O. Lima (eds), *Entre o estético e o político: a mulher nas literaturas de línguas estrangeiras* (Florianópolis: Mulheres, 2006), pp. 163–76.
34. Nichols, *long memoried woman*, p. 21.
35. Ibid., p. 86.
36. Ibid.
37. See Gudrun Webhoffer, *Identity in the Poetry of Grace Nichols and Lorna Goodison* (Lewiston, NY: Edwin Mellen Press, 1996).
38. See also Escudero, 'Race, Gender'.
39. Grace Nichols, *The Fat Black Woman's Poems* (1984; London: Virago, 1994), p. 18. See Brandão, 'Nichols: do fragmento', and Escudero, 'Race, Gender'.
40. See Susan Bordo, 'Anorexia Nervosa: Psychopathology as the Crystallization of Culture', in Irene Diamond and Lee Quinby (eds), *Feminism and Foucault: Reflections on Resistance* (Boston: Northeastern University Press, 1988), pp. 87–117; see also S. Bordo, *Unbearable Weight: Feminism, Western Culture, and the Body* (Berkeley: University of California Press, 1993).
41. See Izabel Brandão, 'Grace Nichols and Jackie Kay's Corporeal Black Venus: Feminist Ecocritical Realignments', in Douglas A. Vakoch and Sam Mickey (eds), *Literature and Ecofeminism – Intersectional and International Voices* (London and New York: Routledge, 2018), pp. 185–96.

42. See Brandão, 'Nichols and the Body'.

43. Nichols, *Fat Black Woman's Poems*, p. 12.

44. In a personal communication (see note 2) Nichols told me that with her fat black woman she was simply having fun and creating 'a larger than life personality who is at home in her fatness'. Furthermore, she stated: 'I doubt that I would have written *The Fat Black Woman's Poems* had I remained in Guyana, for example, because that obsession with body-size doesn't really exist'.

45. Nichols, *Fat Black Woman's Poems*, p. 13.

46. Audre Lorde, 'Uses of the Erotic: The Erotic as Power', in *Sister Outsider: Essays and Speeches* (Freedom, CA: Crossing Press, 1984), p. 55. See also Gaard, 'Hiking without a Map', p. 237.

47. See Gaard, 'Hiking without a Map'.

48. Nichols, *Fat Black Woman's Poems*, p. 27.

49. Nichols, *Lazy Thoughts*, p. 9.

50. Ibid.

51. Ibid., p. 3.

52. Ibid., p. 6.

53. Ibid.

54. See Judith Butler, *Undoing Gender* (New York: Routledge, 2004).

55. See Diana Fuss, *Essentially Speaking* (New York and London: Routledge, 1989).

56. Nichols's *Lazy Thoughts*, p. 7.

57. Ibid.

58. See Stacy Alaimo, 'Trans-corporeal Feminisms and the Ethical Space of Nature', in Stacy Alaimo and Susan Heckman (eds), *Material Feminisms* (Bloomington: Indiana University Press, 2008), pp. 237–63.

59. Nichols's *Lazy Thoughts*, p. 7.

60. Ibid., p. 8.

61. Ibid.

62. Grace Nichols, *Passport to Here and There* (London: Bloodaxe, 2020).

63. Grace Nichols, *Startling the Flying Fish* (London: Virago, 2005); and see Sarah Crown's insightful review, 'Seamstress of the Caribbean', *Guardian*, 16 June 2006.

64. I am deeply indebted to Letícia Romariz and Ib Paulo de Araújo, two of my former students, who were second readers to this essay. Both are currently doing postgraduate research on Grace Nichols.

CRITICAL REFLECTIONS AND FURTHER STUDY

Grace Nichols's poetry has always appealed to me from the very first time I read her, in 1990, and since then her poetry has been a regular part of my teaching. Students are open to her poems for many reasons. First and foremost they are attracted to her concise language, and also because they recognise words from their own cultures in some of these poems: Yemanji, Ogun, Shango and many others. Apart from that, in my practice with Brazilian students, I have always asked them to read each poem out loud so that they can hear and feel the differences between oral and written forms of the language. Exploring the distinctive oral dynamics of Nichols's poetry helps to bring out its musicality and rhythms (which are often crucial to her meanings) while also drawing attention to her creative blending of Caribbean Creole and standard English. In this way, students can share in Nichols's contribution to exorcising a language that was once an oppressive means of imposing colonial traditions and cultural differences. Kenyan writer Ngũgĩ wa Thiong'o is helpful here in emphasising orality in the struggle to 'decolonise the mind' as well as in affirming the value of good storytellers or performers who can bring language to dramatic life in their 'use of words and images and inflexions of voices to effect different sounds' ('From *Decolonising the Mind*', p. 80; see Further Reading).

As far as criticism of Nichols's poetry is concerned, it was very scant in 1990 and remains relatively so today. The first work that comes to mind is Terry Gifford's *Green Voices* (1995), where Nichols is defined as 'a new green voice' that speaks with 'gentle wit' about 'what it means to live with the constructions of nature located in two places' (pp. 159, 161). In her 2020 collection *Passport to Here and There*, Nichols admits in her preface that she has become more 'fluid', identifying her diasporic self with the idea of transit constructed within her Caribbean-British identity. This might be understood in relation to the idea of hybridity as a 'nuanced process of dialogue' in the postcolonial counter-discourse (Poplawski, 'Postcolonial Literature in English', p. 680) and one way of engaging further with Nichols's work would be to explore precisely how her poems reflect such a nuancing in relation to questions of hybridity and diasporic identity.

Of relevance here is Gudrun Webhoffer's 1996 book *Identity in the Poetry of Grace Nichols and Lorna Goodison* (cited in my essay, note 37), which focuses in particular on *The Fat Black Woman's Poems*. For Webhoffer, the two poets discussed 'claim no *one* poetic identity but a plethora of different selves', and Nichols, she suggests, 'demonstrates the notion of writing the body by creating difference on the page: by unconventional layout and style and by the oral quality of her poems' (p. 76). Sarah Lawson Welsh's 2007 book *Grace Nichols* (see Further Reading) delves more generally into the Caribbean poet's life and works. For this scholar, *The Fat Black Woman's Poems* is about 'a longer history of representing the black female body' (p. 40) and Nichols's understanding of women is one that escapes stereotypes and creates its own politics of gender. As suggested in my essay, such a politics includes the notion of an 'anti-woman' and, here, it is the fat black woman who, Nichols argues, 'doesn't represent just fatness per se but rather a largeness of spirit' which 'transcends the limitations put upon her' (see my essay, note 2).

Since Nichols's poetic discourse is gender based, one cannot escape the question of how she addresses women of all races and nationalities. I feel particularly drawn to consider her use of historical figures and how these work in her contemporary realignment of women. For instance, in her references to 'steatopygia' and anthropology, she subtly evokes the South African Saartjie Baartman in her 'Thoughts drifting through the fat black woman's head while having a full bubble bath', suggesting a playful new perspective on this nineteenth-century woman in order to challenge established anthropological and historical views. Similarly, the Mexican Malinche, Cortez's translator and lover, inspires the poem 'And You, Malinche' (*Startling the Flying Fish*); and in *Picasso, I Want My Face Back* (2009) Nichols presents the French photographer Dora Maar, Picasso's lover and inspiration for his painting *The Weeping Woman* (1937). These women are from widely differing backgrounds – a black South African, an indigenous Mexican and a white European – but how familiar or relevant are they to the reader today and why is it important for Nichols to recover and rehabilitate them?

For me, these poems create women who are, as Escudero says, 'the epitome of endurance, vitality and spiritual strength' ('Race, Gender and Performance', 15; cited in my essay, note 11). They are, perhaps, precisely like Nichols's fat black woman, someone who has 'a largeness of spirit, a generosity of being and a sense of unbounded freedom', as the poet told me in 2011. Now, in her latest collection, Nichols reflects in her preface: 'One of the things we do as poets, is to try to preserve experiences, people, places important to us, in an effort to save them from time's erasure'. So be it.

FURTHER READING

Collins, Patricia Hills, *Black Feminist Thought: Knowledge, Consciousness, and the Politics of Empowerment* (New York: Routledge, 2009)

Gifford, Terry, *Green Voices – Understanding Contemporary Green Poetry* (Manchester University Press, 1996)

Grosz, Elizabeth, *Volatile Bodies – Toward a Corporeal Feminism* (Bloomington: Indiana University Press, 1994)

Loomba, Ania, *Colonialism/Postcolonialism* (London and New York: Routledge, 2015)

Ngũgĩ wa Thiong'o, 'From *Decolonising the Mind*', in John Thieme (ed.), *The Arnold Anthology of Post-Colonial Literatures in English* (New York: St Martins Press, 1996), pp. 79–83

Poplawski, Paul, 'Postcolonial Literature in English', in Paul Poplawski (ed.), *English Literature in Context*, 2nd edn (Cambridge University Press, 2017), pp. 619–708

Welsh, Sarah Lawson, 'Caribbean Cravings: Literature and Food in the Anglophone Caribbean', in Lorna Piatti-Farnell and Donna Lee Brien (eds), *The Routledge Companion to Literature and Food* (New York: Routledge, 2018)

Welsh, Sarah L., *Grace Nichols* (Tavistock: Northcote House, 2007)

30 'The All-Purpose Quote': Salman Rushdie's Metacontextuality

JOEL KUORTTI

Abstract

Salman Rushdie (b. 1947 in India) entered the literary field with his novel *Grimus* in 1975. In that science fiction fantasy novel he developed the idea of *all-purpose quotes*, philosophical phrases that would be suitable for all situations. With such quotes, people could bring meaning to their lives, for 'the all-purpose quote increases our awareness of the interrelations of life'.[1] With this idea, Rushdie began an *œuvre* that would be constantly aware of the contextuality of writing.

In this essay I will discuss the way Rushdie emphasises the significance of contextuality. Although Rushdie writes in the fashion of magical realism – that is, mixing the realist with the magical – his works are always (with the exception of *Grimus* and the children's books *Haroun and the Sea of Stories* (1990) and *Luka and the Fire of Life* (2010)) keenly embedded in historical or contemporary contexts. Furthermore, Rushdie, a history graduate from Cambridge, frequently also provides metatextual and metacontextual commentary on the contexts he writes about.

The focus of the essay will be on three of Rushdie's novels that were published after *Grimus* but before the *Satanic Verses* affair: *Midnight's Children* (1981), *Shame* (1983) and *The Satanic Verses* (1988) itself. Together with *The Moor's Last Sigh* (1995), *The Ground beneath Her Feet* (1999) and *The Enchantress of Florence* (2008), these books form what can be called Rushdie's 'India cycle', although the Indian subcontinental context is in many ways relevant also for his other novels. My analysis of Rushdie's novels will consider, among other things, the political history of India and Pakistan, communal violence, religious sectarianism and popular culture. Theoretically, I will be using a postcolonial framework, within which Rushdie's works hold a particularly central place for subcontinental writing, with *Midnight's Children* as *the* key novel.

Midnight's Children: A Tryst with India

There is a metatextual comment for readers and interpreters of *Midnight's Children* (1981) within the novel itself: 'Midnight's children can be made to represent many things, according to your point of view.'[2] Keeping this in mind, I outline some major issues for the contextuality of *Midnight's Children.*

At the beginning of the novel, its first-person narrator Saleem Sinai is in the process of being born. His birth symbolises the birth of the nations of India and Pakistan at the moment of midnight on 14 August 1947. As Saleem attests, 'I had been mysteriously handcuffed to history, my destinies indissolubly chained to those of my country' (p. 9). At that midnight hour, the transfer of power from Britain to India and Pakistan was the culmination of a long struggle for independence. Although there had previously been popular resistance to the colonisers, in effect the concerted struggle had started in 1857 as a rebellion (or 'Sepoy Mutiny') against the British East India Company, and as a consequence the British Raj took over the rule of India from the Company for the next ninety years.[3] When independence was finally gained, the British king remained the symbolic head of state of the new nations – first designated as the Dominion of India and the Dominion of Pakistan – though with no actual power. This remained the case in India until 1950 when a new constitution transformed it into a republic, and in Pakistan until 1956 when it became the Islamic Republic of Pakistan with the administrative provinces of West Pakistan and East Pakistan.

Even though independence was a much coveted goal, it meant, simultaneously, a partition of the country, a tragedy on the advent of the new nations that saw the death of maybe 1 million people, and mass migration of 10 to 15 million (Figure 30.1).[4]

The first prime minister of India, Jawaharlal Nehru, gave a memorable speech when the transfer of power was completed, in which he described this historical event as a 'Tryst with Destiny': 'Long years ago we made a tryst with destiny; and now the time comes when we shall redeem our pledge – not wholly or in full measure, but very substantially. At the stroke of the midnight hour, when the world sleeps, India will awake to life and freedom.'[5] In Pakistan, a similar, if not so memorable, declaration was delivered by the first Pakistani governor general, Muhammad Ali Jinnah. The Partition is not explicitly dealt with in Rushdie's novel, although there is a clear allusion to it when we are told that even *time* was partitioned and, as a result, 'the clocks in Pakistan would run half an hour ahead of their Indian counterparts' (p. 79). However, the secession of East Pakistan from the Republic and the creation of Bangladesh after a civil war in 1971 is described in more detail. The equivalence between Saleem's life and the nations' histories is once more emphasised: 'I remained responsible, through the workings of the metaphorical modes of connection, for the belligerent events of 1971' (p. 351).

Figure 30.1 Migrants on the road following the Partition of India, October 1947.

The hiatus between the beginning and the actual birth of Saleem alludes to Laurence Sterne's novel *The Life and Opinions of Tristram Shandy, Gentleman* (in nine volumes, 1759–67), and especially its eponymous narrator, Tristram. In his meandering short story 'Yorick' (1982), Rushdie makes an explicit reference to Tristram, 'who (although Yseult-less) was neither triste nor ram, the frothiest, most heady Shandy of a fellow'.[6] Very intricately, then, Rushdie weaves together William Shakespeare's *Hamlet* (whose jester Yorick was) and the twelfth-century tragic romance *Tristan and Isolde* (Yseult).

Like Tristram, the 32-year-old Saleem waits a long time to get to tell about his birth. He goes first to the year 1915 in Kashmir, and only in chapter 8 does he describe his birth (while Tristram procrastinates until volume three). Saleem's genealogy thus far narrated is then capsized as we learn that he is a changeling, his identity switched in the hospital with his counterpart, Shiva. With the family line altered, all that has been told about the allegorical association between Saleem and India becomes null and void. It turns out that Saleem's actual (biological) father is a colonial Englishman, William Methwold, who, as Independence approached, sold his estate, comprising four villas, to Saleem's (legal) father-to-be, Ahmed Sinai, on the conditions 'that the houses be bought complete with every last thing in them, that the entire contents be retained by the new owners; and that the actual transfer should not take place until midnight on August 15th' (p. 95). Thus, in an allegorical sense, the actual father of India, and the author of its history, is the British Raj. Methwold slyly comments on his actions to Ahmed: 'Mr Sinai ... you'll permit a departing colonial his little game? We don't have much left to do, we British, except to play our games' (p. 95).

Later Rushdie wrote about the significance of national narratives in his essay 'In God We Trust' (1985) that 'the idea of sequence, of narrative, of society as a story is essential to the creation of nations'.[7] He suggests here an analogous idea to that of Benedict Anderson's influential concept of 'imagined communities' (although Anderson's book by that name was published only after *Midnight's Children*).[8] The novel probes into the question of what happens when the national narrative is shown to be false, or like a perforated sheet through which one cannot perceive the whole but only parts. For Rushdie, such 'wrong' genealogy is not a negative matter. In *The Moor's Last Sigh* (1995), the Moor describes himself as 'a mongrel cur ... a real Bombay mix'.[9] And when Ahmed Sinai brags about his pedigree to Methwold, he says with self-importance: 'Actually, old chap, ours is a pretty distinguished family, too ... Mughal blood, as a matter of fact. ... Wrong side of the blanket, of course; but Mughal, certainly' (p. 110).

The children in the title refer to the 1,001 children born in the first hour of independent India: 'during the first hour of August 15th, 1947 – between midnight and one a.m. – no less than one thousand and one children were born within the frontiers of the infant sovereign state of India' (p. 195). Of these, Saleem and Shiva are born at the exact moment of midnight. All these children are 'endowed with features, talents or faculties which can only be described as miraculous' (p. 195). At the age of 10, Saleem comes to know his own talent, which is the greatest of them all, 'the ability to look into the hearts and minds of men' (p. 200). Later, Rushdie wrote that he ended up with the number 1,001 when he calculated 'what would be a convincing number of children to be born in one hour ... I discovered that a figure of somewhere around 1,000 was not unconvincing for that time. In fact, if anything, it was a little bit low' ('In God We Trust', p. 5).

Within ten years, 420 of the children die, providing another evocative number for readers. If 1,001 points to the stories Scheherazade tells to Prince Shahryar in *The Arabian Nights*, 420 is 'the number associated with fraud, deception and trickery'.[10] The number has colonial origins in the Penal Code of 1860, but in the novel the ironic focus is on the Widow, Prime Minister Indira Gandhi. The novel is severe in its criticism of Gandhi's rule and administration, especially during the Emergency of 1975–7 when, for example, civil rights were suspended and forced mass sterilisations executed. Saleem mentions Gandhi's political slogan – 'India is Indira and Indira is India' – as an example of her 'lust for meaning' (p. 420), being, like Saleem, allegorically handcuffed to the history of India.

It is also worth considering the status of Mohandas 'Mahatma' Gandhi in the novel. Although unquestionably a major figure in the creation of independent India, the Mahatma has a marginal presence in the novel, but he is mentioned in three significant contexts. The so-called Salt March (Dandi Satyagraha) that he organised in 1930 as a non-violent protest against the British salt monopoly is alluded to in 'the long pacifying walk of Mahatma Gandhi' (p. 112) – and then somewhat more attention is given to another protest, the national *hartal* (strike, or lockdown in order to mourn) against the Rowlatt Act of March 1919 which radically restricted basic rights.[11] In Amritsar this led to the Jallianwala Bagh massacre where about 400 people were shot dead and over 1,000 were injured.[12] Rushdie comments critically on Gandhi for trying to homogenise India and on how the country acceded to Gandhi's idea of turning the hartal into a nationalist project:

> *Hartal*! Which is to say, literally speaking, a day of mourning, of stillness, of silence. But this is India in the heyday of the Mahatma, when even language obeys the instructions of Gandhiji, and the word has acquired, under his influence, new resonances.
> *Hartal – April 7*, ... Gandhi has decreed that the whole of India shall, on that day, come to a halt. To mourn, in peace, the continuing presence of the British. (p. 33)

The aftermath of the massacre ultimately led Gandhi, who after his return to India from South Africa in 1915 had been campaigning for social justice, to become involved in politics.

The third instance where the Mahatma is mentioned relates to his assassination, and it underlines Rushdie's constant themes of both the importance of narrative and its simultaneous unreliability.[13] Saleem defines his view of the reliability of memory:

> 'I told you the truth,' I say yet again, 'Memory's truth, because memory has its own special kind. It selects, eliminates, alters, exaggerates, minimizes, glorifies, and vilifies also; but in the end it creates its own reality, its heterogeneous but usually coherent version of events; and no sane human being ever trusts someone else's version more than his own.' (p. 211)

Against this backdrop, it is understandable that Saleem finds an incongruence between his memory and the actual date of the assassination of the Mahatma, which 'occurs, in these pages, on the wrong date. But I cannot say, now, what the actual sequence of events might have been; in my India, Gandhi will continue to die at the wrong time. Does one error invalidate the entire fabric?' (p. 166). In this way, Saleem asserts his control over the narrative which, in his case, is also the narrative of India.

Shame: Miracles That Went Wrong

Two years after the publication of *Midnight's Children*, Rushdie published his third novel, *Shame* (1983). It is set in Pakistan, or rather, as the narrator says: 'The country in this story is not Pakistan, or not quite. There are two countries, real and fictional, occupying the same space, or almost the same space. My story, my fictional country exist, like myself, at a slight angle to reality.'[14] Here again Rushdie brings forth the centrality of narrative truth that might be somewhat contrafactual, yet true.

Shame is not a book about the creation of a nation. The originary story of Pakistan is, however, briefly recounted as a creation of 'a palimpsest on the past ... To build Pakistan it was necessary to cover up Indian history, to deny that Indian centuries lay just beneath the surface of Pakistani Standard Time' (p. 87). The constructed nature of the country is also present in its name: 'It is well known that the term "Pakistan", an acronym, was originally thought up in England by a group of Muslim intellectuals. P for the Punjabis, A for the Afghans, K for the Kashmiris, S for Sind and the "tan", they say, for Baluchistan' (p. 87). In this way, the name of the country had already sown the seeds of discontent within the nation, as the narrator notes in a parenthetical comment: '(No mention of the East Wing, you notice; Bangladesh never got its name in the title, and so, eventually, it took the hint and seceded from the secessionists. Imagine what such a double secession does to people!)' (p. 87). In this way, too, a new theocracy was created: 'Al-Lah's new country: two chunks of land a thousand miles apart. A country so improbable that it could almost exist' (p. 61) (Figure 30.2). And we come here to another of Rushdie's major themes: migration.

The partition and the secession of Bangladesh meant huge mass migrations, estimates suggesting around 10 million in both cases;[15] but Rushdie deals with migration in many other contexts and senses as well. The narrator comments on the adaptation of Pakistani history: 'Who commandeered the job of rewriting history? – The immigrants, the mohajirs. In what languages? – Urdu and English, both imported tongues' (p. 87). The theme of migration runs through most, if not all, of Rushdie's novels. In Rushdie's latest work, *Quichotte* (2019), the authorial voice makes an intervention in the middle of a description of the circumstances in England just before Brexit: 'For we migrants have become like seed-spores, carried

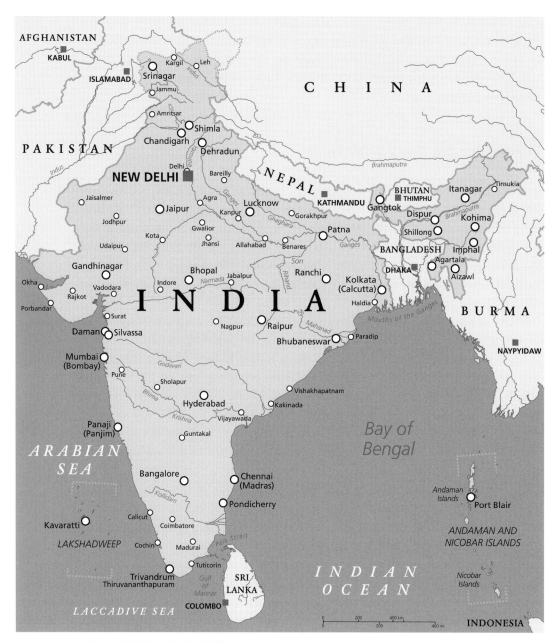

Figure 30.2 Map of India, 2015.

through the air, and lo, the breeze blows us where it will, until we lodge in alien soil, where very often ... we are made to feel unwelcome'.[16] Rushdie speaks for the ubiquity and significance of migration, and against chauvinism and racism. In *Shame*, migration is characterised as translation in a positive sense: 'It is generally believed that something is always lost in translation; I cling to the notion ... that something can also be gained' (p. 29). By emphasising migration, Rushdie contests narrow and imaginary nostalgic ideas of nationalism. Here, and in many other instances in his novels, he also plays with the idea that the narrator is the same as the actual author. When the narrator comments 'I, too, know something of this immigrant business. I am an emigrant from one country (India) and a newcomer in two (England, where I live, and Pakistan, to which my family moved against my will)' (p. 85), it is also a description of Rushdie's own biography. Rushdie's play with autobiographical elements in his novels is a recurring feature, and I shall come back to this question in the next section on *The Satanic Verses*.

If *Midnight's Children* criticised Indira Gandhi, in *Shame* the critical target is the Pakistani political elite, especially General Muhammad Zia ul-Haq and Prime Minister Zulfikar Ali Bhutto (who appear already in *Midnight's Children*), in the novel disguised as Raza Hyder and Iskander Harappa. Bhutto's daughter Benazir, then, appears as Arjumand Harappa, the 'virgin Ironpants' (p. 107). In 1977 Pakistan experienced a military *coup d'état* that established Zia as president, after Bhutto, who was subsequently executed in 1979. This political situation provides the context for *Shame*'s narrative, and Rushdie here employs what Timothy Brennan describes as a characteristic technique of 'third world cosmopolitans' like Rushdie, namely the 'Humorous parody of current and identifiable political villains'.[17] There is clearly a humorous streak in *Shame*, but there is also a more sardonic, darker note in its perception of Pakistan, for example when the narrator comments on the social atmosphere: 'You can get anywhere in Pakistan if you know people, even into jail' (p. 28).

The single word that is the name of the novel, 'shame', is glossed in the text: '*Sharam*, that's the word. For which this paltry "shame" is a wholly inadequate translation' (pp. 38–9).[18] The word presents the novel's central theme: how ruthless authoritarian politics – whether by a supposedly democratic civilian like Bhutto/Harappa or a blatantly anti-democratic military leader like Zia/Hyder – lead to shameful acts. But the socially constructed nature of shame is underlined through a list of sources of shame:

> Shameful things are done: lies, loose living, disrespect for one's elders, failure to love one's national flag, incorrect voting at elections, over-eating, extramarital sex, autobiographical novels, cheating at cards, maltreatment of womenfolk, examination failures, smuggling, throwing one's wicket away at the crucial point of a Test Match: and they are done *shamelessly*. (p. 122)

The items on the list vary from the political to the personal, from the moral to the criminal – with an ironic metafictional comment on the autobiographical elements in the novel itself.

Besides their social and political aspects, there is also an individual side to shame and shamelessness. Iskander Harappa becomes a legend and a martyr after his execution, but his wife Rani describes him as 'world champion of shamelessness; he was international rogue and bastard number one' (p. 108). To refute the emerging glorification of Iskander, she weaves a counternarrative in the form of shawls: 'An epitaph of wool. The eighteen shawls of memory' that she names as 'The Shamelessness of Iskander the Great' (p. 191). Even more pronounced personifications of shame and shamelessness are there in the characters of Raza Hyder's daughter Sufiya Zinobia and a physician Omar Khayyam Shakil. Fatherless Omar had been raised by his (no less than) three mothers not to feel shame, and he lives up to his shamelessness. He marries Sufiya, who, for her part, is the epitome of shame: 'They say the baby blushed at birth' (p. 90). Her shame is attributed to her being 'born the wrong sex' (p. 122), just like Arjumand, who detests her own sex as 'it brings a person nothing but babies, pinches and shame' (p. 107).

Sufiya, the idiot girl, gains central stage in the novel, as the narrator acknowledges: 'This is a novel about Sufiya Zinobia' (p. 59). She functions as a social barometer of a nation that is caught in a web of shame. The narrator/author owns that he made Sufiya an idiot because 'idiots are, by definition, innocent', and that 'she remains, for me, somehow clean (*pak*) in the midst of a dirty world' (pp. 120–1). It is ultimately Sufiya that reveals the root evil in the world: 'Shamelessness, shame: the roots of violence' (p. 116). In the hands of her father and husband she becomes the madwoman in the attic and is 'kept unconscious until further notice', padlocked 'to the attic beams' (p. 236). One night, on the day of the execution of Iskander Harappa, Sufiya escapes from the attic, except that it 'was not Sufiya Zinobia Shakil at all, but something more like a principle, the embodiment of violence, the pure malevolent strength of the Beast' (p. 242). She embodies all the embottled feelings of shame, eyes burning with yellow fire, and begins to rip off the heads of men. She wreaks havoc until Raza Hyder is ousted by his generals and escapes, emasculated, 'in women's clothing' (p. 262). Then Sufiya's raids cease: 'It was as if her hunger had been satisfied; or as though she had never been more than a rumour, a chimaera, the collective fantasy of a stifled people, the collective fantasy of a stifled people' (p. 263).

Early on in *Shame*, the narrator sums up his writing career, linking it with his status as a migrant. If Saleem's connection to India was secured with handcuffs, then this narrator has a similar but less fixed binding: 'I tell myself this will be a novel of leavetaking, my last words on the East from which, many years ago, I began to come loose. ... It is a part of the world to which, whether I like it or not, I am still joined, if only by elastic bands' (p. 28). My last words on *Shame* are to comment on Sufiya's allegorical connection with the not quite Pakistan when 'the edges of Sufiya Zinobia were beginning to become uncertain, as if there were two beings occupying that air-space, competing for it, two entities of identical shape but of tragically opposed natures' (p. 235). Like the Pakistan of the novel, with the real and the fictional occupying the same space, in Sufiya there are two overlapping beings.

Both Pakistan and Sufiya are miracles 'that went wrong' – Pakistan for being 'just *insufficiently* imagined', and Sufiya for being born the wrong sex (p. 87).

The Satanic Verses: An Ultimate Bad Review

Despite the narrator's leave-taking of the East in *Shame*, Rushdie returned again to the orient in *The Satanic Verses* (1988). Rushdie's play with autobiographical elements has already been mentioned, and in this novel there is again a Rushdie lookalike character that appears to one of the two main protagonists of the novel, Gibreel Farishta: 'a man of about the same age as himself, of medium height, fairly heavily built, with salt-and-pepper beard cropped close to the line of the jaw. What struck him most was that the apparition was balding, seemed to suffer from dandruff and wore glasses.'[19] This postmodern metafictional feature could be seen as just that, except that there is a more ominous side to it.

When *The Satanic Verses* was published in September 1988, it did not take long before protests against it were organised. The book was banned in India, Pakistan and Bangladesh immediately in 1988, and many countries followed suit. On Valentine's Day 1989 the so-called Rushdie Affair escalated as Ayatollah Khomeini of Iran issued a *fatwa*, a religious decree condemning to death its author and the publishers.[20] The reason for this outrage was the alleged blasphemy of the novel.

The controversy quickly turned into a battle between liberal and Islamic (and more generally, religious) positions with deep-dug trenches. The publisher, Viking Penguin, and (much of) the literary establishment held that the book was not intended as blasphemous and in their statement on the matter Penguin said that 'we believe that calling the book blasphemous and offensive to Islam is the result in many cases of a failure to read in its entirety what is, after all, a work of fiction.'[21]

The title of the novel refers to an incident which is on the disputed terrain between fiction and fact. The 'satanic verses' (in transliteration from Arabic: 'tilk al-gharaniq al-'ula wa inna shafa'ata-hunna la-turtaja') translates into English as: 'these are exalted females whose intercession is to be desired.'[22] This sentence is said to have been expunged from the fifty-third sura of the Qur'an entitled 'Sūrat-an-najm', 'The Star' (53:19ff.), to exclude the earlier included goddesses al-Lāt, al-Uzzá and Manāt. The historicity of the incident is disputed.

The novel is set mainly in contemporary Britain and medieval Arabia at the time of the birth of Islam (Arabic for 'submission'). In London, the narrative focuses on Indian diasporic people and in Arabia, on Mahound, the Prophet of 'the new religion ... *Submission*' (p. 125). One of Mahound's close immigrant companions is Rushdie's namesake, 'some sort of bum from Persia by the outlandish name of Salman' (p. 101). He is 'the most highly educated of Mahound's intimates owing to the superior educational system then on offer in Persia', and eventually, after many other scribes take down the revelations made to Mahound, Salman is 'made Mahound's official scribe, so that it fell to him to write down the endlessly proliferating rules' (p. 365). This soon leads to a decisive turn for Salman Farsi – and Salman Rushdie. After a while Salman becomes estranged from Mahound as the revelations from Archangel Gibreel are, for Salman's liking, too convenient, and the profusion of rules in the revelations makes him wonder 'what manner of God this was that sounded so much like a businessman' (p. 364). The Jahilians, the people of pre-Islamic Mecca, also do not respect the Prophet and his revelations, which they start 'disrespectfully calling the Rule Book' (p. 385). For Salman, however, the rift between him and Mahound is more severe. He had contested the Prophet for accepting the temptation of the 'satanic verses' and, in becoming his scribe, he begins, 'surreptitiously, to change things' when writing down the revelations (p. 367).[23]

Further supposed evidence that was – in negative assessments – considered an indication of the author's intention to blaspheme comes in the scene where Mahound confronts Salman Farsi after he has figured out that he has been tampering with the texts of the revelations. When Mahound prepares to pronounce his death sentence on Salman, Salman responds by reciting the *qalmah* (the first of the six traditional phrases to confess one's Islamic faith, *kalimat tayyibah*): 'La ilaha illallah! La ilaha!' (p. 374). This does not, however, find favour with Mahound, who comments: 'Your blasphemy, Salman, can't be forgiven. Did you think I wouldn't work it out? To set your words against the Words of God' (p. 374). In another twist to the plot, however, Salman is spared and, eventually, as an educated man, he finds 'work as a letter-writer and all-purpose scribe' (p. 385).

All in all, the *Satanic Verses* affair (often named the Rushdie Affair by Rushdie's critics, to claim authorial accountability) is in many ways a case of the ultimate bad review, based on a not-reading of the novel. The early negative responses, Khomeini's fatwa included, were clearly not founded on a reading of the book but on hearsay and decontextualised passages (if even those). Sentencing an author to death on such a basis is indeed an extreme way of judging any work.

Conclusion: All-purpose Context

Rushdie's writing is notably encyclopaedic, incorporating complex networks of literary, cultural and historical material. In his novel *Grimus*, he talks about all-purpose *quotes*, philosophical phrases that would be suitable for all situations. Such quotes would enable people to bring meaning to their lives, for 'the all-purpose quote increases our awareness of the interrelations of life' (p. 154) – and it is appropriate, then, that in *The Satanic Verses* the Persian Salman Farsi is described as an 'all-purpose scribe' (p. 385), alive to the complex and open-ended 'interrelations of life'. As suggested at the start, Rushdie's postmodernist novels are themselves certainly wide open to multiple interpretations in the spirit expressed by the narrator of *Midnight's Children*, who acknowledges that the interpretation of the text depends on the reader: 'Midnight's children can be made to represent many things, according to your point of view' (p. 200).

Along with their fluid interpretative outlook, Rushdie's novels are deeply embedded in the contextuality of their subject matter, and our reading of them can therefore only be enhanced by a greater appreciation of their many and various material and cultural contexts. Furthermore, the *meta*contextuality of Rushdie's writing implies that the texts are explicitly aware of their contexts, commenting on them. They are themselves characters that play their part in the stories. This is especially so with Rushdie's key spatial contexts Bombay/Mumbai and London, but also his newer location, New York. Rushdie approaches his cities as palimpsests, layered realities consisting of lives that are led separately but that occasionally and suddenly come into contact, revealing our limited understanding of, and control over, the contexts in which we all live.

Rushdie's intended audience does not appear to be figured restrictively as either international or local, but the diasporic *trans*-location of Rushdie's telling embraces both global and local readers, all of whom will feel the resonance of his work for their own lives and contexts, though none of whom will find it easily *trans*-lated (born across) without some loss or gain in the process of translation. The spirit of multiplicity evident in the three novels discussed here (and, indeed, in most of Rushdie's other writings) invites us to adopt what I can now perhaps describe as an 'all-purpose' strategy of contextual and metacontextual reading, whether that relates to the India of *Midnight's Children*, the not-quite-Pakistan of *Shame* or the shifting times and places of transnational migrations in *The Satanic Verses*. In our own reading, we can perceive, under the textual surface, 'all-purpose' layers of signification that may resonate with us.

NOTES

1. Salman Rushdie, *Grimus* (London: Grafton, 1989), p. 154.
2. Salman Rushdie, *Midnight's Children* (London: Picador, 1982), p. 200; subsequent references are incorporated in the main text.
3. See Bipan Chandra et al., *India's Struggle for Independence 1857–1947*, rev. edn (New Delhi: Viking, 2016).
4. The estimates of the casualties – either with or without overall mortality figures – vary immensely, from 20,000 to 2 million. See C. Emdad Haque, 'The Dilemma of "Nationhood" and Religion: A Survey and Critique of Studies on Population Displacement Resulting from the Partition of the Indian Subcontinent', *Journal of Refugee Studies* 8.2 (1995), 185–209 (194); Paul R. Brass, 'The Partition of India and Retributive Genocide in the Punjab, 1946–47: Means, Methods, and Purposes', *Journal of Genocide Research*

5.1 (2003), 71–101 (75); and Robert S. Corruccini and Samvit Kaul, *Halla: Demographic Consequences of the Partition of the Punjab, 1947* (Lanham, MD: University Press of America, 1990), pp. 34–5.

5. Jawaharlal Nehru, '"Tryst with Destiny": Speech on the Granting of Indian Independence, August 14, 1947', in Brian McArthur (ed.), *Penguin Book of Twentieth-Century Speeches* (London: Penguin Viking, 1992), pp. 234–7. See also 'Trust with Destiny', YouTube, www.youtube.com/watch?v=lrEkYscgbqE; and *Midnight's Children*, p. 116.

6. 'Yorick', in Salman Rushdie, *East, West* (London: Jonathan Cape, 1994), pp. 61–84 (p. 64); the story was first published in *Encounter* 59.3–4 (1982), 3–8. See also John Haffenden, 'John Haffenden Talks to Salman Rushdie', *Literary Review* 63 (September 1983): https://literaryreview.co.uk/john-haffenden-talks-to-salman-rushdie; and Catharine Cundy, *Salman Rushdie* (Manchester University Press, 1996), p. 28.

7. Salman Rushdie, 'In God We Trust', in *Imaginary Homelands: Essays and Criticism 1981–1991* (London: Granta, 1992), pp. 376–432 (p. 382).

8. Benedict Anderson, *Imagined Communities: Reflections on the Origin and Spread of Nationalism* (London: Verso, 1983).

9. Salman Rushdie, *The Moor's Last Sigh* (New York: Vintage International, 1997), p. 104; subsequent references are incorporated within the main text.

10. *Midnight's Children*, p. 196; see Srinivas Aravamudan, '"Being God's Postman is no Fun, Yaar": Salman Rushdie's *The Satanic Verses*', *Diacritics* 19.2 (1989), 3–20.

11. See John McLeod, *The History of India* (Westport, CT: Greenwood Press, 2002), pp. 113, 106.

12. These figures are not conclusive: see Joel Kuortti, '"One Thousand Six Hundred and Fifty Rounds": Colonial Violence in the Representations of the Jallianwala Bagh Massacre', *Indi@logs: Spanish Journal of India Studies* 1 (2014), 38–50: http://dx.doi.org/10.5565/rev/indialogs.3.

13. See Salman Rushdie, 'Errata: Or, Unreliable Narration in Midnight's Children', in Britta Olinder (ed.), *A Sense of Place: Essays in Post-colonial Literatures* (Gothenburg: University of Gothenburg, 1984), pp. 98–100; reprinted in Rushdie, *Imaginary Homelands*, pp. 22–5.

14. Salman Rushdie, *Shame* (London: Picador, 1984), p. 29.

15. UNHCR (Office of the United Nations High Commissioner for Refugees), *The State of the World's Refugees, 2000: Fifty Years of Humanitarian Action*, ed. Mark Cutts (Oxford University Press, 2000), pp. 59–61: www.unhcr.org/publications/sowr/4a4c754a9/state-worlds-refugees-2000-fifty-years-humanitarian-action.html; Leszek A. Kosinski and K. Maudood Elahi (eds), introduction to *Population Redistribution and Development in South Asia*, GeoJournal Library 3 (Dordrecht: D. Reidel, 1985), pp. 3–14; and Partha S. Ghosh, *Migrants, Refugees and the Stateless in South Asia* (New Delhi: Sage, 2016), pp. 20–1.

16. Salman Rushdie, *Quichotte* (London: Jonathan Cape, 2019), p. 54.

17. Timothy Brennan, 'Shame's Holy Book', *Journal of Indian Writing in English* 16.2 (1988), 210–27; reprinted in D. M. Fletcher (ed.), *Reading Rushdie: Perspectives on the Fiction of Salman Rushdie* (Amsterdam: Rodopi, 1994), pp. 109–22 (p. 121).

18. See Vijay Mishra, *Salman Rushdie and the Genesis of Secrecy* (London: Bloomsbury, 2019), pp. 141–4.

19. Salman Rushdie, *The Satanic Verses* (London: Jonathan Cape, 1988), p. 318.

20. 'Ayatollah Sentences Author to Death', BBC News, 14 February 1989: http://news.bbc
.co.uk/onthisday/hi/dates/stories/february/14/newsid_2541000/2541149.stm. See also Joel
Kuortti, *Place of the Sacred: The Rhetoric of the* Satanic Verses *Affair* (Frankfurt am
Main: Peter Lang, 1997).

21. Penguin Group statement, n.d. (autumn 1988), repr. in M. Manazir Ahsan and A. R.
Kidwai (eds), *Sacrilege versus Civility: Muslim Perspectives on the Satanic Verses Affair*
(Leicester: Islamic Foundation, 1991), pp. 319–20.

22. *Satanic Verses*, p. 340. Rushdie, who had studied Islamic history at university, follows
here quite closely William Muir's translation in his *The Life of Mohammad from Original Sources* (1923), rev. edn, ed. T. H. Weir (New York: AMS Press, 1975), p. 81.

23. For details on the 'satanic verses', see, e.g., Jaakko Hämeen-Anttila, 'Qur. 53:19, the
Prophetic Experience and the "Satanic Verses" – a Reconsideration', *Acta Orientalia* 58
(1997), 24–34; and Kuortti, *Place of the Sacred*.

CRITICAL REFLECTIONS AND FURTHER STUDY

There are various interpretative lines that have been drawn in studying
Rushdie's works. The latter's encyclopedic nature, rich intertextuality and acute
contextuality encourage such proliferation, not only thematically but also
often in perspectives that can sometimes be inconsistent, contradictory and
controversial. These approaches include language issues, especially the position
of English for postcolonial writing; gender issues; and issues relating to visual
aspects of/in Rushdie's works. In what follows I outline briefly these three
areas with some sources to follow up the discussion. There is a substantial and
growing body of Rushdie criticism, so research material is readily available, and I
list a few general works below to begin with.

FURTHER READING

Eaglestone, Robert, and Martin McQuillan, eds, *Salman Rushdie: Contemporary Critical
Perspectives* (London: Bloomsbury Academic, 2013)

Grant, Damian, *Salman Rushdie, Writers and Their Work* (Tavistock: Northcote House,
1999)

Kuortti, Joel, *The Salman Rushdie Bibliography: A Bibliography of Salman Rushdie's Work
and Rushdie Criticism* (Frankfurt am Main: Peter Lang, 1997)

Kuortti, Joel, 'Bibliography of Rushdie's Works', in Rajeshwar Mittapalli and J. Kuortti (eds),
Salman Rushdie: New Critical Insights, vol. I (New Delhi: Atlantic, 2002), pp. 195–241

Kuortti, Joel, 'Bibliography of the Rushdie Criticism', in Rajeshwar Mittapalli and J. Kuortti (eds),
Salman Rushdie: New Critical Insights, vol. II (New Delhi: Atlantic, 2002), pp. 177–217

Noakes, Jonathan, and Margaret Reynolds, *Salman Rushdie: The Essential Guide*, Vintage
Living Texts (London: Vintage, 2003)

RUSHDIE'S USE OF LANGUAGE

One of the first things a reader of Rushdie's fiction encounters is the peculiarity of its language. Rushdie's play with language, names and intertexts invites interpretations. One term that has been employed to describe Rushdie's use of language is 'chutnification', adopted from *Midnight's Children*: 'the feasibility of the *chutnification* of history; the grand hope of the pickling of time!' (p. 442). Chutnification refers to the way in which Saleem Sinai pickles and preserves stories, the narratives of his life and that of India, but metaphorically it is also the way in which Rushdie uses the English language – a language that was reserved a special place in independent India's constitution – to find a voice for Indian writing in English and a means for Indian writers to create an idiom of their own: 'The language, like much else in the newly independent colonies, needs to be decolonized, to be made in other images, if those of us who use it from positions outside Anglo-Saxon cultures are to be more than artistic "Uncle Toms"' ('The Empire Writes Back with a Vengeance', p. 8). An interesting topic for further study – even though much researched already – would be to consider precisely how Rushdie might be said to 'decolonise' English particularly in relation to how he argues for its continued use for Indian (and other postcolonial) writers.

FURTHER READING

Dwivedi, Om Prakash, 'Linguistic Experiments in Rushdie's *Midnight's Children*', *Transnational Literature* 1.1 (2008): https://bit.ly/3gw8AUN

Giles, Todd, 'Writing and Chutnification in Rushdie's *Midnight's Children*', *Explicator* 65.3 (2007), 182–85: https://doi.org/10.3200/EXPL.65.3.182–185

Langeland, Agnes Scott, 'Rushdie's Language', *English Today* 12.1 (1996), 16–22: https://doi.org/10.1017/S0266078400008749

Rushdie, Salman, 'The Empire Writes Back with a Vengeance', *The Times*, 3 July 1982, p. 8

Rushdie, Salman, 'Damme, This Is the Oriental Scene for You!' *New Yorker*, 23 and 30 June 1997, pp. 50–61

RUSHDIE'S PORTRAYAL OF WOMEN

Rushdie's portrayal of women in his novels has generated a lot of criticism. Although there are strong female characters – such as Padma in *Midnight's Children*, Sufiya Zinobia in *Shame*, Aurora Zogoiby in *The Moor's Last Sigh*, Vina Apsara in *The Ground beneath Her Feet* or Qara Köz in *The Enchantress of Florence* – their status is often seen as secondary in relation to the male characters. Some of the criticism even connects this gender imbalance inappropriately to Rushdie's personal history. Although the early novels have been studied in much detail from the gender perspective, there is a lot of scope for more extensive study. Furthermore, a wider look at gender issues, for example through queer studies, would provide new prospects for research.

FURTHER READING

Ahmad, Aijaz, 'Salman Rushdie's *Shame*: Postmodernism, Migrancy and Representation of Women', *Economic and Political Weekly* 26.24 (1991), 1461–71

Chari, Hema, 'Colonial Fantasies and Postcolonial Identities: Elaboration of Postcolonial Masculinity and Homoerotic Desire', in John C. Hawley and Dennis Altman (eds), *Post-colonial, Queer: Theoretical Intersections* (Albany: State University of New York Press, 2001), pp. 277–304

Cundy, Catherine, 'Rushdie's Women', *Wasafiri* 9.18 (1993), 13–17: https://doi.org/10.1080/02690059308574321

Grewal, Inderpal, 'Marginality, Women and *Shame*', in D. M. Fletcher (ed.), *Reading Rushdie: Perspectives on the Fiction of Salman Rushdie* (Amsterdam: Rodopi, 1994), pp. 123–44

Natarajan, Nalini, 'Woman, Nation, and Narration in *Midnight's Children*', in Janet Price and Margrit Shildrick (eds), *Feminist Theory and the Body* (New York: Routledge, 1999), pp. 399–409

da Silva, Stephen, 'Minor Trouble, Queer Trouble in Salman Rushdie's *The Moor's Last Sigh*', in David A. Powell and Tamara Powell (eds), *Queer Exoticism: Examining the Queer Exotic Within* (Newcastle upon Tyne: Cambridge Scholars, 2010), pp. 141–52

Strandberg, Lotta, 'Images of Gender and the Negotiation of Agency in Salman Rushdie's *Shame*', *NORA – Nordic Journal of Feminist and Gender Research* 12.3 (2004), 143–52: https://doi.org/10.1080/08038740410004641

Weickgenannt, Nicole, 'The Nation's Monstrous Women: Wives, Widows and Witches in Salman Rushdie's *Midnight's Children*', *Journal of Commonwealth Literature* 43.2 (2008), 65–83

FILM AND VISUALITY IN RUSHDIE'S WRITING

The film version of *Midnight's Children* came out in 2012, directed by the Indian-Canadian filmmaker Deepa Mehta. Considering Rushdie's intense interest in film, and his adaptation of cinematic techniques in his writing, it is peculiar that it took so long to produce the film. The main reason behind this hiatus has been the *Satanic Verses* affair, which intimidated producers and discouraged them from taking up Rushdie's texts. As several studies indicate, there is a long and varied focus on film in Rushdie's novels. They refer or allude to numerous films, but they also exploit cinematic language in the narrative. *Midnight's Children* uses the cinematography term 'close-up' to focus on details even though this is not strictly necessary for the narrative; the passage also includes a familiar linguistic feature of Rushdie's writing in its listing of items (sometimes even written together as one word): 'Close-up of my grandfather's right hand:

nails knuckles fingers' (p. 33). Besides film, other forms of visuality – painting, sculpture, photography – often feature in his work.

FURTHER READING

Mendes, Ana Cristina, ed., *Salman Rushdie and Visual Culture: Celebrating Impurity, Disrupting Borders* (New York and London: Routledge, 2012)

Mendes, Ana Cristina, and Joel Kuortti, 'Padma or No Padma: Audience in the Adaptations of *Midnight's Children*', *Journal of Commonwealth Literature* 52.3 (2017), 501–18: https://doi.org/10.1177/0021989416671171

Mishra, Vijay, 'Rushdie and Bollywood Cinema', in Abdulrazak Gurnah (ed.), *The Cambridge Companion to Salman Rushdie* (Cambridge University Press, 2007), pp. 11–28: https://doi.org/10.1017/CCOL0521847192.002

Stadtler, Florian, *Fiction, Film, and Indian Popular Cinema: Salman Rushdie's Novels and the Cinematic Imagination* (New York and London: Routledge, 2013)

Valovirta, Elina, and Joel Kuortti, 'Losing One's Illusions: Affective Sense-Making in Salman Rushdie's *Joseph Anton* and the Popular Media', *Anglia* 134.3 (2016), 491–505: https://doi.org/10.1515/ang-2016-0051

31 Postcolonial Literature and the World, 2017–2019: Contemporary Complexities

ULLA RAHBEK

Abstract

This essay explores some of the directions postcolonial literature seems to be taking in the present moment. It focuses on Diana Evans, Bernardine Evaristo, Guy Gunaratne, Yvonne Adhiambo Owuor, Mohsin Hamid and Helon Habila, and takes a point of departure in three central ideas from the postcolonial theoretical toolbox – (black British) identity, nation and migration. The essay explores how the selected narratives complicate such ideas, by refusing to make identity issues extraordinary or bound up in notions of insurmountable difference, by showing that the nation's promise of unity is compromised by internal and external forces in the past and the present, and by rethinking migration in ways that bear directly on the central topic of our times, the ongoing refugee crisis that peaked in 2015. The overarching argument pursued in the essay is that although the novels discussed engage in familiar postcolonial terrain, they do so in exciting new ways that force readers to rethink and reconsider identity, nation and migration and to reflect on how these postcolonial concepts operate in and impact upon the external world.

In this essay I engage with six recently published postcolonial novels by Diana Evans, Bernardine Evaristo, Guy Gunaratne, Yvonne Adhiambo Owuor, Mohsin Hamid and Helon Habila, with particular focus on how these narratives thematise central ideas from the postcolonial theoretical toolbox.[1] The authors explore identity, especially black British identity, the notion of the nation and the red-hot topic of migration in ways that illuminate the continued critical traction and sustainability of such ideas as they bring them into the contemporary complexities of our globalised and interconnected world. Based on a tentative reading of selected moments and characters in the novels, I argue that the authors can be said, perhaps surprisingly, to supplement, maybe even to theorise anew, the established categories of identity, nation and migration so that they resonate better with the world in which the texts are set – and read.

Complicating Black British Identities: Diana Evans and Bernardine Evaristo

'Literature,' Andrew Bennett and Nicholas Royle write, 'is the space in which questions about the nature of personal identity are most provocatively articulated.'[2] This is especially true of postcolonial literature. Black British literature, read under the rubric of postcolonial studies, has traditionally been invested in exploring what it means to be black and British and thus visibly different compared to the white national majority. Black British literature in the twenty-first century, however, seems less preoccupied with black Britishness as something extraordinary and more focused on black Britishness as something quite ordinary within the nation. According to John McLeod, one 'significant manoeuvre ... in contemporary black writing of Britain is the situated reimagining of the British nation *in toto*, and not primarily for black Britons, within a firmly international frame'.[3] Contemporary black British literature is alert to the fact that in a globalised, interdependent world there has to be a new way of thinking about both personal and national identity that is not rigidly bound up with difference, blackness or Britishness. In *A New Politics of Identity* (2008) Bhikhu Parekh suggests that if we want to 'respond to the challenges of our age, we need to rethink our traditional ... categories'.[4] To this end he puts forward his new politics of identity which sees identity as consisting of three intertwined dimensions, the uniquely personal, the social or communal, and the human, and it is the human dimension of identity – which relies not on our possible sociocultural differences but on what we *share* as human beings – that needs to be activated in the twenty-first century. Diana Evans's *Ordinary People* (2018) and Bernardine Evaristo's *Girl, Woman, Other* (2019) illustrate how black British authors articulate identity in strikingly complex ways that encourage the reader to rethink their preconceived assumptions about black British identities and, by extension, about identity in general.

Ordinary People explores daily routines and middle-class suburban problems, focusing on two London couples – Melissa and Michael and Stephanie and Damian – and their connected stories. Here I will only consider the central quarrel between Melissa and Michael that animates the book from beginning to end. It is a struggle about identity and how identity is bound up with what Kwame Anthony Appiah calls 'scripts': 'narratives that people use in shaping their pursuits and in telling their life stories'.[5] Melissa struggles with post-natal depression and frustrations that are emphatically not specific to black Britishness. On the contrary, after immersing herself in feminist thought, she feels that her frustrations are enmeshed in gender rather than in ethnicity: 'It was the depression of all women, all the oppressed women all over the world, and Michael was no longer Michael but a patriarch, *the* patriarch.'[6] Thus, she increasingly feels that she needs space, and that only when Michael is away can she finally return to her true self (p. 207), having lost track of who she is when with him. Yet she also knows that gender functions as what she labels an 'old script' (p. 246) that leaves her stuck – indeed, one that leaves us all stuck, she insists, presumably referring to all women. Undoubtedly, gender scripts come with expected behavioural patterns that might help us navigate our lives, but, if too tightly scripted, might also hinder our identity constructions. This, as we see, is Melissa's dilemma, and it is exacerbated in her quarrel with Michael.

In the novel, it is typically when routines are broken and the quarrel intensifies that the male characters reflect on their *black* Britishness. At a glitzy work-related social occasion, an uncomfortable Michael feels 'too tall and dark', wondering if he is 'the only black person in the room' and thinking that the other people 'are virtually another species even as they shared his citizenship'; yet at the same time he also realises that 'it was hard to believe' that 'he was still asking himself this question' in 2008, when the novel is set (p. 163). For Michael, blackness is central to his sense of self, and he wants the same for his children. When he explains to Melissa that he needs 'to be around brown people' (p. 232), her heart sinks. As the narrator divulges her thoughts, there is a sense that this problem is the novel's central thematics: For Melissa, her husband's 'reliance on brownness' is a prison that blinds him in the sense that '[c]olour was in his way of all the other colours. It had given him a script for his life ... and he was compelled to follow it' (p. 232). That is why when Melissa tries to see the world from Michael's perspective, it is 'half closed' to her (p. 233). When the couple argue over where to raise their children Michael wants them to *see* black people and not just *feel* their blackness inside, as Melissa insists is enough. Indeed, for Melissa the very words 'blackness, black people, whiteness' are 'crude' and 'contagious', a 'malady' that infects and imprisons people (p. 233). Consequently, she wants to break down such identity-forming prison doors, even if she does not know exactly how to do so.

This domestic conflict at the heart of the narrative might seem to mirror how contemporary society either sees 'race' as central in identity formation or as a burden to overcome in a move towards a supposedly colour-blind world.[7] The novel, however, suggests a different trajectory, towards a world that energises a human identity, 'the most general and the most basic form of self-identification' that rises above 'social roles, status ... and place in society', an identity that can help to promote what Parekh terms 'the spirit of human solidarity'.[8] In *Ordinary People*, it is striking how the 'raced' moments are the exception, and thus stand out, in a novel that is preoccupied with humdrum daily lives and their recognisable routines. Yet the text also simmers with identitarian reflections, as characters are trying to explain to each other that they do not really know who they are (p. 217) in gestures that speak to a familiar *human* condition, and not to a specific black British identity. Indeed, the novel ends with a profoundly recognisable human experience, general to the nation in toto, of two friends eating chips together and agreeing, to quote the last words of the novel: "'These are good chips.' / 'Yes. They are'" (p. 326). There is no exceptional drama in the sheer everydayness of this moment.[9]

The idea of the human identity is also at the heart of *Girl, Woman, Other*, a novel with twelve protagonists, mostly black British women. The text tells the linked stories of these women, framing them by an event that takes place in 2017, the staging of a play by black lesbian playwright Amma. And it is to fifty-something Amma, a card-carrying feminist, that her nineteen-year-old daughter Yazz explains contemporary gendered identity thinking:

> Feminism is so herd-like … even being a woman is passé these days, we had a non-binary activist at uni called Morgan Malenga who opened my eyes, I reckon we're all going to be non-binary in the future, neither male or female, which are gendered performances anyway, which means your women's politics, Mumsy, will become redundant … I'm a humanitarian, which is on a much higher plane than feminism.[10]

To Yazz gender is a script that is too tight, if not downright superfluous. Blackness also seems to be irrelevant to a character whose friends, affectionally called the squad, are white, brown and black. Yazz's identity-thinking is inspired by the influencer Morgan Malenga, described in the novel as Megan/Morgan who dreams of a gender-free world. She is 'part Ethiopian, part African-American, part Malawian, and part English, which felt weird when you broke it down like that because essentially she was just a complete human being' (p. 311), pointing, again, towards how identity is complicated in the novel. Furthermore, Yazz's father, a gay black Briton, adds to his daughter's identity development with his worries about the burden of representation (p. 415) when he 'bemoans the fact that black people in Britain are still defined by their colour in the absence of other workable options' (p. 414). I want to argue that with its diverse gallery of protagonists, the novel demonstrates that both gender and 'race' are limiting identity labels that cannot encompass the complexities of the full human being. Thus, the workable identity option that the novel seems to promote is the kind of human solidarity that transcends a narrow focus on 'race' or ethnic-cultural differences. Indeed, the text helps to *theorise* identity by engaging in the many different ways of identifying as woman or as black woman, but also of being just an ordinary human being. That is why the novel is dedicated at the start to the amazing diversity of 'the human family'. Given her own personal history of growing up in 1960s London as the daughter of a Nigerian father and English mother, Evaristo is, of course, no stranger to the various ways in which discriminatory attitudes can *exclude* people from that family, so this dedication is not lightly or naively made. Evaristo has said that her childhood was shaped by racism, with nothing in the culture of her early life (except the music of Motown) to give her a positive image of blackness. Moreover, her sense of black identity was also conflicted. In a recent radio appearance, she recalled herself thinking as a young girl, 'Do I really fit into any kind of black culture when I have a white mother?' – and, she added, 'I wasn't always welcome, either, in black spaces because I was mixed race'.[11] Thus, while Evaristo's novel can be said to be aiming to transcend 'narrow' ethnic-cultural differences, her own experiences of ethnic exclusion provide a useful critical counterweight to any sense of a naively optimistic humanism here. The novel presents a critique of the limits of identity labels, but it still gives full play to the damaging *effects* of some of those labels.

Be that as it may, the large cast of characters in *Girl, Woman, Other* certainly reflects the diversity of the human family Evaristo refers to in her dedication, even as she specifies their individual histories and problems. In terms of black British identity, Carol is an especially interesting character. She is the aspirational daughter of a Nigerian immigrant who grows up in a working-class council estate, reads maths at Oxford and ends up in the banking business in London's City. Carol is acutely aware of how both gender and 'race' affect her identity. At Oxford, 'nobody talked loudly about growing up in a council flat on a sky-scraper estate with a single mother who worked as a cleaner' (p. 132). When she thinks about dropping out, her mother, Bummi, castigates her, invoking identity in a somewhat confused manner: 'you must go back and fight the battles that are your British birth-right, Carol, as a true Nigerian' (p. 134). Yet when Carol goes on to succeed, her mother tells her that 'there is no point in getting on in this country if you lose who you really are, you are not English or did you give birth to yourself? You are a Nigerian, first, foremost and last-most' (p. 155). And when Carol plans to marry her white boyfriend her mother worries that 'their children will be mixed, and their children will look white, to be wiped out in two generations, is this why we came to England?' (p. 185). To be sure, black Britishness is complicated, and as a unifying script it implodes, Evaristo suggests, not only because of the inherent dialogical nature of identity – as *simultaneously* social and psychological – but also since there are so many different ways of identifying as black British. Bummi is alert to the conundrum of identity, complaining that 'people viewed her through what she did (a cleaner) and not what she was (an educated woman)' (p. 167). It seems to me that Evaristo uses Bummi to voice the worries of an older generation, thinking along established lines of ethnic scripts and expected ways of being in the world.[12] But hers is just one of the multiple stories in this epic novel. Reading Evaristo's sweeping narrative together with Evans's narrow focus on a suburban black British couple exemplifies how black British writers currently complicate identity by exposing how ordinary identity issues are and how typically human it is to ask questions about the self.[13]

Contesting the Nation: Guy Gunaratne and Yvonne Adhiambo Owuor

Postcolonial literature is profoundly intertwined with the notion of the nation. Even if the idea of the nation has been critiqued as derivative and Eurocentric, it has maintained its hegemonic power over many postcolonial writers' imaginations. In *Beginning Postcolonialism*, John McLeod asks an important question in this connection: 'Why does the nation have to be the primary vehicle of collectivity for once-colonised peoples?'[14] Indeed, contemporary postcolonial literature still engages with exactly this question, albeit from many different perspectives and positions in the world. Fully aware of the fact that the nation can never live up to its promise of internal homogeneity and unity, Guy Gunaratne and Yvonne Adhiambo Owuor contest the nation by showing readers how, in a globalised world, the nation is a fragile construct which cannot provide a secure sense of belonging for its disparate inhabitants. Instead, the writers disclose how the world seeps into the nation through its porous borders, giving life to Sara Ahmed's suggestion that the nation and the world – what she calls home and away – names a false opposition. Defining home, or the nation, through 'stasis, boundaries, identity and fixity' as a 'purified space of belonging' is impossible, Ahmed holds, because it is already an impure space; the world is already, as it were, inside the home.[15] Homi Bhabha, too, draws attention to how 'the border between home and the world' is confused; both the nation *and* its national literature are marked by that which is presumed excluded in the traditional idea of the nation as a vehicle for turning 'one out of many', or heterogeneity into homogeneity.[16]

The way that Gunaratne's *In Our Mad and Furious City* (2018) contests the nation is through the world-in-one-city trope, a popular appellation for London as one of the most ethnically diverse cities in the world. Gunaratne exposes the reader to forty-eight violent hours on a Neasden housing estate in the metropolis, a metonymic placement for the nation itself. The murder of the real-life British soldier Lee Rigby in 2013 sets in motion the events of the novel, narrated from the five different perspectives of black British Selvon and his Windrush-generation father, Nelson; Ardan and his Irish Catholic mother, Caroline; and Muslim Yusuf. This internal diversity illustrates the precariousness of the nation's alleged homogeneity. Selvon, Ardan and Yusuf are 'London's scowling youth', 'siblings of rage' with 'an elsewhere in [their] blood, some foreign origin'.[17] In spite of the foreignness in their blood, they feel a sense of belonging within the estate. According to Yusuf: 'Home for me was Estate. Pakistan was some place in fragmented memory ... A world away' (p. 30). Yet he also realises that in a complicated present 'one world had buckled into another' (pp. 30–1) and that national purity is a fiction. What Yusuf witnesses around him is not only 'the city's anger' but also how this fury is part of 'the same slow collapse' (p. 93), the implosion, perhaps, of an outmoded idea of nation as signalling unequivocal belonging and inclusion. For Yusuf the outward signs of this collapse are manifestations of racism and intolerance, both *towards* Britain's Muslims, but also *within* 'the coarser kind of narrative' of the local Muslim community that has replaced the more gentle and tolerant narrative of his late father, the Imam (p. 144). 'Fissures had opened between everyone', Yusuf notices (p. 114), and when his brother, Irfan, tells him that it is the West that has messed him up, Yusuf insists: '"It weren't the West bruv. We are the fuckin West Irfan"' (p. 179), contesting the standard narrative of nations and their reliance on being defined against their binary opposites. Perhaps Yusuf is even contesting what the author himself calls 'this singular vision of England' in the essay 'The Englishness of Street Verse' appended to the novel (p. 296).

This bloody present is undergirded by Nelson's memories from Montserrat and his early years in London. Thus, the past percolates into a complicated present which brings out both differences and similarities between then and now. Nelson's memories unpack a story based on the feeling that 'if this Mother Country is a bitch then I will be a bastard son' (p. 235), and, with his wife, they will 'raise a Londoner of we own' (p. 283), whom they call Selvon. As this allusion to Sam Selvon suggests, Nelson's story also provides Gunaratne with an opportunity to honour the black British literary history that his novel continues and develops. Nelson's relationship with the nation is fraught, but in a different way compared to the young Londoners who have a more aggressive claim to it. Nelson recollects 'the brute savagery of England' (p. 130) and the effect of seeing the sign KBW (Keep Britain White) for the first time: 'To see it there writ across the brick, it have me numb and leave me feeling a sorta deep-down shame. Sorta shame the Lord give you when you love a wretched thing. Was how it feel like when I realise that this Britain here did not love me back, no matter how much I feel for it' (p. 79). Consequently, Nelson intuits that the threat to Britain's growing black population is 'Britain itself, this city' (p. 129), running together nation and capital in a manner characteristic of the entire novel. Indeed, Gunaratne is concerned with the state of the nation, and with the love–hate relationship between the nation and its multi-cultural and multi-ethnic citizens, as we see in the story. As he explained to the *Guardian* in 2019: 'Some people revel in unbelonging because if you're not wholly one thing or another you become a citizen of now, and as a writer I don't think there's anywhere as interesting to be. But I'm concerned that the material conditions of being British are changing, and these things need confronting.'[18]

Owuor's *The Dragonfly Sea* (2019) is a very different novel indeed, but it, too, confronts the notion of belonging and the material conditions of being a problematic part of a nation. It is an epic story that centres on the life of young Ayaana, her mother and adopted father. Central to Ayaana's story is place – the small Kenyan island of Pate and its uneasy relationship not only with the Kenyan nation *in toto* but also with the rest of the world. Since Ayaana has Chinese ancestry she is given a scholarship to study in China, a journey that takes her out into the world and eventually returns her to Pate. It is also a voyage that precipitates questions about nation, belonging, home and away. In the novel, 'Kenya, the restarted country' (upon independence in 1963), is sidelined, and refracted from the position of the inhabitants on the neglected island of Pate.[19] Pate is the place where people come and go – and come back again – and it plays a central part in how Owuor reconfigures the nation through a bifocal lens that looks to the local and the global simultaneously. It is the sea that connects the island to Kenya and to the rest of the world. By focusing on Pate – awkwardly of and not quite of the nation of Kenya – Owuor imagines the nation as small or local and large or global at the same time. Pate is a natural and cultural 'palimpsest' (p. 69), a place where 'all the world's blood flows' (p.156). The nation, in spite of its man-made borders, cannot prevent such complex connectivity, where the external world impacts the internal world of the national home. Borders cannot always be policed. Still, the island of Pate – the hyper-local and a Kenya in miniature – is so small that Ayaana is unable to find it on the map when she wants to locate 'where she was in the world'; consequently, she needs to 'know about places that could be rendered invisible' (p. 43), which is why the novel keeps circling back to Pate, its history and ethnically diverse people. How can such a world-in-miniature exist and not exist (as a place on a map) at the same time, the novel ponders, through the imagination of its central character.

When a DNA test proves Ayaana's Chinese ancestry she is labelled 'the Descendant', and whisked away into the world as 'a bridge' (p. 155) between 'worlds and people' (p. 283). Her fate, she realises, 'had betrothed her small island to an immense nation', namely China (p. 269). In China, Ayaana studies nautical navigation with the intention of learning 'the language of the seas' (p. 288), that connective global conduit in the story, hoping that she will find answers to her questions about how places can be perceived as invisible. Ayaana is daunted by 'the grandeur of this nation's [China's] dreams' (p. 266), even as 'Pate pervaded her dreams' (p. 269). The narrator explains how 'distance amplified' visions and ideals of home (p. 247) describing how Ayaana's imagination becomes increasingly geographically entangled. As home and the world merge in Ayaana, the novel reflects on the idea of the nation, and concomitantly, of belonging, safety and shelter in a globalised world. Exposed to Ayaana's thoughts, the reader realises that the nation has to be understood in the light of Ahmed's and Bhabha's insights, not as a bounded and fixed entity but as an impure, porous and already compromised location where home and away are not binaries but messily and inextricably entangled. In this novel peopled with travelling characters, Owuor also revitalises the theoretical postcolonial staple of 'roots' (or origins) and 'routes' (or journeys), associated with the notion of the nation, too, by exposing these ideas not as a binary but as an inevitable unity, in the sense of roots and routes. Demonstrated

Figure 31.1 A family seeking refuge cross the Croatian border on 20 September 2015, a year which saw at least 1 million people displaced by wars in Syria and Afghanistan.

in the characterisation of Ayaana, Owuor seems to suggest that an activation of our human identity, as advocated by Parekh, is a corollary to this rethinking of the nation as simultaneously small and big, and as encompassing home and away and roots and routes at the same time. Indeed, as Ayaana's adopted globetrotting father tells her: no matter where you go in the world, 'people are people' (p. 60). There is, the novel insists in its contesting of the traditional idea of the nation, 'nothing new or unusual about the arrival and departure of souls from here or elsewhere. It was the warp and weave of existence' (p. 467). Borders are man-made constructions that seem hopelessly outdated in a novel that traverses time and space while remaining firmly anchored to a small island that cannot be located on the map of the world (Figure 31.1).

Conceptualising Migration: Mohsin Hamid and Helon Habila

The phenomenon of migration is central to postcolonial studies. Whether conceptualised broadly as voyages out and voyages in or more narrowly as expatriation or exile, postcolonial theory and literature have always been profoundly engaged with the material and psychological effects of mobility.[20] If migration refers to the movement of people from one place in the world to another with the intention to settle, migrancy signals 'a particular mode of existence' that is not over when the movement is completed and that releases 'new forms of knowledge and being' (McLeod, *Beginning Postcolonialism*, p. 242). Migrancy is often coupled with the notion of diaspora as a way of conceptualising the result of migration and the relocation of communities that maintain a dual allegiance to the old home and the new host nation. Indeed, according to Kevin Kenny, diaspora is 'an idea that helps explain the world migration creates'.[21] Written against the backdrop of the current refugee crisis, Mohsin Hamid's *Exit West* (2017) and Helon Habila's *Travellers* (2019) help us to conceptualise the world that migration creates in newly illuminating ways commensurate with an increasingly intertwined and globalised form of living that cannot be fully captured in established ideas such as diaspora or exile. Indeed, as Hamid's narrator suggests, nowadays it is as if 'the whole planet is on the move' and thus, in one way or another, '[w]e are all migrants through time' even if we do not actually travel.[22] Travelling, to use Habila's preferred concept, is a potentially democratising act that, like Hamid's migration, unites humankind, however disparate its origins. Importantly, however, both authors, as we shall see, couple liberating acts of movement with profound experiences of loss.

Exit West tells the migration story of Saeed and Nadia, and their escape from a formerly colonised nation on the brink of war and 'swollen by refugees' (p. 1). The protagonists move into the world through magical-seeming doors – marking passages that are 'both like dying and like being born' (p. 98) – first to Greece, then to Britain and, finally, to the United States, before returning to the city of their birth at the end of the novel. Although the omniscient yet distant narrator familiarises us with the two named characters, the novel suggests that they can be read as Everyman and Everywoman. Indeed, the narrative seems to insist that *Homo sapiens* is by nature a travelling species and, consequently, as it moves it has profound effects on the planet. In the American section of the novel a Chinese-American woman who has lived in California all her life observes the rapidly changing social world outside her home and feels that 'she too had migrated, that everyone migrates, even if we stay in the same houses our whole lives' (p. 209). Such human migration inevitably changes the natural world too. The foreman of a work camp for migrants in London notices that the workers are somehow caught in between the past and the present, utilising manual labour and technology in such a way that they 'were remodelling the Earth itself' (p. 177). Migration in the Anthropocene exposes man as a devastating geological force whose mobility impacts upon the very planet itself.

Against such planetary and generalising evocations of migration, *Exit West* humanises mobility and its concomitant experiences of loss in the characterisation of the two protagonists. Extroverted Nadia thrives on new social experiences and, unlike introverted Saeed, is not prone to nostalgia. She notices that 'the further they moved from the city of their birth, through space and time', Saeed tries to maintain his connection with it in futile gestures that to Nadia seem like 'tying ropes to the air of an era that for her was unambiguously gone' (p. 187). The character of Saeed illustrates how migration is inevitably coupled with profound experiences of loss. In fact, Saeed embodies the narrator's pronouncement that 'when we migrate, we murder from our lives those we leave behind' (p. 94). In an attempt to tie a rope to the past, Saeed prays. This spiritual ritual develops in the narrative until it becomes a way for Saeed to 'touch his parents, who could not otherwise be touched' (pp. 201–2) since they are both dead and buried in the city Saeed left behind. This filial connection becomes a cord that unites Saeed not only with his parents but, in an affiliative manner, with humankind. When he prays, it seems to Saeed that 'we are all children who lose our parents ... and this loss unites humanity' (p. 202). *Exit West*, I want to suggest, uses Saeed's developing understanding of the ritual of prayer to expose a cumulative pattern at play in the novel. The coiled phenomena of migration and loss that are initially played out in the lives of the two protagonists when they leave behind the city of their birth develops into a description of *humanity*'s mobility and its effect on the planet. Migration thus has to be conceptualised outside of the more traditional framework of diaspora and exile. If we are all migrants, as the novel suggests, then consequently migration has to be democratically and universally reconceptualised as an inherently human characteristic and as an ordinary occurrence even if it may have extraordinary effects on both intimate social bonds and the all-encompassing natural world.

Habila's *Travellers* also elevates migration into something that potentially unites humankind across time and space. This novel begins with the unnamed first-person narrator, a 35-year-old Nigerian immigrant to the United States, and his African-American artist wife, Gina, during a year-long stay in Berlin. Here Gina completes her 'series of portraits she called *Travellers*'.[23] Although she wants to paint 'real migrants' whose faces are right (p. 4), she never paints her migrant husband or his friend Mark, a transgender film student originally from Malawi. Mark realises that he is not the kind of migrant Gina wants to paint, prompting him to ask a German journalist at the party celebrating Gina's art: 'Why ... do white people always assume every black person travelling is a refugee?' (p. 42). This question hovers in the air throughout the rest of the novel, and it signals Habila's unspecified and intriguing way of using the terms 'travel' and 'traveller'. Indeed, it seems to me that Habila wants to disturb our habitual connotative responses to these superficially innocent and quotidian terms. One of the travellers Gina does paint, however, is Manu, a 'real' refugee from Libya, whose story is unfolded in a separate chapter in this novel which relies on staged storytelling as a way of connecting the diverse characters.

Habila uses the unnamed narrator-protagonist as the major conduit for the stories of travel and loss that constitute the novel and he thus helps the reader rethink migration as we eavesdrop on his thoughts when he reflects on the tales he listens to.

His reflections are bound up in the novel's intertextual web, especially in Alfred Lord Tennyson's 'Ulysses' (1833/42) and John Milton's 'Lycidas' (1637).[24] These poems provide a poetic vocabulary of the twinned human phenomena of restless journeying and painful loss. Line 6 from 'Ulysses' – 'I cannot rest from travel' – is used as the novel's epigraph, and Tennyson's heroic Ulysses remains a shadow traveller in the text. Like Ulysses, the protagonist, too, is 'always roaming' (line 12), drifting towards 'that untravell'd world' (line 20). He moves from Nigeria as a PhD student to the United States, then to Berlin and Basle, with a period as a refugee in Italy, before he returns to Nigeria – and he eventually finds himself in London, where the novel ends.

In her 1943 essay 'We Refugees', Hannah Arendt describes the profound confusion of refugees, comparing them to 'Ulysses-wanderers who … don't know who they are' because they refuse 'to keep their identity'.[25] Habila's Ulysses-wanderer, whose personal identity is indeed sketchy to the reader, forms close bonds with fellow African traveller Portia. Portia brings Milton's 'Lycidas' into the suggestive intertexts of the narrative. If 'Ulysses' gives the protagonist a lexicon to explain travel, 'Lycidas' aids Portia's understanding of loss. She is trying to find out what happened to her dead brother, and how his story is interlaced with their father's story of exile. Portia fixates on Milton's lines, 'For Lycidas is dead, dead ere his prime' (line 8) and 'He must not float upon his watery bier / Unwept' (lines 12–13). In the refugee context that forms the background for the novel, these lines powerfully resonate in the reader's response to the chronicles of travel and loss. When Portia tells the protagonist the story of her father's developing experience of exile, that account works both as context to the other stories in the narrative and, by comparison, as an example of how different and dated it is. Portia's father, we learn, first 'develops a taste for exile' before he gradually becomes 'a professional exile' (p. 134). In the end, Portia explains, 'exile was all he knew … Exile was his life. The return killed him' (p. 139). Again, we are reminded that twentieth-century notions of exile and diaspora cannot have the same explanatory traction in a twenty-first-century globalised world of criss-cross travel and technological connections. Trying to make sense of Portia's quest to find out why her brother and father left and died, albeit in very different circumstances, and to comfort her, the protagonist inevitably resorts to a poetic lexicon: 'There was something they wanted, something just beyond the horizon, something outside their grasp, they would keep searching for it till they died' (p. 141). Habila's cast of characters, modern-day Ulysses-travellers, do not fit ready-made patterns and concepts, as they move restlessly from place to place in the narrative. It is travel that unites them, and, according to the author, 'travel is about trying to be understood, I think, and trying to understand others'.[26]

'How is it that the literature of exile has taken its place as a *topos* of human experience alongside the literature of adventure, education, or discovery?' Edward Said asks in the essay 'Reflections on Exile' (2000). For Said, exile is 'an essential sadness', 'a crippling sorrow of estrangement', a state that indexes 'the unhealable rift between … the self and its true home'; indeed, exile is forever marked by 'the loss of something left behind forever'.[27] In Hamid's and Habila's conceptualising of migration they take a point of departure in our traditional understanding of mobility, prompted by Said's reflections, but encourage a rethinking of the figures of the exile, migrant and refugee. Such travellers are no longer the exception, these writers suggest. The authors motivate readers to re-evaluate established connotative associations of the concepts 'migrant' and 'traveller' as they simultaneously democratise the terms' denotations. The loss that accompanies the restless migration of a planet 'on the move' is ordinary people's loss. In fact, the authors claim that migration is a fundamentally human experience that needs to be conceptualised in inclusive and equitable ways in the twenty-first century.

In their *Postcolonial Literatures in English: An Introduction* (2019), Anke Bartels and colleagues argue that literature 'is already inherently conceptual and theoretical' in the many different ways in which it is a world-making activity.[28] To them, literature 'theorises' in the sense of developing ideas about the world and our experiences in it. In this essay I have suggested, albeit in a brief and tentative manner, how contemporary postcolonial literature helps us theorise identity, nation and migration in ways that respond to contemporary complexities. In a globalised and intertwined world, the somewhat outmoded concepts we still use to make sense of our place in the world need to be updated. The six novels I have introduced here suggest how we might go forward without losing a sense of where we have come from. They do so, I insist, by revitalising rather than bankrupting the established postcolonial theoretical toolbox.

NOTES

1. I use the term 'postcolonial literature' to refer to texts written by authors from previously colonised countries or who have migratory connections with such countries.
2. Andrew Bennett and Nicholas Royle, *Introduction to Literature, Criticism and Theory*, 3rd edn (Harlow: Pearson/Longman, 2004), p. 125.
3. John McLeod, 'Extra Dimensions, New Routines', *Wasafiri* 25.4 (2010), 45–52 (50).
4. Bhikhu Parekh, *A New Politics of Identity: Political Principles for an Interdependent World* (London: Palgrave, 2008), p. 2.
5. Kwame Anthony Appiah, *The Ethics of Identity* (Princeton University Press, 2007), p. 108.
6. Diana Evans, *Ordinary People* (London: Chatto & Windus, 2018), p. 93; subsequent references are incorporated in the main text.
7. I put the term 'race' in inverted commas to signal the fact that it is a sociopolitical construct and not a biological fact.
8. Parekh, *New Politics of Identity*, pp. 26–7, 2.
9. Of course, this is not to suggest that the experience of blackness should be categorised as 'exceptional drama', nor that whiteness is somehow unexceptional and not itself 'raced'. Similarly, it is important to note that my point earlier in the paragraph about the novel's

energising of 'human identity' relates closely to Parekh's 'spirit of human solidarity' and should not be confused with the fallacy of a 'colour-blind' approach to identity.

10. Bernardine Evaristo, *Girl, Woman, Other* (London: Hamish Hamilton, 2019), p. 39; subsequent references are incorporated in the main text.

11. *Desert Island Discs*, BBC Radio 4, 20 September 2020. As she grew up, Evaristo nevertheless found a strong sense of unity and belonging in her black identity and, throughout her subsequent career to the present, she has been a tireless activist and advocate for a more diverse and inclusive society, not least within the world of the arts, creative writing and publishing. Among many other things, she co-founded Britain's first black theatre company and was a founding director of Spread the Word, a literature development agency for people from underrepresented groups within the field. Critical of the appropriative tendencies of established white cultural institutions, she has helped to set up many new initiatives, mentoring schemes and prizes to promote black writing, and she is currently curating a new book series for Penguin entitled Black Britain: Writing Back, which is republishing out-of-print works by black writers from the past (the first six appeared in 2021). Her recent memoir, aptly entitled *Manifesto: On Never Giving Up* (London: Penguin 2021), provides a fuller account of her background and beliefs and of her development as a writer. See also the recent television documentary, *Imagine: Bernardine Evaristo – Never Give Up*, presented by Alan Yentob, BBC1, 2 September 2021.

12. Not that such established lines of thinking are limited in their impact to the older generation: they clearly continue to affect the lives of young people too – but, as I say, Bummi's is just one particular perspective here.

13. As this suggests, my intention has been to interrogate and *complicate* ideas of black identity in contemporary British society. It is important therefore not to misconstrue my references to the 'ordinary' and the 'typical' as a denial of the specificity and distinctiveness of black British experience, or as a gesture towards some simplistic notion of a 'universal' human identity, a notion which can easily appear to elide all ethnic-cultural differences while actually continuing to privilege cultural narratives of whiteness as a dominant 'default'.

14. John McLeod, *Beginning Postcolonialism*, 2nd edn (Manchester University Press, 2010), p. 135.

15. Sara Ahmed, *Strange Encounters: Embodied Others and Post-Coloniality* (London: Routledge, 2000), pp. 87–8.

16. See Homi K. Bhabha, 'The World and the Home', *Social Text* 31/32 (1992), 141–53 (141).

17. Guy Gunaratne, *In Our Mad and Furious City* (London: Tinder Press, 2018), pp. 2–3; subsequent references are incorporated in the main text.

18. Claire Armitstead, interview with Guy Gunaratne, *Guardian*, 28 June 2019, www.theguardian.com/books/2019/jun/28/guy-gunaratne-citizen-of-now-interview (accessed 20 April 2020).

19. Yvonne Adhiambo Owuor, *The Dragonfly Sea* (New York: Alfred A. Knopf, 2019), pp. 26–7; subsequent references are incorporated in the main text.

20. See McLeod, *Beginning Postcolonialism*, p. 234.

21. Kevin Kenny, *Diaspora: A Very Short Introduction* (Oxford University Press, 2013), p. 1.

22. Mohsin Hamid, *Exit West* (London: Hamish Hamilton, 2017), pp. 167, 209; subsequent references are incorporated in the main text.

23. Helon Habila, *Travellers* (London: Hamish Hamilton, 2019), p. 4; subsequent page references are incorporated in the main text.

24. The poems can be found in *The Norton Anthology of English Literature*, 8th edn (New York: W. W. Norton, 2006), vol. I ('Lycidas', pp. 1805–11) and vol. II ('Ulysses', pp. 1213–14).

25. Hannah Arendt, 'We Refugees', in Marc Robinson (ed.), *Altogether Elsewhere: Writers on Exile* (Boston: Faber & Faber, 1994), pp. 110–19 (p. 118).

26. Helon Habila, 'On *Travellers*', YouTube, 25 August 2019, www.youtube.com/watch?v=qVLwYzaL0fE (accessed 16 April 2020).

27. Edward Said, 'Reflections on Exile', in *Reflections on Exile and Other Essays* (London: Granta, 2000), pp. 180–92 (pp. 188, 180).

28. Anke Bartels et al., *Postcolonial Literatures in English: An Introduction* (Berlin: J. B. Metzler, 2019), p. 6.

CRITICAL REFLECTIONS AND FURTHER STUDY

In this essay I have been inspired by some recent introductions to postcolonial studies and their revitalisation of the traditional concepts in what I call the postcolonial theoretical toolbox – especially identity, nation and migration. I have also been reading a lot of new postcolonial literature and have developed an interest in how such texts engage with these notions in new and exciting ways. In the essay I approach six recently published novels in a tentative and selective fashion, suggesting how they help us rethink the usefulness of the standard toolkit. Within the confines of a relatively short essay, such an approach, obviously, comes at the expense of in-depth and detailed analyses of the novels. In this section, then, I want to propose some ways in which you can go forward in your own readings of three of the six novels I introduce in the essay, in order to provide more depth to the literary analyses. My suggestions include critical perspectives, readings and questions to consider in your own further studies.

POSTCOLONIAL FEMINISM AND BERNARDINE EVARISTO

It makes good scholarly sense to approach *Girl, Woman, Other* (2019) from a gender perspective. Take a point of departure in John McLeod's 'Postcolonialism and Feminism', chapter 6 of his *Beginning Postcolonialism* (cited in my essay, note 14), and read it together with the novel. Keeping in mind the idea that literature can theorise, consider how the novel takes McLeod's ideas further into the twenty-first century. Explore how it complicates the notion of gender and of what it means to be a woman, not only by engaging in traditionally understood ideas of biological sex and sociological gender but also by incorporating intersectionality, transgenderism and gender fluidity. Evaristo is especially keen on the issue of 'ungendering', as we see in her use of 'womxn' in the novel's epigraph. When you read the novel, consider the characters Yazz and Megan/Morgan in the light of contemporary gender complexities. A useful supplement to your reading would be Robert Young's 'Postcolonial Feminism', chapter 5 of his *Postcolonialism: A Very Short Introduction* (2nd edn, Oxford University Press, 2020). Finally, you might want to include your thoughts on the documentary film *Woman* by Anastasia Mikova and Yann-Arthus Bertrand (Hope Production, 2020), so as to achieve a richer understanding of the central question of *Girl, Woman, Other*: what does 'woman' mean in the twenty-first century?

POSTCOLONIAL LONDON AND GUY GUNARATNE

An illuminating perspective on *In Our Mad and Furious City* (2018) can be gained by combining urban postcolonial studies with human geography. In *Windrush: The Irresistible Rise of Multi-Racial Britain* (London: HarperCollins, 1999), Mike Phillips and Trevor Phillips write:

> The story of how the Caribbean migrants came to this country and became British is a story about cities. It isn't to do with a specific city, although London plays a major part in what happened. It is something to do with the nature of cities ... Their [i.e., the migrants'] colonial relationship with the mother country was the means which gave them a legal and moral permit, but it was the life of the city which called to them and which they had begun to crave ... So, the essential job of the city was to put people together ... it was the character of the city which came to define the identity of the nation. (pp. 382–3, 387)

Use this quotation as an inspirational proposition to help unpack how the novel explores the relationship between the city and its ethnically diverse residents. In this connection, consider also what this relationship suggests about the nation as such. You will find theoretical help in human geographer Tariq Jazeel's *Postcolonialism* (London: Routledge, 2019), especially chapter 4, 'Imperial, Colonial and Postcolonial Cities', and contextual help in John McLeod, *Postcolonial London: Rewriting the Metropolis* (London: Routledge, 2004). You might even want to take a postcolonial urban studies approach with you into the contemporary complexities of the emerging literary genre called BrexLit. In the *Guardian* (27 October 2019), Robert Eaglestone suggests that postcolonial literature makes up one of the five strands of BrexLit that he identifies: 'Postcolonial fiction is part of the movement too, although these texts have been investigating perceptions about race, immigration and national identity in Britain for years – Brexit merely adds a new layer of complexity' (www.theguardian.com/books/2019/oct/27/brexlit-new-literary-genre-political-turmoil-myths-fables). Although the actual setting of *In*

Our Mad and Furious City predates Brexit, can the novel still be read as part of the BrexLit movement?

POSTCOLONIAL INTERTEXTUALITY AND HELON HABILA

Travellers (2019) is rich in intertextual references. Postcolonial literature has always had a love–hate relationship with canonical western literature, and postcolonial theory has, since its inception, explored how postcolonial literature writes back intertextually to the imperial centre. In fact, one of the first postcolonial textbooks, by Bill Ashcroft and colleagues, was called *The Empire Writes Back: Theory and Practice in Post-Colonial Literatures* (London: Routledge, 1989), though perhaps the best introductory resource for intertextual approaches to postcolonial literature is chapter 5 of McLeod's *Beginning Postcolonialism*, 'Re-reading and Re-writing English Literature' (also helpful is Leela Gandhi's 'Postcolonial Literatures', chapter 8 of her *Postcolonial Theory: A Critical Introduction* (2nd edn, New York: Columbia University Press, 2019)).

Intertextuality can be read as both criticism of the hegemonic power of western literature and as homage to the aesthetic power of canonical literature. Read *Travellers* carefully and make a note of explicit and implicit intertextual references that undergird the novel – for example, the epigraph culled from Theodore Adorno's *Minima Moralia: Reflections from a Damaged Life* (1951), or Gerard Manley Hopkins's poem 'Spring and Fall' (1880), which the protagonist reads to his wife Gina. What functions do they serve in the story? What stories do they tell? Do you read criticism or homage – or something else – into this intertextual entanglement? If you become interested in migration (or travel) and intertextual approaches to postcolonial literature then you should explore how the *Refugee Tales* books, edited by David Herd and Anna Pincus (Manchester: Comma Press, 2016, 2017, 2019 and 2021), make thought-provoking use of Geoffrey Chaucer's *Canterbury Tales* in a twenty-first-century refugee context. These tales are very much part of the complexities of contemporary postcolonial literature.

Appendices

PAUL POPLAWSKI

APPENDIX A
Glossary of Critical Terms

Generally, only terms that feature in the volume are included here and then only if they have not already been clearly explained in the immediate context of use in the essays, although I have in some cases deliberately consolidated explanations given in the main text where I felt this might be useful to the reader or might help to accentuate one of the volume's broader themes. There is only room here for a fairly limited number of definitions, and it should go without saying that, with words or terms which have complex histories and meanings, a short dictionary-style definition can only provide a starting point for further enquiry. There are many fuller glossaries of literary terms that can be consulted as a first port of call in pursuing particular topics further. For example M. H. Abrams's long-established *A Glossary of Literary Terms* (first published in 1957) provides very full and clear explanations of almost all terms any literary student will need and each entry has suggestions for further in-depth reading (11th edn, with Geoffrey Galt Harpham, Boston MA: Cengage, 2015). Raymond Williams's classic exploration of the evolution of critical and cultural 'keywords' is also particularly to be recommended for its clear exposition of how words and concepts can develop and change their meanings according to changing times and contexts (*Keywords: A Vocabulary of Culture and Society*, 2nd expanded edn, London: Fontana, 1983).

allegory A narrative with a sustained parallel (or metaphoric) meaning which refers the reader to people or events in the world outside of the narrative itself.

Anthropocene A term coined in relation to geological time divisions (e.g., Pleistocene, Holocene), meaning the 'human epoch' and intended to stress humanity's profound and lasting physical impact on planet Earth and its atmosphere, especially since industrialisation, in terms of things like climate change and the pollution of air, soil and water. While it remains a contentious term for geologists, it has quickly established itself (from around 2016) as a valuable concept within ecocriticism and the environmental humanities generally.

anthropology The systematic study (or science) of humankind. There have been many different traditions and approaches to this study, but cultural anthropology, incorporating sociological and psychological elements, is of most relevance here.

anthropomorphism The attribution of a human form or human nature to animals, gods or things.

anti-Jacobin novel Written from the 1790s onwards by those opposed to the French Revolution and to Revolutionary thought, Anti-Jacobin novels attempted to bolster the status quo and were a response to the Jacobin novels of the 1780s onwards.

biosemiology or biosemiotics The study of signs, communications and meanings among living organisms and biosystems, from the cellular to the animal and human.

bombast A style in which grand words are used for a relatively trivial subject – an equivalent of inflated rhetoric, or misplaced grandiloquence.

chanson (de geste) A medieval French form of epic-heroic literature.

character A participant or agent in the story-world. There is a good deal of critical debate about the theoretical basis of character – whether we conceptualise characters as representations of people, or as functions in the narrative, for example.

canon, canonical The 'literary canon' refers to the body of works traditionally considered to be of high artistic value or merit and thus particularly worthy of study; authors, texts, movements, forms and genres within that body are therefore 'canonical' while those that have been excluded or marginalised in the past are 'non-canonical'. The notion of a canon derives from the rules of the Church, so it is a type of regulatory term. In the context of literary studies, it has often helped to determine the nature of programmes of study. As contemporary critical theories have questioned whether there can ever be wholly objective grounds for determining 'literary value', so the relative – and often ideological – nature of defining a canon has increasingly been recognised over recent decades. On the whole, then, when critics and academics refer to the 'canon', they are invoking a tradition which took for granted a more or less stable body of 'great' writers and texts considered to be particularly worthy of study, but, from the last quarter of the twentieth century to the present, it has become much more common to refer in the same breath to 'canonical and non-canonical' writing in order to signal a general broadening out of the field of study to encompass previously excluded, marginalised or under-represented writers, texts, movements, forms and genres.

chronology A chronology can be seen simply as a timeline, a list or sequence of events or occurrences set out in the order of their dates or in 'chronological order'. However, 'chronology' can also be understood as 'study of time' (*chronos* = 'time' + *-[o]logy* = 'study of') and, for that reason, I think it is a richer and intellectually more provocative term than 'timeline'. In particular, 'chronology' carries with it the implied question of precisely *how* we should study time (or events in time, or history) and this immediately alerts us to the need to remain critical about how (and why) histories are developed. How, exactly, do we organise and make sense of events in time: how do we 'do' history? Even apparently neutral lists of dates linked to events, such as are provided by timelines and chronologies, require critical caution because, inevitably, they will have been guided by some principles of organisation and selection. Chronology is directly pertinent to many of the concerns of this book as well as to its overall organisation into sections which broadly follow traditional literary-historical divisions or periods. The provisional nature of these divisions is emphasised throughout the book and readers are encouraged to 'read across' the different periods to resist any oversimplistic sense of step-by-step historical continuity. Arguably, however, some chronological and critically nuanced understanding of historical developments is often crucial to a fuller understanding of literary texts and their contexts.

circulating library Commercial enterprises that lent books to patrons, typically for an annual or quarterly fee. Normally based in booksellers' shops, they developed out of informal lending arrangements by a handful of booksellers during the later seventeenth century. They flourished from the 1740s onwards.

classical revival The phrase was used by the poet and philosopher T. E. Hulme in his essay 'Romanticism and Classicism' (written in 1911–12, published in 1924), where he suggests that the time is ripe for a return to the classical values of discipline and tradition in both life and literature. It designates a group of modernist poets whose interests were especially invested in the classics, including Ezra Pound, F. S. Flint, Richard Aldington and H. D. (Hilda Doolittle), and is also associated with James Joyce, Wyndham Lewis and T. S. Eliot.

communications circuit This is a term in print culture studies (or book history) which refers to the full complex cycle of how texts come into being and circulate in culture and society, from their first writing through to their reading. Robert Darnton first proposed the term and his classic diagram and explanation of the circuit are reproduced in the Critical Reflections and Further Study section of Essay 14.

concatenation A form of stanza-linking where one line or word at the end of one stanza is repeated, with variation, in the opening line of the next stanza.

context See discussion in the Introduction, pp. 4–5.

corpus Latin for 'body' and often used to denote a 'whole' collection (or body) of texts such as the complete works of an author.

deconstruction A critical approach closely related to post-structuralism and premised on the radical indeterminacy of meaning in texts, which are seen as self-referring sign systems with no objective external reference by which to ground or validate their meanings definitively. Texts in this view are also always dependent on a boundless play of *inter*textuality, or the play of signification across the full social, linguistic and cultural sign system within which they exist. In principle, therefore, any text is open to any number of different, even contradictory, readings. Deconstructive criticism typically provides a close reading of a text 'against the grain' to expose its contradictions, gaps and inconsistencies and essentially to unravel any apparent unity of meaning it may have. *See* post-structuralism.

diachronic Literally 'across time' and usually used together with its opposite term 'synchronic', with the sense of 'at the same time'. These terms became influential in critical theory in the twentieth century because of their reliance on the work of the linguist Ferdinand de Saussure, who used the terms to elucidate his theory of language and how it could be analysed 'vertically' in historic terms or 'horizontally' as it operates as a self-regulating structure or system at any present moment.

discourse Any sustained use of language beyond a sentence; in literary and cultural studies, the term usually suggests some thematically, theoretically or ideologically connected argument or set of arguments; in a broad related sense it can be considered as an ongoing conversation or 'narrative' which gradually develops and consolidates a set of linked ideas.

dramatic monologue A poetic genre in which the poem's speaker makes an extended speech, usually in *implied* interaction with one or more other people (who do not however speak themselves), and in which they inadvertently reveal more about themselves than they intend.

ecocriticism Now a major field of critical theory within the humanities, including literary studies, and, as the word suggests, a form of criticism based on an ecological or environmental perspective. It is a very broad field and 'ecocriticism' is something of an umbrella term, but see Essay 24, pp. 408–9 for a succinct overview.

ekphrasis A verbal evocation of a real, or imaginary, visual art object. Reverse ekphrasis is a graphic representation of verbal art.

epigraph A quotation preceding a literary work, suggestive of its theme, context and tradition, or alternatively, providing an antithesis to it.

essentialism The relevant meaning here, especially in relation to gender identities, is a belief that people have some fundamentally defining or determining 'essences' that give them a fixed identity.

Evangelical novel First becoming popular in the early 1800s, evangelical novels were didactic works that aimed to inculcate the values of Christianity, often via a romance plot.

exegesis Skilful interpretation of a text (originally of sacred texts).

fictionality A kind of rhetorical signalling which indicates to a reader that the situations, actions and persons being discussed are invented.

genre Literally, a 'type' or 'kind' of thing. Once used in reference to classical Greek literature to distinguish comedy, tragedy and epic, and later in reference to European literature to distinguish verse, prose and drama, the term is now quite an elastic one and needs to be understood according to its context of use. It can refer to specific types of fiction or non-fiction (science fiction, biography), or sets of cultural tropes (allegory, magical realism), or it may mark a type of publishing prestige ('she writes literary fiction; he writes genre fiction').

gentry In medieval terms, the knightly class (or those landholders who could be knights) below the rank of nobility but above the freeholding yeomanry.

georgic Originally a didactic poem about farming or pertaining to agriculture and rural affairs, especially associated with the *Georgics* of Virgil (70–19 BCE) and with many imitations in the eighteenth century. Joseph Addison distinguished it from the pastoral in his *Essay on the Georgic* (1697).

Gothic novel The Gothic novel has a prevailing atmosphere of mystery and terror. Often involving complicated and tangled plots, its heyday was the 1790s, although it is usually said to begin with Horace Walpole's *The Castle of Otranto* (1764).

hermeticism (or hermetism) A system of philosophical, religious and occult traditions involving alchemy and astrology which arose from the Hermetic writings attributed to the Hellenic deity Hermes Trismegistos. Through Marsilio Ficino's translation, it influenced the Renaissance; in the late nineteenth century, it also inspired an interest in esotericism, evinced by the members of the Hermetic Order of the Golden Dawn (1887), including Algernon Swinburne, Oscar Wilde and W. B. Yeats.

historicism This can have the simple sense of a method of study which takes a historical perspective and makes careful connections between the past and the present. However, the term can be used in two other somewhat conflicting ways: first, to refer to a theory which maintains that events in a particular period can be interpreted only from the interpretative framework of that period; and, second, to talk of a sense of history as a matter of large-scale 'laws' of progression. 'New Historicism' is a contemporary literary-critical theory which rejects both of those views and which engages with texts and contexts in terms of both their own and our own cultural histories: *see* Essay 9 and Essay 15.

Hundred Years War Despite its famous nineteenth-century title, this was more of a sustained but sporadic series of hostilities and battles fought between England and France between 1337 and 1453. At the heart of the matter was the question of English control of the extended duchy of Aquitaine, a duchy which made the English king a vassal (in this one respect) of the French king, coupled with English claims to the French throne through familial descent. Under Edward III the situation was frequently connected to, and exacerbated by, Anglo-Scottish relations (and vice versa).

intertextuality Affinities, links and relationships between texts. These are often signalled, especially in literary texts, by explicit allusions to or quotations from other texts, but they may also be implicit in a whole range of formal or thematic elements that evoke connections with other texts. It is worth drawing attention here to Emily Thornbury's fascinating discussion (in Essay 1) of '*mouvance*', a particular form of intertextuality that takes place in the interactions between oral and written traditions in the medieval era, especially for its drawing out the lively *mobility* of meanings arising from the changing contexts of every different 'performance' of a text. *See also* paratext.

irony An authorial tone or rhetorical signalling to the reader that a situation or event is not as represented; an understanding between author and reader that the surface truth is somehow misleading, the comprehension of which often provides a wry or amusing twist.

Jacobin novels Written mainly between 1780 and 1805 by British radicals who supported the ideals of the French Revolution. Plots usually attacked the established social and political order.

metafiction A type of fiction that, in various ways, self-consciously steps out of its own fictional 'frame' to reflect back on itself *as* a constructed fiction, encouraging reflection on the relationship between fiction and reality and on the nature of linguistic representation. Metafiction pushes beyond the normal conventions of fiction by which the author contrives to make the reader 'suspend disbelief' in the created fictional world (through, for example, the techniques of realism). Instead, it positively invites a type of critical disbelief or detachment about the fiction, often by referring to matter-of-fact real-world events which break the illusion of the fictional 'reality'. However, this 'frame-breaking' is nevertheless, paradoxically, still part of an overall fiction – that is, of the text that we call a metafiction. The prefix *meta-* has the meanings of 'after', 'over', 'beyond' and 'with', and these all help to suggest the paradoxical layered perspectives of metafiction as a fiction within a fiction or a fiction beyond/over a fiction.

metaphor A figure of speech which, for rhetorical effect, asserts or implies an identity or resemblance between two things which are not literally alike (e.g., 'All the world's a stage').

metonymy A figure of speech which represents something by reference to something closely associated with it – as in 'The pen is mightier than the sword', where 'pen' stands for writing and persuasive ideas and 'sword' stands for brute force.

modernism Traditionally, this term has defined the experimental and innovative art and literature of the period roughly between 1890 and 1939; but it is a much debated term and the emergence in this century of 'new' modernist studies has begun to expand the meaning of the term to take in a much longer period and a wider range of writers.

modernism in religion The intellectual movement at the turn of the twentieth century, stressing freedom of individual conscience and seeking to revise Christian doctrines in the light of modern historical critique, philosophy and psychology.

narrative voice, point of view, focalisation These are key related terms in understanding how any narrative is narrated and, in particular, in understanding the interrelations between narrators, characters, actions and ideas. Crucial distinctions here can be expressed in the form of these simple questions: 'Who speaks?', 'Who sees?' and 'In what ways?' Simply, it is the narrator (the narrating 'persona' created by the author) who 'speaks' – who gives voice to the narrative, introducing characters, scenes, actions, ideas; and it is the 'focaliser' who 'sees' – this might be a character in the narrative ('Jane saw the cat leap') or it may be the narrating persona who focalises the action or scene directly ('The cat leapt on to the table'). The latter situation is common in what is traditionally described as omniscient third-person narration, where the narrator appears to have an all-knowing bird's-eye view on the world of the narrative. This may blur the distinction between speaking and seeing and can be a cause of confusion, but these are in principle *very* different functions and our understanding of the dynamics of any narrative often depends on a proper appreciation of how the writer has negotiated the balance between such speaking and seeing. A narrator 'external' to the narrated world (like the above 'omniscient' narrator who refers to the characters as 'he', 'she' or 'they') may present, and comment upon, that world more or less directly, and in that situation the narrative voice, the persona of the narrator, also tends to control our moral or ideological 'point of view' on the narrative (and here it is another useful distinction to think of point of view or perspective as having a *conceptual* meaning, relating to our opinions, as well as the literal *per*ceptual meaning). On the other hand, such a narrator may present – or focalise – events through the eyes of one or more characters, thus imposing one or more 'limited' points of view. It is then often precisely the play of differences between and among the voice of the narrator and the points of view of the characters through which thematic issues are conveyed and through which we recognise such things as irony or satire. In a first-person narration, where the narrator is a character or participant in the narrated world and speaks as 'I', then that 'I' that speaks is also usually the 'eye' that sees or focalises the action for us (though, even then, the first-person narrator can always temporarily transfer the focalising function to another character). As I think will be evident by now, there are many possible permutations in how narratives are narrated and focalised, but clarifying these latter terms, along with that of 'point of view', can help us to analyse more precisely the specific permutations we find in a particular text. If it is the author speaking in their own name, as in much of non-fiction, it is not the flesh and blood author as they exist in actual life but the author as they present themselves to the reading public; therefore, some call this voice the implied author.

natureculture A coinage in ecocriticism designed to subvert the long tradition which sees human culture as existing on some separate plane from the natural world and stressing instead the inextricable interdependency of the two.

New Historicism *See* Historicism; *see also* Essay 9 and Essay 15.

organicism Obviously related to the meaning of the 'organic' as something living and growing and with connotations of the 'natural' (especially as opposed to the 'mechanical'), 'organicism' is usually used in critical reference to conservative romanticised notions of some past 'organic community' that reflected the 'natural order of things'.

palimpsest Originally, writing material like parchment that has been reused or written over so that there are still visible traces of underlying script; by extension, anything that can be said to have still potentially decipherable layers of significance beneath the surface (somewhat like an old canvas that has had different pictures painted on top of each other).

paradigm shift A term popularised in the wake of Thomas Kuhn's influential book in the philosophy of science, *The Structure of Scientific Revolutions* (1962), in which he explained periodic revolutions in science as a process whereby one dominant conceptual world view, one framework (or paradigm) of assumptions, is replaced by another.

paratext It is helpful to note that the prefix *para-* comes from the Greek for 'beside', 'beyond' or 'against' as the paratext is what is presented to the reader with the text but which is not strictly the text itself. Examples include an epigraph, preliminary materials, back cover blurb, a prize announcement on the cover, the cover art, and, with texts in journals, the various features such as advertisements which might surround the text. All of these, including the author's name, may influence the way a text is received by the reader.

pastoral In a literary context, works relating to the countryside and rural life and, in traditional forms, usually depicting that life in idealised terms of 'natural' peace and simplicity and 'organic' authenticity. Related terms, deriving originally from the classical poets Theocritus and Virgil, are 'idyll' and 'eclogue'.

positionality The social and political contexts that help to define identity in a range of ways.

postmodernism A tendency in literature of the second half of the twentieth century which shares most of the theoretical assumptions of post-structuralism and is characterised by its questioning of the nature and norms of literary representation and by a playful self-reflexivity and metafictionality.

post-pastoral One among many contemporary ecocritical terms that are designed to revise traditional approaches to the natural environment that have tended to idealise or romanticise it and to see it too simplistically as a clear-cut binary opposite to human culture and activity. Terry Gifford first proposed the term and he clarifies its meaning in Essay 24. *See* pastoral.

post-structuralism A critical approach which pushed structuralism to its logical conclusion by pointing out that if, as structuralism argues, all meanings are dependent on an underlying system of signification that is self-contained, with no external grounds of 'objective' truth, then that argument must also apply to structuralism itself. Post-structuralism emphasises the indeterminacy and instability of meaning. If meaning is generated only by language's internal system of differences, not by any positive value or objective 'presence' in the world, then meanings and interpretations are always being deferred along a never-ending chain of signification. In principle, then, the meaning of anything we say or write or argue is open to an infinite number of interpretations because of the constant slippage and play of meaning in the very system of language. Post-structuralism is perhaps not so much a theory of its own as a procedure of deconstructive critique of other theories and discourses, including the discourses of literary texts. Obviously, post-structuralist readings are themselves open to deconstruction and they often therefore exhibit a playful self-reflexivity; and, because of the constant *play* of meanings, because meanings cannot be definitively tied down to any one utterance but are constantly 'disseminated' across the whole field of signification, the concept of intertextuality is also an important element in post-structuralist thought.

See deconstruction, intertextuality, structuralism.

print culture studies A relatively new term for studies in the history of printing and publishing that has come to replace the traditional label of 'book history' in order to encompass the full range of interrelated print materials (such as newspapers, journals and magazines) as well as to acknowledge the full extent and interdisciplinary nature of the 'communications circuit' involved in the production, circulation and consumption of print materials. *See also* communications circuit.

radical A person who advocates thorough or complete political or social change, or a member of a political party or section of a party pursuing such aims. In the context of the late eighteenth and early nineteenth centuries, radicals almost always supported the aims of the French Revolution.

register In phonetics, a tonal range of voice – which helps to define the more relevant sense here of a situationally distinctive variety of language, as in 'legal' or 'scientific' or 'academic' English, for example.

reverse ekphrasis *See* ekphrasis.

romance Chivalry, quest, courtly love, marriage, adventure and supernatural marvels are all notable features of this complex medieval genre which, spreading from twelfth-century France, largely displaced earlier heroic forms of narrative. Arthurian legend became one of the main subjects of romance. *See* Essay 3 for a full discussion.

romanticism A complex cultural movement of the late eighteenth and early nineteenth centuries which challenged the values of classicism and affirmed the creative powers of the imagination, individualism, emotion and spontaneity; it celebrated nature in its sublime and wild aspects and saw possibilities of transcendence through communion with nature.

satire The art of diminishing a subject through ridicule.

semiotics The general science of signs (sometimes also called 'semiology'). Contemporary semiotics are usually said to have been inaugurated by the work of the American pragmatic philosopher Charles Sanders Peirce (1839–1914) and the Swiss linguist Ferdinand de Saussure (1857–1913).

sentimental novel The sentimental novel is an emotionally extravagant novel of a kind that became popular in Europe in the decades between 1740 and 1780 in Europe. Usually thought to begin with Samuel Richardson's *Pamela; or, Virtue Rewarded* (1740), the sentimental novel emphasised the relationships between virtue and sensibility, and foregrounded emotional excess.

stichomythia An emotionally charged dialogue in verse drama, with characters speaking in single alternating lines, repeating one another's words which, however, are used in a different sense and for a witty retort.

stream of consciousness A technique involving at least some degree of mimetic representation of a character's inner consciousness or fragmentary thoughts.

structuralism A formalist critical theory, developed in the 1950s and 1960s, concerned more with *how* structures or systems of meaning work than with what meanings they generate in particular cases. Structuralism based its approach on the structural linguistics of Ferdinand de Saussure who developed a model of language seen as a self-contained system of differential relationships where meanings are generated not by reference to external 'reality' but purely within the system itself through its internal chain of signifying differences. With its focus on socially constructed signifying systems, structuralism is closely aligned with semiotics.

subscription library Libraries financed by membership fees. Unlike public or circulating libraries, access was restricted to the members, but access rights could be (and often were) extended to others, such as students.

synchronic or synchronous Existing or occurring at the same time. *See* diachronic.

text I have already glossed the root meaning of this term in the Introduction, pp. 4–5, but it is worth reflecting a little further on the term, especially in relation to material print culture. Usually, in a study setting, 'text' simply refers to a short piece of writing or to the whole literary 'work' in front of us (novel, poem, play, etc.), usually appearing in the form of a book. However, why do we talk of one apparently singular text when this actually manifests itself in the world in the form of *many* material text*s* (or books)? We talk of *the* text of *Middlemarch*, for example, but this text circulates in very large numbers of 'texts' in the form of physical (or digital) books. Is the singular text something different or somehow separable (or abstractable) from its material manifestations in multiple *texts*? What if some of those texts are different from one another – as we see in revised or differently edited and differently presented versions of the 'same' text? What and where is that 'same' text? Is it the author's original manuscript or typescript or word-processed document? And how has the original piece of writing been turned into a printed text anyway? Who did it? Is it now still the exact 'same' text even though it has become multiple printed texts? If there are versions of a text which differ from one another, how do we decide on the 'authentic' text? Is there just one definitive, authentic or authoritative version of a text, then – and who decides on that? Do readers contribute to the shaping of a text in any way – is there a reader 'in' the text, as some critics have suggested? To what extent

is a text a collaborative *process* rather than just one finished, static entity?

topography Description or representation of place and its physical features especially.

Tory A person who advocates traditionalism and conservatism, and upholds the supremacy of social order. In the eighteenth-century context, Tories opposed the French Revolution and supported the government of the day.

underreading/overreading Both these terms refer to the ways that readers observe evidence, fill narrative gaps and draw conclusions and implications as they read. Underreading means not making good use of all the evidence given in the text; overreading means jumping to conclusions for which one has insufficient evidence.

unreliable narrator A narrator (not necessarily a participant in the story-world) who signals bias, ignorance, prejudice, dishonesty or some other grounds that make their assertions and colourings worthy of doubt.

APPENDIX B
Study Guide: Learning from the Essays

This short study guide is aimed primarily at undergraduate student readers with a view to helping you to make the most of this volume in the course of your studies.

After a brief introduction, I provide some review questions on the content of the essays. These questions are designed to supplement the guidance already provided in the Critical Reflections and Further Study sections which follow the essays and in which the essay authors provide a range of suggestions on how best to engage with the essays and on how you can build on their ideas in your own further reading and research. Following the review questions, I turn to how you might use the essays in the volume as exemplary models of academic writing in the development of your own essay-writing practices. I will draw your attention to some of the key features of the essays and also invite you to analyse them structurally and stylistically for yourself in order to identify writing strategies that you might find helpful in the future.

Initial Orientation

In order to optimise your learning from any book that you intend to use for intensive study, you should first ensure that you are fully familiar with what the book has to offer and, in particular, how it is organised and structured and what special features it may have. For this, especially with a large book like this one, it is always useful to make a first general survey of the book's contents to identify what are its key elements and to note how different parts of the book connect with one another.

It is not a bad thing to start with, simply to flick through the whole book to get an initial sense of the length and nature and layout of its constituent parts, but then the obvious first port of call, in mapping out a volume like this, is to the list of contents. Here, you have quite a long list, so it is well worth spending a few minutes looking through it carefully and in particular noting down the essays that might be of special interest to you. Also, you should not neglect the book's preface. I put it that way because I understand perfectly well that most people *do* neglect preliminary materials like prefaces, forewords and introductions, usually preferring to jump straight into the main text of a book. For many people, such preliminaries are viewed, at best, as purely of technical interest, but there is often genuinely valuable information to be found in these sections and, here, the main purpose of my preface is precisely to provide readers with a clear initial orientation on the aims and structure of the book – so I do recommend at least a quick read of this if you have not read it so far. You should note too that Appendix C provides two alternative contents listings which show the volume's essays organised by genre and theme rather than by chronological period as in the main list of contents. This may help you further in selecting essays that are of special relevance to you. A skim through the index can also be helpful in this, as it may draw your attention to topics that the essay titles themselves may not mention explicitly.

Once you have established an overall idea of the contents and structure of the book, the other introductory material – the Introduction itself and my later introductory notes at the start of each of the essay sections – may also be useful to provide a first engagement with the ideas and arguments presented in the book. However, if you prefer to plunge into the essays directly, these introductory elements will bear returning to later on and could be helpful in future as a convenient way of reviewing your understanding of the main lines of discussion in the essays. A broader sort of background preparation for your reading of the essays would be to refer to the book's parent volume, *English Literature in Context* (2nd edn, 2017), as that book provides clear orientation for this one. The earlier volume has a substantial chapter devoted to each literary period in which a full range of relevant historical contexts for the literary developments of that period are discussed, and each chapter contains many inset text boxes providing definitions or explanations of particular terms, movements, issues and so on. If, therefore, you are an undergraduate student at the beginning of your studies and feel uncertain about the broader historical contexts of English literature, then that volume is a good place to begin as you will then find the essays in this volume easier to grasp in relation not only to their historical periods but, crucially, also in relation to literary critical traditions. Bear in mind, too, that the short readings given there at the end of each chapter can also serve as bite-sized examples of the same sorts of readings as you will find in the longer essays here and, in some cases, there are useful direct continuities (for example, Lee Morrissey's reading of *Oroonoko* could be used to prepare yourself for reading Oddvar Holmesland's extended reading of the same novel here). Additionally, all the chapters provide comprehensive and annotated reading lists which will direct you to further relevant materials for each period.

Reviewing the Content of the Essays

Clearly, the primary form of learning to be derived from these essays is in terms of their subject matter and in terms of gaining an enhanced knowledge and understanding of the texts and contexts they deal with. In addition to my own summary comments in the Introduction and introductory notes to the essays, the contributors have provided some focused ideas on this dimension of their essays in the concluding Critical Reflections and Further Study sections, so I do not intend to discuss the specific contents of the essays in any further detail here. Instead, I provide below a list of review questions, one for each of the essays, which are intended to encourage both careful reflection on your understanding of the essays and some practical application of what you have learnt from them to your present studies.

Review Questions

The numbers of the questions relate to the essay numbers and, although I often refer to the specific texts dealt with in each essay as if you are actually studying them at present, I have tried wherever possible to formulate the questions in such a way as to make them broadly applicable to other similar or related texts. Hopefully, this will allow you to consider the questions in relation to at least some of the texts which you are currently studying on your own particular programme of study.

1. Once you are satisfied that you clearly understand the broadly intertextual concept of *mouvance* that Emily Thornbury discusses in her essay, consider precisely what sorts of *mouvance* might now be in play in your own contemporary reading of *The Dream of the Rood* as your twenty-first-century assumptions and expectations give new voice to an Old English poem from around a thousand years ago.

2. It is often said that a lot is lost in the process of translation, but Filip Krajník's discussion of Chaucer as translator is highly suggestive of a lot that is also *gained* through translation. From your reading of this essay, what do you think were the specific gains of translation for Chaucer and for literary culture generally in Britain at this time? At the same time, choose a short passage from *The Parliament of Fowls* in its original Middle English and (using an appropriate dictionary or drawing on the notes or glossary in your edition of the text) make your own translation into natural flowing modern English and then reflect carefully on the various things you might have 'lost' or 'gained' in this process.

3. In his essay K. S. Whetter suggests that medieval romance 'offered its original authors and audiences a venue in which to explore some of the major social, cultural and political questions of the day'. Look closely at two or three episodes in a medieval romance that you are currently studying and, following Whetter's example, consider how these episodes exhibit the generic conventions of medieval romance and how, through these, they suggest some of the social, cultural or political issues of the day.

4. In the light of Alessandra Petrina's essay, look closely at one of the Renaissance texts that you are currently studying and compile a list of all the traces you can find of cross-cultural influences from Europe (and, possibly, beyond). Try then to assess their relative importance to the text in question.

5. Jane Grogan's essay consolidates Petrina's essay by considering the global horizons of early modern epic with specific reference to Spenser's *The Faerie Queene* and, in particular, Book II of that work. After a careful reading of the essay and its discussion of Spenser's Irish and transatlantic perspectives, go back to one of the other books in Spenser's epic and try to follow Grogan's example yourself by identifying evidence of Spenser's broader horizons beyond just those of England.

6. Christa Jansohn's discussion of *Arden of Faversham* suggests that, among other things, the characterisation in this play represented an important step forwards in the progression of domestic drama towards greater psychological realism. Make a close study of one of the main characters from the play in light of this view and assess the extent to which such a view can be justified.

7. In her essay on *Henry V*, Ina Habermann cleverly sets up a dialogue between text and context in terms of the play of the 'play' and the play of 'history'. In the light of Habermann's discussion and your own experience of the play, what sort of balance would *you* say exists in *Henry V* between the play (as text or performance) and the history?

8. Robert Wilcher discusses the reception of Henry Vaughan's poems at different times in history. Choose one of Vaughan's poems and write three short paragraphs of your own analysing its main themes and any formal features that you feel are important – but (after a little historical research) you should present each paragraph from a different historical perspective: first, imagining yourself as a critic in the 1650s; then as a critic in the mid 1800s; and then as a critic of today.

9. Lee Morrissey's essay is a key essay in this collection for its carefully theorised account of the complexities of reading texts in context. In addition, it provides an inspired reading of Gray's *Elegy Written in a Country Church Yard* as 'a metaphor for literary history seen as a set of buried possibilities ready for rediscovery and reimagining'. After reading his essay and his reading of the *Elegy*, write a short summary of what you now understand about reading English literature in context. If you are studying another work from this period, make some notes on how you might apply such understanding to that text, perhaps, if appropriate, following Morrissey's example in his reading of Gray's *Elegy*.

10. In the light of Oddvar Holmesland's essay and your own reading of *Oroonoko*, write a short paragraph on how *you* view the text's representations of (a) the indigenous Surinamese people, (b) the enslaved Africans, and (c) Oroonoko himself.

11. The contents page of the *British Magazine* reproduced in Richard Jones's essay provides a very vivid sense of the material print context of Smollett's novel *Sir Launcelot Greaves*. From snakes and ploughs to longitude and literature, we can see immediately the sort of everyday discourses that were jostling around the novel as it first appeared in serial form in this magazine. This would have been a very different reading experience from reading the novel as an independently printed volume and we can also see how this context may have influenced the author as he was writing the novel's instalments and thinking of the company they would be keeping. In the light of this latter point, choose a chapter from Smollett's novel and analyse it carefully for any signs of how it might indeed have been influenced in this way.

12. Daniel Sanjiv Roberts's essay provides a rich overview of the many and various responses to India and the orient registered in English literature of the Romantic era. As Roberts covers such a wide range of materials, there is scope for developing some of his analyses further. Therefore, choose one or two of the texts he considers and, following his broad lead, look at them in some more detail in relation to how exactly they represent and respond to the orient.

13. From your reading of Fiona Price's essay, how would you paraphrase the 'debate' she discusses between Scott and Porter over the nature of 'heroism'?

14. Katie Halsey, in her essay, points out that *Northanger Abbey* is the most overtly intertextual of Austen's novels and, while this feature of the novel, especially in relation to its parodying of the Gothic novel, is what makes it so much fun, it also accounts for some of what Halsey calls its 'tonal oddities'. Halsey shows, through a couple of well-chosen examples, how skilful Austen could be in exploiting her intertextual references. However, to what extent do you think Austen was successful in the novel *overall* in balancing her own narrative development with these references to other narratives? Select one or two further scenes which allude to other novels and, following Halsey's example, discuss how effective these are.

15. Paul Wright's essay is poised on a cusp between faith and science, but it is so in a particularly visceral way because of its medical dimension. The engraved image of the brain reproduced in the essay makes clear that this was a time when there was no longer any hiding place for the soul if it existed in any material bodily way. Wright clearly sets out the Keatsian terms of the debate between physical sensation and Romantic intimations of immortality in his analysis of the ode 'To Psyche'. Choose another of Keats's poems and explore this theme for yourself, paying particular attention to the details of the language and assessing the balance Keats strikes between a language of the senses and a language of the soul.

16. The richly allusive satirical cartoon reproduced in Jordan Kistler's essay clearly invites some further research to reveal its full significance, but one of its allusions

seems to be to an essay Darwin had recently published on the subject of worm mould. This is perhaps only a circumstantial detail but it reinforces Kistler's argument that Victorian poetry and culture were highly responsive to scientific developments of the time and were, indeed, in fairly constant and immediate dialogue with those developments. This suggests that it is worth carefully researching the immediate contexts of any Victorian texts which make reference to scientific matters. Therefore, choose one of the poems discussed by Kistler – or another appropriate one among those you are currently studying – and see how much you can find out about the scientific work being carried out at around its time of composition.

17. The life of a writer is by definition a writing life, but Maria Frawley's essay makes us think about how that life is actually written into being. Frawley's own writing is sensitively attuned to that of both Charlotte Brontë and her character Lucy Snowe from *Villette* as she teases out the various ways in which their respective life writings can be understood not just as writings *about* their lives but writings constitutive *of* their lives. Following Frawley's analysis, try to express in a piece of your own writing what sort of life you think Lucy Snowe ultimately writes for herself in *Villette*.

18. With Dickens, and perhaps with Victorian fiction more generally, literature's traditional mission to explore the values of life seems inextricably linked with an exploration of the values of money. But, as Ben Moore's essay suggests, money is merely a *token* of value, and the nature of *that* value is itself elusive and could be said to be merely a token of yet something else. We are thus drawn into something of a hall of mirrors where meanings and values are constantly reflected somewhere else and ultimately recede into infinity. So, does Dickens – and do Gissing and other writers of the era – ever succeed in conveying a sense of human value that is not mixed up with the value of money, and if so, how?

19. After reading Fionnuala Dillane's essay on serial fiction – and drawing on your own experience of reading and of watching screen texts – make a list of all the differences you can think of between reading serially and non-serially. Try then to come up with a list of the main distinguishing features of serial fiction.

20. Sue Asbee, in her analysis of women writers of the *fin de siècle*, draws attention to the way in which we all 'perform' identities in public and to how public spaces can be transformed by changing patterns of identity performance. Choose a work not featured in the essay but by one of the authors Asbee discusses, and follow her example in analysing how it stages this sort of performance of identity.

21. As Stefania Michelucci's essay makes clear, the modernist era was characterised by a 'crisis of representation' which led writers and artists to experiment with new forms of representation, many of which focused on questions of

space – and, in the field of literature, the 'spatial novel' was one manifestation of this trend. From your reading of Michelucci's essay and from your own reading of the novel, try to explain in your own words why Lawrence's *Women in Love* can be viewed as a spatial novel. Consider its overall plot and structure but then also choose one major episode from the novel for more detailed analysis of its language and organisation.

22. Anna Budziak's discussion of T. S. Eliot's use of a classical epigraph for his poem *Marina* focuses attention on the time-layered nature of literary contexts and inevitably brings to mind Eliot's famous notion of 'the mythical method'. Eliot introduced the idea in an essay on James Joyce in 1923 and it came to be closely associated with modernism. Do some research to find out more about the mythical method and then choose another poem of Eliot's through which to make a comparison with *Marina* in terms of Eliot's use of the past to inform the present.

23. Judith Paltin's essay on Virginia Woolf's *A Room of One's Own* is unique in this volume for concentrating entirely on the essay genre. Yet Virginia Woolf's essay is not a conventional one and certainly rather different from the academic essays in this volume. After reading Paltin's essay, go back to Woolf's essay and try to describe exactly what sort of essay it is. What are its main features and how successful do you think it is as an essay and as a piece of writing generally? In fact, why not try to write a short essay of your own on the model of Woolf's, creating your own Beton-like character, in order to answer this question?

24. In his essay, Terry Gifford introduces and explains some ecocritical terms which may be unfamiliar to you. After reading his essay, write down your own explanations of two or three of these terms – such as 'inhabitation', 'natureculture', 'post-pastoral' and 're-enchantment'. Choose an appropriate nature-themed poem by Ted Hughes and read it carefully with these terms in mind and then go back to your written explanations and revise your definitions in the light of what you have just learnt from your chosen poem. Read the poem again and then try writing a poem of your own on a similar theme.

25. From your own reading and book buying (or book borrowing) experience – and judging from the books on your bookshelves (or piled on the floor) – how aware have you been in the past of the influence of publishers and the publishing industry on what sorts of books are available to you? Do you have any books published by feminist imprints like Virago? Choose one of your favourite contemporary books and do some research into its publishing history to see where, exactly, it has come from and what sort of editorial decisions may have been made about it before it was published. Also, do some general research into the nature of the publishing industry at present – which are the dominant companies, who owns what, who are the top executives, what sort of equal opportunities policies do they operate and do they report pay differentials

according to gender, etc.? What evidence can you find to support Catherine Riley's view that women are now far better represented in the publishing world than in the past?

26. Judging from your own experience of contemporary drama, either in performance or through textual study, do you agree that, among the arts, drama is an especially powerful mode of social critique? To what extent does that power depend on the impact of live performance, or can it be felt equally on the page – or does this depend on the type of play involved? Choose two of the plays discussed by Clare Wallace in her essay and compare them in these terms. Do some internet research to see if you can find reviews of the plays which will give you further points of view to add to your own.

27. Fiona Moolla's essay suggests that romance has been a suppressed element in mainstream African fiction in English. Is that a view borne out by your own reading of African novels? If so, how would you account for it? Is it perhaps a feature of a particular period in the evolution of the African novel in English – or a variable feature that has something to do with the gender of authors? Choose two African novels that you are studying and make a careful comparison of them in terms of their respective treatments of romance.

28. After reading Loretta Stec's essay along with her own comprehensive Critical Reflections section, take one of Bessie Head's works that you have studied or are studying and try to come up with your own 'constellation diagram' in which you note all the influences on your thinking about that work. Make a special point of including some reflections on how *your* 'philosophy of everyday life' might inform your reading of the work.

29. As Izabel Brandão's essay suggests, especially in its title perhaps, the poetry of Grace Nichols evades easy categorisation because of its wide range of moods and themes, sometimes obviously serious and politically committed and sometimes apparently light-hearted and simply celebratory of the everyday and the ordinary. Choose two poems by Nichols which seem to you to represent these two aspects of her work and make a close comparison of them. Do they in fact represent two opposite tendencies in her work, or do they perhaps have more in common than first meets the eye?

30. Joel Kuortti talks of how Salman Rushdie's novels carry their contexts with them on open display, as it were. They are both metafictional and, in Kuortti's term, 'metacontextual' novels, acutely aware of their own fictionality but also of their contextuality. Are we then to understand that contexts are in some senses fictional too? Taking the position of a first-person narrator, write an outline plan for a Rushdiesque novel about your own life, indicating which real-world contexts it would be important for you to fictionalise or metacontextualise.

31. Ulla Rahbek presents a wide-ranging discussion of several contemporary novels from a broad postcolonial perspective. How has her essay refined your

understanding of what 'postcolonialism' means? Try to write down a brief definition of what you think is meant by 'postcolonial literature' today in the light of her discussion. Make some notes, too, on how far you think this label that can encompass such a diverse range of texts and writers as Rahbek includes in her essay. Are there any other alternative terms that might be considered?

Reviewing the Structure, Style and Technique of the Essays

The other major form of learning to be derived from your reading of these essays is to do with developing your own essay-writing skills and practice. There are no hard and fast rules for how to write a good academic essay, and like any high-level skill it is not something anyone can teach you overnight or in any simple mechanical way. Although there are of course basic general guidelines, which you are probably only too familiar with already, mainly you have to learn slowly from your own independent regular practice and the feedback it generates from tutors – *and* from the example of others. And that is where this volume can help you above all, in providing a concentrated source of varied and high-quality examples of academic writing on a wide range of literary topics, a good proportion of which will almost certainly overlap in some ways with your own particular programme of studies.

So, here, I am not going to present you with a standard set of general guidelines for essay writing. I am sure you will have been given something like this already by your department and there are many available guides to study skills and essay writing available on the market (see, for example, Gordon Taylor, *A Student's Writing Guide: How to Plan and Write Successful Essays* (Cambridge University Press, 2009)). Instead, as above, I want mainly to encourage you to explore the essays available to you in this book in some careful analytical detail so that you read them not only for what you can learn from their contents but also for what they can teach you about the formal aspects of essay writing. You have in this volume a large number of highly polished essays produced by writers who are not only leading scholars in their fields but also experienced university and college teachers: so, viewed in that light for now, you might like to think of their essays as ways of teaching by example and 'sharing best practice' with you in the art of essay writing.

The structure, style and technique of an essay are clearly interrelated elements and, ultimately, need to be negotiated together – along with the essay's intellectual content – in order to produce a unified and persuasive piece of academic writing. It is nevertheless useful to begin with, in thinking analytically about what makes a good academic essay, to separate out these three elements and to try to identify what are their most important features. I will therefore make some brief general observations about each of them below and will then suggest some further review activities that you might like to undertake for yourself in relation to the volume's essays.

Structure

On the whole, it is the structure of the conventional academic essay which is its most standardised element. The style and technique of an essay can vary quite widely and can be – and, with some important qualifications, possibly *should* be – as unique and individual as the person who is writing it. Along with the quality of its thought and ideas, this latter dimension of the individual 'voice' of an essay is a large part of what makes an essay engaging and effective and, more generally, what gives the essay form, at its best, its creative appeal and vitality. So, structure, we might say, is what imposes the discipline of the form while the less easily prescribed realms of style and technique are where the *play* of expression and individuality comes in – but it needs to be stressed that *both* aspects are equally important. It is no use producing a highly individual and creative essay if it is so poorly organised that the reader cannot make sense of it; and, equally, even the most perfectly structured essay will not succeed if it is devoid of original ideas and expressive interest. For beginning students, it is particularly important to assimilate the academic 'template' of structure as quickly as possible so that you can then concentrate on what is really the more difficult task of developing your own individual writing voice and technique.

The underlying structural principle of an essay is that it should present a clearly developed, rounded and logical *argument* that is supported by appropriate and persuasive evidence from primary and secondary sources. The structure of the essay, that is, should be the structure of a logical argument supported by a reasonable range of *evidence* that demonstrates a genuine engagement with the field of study. The essay should have a clear *introduction* where the essay's main argument is briefly stated in outline; it should then develop the argument more fully in a sequence of logical steps which are more or less clearly signalled by and contained within their own distinct *paragraphs*, so that the route from your introduction to your conclusion is clearly waymarked by what you might think of as 'paragraph steps'. The *conclusion* itself should be a type of elegant variation on the introduction and should sum up the argument that you have presented. Essentially, this is similar to the advice often given for making a speech: tell your readers at the start what you are going to tell them; then tell them; then tell them what you've told them! But, on the page, you have much more scope for elaborating each of these stages and for presenting more detailed and involved evidence to support what you say. On the subject of evidence, all your primary and secondary sources, and any additional material and references that you draw on, should be presented consistently using a standard system of citation (Chicago, Modern Humanities

Research Association (MHRA), Modern Languages Association (MLA), etc.), using either footnotes or endnotes and, depending on the system, a list of works cited or a list of references. What is most important here is not so much which system you use, but that you are consistent in your presentation throughout the whole of your essay. Such systems of citation are often referred to as style systems, and your institution may well have provided you with a style sheet or style guidelines outlining the reference system you should use for all your essays. (Note that this use of the word 'style' is a relatively specialised one and refers primarily to technical matters such as punctuation and spelling and layout; my use of it more generally in this section refers to your whole writing style or style of expression.)

Review Activities

At this point, collect ten or so bookmarks and then mark out the start and end of three essays of your own choice in the volume, keeping a few bookmarks in reserve for marking further pages later on as you work through the following review activities.

a. Ignoring the abstracts for now, skim-read the first and last paragraphs of all three of your chosen essays and then make a list of what you notice about them and try to identify any clear features they have in common.

b. Although the essay abstracts in this volume are not integral parts of the essays, they nevertheless provide a convenient overview of each of the essays and many of them will neatly outline the main structure of an essay. Quickly read through the abstracts of your three essays now and see if you can further abstract them into a simple numbered list of, say, the five key 'steps' in the essay.

c. Some of the essays use subheadings to indicate subdivisions within the argument – units of logic smaller than the whole essay but larger than individual paragraphs. This is of course a useful way of grouping ideas and of signposting the reader along the route of the argument being presented, and it is especially important in longer essays or book chapters. However, you should note that most of these relatively short essays use such subdivisions with restraint. While subsections can indeed break up an argument into manageable units and prevent the reader 'getting lost', there is also a danger that too many such breaks can also break the discursive continuity of the argument so that in too often being asked to break off to look at signposts the reader may at the same time lose the thread of why they are going in that direction in the first place. This is a matter of judgement (and probably as much about technique as structure), but, on the whole, in shorter literary-critical essays it is usually better to concentrate on ensuring a tightly and continuously argued essay than to risk fragmenting it with too many subdivisions. Look at your three essays and, if they have subdivisions, note how many there are and how they are spread out in the essay. Look also at how the writer ends one subsection and begins the next: are there any clear grammatical or linguistic markers of continuity ('as we shall see below', or 'Moving on from this idea, I would now like to …') or is there a sort of skip in the explicit logic as we step from one section to the next?

d. Take some time now to read through the first six or seven paragraphs of one of the essays and try systematically to identify the 'topic' sentences of each paragraph. These are the sentences which most strongly signal the main point being made by the paragraph as a whole, the ones which seem to be announcing the next step or building block in the argument. The topic sentence can often be the very first sentence of the paragraph, but it certainly does not need to be so (and only a fairly simple essay would have *every* paragraph beginning with a topic sentence). As you do this, try also to assess the extent to which the sequence of paragraphs is itself an identifiable 'unit' (or section) of meaning, with individual paragraphs strongly dependent on one another and so slowly building up to a bigger key idea – or whether they are in fact making relatively discrete points individually and so moving the argument on in quick short steps, so to speak. Again, this is a structural element that begins to slip into matters of technique too.

e. Turning to the question of 'evidence' in the essay, look carefully at how the author presents quotations, notes and references and how these are blended into the running argument of the essay. Follow through some of the references, from the note indicator in the main text to the actual endnote, so that you get a feel for how this sort of discursive 'counterpoint' operates. Sometimes, it is purely a technical matter of noting a page reference in a primary or secondary source, but often it is also more genuinely like musical counterpoint in that an idea in the main line of argument is given some further resonance in a second line.

f. Spend a little time now with the actual endnotes, looking carefully at *exactly* what they contain so that you attune yourself to what is normally expected of such notes. In particular, make an analytical note of the key elements that are contained in the book and essay references and how these are presented and punctuated. Try to identify the general pattern.

Style

As mentioned earlier, I am referring here to styles of writing and expression rather than to the more narrow technical sense of 'style' used in relation to the conventions of layout and presentation; and, as also mentioned earlier, this is something much less subject to standardisation than questions of structure and stylistic conventions. Nevertheless, there are certainly *some* standard expectations about styles of expression in academic writing and you need to be very clear about these from the start. Probably the most important general point that needs to be remembered is that we are involved here, as members of an academic community, in a *field* of discourse which is, broadly speaking, a fairly formal and 'elevated' one, to do with the serious pursuit of knowledge, intellectual advancement and academic excellence, including excellence and precision in the use of language. Clearly, then, this is a discursive field – or institutional context – where a relatively high degree of formality is required and where, also, high degrees of precision in thought and expression are expected and highly valued. This does not mean that you must adopt some exaggeratedly stuffy or artificially elevated style of writing in your essays, but it does mean that you generally need to maintain a fairly formal style of expression, using standard written English correctly and accurately, and that you should generally avoid slipping into the more casual forms and styles of language we use in everyday speech. Intersecting the axis of formality–informality is that of objectivity–subjectivity. Again, the field of discourse clearly dictates a high degree of respect for 'objective' and evidence-based discourse as opposed to discourses which are clearly subjective and based on personal opinions or prejudices – so, stylistically, the general expectation in academic writing is that writers should adopt a fairly objective and impersonal style in preference to one that conveys a strong sense of a subjective and personal point of view. Once more, this is not to say that there is no room for *any* subjectivity and personality in academic writing, but simply that this should not be the predominant approach.

Essentially, if we are clear about the context, the field of discourse, in which we are writing, and the expectations of the audience we imagine we are addressing within that field, then everything else should flow from this. But again, examples of best practice are probably the best way to appreciate the full nature of that context and those expectations.

Review Activities

a. Read through the opening few paragraphs of your three chosen essays once more (or choose another three for this set of activities if you prefer), and, as you do this, make notes in which you describe the style of writing in terms of its relative degrees of formality and informality and then also of objectivity and subjectivity. Are there any clear markers of these things in (i) the vocabulary used by the writer, (ii) the grammar or syntax of the sentences, and (iii) the writer's mode of address?

b. Now, read a few more paragraphs of just two of the essays and try to establish a sense of the *tone of voice* of the writer in each case. Compare and contrast the two writing voices and, making a few brief notes in writing, try to describe them as clearly as possible. How do you imagine the writers as 'speakers' of their essays and how do you feel you are being addressed by them? Do you feel 'distant' or 'close' to their voices and/or materials – and what are the specific features of the language on the page that principally determine how you feel?

c. Imagine that you have been given some fragments of pages from these essays so that you had no external evidence of their original context. How might you be able to deduce that context simply from looking at the fragments of language before you? What are the giveaway signs, in the words, phrases and sentences, of the field of discourse they come from? List as many features as you can.

d. From the activities so far, you may have become aware of some patterns of language use in the essays that you might now start to think of as 'typical' of academic literary-critical writing – the use of certain words or types of word, and the use of certain types of phrase or grammatical construction. Look over the essays again and see how many specific examples of such patterns you can identify.

Technique

The distinction between style and technique is not a categorical one and the two things are quite closely interconnected in practice. However, in principle, one might say that style is more to do with the manipulation of the basic elements and structures of language – which words we choose and how we arrange them to make sentences, how we connect and arrange and balance sentences within paragraphs, and so on – while technique is more a matter of the *strategies* we deploy to ensure our writing achieves what it sets out to do, which, in the case of academic essay writing, is to construct an engaging and convincing scholarly argument. As we have already seen, the basic prerequisites for this are a clear structure of argument and the adoption of an appropriate style and tone of voice, but these alone provide no necessary 'force of argument', as it were. The structure provides a framework within which to work and the style provides an appropriately pitched voice through which to present the argument, but that still leaves the work of active persuasion to be done, and this is where some sense of rhetorical technique is needed too, if we are to capture and keep the attention of our readers and then lead them to the conclusions we want them to be persuaded by in the end. Again, there is no quick fix to learning how to write forceful and persuasive academic essays, although we have already established some of the essentials – above all, perhaps, in the terms of Aristotle's three forms of rhetoric (from his fourth-century BCE *Art of Rhetoric*), the fact that the argument must be predominantly *logos*-based, that is, based on logic and reason, and not merely on personal opinion (*ethos*) or indeed on an appeal to the emotions (*pathos*). There is no substitute for logic and evidence and for a clear line of well-reasoned argument, of course, but to develop and sustain such a clear line of argument throughout a complete essay on complex topics is, for most of us, a lot easier said than done. So, let me once more direct you to take a closer look at how the experienced practitioners in this volume have tackled this challenge.

Review Activities

a. As you have already looked at several introductions and conclusions, you should be in a good position to identify some different ways of beginning and ending essays. What are some of the 'gambits' that writers here use for this purpose. Try first to jot down some ideas from memory, but then go back to the essays to see if you have remembered rightly; and then take a look at some more introductions and conclusions in essays you have not so far consulted. Try to identify some useful generic phrases for opening and closing a discussion that you might be able to make use of in your own essay-writing. Finally, write a short introduction to an essay entitled 'How to Write a Good Essay'.

b. Go back to some of the essay paragraphs you considered earlier (or choose a new run of paragraphs in another essay) and analyse carefully how *these* begin and end and how the writer creates a sense of continuity moving from one paragraph to the next. Are there explicit 'cohesion ties' indicated by specific linking words and phrases or does the writer simply *imply* continuity by the logic of the discussion? (Sometimes the repetition of a key word or idea from a previous paragraph will have this effect.)

c. Many writers will use rhetorical questions to make a point and to advance their arguments in that way. Try to find examples of this in any of the essays you have been looking at and then consider how effective a strategy this is for you as a reader.

d. Take any two essays which you have read in their entirety and make a careful comparison of them in terms of the *range of* reference they employ in the course of their arguments and how effective that range is in convincing you of the argument in both cases. Some writers, that is, will restrict their range of reference quite tightly to focus closely on something that may therefore seem to be contextually very narrowly framed, while other writers will seem to have a much more open frame of contextual reference and will draw on very diverse materials to feed their argument. Both strategies can be effective in different ways, depending on the subject and nature of the argument, but see if you can identify how writers handle different perspectives like this and consider which of the two tendencies you feel most drawn to and why.

e. One of the most important skills you need to develop is how to negotiate the tricky business of incorporating primary and secondary sources into your essays in a balanced and convincing way. As I have suggested, these are effectively what provide you with the main 'evidence' for your argument, so it is essential to know how best to present them and how to work them smoothly and convincingly into your discussion. Look closely at how the writers in this volume's essays do this – and, to begin with, look separately at the two types of sources, so that you are clear about their differences and the different approaches that they each sometimes require. Look at two essays at least for this exercise and try to identify what is common in their handling of sources as well as what is different.

f.   Critics will vary quite a lot in how – and how much – they draw on secondary sources and therefore on the views of other critics. Related to this is the variation in how different critics might draw on general thinkers and theorists to inform their arguments. Some writers will very clearly announce that they are working from within a particular theoretical tradition or framework while others might appear to rely solely on their own ideas and forms of analysis. Look now at this aspect of the essays here and consider how the writers 'frame' their discussions and declare their theoretical and/or methodological positions. For this exercise, try to identify two essays which clearly declare a strong theoretical framework and two which appear not to do so.

Coda

The aim of this short study guide has been to encourage you to learn for yourself from the examples set by the essays, drawing on them as inspiration for your own individual 'essays' or experiments in thought and expression. The remarkable thing about essays like those collected here is that, despite the existence of thousands if not millions of other similar essays in the world, and despite the sorts of 'family resemblance' I have noted above, they are all each still pretty much unique. They are, as I have said, as individual as the individuals who have produced them. So, perhaps above all, in facilitating insights into some of the possibilities of the essay form, I hope that this guide will help you eventually to nurture your own unique and creative voice as an essay-writer.

FURTHER READING AND REFERENCE

Acheson, Katherine O., *Writing Essays about Literature: A Brief Guide for University and College Students* (Peterborough, Ontario: Broadview Press, 2010)

Bailey, Stephen, *Academic Writing: A Handbook for International Students*, 5th edn (London: Routledge, 2017)

The Essentials of Academic Writing for International Students (London: Routledge, 2015)

Baldick, Chris, *The Oxford Dictionary of Literary Terms*, 4th edn (Oxford University Press, 2015)

Chatman, Seymour, with Geoffrey Galt Harpham, *A Glossary of Literary Terms*, 11th edn (Boston, MA: Wadsworth Cengage Learning, 2015)

Crystal, David, *The Cambridge Encyclopedia of the English Language*, 3rd edn (Cambridge University Press, 2018)

Griffith, Kelley, *Writing Essays about Literature: A Guide and Style Sheet*, 9th edn (Boston, MA: Wadsworth Cengage Learning, 2013)

Headrick, Paul, *The Wiley Guide to Writing Essays about Literature* (Oxford: Wiley Black-well, 2014)

Littlewood, Ian, *The Literature Student's Survival Kit* (Oxford: Blackwell, 2006)

Manninen, S., Turner, E., and Wadsö-Lecaros, *Writing in English at University: A Guide for Second Language Writers* (Lund: Lund University, 2020); available for download at https://portal.research.lu.se

Taylor, Gordon, *A Student's Writing Guide: How to Plan and Write Successful Essays* (Cambridge University Press, 2009)

Young, Tory, *Studying English Literature: A Practical Guide* (Cambridge University Press, 2008)

APPENDIX C
Essays Listed by Genre and Theme

The following two tables each provide an alternative 'list of contents' for the volume to help readers who might like to read the essays selectively according to either genre or theme (or a mixture of the two). In both cases, but especially in the second list, the groupings of essays should not be seen in too categorical a light: the aim is simply to suggest the *predominant* emphases of each essay and, as will be seen, some essays have a multi-generic focus and most of them range across more than one of the key themes that I have identified here. For this reason, in the second list, I have not hesitated to list essays more than once under different headings where this seemed appropriate (though the fact that an essay is *not* listed under a particular theme does not necessarily mean that it contains nothing of relevance to that theme – just that its principal focus lies elsewhere). The broadly conceived themes I have selected in order to organise this second list are intended roughly to reflect the lines of my introductory discussion to the volume. These are of course only my own interpretative constructs for mapping out what I see as the volume's leading concerns. Different readers may want to make different thematic maps for themselves but I hope that my broad-brush approach here will still leave plenty of scope for this.

Genre

Poetry
1   Finding *The Dream of the Rood* in Old English Literature (Emily V. Thornbury)
2   The Translator as Author: The Case of Geoffrey Chaucer's *The Parliament of Fowls* (Filip Krajník)
3   Arthurian Romance as a Window on to Medieval Life: The Case of *Ywayne and Gawayne* and *The Awntyrs off Arthure* (K. S. Whetter)
5   'Mr Spencer's Moral Invention': The Global Horizons of Early Modern Epic (Jane Grogan)
8   Poems and Contexts: The Case of Henry Vaughan (Robert Wilcher)
9   Periodising in Context: The Case of the Restoration and Eighteenth Century (Lee Morrissey)

Drama

Fiction

Mixed Genre/Non-Fiction

Theme

Global or Transcultural Mobilities

Transhistorical Connections

Thought and Belief

Index

Entries in **bold** refer to major recurrent topics.
Page numbers in *italics* refer to content in figures.